Calendar

	Autumn			Winter		
Aug.	Sep.	Oct.	Nov.	Dec.	Jan.	Feb.
Summer proper	The typhoon season	Autumn proper		Early winter	Winter proper	

— Hot, but fine, weather

Many typhoons

A period of fine, clear weather

The coldest season. Fine, clear weather along the Pacific coast, but heavy snow along the Japan Sea coast.

Sudden drop in temperatures

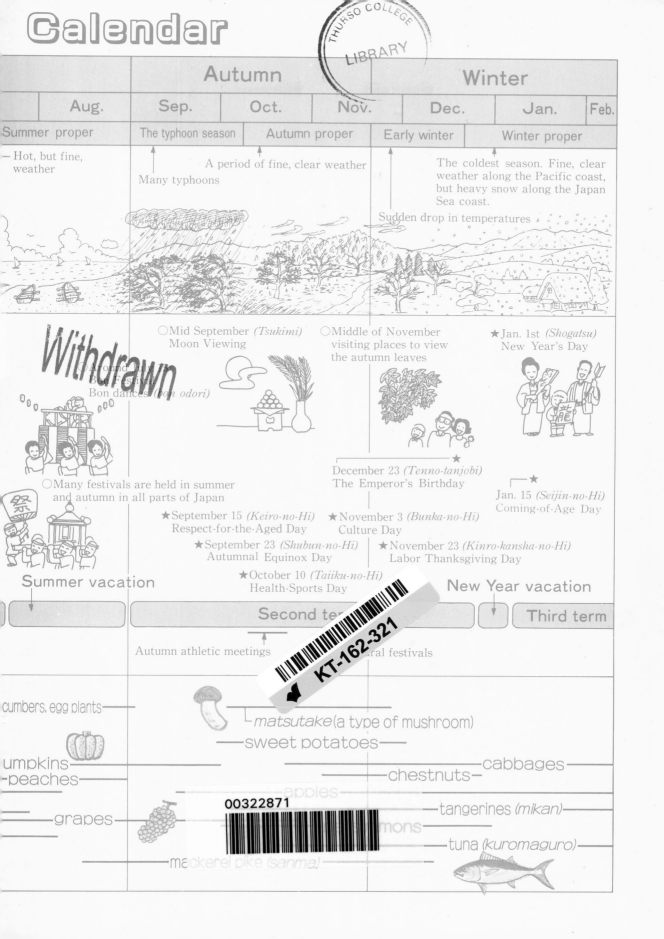

○Mid September *(Tsukimi)*
Moon Viewing

○Middle of November
visiting places to view
the autumn leaves

★Jan. 1st *(Shogatsu)*
New Year's Day

○Around July 13
Bon Festival
Bon dances *(bon odori)*

○Many festivals are held in summer and autumn in all parts of Japan

December 23 *(Tenno-tanjobi)*
The Emperor's Birthday

Jan. 15 *(Seijin-no-Hi)*
Coming-of-Age Day

★September 15 *(Keiro-no-Hi)*
Respect-for-the-Aged Day

★November 3 *(Bunka-no-Hi)*
Culture Day

★September 23 *(Shubun-no-Hi)*
Autumnal Equinox Day

★November 23 *(Kinro-kansha-no-Hi)*
Labor Thanksgiving Day

★October 10 *(Taiiku-no-Hi)*
Health-Sports Day

Summer vacation

New Year vacation

	Second te...		Third term

Autumn athletic meetings

...ral festivals

cumbers, egg plants —

matsutake(a type of mushroom)

— sweet potatoes —

umpkins —

cabbages

peaches —

chestnuts —

apples

— grapes —

tangerines *(mikan)*

...mons

tuna *(kuromaguro)*

mackerel pike *(sanma)*

Pictorial Encyclopedia of JAPANESE CULTURE

The Soul and Heritage of Japan

Gakken

STAFF

Editorial Consultant
    Nakayama Kaneyoshi (Professor of English, Tokoha Gakuen University)
Translator
    Richard De Lapp
English Language Advisors
    Anne Cortese
    Sekimori Gaynor (LOGOSTIKS)
Planning Advisor
    Koyama Yoshihisa
Book Design
    Shimada Takushi
Editorial Staff
    Anzai Tatsuo
    Tachibana Yukio
    Kisu Production
Publishing Manager
    Tachibana Yukio

Jacket photo: Woodblock print *Ichikawa Danjuro I*
                as Sogano Goro uprooting a bamboo
                (Tokyo National Museum Collection)

Pictorial Encyclopedia of JAPANESE CULTURE

Copyright © 1987 by GAKKEN CO., LTD.
All rights reserved, including the right to reproduce this book or portions
thereof in any form without the written permission of the publisher.

Published by GAKKEN CO., LTD.
4-40-5, Kami-ikedai, Ohta-ku, Tokyo 145, Japan

Overseas Distributor : Japan Publications Trading Co., Ltd.
P.O.Box 5030 Tokyo International, Tokyo, Japan.

Distributors:
United States : Kodansha International/USA, Ltd., through Harper & Row,
Publishers, Inc., 10 East 53rd Street, New York, N.Y.10022
South America : Harper & Row, publishers, Inc., International Department
Canada : Fitzhenry & Whiteside Ltd., 195 Allstate Parkway, Markham,
Ontario L3R 4T8
British Isles : International Book Distributors Ltd., 66 Wood Lane End,
Hemel Hempstead, Herts HP2 4RG
Australia and New Zealand: Bookwise International, 54 Crittenden Road,
Findon 5023, South Australia
The Far East and Japan : Japan Publications Trading Co., Ltd., 1-2-1,
Sarugaku-cho, Chiyoda-ku, Tokyo 101

First edition 1987
Eighteenth printing 1992
ISBN : 0-87040-752-X
ISBN : 4-05-151315-7 (in Japan)
Printed in Japan

PREFACE

Worldwide interest in Japan has mounted steadily over the past two decades in proportion to the nation's economic advancement abroad. Inevitably, the primary focus of that interest centers merely on cars, cameras, consumer electronics and other "things". There is, however, an increasing desire among people abroad to get beyond the economic realities of today's Japan and discover more about the soul that underlies the society, culture, customs and history.

Books on these aspects of Japan abound. Regrettably, their tendency to generalization does little to demystify the aura of "inscrutibility" that surrounds the Japanese image, and leaves the reader with the understandable but sadly mistaken impression that the Japanese are, after all, unique, that they do indeed form one large corporate entity, that they are, in truth, economic animals.

Japan is of course unique—just as America, Italy, and South Africa are unique. A strong characteristic of Japan's particular uniqueness is that the nation has held on to its Japaneseness despite a long history of voracious cultural borrowings. Westernized or Americanized though it may appear at first glance, Japan is, at its core, Japan, with deeply entrenched traditions and customs that underlie the surface veneer.

Being a human society, Japan is also quite capable of being understood by non-Japanese. In fact, it is on that very premise that this book was conceived and brought into its present form. In an easy-to-follow format it presents Japan's traditional culture, observances, behavioral patterns and customs, delving into their historical development to provide the reader with a fuller understanding of what constitutes the soul of this nation. To further facilitate meaningful communication with the Japanese, the book offers helpful, practical and necessary information, augmented with illustrations and pictures to enhance understanding.

This book is for all people who have an interest in Japan or who visit Japan on business, for study or for pleasure. It is also ideally suited for Japanese going abroad for similar purposes or on home-stay programs who would like their associates, friends and acquaintances to have a deeper knowledge of Japan.

CONTENTS

CREDITS

We are grateful to the following for cooperation and permission
to reproduce the photographs:

Akama Shrine, Asukamura Board of Education, Bank of Japan, Byodoin, Chishakuin, Chokoji, Chuguji, Communications Museum, Daisenin, Enkakuji, Enryakuji, Fukuoka Board of Education, Gakushuin University, Haga Library, Hakozakigu, Heian Shrine, Horyuji, Idemitsu Art Gallery, Imperial Household Agency, Ise Shrine, Ishiyamadera, Izumo Grand Shrine, Jingoji, Jishoji, Kamakura National Treasure House, Kanagawa Prefectural Museum, Kankikoji, Kasori Shellmound Museum, Katsura Detached Palace, Kenninji, Kishimoto Photo, Kobe City Museum, Kodaiji, Kofukuin, Kofukuji, Koseiji, Kyodo News Service, Kyoto National Museum, Kyoto University, Nagasaki Municipal Museum, Nara National Cultural Properties Research Institute, National Diet Library, National Noh Theater, National Theater, Nezu Art Museum, Meiji Village Museum, Mitoshooku, Miyagi Prefectural Library, Myokian, Omote Senke, Osaka Castle, Oura-tenshudo, Oyamazumi Shrine, Paper Museum, Rokuonji, Ryoanji, Sankeien, Seikado, Shibayama Haniwa Museum, Shinjuan, Shizuoka Municipal Toro Museum, Shofukuji, Shosoin, Shugakuin Detached Palace, Suntory Museum of Art, Takayama Museum of Local History, Taharacho Board of Education, The Fuji Bank Ltd, The Hatakeyama Collection, The Sanwa Bank Ltd, The Tokai Bank Ltd, The Tokugawa Reimeikai Foundation, The Yasukuni Shrine, Todaiji, Tohoku University, Tokeiji, Tokyo National Museum, Tokyo University, Tokyo University of Art, Toshodaiji, Toshogu Shrine, Tsunanmachi Board of Education, Tsurugaoka Hachiman Shrine, Yakushiji, Yamatobunkakan, Zuisenji, others.

THE LAND OF THE RISING SUN

Japanese mythology declares that the deities were born amidst the chaotic time when heaven and earth had just separated. Izanagi and Izanami were respectively the seventh male and female gods. Both of them thrust a halberd from the Bridge of Heaven into the sea. As they withdrew it, droplets trickling off the halberd formed an island. Izanagi and Izanami descended to it and brought forth island after island: Japan was created.

Izanami gives birth to various gods, but is burned to death while delivering the god of fire. After seeing her dead body, Izanagi proceeds to a river to purify himself, whereupon three more deities are born. One is Amaterasu-o-mikami, the sun goddess and queen of the divine country Takamagahara. Another is Tsukuyomi-no-mikoto, the moon god and the ruler of the kingdom of darkness. The third is the rogue Susanoo-no-mikoto, the tyrant of the seas.

Amaterasu-o-mikami sends her grandson Ninigi-no-mikoto down from heaven to the mountain pass called Takachiho to rule over the islands of Japan. His progeny beget the first Japanese Emperor.

Japanese myths are recorded in two historic works of the 8th century: *Kojiki* (Record of Ancient Matters), and *Nihon Shoki* (Chronicles of Japan). Though written with the intent of furthering the cause of the Imperial House, the myths also afford a good understanding of how the people of the time saw the world and nature.

▶**Susanoo-no-mikoto Slaying the Serpent** Japanese mythology relates the following story about Susanoo-no-mikoto. He was such a wild fellow that he was driven out of the divine land of Takamagahara by his sister Amaterasu-o-mikami. He descended to the land of Izumo (present-day Shimane prefecture). Walking along the upper reaches of a river he came upon a young girl crying. When asked why, she explained that the great serpent, Yamata-no-orochi came each year to devour a maiden and that her turn was now at hand. Susanoo-no-mikoto thereupon tricked the serpent into getting drunk, slew him, and married the maiden.

Each autumn in the Izumo area a dance based on this story is performed, one segment of which is shown in the photo.

SHRINES

Shinto—the way of the gods—is the name given to the simple faith possessed by the ancient Japanese. Whether it can also be termed a religion is a matter of debate, for Shinto has no particular teachings or dogmas. It is just a belief in the power of spirits thought to be in man and in elements of nature. This spritual power is what the Japanese call *kami*.

Kami could be all of one's deceased relatives or all of the dead. The sun, mountains, wind, rain, rocks, trees and other natural phenomena were also believed to be indwelt by *kami*. If worshipped, *kami* would be benevolent towards people, but provoked to wrath and possible calamity when neglected. People therefore chose to worship *kami*. That, in brief, is the basis of the faith referred to as Shinto.

Because the ancient Japanese deified and directly worshipped mountains, trees, even the sun as they were found in nature, religious edifices were unnecessary. Eventually, however, structures were built in places where *kami* could be worshipped. Each structure was given a specific name to show its purpose, such as *haiden* for the building where worshippers offer prayers, or *honden* for the building that contains the symbol (often a mirror) of the enshrined deity. Collectively, these structures are called *jinja* (shrines).

▲**Torii** *Torii* mark the entrance to a shrine, indicating that what lies ahead is ground sacred to the gods.

◄**Kasuga Grand Shrine** The family shrine of the politically powerful Fujiwara clan that held power at court from the 7th to the 12th centuries. The shrine was begun around the 8th century, but the present *honden* (main building) dates back about 200 years.

▲ *Goshinboku* (god-tree)   A rice-straw rope (*shimenawa*) tied around the trunk of a tree indicates the spot where the divinities descend to earth.

◀ **Aerial View of Izumo Grand Shrine** This shrine is credited to Okuninushi-no-mikoto, the fabulous ruler of the Izumo region in the mythological age. Along with the Ise Grand Shrine on the next page, it is one of the oldest shrines in Japan.

◀ (above) **Shinto Priest at Prayer** The priest offers prayers of celebration (*norito*) to the gods.

◀ (below) **Priest Making Fire** Fire to be used at shrines is created the natural way through friction.

▲ *Miko* (shrine maidens) **at a Wedding** *Miko* originally played an intercessionary role between man and the deities, relaying the divine will.

▲**Approach to Ise Shrine**　Across the bridge is the *torii* that signals the shrine entrance. In former times, worshippers first purified themselves in the river.

▶**Main Hall of Ise Shrine**　Ise Shrine is divided into "inner" and "outer" shrines. The inner shrine is sacred to Amaterasu-o-mikami, the deity of the Imperial House. Like Izumo Grand Shrine, Ise is one of the oldest shrines in Japan. It is rebuilt every 20 years, but always retaining the same design and form. The most recent rebuilding was in 1973. Despite its dedication to the legendary deity of the Imperial House, the building is a plain structure of Japanese cypress. It is precisely this simplicity, however, that so stirs the faith among the Japanese.

▼**Imperial Messenger to Ise Shrine**　At the forefront is a female member of the Imperial House. The robes of the entourage are fashioned according to those worn at court until 120 years ago.

HARMONIZING WITH NATURE

Earthenware, called Jomon ("rope print") after its decorative patterns, began to be used in Japan some 10,000 years ago. What appear to be the prototypes of the Japanese and their language also fall within the Jomon period: 10,000 B. C.~300 B. C.

Some of the pottery of mid-Jomon times has decorative flame-like shapes that seem to leap as if in praise of the might of heaven and earth, suggesting that for the people of the period, pottery-making was also a way to express a heightened artistic awareness.

A temperate climate has long made the Japanese view nature as a giver of blessings. Harmonizing with nature and becoming one with it is a feeling that lies at the root of Japanese spiritual life.

▲**Earthen Mask** It was probably used at rites invoking the earth's bounty.

▼**Restored Pit Dwellings** They were dug to a depth of about 50cm.

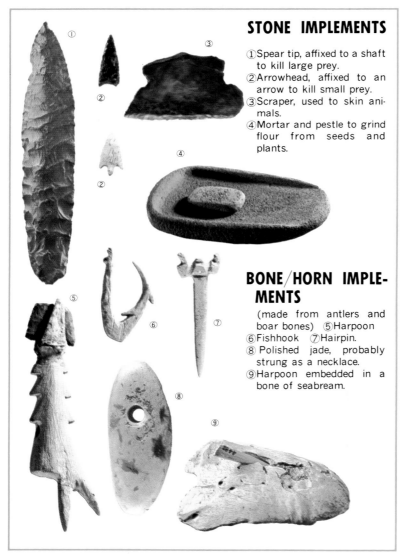

STONE IMPLEMENTS

①Spear tip, affixed to a shaft to kill large prey.
②Arrowhead, affixed to an arrow to kill small prey.
③Scraper, used to skin animals.
④Mortar and pestle to grind flour from seeds and plants.

BONE／HORN IMPLEMENTS

(made from antlers and boar bones) ⑤Harpoon ⑥Fishhook ⑦Hairpin.
⑧ Polished jade, probably strung as a necklace.
⑨Harpoon embedded in a bone of seabream.

One of the oldest pieces of Jomon earthenware.

Sculpture-like pottery from around 5000 B. C. with elaborate ornamentation suggestive of flames. It may have been used as a storage container for precious grains.

* In an age when life was always exposed to nature's dangers, a simple faith in magic was practiced for self-protection and good harvests.

▶ A clay figure in a human-like form was probably thought capable of warding off evil spirits. Tablets and stone idols were used for similar purposes.

▼ **Skeleton** The classic posture for burial in the Jomon period, with arms and legs folded. Theories abound as to why.

13

FARMING-BASED GROUPISM

The technique of wet-rice cultivation came from China and Korea around 300 B. C. Although hunting continued, the onset of farming made life more settled and regular crop production changed Japanese life. Because rice cultivation required more of a group effort than hunting, a more closely-knit social order was necessary. Consequently, the farming culture was the basis for the Japanese tendency to collective action.

Concurrently from China and Korea came metalware of bronze and iron. Bronzeware was mainly used for religious rites, whereas iron was used for making tools.

Earthenware went from the rough vigor of the Jomon epoch to a simpler design. These two tendencies later formed the Japanese aesthetic sense.

The Yayoi period (300 B. C. ~ 300 A. D.) is named for the Tokyo site of the discovery of its pottery. The intrinsic character of Japanese culture flourished as the beliefs, customs and folkways of this period's predominantly agricultural society spread.

▲**Yayoi Earthenware**   First unearthed in Yayoi, Tokyo.

▲**Aqueduct Remains**   A waterway that ran between two rows of wooden supports. (Toro, Shizuoka prefecture)
◄**Pit Dwelling Remains**   Built atop mounded earth. Small center holes were for posts. (Toro)

▼**Reconstructed Pit Dwelling**

◄**Bronze Sword**
A widebladed sword made in Japan for ceremonial use.

►**Bell-shaped Bronze**
Many were buried in small groups in mountains and elsewhere away from settlements, perhaps as treasures to be hidden and saved from marauding groups.

Stone and Bronze Tools

①Stone knife ②Stone ax
③-⑤Bronze spade. Unearthed
at sites in Fukuoka prefecture.

①

⑤

④

③

②

Wood Tools

Farm and everyday
tools from a site
in Toro.
①Rake
②Ladle
③Fire drill (base)
④Fire drill (bow)
⑤Footwear
⑥One-legged fold-
ing table

①

②

③

④

⑤

⑥

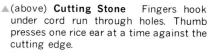

▲(above) **Cutting Stone** Fingers hook
under cord run through holes. Thumb
presses one rice ear at a time against the
cutting edge.

▲(below) **Fire Drill** Vertical motion of
the bar rotates the stick in the hollow of
the wood base to create friction and
flame.

▼Threshing scene depicted on bell-shaped bronze.

▼**Bronze Mirror** A symbol of the sun, not an object for
viewing one's face. A prized treasure held by a chief.
Lettering is visible
on the back.

Haniwa These figures of clay were placed around and atop the burial mound, probably as tableaus in clay of the life of the deceased.

BURIAL MOUND CULTURE

High-mounded graves that first developed in western Japan around 400 A.D. to serve as burial places for political administrators are called *kofun*.

The largest is the mound in Osaka for Emperor Nintoku. Its 486-meter length exceeds even the largest of the pyramids. It would have taken 1,000 workers a day four years to complete it. Only personages of powerful clans had the wherewithal to build such colossal tombs.

The mounds were surrounded by moats and topped with *haniwa* (clay figures of people, houses and animals).

In addition to the body, mirrors and ornaments were buried in the *kofun*. Equestrian paraphernalia increased as the eras evolved. *Kofun* interiors were likely regarded as belonging to the afterlife.

Around the 5th century, characters for writing, called *kan* (China) *ji* (letter) were introduced from China. Many express meaning through form, such as "川" for river or "木" for tree.

▶ **Restored Goshikizuka Tomb** Many of the old tombs extant today are covered with trees. Those in ancient times were entirely covered with stones.

Miko Interceded between man and heaven to convey divine will.

▶**Ear Pendants** Metal with complex design.

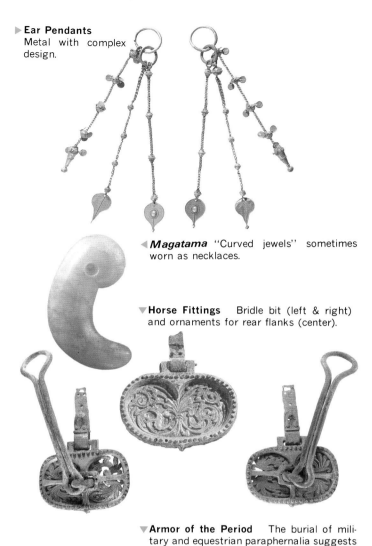

◀**Magatama** "Curved jewels" sometimes worn as necklaces.

▼**Horse Fittings** Bridle bit (left & right) and ornaments for rear flanks (center).

▼**Armor of the Period** The burial of military and equestrian paraphernalia suggests an age in which much fighting occured over unification attempts.

◀**Tomb of Emperor Nintoku** The largest tomb in Japan. It is square at the front and round at the rear. Other tombs come in cubes and domes.

◀**Decorated Tomb** Letters and figures in geometric patterns decorate the stone chamber walls. Many such tombs are found in Kyushu, southernmost major island of Japan.

BUDDHISM'S PROFOUND IMPACT

After its arrival in Japan from Korea in 538 A. D., Buddhism ignited a struggle among powerful clans. Victory by its supporters led to its rapid spread and the building of temples; Horyuji (temple) in Nara is a classic example.

Because Buddhism was the first systematic thought carried to Japan, it influenced all subsequent art, architecture, literature, technology and thought. Temples became centers of higher learning from the continent, and their architecture and statuary captured the hearts and minds of the Japanese.

▲ **Prince Shotoku**   The age's foremost Buddhist thinker to whom the erection of the Horyuji is attributed. A political reformer and regent to the first Empress, Suiko.

◀ **Aerial View of the Horyuji** the world's oldest wooden structure. A number of national treasures of Buddhist statuary and traditional crafts are housed here.

▲ **Miroku (a future Buddha)**   Seemingly lost in contemplation, its facial expression imparts a captivating sense of delicate gentleness. (Chuguji)

◀ **Buddhist Trinity of The Horyuji's Golden Hall**   The faint smile is referred to as "the archaic smile."

◀ Decapitated Buddha Though only the head remains, the robust but gentle-looking features exhibit great charm. (Kofukuji)

▲ Yakushiji Pagoda What appear to be six roofs are actually three due to an architectural technique called *mokoshi*. Pagodas were originally built to house relics of Shaka, the founder of Buddhism. Visible from afar, they now symbolize temples.

▲ Wall Painting at the Horyuji (Copy) Clearly shows artistic influences from Ghandara, Pakistan.

● Takamatsu Burial Mound

While ancient tombs in Japan show influences from China and Korea, differences among them also exist. Distinctive only to Chinese and Korean tombs is the presence of wall paintings depicting the lives of their rulers.

Decorated tombs do exist (see p. 17), but the decorations are extreme abstractions void of human representation. In 1972, however, a tomb was discovered in Asuka, Nara that has realistic wall paintings. The tomb is called the Takamatsu Burial Mound.

The paintings (see photo, right), show groups of men and women, plus animals that symbolize the deities of the four directions. The tomb also contains human remains, wooden coffins of lacquer overlaid with goldleaf, bronze mirrors and other items.

Direct influences from China and Korea are revealed by the artifacts and painting techniques. The tomb itself is thought to date from the mid-7th to 8th century.

THE NARA CAPITAL AND THE GREAT BUDDHA

In 710 A.D. Japan's capital was moved to Nara. Nara was modeled after an early Chinese capital; it extended 4.2 km east to west and 4.7 km north and south. Previous capitals were smaller. Nara was the first full-scale capital. The 70 or so years following its construction are called the Nara period.

Because the emperors of this period were devout Buddhists, Buddhistic culture flourished. The statue in the Todaiji is a classic example. Emperor Shomu built it in the hope of propagating Buddhism as a means in stabilizing the country. It is the world's largest statue of cast metal. Yet the Buddhism of this age stayed within the nobility and did not spread to the masses.

▲**The Todaiji Buddha** Wars and earthquakes damaged the original. Today's statue dates to the late 1600s and stands 14.9m (originally 16m).

▲**Lecture Hall of Toshodaiji** Once a part of government offices within the palace grounds. Despite considerable repairs, it is a good model of the original.

◀**Site of Former Palace** Excavated in the north-central part of the old capital. Yields include items of daily use. The site is now a public park.

▲**Todaiji**   The Hall of the Great Buddha is visible above the treetops.

▶ **Emperor Shomu**   He used the power of Buddhism to reign, built temples throughout the country and had the Todaiji and Buddha constructed.
◀**Zochoten**   One of the four protective deities of Buddhism.

▼**Unglazed Tableware**   Simple and unadorned.

THE SHOSOIN

A treasure house located near the Todaiji in Nara. Its three repositories (north, central, south), were built around 752 A. D. and house some 10,000 items. Many were the personal possessions of Emperor Shomu, while others belonged to the nobility of the Nara period. Still others came from abroad and attest to Japan's cultural contact with the countries such as China, India, Persia some 1200 years ago.

▶ **Temple/shrine register:** Lists descriptions, purposes and givers of gifts.

Treasures of the Shosoin

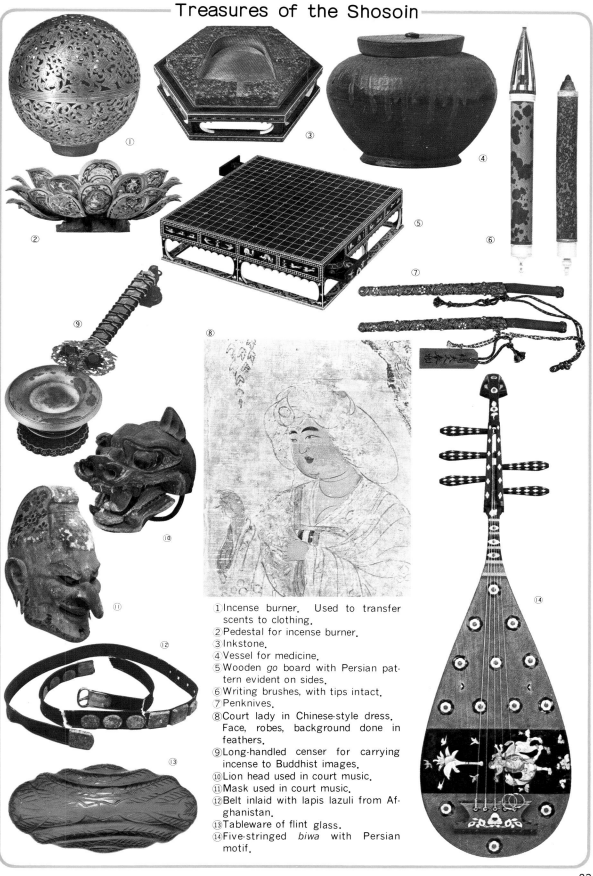

1. Incense burner. Used to transfer scents to clothing.
2. Pedestal for incense burner.
3. Inkstone.
4. Vessel for medicine.
5. Wooden *go* board with Persian pattern evident on sides.
6. Writing brushes, with tips intact.
7. Penknives.
8. Court lady in Chinese-style dress. Face, robes, background done in feathers.
9. Long-handled censer for carrying incense to Buddhist images.
10. Lion head used in court music.
11. Mask used in court music.
12. Belt inlaid with lapis lazuli from Afghanistan.
13. Tableware of flint glass.
14. Five-stringed *biwa* with Persian motif.

BEAUTIFUL OLD KYOTO

Though Buddhism in the Nara period was state-supported and Buddhistic culture flourished, serious abuses occurred when the religion grew so strong that it could exert influence on politics.

Emperor Kanmu therefore founded a new capital in Kyoto in 794 A.D. He named the capital Heian-kyo; he wanted peace (hei) and stability (an) permanently secured. Larger than Nara, it stretched 4.5 km east to west and 5.3 km north and south.

His dreams were not realized, however, as the political war between the nobility raged. Nevertheless, Kyoto continued to develop, and for some 1000 years held supreme authority as capital and cultural center of the nation. Today it is renown as a city of historic traditions, beautiful temples and as a mecca for tourists.

◄**Heian Shrine** Built in 1895 to commemorate the moving of the capital by Emperor Kanmu to Kyoto 1000 years earlier. Its architecture is adapted from a building that was once the capital's political hub.

▶**Marketplace in the Old Capital** There were two: one in the east sector, the other in the west.

▲**Government vs. Northeast Troops** Evidence that the Kyoto government had yet to control the entire nation.

▲**Security Forces in Kyoto** Units patrolled the streets to maintain law and order.

▲**Aoi Festival**   Held every May 15th, this famous Kyoto festival vividly recalls the splendor of the city's past.

●ESOTERIC BUDDHISM AND SECRET RITES

The excesses of the established Buddhist sects were curbed with the arrival on the religious scene of the two priests, Saicho and Kukai. Each had gone to China at the turn of the 9th century to study Buddhism, and upon returning had founded a new sect. Together the two sects, Saicho's Tendai and Kukai's Shingon, became the mainstream of esoteric Buddhism in Japan.

This type of Buddhism had had its start in 7th-8th century India and held that the most profound teachings of Buddha were to be found in secret rites. Through intense prayer, priests were to strive to establish a connection with the spirits present in the universe. To gain this ability to become one with creation required secluding oneself in serene surroundings in the mountains and practicing rigorous self-denial and austerities. Hence the epithet "Mountain Buddhism" was applied to this new school as opposed to the "urban Buddhism" of the older Nara sects.

Such acts of prayer designed to grasp the secrets of the universe contain simultaneously a very primitive aspect and a highly spiritual aspect, a dichotomy that is one of the characteristics making up the culture of Japan.

▶(above) **Mt. Koya**   Here Kukai built the Kongobuji as the headquarters of his sect. There are many esoteric temples deep in the mountains.

▶(below) **Enryakuji**   Saicho built this temple on Mt. Hiei as the head temple of the Tendai Sect.

THE LIFE-STYLE OF THE NOBILITY

The Fujiwara clan was of the nobility and had secured political power in Kyoto by intrigue, taking possession of major offices.

Accompanying their autonomy was the practice of giving their daughters in marriage to emperors as a means of appointing themselves to high positions.

In their disdain for war, nobles immersed themselves in formalities and rituals that required ornate attire. The nobility lived lavishly in this manner on huge incomes from their country estates. Its life-styles created the standard for elegance and culture.

The strong influence Tang China had once exerted during the Nara period was digested and Japanized into truly Japanese models as Japanese aestheticism and culture were fostered.

▲(above) **Temple Visits**   More was involved than religious piety, as such visits constituted the greatest recreation enjoyed by the nobility.

▲(below) **Playing *Go***   Court ladies compete to see who can cover more of the 361 places on the board with stones of their color, either black or white.

◄**Nobleman's Estate**   The manor (*shinden*) is connected by corridor to the family quarters and to those for retainers. A pond big enough for pleasure-boating is in the garden.

▲**Football**   A leather ball is kept in the air by kicking.

▲**Cock-fighting**   A spring ritual in which cocks are goaded into fighting.

▲Musical Diversion Nobles engage in pleasant conversation (above), while on the pond a boat carrying musicians glides by.

▼Noblewoman in Full Dress The wearer's taste was judged by the colors and hues of the layered clothing visible at the sleeve tips.

▲Phoenix Hall of the Byodoin This beautiful structure was built in Uji, Kyoto, by the Fujiwaras as a representation of what they hoped to find in the hereafter.

◀Nobleman in Full Dress A peaked hat, and a wood scepter to maintain dignity.

▲Nobleman's Carriage Shown here is one for the sole use of the Emperor, Empress or others of the highest rank.

THE WORLD OF *GENJI MONOGATARI*

Genji Monogatari (The Tale of Genji) is the most famous work of Japanese literature known abroad thanks in great measure to the English translation of Arthur Waley and, more recently, that of Edward Seidensticker. The original book was written in the early 11th century and contained 54 chapters. Its author was Murasaki Shikibu, a lady-in-waiting to the daughter of Fujiwara Michinaga, who was a high-ranking and powerful figure at court.

The story concerns the amorous adventures of Hikaru Genji, a handsome young noble of imperial descent. In the age in which the story takes place it was not the custom among the upper strata of the nobility to practice monogamy. Instead, a gentleman would visit his lover's house, or simply set up quarters for a lady who had taken his fancy and given her consent, and then call on her at nightfall. The life of Hikaru Genji follows the same pattern, but despite his romantic involvement with various ladies, he is unable to forsake past loves.

Monono aware, the dominant aesthetic that runs through the story, is what the Japanese identify as one of pathos, which expresses the feelings that arise from deep stirrings within the heart as we sense the transience of every event.

The original book was written in a Japanese script called *kana*—phonetic symbols developed by the Japanese based on Chinese characters. This is yet another reason for the important position the book occupies in the cultural history of Japan.

Inspired by the beautiful love story, many an artist has put brush to canvas so that there exists a whole genre of pictures based on the story, the so-called "Genji pictures."

◄ **Genji Shells** An indoor game enjoyed by the gentry. Made up of 54 sets of shells, and played by matching up halves or finding designated scenes.

► **Genji and Child** The child was born to Genji's wife but not sired by Genji. Though painfully aware of the situation, Genji determined to raise him as his own. The picture is from the *Genji Scroll*, painted in the early 12th century.

▲ **Murasaki Shikibu** The daughter of a provincial governor. She later became a lady-in-waiting at court, where her book *Genji Monogatari* proved popular. Fujiwara Michinaga, the most powerful man then at court, had Murasaki become tutor to his daughter, the Empress Shoshi.

▲ **The Aristocracy Amusing Themselves** A scene of members of the nobility enjoying the hospitality of the Emperor. Boats sail about the pond (above and below). At center left are two dancing figures. Painted between the end of the 16th century and the beginning of the 17th.

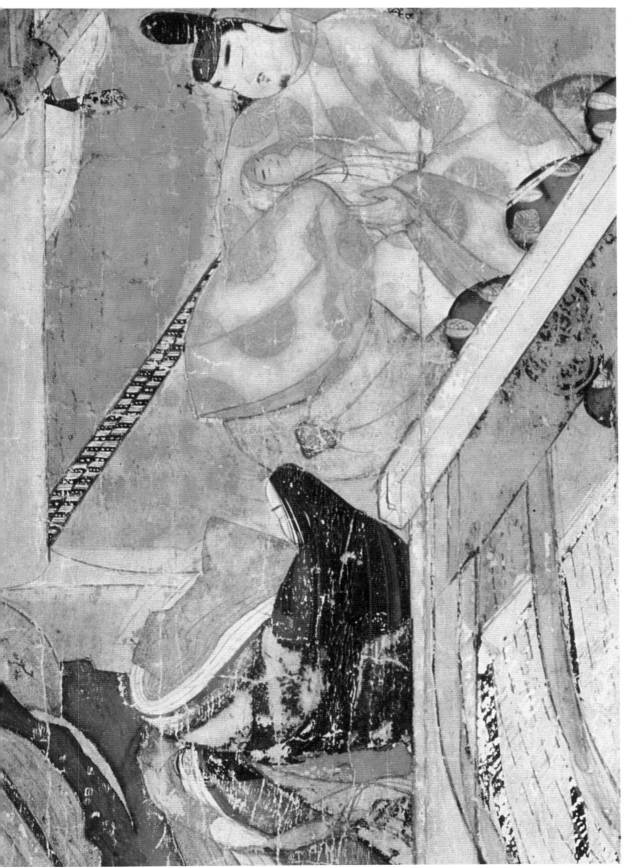

BUDDHIST STATUES

Buddhism is more of a philosophical system of thought centering on the principle of mercy than it is a religion. Its teachings center on how to solve or overcome the problems of life and death, and hold that all things change.

Statues of Shaka, the founder of Buddhism, are objects of worship, as are various other deities sacred to Buddhism. Over the centuries they have come to be stylized into various forms, as shown here:

① Nyorai——A manifestation of the enlightened Buddha.

② Bosatsu (Bodhisattva)——A deity in the process of becoming a Buddha (Nyorai). The highest of Shaka's disciples.

③ Tenbu——Deities in India prior to the advent of Buddhism. They subsequently became believers in and protectors of Buddhism.

④ Myoo——A deity empowered by Nyorai to overcome evil.

⑤ Rakan——Buddha's disciples and high priests.

Distinguishing which deity is which is no easy task. Even the positions and shapes of the arms, hands and fingers have individual significance. The only ones easy to identify are the Nyorai, for they are simply clad in one-layered garments and are unadorned with personal ornamentation such as crowns or necklaces. Having cast off all worldly possessions, they devote themselves wholeheartedly to ascetic practices, a sight that draws the sympathy and admiration of suffering humanity.

▶ *Yakushi* **Triad** This trio of Buddhist statues at the Yakushiji in Nara dates back to the 7th century. In the center in a sitting position is a Nyorai-type statue called Yakushi Nyorai, the healing Buddha. To its left and right are Nikko Bosatsu and Gakko Bosatsu, two typical bosatsu-style attendants. Often there are statues of Kannon (Goddess of Mercy) on both sides of a Nyorai statue, and the arrangement is called a triad. In the case of Yakushi Nyorai, however, Nikko and Gakko bosatsu always appear. Since Nyorai statues represent the enlightened Buddha they are unadorned and in simple dress. Kannon, representing Shaka (Buddha) in youth before enlightenment, has a crown and ornamentation.

31

THE RISE OF THE SAMURAI

The word *samurai* comes from a verb meaning "attend upon a noble." This the samurai did, serving and guarding them and fighting in their stead in wartime.

The provinces politically decayed while the nobles luxuriated in Kyoto. Leading families encroached upon neighboring lands and in some cases attacked government offices. As always, samurai were sent to restore order. Their power accordingly increased and they began to make their voices heard. Two particularly strong clans were the Genji and the Heike.

The two clans were rivals, and at one time the Heike actually curbed the power of the Fujiwara and seized control. However, because the Heike had made their headquarters in Kyoto, they themselves became effete and in turn were defeated by the Genji clan under Minamoto Yoritomo. Later, in 1192, Yoritomo established a military government in Kamakura which eventually ushered in an era centered on the warrior class rather than on the nobility.

▲**Early Warrior and Attendants**　The image of the fighting samurai is not yet evident.

▲**Battle in the Northeast**　This portion of the country was particularly powerful and unheedful of the central government. The Genji were sent to rectify that.

◀**Torching a Manor**　A power-struggle between the nobility and the samurai arose in the latter half of the 12th century. The Heike, led by Taira Kiyomori, were victorious and held control for 25 years thereafter.

▲**Itsukushima**   Refurbished and enlarged by Kiyomori to make it the patron shrine of the Heike clan. (Hiroshima prefecture)

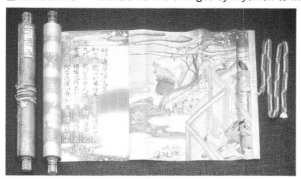

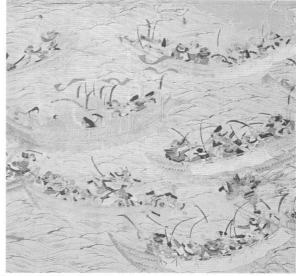

▲**Sutra**   Presented to Itsu-kushima shrine by the Heike in hopes of gaining glory for their clan. Though descended from samurai they followed aristocratic customs.

▶**The Fall of the Heike** The clan was overthrown by the Genji. Antoku, the 8-year-old Emperor of Heike descent, goes to his death in his grand-mother's arms.

▼**Hachiman Shrine in Kamakura**   Venerated by the Genji clan. Its sim-plicity contrasts sharply with the patron shrine of the Heike at Itsuku-shima.

▲**Minamoto Yoritomo**   Became Shogun after defeating the Heike and set up a gov-ernment in Kamakura,far from the Kyoto nobility.

ARMS AND ARMOR

Japanese arms and armor gradually developed in accordance with times and necessities.

For example, early Japanese swords were straight and only used for thrusting until they became curved in the 9th century in order to be used for slashing.

Full armors were perfected in the 10th century for protection of mounted commanders. Commanders also needed doublets and protectors previously used only by foot-soldiers, because in the 13th-14th centuries tactics of warfare intensified to group onslaughts by sword. European influences followed the introduction of firearms in the mid-1500s.

The Tokugawa reign was a 200-year war-free era that permitted extravagance to flourish; instruments of war were embellished in color, craftsmanship and fine design and became appreciated as works of art.

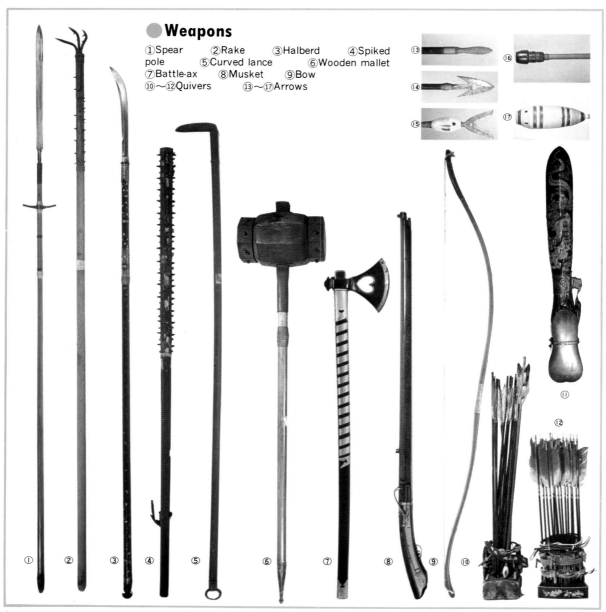

●Weapons
①Spear　②Rake　③Halberd　④Spiked pole　⑤Curved lance　⑥Wooden mallet ⑦Battle-ax　⑧Musket　⑨Bow ⑩～⑫Quivers　⑬～⑰Arrows

THE CULTURE OF THE WARRIOR CLASS

▲Preaching A priest delivers a sermon to those in search of salvation.

The Kamakura military established a government of acknowledged power, but culturally lacking the finesse of Kyoto.

Kamakura's culture evolved from its military's constant readiness, its pride, and its awareness that true power lay with them. The soldiers were virile and valorous; the city was teeming with activity and force which sharply contrasted with the grace and elegance that epitomized the Kyoto nobility.

The atmospheres of Kyoto and Kamakura respectively created the two currents that comprise the stream of Japanese aesthetics —the elegant, the quiet, the refined, versus the rugged and the vigorous.

Buddhism, too, went from complex dogma to teachings understandable to all, and in doing so became internalized and Japanized.

▲Yabusame Shooting at a target from horseback. Such competitions honed military skills. The contest can still be seen in Kamakura today.

▶Warrior's Home Plain in comparison with a nobleman's manor. Above the gate is a defensive fortification.

▲**Todaiji South Gate**　Done in Chinese style. The temple was destroyed by fire in fighting between the Genji and Heike clans, but was rebuilt in 1195.

▶**Laboring to Build a Temple**

◀**Shariden** of the Enkakuji Done in the Chinese *So* style with sharply curved roof edges.

▼**Mongol Invasion and the Kamikaze**　Mongol forces attacked Japan in 1274 and 1281. In the midst of each of the two battles a typhoon struck and delivered fatal blows to the Mongols. This *kami* (god) *kaze* (wind) convinced many that Japan was under divine protection.

▲*Ryutoki* A sculpture alive with the earthy humor of the commoners.
▶*Kongorikishi* In its powerful sturdiness this sculpture well symbolizes the vigor inherent in the culture of the warrior class.

▼*Suigetsu* **Goddess of Mercy** Buddhist statues invited intense prayer and faith, but until this one atop a dais of rocks appeared it was rare for one to project a sense of being at ease.

WABI-AESTHETIC IDEAL

Two cultures of Muromachi period: the sumptuous one exemplified by the Golden Pavilion (Kinkakuji) and the elegantly refined one exemplified by the Silver Pavilion (Ginkakuji). China and Zen Buddhism exerted a profound influence, the arts flourished and, along with industry and education, spread to the clergy and military under the autonomous rule of the warring *Daimyo*.

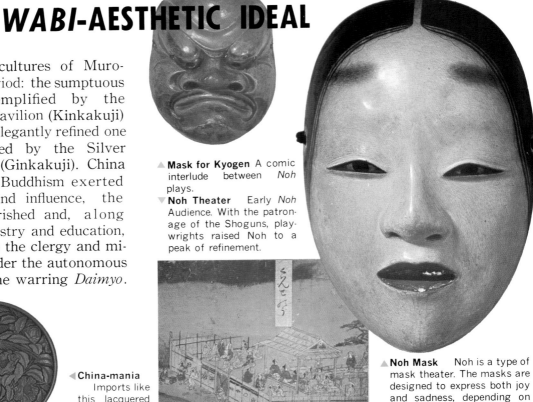

▲ **Mask for Kyogen** A comic interlude between *Noh* plays.

▼ **Noh Theater** Early *Noh* Audience. With the patronage of the Shoguns, playwrights raised Noh to a peak of refinement.

◄ **China-mania** Imports like this lacquered tray were highly prized.

▶ **Noh Mask** Noh is a type of mask theater. The masks are designed to express both joy and sadness, depending on the requirements of the scene.

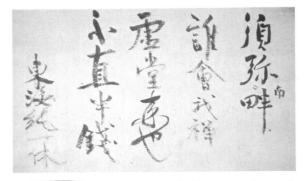

▲ **Five-Temple Literature** refers collectively to the copious output of writings by Zen priests (mainly of the Rinzai Sect) which, during the Muromachi period, contributed much to the literary arts and learning. (writing of Priest Ikkyu.)

◄ **Celadon Porcelain from China.**

▲ **Kinkakuji** Destroyed by fire in 1950: rebuilt in 1955.
▼ The Ryoanji's roofed wall is made of oil-impregnated soil; thatched shingles of the overhang have been restored.

Flower Arrangement
Forms were laid down
in this period and in
vogue among all classes. (page in 1529
manual.)

▲Room used by Shogun Yoshimasa as a study.
▶**Ginkakuji** A chapel above,
a study below. Death halted
the Shogun's plans to gild it
with silver.

▼Eating habits and diet improved in this period. Daily
meals rose to three; foodstuffs
increased; culinary arts
advanced; Japanese cuisine
became fixed.

■ **Tea Ceremony** Implements range from whisks
to kettles. Choice Chinese
bowls were often used. The
system of appreciating
both the tea and the implements dates from this
period.

▲**Tea bowl from China**
▼**Ink Painting** Winter scene
from a scroll by Sesshu,
who Japanized the original Chinese technique.

▲**Maki-e** a unique Japanese art also
exported to China. (*maki-e* box
favored by Shogun Yoshimasa.)

▲**Chinese Kettle**

THE BEAUTY OF NOH

Noh, based on an old folk art and perfected in the 14th century, is one of the oldest traditional arts in Japan. It could well be called a kind of dance-drama performed through song and dance.

The Noh player speaks and chants his part, while scenic description is provided by a chorus of 8 or 10 persons. A story teller gives the story development, and there is musical accompaniment by one flute and two, sometimes three, drums.

Another of the singularities of Noh is its mask drama. Through the use of swift changes the performer can instantly transform from, say, a young woman to an evil spirit.

The central characters in a Noh play are not ordinary human beings. In some cases they are not human at all. Lost souls, crazed women, evil spirits, even plants and animals are some of the supernatural characters that stalk through this theater of the fantastic. Stripping away the veil of life's conventionalities, Noh reveals through dance the web of unfulfilled resentments behind the face of man, the crushing agony of the dark desires that smolder in the deep recesses of the human heart. It is, so to speak, a drama of human alienation.

Noh brims with deep insights into the human spirit. What we come to sense within its simplified expressions and symbolic movements is a highly esoteric awareness of beauty. More than just a traditional type of theater, Noh has about it much of the avant-garde.

▲▶ **The Noh Stage**   The Noh stage, unlike the standard pictureframe type in the West, allows for an audience on its left in addition to its front. Props are minimal, and scenery is a single pine painted on a backdrop. Performances take place towards the rear part of the stage to the accompaniment of a flute and various-sized drums. Story narrations are sung by chanters at stage right. Upper photo shows a scene from "Shakkyo Old Style", with two lions frolicking among the peonies. At right is a scene from "Kakitsubata", a play about a woman longing for her dead lover.

▲ **Takigi Noh**   Fire consecrated to the gods is made by burning *takigi* (firewood). *Takigi* Noh originally meant "Noh performances for the gods". Now it refers to outdoor performances by torchlight.

▶ **Noh Robes**   Elaborately designed and carefully made.

● Noh Masks

● Kyogen Masks

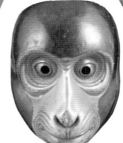

Ko-ushi
(old man)

Hannya
(devil)

Muko-zaru
(monkey)

Hana-hiki
(old man)

Fukure
(old woman)

Waka-onna
(young woman)

▶ **Kyogen Performance**   "Kyogen" literally means "deviant words". It is a farce-comedy performed between Noh plays. It sometimes makes use of masks. Pictured is a scene from "Hanago", in which a man boasts of having come to see his lover, not recognizing that the person in night–clothes is actually his wife.

ZEN AND MEDITATION

Zen, as a way for Zen Buddhists to attain spiritual enlightenment, is a practical method of soul-searching that stresses the practice of meditation. To sit in meditation, and through the stilling of the mind to try to grasp the truth of the universe (the nothingness of the absolute) is by no means restricted to Buddhists or priests. Practitioners include business people, athletes, and many people in other lands.

Zen's fundamental teaching is that in the pursuit of truth one must not rely on words. That is, truth transcends the limits set by rational thought, so one must grasp truth directly through meditation. Since man has a latent intuitive power, the object of meditation is to rouse it by turning the mind over to its unconscious, involuntary actions.

Japanese priests who studied Zen in China brought it to Japan in the 12th-13th centuries where it spread mainly among the military class. Japanese culture's strong preference for the meditative and the silent is due greatly to the influence of Zen. Stone gardens, ink paintings, the tea ceremony, and flower arrangement are all cultural heirs of the Zen spirit. Often-heard complaints that the Japanese are not logical in what they say or that it is difficult to tell what a Japanese is thinking may well be attributed to the many points on which Japanese thought harmonizes with the spirit of Zen.

▲**Dogen** Zen teachings were brought to Japan by Eisai and Dogen in the 12th and 13th centuries.

▶(above) **Monks in Meditation** Done once in the early morning, once again in the evening. When concentration falters, a trainer (*jikido*) strikes the monk's shoulder sharply with an oakwood pole to correct him.

▶(below) **Novitiates Clean the Temple** Cleaning and cooking are important practices in the search for enlightenment.

44

▲**Ink Painting**   Nature's grandeur is captured by simple ink-shadings. Ink paintings reflect the Zen spirit of quiet and meditation. (Ama-no-Hashidate by Sesshu; early 16th century.)

▼**A Rock Garden**   Gardens that liken stones to mountains and islands, sand to seas, are, like Zen, seeing the world in a grain of sand. (Daiseninshoin, Kyoto)

▲**Zen Monks Seeking Alms**   Chanting sutras while making the rounds of homes to solicit alms is an important part of training for monks.

45

PUBLIC ENTERTAINMENTS

Towns had mainly flourished around seats of the government. But in the 15th-16th centuries towns in their true sense formed through the commerce and industry of their inhabitants. Burghers were merchants who enjoyed self-rule in these towns. These bourgeois began or revived the Doll Festival, the Star Festival, the Gion Festival of Kyoto, and created much of the liveliness of contemporary town life.

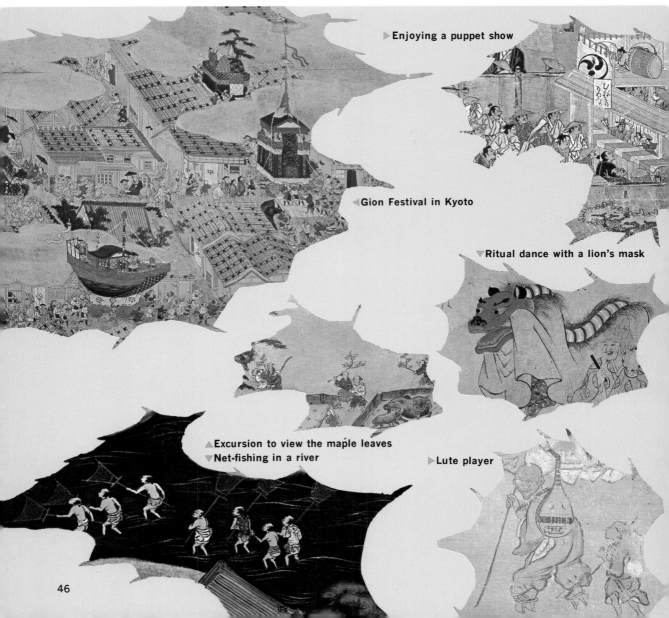

► Enjoying a puppet show

► Gion Festival in Kyoto

► Ritual dance with a lion's mask

▲ Excursion to view the maple leaves
▼ Net-fishing in a river

► Lute player

●Fairy Tale Books

Easy-to-read, illustrated books for the bourgeois. Books prior to the 15th-16th centuries were only for nobles, clergymen or samurai. These delightful animal, ghost, or success stories form the basis for many of today's well-loved nursery tales.

▶Scene from a tale about a sparrow.

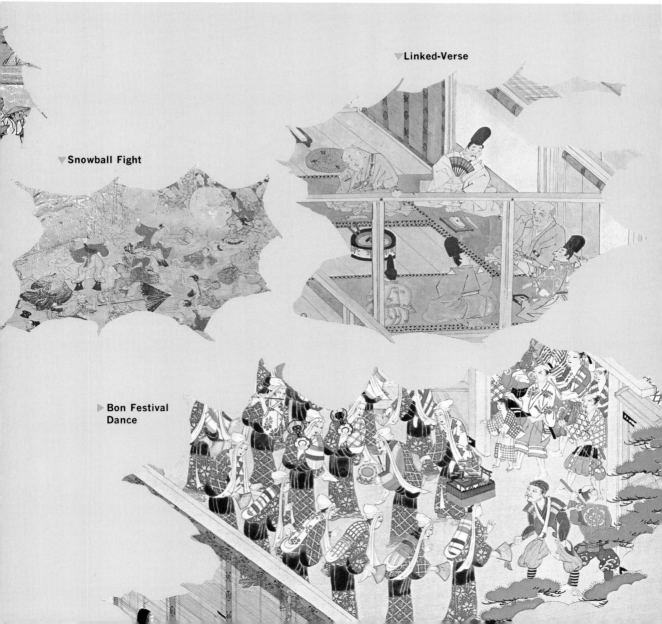

▽Linked-Verse

▽Snowball Fight

▶Bon Festival Dance

CURRENCY
OLD AND NEW

⑪Keicho Koban   1601; model for later koban
⑫Bunsei Nibukin   1818 ⑬Tenpo Nishukin   183.
⑭Bunsei Isshukin   1824 ⑮Keicho Ichibukin   160
⑯Tenpo Ichibugin   1837 ⑰Meiwa Nishugin   177
⑱Kaei Isshugin   1854 ⑲Meiwa Gomonmegin   176

NAME	DATE ISSUED (A.D.)
①Wado Kaichin	708 Oldest silver coin
②Wado Kaichin	708 Oldest copper coin
③Kaiki Shoho	760 Oldest gold coin
④Jingo Kaiho	765
⑤Kaigen Tsuho	621 From China; model for later coinage
⑥Taikan Tsuho	1107 From China
⑦Eiraku Tsuho	15th C.; From China
⑧Kanei Tsuho	1636
⑨Tenpo Tsuho	1835
⑩Ibanashisen	1860 Directly from its cast

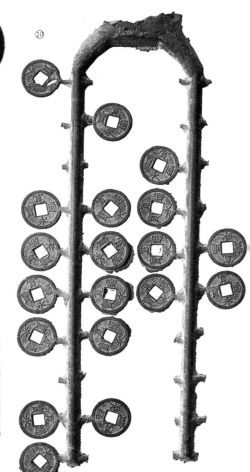

48

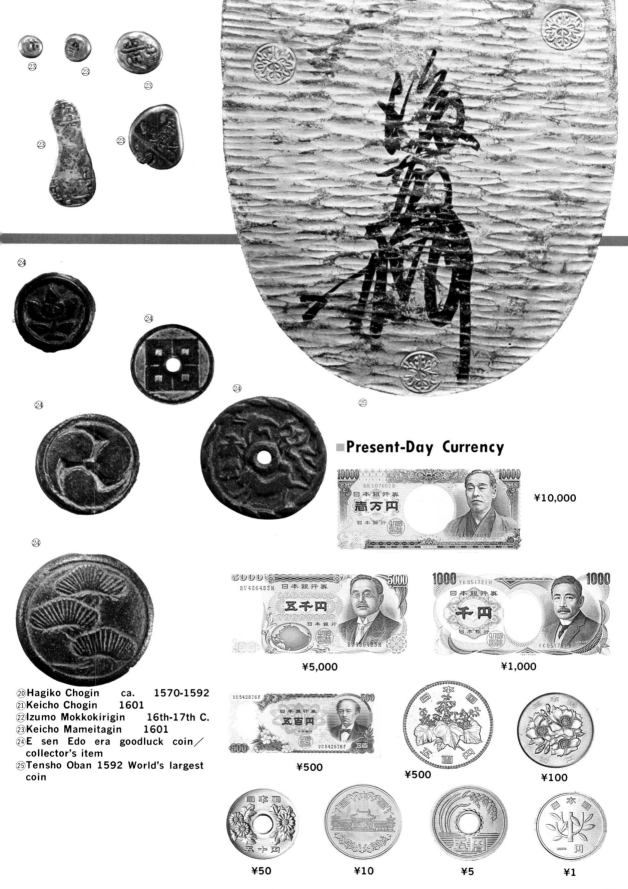

■Present-Day Currency

¥10,000

¥5,000

¥1,000

¥500

¥500

¥100

¥50

¥10

¥5

¥1

⑳Hagiko Chogin ca. 1570-1592
㉑Keicho Chogin 1601
㉒Izumo Mokkokirigin 16th-17th C.
㉓Keicho Mameitagin 1601
㉔E sen Edo era goodluck coin/
  collector's item
㉕Tensho Oban 1592 World's largest
  coin

Courtesy of Bank of Japan／Fuji Bank／Sanwa Bank／Tokai Bank

ENCOUNTERS WITH THE WEST

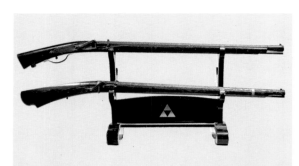

Muskets Called "Tanegashima arms" after the place of their introduction by the Portuguese. Domestic make (top). Portuguese make (bottom).

Musket Manual Marksmanship followed the introduction of muskets, and students received confidential manuals. (Inatomi School)

The European prominence began in the 16th century when a Chinese ship with Portuguese aboard shipwrecked at Tanegashima in southern Kyushu in 1543. The event had great impacts on Japan.

First, trade was started, for other Portuguese and succeeding Spanish ships anchored on Japan's coasts. Next, firearms were introduced.

Muskets brought by the Portuguese were welcomed as a new type of weapon which quickly spread among daimyo (feudal lords), and necessitated changes in warfare as well as castle construction. Finally, St. Francis Xavier made Christianity known in 1549. It spread rapidly. Some trade-minded daimyo protected its propagation while others, the so-called "Christian daimyo", even became converts.

New elements were thus added to the culture of Japan, though they did not necessarily survive intact. Indeed, Japan's 200 year policy of seclusion 90 years later so cut it off from the world that by the mid-17th century even the muskets were gone. A re-introduction of Western culture had to wait upon the forcible opening of the country in the latter half of the 19th century when Commodore Perry arrived.

St. Francis Xavier

"Temple" Interior Christian churches were referred to as "temples of the southern barbarians". They were built in Kyoto, Yamaguchi and elsewhere.

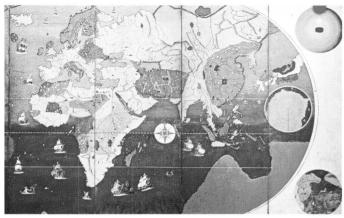

Folding Screen A number of pieces of *namban* (southern barbarian) art have survived and are valuable sources for historical research. Visible in the above painting are missionaries in clerical garb and black porters.

◄**World Map** The fact that many folding screens like this were made attests to the heightened Japanese awareness and increased knowledge of lands abroad. Although copied and enlarged from a map obtained from a European, this screen is surprisingly accurate.

●EUROPEAN INFLUENCES

European culture brought many a change to Japanese life. One such was the performing of surgery at hospitals attached to the church. Furthermore, European printing presses were imported and books were printed in Roman letters.

◄**Saddle inscribed with Roman letters**

▼**Gunpowder container with Portuguese motif**

▲*Tale of the Heike* in Roman letters

MISSION TO ROME

In 1582 three Christian daimyo (Otomo, Omura, Arima) under the urging of Fr. Valignano sent a mission of four young men to the Pope in Rome: Ito Mansho, Chijiwa Michael, Hara Martino, and Nakaura Julian, all 13-14 years old. They arrived in Rome three years and two months later to a tumultuous reception by the Pope and city. In 1590 they returned to Japan. The ruler at that time, Toyotomi Hideyoshi, summoned and had them perform some Western music for him, but since Christianity was by then proscribed, the four could not use the knowledge they'd gained abroad and led the remainder of their lives in obscurity.

THREE LEADERS OF THE SAMURAI

Feudatories waged fierce wars with one another from the late 1400s to the early 1600s, an epoch now known as the Era Of The Nation At War.

Because no one among the military was powerful enough to subdue the country for him, the emperor became but a symbol.

The incessant warfare of this epoch caused injustice to prevail; law and order decayed; the strong preyed upon the weak. Conversely, they were also vibrant times when abilities could be used to the fullest.

Order from the chaos was achieved by the power of three warriors: Oda Nobunaga, his vassal Toyotomi Hideyoshi, and his ally Tokugawa Ieyasu. They quelled the upheaval and made the country one.

The attributes these leaders displayed are highly admired by today's Japanese top management: Nobunaga was of stern temperament, but open to new ideas; Hideyoshi was well respected by his men as a student of human nature; Ieyasu was commedable for his long-suffering and endurance, regardless of the adversity.

▲Oda Nobunaga

▲Toyotomi Hideyoshi

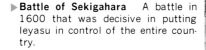
▶Battle of Sekigahara   A battle in 1600 that was decisive in putting Ieyasu in control of the entire country.

▲Ieyasu takes to the field astride his black mount.

▲ Battle of Nagashino Here in 1575 Nobunaga allied with Ieyasu to fight the Takeda army. The battle is famous for Nobunaga's clever use of matchlocks. Lining up his men in three ranks he had each row fire in turn, thus devastating the enemy.

▲ The Siege of Osaka Ieyasu slew Hideyoshi's son Hideyori when he attacked Osaka in 1615. This event broke the last resistance to the Tokugawa's, ended the age of war, and ushered in the era of the Tokugawa Shogunate.

OPULENT ART OF MOMOYAMA

In his later years, Hideyoshi built and lived in Fushimi Castle, Kyoto. This move inspired what later was called Momoyama culture. Its aura of grandeur and opulence reflected the tastes of the newly-risen daimyo who had succeeded to power as well as wealthy merchants.

Flowers, birds and even Chinese lions were painted in rich bold colors on goldleaf folding screens or heavy sliding panels to adorn castles or the homes of the military. Numerous screens depicted people enjoying such contemporary Japanese pastimes as shrine or temple observances, excursions to view the cherry blossoms or outings to enjoy the autumn leaves.

Distinctive to the arts of this era is their magnificent grandeur which sharply contrasts with the mental serenity so highly valued in Zen or Noh.

◀ **Kodaiji _Maki-e_** The temple was erected in memory of Hideyoshi by his wife, Kita-no-Mandokoro. It is renowned for its _maki-e_ (a design made by applying sprinkled powder of gold or silver to lacquer while it is still damp)

▼ **Maple Panels** A classic example of large-paneled work on gold lacquer. The varied hues of autumn leaves are shown at their zenith, with emphasis on the maple.

Chinese Lions A folding screen attributed to Kano Eitoku and said to have belonged to Hideyoshi. Its opulent ethos is typical of Momoyama art.

Maple-viewing at Takao A forerunner of folding screens that depicted customs in vogue during the Momoyama era. Takao was (and is) a place near Kyoto noted for its fall leaves. Those who went to admire them included the military, the clergy and the townsfolk.

Early Kabuki Performance The first Kabuki was originated by women of easy virtue. One of the performers is shown wearing a crucifix.

CASTLES

Castles were originally strongholds against enemy invasion. Crude fortifications of stones piled one atop another on the slopes or tops of high hills were of course known from ancient times, but it was not until around the 15th century that the word *shiro* (castle) was brought into use.

In the 15th-16th centuries when internal warfare raged throughout the country, most castles were situated on hilltops for the obvious purpose of making attack difficult. After the 250 years of internal warfare were finally brought to an end, a major change in the nature of castles took place. Rather than being a place for waging war, they became a means of maintaining peace by securing themselves as administrative hubs which governed the people within their territories. Castles thus descended the mountains and became centers of communication which promoted castle towns.

The focal point of a Japanese castle is its *tenshukaku*, or what in the West would correspond to a keep. This towering, uppermost section of the castle was not only a symbol of the power of the daimyo who resided there but it also served as a symbol of the castle town. As such, it could be—and often was—artfully decorative. At present there are only 12 original *tenshukaku* remaining in Japan.

▼**Himeji Castle** Completed in 1610 when castle architecture was at its peak. Variations in the roof patterns create a beauty of their own.

▶**Matsumoto Castle** Built in the early 17th century. Its darkness makes it conspicuous against the whiteness of the snow. In the far distance are the Japan Alps.

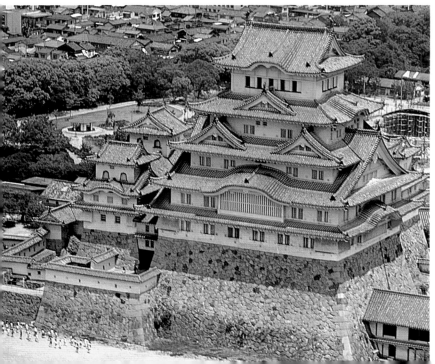

TEA CEREMONY AND FLOWER ARRANGEMENT

The tea ceremony and flower arrangement, both influenced by Zen Buddhism, are classic examples of how everyday things in life can be elevated to an art. The tea ceremony, begun in the latter half of the 15th century, was perfected a century later by Sen no Rikyu, and today it is called *chado*. It is, simply put, no more than the making of *matcha* (powdered green tea) for a guest. It is, however, an artistic accomplishment that distills the beauty of life in its multi–faceted forms, and demands the utmost mental attitude and manners. The spirit underlying the tea ceremony is that of discovering beauty in the commonplace things of everyday life, taking the plain and simple as a principle.

Utter simplicity also governs the etiquette, utensils and décor.

Flower arrangement is another artistic accomplishment arising from daily life. It developed into an art form in the late 15th century. It is, on the surface, no more than simply arranging flowers attractively in a vase or other receptacle, as people anywhere in the world might do. However, to lovingly prolong the beauty of the fleeting life of a flower is also to bring about renewal in the heart of the arranger. Nature and the arranger thus become one, expressing therein a harmony between heaven, earth and humanity that is, in essence, the true art of flower arrangement (ikebana).

▲**Sen no Rikyu**　The 16th-century perfecter of the tea ceremony, still regarded as the greatest of the tea masters.

▲*Akaraku* **Tea Bowl**　One of the bowls favored by Sen no Rikyu. Like this one, tea bowls are simple but have something deep.

▲*Myokian-Taian*　A tea hut built by Sen no Rikyu in southern Kyoto. Although the tea room is small (3.3m²), Rikyu enjoyed its rich spiritual atmosphere.

▲Tea Ceremony Detailed rules govern tea ceremony etiquette and movements. Depicted here is the return of the cup to the host after the guest has finished drinking.

▲Tea Hut Exterior Tea huts are usually made of plain wood. The path outside the entrance is laid with stepping stones. (Sankeien, Yokohama)

▶ Tea Implements A proper tea ceremony requires implements as these shown. Antique or hand-made utensils are treated like valuable objects of art.

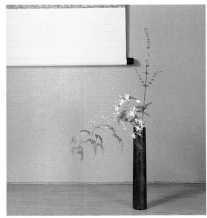

◀Flower Arrangement
(above) Flowers arranged in the *tokonoma* (alcove) of a Japanese house. Arrangements for tea ceremonies are simple.
◀(below) Table piece for a Western-style house.

▲ Flower Arrangement Students Like the tea ceremony, flower arrangement is best done on *tatami* (mat) flooring. Nowadays it is often done while seated on a chair, and people abroad are showing increasing interest.

THE AGE OF THE SHOGUN

Tokugawa Ieyasu quelled the internal warfare, unified most of the country, and in 1603 became shogun, establishing his government in Edo (now Tokyo). This Edo-based shogunate lasted some 265 years and is called the Edo period.

Japan was divided into some 300 fiefs, each headed by a lord. These lords (daimyo) were required to live every other year in Edo. The idea was to force each daimyo to expend huge sums on travel and the maintenance of two estates so that he would be unable to accumulate the economic wherewithal to oppose the shogun. Wives and children always remained behind in Edo, much like hostages.

Since there were no major battles in this era, vassals could no longer demonstrate their loyalty to their lord under actual fighting conditions. To buttress the concept, a form of conduct arose whereby loyalty could be demonstrated. In extreme cases responsibility was assumed through hara-kiri if, for example, the lord died of illness or the vassal fell into disfavor. Such a moral code of loyalty and honor was called *bushido*. However, few samurai performed harakiri, and the shogunate soon issued a proclamation prohibiting it.

▼**Daimyo and Retinue**   On various occasions, especially on the way to or from a compulsory stay in Edo, the daimyo would form a huge procession of vassals to display his authority.

◀ **Yomei Gate at Nikko Shrine**
Ieyasu was enshrined in Nikko upon his death but the shrine itself was built in the time of his grandson Iemitsu (the third shogun). In the architecture of the gate the vestiges of the grandeur of Momoyama art are particularly evident.

▲ **Drawing of Edo Castle** The original built by Ieyasu was destroyed in a fire. What remains is now part of the Imperial Palace.

▶ **Martial Arts** Warriors at outdoor practice. In the warless Edo period, stress was put on the cultivation of the mind and the attitude towards the sword and bow rather than on prowess in them.

THE CLOSING OF THE COUNTRY

The shogunate banned Christianity as being harmful to feudality while it simultaneously connived at its dissemination because it promoted trade. However, its suppression was later intensified and all missionary work forbidden when English and Dutch Protestants warned the government of the Spanish and Portuguese Catholics' territorial ambitions. In 1641 relations with all countries were cut off except for trade with Holland and China at Nagasaki. This reaction not only severed the influx of Christianity, but also gave the government a monopoly on trade. Japan incubated its indigenous life-style and culture in the succeeding 200 years of seclusion.

▲ **The 26 Martyrs** Crucified in 1596, these converts and missionaries became the church's first martyrs in Japan. All were later elevated to sainthood by Rome.

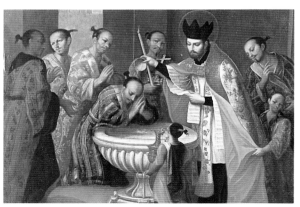

▲ (Above left) **Trading Ships (Shuinsen)** Such ships plied among the nations of S. E. Asia prior to the closure of the country.

▲ (Above right) Japanese warrior, Hasekura Tsunenaga, baptized at Rome before the edict closing the nation.

◄ **The Shimabara Revolt** Both the land and people of the Shimabara region were poor. The peasants sought salvation in Christianity, but the local lords suppressed it and imposed heavier taxes. In 1637 the peasants rioted, entrenched themselves in Hara Castle and inflicted heavy damage on the attacking armies.

▲**Virgin Mary** Believers who had only pretended to renounce Christianity made and worshipped statues of Mary in the likeness of Kannon, the Buddhist Goddess of Mercy, and were called "hidden Christians."

▶**Dejima** A tiny man-made islet in Nagasaki harbor where the Dutch conducted trade and from which they were forbidden to leave.

◀▶***Fumi-e* Plaque and Procedure** People had to tread on an image of Christ or Mary. To hesitate or refuse meant guilt.

▼**Trade at Dejima** All trade with Holland was conducted here.

▲**Temple Registry** Those whose names were unlisted were suspected of being Christians and arrested.

PEASANT-BASED WORK ETHIC

The Edo era's warrior class controlled the peasant class which constituted 80% of the population.

Peasants were harshly treated. Warriors demanded that 50% to 60% of their harvests be yielded as annual taxes. If one family in a group of five could not pay, the others had to balance the difference. This is a good example of the warrior class making use of the Japanese tendency toward groupism.

The government, for its part, directed detailed edicts at the peasants: "Divorce a luxury-loving wife, even if she be comely." "Rise early, work late." "Make simplicity your cloth."

High taxes and land rent forced the peasants to labor long and hard on small plots. Harvests were directly tied to how hard a person toiled, and most work was done by hand. Such a heritage has been a major source of Japanese industriousness.

●RICE-GROWING

▲**Transplanting**　Seedlings are set out in the paddies, usually in June.

▲**Harvesting**　A collective effort that begins in fall.

▲**Annual Taxes**　Taxes levied on the village are carted off to storage.

▲**Farmhouse Interior**　A well-to-do farmer's house of the early 18th century contained a hearth around which the family sat doing indoor chores.

▲**Peasants at Play**　Harvest festivals provided one of the few non-working days available to peasants and were celebrated with much eating and drinking.

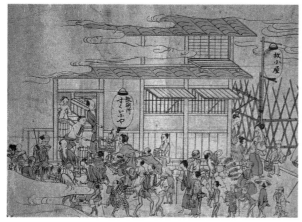

▲**Soup Line** Peasants at the mercy of the weather were at times beset by misfortune. When there was no rice to eat, authorities made and distributed gruel.

▲**Farmhouse Yards** Peasants labor in a Kyoto village.
◀**Rice Riot** In times of poor harvests peasants demanded reductions in rice taxes; poor townspeople plundered rice shops in retaliation for exorbitant prices.

●EDUCATION FOR THE MASSES

There was no national educational system in the Edo era. However, various educational systems for commoners did exist. One such arrangement was the temple school. All over the country, teachers (priests, warriors, doctors) used temple facilities to teach groups of 20-30 students. The number of schools rose sharply around the mid-1700s. By the end of the era they reportedly reached some 15,000, a surprising figure when compared with today's 25,000 primary schools under the compulsory school system. Practical courses of reading, writing and calculation were taught.

For the children of the military class, there were schools on each fief. To develop the right mind-set, emphasis was initially put on the Chinese classics since their aim was to produce able administrators. Later, other subjects deemed useful to the clan were added: mathematics, medicine, Western studies, military science, etc. The shogunate had its own schools, which later formed the nucleus for Tokyo University.

▶(above) **Temple School** Play-minded scholars have a lesson.
▶(below) **Clan School** This one in Yamaguchi prefecture educated many of Japan's 19th century leaders.

A TALE OF THREE CITIES
(EDO, OSAKA, KYOTO)

Cities and castle towns were established nationwide from the latter half of the 16th century to the turn of the 17th. The three most populous—Edo, Osaka, Kyoto, known as "The Big Three"—were under the direct control of the government.

Edo, the government seat and political center, devoted some 60% of its area to districts for the warrior class. Hordes of merchants catered to their needs. By the 18th century, Edo's one million people made it the largest city in the world.

Osaka was the collection site for taxes and the clearinghouse for goods. It had a population of 350,000, an active money-lending business, and scores of business tycoons.

Kyoto had the court, a resplendent culture and approximately 400,000 people. It was the production center for high-grade weaving and crafts.

▲**Nihonbashi in Edo**   The first Shogun reclaimed this part of the coast and built this bridge. It marks the point from which all distances were measured.

▶**Festival in Kanda**   Dates from the Genroku era and is a source of pride for its inhabitants. Revelers carrying a portable shrine proceeded into the castle grounds for the Shogun's amusement.

▼ **Interior of Moneychanger's Shop**   Eastern Japan centered on Edo and used gold. But western Japan centered on Osaka and used silver. Brokers facilitated currency exchanges. Also in use were copper coins of small denominations.

Trading Ship This type of ship ran along the coast between Edo and Osaka. Cargo consisted mainly of cotton, oil, vinegar and sake.

◀ **Messengers** Hikyaku (runners) carried letters, documents and messages between distant places. The 560 km separating Edo and Osaka required one week.

▲ **Osaka Waterfront** The mouth of the Aji River was a busy terminus for the great shipping activity between Edo and Osaka.

▶ **Kyoto Pleasure-dome** The *Sumi-ya* in the Shimabara district. Once at the top of Kyoto's night life, it now is preserved as a cultural structure.

▼ **Kyoto Street Scene** Included are (right) a rich merchant's home, and (left) an umbrella maker's, a lacquerware shop and a writing-brush shop.

GENROKU BOURGEOIS CULTURE

From the late 17th century to the turn of the 18th, the Japanese economy surged; and townsmen, in the course of spending their money, created a colorful culture called Genroku (1688-1703).

Such an affluent burgeois culture was a new, unique phenomenon. It flourished primarily among the middle-class of Kyoto, Osaka and its vicinities.

The common people now ventured into literature and art. There were writers like Ihara Saikaku, Matsuo Basho and Chikamatsu Monzaemon who gained popularity for portraying people realistically or writing boldly of love.

Art, too, brimmed with a sumptuousness that reflected the liberal spending power of the prosperous bourgeoisie.

▲**Kabuki** An escalation in popularity in this era made it the top entertainment of the townspeople. Audiences ate and drank while enjoying the performances.

▲**Matsuo Basho** A grand master of *haiku* poetry who refined it to an art.
▲(right) **Ihara Saikaku** Wrote about money and sex.

▼**Katsura Rikyu (Detached Palace)** A pinnacle in Japan's landscape gardens. Built in 1620 for Emperor Goyozei's brother Prince Toshihito. Taut, a German architect, promoted its fame abroad after a 1933 visit.

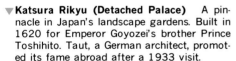

▲*Mikaeri Bijin* By Moronobu. An original painting, not a *ukiyo-e* print.

Irises Decorative folding screens were greatly prized by prosperous merchants. Ogata Korin, the painter of this one, was born into the family of a well-to-do cloth merchant and is famous for his freshness of design.

Wind Deity Right side of a folding screen (left shows the deity of thunder) painted by Tawaraya Sotatsu. The grand scale probably appealed to the wealthy merchants.

● Genroku at a Glance

Genroku culture arose particularly from the lively enterprising towns-people of Kyoto and Osaka. Frugality conceded to an extravagance visible in every facet of their lives.

▼ **Short-sleeved Kimono with Fall Flowers on White Cloth**

▶ **Mt. Yoshino Painted on Tea Jar (Nonomura Ninsei)**
▼ ***Maki-e*-style Writing Box with Arched Bridge (Honami Koetsu)**

▲ **Decorative Comb**

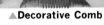

▲ ▼ **Hairpin**

KABUKI AND BUNRAKU

Noh, Kabuki and Bunraku are the major traditional performing arts. Noh developed in the latter half of the 14th century as entertainment for the shoguns and the military caste, whereas Kabuki and Bunraku developed from the 17th century as entertainment for the masses.

The essence of Kabuki can be found in the beauty of its traditional Japanese dancing. Accordingly, in its performance much stress is placed on stylized movements. Kabuki plays have a story, stage settings, musical accompaniment and dialog for the actors. The scenery and costumes, however, are eye-catchingly elaborate, and the actors' gestures and deliveries are highly exaggerated. As opposed to theater in the West, which is more or less grounded in realism, Kabuki tends to deal with the imaginary world. As in opera, Kabuki devotees enjoy the performance or interpretation of a particular actor in a particular role.

Perhaps Kabuki's greatest distinctness is its male enactment for both male and female roles. Kabuki was originally performed exclusively by females until allegations of morally disruptive behavior impelled an all-male cast.

Bunraku is a kind of puppet theater. A *tayu* (male reciter) is seated on a revolving dais next to the puppets' stage. A *shamisen* player sits by him. The tayu chants the narration and all the puppets' lines as the shamisen is played. Stories and plots mainly treat such themes as the love-vs.-duty conflicts that arise from the contradictions inherent in a feudal society. The movements of the dolls are synchronized with the melodious, deep-toned strumming of the shamisen and reciting. The dolls, about one meter (3 feet) tall, require three operators each. The first manipulates the head and right arm; the second operates the left arm, and the third operator manipulates the legs and feet. Although incapable of altering their facial expressions, the dolls are so skillfully manipulated to express emotions ranging from grief to laughter that they seem to be imbued with the very breath of life, much to the delight of the audience.

Stage with *Hanamichi* A raised runway that cuts through the audience on the left to join the stage at a right angle. It heightens the sense of audience participation.

Kabuki Makeup The actor's face is made up with *kumadori* paint to highlight the character, in this case the violent and powerful nature of a demon.

▲ *Oyama* Kabuki is performed entirely by male actors. Those who play female roles are called *oyama*, and outdo women in expressing stylized concepts of femininity.

▲Stage Properties The Kabuki stage uses a variety of props. The huge toad would certainly be a surprise to any first-timer.

▲Striking a Pose At a peak moment in a performance an actor will strike an exaggerated pose (*mie*). This brings on audience applause and the yelling out of the actor's stage name by aficionados.

▲Bunraku Doll A scene from Chikamatsu's Joruri, *The Love Suicide at Sonezaki.* The dolls express such subtle emotions that they seem imbued with life.

▼*Tayu* and *Shamisen* Player The *tayu* narrates the story; the player provides the musical accompaniment. Both are to stage left.

▲Dolls and Operators One doll requires three operators. The assistant operators wear black masks, but the chief operator is sometimes bare-faced.

MARTIAL ARTS AND SUMO

The strategy in combative sports in Japan is to passively take advantage of an opponent's power by making it work against him.

The principal technique of the martial arts is that of pulling: the tugging of one's opponent in judo, the pulling motion on the sword in kendo, the pulling actions in karate, etc. It is supposedly the same motion used when tilling a field with a hoe. It is also contrary to the Western approach of charging aggressively forward: the lancing of the sword in fencing, the thrusting of the fists in boxing, etc. The latter motion is used by men and animals when they fight.

Judo, kendo, archery, karate and other Japanese martial arts were originally to protect oneself from personal attack. Later they developed into disciplines of the mind and body under the influences of Buddhism and Confucianism. These martial arts thus possess both a physical, practical aspect —the techniques and methods of defense —and a spiritual aspect—ethics and morals. As in all sports, martial arts teach the meaning and importance of fair play, loyalty, and honor. They have now come to be enjoyed like most other sports.

Japan's national and most popular sport is sumo. In olden times, sumo was associated with the art of divination; the winner's village was supposedly favored with a good harvest.

Nowadays, sumo is a sport only. Over the past two decades a handful of foreign participants have climbed into the sumo ring, and two of them, Takamiyama, and Konishiki, natives of Hawaii, attained high sumo ranks.

▲**Sumo Arena**　A display of wrestlers gets underway in the ring prior to the day's bouts at Tokyo's Sumo Wrestling Amphitheater. 15-day tournaments are held six times a year.

▲**Sumo Match**　Two wrestlers vie in each bout. The loser is the one pushed out first or who touches any part of the ring with any part of his body other than the soles of his feet.

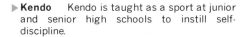

▲**Kyudo** The archer learns to respect and understand his limitations and potentials.

▶**Kendo** Kendo is taught as a sport at junior and senior high schools to instill self-discipline.

▲**Karate** A combative technique that uses no weapons. It is generally believed to have originated in Tang China, but some theories favor Korea or even Okinawa.

◀**Judo** Judo is another form of unarmed combat, differing from karate in that it employs throws and holds whereas karate uses hands and feet. Judo originated in Japan, but is now a worldwide sport. Since the 1964 Tokyo Olympics it has been a regular Olympic event.

KASEI CULTURE AND UKIYO-E

From the mid-1700s to the beginning of the 1800s, the economic center of the Edo era gradually shifted from the Kyoto-Osaka area to Edo. The cultural capital accordingly re-established in Edo. This relocation marked a new cultural era called Kasei, for it combines two eras that comprise it: Bun*ka* (1804-1817) and Bun*sei* (1818-1829).

Kasei culture penetrated beyond the prosperous middle classes of the Genroku era to the lower classes. Books therefore began employing simple sentences written in the vernacular; they were illustrated and frequently focused on humorous themes.

Ukiyo-e prints became popular and expanded beyond images of actors and beautiful women to include landscapes. It is from this period that much of popular culture springs.

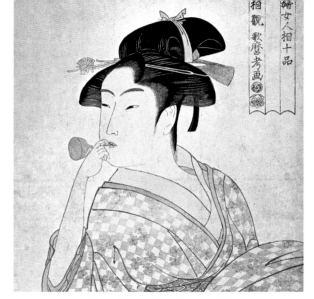

▲**Woman with Glass Toy** By Kitagawa Utamaro, famous for his prints of beautiful women. Early ukiyo-e prints were done in one color or two but by this period many colors were used.

▶**Akasaka Stage of the Tokaido** The artist, Ando Hiroshige, was the foremost portrayer in ukiyo-e of Japanese-style landscapes.

▼**The 47 Samurai** The story of a lord whose conduct brings on his forced suicide (*harakiri*). Later, his vassals slay the instigators. This 1702 event was performed as a kabuki play in 1748 and remains a favorite tragedy since it appeals to the sympathy traditionally shown to unfairly treated people who die tragic deaths.

▲**Electric Generator** Hiraga Gennai, an inventor, repaired this generator obtained from a Hollander and succeeded in making it work. A budding scientific spirit was astir in the era.

▲**Actor** In bold strokes, Sharaku captured an actor's personality.

▶**Wave at Kanagawa** Hokusai's originality of expression influenced even the French impressionists.

◀**Ryogoku Area** Aodo Denzen studied Western art and became proficient in the depiction of perspective.

▶**Hippocrates** "The Father of Medicine" by Watanabe Kazan, a student of Dutch learning.

●Personal Possessions of the Townspeople

People in the Edo era owned things of a rather extravagant nature. Made by the hands of expert craftsmen they are precious in contrast to the mass-produced items of today.

▲*Inro* A pill box worn at the sash.

▶**Lantern** Thin paper outside, a candle within.

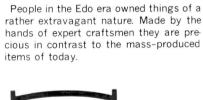

▲**Smoking Needs**

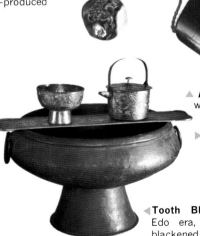

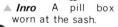

◀**Tooth Blackener** In the Edo era, wives commonly blackened their teeth.

JAPANESE GARDENS

The Japanese have a great fondness for gardens, stemming perhaps from a sense of having lived in harmony with nature for so long. They tend to fill any open spaces on their plots with trees or plants no matter how small these spaces may be. At the same time as the Japanese seek the quiet repose of nature in a garden, they also try to create there a kind of universe in miniature. This practice goes as far back as the Heian era when nobles incorporated into their gardens the imagery of a perfect world (paradise). Later, in the Kamakura and Muromachi eras, Zen priests created rock gardens in which stones were likened to mountains or Buddhist images, sand to oceans, and so on.

There are of course many gardens enjoyed solely for their natural beauty. In the Edo era (1603-1868) feudal lords often built huge rambling gardens for strolling in, some of which survive today in the form of public or private parks.

Garden construction reflects the Japanese ideal of beauty. Japanese gardens differ from Western gardens in that the former, instead of symmetrical, orderly arrangements, prefer more abstract, natural ones that display nature's many facets as they are, emphasizing unbalanced gracefulness.

▶**Kenrokuen**   Used to be the garden of Lord Maeda, whose fief in Kaga yielded the largest amount of harvest excluding that of the Tokugawa shoguns. From the early 17th century to the early 19th, repeated expansion and restoration made the garden what it is today. It is an excellent example of the strolling-type of garden. The pond in the center and the stone lantern nearby present a scene of beautiful harmony in their covering of snow. (Kanazawa, Ishikawa pref.)

▲**Ritsurin Park**　Formerly the garden of Lord Matsudaira, ruler of the province of Takamatsu in Shikoku. Clusters of stones form islands in the six ponds spanned by gracefully curved wooden bridges. (Takamatsu, Kagawa pref.)

▲**Shugakuin Detached Palace Garden**　Built in the late 17th century for Emperor Gomizunoo at his Kyoto villa. Incorporates court refinement.

▲**Zuisenji Garden**　The original, built in the middle of the 14th century, was long neglected until restored in 1970. The pond was created by excavating the foot of a hillside. (Kamakura, Kanagawa pref.)

Daisenin Garden A mid-16th century Zen garden in Kyoto, part of the one on p. 45 lower right. White sand represents a large river and two islands.

Korakuen Once the garden of Lord Ikeda who ruled the Okayama fief. Completed in 1701, it is one of Japan's top three gardens.

TRADITIONAL HOUSES

A traditional Japanese house is made of wood and paper, and provides good ventilation. The essential structure is of wood.

The sliding partitions are called either *fusuma* (a solid paper partition on a wooden frame), or *shoji* (a paper-windowed partition on a wooden frame). They are miscalled "doors" by Westerners; actually, they are a kind of room divider.

Susceptibility to fire is a drawback for such houses, but their suitability to Japan's humid summers and their resiliency to earthquakes are definite advantages. The fact that the Horyuji, a 7th-century wood structure, is still standing, says much for the excellence of wood as a building material.

The biggest difference between Western and Japanese houses is probably in the concept of rooms. In Japan, rooms are divided by the afore-mentioned *shoji* and *fusuma* and have no locks. Also, each room can function as living room, dining room, or bedroom, and removing the *shoji* or *fusuma* partitions results in one big room. In comparison with a Western house, where each room is independent and has but one function, the Japanese house is multi-functional in construction and highly versatile. The adaptability of a Japanese house likely accounts for the West's misconception that a Japanese cannot maintain any privacy at home and is afforded little personal independence.

In the past few decades, houses built of concrete have increased in number, but the touch of wood is something the Japanese are unwilling to forsake. Most of the interiors of concrete houses are consequently of wood, even if it is only wood paneling.

▲**Former Nara Family Home**   Built in the latter half of the 18th century. The roof, as befits a house in a farming village, is thatched, but spectacularly so. A rich farmer's house of the first rank in the northeast. (Akita prefecture)

▲**Nara Home Interior**   The special parlor where relatives gathered at such times as New Year's to exchange formalities with the family head. *Shoji* to the left, *fusuma* to the right, *irori* (a hearth) is in the center. *Tatami* flooring is unusual for a room with *irori*.

▲**The Osumi Home** Late 17th-century home of upper-class merchant built along a main road in Shiga prefecture. It served as both a pharmacy and a lodging house for daimyo. The woodwork under the eaves is especially noteworthy.

▲**The Kometani Home** A mid-18th century merchant's home in Imai, Nara prefecture. The walls were stuccoed and windows kept few as a precaution against fire. Imai is a famous town of old merchant homes.

▶**The Toyoda Home** Merchant's house built in the latter half of the 17th century. A big crest of a tree adorns this home of Edo era lumber dealers. The second-story lattice-work is decorative. (Imai)

▼**The Sasagawa Home** The family, major landowners in the Niigata plains and the Edo era's major rice producers, also served as village officials. They thus adopted features of military-class homes such as the entryway construction to the left.

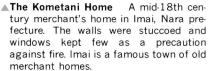

MODERNIZATION-CUM-WESTERNIZATION

Despite its massive importation of Chinese culture in earlier epochs, Japan never lost its Japaneseness. What was imported was not always adopted, and what was adopted was nearly always adapted or Japanized to suit Japanese life. Continental culture was considered important but not the absolute standard.

Accordingly, in the 19th century when Western imperialism was on the march and came knocking on Japan's gates in the form of Commodore Perry in 1853, Japan had only to look at China being carved up by the Western powers to realize that the only way to save itself from the same fate would be to end its 200-year policy of seclusion, open its doors to the West, and again import, evaluate and adapt. The process, however, was often limited to the outward forms and manifestations of Western civilization rather than its spirit which, being based on a long tradition of Christianity, was unsuitable for the Japanese to absorb.

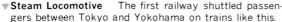

▲**Rokumeikan Ball** To show the West that Japan was equally modern, the government constructed this building to hold balls to which the entire diplomatic corps was invited.

▼**Steam Locomotive** The first railway shuttled passengers between Tokyo and Yokohama on trains like this.

▶ **Rickshaws** Made in the late 19th century, they soon became popular.

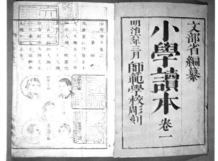

▶**1870s Primer**

●Objects of Interest

Interest in things foreign ranged from items of daily use to Western-style clothes.

▲ **Brick Building** Few remain in today's Tokyo.

◀ **Barber shop** To abandon the traditional topknot for a Western-style cut was a mark of a cultured man.

▲ **Stein**

◀ **Mantle Clock**

▲**Lamp**

THE DAWN OF MODERN CULTURE

Japan's Westernization was too rapid to be anything but superficial. Old temples were suddenly considered worthless; pagodas that today are national treasures stood in danger of being torn down; ukiyo-e prints, looked upon as mere craftwork, were disposed of like so much wastepaper. Indeed, the first to recognize their value and preserve them were the art historians of the West.

A counterreaction against this rapid Westernization set in around 1887. It was not so radical as to draw the nation back into its isolationist shell, for the Japanese appreciated Western civilization's strengths. It was instead a stabilizing period Japan needed in order to harmonize the Japanization of Western adaptations with existing Japanese traditions. The fusion of the two created a new modern culture.

Western techniques in art, for example, were applied to Japanese themes; Western music was introduced into school curriculums, and similar advances were made in the natural sciences.

▲*MUGA* (selflessness), by Yokoyama Taikan

▲*ROEN* (old monkey), by Takamura Koun, who created modern, realistic works using Japanese techniques of wood carving.
◄*HIBO KANNON* (Merciful Mother) by Kano Hogai

▲ *BUGI* (Dancing Girl) by Kuroda Seiki
◀ *"Japanese* Woman" by Ragusa, an Italian sculptor invited to Japan to teach at a college of fine arts.

◀ **Meiji Era**   Japan's Westernization occured mainly in the large cities. Elsewhere, basically little changed from the previous era except perhaps hairstyles.

● WESTERN STYLE ARCHITECTURE

Western architectural concepts were rapidly introduced. Though initial results were an irregular intermingling when blended with Japanese architecture, full mastery was eventually achieved with the help of foreign technicians.

▲ **Residence of Saigo Tsugumichi**

▲ **Former Akasaka Detached Palace**   Now used as a state guest house.

THE PACIFIC WAR AND ASIANISM

Following the opening of the country, top priority was given to strengthening the nation, and European systems were enthusiastically incorporated to that effect; thus Japan became the first Asian nation with a modern constitution and parliament.

But this governmental achievement encouraged unfavorable actions. Japan's successes emboldened it to invade a weakened China in the 1920s. Japan thereafter believed its destiny was to liberate Asia from the yoke of Western imperialism, so set out to dominate Asia under the motto "Asia for the Asiatics". This led to the Pacific War in December, 1941. By this time the Japanese were unable to stop the rampant militarism of its war machine, and paid for that inability in the atomic bombing.

Japan rid itself of every vestige of ultranationalism after its defeat. It started afresh as a democratic state, constructing a cultural and economically-based nation.

▲The rising sun flag floating high in Singapore

▲**Tokyo in Ashes** Repeated bombings, especially the major one in March, 1945, left Tokyo in ruins.

▲**Wartime Citizens of Tokyo** Aerial bombings were intensified from the end of 1944 and air-raid drills became more frequent.

▼**Wartime Civilian Garb** Steel helmet on the back was worn during air raids.

▲**Women's Wartime Wear** Baggy pants (monpe) were worn instead of banned skirts. The hood was for air raids.

A Practical Guide to
THE LIVING TRADITIONS OF JAPAN

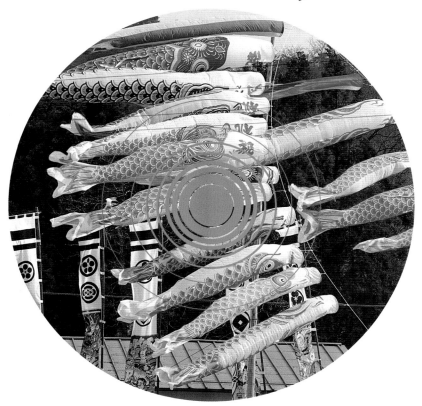

JAPANESE RITES OF PASSAGE

The hope of having a healthy and happy life is a universal one that remains unchanged from ancient times.

Upon reaching each of life's milestones, the Japanese give thanks for arriving thus far and ask for future blessings through prayer. The most numerous rites of passage are those arising from the wish of parents for the healthy growth of their children.

The figures for life span during the 1890s were 42.8 years for men and 44.3 years for women; the infant mortality rate was high. Therefore it is not surprising that so many celebrations exist for a child's safe transition from one stage of life to another. Japan's most colorful ritual is the wedding ceremony. Customs differed from locality to locality until about 200 years ago, but presently either Buddhist, Shintoist, or Christian weddings are performed. Common rituals throughout the country are given here.

▲**First Shrine Visit** Boys are taken 30 days after birth, girls 31. As a rule the mother's family provides the finery, and the paternal grandmother carries the baby.

▲**Shichi-Go-San (7-5-3 Festival)** Girls three and seven, and boys five, dress up in new outfits on November 15th and visit shrines to pray for their safe and healthy future.

▲**Starting School** The school year begins in April. Parents usually accompany their children to the entrance ceremony.

▲**Coming-of-Age Day** On January 15th, a national holiday, those who have attained the age of 20 are recognized as adults. Towns and villages sponsor various events.

◀**Wedding Ceremony** A peak among life's many rites of passage. The average age for the groom is 27, for the bride 23. Most weddings are conducted according to Shinto rites, but there are also Buddhist and Christian services. There are some 730,000 weddings each year and 180,000 divorces.

▶**Wedding Reception** The actual wedding is witnessed only by the go-betweens and the parents and relatives of the bride and groom. The reception that immediately follows is attended by the above and invited guests and lasts two to three hours.

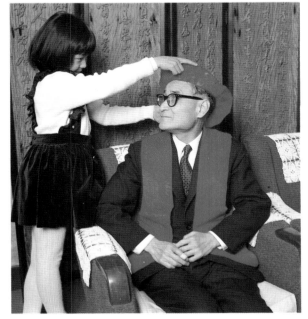

▲*Kanreki* A celebration for those who attain their 61st calendar year. It marks the completion of one full cycle of the Ten Calendar Signs and the Twelve Zodiacal Signs so that a person figuratively enters a ''second childhood''. To celebrate, a red cap and vest (*chanchanko*) are worn.

▲**Funeral** Weddings mainly follow Shinto rites, but funerals are mostly conducted according to Buddhist ritual. Only 10% are performed along Christian or Shinto lines. Undertakers handle arrangements, and Buddhist priests conduct religious services.

ANNUAL EVENTS

The fact that the Japanese are able to keep alive so many traditions is due in good part to the various celebrations that take place throughout the year. One such observance—the year's biggest—is New Year's, which lasts from January 1st to 3rd.

Preparations start getting underway toward the close of the old year. Government offices, private businesses and industries begin closing down around the 29th of December. There then follows a mass exodus from the cities as people stream back to their home towns, overloading every available means of transportation in the process. Meanwhile, homes are thoroughly cleaned inside and out so that the New Year will get off to a fresh start; pine branches are arranged at the front gate or door, sacred straw festoon are hung, and traditional foods to be eaten during the holidays are prepared. On New Year's Eve, many families sit down to a bowlful of a long, slender-type of noodle as a symbolic wish for a long life.

At midnight, temples throughout the nation slowly ring their bells 108 times in order to expiate what Buddhism considers the 108 inherent evil desires one must rid oneself of to live a wholesome life. Many people go to temples or shrines on the following days to pray for health and prosperity.

At home they enjoy traditional foods (*ozoni*) and amuse themselves with one or another of the many New Year's games. Children, meanwhile, receive gifts of money called *otoshi-dama* in traditional envelopes from family and relatives.

▲ *Kadomatsu* These decorations of pine and bamboo adorn both sides of entryways at New Year's. Pine and bamboo symbolize longevity.

▲ **Battledore** Decorated paddles keep aloft a shuttlecock with a tiny bell affixed to it. A classical New Year's game for girls that is gradually disappearing.

▲ **First Prayer** People go to shrines to pray for a good year. Some buy paper fortunes there, as these young ladies have done.

▲**Kite-flying** Flying kites used to be a popular activity for boys at New Year's. However, the decrease in open areas and the proliferation of telephone lines have placed this traditional pastime in danger of disappearing.

▲**Kaki-zome** The year's first formal writing with a brush, usually on January 2nd. Students are often assigned this as homework to improve their writing. Here it is done at a shrine, though home is the usual place.

●KARUTA AND HYAKU-NIN-ISSHU

Karuta and *Hyaku-nin-isshu* are typical indoor games enjoyed during the New Year holidays. *Karuta* takes its name from a game introduced from Portugal in the 16th century. The game itself has since become thoroughly Japanese. It is played with a deck of 100 cards divided into 50 with pictures and 50 with short phrases or proverbs on them. The picture cards visually depict the ideas expressed on the word cards, and are laid out faceup on the playing surface in random order. From the stack of 50 word cards a reader draws and reads aloud one card. The other players then vie to see who can first take up the picture card that corresponds to the verse. The person with the most cards at the end of the game is the winner.

Hyaku-nin-isshu is similar to *karuta*. On the cards, however, are poems by famous poets from the 7th to the 13th centuries. Word cards have the entire poem plus a likeness of the poet. The matching cards bear only the concluding verse. When the reader begins to read out the first lines of the poem, the players recalling the ending verse try to be the first to locate and take that card.

In the eras when the 100 poets were active it was conventional for the nobility and upper classes to quote poetry in their conversations and correspondence. Skill at this for both men and women was a barometer of how cultured they were. A more suitable game to evoke the elegant atmosphere of those bygone days would be hard to find. Some of the card sets are beautiful enough to be called works of art.

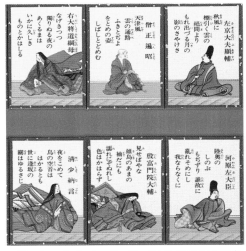

▲ *Hyaku-nin-isshu* **Cards** Each card has on it a poem from ancient times and a likeness of the poet.

▶*Hyaku-nin-isshu* **game** As shown by these players in old court attire, this play-at-home game is also enjoyed at shrines during New Year's.

Many events take place throughout the year. Some are celebrations that now occur only in limited regions, although the ones given here are common events observed nationwide.

One celebration that probably differs from those abroad is *Kodomo-no-Hi*, Children's Day (May 5th). Originally an old traditional ceremony to mark the growth of a son, May 5th was not officially designated a national holiday until after the Second World War. The fact that a day exists solely for children suggests the degree to which family life in Japan is child-centered, as opposed to the more adult-centered family in the West. Other red-letter days include Mother's Day (the second Sunday in May) and Father's Day (the 3rd Sunday in June.)

▲**Setsubun** The day before the first day of spring (by the old calendar), either the 3rd or 4th of February. People throw parched beans within the home to drive demons out and bring good fortune in. The day is also observed at temples and shrines.

▼**Hina-Matsuri (Doll Festival)** A March 3rd fete to wish girls happiness. Court dolls are displayed at home and special food is eaten. Peach trees are in bloom at this time, so it is also called "Peach Festival".

Flower Festival April 8th, Buddha's birthday. Temples observe a ritual in which sweet tea (symbolizing the birth bath) is poured over small statues of Buddha.

Boy's Festival May 5th has long been the day for boys. Military dolls are displayed so that boys will grow up to possess the Japanese ideals of manhood.

Hana-mi From late March to early April the cherry blossoms bloom and people hold parties with picnics and merrymaking beneath the boughs at night as well as in the daytime to welcome the coming of spring.

Koi-Nobori (Carp Streamers) These cloth streamers, flown on and around May 5th, express the hope that sons will be as vigorously healthy as the carp that swim against the stream. May 5th is also called Kodomo-no-Hi (Children's Day) because it is now celebrated for girls as well.

93

▲**Tanabata**　A July 7th star festival, Chinese in origin, to celebrate the annual tryst of Altair and Vega, stars separated by the Milky Way. People decorate bamboo branches with paper ornaments and prayer cards, and place them in the garden or hang them from eaves.

▶**Shopping Mall Tanabata**　Commercialization has made tourist attractions out of some shopping districts.

▲**Fireworks Display**　Fireworks extravaganzas are held in most localities on July and August nights.

▲**Bon Odori** The week around July 15th (August 15th in some areas) is called *o-bon*, a time for consoling the spirits of the dead. Neighborhood groups gather for dancing (*odori*) to the music of flutes and drums.

▲**Cemetery Visits** The spring and fall equinoxes are times for remembering ancestors. Because of such religious awareness, the Japanese faith is sometimes referred to as "ancestor worship".

◀**Maple Viewing** Autumn's counterpart to spring's cherry-blossom viewing. The custom is especially noticeable in Kyoto, where there are many places renowned for autumn maple leaves.

▼(lower left) **Chrysanthemum Dolls** Mums are about as Japanese as cherry blossoms. Dolls crafted from them are a common sight in fall. Themes are often taken from Kabuki.

▼(lower right) **Battledore Fair** At the end of December, fairs selling New Year goods are held at shrines. Paddles sold are often for decoration, not actual use.

THE IMPERIAL INSTITUTION

Except for the period of national consolidation from the 4th through the 7th centuries, the emperors of Japan have almost never held political power and therefore have rarely been directly involved in political strife. This peaceful image and the aura of historical tradition and sanctity surrounding him have firmly embedded the concept of the emperor as the focus of unity in the minds of the Japanese people.

Under state-fostered Shinto from the time of the Showa Emperor's grandfather, and in the period prior to World War II when ultranationalistic thought swept Japan, the Emperor was called a "living man-god" and the nation treated as one family with the Emperor at its head. In 1946, however, the Showa Emperor renounced this mystique of divinity, and under the present constitution has become a symbol of the unity of the people.

From the historical perspective, the imperial institution has been maintained through the hereditary transmission of religious authority. Festivals and rites for bountiful harvests were ritualized and institutionalized, always with the emperors acting as high priests. The system thus had its beginnings with the emperor acting as the head of a primitive state in which his prayers determined courses of action. Vestiges of this role can still be seen today in the ceremonial transplanting and harvesting of rice that the Emperor performs within the palace grounds each year.

The personal name of the Showa Emperor is Hirohito. His ascension to the throne took place in 1926, which made him the longest-reigning emperor in the nation's history.

The recent demise of emperor Hirohito marks the end of the longest imperial reign in Japanese history. The new emperor, Akihito, is the 125th in the imperial line.

The new empress, Michiko, who is not of imperial birth, married Akihito in April, 1959.

The Emperor and Empress visiting a health clinic for mothers and children The imperial couple take delight in the welcome of the children. In the background is a collage of the seabed the children have made.

The new Emperor carrying out his official duties The new Emperor has declared to the nation that he will promote pacifism on the basis of the Japanese Constitution.

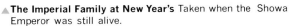
▲**The Imperial Family at New Year's** Taken when the Showa Emperor was still alive.

▼**The Present Emperor and Family** In April, 1959, the present Emperor delighted the nation when he married Shoda Michiko, who is not of imperial birth.

▲**Visiting a Home for the Elderly** The present Emperor and Empress are here accompanied by their youngest daughter, Nori-no-miya.

▲**Hiro-no-miya Inspecting a TV Studio** The youthfulness and unreserved manner of the Crown Prince have won him the affection of the Japanese people.

TRADITIONAL JAPANESE COOKING

When we examine the dietary life of the modern Japanese, we find an enormous diversity, with traditional Japanese cooking existing side by side with, and sometimes incorporating, cooking from around the world adapted to the Japanese taste. The gustatory preferences of the Japanese have clearly changed. Nevertheless, the special form and spirit of traditional cooking and dietary life remain deep-rooted.

We can distinguish three main features in traditional cooking. Firstly, premium is placed upon freshness and innate flavor, which are brought out to the full in the cooking. Secondly, the Japanese aesthetic sense is displayed in the arrangement of the food and in the choice of receptacles for serving it. A sense of season, a feeling for nature, and an eye for color are skilfully incorporated. Thirdly, Japanese cooking derives from a non-meat eating culture. The staple food is rice, with fish and vegetables forming the nucleus of the side dishes.

These features together form a harmonious whole and have made Japanese cooking what it is.

▲ A splendid harmony between the simplicity of the herring and the brilliant yellow of the dish.

▲ An elegant combination of the red, yellow, green, brown, and white of the food in a bowl suggesting the sun and the moon.

▲ A shrimp in the form of a chrysanthemum flower. Tranquillity within flamboyance.

◀ Cool and refreshing food in a clear dish. A masterly suggestion of summer.

A Historical Look at Japanese Cooking
● Shojin ryori (vegetarian cooking)

The Zen sect of Buddhism was spread in Japan from around the beginning of the 13th century by the efforts of two monks, Eisai (1141-1215) and Dogen (1200-1253), and a large number of Zen temples were built. The daily diet in these temples was vegetarian, and with the popularization of the Zen sect, *shojin ryori* (vegetarian cooking) permeated the eating habits of the people at large, partly because it was served at Buddhist memorial services.

Buddhist influence in Japan from early on had established the custom that meat was not generally eaten. *Shojin ryori* went to the logical extreme, derived as it was from Buddhist bans on the killing of living things and the consumption of alcohol. It became a virtue to be satisfied with simple, even coarse, food.

In *shojin ryori* vegetable protein, oils and fats are skilfully incorporated so that even from the point of view of modern dietetics, it provides a healthy well-balanced diet.

●Receptacles and the Arrangement of Food

It has often been said that Japanese cooking is "a feast for the eyes." It is to that extent that great care is taken in the choice of bowls and dishes, and the arrangement of food, as well as in the beauty of the food itself.

Dishes and bowls, in their color, shape and texture, should harmonize with, and enhance, the cooking. The food should look refined as well as delicious so that the color and shape of the bowls in which it is served must also be refined. The arrangement of the food takes into account both the season, and the harmony and balance of the food with the dishes to be used. A sense of space and suggestiveness should pervade the clearly-defined arrangement.

▲ Elegant pale blue porcelain contrasting with the bright red and white. An impression of balance between movement and stillness.

▲ The red maple is redolent of the quiet deep in the mountains, and the food suggests the autumn harvest.

◀ Ordinary ingredients go into making this food, served in an ornate dish decorated with gold and flowers. The greenery on top is also striking.

▶ The gold and the butter, and the celadon and the green pepper set each other off to perfection, engendering a strange charm.

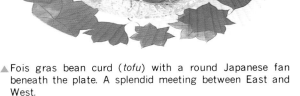

▲ Fois gras bean curd (*tofu*) with a round Japanese fan beneath the plate. A splendid meeting between East and West.

●Honzen ryori (formal banquet-style cooking)

Cooking developed into an art in the 14th century. It was a time when there was much interaction between the court aristocracy and the new warrior ruling class. The code of manners for the warriors was strictly enforced, and even the way food was to be prepared for, and served to, guests was laid down both in form and content.

The refined cuisine which developed out of the formal styles of those times was developed further in the Edo period (1603-1868) as *honzen ryori* (literally, "main table") by the high-class restaurants of the time. *Honzen ryori* is the basis of Japanese cooking in form and etiquette.

Honzen ryori is served on small low individual tables called *zen* which look like four-legged trays. The tables are named for the order in which they appear: *honzen* (main table), *ni no zen* (second table), *san no zen* (third table), and so on. A completely separate table called the *suimono zen* is used for serving *sake*.

●AN OUTLINE OF JAPANESE COOKING

Here we shall mention some of the types of Japanese cooking that are popular both within and without Japan. They are all integral components of modern cuisine, old and familiar dishes well-loved by the Japanese, and each exhibits the characteristics of Japanese cooking.

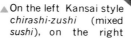

▲On the left Kansai style *chirashi-zushi* (mixed *sushi*), on the right Tokyo style *nigiri-zushi* (hand-formed *sushi*). The distinctive harmony between the fish and the vinegared rice is a typically Japanese taste.

▲**Sashimi** Fresh, uncooked seafood. The taste varies with the skill with which the knife is used in cutting the fish. Here, *fugu-sashi* (balloon fish sashimi) is arranged on a large plate in the shape of a chrysanthemum.

◀**Tempura** Its origins reputed to stem from the Portuguese cooking introduced in the 17th century, *tempura* is deep-fried fresh seafood and vegetables. One of the favorite Japanese foods abroad.

●Chakaiseki (tea ceremony cuisine)

The tea ceremony was formalized by Sen no Rikyu (1522-1591) in the latter half of the 16th century. *Chakaiseki* is the food served before the powdered green tea (*matcha*) appears during the tea ceremony. It is plain and simple, just enough to help an empty stomach endure.

Originally it was the custom that the person who gave the tea ceremony also prepared the food himself. However, by the middle of the 19th century special shops catering for the tea ceremony had made their appearance, and today in most cases it is such specialists who continue to exercise their talent. In the circumstances, the simple *chakaiseki*, which at first consisted only of one soup and two or three side dishes, gradually became more lavish.

Today, the standard menu has become two dishes added to the basic one soup and three side dishes. A further two or three dishes, such as a soy-flavored or a vinegared dish, may be added.

▶ **Sukiyaki** A dish special to Japan comprising meat, vegetables, bean curd, etc. simmered in a sauce of which soy sauce and sugar are the main ingredients. *Sukiyaki* is representative of the many varieties of one-pot table cooking (*nabemono*) and is famous the world over.

▶ **Two Dishes Made from Bean Curd (tofu)** In recent years bean curd has been gaining attention abroad as a health food. Its attraction is its lightness and simplicity, together with its rich and nourishing taste. It has a deep-rooted popularity in Japan.

▲ **Japanese Sweets (wagashi)** Sweets in Japan are intended to satisfy both the sight and the taste. There is also pleasure in the seasonal feeling they evoke.

▲ **Oden** An example of nabemono popular in Japan since the Edo period. Two main types are recognized: one made on a broth based on soy sauce, the other made on a broth based on *miso* (fermented bean paste). It is a style of cooking growing popular overseas.

● Kaiseki ryori (informal banquet cooking)

Japanese cooking reached maturity during the Edo period, supported by the development of restaurants and by the existence of other cooking traditions such as the European (*nanban ryori*, mainly Dutch, Spanish and Portuguese) and the Chinese.

With the existence of restaurants and the growth in the social influence of urban dwellers (*chonin*), relaxed and informal dinner parties became very popular, and the food served at them incorporated the forms and content of both *honzen ryori* and *chakaiseki*, though taste was emphasized over the formalities. This newly developed, independent form of cooking was called *kaiseki* (banquet) *ryori*.

By the end of the Edo period, when restaurants had become firmly established in the culture, both the food and the number of courses served became more sumptuous. The small tables on which the food was served (*zen*) changed also, becoming legless trays called *kaisekizen*.

●Gyoji ryori (food associated with annual events)

Since ancient times, special food has traditionally been prepared for festivals and celebrations. The assortment of food called *osechi ryori*, cooked ahead and served in special lacquered boxes, and the special soup called *ozoni* appear at the New Year, and the boxed food (*orizume*) is served at celebrations and ceremonies. Even today, when the national diet is so much richer and more varied than that of people of the past, the Japanese retain a special affection for the food that in the past contrasted strongly in its extravagance with the simple food of every day.

▲*Osechi ryori* Sumptuous New Year's food. Traditionally the food has been arranged as shown in five-layered lacquer boxes called *jubako*. The norm nowadays however is for only two or three layers. There are many local traditions in *osechi ryori*; the type shown here is from Tokyo.

▼(right) **Boxed Food** The items, of an auspicious uneven number, are packed in a box, which is wrapped with thick ceremonial paper, and tied with strands of decorative string dyed red and white.

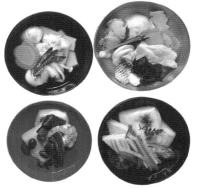

▲*Ozoni* A soup integral to the cooking that celebrates the New Year. It is essentially a soup containing glutinous rice cakes called *mochi*, garnished with a variety of other ingredients. Different regions have different ways of shaping the *mochi*, of selecting the other ingredients and of seasoning. The photograph shows four different types rich in local color.

▲**Boxed Food** The sea bream cooked whole and the red rice (*sekihan*) are the core of celebratory food. Here, they are packed to be taken home with the guest. Red rice is made by steaming small red *azuki* beans with glutinous rice.

●Modern Japanese Cooking

We cannot speak of modern Japanese cooking without considering the ubiquitous role of the restaurant in Japanese culture. It is not an exaggeration to say that traditional forms and dishes are now the preserve of high-class restaurants and inns, or are served only on ceremonial occasions, such as wedding banquets.

Nevertheless, a new type of Japanese cooking style has emerged which in its modern outlook sensitively reflects the spirit of the times. While taking into account traditional methods of preparation, it has adopted new ingredients, as well as an eclectic style which brings out the best in Western and Chinese cooking.

Of course there are many specialty restaurants serving well-loved traditional dishes, such as sushi, tempura, unagi (eel), soba and udon (two types of noodles). At the same time restaurants in general today are the setting for the diversification and internationalization of Japanese cooking. Large numbers of Western and Chinese restaurants, as well as fast-food outlets, compete with each other and with the traditional Japanese places, acting as a spur to one another. Japan must be the leading country in the world for multi-cultural cooking.

The table of the average family is, at least in the metropolitan areas, similarly diversified and multifaceted, and traditional home cooking is gradually being eroded.

▲**Packed lunch** *(bento)* One type is used for taking on excursions, etc. and another for formal dining. The type pictured is the *Shokado bento*, most often eaten at tea ceremonies as *kaiseki*. Seasonal food is delicately wrought and arranged.

●Eating Etiquette

When eating traditional food, such as formal *chakaiseki* or *honzen*, the etiquette and the rules are strict and detailed. From how to set down the lid of your soup bowl and how to place your chopsticks on the table to the order of consumption of the dishes and the way to bring the meal to a finish, everything has a particular formality.

However, when enjoying ordinary food, this formality tends to be little regarded, and the enjoyment of the cooking itself is foremost. Rather than learning formal etiquette, what is more important is the spirit in which the food is served, as expressed in the cooking, and the effort given to sincere appreciation of the beauty and the taste of the food. Here are some basic pointers which presuppose such a frame of mind.

Firstly, eat what is supposed to be hot while it is still hot, and do not let what is supposed to be cold get warm. That is both politeness to the cook and appreciation of the food at its best.

Japanese food is to be consumed by the eyes as well as the tongue. Before and while eating, take your time to appreciate the beauty, the freshness and the smell of the food.

Slurping your soup is not necessarily rude, but avoid talking with your mouth full.

Cultural differences in eating and cooking may mean that some food does not agree with you. Nevertheless, as far as possible, try not to leave any food.

Eating is a pleasure, and conversation is a part of that pleasure. It is good to be stimulated by conversation, but be careful not to let it dominate your meal, and not to speak in such a loud voice that it disturbs people at other tables.

These are merely some ways to make the meal more pleasant; there is no need to think of them in over-formal terms.

●The Use of Chopsticks and Japanese Cooking

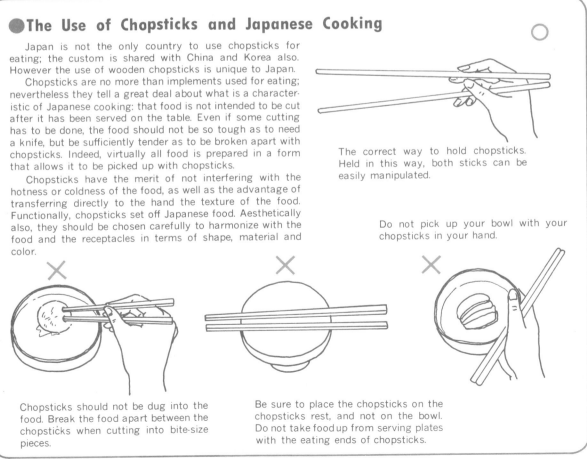

Japan is not the only country to use chopsticks for eating; the custom is shared with China and Korea also. However the use of wooden chopsticks is unique to Japan.

Chopsticks are no more than implements used for eating; nevertheless they tell a great deal about what is a characteristic of Japanese cooking: that food is not intended to be cut after it has been served on the table. Even if some cutting has to be done, the food should not be so tough as to need a knife, but be sufficiently tender as to be broken apart with chopsticks. Indeed, virtually all food is prepared in a form that allows it to be picked up with chopsticks.

Chopsticks have the merit of not interfering with the hotness or coldness of the food, as well as the advantage of transferring directly to the hand the texture of the food. Functionally, chopsticks set off Japanese food. Aesthetically also, they should be chosen carefully to harmonize with the food and the receptacles in terms of shape, material and color.

The correct way to hold chopsticks. Held in this way, both sticks can be easily manipulated.

Do not pick up your bowl with your chopsticks in your hand.

Chopsticks should not be dug into the food. Break the food apart between the chopsticks when cutting into bite-size pieces.

Be sure to place the chopsticks on the chopsticks rest, and not on the bowl. Do not take food up from serving plates with the eating ends of chopsticks.

FORETHOUGHT AND MINIATURIZATION

Forethought

Forethought is a distinctive feature of Japanese behavior. What the word expresses is a variation on the Golden Rule: to do unto others—usually for their benefit—before being asked to do so. Typical examples will clarify how it works.

◇ **A Lockless Culture** Western-style doors have locks on them, as do Japanese doors that open to the outside. But *fusuma* and *shoji*—the room dividers in a Japanese house—are not so equipped. Neither is it a conventional practice in Japan to ask permission each time one wishes to enter a room. Faced with a closed *fusuma*, the only recourse for the would-be entrant is to employ forethought to interpret whether the closed *fusuma* means "Keep Out", "Knock First", or "Ask". Without such forethought, *fusuma* would be unable to fulfill its function as a boundary marker.

◇ **Non-Verbal Communication** Rather than use words or argument to gain another's understanding, the Japanese prefer to convey their intentions or feelings through subtle signals using a minimum of verbal communication. Words, say the Japanese, are merely signals that indicate directions and function no more than signs do. This is particularly evident in the family, where, among people who understand one another, outward demonstrations of affection such as hugging, kissing or verbal reassurances of love are neither the norm nor missed.

Even at the work place, associates of long standing most often convey their feelings through such non-verbal methods as head movements or altering facial expressions, and refrain from any long stream of personal questions. For people in close rela-

● **Determining attitude based on circumstances**

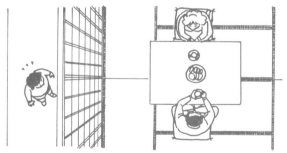

▲ "My brother has his girlfriend with him in his room; we'd better not call out to him."

● **What can be understood without words should not be voiced.**

▲ "Dad loves mom, but he has never once said 'I love you.' to her."

● **Something small which represents the whole world**

▲ This garden is a miniature of the universe. Small as it is, it contains mountains and seas.

● **Small is efficient.**

▲ Ever since the small but efficient transistor radio was put on the market in August 1955, a great variety of miniaturized products have made their appearance.

tionships, this is deemed sufficient to convey the message.

Small is Better

There are those who say that Japan is a country of the miniature culture; that is, a culture that makes small things—or makes things small. The Japanese, to be sure, have often enough failed when attempting expansion; but they have attained great success when it comes to reduction. Even traditional culture offers examples of this, as in *bonsai*. It is, so to speak, a knack the Japanese have for utilizing limited space as if it were limitless.

◇**Mechanical Miniatures** The first item successfully miniaturized in the postwar industrial period was the portable radio. Next came the radio-cassette, then the miniaturized cassette tape-recorder, followed by a long list of small or compact items that includes the "Walkman", pocket calculators, TVs, cameras, cars and personal computers.

Haiku and Tanka

Haiku and *Tanka* are two traditional forms of poetry. *Haiku* is made up of 17 syllables, *Tanka* 31. These ever-popular art forms are enjoyed by young and old, male and female in all walks of life. To create an image in only 17 or 31 syllables requires that the words used be carefully chosen for their succinctness, be pared down to bare essentials, and be symbolically expressive of the feeling to be evoked:

> Matsushima ya
> Ah, Matsushima ya
> Matsushima ya

By the simple repetition of the name "Matsushima", treating it almost like an interjection, the poem attempts to capture the scenic beauty of the Matsushima area, which is well-nigh impossible to put into words.

●**The *haiku*—a poem in seventeen syllables**

荒 海 や（5 syllables）
あら うみ

Ah, the rough sea!

佐 渡 に 横 た う（7 syllables）
さ ど よこ

And, stretching over Sado Island,

天 の 河（5 syllables）
あま がわ

the, Galaxy.

▲Matsuo Basho (1644-1694), the most famous of the *haiku* poets, brought the world's vastness into a short poem of seventeen syllables.

●BONSAI

Bonsai is nature in a small package. Interest in bonsai among gardening enthusiasts abroad is such that the word now has an international currency.

Bonsai is the attempt to portray the macro cosmos on a micro scale. A solitary pine or other tree, or a grouping of various plants is placed in a pot, tray or some such container along with rocks, soil or sand. A tiny stand of trees can thus be likened to the grandeur of nature's own forests—an exquisite miniature intended to expand in the mind's eye. It is the Japanese mind trying to find the mystery of the universe within the limited space of a tiny garden.

GESTURES AND ACTIONS

Pulling And Pushing

Gestures intended to convey the same meanings often differ greatly from country to country, as is evident even in the motions of pushing and pulling. It is said the basic movement in the West, whether in the use of tools or in gestures, is one of pushing. In Japan, the basic movement is one of pulling. Typical examples are the ways in which tools such as saws and planes are used. In Japan they are pulled to cut; in the West they are pushed.

Actions Easily Misunderstood

A cautionary word should be said in connection with some of the actions peculiar to Japan. In conversation, it is common for the listener to nod and utter approving sounds. These do not, however, necessarily mean consent or agreement. In fact, in most cases they signal only that the listener is receiving input; that the physical act of hearing is taking place.

Another potential source of misunderstanding is smiling. A Japanese, like most other people, will usually have a smile on his or her face when happy or amused. The problem is that the smile is sometimes there even when the person is sad or embarrassed. This may be due to mild or intense embarrassment, or to the fact that the person does not wish to reveal the extent of emotions raging within. According to Japanese thinking, disclosing such emotions would be to foist off one's problems onto another, to burden the listener and thereby show a lack of consideration.

Nodding and smiling in conversation are no more than long-established paralingual habits and should not be construed as malevolent or anything other than normal actions for a Japanese.

●The Cutting Motion with Japanese Implements

▲Japanese saws and planes are used with the blade edge facing toward the body and consequently the cutting motion toward the user, in contrast to the Western style of usage. Likewise, the Japanese sword does not cut in a thrusting motion like the European sword, but in a swing-draw motion.

●Counting on the Fingers

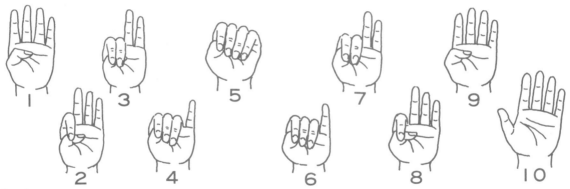

▲For the numbers 1 to 5, the fingers are bent in the order thumb to little finger, and for the numbers 6 to 10, the fingers are raised in the order little finger to thumb.

●Indicating Numbers to Others

▲With the elbow bent, the hand raised, and the fingers bent as shown in the diagram. One hand is used for the numbers 1 to 5, and two hands when counting from 6 to 10.

●Indicating Oneself

▲When inquiring whether something is theirs, or indicating themselves, the Japanese point to their nose with their finger.

●Beckoning Someone

▲The palm of the hand faces downwards, the fingers are extended slightly, and the hand is waved several times in a beckoning motion towards the body of the beckoner. This is not a gesture that is performed toward a superior.

●Banzai

▲Equivalent to the English "three cheers," the word *banzai* is shouted three times in unison to the accompaniment of raised arms when someone has won a contest, when there is something to be celebrated, or when a party comes to a close.

●Maru and Batsu

▲Maru, the sign of a circle, indicates that something is correct. Its positive image contrasts with the negative of the batsu sign, a cross, which indicates that a mistake has been made.

●Shaking Hands and Bowing

▲The Japanese bow contrasts with the European and American custom of handshaking in that, instead of being based on the thrusting motion of the hand toward the greetee, the head is bowed and the body bent forward and withdrawn in modesty.

●WINKING

Like most nonverbal signals, winking has a significance that varies from society to society. In Japan's case, winking is not even a custom, so that the chances of observing one in action are just about nil. However, as observers of Western culture, many Japanese feel they understand the meaning of the wink. As the following story suggests, this assumption is open to question. A young Japanese girl on vacation in California was winked at by a handsome young man. Taking it to be a sign that he was personally interested in her, she had mixed feelings to discover that the wink he'd given her was simply a kind of conditioned reflex he would give to any attractive young girl, meaning no more than a visual way of saying a friendly hello.

GUESTS AND GIFTS

Entertaining Guests

The desire to do one's best when entertaining guests is universal. The considerable differences that exist across borders are only in regard to ways and methods. In the West, entertaining guests in the warmth of the home and serving them a home-cooked meal is usually preferred. Just the opposite is true in Japan where tradition prescribes that a meal prepared by a superb chef at a spacious and impressive restaurant is by far the superior way to treat a guest. However, nowadays it is becoming more common to invite people to one's home as in the Western fashion.

Japanese-Style Hospitality

In Japan, seeing to a guest's needs is an important part of serving as host. A host will try to anticipate what a guest might want or need. Coffee or tea, for example, will sometimes promptly be served a visitor automatically, and it would not be thought unusual if drinks or even a meal were brought out.

O-shibori, the small dampened cloth offered to guests at private homes, inns, restaurants and practically everywhere else, falls within this category of hospitality. Chilled in summer and warmed in winter, *o-shibori* provides a refreshing prelude to a meal, drinks, or conversation.

Gift-Giving

On even the simplest occasion a gift (o-miyage) is customarily taken along and presented as an expression of the giver's respect and goodwill.

Seasonal gifts are an important aspect of Japanese culture. O-chugen (mid-year gifts) is usually given to one's superiors from early June to mid July. O-seibo (year-end gifts) is presented as an expression of appreciation for favors received in the past year. Those in a socially superior position, such as a family doctor, or a teacher of flower arrangement are typical recipients. Today these gifts are delivered by stores or sent through the mail. Gift sets of seasonal foods and drinks, soap sets, and flowers are only some of such gifts. O-toshidama (New-Year's gift) which had religious meaning in the past connected with Shinto or Buddhism is now always given to children in cash by parents and close relatives or by neighbors as a New Year's gift. Gift-giving is part of a larger system of social exchange.

●Some situations to be careful about

▲Do not take gifts that have roots attached, such as potted plants, when visiting a sick person. The Japanese dislike to receive anything that reminds them of "taking root," since it implies that the illness will be prolonged.

▲Do not open a present immediately upon receiving it. The Japanese have traditionally considered such behavior to be bad manners.

▲Whereas in Europe and America the custom is that neighbors welcome a newly arrived person with a gift, in Japan, the person who has moved in is expected to take a present to his or her new neighbors.

Significant stages in human life such as birth, coming of age, and marriage, as well as funerals and partings require gifts. Gifts are often given out of a sense of obligation and in turn require a return gift (O-kaeshi).

Saying Thank You

It may be considered rude for a receiver of another's hospitality (be it a meal, drinks or gifts) to thank his or her benefactor only once. "Arigato gozaimasu" (the polite form of "Thank you") is first said upon receiving them. Gratitude is expressed again when the recipient next meets the giver. This custom of saying "Thank you" several times conveys a perpetual rather than a transitory relationship between them.

● **Sitting on *tatami* floors**

· *Seiza*

▲*Seiza* is the formal way of sitting on *tatami*. Since the legs are tucked under one's body, they tend to fall asleep.

· Informal Sitting Styles

▲Men may sit cross-legged in informal situations, but women must sit with the legs tucked back on one side of the body or the other.

● **Bowing in the Japanese fashion**

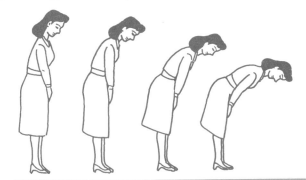

The basic form of greeting in Japan is the bow. When standing, bring the legs together, bend the body forward from the waist, and lower the head. The angle at which the head is lowered indicates the degree of politeness of the bow. When sitting on *tatami* matting, bow from the *seiza* position bending the whole body forward, placing both hands on the floor in front and lowering the head.

● **Direct Ordering of Local Products**

Gift-giving as an expression of thanks at prescribed seasons, known as *o-chugen* in mid-year and *o-seibo* at the year end, is a thriving custom in Japan. Such gifts may be given personally to the recipient, although in the majority of cases they are delivered by the department store with whom the order was placed. Since, however, there is little variation among the goods offered by the various department stores, the choice has tended to become stereotyped. In addition, many restrictions apply when sending fresh foodstuffs.

What has become popular in recent years is having local goods sent directly from the place of production by placing a telephone call, thus ensuring the freshness of the product. Since the early sixties such direct ordering has gained a following as a way of lowering costs by avoiding the usual distribution network of wholesaler and retailer, and a means by which health foods (e. g., those on which agricultural chemicals have not been used) may be obtained. It has only been more recently, however, that direct ordering of fresh foodstuffs or distinctive local products has been applied to the buying of seasonal gifts. The popularity of such direct ordering is gradually increasing, suiting as it does the Japanese national characteristic of love of fresh natural foods which suggest a particular season.

▲A variety of products bought by direct order

SEASONAL VARIATIONS AND HARMONY WITH NATURE

Seasonal Changes

Japan's seasons are clear-cut. Since the archipelago runs north and south some 3000 kilometers it encompasses both a semi-tropical and semi-frigid zone, providing the nation with weather of almost every sort: rainy, dry, snow, typhoons and most things in between.

Such a varied climate has fostered among the people a keen awareness of nature, as can be seen in various arts and customs. Nature, for example, is always an important theme in classical literature, with seasonal elements incorporated as essential background. And in the 17-syllable type of poetry known as *haiku*, words that indicate the seasons are indispensable components.

Endowed with a relatively mild marine climate and surrounded by sea, Japan, an island country, was shielded from a magnitude of calamities, natural or man-made. This fact has greatly influenced Japanese life and even formed the inclination referred to as "insular narrowness".

Nature in its Cultural Perception

The tea ceremony, flower arrangement, garden construction and many other arts exemplify the Japanese outlook toward nature. The essence of such arts is a reduced reproduction of nature as it is. Even in the martial arts the Japanese perception of nature can be seen. In judo, for example, the

●Traditional kimono patterns reflecting the seasons

Japanese kimonos are known the world over for the beauty of their patterns, which are abstractions of natural phenomena through the four seasons. Such patterns perfectly reflect the cast of the Japanese mind which delights in nature and feels close to it.

▼A spring kimono

▼A summer kimono

▼An autumn kimono

▼A winter kimono

opponent is brought down not by matching strength with strength, but by yielding to his strength and utilizing it so that the opponent falls from his own force.

Nature and the Commonplace

The attitude of harmonizing with nature is clearly evident in the daily things of life. A traditional Japanese house, for example, is made of wood, floored with *tatami*, and divided into rooms by *fusuma* and *shoji* partitions made of wood and paper. This is not inconvenient though it might at first seem so. Actually, it is the ideal construction given Japan's humid summer climate, as it allows for air circulation throughout the house and thus aids in controlling mold and mildew.

In regard to food there is much that, like *sashimi*, is eaten raw, and when food is cooked, great efforts are taken to preserve its natural appearance and flavor.

As Japanese life becomes more and more Westernized and urbanized there is a corresponding lessening of the spirit of harmonizing with nature. Houses these days are of concrete more often than not—albeit with Japanese adaptations—and processed and artificially grown foods rob the seasons of their unique offerings. Even so, given their preference, most Japanese would still opt for nature's way.

●Seasonal variation between north and south

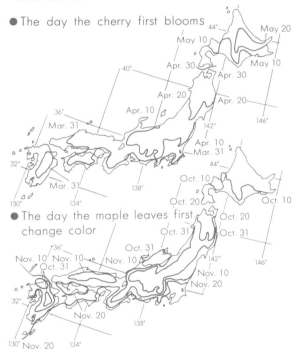

●The day the cherry first blooms

●The day the maple leaves first change color

Though Japan is a small country, it stretches some 3,000 kilometers north to south, over twenty-five degrees of latitude. As a result, there is a great difference in temperatures between north and south, and a forty-day variation between the times the cherry first blooms and between the times the maple leaves change color. Nevertheless, though the season may vary at any one time from place to place, cherry blossoms and maple leaves are to be found in every part of Japan, and Japanese people, wherever they may live in the archipelago, have a common feeling for nature, that the cherry is the symbol of spring and the maple the symbol of autumn.

●BATHING

The Japanese are a bath-loving people. There is, however, a difference in the way they take baths. All soaping, scrubbing and rinsing of the body is done outside the tub and usually while perched atop a tiny stool. Water disappears via a drain in the floor, which is usually of tile. Only after the body is thoroughly clean will a Japanese submerge neck-deep in the hot water of a deep tub to soak and relax. Though a shower might suffice in the West for the practical purpose of cleansing the body, a bath—a Japanese-style bath—is something no Japanese would willingly do without.

It is also the norm in Japan to bathe in the evening, usually before retiring. Again this is quite in contrast to the common Western practice of showering in the morning before leaving for the day's activities. Traditionally, the Japanese have believed that a morning bath is not suitable for the diligent. This idea has even found expression in an old folksong that bemoans the fate of one who loses everything because of being too fond of sleeping, drinking and bathing in the morning.

And yet when on vacation at a hot springs resort some Japanese do enjoy a morning bath—irresistibly nice! Due to numerous volcanoes throughout the nation spas have long abounded. Some even have facilities for open-air bathing. This allows the bather to relax both body and soul in natural surroundings while enjoying the scenic beauty. Such a style of bathing also underscores the Japanese predilection for harmonizing with nature. Meanwhile, there has been a decrease in the number of *sento*—the public bathing facilities that used to dot each neighborhood. Nevertheless they are still used as a kind of meeting-place for gossiping. Increasing numbers of foreign residents in Japan use these public baths.

▲Open-air bathing

LIFE OF A SALARIED EMPLOYEE

Many people abroad are under the impression that the average Japanese willingly slaves at the workplace. Are the Japanese truly such a hardworking people? History indicates that their ancestors were, since hard work was the only alternative for farmers who wanted the biggest harvests possible from their meager plots of land. Such historical factors conform well with today's emphasis on prosperity and success.

Due to the lifetime employment system, the corporate worker has a strong identification with the company. This in turn contributes to stability in management, for the company and employee both feel as if they are in the same boat. It is against this kind of background that Japan achieved its phenomenal economic growth in the 1960s.

Workaholics in Rabbit Hutches?

In view of their hard work it would seem that the Japanese are now enjoying "the good life". Young working singles can, it is true, indulge themselves in clothes and travel; but once married, they too come smack up against economic realities. Japan's status as a country with a huge trade surplus cannot erase the smallness of the nation's land or the scarcity of its natural resources. Japan's economy rests on a surprisingly fragile foundation. Its inadequacies compel the Japanese to be "workaholics". The epithet of affluence is belied by poor social welfare and unsatisfactory infrastructure, with personal assets comparatively lower than in Western countries. Under such circumstances the word "affluent" seems a misnomer. Housing—or more precisely its inadequacy—is a glaring example. Even to obtain what has jokingly been referred to as a "rabbit hutch" takes a lifetime of hard work for urban Japanese. With the price of land in metropolitan areas sky-rocketing, the dream of owning a home continues to be nothing more than just a dream.

A Day in the Life of a Salaried Man

Many workers in big cities spend over an hour commuting to their jobs each day on

●OCCUPATIONS AND CLOTHING

At one time in Japan, clothing specific to an occupation came about naturally by the wearers themselves. This has now all but disappeared and workers wear clothes more in keeping with the times and in tune with the rest of the world. In contrast, nurserymen, carpenters and a few other workers (see below) continue to wear traditional work clothes.

▶ salaried worker

▲ doctor

▲ policeman

▼ hairdresser

▼ sushi shop employee

▼ greengrocer

▲ fish dealer

▲ nurseryman

▲ carpenter

▲ farmer

▲ fisherman

jam-packed trains. Once at the office they hear a morning pep talk or perhaps loudly chant the company's motto as a prelude to the day's work.

Employees often work overtime and without taking their alloted annual vacations. After work, they often stop off for a drink with colleagues to relax, exchange small talk and information, and get rid of the day's stress, all of which is considered helpful in business.

Nighttime can also mean entertaining company clients. This often involves bar-hopping and singing at *karaoke* (sing-along) bars.

Company Parties

Every year in April companies hire a new crop of employees, and each department or section holds drinking parties to welcome them. Such parties deepen the sense of belonging and help bond the newcomers to the group.

All of the year's frustrations, failures and disappointments are forgotten and only its pleasant memories are reminisced and toasted to at parties called *bonenkai* (year-end party). Such parties are usually held in mid-December. Their festive atmosphere

▲Rush hour in Shinjuku station, Tokyo.

fosters a mutual desire to work together in the coming year.

The Pursuit of Leisure

During the industrial boom until some years ago, intensive production made it necessary for workers to dedicate much of their time to their jobs and the Japanese generally felt work was what made life worth-while. They spent their limited free time relaxing in front of the TV or playing a Japanese form of pinball called *pachinko*.

Nowadays, however, especially among the young, a strong shift towards active enjoyment of one's leisure hours in a more positive manner has occurred. Tennis and skiing are popular among the young set, while those in middle age and above find enjoyment and pleasure in such pursuits as golf, jogging, and weekend carpentry.

●Weekly working hours in industry (1984)

	hours
W. Germany	31,3
France	31,7
USA	37,0
England	37,4
Japan	41,7

●Hourly wage in industry (1984)

	yen
W. Germany	2,180
USA	1,403
Japan	1,293
England	1,167
France	812

●Number of days off

Total Employed (average)	two days a week			one day a week	monthly	not fixed	un-known
	every week	every two weeks	once a month				
1950		8	13	46%	10	23	0
1955	12	13	5	43	5	20	2
1960	13	12	7	39	5	21	3
clerical, technical workers							
1950		10	24	58		4	4 0
1955	15	21	8	46	3	5	1
1960	20	18	16	34	5	6	1

●Distribution of commutation time (weekdays)

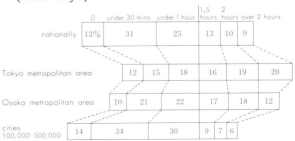

	0	under 30 mins	under 1 hour	1.5 hours	2 hours	over 2 hours
nationally	13%	31	25	13	10	9
Tokyo metropolitan area		12	15	18	16	19	20
Osaka metropolitan area		10	21	22	17	18	12
cities 100,000-500,000		14	34	30	9	7	6

EDUCATION IN JAPAN

High Educational Level

Japan's high level of education has enabled it to become a prominent economic power despite its small size and lack of natural resources. Moreover, Japan can boast of being one of the most highly educated countries in the world, for at present school enrollment and literacy rates are 100%.

Japan's modern system of education had its beginnings in 1872 following the Meiji Restoration. But Japan's tradition of popular education goes back even further. In the latter half of the 18th century when the Tokugawa shoguns ruled the country, there was already a fairly developed system of private schools for the children of the warrior class and "temple schools" for the commoners. Around the middle of the 19th century, approximately 45% of male children and 15% of female children could read and write. These figures put Japan in proximity to the advanced countries of that era.

Nine Years of Mandatory Education

Primary learning was limited to four years when the compulsory education system was first established. It was later extended to six years and then to nine years after the Pacific War in 1947. Japan's present educational system requires six years of elementary school and three years of junior high school for a total of 9 years of compulsory learning. Enrollment is 100%. Although high school is not a part of mandatory education, Japan's competitive society makes it as if it were so. About 94% of junior high graduates go on to high school.

Above high school is the university, which offers four years of study. There are more than 460 universities; 95 are state institutions and 34 are public. Junior colleges, with two-year terms, number about 540. Some 37% of high school graduates go on to higher education. The four-year universities offer Graduate School Programs and have an enrollment of around 55,000 students.

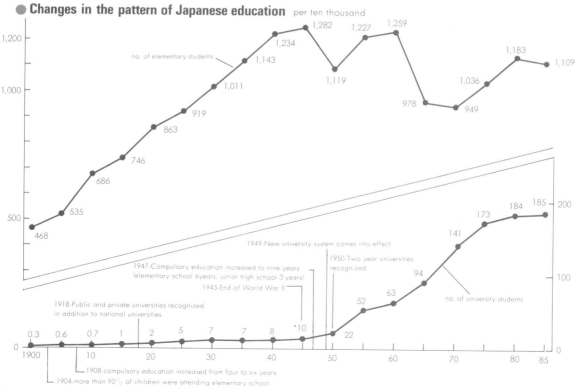

● **Changes in the pattern of Japanese education** per ten thousand

no. of elementary students

1,282
1,259
1,234
1,227
1,200
1,183
1,143
1,119
1,109
1,036
1,011
978
949
919
863
746
686
535
468

1949-New university system comes into effect.
1950-Two year universities recognized.
1947-Compulsory education increased to nine years (elementary school 6years; junior high school 3 years).
1945-End of World War II
1918-Public and private universities recognized in addition to national universities.

185 — 200
184
173
141
94
no. of university students
63
52
100
22
0.3 0.6 0.7 1 2 5 7 7 8 '10
0
1900   10   20   30   40   50   60   70   80 85   0

1908-compulsory education increased from four to six years.
1904-more than 90% of children were attending elementary school.

All schools begin in April, although a September entry is also being pursued in view of the need to accommodate numerous students from abroad and returning Japanese students.

"Examination Hell" and the "Juku" Boom

Japanese children must be among the busiest in the world, for many, if not most, attend "juku"(private tutoring schools) in addition to their regular studies. The reason for all this schooling is due to the difficult university entrance examinations.

Japan has long been a society that takes a person's academic background seriously. A person's alma mater (university) can be a determining factor in employment by a big-name firm, appointment to a high government position, or even assure promotion. Therefore entrance examinations to top-rated universities are so difficult that they are referred to as sheer "hell". Many parents send their children to "juku" which offer lessons in the academic subjects that are important in school entrance examinations, primarily English, mathematics, and Japanese. The rigorous "juku" require hard-er work and longer hours than ordinary schools. Japanese children are under great pressure in the present educational system. As a matter of fact some parents even believe that a good kindergarten is necessary to assure admission to a good elementary school and so on up the line.

Except for the positions of high-ranking government officials, the significance of one's academic background is gradually diminishing as more and more weight is being given to a worker's ability. The Japanese system of seniority is not actually employed to the extent believed abroad. Even so, many parents still think it best to enroll their children in good schools.

Youth in Search of Vocational Training

Increasing numbers of young people are forsaking a university education to study at professional or other specialty schools ranging from computer technology to cooking. Others attend university classes during the day and study at technical schools at night, a phenomenon referred to as "Double School".

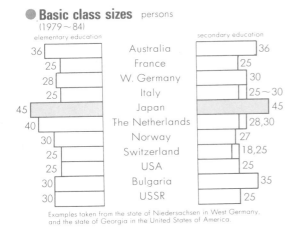

● Basic class sizes persons (1979~84)

Examples taken from the state of Niedersachsen in West Germany, and the state of Georgia in the United States of America.

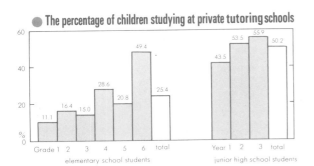

● The percentage of children studying at private tutoring schools

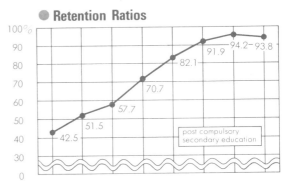

● Retention Ratios

The percentage of junior high school graduates who continue on to study in senior high school.

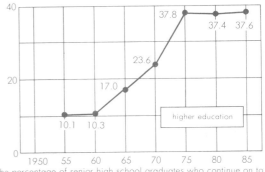

The percentage of senior high school graduates who continue on to study in four or two-year universities.

THE JAPANESE GOVERNMENT

Three Divisions of Power

Over the years a number of words or phrases about Japan have gained currency abroad, such as "harakiri" of the samurai, "kamikaze" of the Second World War or the "economic animal" of the '60s and '70s. Taken in the aggregate these terms would seem to suggest that Japan is a nation unsettled or exotic—whereas in truth it is the most stable democracy in Asia.

The organization of the Japanese government is patterned after the English parliamentary system. Political power is shared by three branches of government: the legislative power of the Diet, the administrative power of the cabinet, and the judicial power of the judiciary.

The Diet

The Diet is the most prominent of the three powers of government. It is made up of the House of Representatives (512 members serving four years) and the House of Councillors (252 members serving six years). Both houses are entirely elective. Although the powers of the two houses are similar, higher authority resides in the House of Representatives which can, for example, repass a bill rejected by the Councillors and announce it as the decision of the entire Diet. The House of Representatives can also initiate a non-confidence motion in the cabinet. Should it be passed, the cabinet must then resign en bloc or the House of Representatives be dissolved. In the latter case, the incumbency of the members terminates at that point.

The Cabinet

The Prime Minister heads the cabinet. He or she is elected by the members of the Diet. Since members ordinarily vote for the head of the party they are affiliated with, the head of the party holding the largest number of seats becomes Prime Minister. The Prime Minister represents Japan at important international conferences as the Emperor is only the symbolic head of state. Unlike the President of the United States, the Prime Minister is not elected directly by the people but indirectly through the strength of a political party.

Political Parties

The major political parties in Japan are the Liberal Democratic Party (LDP), the Social Democratic Party of Japan (SDPJ), the Komei Party, the Democratic Socialist Party, the Japan Communist Party (JCP), and the United Social Democratic Party. The conser-

▲The Diet Building

● Distribution of seats by party, House of Representatives (as at election)

date of election							full number
1958. 5	The Liberal Democratic party 287		Japan Socialist party 166		Japan Communist party 1 / Other 13		467
1960.11	296		145	Democratic Socialist party 17	3	6	467
1963.11	283		144	23	5	12	467
1967. 1	277		140	Komei party / 30	5 25	9	486
1969.12	288		90	31 14	47	16	486
1972.12	271		118	19 38	29	16	491
1976.12	249	New Liberal Club 17	123	29 17	55	21	511
1979.10	248	4	107 35	United Social Democratic party 2 / 39	57	19	511
1980. 6	284	12	107	32 29	33	11	511
1983.12	250	8	112	38 26	58	3 16	511
1986. 7	300	6	85	26 26	56	4 9	512

The New Liberal Club disbanded in August 1986; most of its members joined the Liberal Democratic party.

vatives are the LDP, the progressives the SDPJ and the JCP, and the middle-of-the-roaders are the others. The LDP was formed in 1955 by the merger of earlier conservative parties and has had a majority in the Diet ever since. The Prime Minister has, accordingly, always come from the ranks of the LDP. Although this party has enjoyed a monopoly of power in postwar politics, it has also consistently adapted to the demands of the times following wide-ranging policies in pragmatic ways and is an ongoing contributor to the stability of the nation.

Party Factions

A peculiarity of Japanese politics is the existence of factions within the party. The LDP contains five large ones, each formed mainly according to personal affiliations rather than major differences in policies or viewpoints. Faction leaders distribute funds to followers at election time and help loyal members obtain important positions within the party and cabinet. The faction leaders must be ardent fund-raisers and often place the interests of their constituencies above those of the nation at large. That such a conventional and premodern political mechanism should be so successful in creating one of the world's leading modern states is a matter of great interest.

●POLICE BOXES AND "SHAME CULTURE"

Crime usually rises as industrialization and urbanization progress, but such is not the case in Japan. Its crime rate in 1982 was at 1.2% as compared to 6% in the U.S. and other Western countries. Japan's criminal arrests were at nearly 60%, three times higher than in the U.S.

One contributing factor is Japan's "shame culture". The Japanese try to live up to an ideal image of themselves and when they fail, they feel ashamed of themselves in their own eyes as well as others'. Shame is a reaction to the feeling that one has disgraced one's own self-image. More practically, crime reduction is largely due to the low unemployment rate and the police box system. Scattered throughout cities and towns, police boxes consisting of one to five policemen form a system in which officers are able to immediately respond to situations because they routinely patrol their areas.

Police also kindly assist people who have lost their way or their belongings, and sometimes look after lost children, etc.

▲Police box

●The Japanese Political System

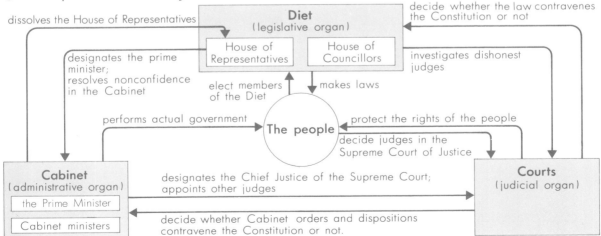

- Since the Cabinet is formed by the majority party, the people can, when dissatisfied with the Cabinet, express their will by not returning the majority party to power in elections.
- The House of Representatives has the power to designate the Prime Minister. Its authority exceeds that of the House of Councillors to vote for bills and the budget and to approve treaties.

MASS MEDIA

Newspapers Three characteristics of Japanese newspapers are the following: (1) Some are nationwide. (2) A clear-cut stance in regard to articles is avoided. (3) The publisher (not the reporter) assumes responsibility for published contents.

◇**Nationwide Newspapers** Japan's size makes news coverage easy. Since so much news is common to the country as a whole, nationwide papers play an important role. The three major national papers and their circulations (morning and evening editions combined) are: the *Yomiuri Shimbun* (13, 740,000), the *Asahi Shimbun* (12,200,000), and the *Mainichi Shimbun* (6,400,000). Both the *Yomiuri* and the *Asahi* boast circulations extraordinarily high for privately-owned newspapers, surpassing the 10,000,000 circulation of the Soviet Union's *Pravda*. Local newspapers in Japan, on the other hand, cover local news in detail but have limited scope and influence.

◇**Factual Reportage Only** Newspaper reports, as opposed to those on TV, can express the views of a paper through the arrangement of editorials and columns. Generally speaking, however, Japanese newspapers avoid stating any clear-cut position on issues. This is because the pages of a newspaper are looked upon as a public forum and news as public property. Insistence on one's own views in such a situation is not something the Japanese public would be able to easily accept. This contrasts with the U.S., where newspapers are expected to clearly express where they stand on issues.

◇**Dubious Responsibility** Due to the public nature of newspapers, subjective reporting is avoided. Basically, each and every article is a neutral statement by the publisher. Criticism from the public is thus directed against the publisher, not the reporter. Though freed from the brunt of public censure, the reporter must, by the

● **Major newspapers worldwide and their circulation** (1985)

country	newspaper	circulation (in 1000s)
Japan	Yomiuri Shimbun	morning paper 8 924
"	Asahi Shimbun	" 7 591
"	Mainichi Shimbun	" 4 180
USA	New York Daily News	" 1 353
"	The New York Times	" 963
England	Daily Mirror	" 3 169
"	Daily Express	" 1 883
"	Daily Mail	" 1 829
"	Times	" 458
France	France Soir	evening paper 433
W. Germany	Bild	morning paper 6 346
Italy	Corriere della Sera	" 583
USSR	Izvestia	evening paper 7 000
"	Pravda	morning paper 10 700
China	Renmin Ribao	" 5 700

Most newspapers in other countries tend to be either morning or evening papers. In Japan, however, the majority of newspapers put out both morning and evening editions. The circulations of evening editions of major newspapers are: Yomiuri Shimbun (4.82 million), Asahi Shimbun (4.61 million) and Mainichi Shimbun (2.21 million).

● **Number of publications issued** 100 millions

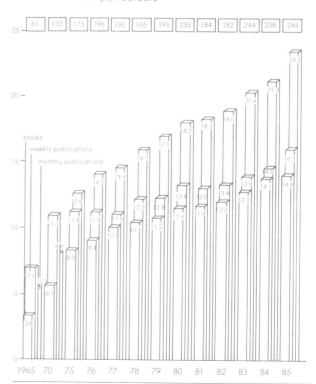

same token, work within the framework of editorial policy.

Weekly Magazines Weekly magazines rank with newspapers as print media. They can roughly be divided into socio-political magazines and entertainment magazines. The personal opinions expressed in the socio-political weeklies actually complement newspapers. Entertainment weeklies, on the other hand, sensationalize topics of personal interest and tend to be vulgar. Photo weeklies are a new kind of magazine. They purport to reveal the truth through articles composed of a single photo and a bit of sarcasm. Despite their spectacular popularity, their publishers are being called into question for their doubtful methods of gathering news and the flagrant way they cater to the public in their intense competition for sales.

Television Television broadcasting is conducted by the Nihon Hoso Kyokai (NHK) and commercial stations. Programs via NHK can be viewed nationwide.

Unlike commercial stations, NHK uses funds collected through users' fees based on a quasi-mandatory contract between all TV owners and NHK. An inevitable result of this operational framework is that the commercial stations cater to the masses.

Regulations governing program content are not excessively strict, so that sex and violence easily find their way over the airwaves.

In Tokyo, NHK has two channels: one for general programming, the other for programs of an educational nature. Commercial stations account for five channels: NTV, TBS, FUJI, TV ASAHI, and TV TOKYO.

Radio Radio broadcasting, like television, is conducted by NHK and commercial stations. Programs that teach conversational French, German, Chinese, Korean and other foreign languages are broadcast daily, with a particularly high audience rating for the Introductory English Conversation program. Late-night broadcasting by commercial stations finds a receptive audience among young people. Radio's portability also makes it a widely-used medium.

● **Number of books published (worldwide)** (1983) units

country	total	country	total
USSR	82 589	China	31 602
USA	76 976	Brazil	19 179
W. Germany	58 489	Canada	19 063
England	50 981	Italy	13 718
Japan	42 977	The Netherlands	13 324
France	37 576	Switzerland	11 405
Rep. of Korea	35 512	Yugoslavia	10 931
Spain	32 138	India	10 649

A unit is a single title. Periodicals are excluded.

● **Breakdown of television programs**
(1986)

NHK (general television): news 38.0% | general culture 27.0% | entertainment 22.1% | 12.9% education

NHK (educational television): 20.1% | education 77.9% | news 2.0% | general culture

commercial television: news 16.6% | 23.7% | entertainment 41.9% | education 12.1% | general culture | 5.7% other

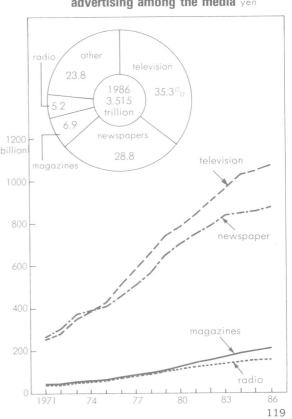

● **Changes in the distribution of advertising among the media** yen

1986 3.515 trillion

radio | other 23.8 | television 35.3%
5.2
6.9
magazines | newspapers 28.8

119

JAPANESE

Japanese is written in three styles of letters: *kanji*, *hira-gana*, and *kata-kana*.

Kanji

Kanji are characters borrowed from China, and each of them has its own meaning. Many *kanji* have meanings that derive from their shape. For example, 【日】 (sun) originated from a crude shape of the sun 【 ☼ 】. 【木】 (tree) came from 【 🌳 】. The character 【東】 (east) is a combination of the sun behind a tree 【 🌳 】, and 【田】 (rice paddy) is derived from four small fields 【 ▦ 】. The character for man 【男】 came from the idea of a man supporting a field. The *kanji* for person 【人】 was taken from the pose of a standing man 【 🧍 】. In appearance it looks as if two bars are supporting each other. This character 【人】 symbolizes the idea that life is led in cooperation with others, that no one can live without the help of others, for if one bar is removed, the other falls.

Kanji are said to number about 50,000. Of these, 1,945 have been chosen as characters for everyday use. These are the ones that appear in newspapers, business letters, or official publications. However, there are other *kanji* that are used in personal and place names, so a knowledge of about 3,000 *kanji* is actually required.

Hira-gana and Kata-kana

Both *hira-gana* and *kata-kana* are phonetic syllabic scripts made from *kanji*. *Hira-gana* are actually simplified versions of selected *kanji*. *Kata-kana*, on the other hand, are segments extracted from whole *kanji*. Further information is provided in the chart on the facing page. Both *hira-gana* and *kata-kana* are original Japanese characters created in the 10th century. Each group has 46 basic letters, representing the basic sounds of the Japanese language.

Aspects of Japanese

Particles indicate the function of each word in a sentence. Although the subject of the sentence usually comes first and the predicate must come last, particles enable Japanese word order to be less rigid than that of English.

● The formation of *Kanji* (Chinese characters)

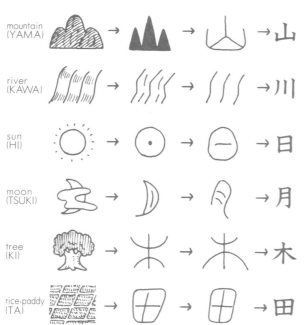

mountain (YAMA)

river (KAWA)

sun (HI)

moon (TSUKI)

tree (KI)

rice-paddy (TA)

Characters derived from pictorial representation

●A character formed by combining two simple characters

• 田 ＋ 力 ＝ 男 (OTOKO)

rice-paddy   strength   man

"Man," defined as one who works hard in the ricefields, is represented by a combination of the characters for "paddy" and "strength."

• 木 ＋ 木 ＝ 林 (HAYASHI)

tree   tree   woods

• 木 ＋ 木 ＋ 木 ＝ 森 (MORI)

tree   tree   tree   forest

A few trees make a wood, many a forest.

• 女 ＋ 家 ＝ 嫁 (YOME)

woman   house   bride

A bride is a woman who enters another family (house).

The formation of *kata-kana*

n	wa	ra	ya	ma	ha	na	ta	sa	ka	a
尓→ン→ン	和→ワ→ワ	良→ラ→ラ	也→セヤ→ヤ	末→マ→マ	八→ハ→ハ	奈→ナ→ナ	多→タ→タ	散→サ→サ	加→カ→カ	阿→阝ア→ア
		利→リ→リ		三→ミ→ミ	比→ヒ→ヒ	二→ニ→ニ	千→チ→チ	之→シ→シ	幾→キ→キ	伊→イ→イ
	由→ユ→ユ	流→ル→ル		牟→ム→ム	不→フ→フ	奴→ヌ→ヌ	川→ツ→ツ	須→ス→ス	久→ク→ク	宇→宀ウ→ウ
		礼→レ→レ		女→メ→メ	部→ヘ→ヘ	祢→ネ→ネ	天→テ→テ	世→セ→セ	介→ケ→ケ	江→エ→エ
呼→シ→ヲ	呂→ロ→ロ	与→チ→ヨ	毛→モ→モ	保→ホ→ホ	乃→ノ→ノ	止→トト→ト	曽→ソ→ソ	己→コ→コ	於→オ→オ	

Kata-kana were formed from one part of a Chinese character.

The formation of *hira-gana*

n	wa	ra	ya	ma	ha	na	ta	sa	ka	a
无→え→ん	和→わ→わ	良→ら→ら	也→せ→や	末→ま→ま	波→は→は	奈→な→な	太→た→た	左→さ→さ	加→か→か	安→あ→あ
		利→わ→り		美→み→み	比→ひ→ひ	仁→に→に	知→ち→ち	之→し→し	幾→弐き→き	以→い→い
	由→ゆ→ゆ	留→る→る		武→む→む	不→ふ→ふ	奴→ぬ→ぬ	川→つ→つ	寸→す→す	久→く→く	宇→う→う
		礼→れ→れ		女→め→め	部→へ→へ	祢→ね→ね	天→て→て	世→せ→せ	計→け→け	衣→え→え
遠→遠→を	呂→ろ→ろ	与→よ→よ	毛→も→も	保→ほ→ほ	乃→の→の	止→と→と	曽→そ→そ	己→こ→こ	於→れ→お	

Hira-gana were formed by simplifying the forms of Chinese characters.

●SET EXPRESSIONS

Words of salutation such as *dozo yoroshiku* (I'm pleased to meet you.), or *o-sewa-ni-narimasu* (Please take care of me.), or *kochira koso* (I expect your kindness, too.) are but three of the many set phrases frequently spoken by the Japanese. No particular requests are made by the people involved; the speakers are simply acknowledging a relationship of mutual dependency.

Oftentimes important words are omitted in many Japanese set phrases. In *sayonara*, for example, which literally means "If so, then...", the idea of "I will see you again" is understood but not stated. The same is true for *kon-nichi-wa*, (literally, "this day"), used as a form of greeting. The full expression is "<u>This day</u> is a nice day."

And when a host serves food or drinks to company at home, he or she will say, much to the surprise of a foreign guest, "Nani mo arimasen ga, dozo meshiagatte kudasai"(This is nothing, but I hope you accept it.) What is understood but not spoken is, "This is nothing <u>THAT I CAN BRAG ABOUT</u>, but..." Set phrases like these express an attitude of modesty.

Nanimo arimasenga, dozo meshiagatte kudasai.

This is nothing, but I hope you accept it.

A Japanese lady

A foreign guest

A Japanese boy who speaks poor English.

Glossary of Culture and History

Asuka culture

The culture associated with Asuka, a region in the southern Yamato plain. It lasted from the middle of the 6th century, when Buddhism was transmitted to Japan, until the middle of the 7th century, the time of the Taika Reform. At its center was the Buddhism made popular by the regent Prince Shotoku (574-622), and it also exhibits Chinese, Indian and Hellenistic influences. The major artifacts extant from the time include the Horyuji, the Shakyamuni triad made by the sculptor Tori Busshi, the Kudara Kannon statue and the Tamamushi Portable Shrine.

Buddhism

The religion and a philosophical system of thought founded in the 6th century B. C. in India by Shakyamuni. Having realized enlightenment, Shakyamuni was called the Buddha ("the Enlightened One"), and his teachings on how to achieve a similar realization gradually spread throughout India, and south-east and east Asia. Buddhism teaches that to escape the delusion of this world it is necessary to possess both wisdom and compassion. It was transmitted from continental Asia to Japan in the 6th century and eventually extended its influence widely on politics and culture.

Bunjinga

Literati painting. A form of painting using ink and light colors, which was popular in the 18th and 19th centuries among scholars and writers. The style, poetic and unworldly, was much admired by the intellectuals of the time. Famous proponents of the form were Ike no Taiga (1723-1776), Yosa Buson (1716-1783) and Tanomura Chikuden (1777-1835).

Bushido

(lit. "the way of the warrior") A moral system taught among samurai, members of the warrior class, during the Edo period. It derived from the practical ethics held in common by samurai, such as the importance of loyalty, bravery, propriety, and frugality. It became theorized in the Edo period under the influence of Confucianism, especially the Neo-Confucianism of the Chu Hsi school, and established as the ethical ideal. Bushido, stripped of the most extreme of its militaristic, antimodern aspects, was once presented as a vehicle to define for Western people all that was most admirable in the Japanese tradition in politeness, generosity, honor, loyalty and self-control. Bushido's strong spiritualism, however, led Japan into becoming, in a

sense, an ultranationalistic state in the modern warring period. Some go as far as to say that Bushido represents all that was most despicable in Japanese wartime behavior. Most Japanese disowned Bushido as part of the ideological equipment of the militarists who had led Japan to defeat and humiliation in World War II and as incompatible with their postwar democratic society.

Byodoin

A temple at Uji, southeast of Kyoto, known particularly for its Amida Hall, popularly called the Phoenix Hall. It was originally the site of a country retreat on the banks of the Uji river, and was converted into a temple by the powerful statesman, Fujiwara no Yorimichi (992-1074), in 1052. The popular name of Phoenix Hall was given to the Amida Hall because of the Phoenix shape of its plan, and the ornaments in the shape of a Phoenix that decorate the roof. Built in 1053, the hall enshrines a statue of the Buddha Amitabha as the central image.

Castles

Military fortifications for protection against the attack of enemies. The number built in Japan increased rapidly after the 14th century, when local conflicts grew more and more widespread. Castles of that period were built on hill-tops, utilizing natural formations. As a result of developments in military techniques, in the 15th and 16th centuries large castles came to be built on the plains as well. They were surrounded by high stone walls and by moats, and became the center for the development of surrounding settlements, called castle towns.

Confucianism

A philosophical tradition attributed to the Chinese teacher Confucius who lived in the 6th century B. C. Confucius advocated that the state should be governed according to an ethical system that all people should uphold. His teachings flourished during the Han dynasty (202 B. C.-220 A. D.), when they were raised to the position of a state cult. A Neo-Confucian movement developed later, the Chu Hsi school during the Sung dynasty (960-1279), and the Wang Yang-ming school during the Ming dynasty (1368-1644). Confucianism exerted an enormous influence on the warrior class, and it was the ethical system that supported the feudal system of the Edo period.

Daimyo

Land-holding lords. The daimyo emerged as vassals of provincial governors in the

● Castles

Kumamoto Castle

Kochi Castle

Nagoya Castle

Kamakura period. During the civil war period of the 15th and 16th centuries, they assumed direct control of their territories. Though warfare, both offensive and defensive, was a way of life for the daimyo, they also encouraged local development by expanding agriculture and permitting the growth of settlements around their castles, the embryo castle town. During the Edo period, a daimyo was a member of the military class who had holdings worth more than 10,000 *goku* (one *koku*=180 liters). There were three types: the *shimpan*, close relatives of the Tokugawa, the *fudai*, hereditary vassals, and the *tozama* (lit. "outside lords"), those who had previously been vassals of Nobunaga or Hideyoshi and who had sworn allegiance to the Tokugawa after 1600. In the early part of the Edo period many had their holdings reassigned. All *daimyo* were placed under the provisions of the Laws for Military Houses (*Buke Shohatto*) and were required to accede to the requirement of alternative attendance (*sankin kotai*); consequently their autonomy was circumscribed and they were subject to much shogunal intervention and control.

Edo Castle
The residence of fifteen generations of Tokugawa shoguns in what is now Tokyo. A small fortification had been built on the site by a local power holder, Ota Dokan (1432-1486) in the 15th century. In 1590 Tokugawa Ieyasu took possession of the castle at the order of his overlord, Toyotomi Hideyoshi, and began massive extensions. The Tokugawa surrendered it to imperial forces in 1868, and the following year it became the Imperial palace.

Emakimono
A scroll depicting a story in both pictures and words. It may be considered a type of Yamato-e (Yamato Painting), and was a popular art form in the 12th and 13th centuries. Famous examples include the *Genji Monogatari Emaki* (The picture scroll of the Tale of Genji) and the *Choju Giga* (The Scroll of the Frolicking Animals).

Esoteric Buddhism (Mikkyo)
A form of Buddhism that emphasizes the direct transmission of the teachings to attain enlightenment from master to disciple. These teachings attach great importance to demanding ascetic practice, prayers and incantations. Esoteric Buddhism rose in India in the 7th and 8th centuries and was brought to Japan early in the 9th century from T'ang China by the Japanese monks Kukai and Saicho. The former made esoteric teachings the center of his Shingon sect, and the latter incorporated them into his Tendai sect.

Fusuma-e
Pictures painted on *fusuma* (wooden sliding partitions), walls and *shoji*. The form was developed during the Momoyama period as internal decoration of castles and mansions. Members of the Kano school of painting in particular were responsible for flamboyant works using bright colors on a background of gold leaf.

Genroku culture
The culture that bloomed during the Genroku era (1688-1704). The newly rich and influential merchants of the Osaka, Kyoto regions were the driving force behind the vigorous and showy culture that combined the cultural traditions of Kyoto and the money of Osaka. The illustrated novels of Ihara Saikaku (1642-1693), the *joruri* scripts of Chikamatsu Monzaemon (1653-1724), and the *haikai* of Matsuo Basho (1644-1694) were all a product of this time. The culture eventually spread throughout the country.

Ginkaku
The Silver Pavilion. A two-storied building, part of the summer retreat erected in the Higashiyama district of Kyoto by the 8th Muromachi shogun, Ashikaga Yoshimasa (1436-1490), in 1489. Its name derives from the fact that original plans were for it to be covered with silver leaf. The lower storey is in the *shoen* style, and the upper is the Zen temple-hall style. With its surrounding garden, it is the epitome of Higashiyama culture. After Yoshimasa's death in 1490, the retreat was converted into a Buddhist temple, Jishoji.

Haikai
A poetic form derived from the classical thirty-one syllable verse form (*tanka*) and the prototype of the *haiku*. It grew out of the opening stanza (*hokku*) of linked verse (*renga*), and consists of three lines and seventeen syllables in the pattern 5-7-5. Despite its being very popular, it was considered slightly vulgar until refined by Matsunaga Teitoku (1571-1653), though with some loss of its original humor and spontaneity. Matsuo Basho brought the form to maturity in the late 17th century. (see also *haiku*)

Haiku
A poetic form also known as *haikai*. The term *haiku* was popularized by the poet Masaoka Shiki (1867-1902) and it is now used to designate the independent 5-7-5 syllable verse. It follows certain conventions, such as the use of a seasonal expression. Matsuo Basho combined the spontaneity of the *haikai* with artistic refinement and sensibility. He also introduced to it the aesthetic value of *sabi* (austere beauty). Other important poets were Yosa Buson

●Edo Castle

now Imperial palace

●Ginkaku

(1716-1783), Kobayashi Issa (1763-1827) and Masaoka Shiki. The form remains widely popular today.

Heiankyo

The original name of Kyoto, and the site of the capital of Japan, the center of government and the location of the imperial court for approximately 1100 years from its founding in 794, when the Emperor Kammu moved the capital there in an effort to reinvigorate the system of government based on the centralization of administration and taxation that was adopted after the Taika Reforms, until 1868 when the capital was shifted to Tokyo.

Patterned after the Chinese capital of Ch'ang-an, Heiankyo measured 4.5 kilometers from east to west and 5.3 kilometers from north to south, somewhat larger than the previous capital of Heijokyo (Nara). The emperor's residence and the government offices were to be located in the center of the city, the main avenues constructed on a grid system and the smaller streets also built to follow the same basic plan. However construction was brought to a halt in 805, and the city never achieved the form of the original plan.

Heijokyo

The capital built by the Empress Gemmei in what is now the western part of the city of Nara, patterned after the grid pattern of the Chinese capital of Ch'ang-an. For seventy-four years (710-784) it flourished as the center of government and culture. It measured about 4.2 kilomters from east to west, and about 4.7 kilometers from north to south. The residence of the emperor and the government offices were located in the northern part of the city and the main east-west and north-south avenues intersected like the lines of a checker board. With their red pillars, white walls and tiled roofs, the buildings belonging to government offices, mansions of the nobility and temples gave the city a color and beauty that was extolled in song.

Higashiyama culture

The culture of the middle part of the Muromachi period (1338-1573). The name is taken from the country retreat that the 8th Ashikaga shogun, Yoshimasa, built in the Higashiyama district of Kyoto as a refuge from the ravages of the Onin war (1467-77). There, following the example of Ashikaga Yoshimitsu, the third shogun, he built the Silver Pavilion. His encouragement of the arts gave the period its flourishing culture. Chinese studies (centering on the writings of the Sung period) were undertaken by monks of the Gozan Zen monasteries, while linked verse poetry (*renga*) was promoted by Sogi (1421-1502) and ink painting by

Sesshu (1420-1506). The *shoin* style was adapted from Zen temples for the domestic architecture of the warrior class, and the arts of tea ceremony and flower arrangement gained in popularity.

Himeji Castle

One of the best surviving examples of a Japanese castle, located in Himeji in Hyogo prefecture. It was completed in 1610 by the daimyo Ikeda Terumasa (1564-1613), a son-in-law of Ieyasu. It is a castle of the "plain" type, erected on a small hill. The central keep, five stories high on the outside and seven stories high inside, is connected with three smaller keeps. The castle is also known as Shirasagi (Egret) Castle because of the beauty of its white walls.

Horyuji

A temple erected in 607 by Prince Shotoku (574~622), located at Ikaruga near Nara. Destroyed by fire in the middle of the 7th century, it was reconstructed some time after that, and is today the oldest wooden construction in the world. It is strongly influenced by Chinese culture, and in the wooden columns of the inner gate and corridor may be discerned curved shafts like those of Greek Doric columns. The layout of the temple compound, with the main hall (*kondo*) and the five-storied pagoda side by side, is a Japanese innovation, not a Chinese design. Horyuji epitomizes the first great period of Buddhist culture in Japan. Among its treasures are the Shakyamuni triad made by the sculptor Tori Busshi in 623, and the minature Tamamushi shrine, dating back to the late 7th century.

Ikebana

Flower arrangement ranks with the tea ceremony as one of the characteristic arts of Japan. It is also termed the way of flowers (*kado*). During the Muromachi period it was called *rikka* ("standing flowers"). It became valued as an art of appreciation, and was especially popular among the nobility and the Buddhist priests.It spread throughout all classes of society during the Edo period, when various schools proliferated.

Ink Paintings (*Suibokuga*)

Monochrome pictures using only contrastive shades of black ink. They originated during the T'ang dynasty (618-907) in China, and were perfected in the Sung dynasty (960-1279). Ink painting was developed in Japan during the Kamakura and Muromachi periods, under the influence of Sung and Yuan (1271-1368) techniques and styles. It was the painter Sesshu (1420-1506) who brought to perfection a Japanese style of ink painting.

●Himeji Castle

●Horyuji

Kondo

●Ikebana

Nageire

Joruri

Narrative chanting that originated during the Muromachi period and gained in popularity during the Edo period. Towards the end of the 16th century, the *shamisen* was introduced from Okinawa as an accompaniment for voice. The form developed when puppets were introduced to illustrate the chanting. During the Genroku era, the chanter Takemoto Gidayu (1651-1714) perfected the *gidayu-bushi* style, which is still used in the puppet theater today. In Edo, *gidayu* was joined to Kabuki, and further styles of chanting, such as *tokiwazu-bushi* and *kiyomoto-bushi*, came into existence.

Kabuki

A popular form of stage entertainment which was developed during the Edo period. It originated in the performances of dancing and light drama (*kabuki-odori*) enacted by a woman, Okuni, and her group in Kyoto at the beginning of the 17th century. When this "women's Kabuki" was banned in 1629, its place was taken by *wakashu kabuki*, performances by young men, and then after 1652, when that in turn was forbidden, by *yaro kabuki*, "men's kabuki." Kabuki was brought to maturity as a dramatic form with the appearance of excellent scripts and the development of women's roles taken by specialist male actors called *onnagata* or *oyama*.

Kana

Simple syllabic writing systems developed in Japan early in the Heian period for convenience of writing. The term *kana* means "not regular" in contrast to the "real writing" (*mana*) of Chinese characters (*kanji*). *Hiragana* (rounded letters), also known as *sogana* (cursive letters), is a system derived from simplified versions of the cursive style of Chinese characters, and originally was used largely by women. The second of the syllabaries used today is *katakana* (fragmented letters). It dates from the end of the Nara period, when various elements of Chinese characters were employed as phonetic symbols to aid Buddhist priests in reciting texts written in Chinese.

Kanji

Chinese ideographs. The oldest known of these characters are to be found engraved on tortoise shells excavated from the site of the capital of the Yin (Shang) dynasty (c. 1400-1027 B. C.). The Chinese writing system was brought to Japan during the 5th century, and used originally by immigrants from the continent for compiling court records and composing letters to be sent abroad. Gradually characters came to be used more and more widely among the Japanese themselves. They are termed "real writing" (*mana*) in contrast to the "nonregular" *kana* (see above).

Kasei culture

The designation given to the brilliant culture of the final years of the Tokugawa period, taking its name from the two eras (Bunka and Bunsei) that covered the first three decades of the 19th century. At that time the center of culture shifted to Edo from the Osaka-Kyoto region, and from the rich merchants to the townsmen in general. In content also, the culture became more popular and was widely disseminated. However, the vitality of the culture was weakened by social dislocation and strict shogunal control and the suppressed vigor was diverted to satire. The ideals of understated but perfect taste (*iki*) and connoisseurship (*tsu*) were stressed.

Katsura Detached Palace (*Katsura Rikyu*)

A villa on the banks of the Katsura River west of Kyoto dating from the middle of the 17th century. Built by Prince Hachijo no Miya Toshihito (1579-1629), the younger brother of the Emperor Goyozei, it is a skilful harmonization of buildings and strolling garden, a place of simple beauty.

Kinkaku

The Golden Pavilion. A splendid three storey building that was originally part of the country retreat that the third Muromachi shogun, Ashikaga Yoshimitsu (1358-1408), built at Kitayama in Kyoto in 1397. It is so called because its walls and pillars were gilded. It is a typical example of the Kitayama culture, with a continental Zen temple style incorporated with the traditional *shinden-zukuri* architectural style. The retreat was converted into a Buddhist temple, Rokuonji, after Yoshimitsu's death in 1408. Destroyed by arson in 1950, it was rebuilt in 1955.

Kitagawa Utamaro

(1753-1806) *Ukiyo-e* artist. Trained in the Kano school tradition and in the techniques of print-making. Influenced by the work of Katsukawa Shunsyo (1726-1792) and Torii Kiyonaga (1752-1815), he perfected the print depicting popular beauties. His work is characterized by the half-torso figure, and his expression of individualistic female beauty through concentration on the face and the hands. He brought about a golden age in the representation of women in prints.

Kitayama culture

The culture of the early part of the Muromachi period (1338-1573). It is typified by the Golden Pavilion (*Kinkaku*) built by the third Muromachi shogun, Ashikaga Yoshimitsu, at Kitayama in the northern part of Kyoto. A special feature of the culture is that it encompasses both the Japanese cultures of the warrior class and the court

● **Kabuki**

"Sukeroku"

● **Kinkaku**

● **Kitagawa Utamaro**

"Musume-hidokei"

nobility and the Zen-influenced Chinese culture. The Five Mountains (*Gozan*) literature and monochrome ink painting (*suibokuga*) were developed at this time, and the Noh drama was perfected by Kan'ami (1333-1384) and his son Zeami (1363-1443)

Kojiki

"Record of Ancient Matters," the oldest extant history of Japan. The Emperor Temmu (r. 673-686) initially ordered its compilation, but interruptions occurred and it was the Empress Gemmei (r. 707-715) who saw to the completion of the work, undertaken by Hieda no Are and O no Yasumaro and presented to the Empress in 712. In three sections, the *Kojiki* covers the mythological beginnings of Japan, its legends, and the reigns of its Emperors, using Chinese characters.

Kokugaku (National Learning)

An intellectual tradition of the Edo period that emphasized the importance of the native Japanese tradition especially in thought and literature. In rejecting what was not Japanese, in particular Chinese and Buddhist, National Learning undertook the historical study of old texts to find what was truly Japanese. Kamo Mabuchi (1697-1769) studied the *Manyoshu* and extolled it as the true expression of Japanese feeling. The studies of Motoori Norinaga (1730-1801) of the *Kojiki* and *The Tale of Genji* gave the movement a new classical tradition independent of Chinese or Buddhist influence. An off-shoot of National Learning was the Shinto revival of Hirata Atsutane (1776-1843) and others. Hirata attempted to rouse the national consciousness of the Japanese as Japanese. This in turn influenced the promoters of Imperial restoration, and had an effect on Meiji policy in the first few years of the new government.

Kyoka

(lit. "mad verse") A literary form that was popular during the 18th century. It employs the thirty-one syllable form of the traditional Japanese poem (*waka*) but depends on humor and punning for its effect. It had an appeal that crossed classes, involving both samurai and townsmen. Many of the *kyoka* satire political and social events of their time. One of the best known of the *kyoka* poets was Ota Nampo (1749-1823).

Kyogen

Light comic plays that are performed between separate Noh plays. Thus they are also called *Nohkyogen*. As Noh developed out of the earlier *sarugaku* tradition in the Muromachi period, certain comic roles that had existed in that popular entertainment came to be emphasized. Many *kyogen* have as their subject matter the everyday life of

the common people, and there are also a large number which lampoon the samurai and the Buddhist priests.

Manyoshu

The oldest collection of Japanese poetry, compiled during the Nara period. Divided into twenty sections, it contains about 4,500 *waka* (poems) written by a wide range of people including emperors, nobles, priests and farmers. Famous poets represented include Kakinomoto no Hitomaro, Yamabe no Akahito, Yamanoue no Okura, Otomo no Tabito, Otomo no Yakamochi and Princess Nukada. The name of the compiler is unclear, although the collection has been attributed to Otomo no Yakamochi.

Matsuo Basho

(1644-1694) A *haiku* poet. Originally a retainer of the Todo family of Iga (Mie prefecture), he studied the *haikai* in Kyoto, and moved to Edo on the death of his lord, at which time he gave up his position as a samurai. He continued to devote himself to his poetry, and spent much of his time on journeys, which became the subject matter for original *haiku*. He raised the *haikai* form to unprecedented heights. His collection of verse and anecdotes, *The Narrow Road to the Deep North* is famous.

Meiji Restoration

The restoration of Imperial rule under Emperor Meiji in 1868. The leaders of the restoration movement were largely members of the samurai class from the "outer," non-Tokugawa domains. Though the new government at first contained many who were the ideologues of Shinto restoration, and was supported by the proponents of the *sonno joi* slogan, the emergent leaders showed a willingness to try new ideas, which led to wholesale importation of Western modes, moderation in their ability to resist the demands of ideology in favor of the practical, and an appreciation of traditional ideals.

Momoyama culture

The culture of the Azuchi-Momoyama period (1573-1603). The flamboyant culture with its strong decorative element took form based on the economic strength of the new daimyo class, typified by Nobunaga and Hideyoshi, and of the rich merchants of the Osaka area. In contrast to previous cultural expressions, the art of this time was little influenced by Buddhism. It was rather a secular culture set firmly at the human level. It was heavily influenced by the Western artifacts of the *Namban* culture.

Mono no aware

An aesthetic term denoting sensitivity to the pathos of things as they constantly undergo change. It has become almost syn-

●Matsuo Basho

●Meiji Restroation

Emperor Meiji

onymous with the artistic and literary ideals of the Heian period. *Aware*, which originally signalled some kind of intense emotion, was used by the Heian nobility to express what was elegant, refined, but ephemeral. The Buddhist teachings of impermanence seem to have influenced the notion.

Murasaki Shikibu
(ca. 978-1016) Author, born into the middle nobility. She began to write *The Tale of Genji* after her husband's death. As a result she became well-known and was summoned to court to attend the Empress, Shoshi, the daughter of Fujiwara no Michinaga and wife of the Emperor Ichijo.

Namban culture
The culture brought by Europeans during the latter half of the 16th century. Much of it was connected directly with Christianity, though it was multifaceted, including astronomy, the calendar, geography, medicine, techniques for movable type printing, oil painting and engraving, food and dress.

Nihon Shoki
"Chronicles of Japan." An historical work completed in 720 compiled at the order of the Emperor by Prince Toneri and O no Yasumaro. It is basically an Imperial history from the mythical age to the reign of the Empress Jito. It was written in classical Chinese and organized according to the Chinese histories. It is, with the *Kojiki*, an important source for the study of early Japanese history.

Noh
One of the classical art forms of Japan. It is a form of drama which developed out of the popular entertainment current since the Heian period, *sarugaku* and *dengaku*, and became perfected as an elegant performing art by the actor and dancer Kan'ami (1333-1384) and his son Zeami (1363-1443) in the 14th and 15th centuries under the patronage of the shogun Ashikaga Yoshimitsu (1358-1408). Five schools now exist: the Kanze, the Hosho, the Kongo, the Kita and the Komparu. Though widely known as Noh, it has officially been called *nohgaku* since the Meiji period.

Oda Nobunaga
(1534-1582) The first of the great reunifiers of Japan after the period of civil war in the 15th and 16th centuries. A daimyo from the province of Owari (the present Aichi prefecture), he defeated the powerful daimyo Imagawa Yoshimoto at the Battle of Okehazama in 1560 and then proceeded to pacify the neighboring province of Mino (Gifu prefecture). In 1568 he installed Ashikaga Yoshiaki as shogun in Kyoto and took control of the government. Yoshiaki took up arms against Nobunaga in 1573, but was defeated and sent into exile, bringing to an effective end the Muromachi shogunate. Nobunaga then subjugated the five provinces of the capital region, and the provinces along the Japan Sea and Pacific Ocean coasts. He built Azuchi Castle in the present Shiga prefecture as his residence. He was assassinated in 1582 by Akechi Mitsuhide at the temple of Honnoji in Kyoto.

Osaka Castle
Erected on the site of the temple, Ishiyama Honganji, by Toyotomi Hideyoshi in 1583. Its construction took three years and the labor of tens of thousands of conscripted workers. After Hideyoshi moved to Fushimi castle near Kyoto, Osaka Castle was put under the control of his young son, Hideyori. It was burned when it fell to the Tokugawa in 1615, but was soon restored by the shogunate. The present keep is a reconstruction dating from 1931.

Otogi-zoshi
Short moral tales written between the 14th and 17th centuries. A large number were composed during the Muromachi period (1338-1573) and were read by townspeople. Tales such as *Monogusa Taro* and *Issun Boshi* have become the basis for modern nursery stories.

Pure Land Buddhism
A general term for those Buddhist doctrines which teach that people can attain rebirth in the Pure Land of a Buddha, Amida (Amitabha) in particular. In Japan they remained for a long time an element of existing sects, but nevertheless dominated Japanese religious thought from the 11th century, and influenced religious art and architecture to a large degree. Pure Land doctrines were brought from China to Japan by various monks during the Heian period and systematized within the Tendai school in particular, from which emerged Genshin (942-1017), who wrote the important treaties on Pure Land faith and practice, *Ojo Yoshu* (Essentials of Rebirth), Honen (1133-1212), who encouraged the single practice of the oral invocation as the only way to salvation and founded the first independent Pure Land sect, the Jodo, and Shinran (1173-1262), who stressed the importance of faith and founded the Jodo Shin sect.

Renga
Linked verse. Consists of alternating stanzas composed by different people based on the two parts of the classic thirty-one syllable poem: the "upper" (*kami no ku*) of three lines and the "lower" (*shimo no ku*) of two lines. Linked verse can continue for fifty or a hundred stanzas. The form originated during the Nara period, and was a type of

●Noh

"Sumidagawa"

●Oda Nobunaga

●Osaka Castle

entertainment among the nobles during the Heian period. Its form was regulated during the Muromachi period, when it spread among the common people and steadily gained in popularity. The poet Sogi (1421-1502) was an acclaimed master of the technique.

Rokumeikan

(lit. "Deer Cry Pavilion") A building constructed in 1883 by the English architect Josiah Conder (1852-1920) in the Hibiya district of Tokyo as a social forum for the upper classes. It reflects the Europeanization of society at the time when Japan was trying to secure the revision of the Unequal Treaties. It was intended to show the world the results of Westernization.

●**Rokumeikan**

Sabi

An aesthetic term denoting pleasure in austere beauty, in what is faded or imperfect. A coarse but often-used tea-bowl of uneven glaze, cracked and mended, may denote it, as may a fallen flower or a moss-covered rock. There is no melancholy engendered, and in this *sabi* contrasts to the *mono no aware* of the Heian period. Basho's *haiku* epitomize the ideal of *sabi*.

Sakoku

The policy of isolation imposed on Japan in the middle of the 17th century by the Tokugawa shogunate. To enforce the ban on Christianity and to ensure shogunal control of overseas trade, Japanese were forbidden to travel abroad and the entry of foreign vessels into Japanese ports was strictly limited. Japanese were forbidden to leave the country in 1635, and in 1639, following the Shimabara Rebellion, in which (Roman Catholic) Christianity had been implicated, Portuguese ships were denied entry to ports. After that, the only foreign trade that was allowed had to be done through the southern port of Nagasaki, and was limited to two countries only, China and Holland.

Sen no Rikyu

(1522-1591) The great tea-master of the Azuchi-Momoyama period. Born in Sakai (near Osaka), the son of a wealthy merchant family, he served both Oda Nobunaga and Toyotomi Hideyoshi, officiating at tea-ceremonies. He brought the tea-ceremony to perfection based on his ideals of simplicity and ordinariness. He was forced to commit suicide after having incurred Hideyoshi's anger.

Senryu

A literary form popular during the latter half of the Edo period. It is composed of seventeen syllables in three lines of five, seven and five. Most *senryu* are a satire of society or a parody of human nature. Since the publication of the immensely popular collection of these verses, *Yanagidaru*, by the poet Karai Senryu (1718-1790) they have come to be called generally by his name.

Sesshu

(1420-1506) A monk-painter during the Muromachi period, the most famous painter of ink paintings (*suibokuga*). He became a monk in the Zen sect at the age of ten, and studied painting. In 1467 he travelled to China and after his return in 1469 perfected a Japanese style of ink painting. Representative of his work are *Landscape of the Four Seasons, Autumn and Winter Landscapes*, and *Landscape on a Long Scroll*.

Shell mounds

Mounds made from piles of shells discarded by people of the Stone Age (corresponding to the Jomon period in Japan). Discarded stone and clay utensils, and animal bones have also been excavated from them. They are thus important in terms of archeology. Many have been discovered along the Pacific Coast in particular. The first systematic excavation of a shell mound in Japan was undertaken by the American zoologist Edward Morse (1838-1923) in 1877 at Omori in Tokyo.

Shinden-zukuri

A style of domestic architecture for the nobility perfected in the Heian period. Its central feature was the main hall (*shinden*), to which was connected in the east, west and north annexes (*tainoya*) and pavilions (*tsuridono* and *izumidono*). Each building was joined by passageways (*watadono*). The main hall was fronted by a formal garden of ponds and artificial hills.

Shinran

(1173-1262) A Buddhist priest who lived at the beginning of the Kamakura period (1192-1333). He studied first at the Tendai complex on Mt. Hiei near Kyoto, and then became a follower of the monk Honen, who had left Mt. Hiei to establish a practice of faith in the Buddha Amitabha, based upon the recitation of the *nembutsu* invocation. Exiled to the present Niigata prefecture, Shinran went a step further than his master and founded the Jodo Shin sect, also called the Ikko (Single-minded) sect. He taught that anybody at all can be saved, if they have absolute faith in Amitabha. In particular he advocated that it is particularly the evil man who has the capacity for rebirth. After spreading his teachings widely through the Kanto area, he eventually returned to Kyoto.

Shoin-zukuri

An architectural style used in the construction of the residences of the warrior class during the Muromachi and Azuchi Momoyama periods. Characteristic elements of the style are the *genkan* (entrance hall), the *tokonoma* (alcove), the *chigaidana* (staggered shelving), the *shoin* (built-in desk), and the use of *fusuma* (sliding screens), *shoji* (latticed paper sliding partitions) and *tatami* (matting for floors). It represents an adaption of elements from Zen architecture to the domestic architecture of the warrior class, and is the basis for the modern domestic style.

Shosoin

An ancient storehouse in the compound of Todaiji, a temple in Nara, now under the jurisdiction of the Imperial Household Agency. It is built in the *azekura* style, walls made of interlocking logs. The term *sho-so* was originally applied to the principal storehouses of local authorities and temples, but now it indicates only the storehouse located north-west of the Great Buddha Hall at Todaiji. It is a treasure house of Tempyo culture, containing articles formerly belonging to the Emperor Shomu (8th century), Buddhist implements, and documents.

Tale of Genji (*Genji Monogatari*)

The best-known, as well as one of the earliest examples, of Japanese prose literature, written early in the 11th century by the court lady, Murasaki Shikibu. It is a very long work, of fifty-four chapters, and over a thousand pages in translation. The first part of the work, up till the 41st chapter, paints the colorful "world of the Shining Prince," the life of the court nobility with the hero, Hikaru Genji, as the central figure. The second part of the Tale is more somber, dealing with the dark fate of Kaoru, supposedly Genji's son.

Tea ceremony (*chanoyu*)

The etiquette surrounding meetings for the drinking of tea. It is also called the Way of Tea (*chado*). It is said to have been brought from China in the Nara period, but it was in the Kamakura period that the powdered green tea used in the ceremony was recommended by Buddhist monks to people as medicine. Tea drinking became naturalized during the Muromachi period, and turned into an accomplishment of refined elegance. The procedure was simplified by Murata Juko (1422-1502), and made into a supreme art by Sen no Rikyu (1522-1592).

Tempyo culture

The culture of the Nara period (710-784). It flourished particularly during the Tempyo era (729-749) when the Emperor Shomu was on the throne. It was an aristocratic culture with Buddhism at its center, and heavily influenced by the culture of the Chinese T'ang dynasty. Also apparent is the influence of western Asian and Indian cultures. Typical of the culture are the Buddhist statues of Todaiji in Nara and the treasures of the Shosoin.

Terakoya (Temple school)

Popular schools during the Edo period. Here the children of townsmen and farmers were taught reading, writing and the use of the abacus by teachers who may have been *ronin* (masterless samurai), Buddhist or Shinto priests, or doctors. Texts such as the *Teikin Orai* (a collection of models for letter writing) were used.

Todaiji

A temple built during the Nara period as the foremost of the national temples (*kokubunji*) by the Emperor Shomu. The dedication ceremony of the main image, the Great Buddha, a statue of the Buddha Mahāvairocana, was conducted in 752. The present Great Buddha Hall is a construction of the Edo period, and is only seventy percent of the dimension of the original; nevertheless it is the largest wooden building in the world.

Tokugawa Ieyasu

(1542-1616) The first Tokugawa shogun. Born the eldest son of Matsudaira Hirotada, the lord of Okazaki Castle (in the present Aichi prefecture). As a child he was sent as hostage to the Oda and Imagawa families. Later, in alliance with Nobunaga, he extended his power, and was a party to the unification of Japan under Toyotomi Hideyoshi. He moved to Edo in 1590 when he was granted the Kanto plain as fief. At the Battle of Sekigahara in 1600 he defeated Ishida Mitsunari and his allies. In 1603 he established his shogunate in Edo, but two years later resigned his position in favor of his son Hidetada. Neverthless he continued to wield actual power from his retirement.

Toro site

Archeological site which is a good example of Yayoi period (ca. 300 B. C.-300 A. D.) remains. It is located in marshland on the eastern bank of the Abe river in the southern part of the city of Shizuoka. It was discovered in 1943, and excavations were undertaken between 1947 and 1950. Archeologists made rich finds: dwellings, storehouses with raised floors, the remains of paddies, and wooden farming implements such as paddy-clogs (*tageta*), looms, and pestles. It was designated a special historical site in 1952.

Toshogu Shrine (Nikko Shrine)

A Shinto shrine in Nikko, Tochigi prefecture, dedicated to Tokugawa Ieyasu. After Ieyasu died, his remains were interred on Mt. Kuno (Shizuoka prefecture). Hidetada, according to his father's wishes, removed the remains to a mausoleum in Nikko, which was completed in 1617. The third

●Tokugawa Ieyasu

●Toro site

shogun, Iemitsu, undertook large-scale extensions, which resulted in the shrine as we know it today. The buildings are flamboyantly decorated with ornate carving, gold-leaf and painted designs. The Yomeimon (1636), the main gate, is a good example of the architecture of the period.

Toyotomi Hideyoshi

● Toyotomi Hideyoshi

(1536-1598) A general who brought all Japan under his control in the late 16th century. He was born Kinoshita Tokichiro in the province of Owaki (Aichi prefecture). A retainer of Nobunaga, he was given posts of increasing importance, until he became the lord of Nagahama Castle in Omi (Shiga prefecture) with the name Hashiba Hideyoshi. He heard of Nobunaga's assassination while campaigning in western Japan. Having beaten the assassin, Akechi Mitsuhide, in battle, he assumed the position of successor to Nobunaga. Later he reached a settlement with Tokugawa Ieyasu and by 1590 had united the whole country. In 1585 he had received the title of *Kampaku* (an Imperial designation) and the following year the surname Toyotomi from the Emperor. His cadastral survey and his Sword Hunt (which forced any one not a samurai to turn in his weapons) laid the foundations for a feudal society. His last years were darkened by the failure of his plans to conquer Korea.

Ukiyo-e

(lit. "pictures of the floating world") A form of art depicting the life of the common people very popular during the Edo period. It had its origins in the latter part of the 17th century in the work of Hishikawa Moronobu (d. 1694). Moronobu at first produced ukiyo-e in the form of painting, but soon moved on to the design of woodblock prints and developed the technique of multicolored printing called *nishiki-e*. The golden age of *ukiyo-e* was the first three decades of the 19th century, with the collections depicting popular beauties by Kitagawa Utamaro (1753-1806), the studies of *Kabuki* actors by Toshusai Sharaku (dates unknown) and the landscape prints of Katsushika Hokusai (1760-1849) and Ando Hiroshige (1797-1858).

● Ukiyo-e

"36 Views of Mt. Fuji" by Hokusai

Wabi

An aesthetic term denoting what is serene and austere. During the turmoil and disruption that marked the Kamakura and Muromachi periods, poverty and simplicity took on a positive value, and were extolled by writers as Kamo no Chomei (*Hojoki*, "An Account of My Hut"). The aesthetic was prized by the tea-masters of the 16th century, and emphasized particularly by Sen no Rikyu (1522-1591). *Wabi* tends to

"53 Stations of the Tokaido road" by Hiroshige

denote a way of regarding things, and contrasts to *sabi*, which is closer to an artistic or poetic ideal.

Yamato-e

Japanese style painting, which emerged around the middle of the Heian period. When the embassies to China were terminated, the predominant Chinese styles of painting were replaced by paintings of a Japanese flavor, of soft lines and bright colors, depicting scenery and customs. At first it was used in the decoration of screens (*byobu-e*) but by the end of the Heian period it had developed into the picture scroll (*emakimono*), with works such as the illustrated *Tale of Genji*.

Yogaku

(lit. "Western learning") The general name given Western studies, particularly science, during the Edo period. Things European were first known through the Portuguese and the Spanish traders and missionaries, and later through the Dutch and English merchants, but after the seclusion policy came into effect, all knowledge of the West came through the Dutch at Dejima, and the study of the West was called Dutch Learning (*Rangaku*). The term *Yogaku* came into use in the 19th century when languages other than Dutch came to be studied. European influence was felt in the early period in medicine, firearms, shipbuilding, engraving, etc. and from the 17th century interest centered around medicine, astronomy, geography and military science.

Yokyoku

The chants composed in the Muromachi period, which acted as the script for Noh plays. Zeami (1363-1443) is the best known of the composers of *yokyoku*. During the Edo period it is said some three thousand were composed.

Zen

A sect of Buddhism. It professes not to place weight on the Buddhist scriptures or on ritual, but says that enlightenment can be gained through meditation (*zazen*). The two best known of its schools in Japan are Rinzai transmitted from China by Eisai (1141-1215), and Soto, transmitted by Dogen (1200-1253). Zen teachings spread widely during the Kamakura and Muromachi periods.

Chronology of Japanese

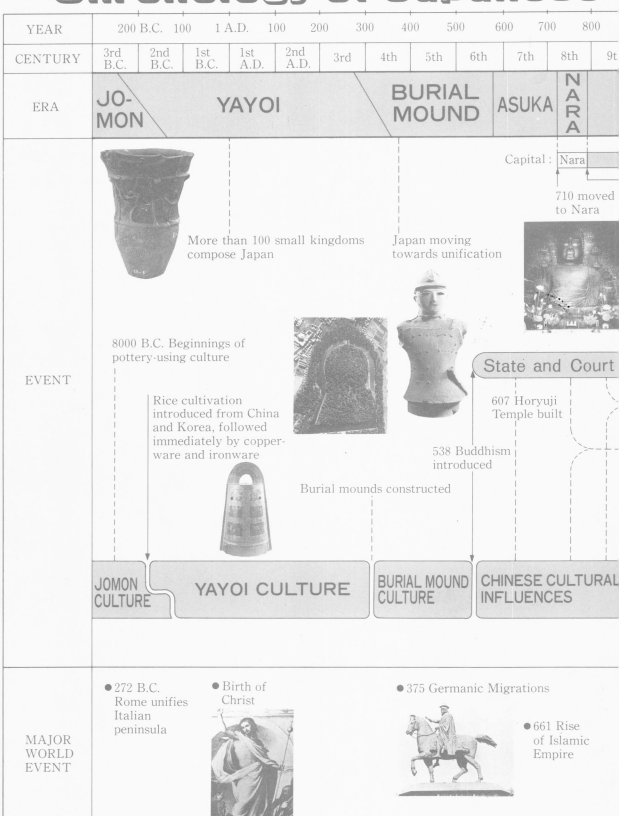

YEAR	200 B.C. 100 1 A.D. 100 200 300 400 500 600 700 800
CENTURY	3rd B.C. / 2nd B.C. / 1st B.C. / 1st A.D. / 2nd A.D. / 3rd / 4th / 5th / 6th / 7th / 8th / 9t
ERA	JO-MON / YAYOI / BURIAL MOUND / ASUKA / NARA

EVENT

Capital : Nara

710 moved to Nara

More than 100 small kingdoms compose Japan

Japan moving towards unification

8000 B.C. Beginnings of pottery-using culture

Rice cultivation introduced from China and Korea, followed immediately by copper-ware and ironware

State and Court

607 Horyuji Temple built

538 Buddhism introduced

Burial mounds constructed

JOMON CULTURE — YAYOI CULTURE — BURIAL MOUND CULTURE — CHINESE CULTURAL INFLUENCES

MAJOR WORLD EVENT

● 272 B.C. Rome unifies Italian peninsula

● Birth of Christ

● 375 Germanic Migrations

● 661 Rise of Islamic Empire

THE POP LARKIN CHRONICLES

H. E. BATES

THE POP LARKIN CHRONICLES

THE DARLING BUDS OF MAY

A BREATH OF FRENCH AIR

WHEN THE GREEN WOODS LAUGH

OH! TO BE IN ENGLAND

A LITTLE OF WHAT YOU FANCY

GUILD PUBLISHING

LONDON · NEW YORK · SYDNEY · TORONTO

This edition published 1991 by
Guild Publishing by arrangement with Michael Joseph

Printed in England by Clays Ltd, St Ives plc

A CIP catalogue record for this book is available from the British Library

CN 9741

·CONTENTS·

·THE DARLING BUDS ·
· OF MAY ·

· 1 ·

After distributing the eight ice-creams – they were the largest vanilla, chocolate, and raspberry super-bumpers, each in yellow, brown, and almost purple stripes – Pop Larkin climbed up into the cab of the gentian blue, home-painted thirty-hundredweight truck, laughing happily.

'Perfick wevver! You kids all right at the back there? Ma, hitch up a bit!'

Ma, in her salmon jumper, was almost two yards wide.

'I said you kids all right there?'

'How do you think they can hear,' Ma said, 'with you revving up all the time?'

Pop laughed again and let the engine idle. The strong May sunlight, the first hot sun of the year, made the bonnet of the truck gleam like brilliant blue enamel. All down the road, winding through the valley, miles of pink apple orchards were in late bloom, showing petals like light confetti.

'Zinnia and Petunia, Primrose, Victoria, Montgomery, Mariette!' – Pop unrolled the handsome ribbon of six names but heard only five separate answers, each voice choked and clotted with ice-cream.

'Where's Mariette? Ain't Mariette there?'

'I'm here, Pop.'

'That's all right, then. Thought you'd fell overboard.'

'No, I'm here, Pop, I'm here.'

'Perfick!' Pop said. 'You think I ought to get more ice-creams? It's so hot Ma's is nearly melted.'

Ma shook all over, laughing like a jelly. Little rivers of yellow, brown, and pinkish-purple cream were running down over her huge lardy hands. In her handsome big black eyes the cloudless blue May sky was reflected, making them dance as she threw out the splendid bank of her bosom, quivering under its salmon jumper. At thirty-five she still had a head of hair like black silk cotton, curly and thick as it fell to her fat olive shoulders. Her stomach and thighs bulged like a hopsack under the tight brown skirt and in her remarkably small delicate cream ears her round pearl drop earrings trembled like young white cherries.

'Hitch up a bit I said, Ma! Give father a bit o' room.' Pop Larkin, who

9

was thin, sharp, quick-eyed, jocular, and already going shining bald on top, with narrow brown side-linings to make up for it, nudged against the mass of flesh like a piglet against a sow. 'Can't get the clutch in.'

Ma hitched up a centimetre or two, still laughing.

'Perfick!' Pop said. 'No, it ain't though. Where'd I put that money?'

Ice-cream in his right hand, he began to feel in the pockets of his leather jacket with the other.

'I had it when I bought the ice-creams. Don't say I dropped it. Here, Ma, hold my ice-cream.'

Ma held the ice-cream, taking a neat lick at a melting edge of it with a red sparkling tongue.

'All right, all right. Panic over. Put it in with the crisps.'

Packets of potato crisps crackled out of his pocket, together with a bundle of pound notes, rolled up, perhaps a hundred of them, and clasped with a thick elastic band.

'Anybody want some crisps? Don't all speak at once! – anybody –'

'Please!'

Pop leaned out of the driving cab and with two deft backhand movements threw packets of potato crisps into the back of the truck.

'Crisps, Ma?'

'Please,' Ma said. 'Lovely. Just what I wanted.'

Pop took from his pocket a third packet of potato crisps and handed it over to Ma, taking his ice-cream back and licking the dripping underside of it at the same time.

'All right. All set now.' He let in the clutch at last, holding his ice-cream against the wheel. 'Perfick! Ma, take a look at that sky!'

Soon, in perfect sunlight, between orchards that lifted gentle pink branches in the lightest breath of wind, the truck was passing strawberry fields.

'Got the straw on,' Pop said. 'Won't be above anuvver few days now.'

In June it would be strawberries for picking, followed by cherries before the month ended, and then more cherries through all the month of July. Sometimes, in good summers, apples began before August did, and with them early plums and pears. In August and again in September it was apples. In September also it was hops and in October potatoes. At strawberries alone, with a big family, you could earn fifteen pounds a day.

'See that, kids?' Pop slowed down the truck, idling past the long rows of fresh yellow straw. 'Anybody don't want to go strawberry-picking?'

In the answering burst of voices Pop thought, for the second time, that he couldn't hear the voice of Mariette.

'What's up with Mariette, Ma?'

'Mariette? Why?'

'Ain't heard her laughing much today.'

'I expect she's thinking,' Ma said.

Lost in silent astonishment at this possibility, Pop licked the last melting pink and chocolate-yellow cream from its paper and let the paper fly out of the window.

'Thinking? What's she got to think about?'

'She's going to have a baby.'

'Oh?' Pop said. 'Well, that don't matter. Perfick. Jolly good.'

Ma did not seem unduly worried either.

'Who is it?' Pop said.

'She can't make up her mind.'

Ma sat happily munching crisps, staring at cherry orchards as they sailed past the truck, every bough hung with swelling fruit, palest pink on the sunnier edges of the trees.

'Have to make up her mind some time, won't she?' Pop said.

'Why?'

'Oh! I just thought,' Pop said.

Ma, who had almost finished the crisps, poured the last remaining golden crumbs into the palm of her left hand. Over the years, as she had grown fatter, the three big turquoise and pearl rings she wore had grown tighter and tighter on her fingers, so that every now and then she had to have them cut off, enlarged, and put back again.

'She thinks it's either that Charles boy who worked at the farm,' Ma said, 'or else that chap who works on the railway line. Harry somebody.'

'I know him,' Pop said. 'He's married.'

'The other one's overseas now,' Ma said. 'Tripoli or somewhere.'

'Well, he'll get leave.'

'Not for a year he won't,' Ma said. 'And perhaps not then if he hears.'

'Ah! well, we'll think of something,' Pop said. 'Like some more crisps? How about some chocolate? Let's stop and have a beer. Got a crate in the back.'

'Not now,' Ma said. 'Wait till we get home now. We'll have a Guinness then and I'll warm the fish-and-chips up.'

Pop drove happily, both hands free now, staring with pleasure at the cherries, the apples, and the strawberry fields, all so lovely under the May sunlight, and thinking with pleasure too of his six children and the splendid, handsome names he and Ma had given them. Jolly good names, perfick, every one of them, he thought. There was a reason for them all.

Montgomery, the only boy, had been named after the general. Primrose had come in the Spring. Zinnia and Petunia were twins and they were the flowers Ma liked most. Victoria, the youngest girl, had been born in plum-time.

Suddenly he couldn't remember why they had called the eldest Mariette.

'Ma,' he said, 'trying to think why we called her Mariette. Why did we?'

'I wanted to call her after that Queen,' Ma said. 'I always felt sorry for that Queen.'

'What Queen?'

'The French one, Marie Antoinette. But you said it was too long. You'd never say it, you said.'

'Oh! I remember,' Pop said. 'I remember now. We put the two together.'

Ten minutes later they were home. With pride and satisfaction Pop gazed on home as it suddenly appeared beyond its scrubby fringe of woodland, half filled with bluebells, half with scratching red-brown hens.

'Home looks nice,' he said. 'Allus does though, don't it? Perfick.'

'Lovely,' Ma said.

'We're all right,' Pop said. 'Got nothing to worry about, Ma, have we?'

'Not that I can think of,' Ma said.

Pop drew the truck to a standstill in a dusty yard of nettles, old oil drums, corrugated pig-sties, and piles of rusty iron in which a line of white ducks, three grey goats, and a second batch of red-brown hens set up a concerted, trembling fuss of heads and wings, as if delighted.

'Just in time for dinner!' Pop said. It was almost four o'clock. 'Anybody not hungry?'

He leapt down from the cab. Like him, everybody was laughing. He knew they were all hungry; they always were.

'Down you come, you kids. Down.'

Letting down the back-board and holding up both arms, he took the youngest children one by one, jumping them down to the yard, laughing and kissing them as they came.

Presently only Mariette remained on the truck, wearing jodhpurs and a pale lemon shirt, standing erect, black-haired, soft-eyed, olive-skinned, and so well-made in a slender and delicate way that he could not believe that Ma, at seventeen too, had once looked exactly like her.

'It's all right. I can get down myself, Pop.'

Pop held up his arms, looking at her tenderly.

'Ah! come on. Ma's told me.'

'Let me get down myself, Pop.'

He stood watching her. Her eyes roamed past him, flashing and dark as her mother's, searching the yard.

It suddenly crossed his mind that she was afraid of something, not happy, and he half-opened his mouth to comment on this unlikely, disturbing, unheard-of fact when she suddenly shook her black head and startled him by saying:

'Pop, there's a man in the yard. There's a man over there by the horse-box. Watching us.'

Pop walked across the yard towards the horse-box. He owned two horses, one a young black mare for Mariette, the other a piebald pony for the other kids. Mariette, who was crazy about horses, rode to point-to-points, sometimes went hunting, and even jumped at shows. She was wonderful about horses. She looked amazing on a horse. Perfick, he thought.

'Hullo, hullo, hullo,' he said. 'Good morning, afternoon rather. Looking for me?'

The man, young, spectacled, pale-faced, trilby-hatted, with a small brown tooth-brush moustache, carried a black brief-case under his arm.

'Mr Sidney Larkin?'

'Larkin, that's me,' Pop said. He laughed in ringing fashion. 'Larkin by name, Larkin by nature. What can I do for you? Nice wevver.'

'I'm from the office of the Inspector of Taxes.'

Pop stood blank and innocent, staggered by the very existence of such a person.

'Inspector of *what?*'

'Taxes. Inland Revenue.'

'You must have come to the wrong house,' Pop said.

'You are Mr Sidney Larkin?' The young man snapped open the brief-case, took out a paper, and glanced at it quickly, nervously touching his spectacles with the back of his hand. 'Sidney Charles Larkin.'

'That's me. That's me all right,' Pop said.

'According to our records,' the young man said, 'you have made no return of income for the past year.'

'Return?' Pop said. 'What return? Why? Nobody asked me.'

'You should have had a form,' the young man said. He took a yellow-buff sheet of paper from the brief-case and held it up. 'One like this.'

'Form?' Pop said. 'Form?'

Ma was crossing the yard with a box of groceries under one arm and a bag of fruit in the other. Three big ripe pineapples stuck cactus-like heads from the top of the huge paper bag. The twins loved pineapple. Especially fresh. Much better than tinned, they thought.

'Ma, did we have a form like this?' Pop called. 'Never had no form, did we?'

'Never seen one. Sure we never.'

'Come over here, Ma, a minute. This gentleman's from the Inspector of Summat or other.'

'I got dinner to get,' Ma said and strode blandly on with groceries and pineapples, huge as a buffalo. 'You want your dinner, don't you?'

Pop turned with an air of balmy indifference to the young man, who was staring incredulously at the receding figure of Ma as if she were part of the menagerie of hens, goats, ducks, and horses.

'No, never had no form. Ma says so.'

'You should have done. Two at least were sent. If not three.'

'Well, Ma says so. Ma ought to know. Ma's the one who does the paper work.'

The young man opened his mouth to speak and for a moment it was as if a strangled, startled gurgle came out. His voice choked itself back, however, and in reality the sound came from a drove of fifteen young turkeys winding down from the strip of woodland.

'Won't hurt you,' Pop said. 'How about a nice hen-bird for Christmas? Put your name on it now.'

'This form has to be returned to the Inspector,' the young man said. 'There is a statutory obligation –'

'Can't return it if I ain't got it,' Pop said. 'Now can I?'

'Here's another.'

As he recoiled from the buff-yellow sheet of paper Pop saw Mariette walking across the yard, slender, long-striding, on her way to the wooden, brush-roofed stable where both pony and horse were kept.

'I got no time for forms,' Pop said. 'Gawd Awmighty, I got pigs to feed. Turkeys to feed. Hens to feed. Kids to feed. I ain't had no dinner. Nobody ain't had no dinner.'

Suddenly the young man was not listening. With amazement he was following the progress of Mariette's dark, yellow-shirted figure across the yard.

'My eldest daughter,' Pop said. 'Crazy on horses. Mad on riding. You do any riding, Mister – Mister – I never caught your name.'

'Charlton.'

'Like to meet her, Mister Charlton?' Pop said. The young man was still staring, mouth partly open. Between his fingers the tax form fluttered in the breezy sunlit air.

'Mariette, come over here a jiff. Young man here's crazy on horses, like you. Wants to meet you. Comes from the Ministry of Revenue or summat.'

In astonished silence the young man stared at the new celestial body, in its yellow shirt, as it floated across the background of rusty iron, pigsties, abandoned oil-drums, goat-chewn hawthorn bushes, and dusty earth.

'Mister Charlton, this is my eldest, Mariette. The one who's mad on horses. Rides everywhere. You've very like seen her picture in the papers.'

'Hullo,' Mariette said. 'I spotted you first.'

'That's right, she saw you,' Pop said. 'Who's that nice young feller in the yard, she said.'

'So you', Mariette said, 'like riding too?'

The eyes of the young man groped at the sunlight as if still unable correctly to focus the celestial body smiling at him from three feet away.

'I say every kid should have a horse,' Pop said. 'Nothing like a horse. I'm going to get every one of my kids a horse.'

Suddenly the young man woke from mesmerism, making a startling statement.

'I saw you riding over at Barfield,' he said. 'In the third race. At Easter. You came second.'

'I hope you won a bob or two on her,' Pop said.

Again he laughed in ringing fashion, bringing from beyond the stable an echo of goose voices as three swaggering grey-white birds emerged from a barricade of nettles, to be followed presently by the half-sleepy, dainty figures of a dozen guinea-fowl.

'Pity we didn't know you were coming,' Pop said. 'We're killing a goose tomorrow. Always kill a goose or a turkey or a few chickens at the weekend. Or else guinea-fowl. Like guinea-fowl?'

If the young man had any kind of answer ready it was snatched from him by the voice of Ma, calling suddenly from the house:

'Dinner's nearly ready. Anybody coming in or am I slaving for nothing?'

'We're coming, Ma!' Pop turned with eager, tempting relish to the young man, still speechless, still struggling with his efforts to focus correctly the dark-haired girl. 'Well, we got to go, Mister Charlton. Sorry. Ma won't have no waiting.'

'Now, Mr Larkin, about this form –'

'Did you see me at Newchurch?' Mariette said. 'I rode there too.'

'As a matter of fact, I did – I did, yes – But, Mr Larkin, about this form –'

'What form?' Mariette said.

'Oh! some form, some form,' Pop said. 'I tell you what, Mister Charlton, you come in and have a bite o' dinner with us. No, no trouble. Tons o' grub –'

'I've eaten, thank you. I've eaten.'

'Well, cuppa tea then. Cuppa coffee. Bottle o' beer. Bottle o' Guinness. Drop o' cider.'

The entire body of the young man seemed to swirl helplessly, as if half-intoxicated, out of balance, on its axis. 'Oh! yes, do,' Mariette said and by the time he had recovered he found himself being led by Pop Larkin towards the house, from which Ma was already calling a second time:

'If nobody don't come in three minutes I'll give it to the cats.'

'Know anybody who wants a pure white kitten?' Pop said. 'Don't want a pure white kitten, do you?'

'So you were at Newchurch too,' Mariette said. 'I wish I'd known.'

A moment later Pop threw up his hands in a gesture of near ecstasy at the overpowering beauty, which suddenly seemed to strike him all afresh, of the May afternoon.

'Beautiful, ain't it?' he said. 'Perfick. I got a beautiful place here. Don't you think I got a beautiful place here, Mister Charlton?'

In the kitchen a radio was loudly playing jazz. In the living-room next door, where the curtains were half-drawn, a television set was on, giving to the nine faces crowded about the table a grey-purple, flickering glow.

'Have just what you fancy, Mister Charlton,' Pop said. 'If you don't see it here, ask for it. Bottle o' beer? Glass o' sherry? Pass the vinegar, Ma.'

Soon the young man, arms crooked at the crowded table, was nursing a cup of tea. In the centre of the table stood the three pineapples, flanked on all sides by plates of fish-and-chips, more coloured blocks of ice-cream, pots of raspberry and strawberry jam, bottles of tomato-ketchup and Guinness, bottles of Worcester sauce and cups of tea, chocolate biscuits and piles of icy buns.

'Perhaps Mister Charlton would like a couple o' sardines with his tea?' Pop said. 'Montgomery, fetch the sardines.'

Mr Charlton, bemused by the name of Montgomery, protested faintly that he did not like sardines.

'Mister Charlton saw Mariette riding at Barfield,' Pop said.

'And at Newchurch,' Mariette said.

'Funny we didn't see you there,' Ma said, 'we was all there.'

'Mister Charlton', Pop said, 'loves horses.'

'Turn up the contrast,' Ma said, 'it's getting dark.'

In the television's flickering purplish light the young man watched the faces about the table, as they munched on fish-and-chips, ice-cream, tomato-ketchup, and jam, becoming more and more like pallid, eyeless ghouls. Pop had placed him between Ma and Mariette and presently he detected under the great breathing bank of Ma's bosom, now mauve-salmon in the flickering light, the shape of two white kittens somehow nestling on the bulging precipice of her lap. Occasionally the kittens miaowed prettily and Ma fed them with scraps of fish and batter.

Above the noise of jazz, television voices, kittens, geese hawking at the kitchen door, and the chattering voices of the family he found it hard to make himself heard.

'Mr Larkin, about this form. If you've got any difficulties I could help you fill it in.'

'All right,' Pop said, 'you fill it in.'

'It's still too dark,' Ma said. 'Turn it up a bit. It never stays where you put it nowadays.'

'I'll give the damn thing one more week to behave itself,' Pop said. 'And if it don't then I'll turn it in for another.'

Mr Charlton spread the yellow-buff form on the table in front of him and then took out his fountain pen and unscrewed the cap.

'Ma, is there any more ice-cream?' Primrose said.

'In the fridge,' Ma said. 'Big block o' strawberry *mousse*. Get that.'

'Full name: Sidney Charles Larkin,' Mr Charlton said and wrote it down. 'Occupation? Dealer?'

'Don't you call him dealer,' Ma said. 'I'll give you dealer. He owns land.'

'Well, landowner –'

'Farmer,' Pop said.

'Well, farmer,' Mr Charlton said. 'I'm very sorry. Farmer.'

'Mariette, cut the pineapple,' Ma said. 'Montgomery, go into the kitchen and fetch that pint jug of cream.'

While Mr Charlton filled in the form Mariette stood up, reached for the bread knife, and started to cut the pineapples, putting thick juicy slices on plates over which Ma poured heavy yellow cream.

'Real Jersey,' Ma said. 'From our cow.'

Every time Mariette reached over for another plate she brushed the sleeve of Mr Charlton, who either made sketchy blobs on the tax form or could not write at all.

'How many children?' Mr Charlton said. 'Six? Is that right? No more?'

'Well, not yet, old man. Plenty o' time though. Give us a chance,' Pop said and again laughed in ringing fashion.

'Gone again,' Ma said. 'You can't see a blessed thing. Montgomery,

Primrose – switch it off and change it for the set in our bedroom.'

In the half-darkness that now smothered the room Mr Charlton felt something smooth, sinuous, and slender brush against his right calf. For one shimmering, unnerving moment he sat convinced that it was Mariette's leg entwining itself about his own. As it curled towards his thigh he felt his throat begin choking but suddenly he looked down to realize that already the geese were under the table, where Ma was feeding them with scraps of fish, half-cold chips, and crumbled icy buns.

Unnerved, he found it difficult to frame his next important question.

'Of course this is confidential in every way,' he said, 'but at what would you estimate your income?'

'Estimate, estimate?' Pop said. 'Income? What income?'

Montgomery and Primrose, who had carried one television set away, now brought in another, larger than the first.

'Steady there, steady!' Ma said. 'Watch where you're looking. Mind the cocktail cabinet.'

'Hear that, Ma?' Pop said. 'Income!'

Ma, as she had done in the truck, started laughing like a jelly.

'Outcome more likely,' she said. 'Outcome I should say.'

'Six kids to feed and clothe,' Pop said. 'This place to run. Fodder to buy. Wheat as dear as gold dust. Pig-food enough to frighten you to death. Living all the time going up and up. Vet's fees. Fowl pest. Foot-and-mouth. Swine fever. Birds all the time dying. Income, old man? *Income?* I should like some, old man.'

Before Mr Charlton could answer this the second television set threw across the room its pallid, unreal glow, now in a curious nightmare green. At the same moment the twins, Zinnia and Petunia, demanded more pineapple. The geese made shovelling noises under the table and Mariette, rising to cut fresh slices, suddenly turned to Mr Charlton with modest, almost whispered apology.

'I'm awfully sorry, Mr Charlton. I didn't offer you any pineapple. Would you like some?'

'No thanks. I'm not allowed it. I find it too acid.'

'What a shame. Won't you change your mind? They're nice ripe ones.'

'Ought to be,' Ma said. 'Cost enough.'

'I'm afraid I'm simply not allowed it,' Mr Charlton said. 'I have to go very carefully. I have to manage mostly on eggs and that sort of thing.'

'Eggs?' Pop said. 'Eggs? Why didn't you say so? Got plenty of eggs, Ma, haven't we? Give Mister Charlton a boiled egg or two wiv his tea.'

'How would you like that?' Ma said. 'A couple o' boiled eggs, Mister Charlton? What do you say?'

To the delight of Ma, Mr Charlton confessed that that was what he really wanted.

'I'll do them,' Mariette said. 'Three minutes? Four? How long?'

'Very light,' Mr Charlton said. 'Three.'

'Nice big 'uns! – brown!' Pop called to Mariette as she went into the kitchen, where the geese presently followed her, brushing past Mr Charlton's legs again as they passed, once more to give him that shimmering, shocking moment of unnerving ecstasy.

'About this income,' Mr Charlton said. 'Can you give me an estimate? Just an estimate.'

'Estimate it'll be an' all, old man,' Pop said. 'Lucky if we clear a fiver a week, ain't we, Ma?'

'Fiver? I'd like to see one,' Ma said.

'We want boiled eggs, too!' the twins said, as in one voice. 'Can we have boiled eggs?'

'Give over. Can't you see I'm cutting the pineapple?' Ma said.

Everybody except Mr Charlton had large second helpings of pineapple, with more cream. When Ma had finished ladling out the cream she poured the remainder of it into a tablespoon and then licked the spoon with her big red tongue. After two or three spoonsful she cleaned the spoon with her finger and fed one of the white kittens with cream. On the television screen a posse of cowboys fired thirty revolvers into a mountainside and Mr Charlton said:

'I'm afraid we have to know what your income is, Mr Larkin. Supposing –'

'All right,' Pop said, 'that's a fair question, old man. Fair for me, fair for another. How much do *you* get?'

'Oh! well, me, not all that much. Civil servant, you know –'

'Nice safe job, though.'

'Nice safe job, yes. I suppose so.'

'Nothing like a nice safe job,' Pop said. 'As long as you're happy. Do you reckon you're happy?'

Mr Charlton, who did not look at all happy, said quickly:

'Supposing I put down a provisional five hundred?'

'Hundred weeks in a year now, Ma,' Pop said, laughing again. 'Well, put it down, old man, put it down. No harm in putting it down.'

'Now the names of children,' Mr Charlton said.

While Pop was reciting, with customary pride, the full names of the children, beginning with the youngest, Zinnia Florence and Petunia Mary, the twins, Mariette came back with two large brown boiled eggs in violet plastic egg-cups to hear Pop say:

'Nightingales in them woods up there behind the house, Mr Charlton. Singing all day.'

'Do nightingales sing all day?' Mr Charlton said. 'I wasn't aware –'

'All day, all night,' Pop said. 'Like everything else in the mating season they go hell for leather.'

The plate holding the two eggs was embroidered with slices of the thinnest white bread-and-butter. Mariette had cut them herself. And now Mr Charlton looked at them, as he looked at the eggs, with reluctance and trepidation, as if not wanting to tamper with their fresh, neat virginity.

'I've been looking at you,' Ma said. 'I don't think you get enough to eat by half.'

'I live in lodgings,' Mr Charlton said. 'It's not always –'

'We want to have some of your egg!' the twins said. 'Give us some of your egg!'

'Now you've started summat,' Pop said.

A moment later Mr Charlton announced the startling discovery that the twins were just alike; he simply couldn't tell one from the other.

'You're quick,' Pop said. 'You're quick.'

'It's gone dark again,' Ma said. 'Turn up the contrast. And Montgomery, fetch me my Guinness. There's a good boy.'

Soon, while Ma drank Guinness and Pop spoke passionately again of nightingales, bluebells that clothed the copses, 'fick as carpets, ficker in fact,' and how soon it would be the great time of the year, the time he loved most, the time of strawberry-fields and cherries everywhere, Mr Charlton found himself with a twin on each knee, dipping white fingers of bread and butter into delicious craters of warm golden egg-yolk.

'I hope the eggs are done right?' Mariette said.

'Perfect.'

'Perfick they will be an' all if she does 'em, you can bet you,' Pop said. 'Perfick!'

Mr Charlton had given up, for the time being, all thought of the buff-yellow form. A goose brushed his legs again. Outside, somewhere in the yard, a dog barked and the drove of turkeys seemed to respond in bubbling chorus. Far beyond them, in broken, throaty tones, a cuckoo called, almost in its June voice, and when it was silent the entire afternoon simmered in a single marvellous moment of quietness, breathlessly.

'If you don't mind me saying so,' Ma said, 'a few days in the country'd do you a world of good.'

'What are we having Sunday, Ma?' Pop said. 'Turkey?'

'What you like. Just what you fancy.'

'Roast pork,' Montgomery said. 'I like roast pork. With them brown onions.'

'Or goose,' Pop said. 'How about goose? We ain't had goose since Easter.'

In enthusiastic tones Pop went on to ask Mr Charlton whether he preferred goose, turkey, or roast pork but Mr Charlton, bewildered, trying to clean his misty spectacles and at the same time cut into thin fingers the last of his bread-and-butter, confessed he hardly knew.

'Well, I tell you what,' Ma said, 'we'll have goose *and* roast pork. Then I can do apple sauce for the two.'

'Perfick,' Pop said. 'Perfick. Primrose, pass me the tomato-ketchup. I've got a bit of iced bun to finish up.'

'Dinner on Sunday then,' Ma said. 'About two o'clock.'

Mr Charlton, who was unable to decide from this whether he had been invited to dinner or not, felt fate softly brush his legs again in the shape of a goose-neck. At the same time he saw Mariette smile at him with intensely dark, glowing eyes, almost as if she had in fact brushed his leg with her own, and he felt his limbs again begin melting.

Across the fields a cuckoo called again and Pop echoed it with a belch that seemed to surprise him not only by its length and richness but by the fact that it was a belch at all.

'Manners,' he said. 'Pardon,' and beat his chest in stern, suppressive apology. 'Wind all of a sudden.'

'What's on now?' Ma said. On the television screen all shooting had died and two men on horses, one a piebald, were riding up the valley, waving farewell hands.

'Nobody's birthday, Sunday, is it?' Pop said.

'Nobody's birthday before August,' Ma said.

'Then it's mine,' Mariette said. 'I'll be eighteen.'

'Pity it ain't nobody's birthday,' Pop said. 'We might have had a few fireworks.'

Suddenly all the geese were gone from the kitchen and Ma, marvelling at this fact, started laughing like a jelly again and said:

'They did that once before. They heard us talking!'

'Tell you what,' Pop said, 'if you've had enough, Mister Charlton, why don't you get Mariette to take you as far as the wood and hear them nightingales? I don't think you believe they sing all day, do you?'

'Oh! yes, I –'

'Shall we ride or walk?' Mariette said. 'I don't mind the pony if you want to ride.'

'I think I'd rather walk.'

'In that case I'll run and change into a dress,' she said. 'It's getting a bit warm for jodhpurs.'

While Mariette had gone upstairs the twins abandoned Mr Charlton's egg-less plate and fetched jam-jars from the kitchen.

'Going to the stall,' they said. 'Think we'll put honeysuckle on today instead of bluebells.'

As they ran off Pop said:

'That's the flower-stall they keep at the corner of the road down there. Wild flowers. Tuppence a bunch for motorists. Everybody works here, y'know.'

'I think I passed it,' Mr Charlton said, 'as I walked up from the bus.'

'That's the one,' Pop said. 'Everybody's got to work here so's we can scratch a living. Montgomery, you'd better get off to your goats and start milking 'em.'

Presently Ma, concerned at Mr Charlton's air of retreat, uncertainty, and fatigue, spread hands like lardy legs of pork across her salmon jumper and said with earnest kindness:

'Taking your holiday soon, Mr Charlton? Where do you usually go?'

'I hadn't –'

'You should come strawberry-picking with us,' Ma said. 'Do you the world of good. Else cherry-picking. Best holiday in the world if the weather's nice. Make yourself a lot o' money too.'

'Perfick,' Pop said. 'Don't cost nothing either. Here's Mariette. Perfick, I tell you.'

Mr Charlton rose from the table to find himself stunned by a new astral body, now in a lime green dress with broad black belt, a flouncing skirt, loose neck, and short scalloped sleeves. Her beautiful dark eyes were smiling at him splendidly.

'Is that your shantung?' Ma said. 'You'll be warm enough in that, dear, will you?'

'Oh! it's hot,' Mariette said. 'It's nice to feel the breeze blowing round my legs again. You ready, Mr Charlton?'

Mr Charlton, the buff-yellow form forgotten, turned and followed Mariette, who actually stretched out a friendly hand. As they crossed a yard noisy with hawking geese, mumbling turkeys, and braying goats being led to milking by Montgomery Pop called:

'Remember about Sunday, Mr Charlton, won't you? Don't forget about Sunday.'

'You really mean it?' Mr Charlton halted and turned back, amazed. 'Are you quite sure?'

'Sure?' Pop said. 'Blimey, old man, I'm going to kill the geese any minute now.'

'Thank you. Thank you very much.'

'One goose or two, Ma?' Pop called. 'Two geese be enough? or shall we have three?'

Mr Charlton, still stunned and amazed, turned to face the waiting figure of Mariette and saw it miraculously framed against piles of junk, rampant nettles and, in the near distance, deep strips of bluebells fenced away, in the strip of woodland, from flocks of brown marauding hens. Her legs, in pale beige silk stockings, were surprisingly shapely and slender. Her breasts protruded with grace from the soft lime shantung.

He could not believe in this figure. Nor, five minutes later, could he believe that the yard of nettles and junk, Pop's beautiful, incredible paradise, lay only a hundred yards away, screened by thickets of hornbeam and hazel, oaks in olive flower and may-trees carrying blossom as rich and thick as Ma's lavish Jersey cream.

'You didn't really believe about the nightingales, did you?'

'No.'

'Listen,' she said. 'You will.'

Walking along the woodland path, Mr Charlton could hear only a single untangled chorus of evening bird-song, unseparated into species, confusing as the tuning of orchestra strings.

'Let's stand here by the gate and listen,' Mariette said. 'Let's stand and listen here.'

Mr Charlton, transfixed, utterly bemused, stood by the gate and listened. Patches of evening sunlight, broken gold, sprinkled down through oak-branches, like delicate quivering translations in light of the bird-notes themselves.

'No, not that one,' Mariette said. 'That's a blackbird. Not the one over there, either. That's a wren. Now – that one. The one in the chestnut up there. The one with the long notes and then the long pause. Can you hear it now? That's a nightingale.'

Mr Charlton listened, hardly breathing, and heard for the first time in

23

his life, in a conscious moment, the voice of a nightingale singing against a May evening sky.

Enthralled, still hardly believing it, he turned to see the deep black eyes holding him in utter captivation and heard her say again:

'You really didn't believe it, did you?'

'I must say I didn't.'

'I tell you something else you didn't believe either.'

'What was that?'

'You didn't believe about me, did you?' she said. 'You didn't believe I was the same girl you saw riding at Easter, did you?'

'No,' he said. 'How did you know?'

'I guessed,' she said. 'I could see it in your eyes. I was watching you.'

She lifted her hands and held them suddenly against his cheeks without either boldness or hesitation but with a lightness of touch that woke in Mr Charlton's legs exactly the same melting, unnerving sensation as when the geese had brushed against him under the table. A moment later he saw her lips upraised.

'Who did you think I was?'

Mr Charlton made a startling, embarrassed confession.

'I thought – well, I was actually told you were someone else in point of fact – that you were a niece of Lady Planson-Forbes – you know, at Carrington Hall –'

Mariette began laughing, in ringing tones, very much like her father.

'Now you've just found I wasn't.'

'Well, yes –'

'You feel it makes any difference?'

'Well, in point of fact –'

'I'm just the same, aren't I?' She smiled and he found his eyes level with her bare, olive shoulder. 'I'm just me. The same girl, Just me. Just the same.'

Again she touched his face with her hands and Mr Charlton took hurried refuge in a sudden recollection of the buff-yellow form.

'By the way I mustn't forget to get your father to sign that form before I go –'

'You'll have to sign it for him,' she said, 'or Ma will. He can't write his name.'

She laughed again and Mr Charlton, his limbs melting once more as she lifted his hand to her bare warm shoulder, heard consciously but dizzily, for the second time in his life, a passionate burst of song from the nightingales.

At the same moment, back in the house, Pop returned to the kitchen after wringing the necks of three fat geese and poured himself a much-needed glass of beer.

'A few days like this, Ma,' he said, ''ll put a bit o' paint on the strawberries.'

Ma was raking the kitchen fire, putting on to it empty ice-cream cartons, scraps of fish-and-chips, egg-shells, pineapple tops, and Mr Charlton's buff-yellow paper.

'I don't know as I shan't get a few bottles o' port wine in for Sunday,' Pop said, 'so we can celebrate.'

'Celebrate what?'

'Well,' Pop said, 'what about Mariette?'

Ma laughed again, jumper shaking like a salmon jelly.

'The only thing is,' Pop said, 'I hope he won't want to take her away from here.' He carried his beer to the kitchen door and from there contemplated, almost with reverence, the paradisiacal scene beyond. 'Gawd A'mighty, Ma, you know we got a beautiful place here. Paradise. I don't know what we'd do if she were took away from here.'

Standing in the evening sunlight, gazing across the pile of junk, the nettles, the rusting hovels, and the scratching, dusty hens, Pop sighed loudly and with such content that the sound seemed to travel with perfect definition across the surrounding fields of buttercups and may, gathering its echo at last from the mingled sounds of the remaining geese, the voices of cuckoos calling as they flew across the meadows and the small, passionate, invisible nightingales.

'Perfick,' Pop said. 'You couldn't wish for nothing more perfick nowhere.'

· 2 ·

When Mariette and Mr Charlton came down from the bluebell wood an hour later, Mariette carrying a bunch of bluebells and pink campion, Mr Charlton bearing in his palm, with the tenderest care, two blue thrushes' eggs a bird had dropped in the grass at the woodside, Pop was washing pig-buckets under the tap in the yard.

'Pigs look well,' Pop said. 'I think we'll kill one. Hear the nightingales?'

Mr Charlton had not a second in which to answer this question before Pop said:

'Wondering where you two had got to, Mister Charlton. Tea's ready. Just in time.'

A searching odour of frying kippers cut almost savagely through the warm May air.

'I thought we just had tea,' Mr Charlton said.

'That was dinner.'

'I ought to catch my bus,' Mr Charlton said. 'I must. The last one goes at eight o'clock.'

'Ma won't hear of that,' Pop said. 'Will she, Mariette? Daresay Mariette won't either. Like to wash your hands? What you got there?'

Mr Charlton revealed the thrushes' eggs, brilliant blue in his office-pale hands, and Mariette gave him a small dark smile of fascination that held him once more transfixed and speechless.

'Always run you home in the truck,' Pop said. 'Next time you come out you must bring your car. What kind of car you got, Mister Charlton?'

Mr Charlton confessed that he had no car. Pop was stunned.

'No car, no car?' he said. 'That'll never do. Can't have that. Hear that, Mariette? Mister Charlton ain't got no car.'

'I don't think I'll have the time to come out again,' Mr Charlton said. 'Do you think we could go into the question of the tax form before I go? It's very important.'

'Tea first,' Pop said. 'Must have a cuppa tea first. Don't want to make Ma mad, do you?'

Pop finished drying his hands and gave Mr Charlton the towel. Mr

26

Charlton put the two thrushes' eggs into his pocket and ran tap water over his hands, washing them with a gritty cake of purple soap. Mariette gave him another intimate, flashing smile and then went towards the house, calling that she was going to powder her nose, and Mr Charlton, completely captivated by the delicate vision of green shantung retreating in the golden evening sunshine, forgot the thrushes' eggs and said:

'I don't know if you appreciate how severe the penalties are for not making a tax return, Mr Larkin.'

'Ma's calling,' Pop said.

Mr Charlton listened but couldn't hear a sound.

'I shall have to make some sort of report to my office,' Mr Charlton said. 'Then if you don't cooperate it'll be taken out of my hands and after that –'

'Beautiful evening, ain't it?' Pop said. Once again, caught in his own web of enchantment, he turned to stare at an evening distilled now into even deeper gold by the lower angle of light falling across still seas of buttercups and long-curled milky waves of may.

'I strongly recommend you –'

'Pair o' goldfinches,' Pop said, but Mr Charlton was too slow to see the birds, which darted past him like dipping sparks of scarlet, black, and gold.

In the kitchen Ma was frying a third batch of four fat tawny kippers in a brand new aluminium pan while Mariette powdered her face over the sink, looking into a heart-shaped mirror stuck about with little silver, pink, and violet seashells.

'How'd you get on with Mr Charlton, duckie?'

'Slow,' Mariette said. 'He's very shy.'

'Well, he mustn't be shy,' Ma said. 'That won't get you nowhere.'

'He would talk about horses.'

'You'll have to find something a bit better than that to talk about, won't you?' Ma said. 'Bit more stimulating.'

Mariette, who was busy making up her lips with a tender shade of pink, not at all unlike the pink of the rose campion, that went well with her dress of cool lime shantung, did not answer.

'I think he looks half-starved,' Ma said. 'No blood in him. Wants feeding up. I'll find him a good fat kipper.'

Mariette was wetting small wisps of short hair with her finger-tips and winding them about her ears like black watchsprings.

'Put some of my Goya on,' Ma said. 'The gardenia. Or else the Chanel. They both stand by my jewel-box in our bedroom.'

While Mariette went upstairs to dab perfume behind her ears and in soft hollows of her legs, Mr Charlton and Pop came in from the yard to join Montgomery, Primrose, Victoria, and the twins, who sat at the table licking thick bars of choc-ice and watching a television programme in which three men, a clergyman, and a woman were discussing prostitution and what should be done about it all.

'Strawberry-picking on Monday over at Benacre, Pop,' Montgomery said. 'I heard from Fred Brown.'

'That's early,' Pop said. 'Earliest we've ever been. I said this wevver'd soon put the paint on 'em.'

Ma came in bearing a big dish of stinging hot kippers running with fat dabs of butter and on the television screen the woman shook a condemnatory finger at the gaping children and said: 'The women are, on the whole, less to be blamed than pitied. It is largely the fault of man.'

'Ma,' Pop said. 'Strawberry-picking Monday. Better get that deep-freeze, hadn't we?'

'Sooner the better,' Ma said. 'Better go in first thing tomorrow. It's Saturday.' She began to serve kippers. 'Start pouring tea, Primrose. Kipper, Mister Charlton? Here we come. Nice fat one. Help yourself to more butter if you want to.'

While Ma served kippers and Primrose poured tea Pop rose from the table and fetched a bottle of whisky from the cocktail cabinet.

'Milk?' he said to Ma.

'Please,' Ma said. 'Just what I need.'

Pop poured whisky into Ma's tea, then into his own, and then turned to Mr Charlton, the bottle upraised.

'Drop o' milk, Mister Charlton?'

'No, no, no. No really. Not for me. No really not for me.'

'Relieves the wind, frees the kidneys, and opens the bowels,' Pop said blandly.

'No, no. No really. Not at this time of day.'

'Do you all the good in the world, Mister Charlton.'

Pop, after filling up Mr Charlton's tea-cup with whisky, stood for a moment staring at the television screen and said:

'What the ruddy 'ell are they talking about? Kids, how much money you make on the stall?'

'Eighteenpence. There was a policeman on a motor-bike come along.'

'Pity he hadn't got summat else to do,' Pop said.

With elbows on the table Victoria, who was trying to eat kipper with a spoon, said in a shrill quick voice:

'I don't like kippers. They're made of combs.'

'Now, now,' Pop said. 'Now, now. Manners, manners. Elbows!'

'Pop'has 'em at a word,' Ma said.

Mr Charlton sat held in a new constriction of bewilderment made more complex by the arrival of Mariette, fresh and lovely with new pink lipstick, face powder, and a heavy fragrance of gardenias that overwhelmed him in a cloud of intoxication as she came and sat at his side.

As if this were not enough she had brought with her the bluebells and the rose campion, arranged in an orange and crimson jar. She set the jar in the centre of the table, where the flowers glowed in the nightmare marine glow of the television light like a strange sheaf of sea-weed. The bluebells too smelt exquisitely.

'Sorry I'm late,' she whispered to Mr Charlton and he could have sworn, in another moment of shimmering agony, that her silky legs had brushed his own. 'Just had to make myself presentable.'

'By the way, Mister Charlton,' Pop said, 'what's your other name? Don't like this mistering.'

'Cedric.'

Ma started choking.

'Kipper bone!' Pop said. 'Happened once before.'

He rose from the table and struck Ma a severe blow in the middle of the back. She boomed like a drum.

'Better?' Pop said and hit her a second time, rather more robustly than the first.

Except for bouncing slightly Ma did not seem to mind at all.

'Worst of kippers,' Pop said. 'Too much wire-work. Fetched it up?'

On the television screen a man in close-up stared with steadfast earnestness at Mr Charlton and the eight Larkins and said: 'Well, there it is. We leave it with you. What do you think? What is to be done about these women? Is it their fault? Is it the fault of men? If not, whose fault is it?' and once again, for the third time, Ma started laughing like a jelly.

'Play crib at all, Mister Charlton?' Pop said.

Mr Charlton had to confess he had never heard of crib.

'Card game,' Pop said. 'We all play here. Learns you figures. Mariette plays. Mariette could show you how.'

Mr Charlton turned to look shyly at Mariette and found his vision, already blurred by the curious light from the television screen, clouded into more numbing and exquisite confusion by the thick sweet fragrance of gardenia. In return she gazed at him with dark silent eyes, so that he could not help trembling and was even glad when Pop said:

'Like billiards? Or snooker? Got a nice table out the back there. Full size. We could have a game o' snooker after tea.'

'You know,' Mr Charlton said, 'I'm really awfully sorry, but I must catch this eight o'clock bus.'

'No eight o'clock bus now,' Montgomery said. 'They knocked it off soon after petrol rationing started.'

'That's right,' Ma said. 'They never put it back again.'

Mr Charlton half-rose from the table, agitated.

'In that case I must start walking. It's eight miles.'

'Walking my foot,' Pop said. 'I said I'll run you home in the truck. Or else Mariette can take you in the station wagon. Mariette can drive. Mariette'll take you, won't you, Mariette?'

'Of course.'

Mr Charlton sat down, mesmerized.

'Why don't you stay the night?' Pop said. 'That's all right, ain't it, Ma?'

'More the merrier.'

'Perfick,' Pop said. 'Ma'll make you a bed up on the billiard table.'

'No, really –'

'It's so simple,' Mariette said. 'After all tomorrow's Saturday. You don't have to go to the office Saturday, do you?'

'Course he don't,' Pop said. 'Offices don't work Saturdays. They don't none of 'em know what work is no more.'

'That's settled then,' Ma said. 'I'll put him on that new super-foam mattress Mariette has for sun-bathing.'

'Oh! that mattress is marvellous,' Mariette said. 'You sink in. Your body simply dreams into that mattress.'

In another unnerving moment Mr Charlton saw the girl, hands raised to her bare shoulders, luxuriously enact for him the attitudes of dreaming into the mattress. As her eyes closed and her lips parted gently he struggled to bring himself back to reality, firmness, and a state of resistance and he said:

'No, I'm sorry. I really must be adamant –'

Pop stared with open mouth, powerfully stunned and impressed by this word. He could not ever remember having heard it even on television.

'Quite understand,' he said.

In a single moment Mr Charlton was raised greatly in his estimation. He looked at him with awe.

'Oh! won't you stay?' Mariette said. 'We could ride tomorrow.'

Groping again, struggling against the dark eyes and the fragrance of gardenia, powerful even above the penetrating sting of kippers, Mr Charlton began to say:

'No, really. For one thing I've nothing with me. I've no pyjamas.'

'Gawd Almighty,' Pop said. 'Pyjamas?'

His admiration and awe for Mr Charlton now increased still further. He was held transfixed by the fact that here was a man who spoke in words of inaccessible meaning and wore pyjamas to sleep in.

'Sleep in your shirt, old man,' he said. 'Like I do.'

Pop had always slept in his shirt; he found it more convenient that way. Ma, on the other hand, slept in nylon nightgowns, one of them an unusual pale petunia-pink that Pop liked more than all the rest because it was light, delicate, and above all completely transparent. It was wonderful for seeing through. Under it Ma's body appeared like a global map, an expanse of huge explorable mountains, shadowy valleys, and rosy pinnacles.

'I wear pyjamas,' Mariette said. 'I'll lend you a pair of mine.'

'No, really –'

Mr Charlton became utterly speechless as Ma got up, went into the kitchen and brought back four tins of whole peaches, which she began to open with an elaborate tin-opener on the sideboard.

'Save some of the juice, Ma,' Pop said. 'I'll have it later with a drop o' gin.'

'I think you're about my size,' Mariette said, as if everything were now completely settled, so that Mr Charlton found himself in the centre of a shattering vortex, trapped there by the torturing and incredible thought that presently he would be sleeping in Mariette's own pyjamas, on her own dreaming bed of foam.

Before he could make any further protest about this Primrose poured him a second cup of tea and Pop, leaning across the table, filled it up with whisky.

'You ought to come strawberry-picking,' Pop said. Mr Charlton suddenly remembered the tax form. It mustn't be forgotten, he thought, the tax form. On no account must it be forgotten. 'This is very like the last summer we'll ever go strawberry-picking, Mister Charlton. We, you, anybody. You know why?'

Tax form, tax form, tax form, Mr Charlton kept thinking. Tax form. 'No. Why?'

On the television screen a voice announced: 'We now take you to Fanshawe Castle, the home of the Duke of Peele,' and Ma, ladling out the last of the peaches, crowned by thick ovals of cream, said:

'Turn up the contrast. I want to see this. It's got dark again.'

'Because,' Pop said, 'the strawberry lark's nearly over.'

Tax form, tax form, tax form, Mr Charlton thought again. How was it the strawberry lark was nearly over? Tax form.

'Disease,' Pop said. 'Sovereigns are finished. Climax is finished. Huxleys are finished. Soon there won't be no strawberries nowhere.'

Tax form. 'You mean that in this great strawberry-growing district –'

'This districk. Every districk. In two years the strawberry lark'll be over.'

'Well, myself, I actually prefer raspberries –'

'The raspberry lark's nearly over as well,' Pop said. 'Mosaic. Weakening strain. And the plum lark. And the cherry lark. And the apple lark. They can't sell apples for love nor –'

'We're in the library,' Ma said. 'Pop, look at the library.'

Tax form – Mr Charlton, with piteous desperation, struggled with the power of all his declining concentration to see that the tax form was remembered. 'I've got to go home,' he thought. 'I've got to start walking.' Something brushed his leg. 'I must remember the tax form.' He was startled into a sudden shivering catch of his breath and a moment later the white kitten was on his knee.

'Gawd Almighty,' Pop said. 'What are all them on the walls?'

'Must be books,' Ma said.

In mute staring concentration Pop sat involved by the picture on the television screen, noisily eating peaches and taking an occasional quick-sucked gulp of whisky and tea.

'Never,' he said. 'Can't be.'

'Beautiful home,' Ma said. 'I like the pelmets. That's what we want. Pelmets like that.'

Tax form! Mr Charlton's mind shouted. Tax form –!

'Books?' Pop said. '*All* books?'

'I'll go and find the pyjamas and get them aired,' Mariette said. Mr Charlton emerged from a moment of acute hypnosis to feel her hand reach out, touch him softly, and then begin to draw him away. 'Coming? We could try them against you for size.'

'The man who owns that owes five million tax,' Mr Charlton said desperately and for no reason at all. 'Mr Larkin, that reminds me – we mustn't forget that form –'

'Perfick place,' Pop said. 'On the big side though. Suppose they need it for the books.'

'Oh! the carpets. Look at the carpets,' Ma said. 'There must be miles of carpets. Acres.'

'He'll have to give it all up,' Mr Charlton said. 'The State will take it for taxes. You see what can happen –'

'Come on,' Mariette said and Mr Charlton, struggling for the last time against the flickering, rising tides of sea-green light rolling across the table in mesmeric, engulfing flow, followed the girl blunderingly into the kitchen, the white kitten softly brushing his legs as he went, the thick night-sweet scent of gardenia penetrating to his blood, seeming to turn it as white as the flower from which it sprang.

· 3 ·

At half past ten, just before television closed down for the night, Pop, Ma, and Mariette were still trying to teach Mr Charlton the mysteries and arithmetic of crib. Utterly baffled – the only coherent thing he had been able to do all evening was to telephone his landlady to say that he wouldn't be coming home that night – Mr Charlton found it quite impossible to understand the elements of the game, still less its language and figures.

'Fifteen-two, fifteen-four, fifteen-six, pair's eight, three's eleven, three's fourteen, and one for his nob's fifteen.'

Pop dealt the cards very fluidly; he counted like a machine.

'I don't understand one for his nob.'

'Jack,' Pop said. 'I told you – one for his nob. Two for his heels. Your deal, Ma.'

Ma dealt very fluidly too.

'Got to use your loaf at this game, Mister Charlton,' Pop said. 'I thought you was office man? I thought you was good at figures?'

'Rather different sort of figures,' Mr Charlton said.

'Oh?' Pop said. 'Really? They look all the same to me.'

Pop picked up the cards Ma had dealt him, took a quick look at them, and said smartly:

'Mis-deal. Seven cards. Bung in.'

'Pick 'em up!' Ma said and threatened him with a hand as large as a leg of lamb. 'Don't you dare.'

'Wanted a Parson's Poke,' Pop said.

'No more Parson's Pokes,' Ma said. 'Get on with it. Make the best with what you've got.' Ma kicked Mr Charlton playfully on the shins under the table, laughing. 'Got to watch him, Mister Charlton, playing crib. Parson's Poke, my foot. Sharp as a packet o' pins.'

'Twenty-two, nine'll do. Twenty-five, six's is alive. Twenty-eight, Billy Wake. Twenty-seven, four's in heaven. Twenty-three, eight's a spree.'

In the combined turmoil of counting and the glare of the television Mr Charlton felt a certain madness coming back.

'What you got, Pop?'

'Terrible. What Paddy shot at.'

'See what I mean?' Ma said. She kicked Mr Charlton a second time on the shins, just as playfully as the first. 'Mis-deal my foot! No wonder he says you got to use your loaf at this game. Your deal next, Mr Charlton. Your box.'

Mr Charlton, as he picked up the cards, was beginning to feel that he had no loaf to use. He felt awful; his loaf was like a sponge.

'Let's have a Parson's Poke!' Pop said.

'No more Parson's Pokes,' Ma said. 'Too many Parson's Pokes are bad luck.'

'Your box, Mr Charlton. Give yourself a treat.'

'Let him play his own game!' Ma said. 'Play your own hand, Mr Charlton. Use your own loaf. What's on telly now?'

'Something about free speech,' Mariette said. 'Freedom of the press or something.'

Pop turned his head, looking casually at the flickering screen. On it four heated men were, it seemed, about to start fighting.

'Wherever conditions of uniform tolerance may be said to obtain –'

'Barmy,' Ma said. 'Want their heads testing.'

'The trouble with telly,' Pop said, 'it don't go on long enough.'

'You miss it when you're talking,' Ma said. 'You feel lost, somehow. Don't you think you feel lost, Mr Charlton.'

Mr Charlton had to confess he felt lost.

'I like this set better than the other,' Ma said. 'Better contrast.'

'Thirsty, Ma?' Pop said. 'I'm thirsty.'

During the evening Pop had drunk the remainder of the peach-juice, laced with gin, two bottles of Guinness, and a light ale. Mr Charlton had drunk two glasses of beer. Ma and Mariette had been drinking cider.

'I'll mix a cocktail,' Pop said. 'Mister Charlton, what about a cocktail?'

'You don't want no more,' Ma said. 'You'll want to get out in the night.'

'I'm thirsty,' Pop said. 'I'm parched up.'

'You'll be pickled.'

Pop was already on his feet, moving towards the expensive glass and chromium cocktail cabinet that stood in one corner. 'Sit down and play your hand.'

Pop stood by the cabinet, his pride hurt and offended.

'Never been pickled in me life,' he said. 'Anyway not more than once or twice a week. And then only standin'-up pickled.'

Was there some difference between that and other forms? Mr Charlton wondered.

'Layin'-down pickled,' Pop said, 'of course.'

'I'm getting tired of crib,' Mariette said. 'It's hot in here. I'm going to cool off in the yard, Mr Charlton.' Like her father she found it difficult to call Mr Charlton by his Christian name. 'Like to come?'

'After he's had a cocktail,' Pop said. 'I'm going to mix everybody a special cocktail.'

While Mariette packed up the cards, the pegs, and the pegboard Pop stood by the cocktail cabinet consulting a book, *A Guide to Better Drinking*, given him by Montgomery for Christmas. It was the only book he had ever read.

'Here's one we never tried,' Pop said. 'Rolls-Royce.'

'That sounds nice,' Ma said.

'Half vermouth, quarter whisky, quarter gin, dash of orange bitters.'

'Dash you will too,' Ma said, 'with that lot. It'll blow our heads off.'

'Blow summat off,' Pop said. 'Not sure what though.'

Once again Ma started laughing like a jelly.

'How do you like our cocktail cabinet, Mister Charlton?' Pop said. 'Only had it at Christmas. Cost us a hundred and fifty.'

'Hundred and eighty,' Ma said. 'We had that other model in the end. The one with the extra sets of goblets. The brandy lot. You remember. And the silver bits for hot punch and all that.'

With confusion and awe Mr Charlton stared at the cocktail cabinet, over which Pop hovered, mixing the drinks, in his shirt sleeves. The cabinet, he realized for the first time, seemed shaped like an elaborate glass and silver ship.

'Am I mistaken?' he said. 'Or is it a ship?'

'Spanish galleon,' Pop said. 'Heigh-ho and a bottle o' rum and all that lark.'

When the cocktail was mixed Pop poured it into four large cut-glass tumblers embellished with scarlet cockerels. He had mixed it double, he said. It saved a lot of time like that.

'Try it first,' Ma said. 'We don't want it if it's no good, Rolls-Royce or no Rolls-Royce. Besides, you might fall down dead.'

Pop drained the shaker.

'Perfick,' he said. 'This'll grow hair.'

'By the way,' Ma said, 'talking about Rolls-Royce, did you do anything about that one?'

'Sunday,' Pop said. 'The chap's a stock-broker. Colonel Forbes. He's only down week-ends.'

'Pop's mad on a Rolls,' Ma explained to Mr Charlton.

'By the way, Mister Charlton,' Pop said, 'what was that about that feller on telly owing five million tax? Was that right?'

'Perfectly correct.'

'What for?'

'Death duties.'

'Deaf duties!'Pop said. 'Deaf duties! I feel like murder every time I hear deaf duties!'

Pop, snorting with disgust and irritation, struck the table with the palm of his hand and as if by a pre-arranged signal the light in the television went out. Ma uttered a sudden cry as if something terrible had happened. Mariette got up suddenly and switched the set off and there floated by Mr Charlton's face, as she passed, a fresh wave of gardenia, warm as the evening itself, disturbed and disturbing as she moved.

'That made my head jump,' Ma said. 'I thought a valve had gone.'

'Closing down, that's all,' Pop said. 'Eleven o'clock and they're closing down. Hardly got started.'

Pop, giving another snort of disgust about death duties and the brief and contemptible daily compass of television, handed round the cocktails.

'Cheers, everybody,' he said, raising glass. 'Here's to the strawberry lark. Roll on Monday.'

Mr Charlton drank. A wave of pure alcohol burned the roots off his tongue. He was utterly unable to speak for some moments and could only listen with undivided and searing agony to a question, first from Pop and then from Mariette, about whether he could be with them on Monday for the strawberry lark.

'I – I – I –'

A sensation as of a white-hot stiletto descending rapidly towards Mr Charlton's navel prevented the sentence from developing beyond a single choking word.

'Make yourself fifteen or twenty quid in no time,' Pop said. 'All the strawberries you can eat. And a pound free every day. You can gather a hundred and fifty pounds a day.'

'I – I – I –'

Burning tears came into Mr Charlton's eyes. He succeeded in murmuring at last, with a tongue cauterized of all feeling and in a voice that did not belong to him, something about work, office, and having no leave.

'You could always come in the evening,' Mariette said. 'Plenty of people do.'

As she said this she again turned and looked at him. The eyes seemed more tenderly, intensely, darkly penetrative than ever and he began flushing deeply.

'It's lovely in the evenings,' Mariette said. 'Absolutely lovely.'

Another draught of alcohol, snatched by Mr Charlton in another desperate moment of speechlessness, injected fire into remote interior corners of his body that he did not know existed.

'My God, this is a perfick pick-me-up,' Pop said. 'We must all have another one of those.'

Mr Charlton despaired and passed a groping hand over his face. His mouth burned, as from eating ginger. He heard Ma agree that the cocktail was a beauty. He actually heard her say that they owed everybody in the neighbourhood a drink. 'What say we have a cocktail party and give them this one? This'll get under their skin.'

That, Mr Charlton heard himself saying, was what was happening to him, but nobody seemed to hear a voice that was already inexplicably far away, except that Ma once again began laughing, piercingly, the salmon jumper shaking like a vast balloon.

'A few more of these and you won't see me for dust,' she said.

'A few more?' Mr Charlton heard himself saying. 'A few more?'

'First re-fill coming up, Mister Charlton. How do you like it? Ma, I bet this would go well with a bloater-paste sandwich.'

Something about this remark made Mr Charlton start laughing too. This enlivening development was a signal for Pop to strike Mr Charlton a severe blow in the back, exactly as he had done Ma, and call him a rattlin' good feller. 'Feel you're one of the family. Feel we've known you years. That right, Ma?'

That was right, Ma said. That was the truth. That was how they felt about him.

'Honest trufe,' Pop said. 'Honest trufe, Mister Charlton.'

A wave of unsteady pleasure, like a flutter of ruffling wind across water on a summer afternoon, ran through Mr Charlton's veins and set them dancing. He drank again. He felt a sudden lively and uncontrollable desire to pick strawberries on warm midsummer evenings, no matter what happened. 'My God, this is great stuff,' he told everybody. 'This is the true essence –'

Nobody knew what Mr Charlton was talking about. It was impossible to grasp what he meant by the true essence, but it set Ma laughing again. Somewhere behind the laughter Mr Charlton heard Pop mixing a third, perhaps a fourth, re-fill, saying at the same time 'Only thing it wants is more ice. More ice, Ma!'

Mr Charlton, for no predetermined reason, suddenly rose and struck himself manfully on the chest.

'I'll get it,' he said. 'That's me. I'm the ice-man.'

When Mr Charlton came back from the kitchen, carrying trays of ice, Pop mixed the new drink and tasted it with slow, appraising tongue and eye.

'More perfick than ever!'

Everything was more perfick, Mr Charlton kept telling himself. The scent of gardenia was more perfick. It too was stronger than ever. He laughed immoderately, for no reason, and at length, looking for the first time straight into the dark searching eyes of Mariette with neither caution nor despair.

'Mariette,' he said, 'what is the scent you're wearing?'

'Come and sit over here and I'll tell you.'

Mr Charlton moved to sit on the other side of the table. Rising abruptly, he stood stunned. It seemed to him that something remarkable had happened to Pop. Pop, it seemed to him, had disappeared.

'I didn't see Pop go out,' he said. 'Where's Pop gone?'

Ma began shrieking.

'I'm under here!' Pop said.

'Under me! I'm sitting on his lap,' Ma said. 'Why don't you ask Mariette if she'll sit on yours?'

Mariette, who needed no asking, sat on Mr Charlton's lap. The illusion of being caressed in a silken, sinuous, maddening way by the goose's neck returned to Mr Charlton as he felt her silken legs cross his own. A sensation that for the second time his blood was turning white, while being at the same time on fire, coursed completely through him. The soles of his feet started tingling. The scent of gardenia overwhelmed him like a drug.

'Tell me what the scent is,' Mr Charlton said.

'Gardenia.'

'Gardenia? Gardenia? What's gardenia?'

'It's a flower. Do you like it?'

'Like it? Like it?' Mr Charlton said madly. 'Like it?'

With extraordinarily soft hands Mariette took his own and held them high round her waist, just under her breasts. With stupefying tenderness she started to rock backwards and forwards on his knee, with the result that Mr Charlton could not see straight. His eyes were simply two quivering balls revolving unrestrainedly in the top of his head.

'Well, getting late,' Pop said. 'Hitch up a bit, Ma, and I'll mix another before we go to shut-eye.'

Pop reappeared presently from underneath the salmon canopy of Ma and announced that he was going to mix a new one this time.

'How about a Chauffeur? Dammit, the Rolls has to have a Chauffeur,' he said. He stood earnestly consulting the *Guide to Better Drinking*. 'One third vermouth, one third whisky, one third gin, dash of angostura. Sounds perfick. Everybody game?'

Everybody was game. Mr Charlton was very game. He said so over and over again. Mariette held his hands more closely against her body and a little higher than before and Mr Charlton let his head rest against the velvety, downy nape of her dark neck.

'You're my goose. My gardenia,' he said.

'Wouldn't you think', Mariette said, 'that it was soon time to go to bed?'

Some moments later Mr Charlton had drained the Chauffeur in two gulps and was addressing Ma and Pop in what he thought were solid, steadfast tones of gratitude.

'Can never thank you. Never thank you. Never be able to thank you.'

He shook on his feet, grasped at air with aimless hands, and started jiggling like a fish.

'Should be a cocktail called gardenia! A sweet one –'

'I'll make one,' Pop said. 'I'll think one up.'

'And one called Mariette,' Mr Charlton said. 'Sweet one too! –'

He staggered violently and some time later was vaguely aware of walking arm in arm to the billiard-room with Mariette. There was no light in the billiard-room. He felt filled with inconsolable happiness and laughed with wild immoderation, once again feeling her legs brush against him like the goose-neck, in the darkness. Once again too he called her a gardenia and stretched out groping hands to touch her.

Instead, unsurprised, he found himself kneeling by the billiard table, caressing in the corner pocket a solitary, cool abandoned ball.

'Where are you? Where are you?' he said. 'Mariette –'

Mr Charlton got up and fell down, breaking the thrushes' eggs in his pocket as he fell.

'Climb up,' Mariette said. Mr Charlton found it impossible to climb up and Mariette started pushing him. 'Upsadaisy. Up you go. I'll get your collar off.'

Meanwhile Pop, who was sitting up in bed in his shirt, thinking of the evening sunshine, the meadows shining so beautifully and so golden with buttercups and the prospect of summer growing to maturity all about his paradise, decided that the only thing to make the day more perfick was a cigar.

'I'm the same as Churchill,' he said. 'Like a good cigar.'

He lit the cigar and sat watching Ma undress herself. The thing he really loved most about Ma, he had long since decided, was that she didn't have to wear corsets. She didn't need them; her figure was all her own; pure and natural as could be.

'Ma, I've been thinking,' he said, 'when does Mariette expect this baby?'

'She can't make up her mind.'

'Well, she'd better,' Pop said.

'Why?' Ma said.

From the depths of her transparent petunia canopy, as it floated down over the global map of her white, wide territory, Ma spoke with her customary air of unconcern.

Smoking his cigar, gazing thoughtfully through the open window to a night of warm May stars, as if pondering again on summer and the way it would soon embroider with its gold and green his already perfick paradise, Pop made a pronouncement.

'I'm a bit worried about Mister Charlton. I don't think that young man's got it in 'im,' he said. 'At least not yet.'

· 4 ·

Mr Charlton woke late and to a dark, disquieting impression. It was that he was lying alone in the centre of a large flat green field. A cold storm was raging about him. Overhead drummed peals of thunder.

Agony taught him some minutes later that the thunder rolled from somewhere inside his own head and that the field was the billiard table, from which he was about to fall. He got up off the table and groped with uncertain agony about the semi-darkened room, white hands limp at his sides, stringy and strengthless, like portions of tired celery.

He was wearing Mariette's pyjamas, which were silk, of a pale blue colour, with a pattern of either pink roses or carnations all over them – he was too distraught to tell which. He could not remember putting the pyjamas on. He could only suppose Mariette had put them on. He could not remember that either.

Presently, after managing to pull on his trousers over his pyjamas, he groped his way out of the billiard-room. In the kitchen the apparition of Ma, now wearing a parma-violet jumper instead of the salmon one, overrode all other objects, like a circus elephant. She was making toast and frying eggs and bacon. His hands trembled as they grasped a chair.

'Ah! there you are, Mister Charlton. One egg or two?' Ma, in her customary fashion, started laughing like a jelly, her voice a carillon. 'Two eggs or three? Sleep all right?'

Mr Charlton sat down and thought that even if wild dogs had begun to chase him he would never again have the strength to move.

'Cuppa tea?' A heavy weight, like a descending pile-driver, hit the table, shaking cups and cutlery. It was a cup. 'Like a drop of milk in it?' With shaking bosom Ma roared happily again. 'Cows or Johnny Walker?'

Mr Charlton prayed silently over the comforting fumes of tea.

'Mariette waited for you but you didn't seem to come so she's gone for a ride now to get her appetite up,' Ma said. 'She'll be back any minute now. Pop's feeding the pigs. He's had one breakfast. But he'll want another.'

Life, Mr Charlton felt, was ebbing away from him. In his cup large tea-leaves swam dizzily round and round, the black wreckage of disaster.

42

'You never said how many eggs,' Ma said. 'One or two? How do you like 'em? Turned over?'

'I –'

A moment later a rough sledge-hammer hit Mr Charlton in the middle of the back.

'How's the tax-man?' Pop said. 'How's my friend? All right, old man? Sleep well? Perfick morning, ain't it?'

Whereas overnight Mr Charlton's veins had run white, in crazy, voluptuous courses, he now felt them to be some shade of pale, expiring green. There was something seriously wrong with his intestines. They were dissolving under waves of acid. He could no longer claim them for his own.

'I don't think Mr Charlton feels very well,' Ma said.

'No?' Pop said. 'Pity. Didn't sleep very well? Potted the white, eh?' Pop barked with violent laughter at his joke. 'Hair of the dog I should say.'

Mr Charlton had never heard of hair of the dog. Pop sat down at the table and drummed on it with the handles of his knife and fork, whistling *Come to the cook-house door, boys* through his teeth.

'What's your programme this morning, old man? Like to come with me and take the pig over to the bacon factory?'

'I think I shall have to go home.'

Faintly Mr Charlton spoke for the first time, his voice full of pallid distress. Echoes of his words rang through his head in hollower tones, as through a sepulchre.

'Don't say that, old man,' Pop said. 'We was looking forward to having you the whole week-end. I want to show you the place. I got thirty-two acres here altogether. Lovely big medder at the back. Beautiful stretch o' river. Perfick. Do any fishing?'

While Pop was speaking Ma set before him a plate of three eggs, four six-inch rashers of home-cured bacon, three very thick brown sausages, and a slice of fried bread. Pop attacked this with the precipitate virility and desperation of a man who has not seen food for some long time. In an excruciating moment the last of Mr Charlton's intestines got ready to dissolve.

Suddenly Pop slapped down his knife and fork, troubled.

'Something wrong?' Ma said.

'Don't taste right.'

'You forgot the ketchup, you loony, that's why.'

'Gorblimey, so I did. Knowed there was summat wrong somewhere.'

Pop reached out, grabbed the ketchup bottle, and shook an ocean of scarlet all over his breakfast.

Mr Charlton shut his eyes. This grave mistake made him think that he was on the deck of a sinking ship, in a hurricane. He opened his eyes with great haste and the deck came up at him.

'Hullo there, bright eyes. Good morning. How are we this morning?'

The astral figure of Mariette, fresh in yellow shirt and jodhpurs, was all that Mr Charlton felt he needed to set him weeping. The pristine, cheerful voice was beyond his range of thought. He tried to say something and failed, faintly.

'Mister Charlton doesn't feel all that well,' Ma said. 'He says he might have to go home.'

Pop belched with enormous pleasure, as usual surprising himself.

'Manners. Early morning breeze. Pardon me.' He struck his chest with the handle of the fork, as if in stern reproval. 'Home, my foot. Stop worrying, old man. That's the trouble with you office fellers. You all worry too much by half. After all, here today and gone tomorrow.'

It was not tomorrow, Mr Charlton thought, that he was worried about. Unless he could find some speedy, drastic remedy he would, he was convinced, be gone today.

'Heavens, I'm hungry,' Mariette said.

She sat down at the table, stirred a cup of tea, and started laughing. Her voice put stitches into Mr Charlton's head: stabbing lines of them, on hot needles.

'See something funny out riding?' Pop said. 'Like the Brigadier's sister?'

'I was just smiling at Mr Charlton. He's still got the pyjamas on.' She started laughing again and Mr Charlton could not help feeling there was some sinister, hidden meaning in the word smiling. 'Oh! that was a laugh, getting them on last night. First we couldn't get one lot of trousers off and then we couldn't get the other lot on. Oh! Mr Charlton, you were a scream. Absolute scream.'

Mr Charlton, who began to feel among other things that he was not grown up, did not doubt it. Everything was a scream. His whole body, his entire mind, and his intestines were a scream.

'Most of the time you were making love to a billiard ball in the side pocket.'

Pop started choking.

'I said you potted the white, didn't I?' he shouted. 'Ain't that what I said, Ma?' With immense glee Pop beat a tattoo on the table-cloth with the handles of his knife and fork. 'Potted the white. Damn funny. Just what I said.'

'Tonight I'll make you a proper bed up,' Ma said. 'In the bottom bathroom. Nobody uses it very much now we've got the new one upstairs.'

'I really think', Mr Charlton said, his voice limp, 'I'd better go home.'

In a sudden gesture of fond solicitude Pop put an arm round Mr Charlton's shoulder.

'You know, Charley boy,' he said, 'I wish your name was Charley instead of Cedric. It's more human. I can't get used to Cedric. It's like a parson's name. Can't we call you Charley? – after all it's short for your other name.'

'Please call me Charley if you wish,' Mr Charlton said and felt once again like weeping.

'What I was going to say, Charley boy,' Pop went on, 'is this, old man, I think you need a Larkin Special.'

Mr Charlton had no time to ask what a Larkin Special was before Pop was out of the room, across the passage, and into the living-room on the other side. Presently there were noises from the Spanish galleon, the monster cocktail cabinet that could have only been moulded, Mr Charlton thought, by a man of evil, demoniac designs.

'That'll put you as right as a lamplighter in no time,' Ma said. 'Acts like a charm.'

'A nice walk after breakfast,' Mariette said, 'and you'll be on top of the world.' Mr Charlton felt sure that that in fact was where he was, but in the act of falling. Mariette was now eating bacon, eggs, large burnished brown sausages, and fried bread. 'We could walk across the meadow and have a look at the motor-boat if you like.'

'Motor-boat?' At the same moment some curious reflex of thought made Mr Charlton remember the buff-yellow tax form. He hadn't seen it since sharing his boiled eggs with the twins the previous day. 'You've got a motor-boat?'

'Nice one. Little beauty. We keep it in the boathouse on the other side of the meadow.'

'Pop took it in exchange for a debt,' Ma explained.

'Mrs Larkin,' Mr Charlton began to say. He felt suddenly, in a guilty fashion, that he ought to make some sort of atonement with himself for all that had happened. He was actually bothered by a sense of duty. 'I don't suppose you've seen that buff-yellow form –'

'Coming up, coming up, coming up,' Pop said. 'There you are, Charley, old man. Larkin Special. Don't ask what's in it. Don't stare at it. Don't think. Just drink it down. In ten minutes you'll feel perfick again.'

Pop set before a demoralized Mr Charlton, on the breakfast table, what Mr Charlton could only think was a draught of bull's blood.

'I think I should go and lie down –'

'Don't think a thing!' Pop said. 'Drink it. Say to 'ell wiv everything and drink it.'

Mr Charlton hesitated. His intestines rolled.

'I can vouch for it,' Ma said.

The soft dark eyes of Mariette smiled across the table. The familiar astral vision of cool olive skin against the light lemon shirt, of dark hair and the firm treasured breasts that Mr Charlton had almost clasped the previous evening, revived an inspiring, momentary recollection of his lost white fire.

He ducked his head and drank.

'Now I must get cracking,' Pop said. 'I got a bit of a deal to do about some straw. I got the new deep-freeze to pick up. And the pigs. And the port.'

With fond assurance he laid a hand on Mr Charlton's shoulder.

'Charley, old man,' he said, 'by the time I get back you'll feel perfick.'

For some time Mr Charlton sat in tentative silence, reawaking. A feeling of slow intestinal restoration made him give, once or twice, a tender sigh. He grasped slowly that the thunder in his head had now become mere singing, like distant vespers in a minor key.

'Feeling more yourself now?'

Mariette was eating toast and golden marmalade. As she opened her mouth to eat he saw, for the first time, how beautifully white her teeth were and how pink, in a pure rose-petal shade, her tongue now appeared as it darted out and caught at golden shreds of marmalade.

He even found himself thinking of gardenia, its compelling, torturing night-scent and the pure whiteness of its flower.

'It's absolutely wonderful in the woods this morning,' Mariette said. 'All the bluebells out. Millions of them. And the moon-daisies. It's hot too and the nightingales had already started when I was coming back. You're not really going home today?'

A lyrical wave passed over Mr Charlton. With distaste he remembered his office: the in-tray, the out-tray, the files, the other chaps, the ink-stained desks, the chatter of typewriters.

'If you're sure it's no trouble –'

'Trouble!' Ma said. 'We *want* you. We love to have you.'

'I've finished,' Mariette said. 'Like to get a breath of air?'

Mr Charlton went to the door and stood in the sun. With reviving heart he stared across Pop's paradise of junk, scratching hens, patrols of geese, and graveyards of rusty iron, in the middle of which Montgomery was milking goats under a haystack. Over all this a sky as blue as the thrushes' eggs that had come to disaster in his pocket spread with unblemished purity. The near fringes of meadows had become, overnight, white with moon-daisies, drifts of summer snow. A cuckoo called and was answered by another, the notes like those of tender horns, the birds hidden in oak-trees, among curtains of thickest olive flower.

'How do you feel now?' Mariette said.

The pale face of Mr Charlton broadened into its first unsteady daylight smile.

'A little more perfick than I was.'

By Saturday night the deep-freeze was installed. By Sunday morning, three nine-pound geese, well-stuffed with sage and onion, were sizzling in a pure white electric oven that could have spoken, Mr Charlton thought, if spoke to. A light breeze drove with frailest spinnings of air through the bluebell wood and bore across the hot yard the delicious aroma of roasting birds.

Ma, who loved colour, cooked in a canary yellow pinafore with big scarlet pockets and at intervals shouted across the yard, either to Pop or Mariette, Mr Charlton or the children, or whoever happened to be there, a demand for instructions about the meal.

'What sort of vegetables do you fancy? Asparagus? I got green peas and new potatoes but shout if you want anything different.' It turned out that Montgomery wanted brown braised onions, the twins Yorkshire pudding, and Primrose baked potatoes. 'Fair enough,' Ma said, 'as long as we know.'

At eleven o'clock, by which time Pop was no longer in the yard, Ma shouted that it was already so hot in the kitchen that she'd be sick by the time the meal was served.

'What say we have it outside?' she called. 'Under the walnut tree?'

By noon Mariette, dressed in neat sky-blue linen shorts and an open-necked vermilion blouse, her legs bare, was laying a white cloth on a long table underneath a walnut tree that overshadowed, like a faintly fragrant umbrella, the only civilized stretch of grass near the house, on the south side, beside which Ma would later grow patches of petunia and zinnia, her favourite flowers. It was cool and dark there under the thickening walnut leaves, out of the sun, and Mr Charlton helped her by bringing cutlery from the house on papier-mâché trays brightly decorated with hunting scenes, race-meetings, or pointers carrying birds.

Perfick, Perfick!

At half past twelve Pop startled everybody by driving into the yard in a Rolls-Royce, a pre-war landaulette in black, with straw-coloured doors that actually looked as if they had been made of plaited basket-work. The horn, sounding with discreet harmonious distinction, brought everybody running to the centre of the rusty, dusty graveyards of junk and iron.

Pop stopped the car and dismounted with triumphant, imperial pride.

'Here it is!' he shouted. 'Ourn!'

Before anyone could speak he leapt down to the doors, proudly pointing.

'Monogram,' he said. 'Look, Ma – monograms on the doors.'

'Royal?' Ma said.

'Duke, I think,' Pop said. 'The feller didn't know. Anyway, duke or viscount or some toff of some sort.'

Ma was dazzled. She took several paces forward and touched the gleaming body-work.

'All in!' Pop said. 'Everybody in! Everybody who wants a ride get in!'

Everybody, including Mr Charlton, got into the Rolls-Royce. On the wide spacious seats of dove-grey upholstery, upon which heavy cords of tasselled yellow silk hung at the windows, there was plenty of room for everybody, but the twins sat on Mr Charlton's lap. Ma herself sat in the centre of the back seat, her pinafore spread out crinoline-wise, almost in royal fashion, her turquoise-ringed hands spread on her yellow pinafore.

Soon an entranced look crept like a web across her face, only her eyes moving as they rolled gently from side to side, taking in the smallest details.

'I wish I had my hat on,' she said at last. 'I don't feel right without my hat on.'

'Got a big picnic basket in the boot,' Pop said. 'Corkscrews an' all.'

'It's got vases for flowers,' Ma said. She leaned forward and fingered with delicacy a pair of silver horn-like vases fixed below the glass screen that divided the back seat from the front.

'Notice anything else?' Pop called. 'Have a good dekko. All round. Want you to notice one more thing, Ma. Have a good dekko.'

After several seconds of silence, in which Ma's eyes revolved on a slow axis of exploration, in pure wonderment, Ma confessed that she saw nothing more.

'That thing like the bit off the end of a carpet sweeper!' Pop yelled. In his own delight he laughed in his customary ringing fashion. 'Mind it don't bite you.'

'No,' Ma said. 'No.' Her mouth expired air in a long incredulous wheeze. 'No –'

'Speakin' tube!' Pop said. 'Pick it up. Say something down it. Give me order. Say "Home James!" – summat like that.'

Ma, in possession of the end of the speaking tube, sat utterly speechless.

'Give me order!' Pop said. 'I can hear whatever you say perfickly well in front here. Go on, Ma. Give me order!'

Ma breathed into the speaking tube in a voice pitched in a minor key of desolation.

'I don't know whether I like it,' she said. 'They'll be putting the price of fish-and-chips up when they see us roll up in this.'

'Never!' Pop said. 'They'll be paying *us*.'

The receiving end of the speaking apparatus was just above the head of Mr Charlton, who was sitting next to Pop in the driving seat. The voices of Victoria and Primrose began to shriek into his ears like a gabble of excited young ducks.

'Take us for a ride! Take us for a ride! Take us for a ride!'

Pop let in the clutch and started to steer a course of slow elegance between a pile of discarded oil-drums and a big galvanized iron swill-tub. No breath of sound came, for a full minute, from either the Rolls or its passengers.

Then Ma said: 'Like riding on air. Not a squeak anywhere. Must be paid for.'

'Cash down!' Pop said.

He pressed the horn. An orchestration of low notes, harmonious, smooth as honey, disturbed into slight flutterings a batch of young turkeys sunning themselves in the lee of the pig-sties.

'That's the town one,' Pop explained. He flicked a switch with a finger-nail. 'Now hark at this. Country. Open road.'

A peremptory, urgent snarl, like the surprise entry of symphonic brass, tore the peaceful fabric of the yard's livestock to pieces. A whole flotilla of white ducks sprang into the air and raced like hurdlers over rusty junk, empty boxes, and feeding troughs. Brown hens flew like windy paper-bags in all directions, shedding feathers.

'Special fittin',' Pop explained. 'Chap who owned it once lived in Paris or somewheres.'

He completed with slow imperial pride the course of the yard, now blowing the town horn, now the snarl.

'Comfortable in the back, ain't it, Ma? Make a nice bed, don't you think?'

Ma, who had recovered equilibrium, now spoke down the speaking-tube, shaking like a jelly.

'Home, James. Else them geese'll burn.'

Pop responded with the honeyed notes of the town horn and the Rolls, like a ship gliding to anchorage in smooth waters, skirted with a final swing of silent elegance past a strong black alp of pig-manure.

'Perfick, ain't it?' Pop said. 'Ain't it perfick?'

Ma, who had stopped laughing, breathed hard before she spoke again.

'I got to have flowers in the vases,' she said, her voice full of a pleasure so deep that it was at once loving and lovable in humility. 'Every time we go out we got to have flowers.'

Back at the house everybody alighted and Ma once again stroked, with touching affection, the shining chariot wings, her huge body reflected in their black curves with a vast transfiguration of yellow and scarlet, distorted as in a comic mirror at a fair.

'Gorblimey, I must run,' she said suddenly. 'I haven't even started the apple sauce.'

As Ma ran towards the house Mariette remembered the table under the walnut tree and took Mr Charlton's hand. Pop remembered the port and called after a dutifully retreating Mr Charlton:

'Charley boy, like to do summat for me while you're helping Mariette? Put the port on ice, old man, will you? Three bottles. Two red and one white. You'll find two ice buckets in the cocktail cabinet. Give 'em plenty of ice, old man.'

At the same time Montgomery stood staring across the yard in the direction of the road.

'Pop,' he said, 'I think we got a visitor. I think it looks like the Brigadier.'

Across the yard a straight, six-foot human straw was drifting. It was dressed in a suit of tropical alpaca, once yellowish, now bleached to whitish fawn, that looked as if it had recently been under a steam-roller.

It was the Brigadier all right, Pop said, and leaned one hand on the front wing of the Rolls with casual pride, raising the other in greeting. He wondered too what the Brigadier wanted and where his sister was and said he betted the old whippet had left him for the day.

'General!' he called. 'What can I do you for?'

'Hail,' the Brigadier said. The voice was low and cryptic. 'Well met, Larkin.'

At closer range it was to be seen that the Brigadier's elbows had been patched with squares of paler coloured material that appeared to have been torn from pillow-slips. The cuffs of his jacket sleeves had been trimmed more or less level with scissors and then sewn back. His socks were yellow. The hat worn on the back of his head resembled more than anything a frayed bee-skip and seemed to be worn so far back in order to avoid his extraordinary extensive white eyebrows, altogether too large for the rest of his cadaverous face, which stuck above his pale blue eyes like two salty prawns.

These prawns were repeated on his upper lip in stiff moustaches, which contrasted sharply with cheeks consisting entirely of purple veins. The chin was resolute and looked like worn pumice stone. The neck was long and loose and held entirely together by a rigid bolt of fiery crimson, the Adam's apple, which seemed over the course of time to have worn the soiled shirt collar to shreds.

The Brigadier shook hands with Pop, at the same time recognizing in Pop's demeanour the divinity of new possession. He held the Rolls-Royce in flinty stare.

'Not yours?'

'Just got it.'

'Good God.'

Pop made breezy gestures of pride. He wanted instantly to reveal possession of the monograms and then decided against it. It was too much all at one time, he thought.

'Hellish costly to run?'

'Well, might be, can't tell, might be,' Pop said. 'But worth it. Always flog it.'

Sooner or later, in his energetic way, Pop flogged most things.

'Good God.' The Brigadier looked at the car with closer, microscopic inspection. 'What's all this?'

'Monogram.'

'Good God.' In moments of humour the Brigadier drew on dry resources of solemnity. 'No crown?'

The remark was lost on Pop, who was dying to demonstrate the horn's orchestral variations.

'Well,' the Brigadier said, 'I mustn't linger. Down to staff work.'

Pop laughed in his usual ringing fashion and said he betted a quid the General wanted a subscription.

'Wrong,' the Brigadier said. 'Not this time.'

'Well, that's worth a drink,' Pop said. 'What about a snifter?'

'Trifle early, don't you think?' the Brigadier said. 'Not quite over the yard-arm yet, are we?'

'When I want a drink,' Pop said, 'I have a drink. Wevver it's early or wevver it ain't.'

The Brigadier, after a minor pretence at refusal, chose to have a whisky-and-soda. Pop said first that he'd have a Guinness and then changed his mind and said he'd have a beer called Dragon's Blood with a dash of lime instead. The Brigadier looked astonished at this extraordinary combination but followed Pop into the house without a word.

In the sitting-room he found it hard to concentrate even on the whisky-and-soda because of powerful, torturing odours of roasting geese that penetrated every corner of the house, delicious with sage and onion stuffing. He sat most of the time with his glass on his right knee, where it successfully concealed a hole that mice might have gnawed.

'Might as well come straight to the point,' the Brigadier said. 'Fact is, Larkin, I'm in a God-awful mess.'

'Wimmin?'

The Brigadier looked extremely startled. The prawns of his eyebrows seemed to leap out. He seemed about to speak and then drank with eagerness at the whisky-and-soda instead.

'No, no, no,' he said eventually. 'Bad enough, but not that bad.'

Pop knew that the Brigadier's sister, who resembled more than anything a long hairpin on the top of which she generally wore a cloche hat that looked like a pink thimble, was presumed to lead him a hell of a dance on most occasions and in all directions. Among other things he felt that she never gave the Brigadier enough to eat: a terrible thing.

'No, it's this damn Gymkhana,' the Brigadier said. 'That Bolshie Fortescue had a God-awful row with the committee Friday and has withdrawn from the field.'

'Always was a basket.'

'Not only withdrawn *from* the field,' the Brigadier said, 'but withdrawn *the* field.'

'Means you've got nowhere to hold the damn thing.'

'Bingo,' the Brigadier said.

In a soft voice Pop called Mr Fortescue a bloody sausage and remembered Mariette. The gymkhana was in a fortnight's time. It might be the last chance she'd ever get to ride in the jumps before she had the baby. She was mad on jumping; her heart was set on horses and all that sort of thing.

'Nothing to worry about,' Pop said. 'You can hold it in my medder.'

'Don't let me rush you into a decision, Larkin,' the Brigadier said. 'You don't have to decide –'

'Good grief,' Pop said. 'Nothing to decide. The medder's there, ain't it? All I got to do is get the grass cut. I'll get the grass cut this week and things'll be perfick.'

The Brigadier was so much touched by this that he nervously held his glass in his left hand and started poking a finger into the hole in his right trouser knee, a habit about which his sister had already scolded him acidly twice at breakfast.

'Can't thank you enough, Larkin,' he said. He several times used the words 'eternal gratitude' in low muttered voice, as in prayer. He coughed, drank again, poked at the hole in his knee, and called Pop a stout feller. He knew the committee would be eternally grateful. 'Never be able to thank you.'

Out of politeness he rose to go. Before he was on his feet Pop was insisting on another snifter and Ma, hearing the tinkle of ice in glasses, called from the kitchen:

'What about one for the old cook in here? What's she done today?'

The Brigadier, under indeterminate protest, had a second whisky-and-soda. Pop had a change of mind and had a whisky-and-soda too. Ma ordered beer because she was parched from cooking and came to the sitting-room door to drink it from a big glass that spilled foam down her hands.

'Bung-ho,' she said to the Brigadier. 'How's your sister today?'

'Gone to see an aunt,' the Brigadier said. Now that Ma had opened the kitchen door the smell of browning goose-flesh was attacking him in even more frontal, more excruciating waves. 'Over in Hampshire. Day's march away.'

'Sunday dinner all on your lonesome?' Ma said.

'Not quite that bad.' Torturing waves of sage-sharp fragrance from the roasting geese made him suddenly feel more heady than even the whisky-and-soda had done on his empty stomach. 'I shall waffle down to the pub and grab a bite of cold.'

'Cold on Sundays?' Ma was deeply shocked. 'You wouldn't catch Pop having cold on Sundays. Why don't you stay here and eat with us?'

'No, no, really no. No, thanks all the same, really –'

'Encore,' Pop said. 'More the merrier. Perfick.'

'Bless my soul, with all your brood –'

'Of course,' Ma said. 'Cold, my foot.'

'Ma,' Pop said, 'pity you didn't put that leg o' pork in after all.' Ma had calculated that, within reason, three nine-pound geese ought to be enough. 'Too late now I suppose?'

He seemed quite disappointed as Ma said, 'Not unless you want to eat about five o'clock,' and went away kitchenwards. He hated having to skimp on joints and things; it made it hard work for the carver.

From the kitchen Ma called a minute later:

'Come here a minute, Pop, I want you. Lift the geese out of the oven for me, will you? I want to baste them.'

Pop went into the kitchen, realizing as soon as he went through the door that the call was after all merely a ruse to get him away from the Brigadier. Ma was standing by the window, arms folded like huge white vegetable marrows across her bolstered bosom, looking towards the walnut tree.

'Take a look at that,' she said.

Under the tree, at the dinner table, cloth and cutlery having been laid, Mariette and Mr Charlton were coolly sitting some distance apart from each other, absorbed in the Sunday papers.

Ma made noises of puzzled disgust, which Pop echoed.

'What's wrong with 'em?'

'Wrong? Don't he know his technique?' Ma said.

'Very like do better on the boat this afternoon,' Pop said. 'There's some very good quiet places up the river.'

Ma, as if she could not bear the sight any longer, turned away to stir the apple sauce with a wooden spoon as it simmered away in a new bright aluminium pan. After looking at it critically she decided it needed a touch of something and dropped into the steaming olive-yellow purée a lump of butter as big as a tennis ball.

'Brigadier looks seedy, I think, don't you?' she said. Pop agreed. He felt immensely sorry for the Brigadier. 'Trouble with these people they never get enough to eat. Like Mr Charlton. Half-starved.'

Pop agreed with that too. 'Cold at the pub Sundays,' he said, as if this was the depths of deplorable gastronomic misery. 'Can you beat it?'

Ma said she could. 'Because if I know anything about it he wasn't going near the pub. He was going home to a Marmite sandwich and a glass o' milk. Perhaps even water.'

A moment later she turned to reach from a cupboard a new tin of salt and Pop, watching her upstretched figure as it revealed portions of enormous calves, suddenly felt a startling twinge of excitement in his veins. He immediately grasped Ma by the bosom and started squeezing her. Ma pretended to protest, giggling at the same time, but Pop continued to fondle her with immense, experienced enthusiasm, until finally she turned, yielded the great continent of her body to him and let him kiss her full on her soft big mouth.

Pop prolonged this delicious experience as long as he had breath. He always felt more passionate in the kitchen. He supposed it was the smell of food. Ma sometimes told him it was a wonder he ever got any meals at all and that he ought to know, at his age, which he wanted most, meals or her. 'Both,' he always said. 'Often.'

This morning, against the shining white stove, the glistening aluminium pans and the background of sunlight on the young coppery green leaves of the walnut tree, he thought she looked absolutely lovely. She was his dream.

He started to kiss her passionately again. But this time she held him away. The Brigadier, she said, would be wondering what was happening. He was to go back to the Brigadier. 'The twins'll be back with the ice-cream any moment too,' she said. The twins had gone to the village, a quarter of a mile down the road, with orders to bring back the largest blocks of strawberry and chocolate *mousse* they could buy.

'Take the Brigadier a few crisps,' Ma said. 'They'll keep him going for half an hour.'

With reluctance Pop went back to the Brigadier, who sat staring into an empty glass, elbows on his knees, his trouser legs hitched up so that his socks and thin hairy shins were revealed. Pop saw now that the socks were odd, one yellow and one white, and that both had potatoes in the heels.

'Crisp, General?' he said and held out a big plastic orange dish of potato crisps, glistening fresh and salty.

The Brigadier, who belonged to two London clubs that he used only twice a year and spent most of the rest of his time wearing himself to a skeleton chopping wood, washing dishes, clipping hedges, mowing the lawn, and cleaning out blocked drainpipes because he couldn't afford a man, accepted the crisps with formal reluctance that actually concealed a boyish gratitude.

Pop also suggested another snifter.

'No, no. Thanks all the same. No, no,' the Brigadier said. 'No really,' and then allowed his glass to be taken away from him with no more than dying stutters of protestation.

Half an hour later two of the three geese were lying side by side, browned to perfection, deliciously varnished with running gravy, in a big oval blue meat dish on the table under the walnut tree. Other blue dishes stood about the table containing green peas and new potatoes veined with dark sprigs of mint, baked onions, asparagus, roast potatoes, Yorkshire pudding, and broad beans in parsley sauce. There were also big blue boats of apple sauce and gravy.

There had been times in his life when the Brigadier would have been prompted, out of sheer good form, social constraint, and various other preventive forces of up-bringing, to describe the sight of all this as rather lacking in decency. Today he merely sat with restrained bewilderment, tortured by odours of goose-flesh and sage-and-onions, watching the faces of Pop, Ma, Mister Charlton, and the entire Larkin brood while Pop carved with dextrous ease at the birds, themselves not at all unlike brown laden galleons floating in a glistening gravy sea.

Even the stiff prawns of his eyebrows made no quiver of surprise as Pop, flashing carving knife and steel in air, suggested that if Charley boy wanted to help he could pour the port out now.

Mr Charlton put the port on the table in its champagne bucket, all beady with ice dew.

'Mix it,' Pop said. 'It makes a jolly good drink, red and white mixed together.'

Mr Charlton went round the table, pouring and mixing port. He had been introduced to the Brigadier by a more than usually facetious Pop as 'a late entry – chap on the tax lark'.

'Actually a real pukka tax-gatherer you mean?' the Brigadier said, as if astonished that there could be such a person.

'Inspector's office,' Mr Charlton said.

'Tried to rope *me* in on that swindle yesterday,' Pop said. He laughed derisively, in his customary ringing fashion. 'I should like, eh, General? What do you say?'

The Brigadier confessed, with a certain sadness, that he paid no tax. At least, hardly any.

'And rightly so!' Pop thundered.

Succulent pieces of bird were now being carved and dispatched about the table with breezy speed.

'That all right for you, General?' The Brigadier found himself facing an entire leg of goose and a large mound of sage-and-onions.

'Start!' Pop ordered. 'Don't let it get cold, General!' To the goose Mariette came to add peas, beans, Yorkshire pudding, and two sorts of potatoes, so that finally, when gravy and apple sauce had been ladled on, no single centimetre of naked plate could be seen.

A moment later the Brigadier, faced with superior forces and not knowing where to attack, saw Ma, like some huge yellow and scarlet butterfly glowing in the walnut shade, come up on his flank, bearing a deep dish of fat and buttery asparagus. With dry humour he started to confess to being out-numbered, a problem that Ma at once solved by placing the dish between the Brigadier and the head of table, where she herself now sat down.

'We'll share, shall we, General?' she said. 'Help yourself from the dish. Everybody else has had some.'

It was some moments before the Brigadier, deeply touched and painfully strung up by the first delicious tortures of eating, could relax enough to remember formality and lift his glass to Ma.

'Mr Charlton, I think we should raise a glass to our hostess.'

'	'Ear, 'ear,' Pop said. 'Cheers to Ma.'

The Brigadier bent upwards from the table, raising his glass to Ma. Mr Charlton also half-rose and raised his glass and at the same moment Victoria said, pointing to the Brigadier:

'You got potatoes in your socks, I saw them.'

'Now, now,' Pop said. 'Manners. Elbows!'

Victoria was silent.

'Pop's got 'em at a word,' Ma said proudly. 'And now *eat* your potatoes,' she said to Victoria. 'Never mind about the General's.'

'This is most superb cooking,' the Brigadier said. 'Where did you learn to cook, Mrs Larkin?'

'She learned at The Three Cocks hotel at Fordington,' Pop said. 'That's where she learnt. I can tell you. And it's never been the same since she left there.'

'I can only say the cock's loss is your gain,' the Brigadier said, a remark that Ma found so amusing that she started choking again, her mouth jammed by a piece of asparagus.

'Hit her, General!' Pop said. 'Middle o' the back!'

The Brigadier was utterly startled by this sudden and unnatural order. He moved vaguely to action by putting down his knife and fork, but a second later Ma had recovered.

'All right, Ma?' Pop said. 'Drink a drop o' wine.'

Ma, sipping wine, said thanks, she was all right again.

'Ma's got a very small gullet,' Pop explained to the Brigadier, 'compared with the rest of her.'

'Have you told the children about the Gymkhana, Larkin?' the Brigadier said.

'Good God, went clean out of my head,' Pop said. Waving a dripping wing-bone, which he had been busily sucking for some moments past, he informed the entire table in proud, imperial tones: 'Going to hold the Gymkhana in the medder, kids. *Here.*'

Before anyone could speak an excited Mariette was on her feet, running round the table to Pop, whom she began kissing with great fervour on the lips, hardly a degree less passionately than Pop, in the kitchen, had kissed Ma.

'Lovely, lovely man. Lovely, lovely Pop.'

Mr Charlton sat tremulous, completely shaken. A curious wave of emotion, at first hot, then cold, lapped entirely through him from the small of his back to his brain. Unaccountably he found himself both jealous, then afraid, of the unquenchable demonstration that had left Pop, laughing loudly, hugging Mariette in return. He was not used to unquenchable demonstrations.

'That's the loveliest, loveliest news. Don't you think so, Mr Charlton?'

'You should really thank the General,' Pop said. 'His idea.'

'Committee –'

The word had hardly broken from the lips of the Brigadier before Mariette was at his side, kissing him too. The Brigadier, looking formally delighted, began to wipe his mouth with his serviette, but whether to wipe away kiss or asparagus butter it was not possible to say. He was still dabbing his mouth when Mariette kissed Ma, who explained to the Brigadier: 'Mad on horses, General. Absolutely stark raving mad on horses,' and then came round the table to where Mr Charlton sat concentrating with every nerve on scraping the last tissues of goose-flesh from a leg bone.

Mr Charlton was all mixed up. He was fighting to concentrate. He was fighting to disentangle one thought, one fear, from another. There had crossed his mind, for no sensible reason at all, the uneasy notion that the goose he was now eating might well be part of the same living bird that had so sinuously, shimmeringly wrapped its neck about his legs the previous day, with the shattering sensation of their being caressed by silk stockings. It was the most disturbing thought of his life and he knew that he was blushing. He knew he was afraid.

'Oh! Mr Charlton, I'm so happy I think I'll kiss you too.'

Mariette, to the unconcealed delight and satisfaction of Ma and Pop, bent and kissed Mr Charlton briefly, but with purpose, full on the lips. Mr Charlton recoiled in a crimson cloud, hearing about him trumpets of disaster. Everyone was laughing.

When he came to himself he knew he could never forget that moment. He was trembling all over. It was impossible to describe what the full soft lips of Mariette had felt like against his own except that it was, perhaps, like having them brushed by the skin of a warm firm plum, in full ripeness, for the first time.

While Mr Charlton was still blushing Pop retired to the kitchen and fetched another goose. He began to carve for the Brigadier several thin extra-succulent slices of the breast. This one, he started saying, as he slid the knife across the crackling dark golden skin, was the tenderest of them all and a moment later confirmed Mr Charlton's worst fears by laughing uproariously:

'This must be the joker that was under the table yesterday and heard us talking. Eh, Ma? Think o' that.'

'Knowing birds,' Ma said and turned to the Brigadier to ask: 'What was it you was going to say, General, about the Committee?'

'Oh! merely that I was elected to be spokesman. To ask your husband –'

'Who's on the Committee?' Ma said.

'Well, Edith is secretary. Edith Pilchester. I expect she'll be coming to see you.'

'Oh! I love old Edith,' Pop said. 'Edith's a sport.'

'You be careful she don't love you,' Ma said. 'I wouldn't put anything past her.'

'Ah! perfickly harmless,' Pop said.

'Splendid organizer,' the Brigadier said.

'That's what she thinks. She fancies she could organize a stallion into having pups,' Ma said, 'but that's where she's wrong,' and once again, as she did so often at her own jokes, laughed with jellified splendour.

'Then there's Mrs Peele and George Carter,' the Brigadier said.

'Still living together I suppose?' Ma said.

'I understand the arrangement still holds.'

'Disgusting.'

Ma made tutting noises as she sucked a final piece of asparagus. Pop belched with sudden richness and said 'Manners.' It was terrible the way people carried on, Ma said and Pop agreed.

'Then there's Freda O'Connor.'

'She's another tart if you like,' Ma said. 'Showing off her bosom.'

'And Jack Woodley.'

'That feller's another So-and-so,' Pop said. 'Just like Fortescue. A complete b –'

'Not in front of the twins,' Ma said. 'I don't mind Victoria. She's not old enough to understand.'

'And then Mrs Borden. That makes the lot.'

Ma, eating the last of her peas with a tablespoon, made more noises of disgust and asked if Mrs Borden was still keeping as sober as ever? Supposed she was?

'With the same fish-like capacity I understand,' the Brigadier said.

'Terrible,' Ma said. 'Shocking. Terrible state of affairs when you let drink get you down like that.'

'Disgusting,' Pop said. 'Disgusting.'

It was time for ice-cream. Mariette rose to fetch it from the kitchen, together with a jug of real Jersey, hoping that Mr Charlton would seize so good an opportunity and come with her, but Mr Charlton was still all mixed up. The day had grown exceptionally humid and warm, the air thick with the stirring breath of growing leaves and grasses. Mariette felt the sweetness of it tingling madly in her nostrils and remembered the kiss she had given Mr Charlton. She was sorry for Mr Charlton and wondered if it would ever be possible to make love with him. Making love might ease his mind. In the meadow beyond the house she had noticed how high the buttercups were growing, thick and sappy and golden among the grasses' feathery flower, and she wondered what it would be like to make love to Mr Charlton in a buttercup field. She thought she could but try. She was growing fonder and fonder of Mr Charlton. His eyes were soft, endearing, and sometimes even sad and she found herself fascinated by their brown, delicate paintbrush lashes.

'Cuppa tea, General?'

After the ice-cream Ma was sitting back with a great air of content, as if really getting ready to enjoy herself.

'No, no, no. No really, thank you.'

'No trouble. Always have one after dinner.'

The thought of tea after two plates of goose, asparagus, sage-and-onions, ice-cream, and everything else provoked in the Brigadier's stomach a restless thunderstorm. He suppressed a belch of his own. Pop was not so successful and a positive bark leapt out, causing Primrose to say:

'I love sage-and-onions. You keeping having a taste of it all afternoon. And sometimes all night too.'

Mariette went away to the house to make tea, hoping again that Mr Charlton would go with her, but Mr Charlton was still battling for courage and concentration. Ma hoped so too and made pointed remarks about the heaviness of cups and trays. Mr Charlton, soporific as well as fearful, made no hint of a move and Ma gave it all up, at last, in disgust. He just didn't know his technique, that was all.

When at last Mariette came across the garden with the tea the Brigadier was moved to admiration of the dark, delicious little figure advancing with shapely provocation under the pure hot light of early afternoon.

'Remarkably pretty she looks,' he told Ma, who agreed with surprisingly energetic warmth, saying:

'I'm glad somebody thinks so. She's been hiding her light under a bushel long enough.'

'Well, I don't know', Pop said, 'as you can say that.' He was thinking of the news Ma had told him two days before. Well, he supposed it was hiding her light in a way. Keeping it dark anyway.

Everybody except the Brigadier had tea, which Mariette poured out thick and strong, with Jersey cream. To Mr Charlton's surprise nobody suggested Johnny Walker milk, though Pop stirred into his own cup two teaspoonfuls of port. It was still icy.

'Helps to cool it down,' he explained. 'Ma can't do with it in a saucer.'

An afternoon of delicious golden content folded its transparent envelope more and more softly about the paradisiacal Larkin world, over the outlying meadow scintillating with its million buttercups and the shady fragrant walnut tree. Pop sighed and remarked how perfick it was. If only the Gymkhana was as perfick it would be marvellous, he said. Should they have fireworks? 'Tell the Committee I'll provide the fireworks,' he said to the Brigadier. 'That'll make it go with a bang.'

The Brigadier, who did not answer, was almost asleep. The twins and the younger children had already slipped away. Ma was falling slowly asleep too, her head falling sideways, so that she was now less like a bright expansive butterfly than a vast yellow parrot tucking its head under its sleepy wing.

'Look at that sky, Charley,' Pop said and indicated with the tip of an unlighted cigar the exquisite expanse of all heaven, blue as flax-flower. 'There's summat worth while for you. Perfick. Blimey, I wonder how you fellers can work in offices.'

Mr Charlton was beginning to wonder too.

'Cigar?'

Mr Charlton declined the cigar with low thanks.

'Ought to have given the General one,' Pop said. The Brigadier was now fast asleep. Bad manners to have forgot the General, he thought. He liked the General. The old sport might not live very grand but he was unmistakably a gent. Not like George Carter and Jack Woodley and a few other baskets he could name. Nor Freda O'Connor and Mrs Battersby and Molly Borden and that crowd. They didn't think much of people like him and Ma. That's why they'd sent the General along as spokesman. He knew.

He liked Edith Pilchester though. Edith was a sport. He laughed softly as he thought that if they had fireworks at the Gymkhana he would put one under Edith's skirts, just to see what happened. 'Probably never turn a hair,' he thought. 'Probably get a thrill.'

'Put the cigar on the General's plate, Charley,' he said to Mr Charlton, 'when you get round to going.'

'I think we're going now,' Mariette said to Mr Charlton, 'aren't we?'

Perfick, Perfick!

Mr Charlton, who had been in a mix-up all afternoon, abruptly fumbled to his feet, expressing agreement by taking the cigar and laying it beside the Brigadier's head, reclining now in flushed oblivion on the table.

'Going on the boat?' Pop said.

'Might do,' Mariette said. 'Might not get that far.'

'Perfick anyway,' Pop said, 'wherever you go.'

As they crossed from the garden to the big meadow beyond Mariette took Mr Charlton's hand. In the startled fashion of a young colt he almost jumped as she touched him. A wave of fragrance blew on the lightest breath of wind from the direction of the river, driving into her quickening nostrils odours of hawthorn bloom, clover, an entire valley of rising grasses, and distant invisible fields of early may.

It was so exquisitely strong that suddenly she bent down, took off her shoes, and started running.

A moment later, Mr Charlton, running too, realized how pretty, how exciting, her naked feet were.

· 5 ·

That evening Pop, after a half hour of twilight spent with Ma in the bluebell wood, listening to a whole orchestra of nightingales, came back to the house to urge on Mr Charlton the virtues of a little sick leave.

'Ma and me don't think you look all that grand,' he said.

Ma followed this up by saying that she didn't like the look round Mr Charlton's cheek-bones. There were white spots on them. White spots were a bad sign, but of what she didn't say.

Pop went on to urge on Mr Charlton to use his loaf and take proper advantage of what he called 'the National Elf lark', a service which, after all, Mr Charlton paid for. Pop was certain Mr Charlton had already paid out millions to this swindle in weekly contributions. It must have cost him a fortune in stamps. With warmth he urged Mr Charlton not to be a mug about it. It was, after all, the State that had started this lark – why not go sick, he urged, and have a bit of fun?

Mr Charlton might have resisted these arguments if it hadn't been that, just before midnight, Mariette pinned him up against the newel post of the dark stairs, kissed him again, and said his hands were hot. Like white spots on the cheek-bones, hot hands were a bad sign. Mr Charlton tried to protest that his hands were invariably hot, especially at that time of year, but Mariette kissed him again, pressing her warm plum-like mouth for a long time against his lips, leaving him in another terrible turmoil of divided emotions about the buttercup field, the nightingales, and the affair of the goose-neck entwining his leg.

'You could stay a week, lovey,' she said. She had begun to call him lovey in the buttercup field. 'And then all next weekend.'

Mr Charlton tried to explain that he had a vast and frightful number of papers on his desk at the office that had to be attended to and how there would be an awful stink if he didn't get back.

'Think if you broke your leg,' she said.

Mr Charlton said he didn't want to think of breaking his leg. He was talking about loyalty, duty, pangs of conscience, and that sort of thing.

'Sounds silly,' Mariette said and Mr Charlton, trembling on the dark

63

stairs, under the influence of the pressing, plum-like lips, was bound to admit that it did.

The result was that he got up next morning to a massive breakfast of two fried eggs, several slices of liver and bacon, much fried bread, and enormous cups of black sugary tea.

Pop was already breakfasting when he arrived at table. Poised heartily above a sea of tomato-ketchup, under which whatever he was having for breakfast was completely submerged, he praised for some moments the utter beauty of the first young strawberry morning. It was going to be a perfick day, he said. The cuckoo had been calling since four o'clock.

The only thing that troubled Mr Charlton as he ate his breakfast was that he felt there was absolutely nothing wrong with him. He could honestly complain of neither sickness nor exhaustion. He had never felt better. 'I don't know what to tell the office,' he said. 'Honestly there's nothing wrong with me.'

'Then you must make summat up,' Pop said, 'mustn't you? Like lumbago.'

Mr Charlton protested that he had never had lumbago in his life, and was not likely to have.

'Oh! yes you are,' Pop said and laughed in hearty, ringing fashion. 'You'll have it chronic tonight. After the first day in the strawberry field.'

At eight o'clock Mr Charlton found himself sitting in the back of the gentian-blue, home-painted truck, together with Mariette, the twins, Montgomery, Victoria, and Primrose. Ma and Pop sat in the cab in front and Ma, who was in great spirits and was dressed in enormous khaki denim slacks with an overall top, laughed and said it was a pity they couldn't all go in the Rolls, just to shake everybody. Mariette was in slacks too, bright salvia red ones, with a soft blue shirt and a spotted red-and-white kerchief over her hair. Over the khaki overalls Ma was wearing the salmon jumper, just because the ride might be cool in the morning air, and a great pudding-bag of an orange scarf on her head.

'Everybody all right in the back there?' Pop yelled and got his customary handsome ribbon of voices in answer. 'Hang on by your toe-nails you kids!'

The truck had hardly rolled out of the yard before everyone began singing. It was Pop who started the song, which was *We Ain't Got a Barrel o' Money*, and everyone took it up in shrill voices. Mr Charlton was embarrassed. He had never ridden in the back of a truck before. Still less had he ever sung in a truck on a public highway.

He wondered what on earth would happen if he was seen by someone who knew him, someone perhaps from the office. It would be terrible to be seen by any of the chaps.

Half a mile down the road the truck drew up with a sharp whistle of brakes and everyone stopped singing and started shrieking loudly instead. Mr Charlton looked over the side-board of the truck to see what the trouble was and saw Pop in the road, lifting up in his arms the tiniest woman Mr Charlton had, outside a circus, ever seen.

'Room for a little 'un?' Pop said and threw the little lady up into the truck. She shrieked like a laughing doll as she landed between the twins and Mr Charlton. 'That Little Two-penn'orth', Pop explained, 'is Aunt Fan.'

Aunt Fan to whom? Mr Charlton wondered but never discovered. His immediate impression was that The Little Two-penn'orth had a face like a small brown shell-fish of the winkle sort. It was all round and crinkled and twisted up. She too was wearing slacks, tiny dark maroon red ones, and a man's grey tweed cap on her head, fixed there by two large pearl hatpins. Her ginger-brown eyes shone like shoe-buttons and her chest was flat.

'Everybody all right in the truck there? Hang on, Aunt Fan!'

Once again everybody, including The Little Two-penn'orth, started singing. By this time the sun was well above the miles of surrounding orchards, chestnut copses, and fields of rising oats and barley, and as it shone down on the truck and on the laughing, singing faces, Mr Charlton saw a tiny creature popping in and out of Aunt Fan's mouth, exactly like a pink mollusc emerging from its shell. This was The Little Two-penn'orth's tongue and it helped to work the shrillest voice he had ever heard. It was a voice like a wild train-whistle shrieking to be heard on a far mountain top.

'Don't you sing, mister?' she said.

Mr Charlton, grinning feebly, did not know what to say. His hair was flying about in all directions. The truck was wildly bumping over a hard clay track, jolting Aunt Fan and the children to new laughter. Mr Charlton did sing. He flattered himself, excusably, that he sang rather well. His voice, belying his bony, very average physique, was a deep, soft baritone. But now his mouth and throat felt like pumice-stone and he was not sure, with the wild bouncing of the truck, quite where his breakfast was.

'You're new, ainyer?' The Little Two-penn'orth said.

Mr Charlton confessed that he was new.

'Thought you was. On 'oliday?'

'Sort of,' Mr Charlton said.

Another mile of this, he thought, and he wouldn't need an excuse for the National Health lark. His breakfast would be up.

To his great relief the truck came to a halt, two minutes later, between a copse of tall chestnut saplings and a big open strawberry field. A sudden sensation of dizziness found Mr Charlton unready as he jumped from the truck. He groped at the air and was suddenly surprised to see The Little Two-penn'orth flying down from the back of the truck, straight into his arms.

He clasped at the toy-like body instinctively, as at a ball. The Little Two-penn'orth landed straight on his chest, winding him temporarily. Everyone began laughing and The Little Two-penn'orth shrieked with delight. Ma started shaking like a jelly and Pop warned Mr Charlton that he'd better watch out or else Aunt Fan would have him on the floor in no time.

'Just what I'd like on a nice warm day,' The Little Twopenn'orth said. 'Just what I bin waiting for.'

Mr Charlton did his best to focus the shimmering strawberry field. He was now convinced that a terrible day lay in front of him. The sun was clear and hot under the shelter of the barrier of woodland; by noon it would be blistering down. Yesterday had been the hottest thirtieth of May, so the papers all said, for forty years. Today would be hotter even than that.

'You can eat all the strawberries you like,' Mariette said. 'But you'll soon get tired of that.'

Mr Charlton did not feel at all like eating strawberries. He longed to be able to sit down, if possible to lie down, in some cool quiet place under the chestnut saplings.

'Keep near me,' Mariette said and gave him a dark low stare which he was too sick to appreciate or return.

He followed her, the rest of the family, and The Little Two-penn'orth into the strawberry field. Already, along the yellow alleys of straw, twenty or thirty girls and women, with an odd man or two, were picking. Flagwise a strange assortment of shirts and blouses, yellow and red and green and brown and even violet, was strung about the field. A green canvas tent, towards which Mr Charlton looked with pitiful desperation, as at an oasis, stood in the centre of the field, piled about with fresh white chip baskets.

Bending down, Mr Charlton started to pick strawberries, deciding at the same time that he would never again eat pig's liver and bacon for breakfast. The hot summery distances were full of calling cuckoos. The field trembled like a zither with chattering women's voices. A man decided to strip his shirt off and the sudden sight of his pure naked torso set every female voice laughing, cat-calling, or simply whistling in admiring wonder.

'Why don't you do that, lovey?' Mariette said. 'You'd be all that much cooler. In time you'd get marvellously brown.'

'I think I'll try and get acclimatized first,' Mr Charlton said.

The process of getting acclimatized took him through a sickening forty minutes of sweat. His spectacles misted over. The Little Two-penn'orth's voice, piercing as a drill, cut the hot air about him, as it seemed, every several seconds. Broad belts of Ma's quivering laughter slapped across the field.

Lying on their fresh beds of straw, the squarish fat crimson strawberries shone in the sun with a too-perfect beauty: exactly, as Pop said, as if painted, and now and then Mr Charlton looked up to see the lips of Mariette parted half in laughter, half in the act of biting into some glistening arc of lovely dark ripe flesh.

'Heavens, I'm getting hungry,' she told him several times. 'I hope Ma brought the rest of the cold roast goose for dinner.'

He was very slow, he presently discovered, at the picking. Mariette could fill, with swift deft ease, three punnet-baskets to his one.

'You're not very fast, are you?' she said. 'Don't you feel very well?'

Mr Charlton confessed with a small wry smile that he was not quite a top note.

'I thought as much,' she said. 'It's just what we were telling you yesterday. You need some sick leave. Come on – let's go along to the tent and get the baskets weighed. You have to get them weighed and checked there.'

It turned out that this, the tent, was Mr Charlton's salvation. Pop, who was also at the tent getting his first baskets checked, introduced him to the foreman, a youngish energetic man in khaki shirt and slacks, as 'Charley boy. Friend of ours, Mr Jennings. Office feller from the tax-lark.'

Mr Jennings appraised Mr Charlton, of the tax-lark, with interested swiftness. You didn't often get office fellers in the strawberry field.

'Chap I'm looking for,' he told Mr Charlton. 'What about sitting here and doing my job? All you do is weigh and book the baskets. How about it? I got a million things to do besides sit here and check these ruddy women.'

'There y'are, Charley boy,' Pop said, clapping him on the shoulder and laughing in ringing fashion. 'Got you promoted already.'

Mr Charlton felt intensely relieved. To his astonishment Pop shook his hand.

'Well: got to run along now, Charley boy. Got to see a man about some scrap iron. Don't do anything I wouldn't do. See you all about five.'

Pop departed across the field to the truck and Mr Charlton, sitting down at the table in the green shade of the tent, at once felt much more himself, much more at home. With a chair under his bottom it was almost like being back in the office again.

'It's pretty simple,' Mr Jennings said, and went on to explain what he said was the easy, straightforward procedure of checking, weighing, and recording the baskets. Mr Charlton thought it was simple too. 'Nothing to it,' Mr Jennings said. 'You just got to keep a record in the book here, with the names, that's all, so we can pay out at the end of the day.'

Mr Jennings departed too after saying that he'd come back in an hour or so to see how Mr Charlton was getting on, though he didn't think, on the whole, he'd have any trouble at all.

'One or two of the old faggots might try a bit of cheek on you,' he said, 'but if they do, be firm. Don't let 'em spit in your eye.'

Mr Charlton said he thought he had it taped all right and sat back and cleaned his glasses and combed his hair. Across the field he could see all kinds of women, fat ones, scrawny ones, pretty ones, old ones, very young ones, together with children, bending and laughing in the long strawberry rows, their blouses and slacks stringing out flag-wise, in brilliant colours, under a hot cloudless sky. It was a very pleasant, peaceful, pastoral scene, he thought, and there was a delicious fragrance of ripe strawberries in the air.

'Forgotten me?'

He was startled. He had utterly forgotten Mariette, who had been standing behind him all the time.

'Afraid I had. So absorbed in the new job and all that –'

'Well, don't,' she said, 'or I'll be miserable.' She kissed him lightly on the cheek. 'Feeling better now?'

'Absolutely all right.'

'You see, I told you,' she said. 'All you want is rest and fresh air and good food and you'll be as right as rain.'

She stood at the door of the tent, so prettily framed against the clear sky beyond that Mr Charlton wished he were back with her in the buttercup field.

'See you soon,' she said. 'And mind what you're up to. Don't get mixed up with other women.'

Mr Charlton, who had no intention whatsoever of getting mixed up with other women, started to apply himself earnestly to the task of checking and weighing the baskets of fruit as they came in. It seemed that he got on very well for a time. All the women seemed very polite and some actually called him 'Duckie'. They spelt their names out carefully when he wasn't quite sure of them. They said how hot it was and one of them, a big sloppy woman named Poll Sanders, with gold-filled teeth and small gold earrings, laughed in a voice like a street-trader selling mackerel and said:

'Sweat – I can feel it running down my back. Goes on like this we'll have to strip out again – like we did that 'ot year afore. Remember that, Lil?'

Lil remembered. 'And that wasn't as 'ot as this though.' Lil was tall, yellow, and hollow-faced. She too had small gold earrings. She was much thinner than Poll but this made no difference. She sweated as much as Poll did. 'Runs orf yer like water.'

Mr Charlton wrote in the book that Poll Sanders had brought in two dozen baskets and then, looking up, saw that Lil had gone. He realized that he had forgotten exactly how many baskets Lil had brought in. He dropped his rubber-tipped pencil on the table and ran after her, catching her up twenty yards across the field.

He said he was frightfully sorry but he had forgotten the number of baskets.

She gave him a look as hard as flint and her mouth opened and shut like a spring trap.

'Two dozen,' she said.

'That's what I thought,' he said and she gave him another look, harder than the first, and he left it at that.

'You want to get your arithmetic working,' she said.

His arithmetic wasn't working very well with Poll Sanders either. When he got back to the tent and sat down to write Lil's figures he discovered he had pencilled down three for Poll Sanders instead of two. Poll had disappeared.

He was so sure the figure was two that he ran after her too.

'Three,' she said. She too gave him that same flat, unflinching look he had seen on the face of Lil. 'I was standing there when you writ it down, wasn't I? Use your loaf, man.'

He decided he'd better use his loaf as much as possible, but he was soon over-busy and it was very stifling in the little tent. He had to keep a sharper, keener eye on the figures as the women came in, bringing scores of baskets. Once The Little Two-penn'orth came in, beht double by two dozen baskets in boxes almost as large as herself, so that they hung from her little hands like overladen panniers from the sides of a tiny grey donkey. The entire Larkin family also came in, all of them eating potato-crisps and big orange lollipops on sticks, except the twins, who were eating pea-nuts, strawberries, and bread-and-jam.

Ma offered Mr Charlton an orange lollipop on a stick and seemed surprised, even pained, when he said no thanks, he didn't think so.

'You'll be glad of it,' she said. 'You ain't had nothing since breakfast.'

Mr Charlton still had moments when he found it impossible to remember breakfast with anything but pain. 'Anyway I'll leave it here on the table. You might be glad of it later.'

'Toodle-oo,' the twins said, 'if you don't want it we'll eat it next time we come,' and ran after Ma, begging for ice-creams.

Mr Charlton looked up, sometime later, to see a pretty, fair-haired, well-made girl standing in the tent. She was wearing tight black jeans and an even tighter thin black woollen sweater. The outlines of her breasts under the sweater were as pronounced as if carved. Her hair was tied up in a long shining horse-tail, the fluffy sun-whitened ends of it brushing her bare shoulders.

'Pauline Jackson,' she said, 'two dozen.'

Her eyes were big and blue. Her very smooth skin was deep brown from working in the fields. Her forearms were covered with tender, downy golden hairs. Her tongue played on her straight white teeth when she had finished speaking.

While Mr Charlton was writing in the book she said:

'New here, aren't you? Never seen you here before.'

'Sort of on holiday,' Mr Charlton explained.

'Nice to be some people.'

She had a slow, drowsy way of talking. It somehow matched the way her tongue remained playing on her lips and the way her hair fell on her shoulders.

'Mind if I ask you something?' she said.

'No,' Mr Charlton said. 'What would that be?'

'Is your name Cedric? They all say your name's Cedric out there.'

The blush that ramped through Mr Charlton's face and neck made every pore of his body break with sweat.

'Oh! no,' he said. 'Goodness, no. Who told you that one?'

'That's what they all say. I said there was no such name.'

She was laughing at him, he thought, in her drowsy, large-eyed way.

He was sure of that. He fumbled about nervously with book, baskets, and papers and said:

'Good Lord, no. Charley. That's me.'

She reached out a brown long-fingered hand and took a strawberry from a basket. She bit into it and then stood staring at the white-crimson juicy inner flesh.

'Don't you like strawberries?' she said.

'Ask the Larkins,' he said. 'Ask Mariette. They all call me Charley.'

'Oh! her. She knows you, does she?'

She put the rest of the strawberry in her mouth and pulled out the clean, white plug.

'Last feller who was here did nothing but eat strawberries. Every time you came in here that feller was bolting strawberries.'

Mr Charlton, confused again, murmured something about having no time. Having something else to do.

'Such as what?'

Mr Charlton didn't know.

She moved nearer the table to pick up another strawberry and then changed her mind and picked up Ma's orange lollipop instead.

'Don't you like these either?'

'Not frightfully –'

'Don't like anything, do you?' She laughed, her voice drowsier than ever in her throat, the tongue drifting idly across her mouth. 'Not much!'

A moment later she started twisting the lollipop round and round in her brown fingers.

'Suppose you'd think I was greedy if I asked you whether I could have it?'

'Oh! no please,' Mr Charlton said. 'Take it if you want. By all means.'

'Thanks.' She laughed again, once more with that drowsy softness that made Mr Charlton feel dreadfully congested, sweating, and messy, sure that she was mocking him. 'That's the way to be nice to anybody. First time.'

Unaware of it Mr Charlton said an extremely foolish thing:

'Aren't people always nice to you first time?'

'Depends.'

Mr Charlton, unaware of it again, said another foolish thing:

'Depends on what?'

She turned sideways, so that for the second time in his life Mr Charlton found himself confronted by an astral body of alarming shape, this time as firm and dark as ebony.

'On whether I let them.'

She had already started to peel the tissue paper from the orange lollipop when Mariette came in, carrying two baskets.

'Oh! company,' the girl said.

Peeling the last of the tissue paper from the orange lollipop, she stared with flat cool eyes at Mariette. Mr Charlton thought Mariette's eyes looked, in reply, like two infuriated black bees.

'Well, I'll push off,' the girl said. 'See you later, Charley.' She tossed her hair from one side of her shoulders to another, at the same time giving Mr Charlton a glad, cool, backward look. 'If not before.'

She was hardly out of the tent before Mariette banged the two baskets on the table and shouted 'Tart!'

Mr Charlton was very much shaken.

'Steady,' he said. 'She'll hear –'

'She's meant to, the so-and-so, isn't she?'

'I really didn't want the thing,' Mr Charlton said. 'I told her to take it –'

'She'd take anything. She'd take the skin off your back – and a bit more if you let her!'

He had never seen Mariette angry before. Her voice sounded raw.

'She's nothing but a –' Mariette choked at some impossible word and then decided Mr Charlton wouldn't understand it. 'No, I won't say it. It's too good. I'll bottle it in. She's no virgin though!' she shouted, 'everybody knows that!'

Mr Charlton, who was not accustomed to hear the word virgin bandied about very much, especially in public, was relieved to see two more women approaching the tent, but was disappointed a moment later to see that they were Poll and Lil. He had made up his mind to remonstrate as tactfully as possible with Poll about rubbing out and altering the figures in the book from two to three and thus twisting him. He was convinced that that was what had happened.

But when he saw the two earringed women, one tall and scrawny as a scarecrow, the other brawny as a bare-armed fish-wife, both as brown as gipsies, he suddenly lost heart and said to Mariette:

'Don't go for a minute. Stay until these two have gone. I want to talk to you –'

'I've got to cool off!' Mariette said. 'I'm going into the wood to cool off!'

'Wait just a minute –'

'I've got to cool off! That's where I'll be if you want me.'

A moment later he was alone with Poll and Lil, who had been having a conference as to whether they could twist him a second time so soon or whether they should leave it for a while and do a double twist next time. Between them they knew a few good ones and they generally worked better, for some funny reason, in the afternoon.

'Hullo, duckie,' they said. 'Here we are again.'

By the middle of the afternoon it was so hot that Mr Charlton got Montgomery and the twins to bring him a bucket of water drawn from a stand-pipe by the gate of the field. He drank a big draught or two of water and then plunged his head several times into the bucket and then dried his face on his handkerchief and combed his wet, cooled hair. After this he cleaned up his spectacles, polishing them on the driest piece of his shirt he could find, and went to stand at the door of the tent, slightly refreshed, to get a breath of air.

The sun hit the crown of his head like a brass cymbal. He had never known it so hot in May. It seemed to affect his eyesight for a moment and when he looked across the strawberry field he was astonished to see a startling change there.

Almost all the women had done what Poll and Lil had said they would do. They had stripped off their blouses and shirts in the heat and were working in nothing but bodices and brassieres. The effect was that the lines of coloured flags had now become like lines of white washing hung out in the blazing sun to dry.

Mr Charlton went back into the tent and tried to satisfy his curiosity about what Pop called the strawberry lark by adding up how many pounds of strawberries had been in and out of the tent that day. He calculated, astonishingly, that he had checked in more than a ton. That meant, he reasoned, a pretty fair lump for the pickers.

His trained mind wondered what the tax position about *that* was. He would have to ask Pop. He was sure Pop would know.

He was still thinking of this when he looked up and saw Pauline Jackson standing in the door. She was not wearing a black sweater now. Like the rest of the women she had stripped down to her brassiere. She had very fine sun-tanned arms and shoulders but the lower part of her deep chest was as white as the inside of a young apple by comparison.

It was this startling whiteness that made his heart start bouncing. She smiled. She came to the table and said in her lazy way:

'Not much cooler, is it?'

She put twenty-four pounds of strawberries on the table. He started to

fumble with pencil and paper, his eyes downcast. She leaned forward as
if to see what he was writing down and said:

'How many does that make for me today? Eight dozen?'

He started to say 'I've got an idea it's more than that, Miss Jackson,'
determined to keep it as formal as possible, and then looked up to see, not
ten or twelve inches from his face, most of her bared, white, perfectly
sculptured bust, blazingly revealed, heaving deeply.

Like Ma, Miss Jackson did not seem unduly perturbed.

'Two more dozen,' she said, 'and I think I'll pack it up for the day.'

'I see. Are you paid every day, Miss Jackson, or do you leave it till the
week-end?'

'What makes you keep calling me Miss Jackson?'

He started to write in the book again when she said:

'What time are you knocking off? Going back to Fordington? If you are
I could give you a lift on my Vespa.'

Where on earth did these people get the money from? Mr Charlton
started thinking. He supposed –

'What about it?' she said.

Too nervous to think clearly, Mr Charlton said:

'I don't know what time I'll finish. I did want to go to Fordington to fetch
some clothes from my room, but –'

'Might go on and have a swim at the pool', she said, 'afterwards. How
about that?'

He said: 'Well –'

'I could wait.' The sculptured breasts rose and fell heavily and came an
inch or two nearer, their division so deep and the pure whiteness so sharp
in the shade of the tent, against the dark brown upper flesh of her
shoulders, that Mr Charlton was utterly mesmerized. 'No hurry for half
an hour one way or the other. Just tell me when.'

She swung her body away. He saw the splendid curves turn full circle
in such a way that he was dizzy in the heat. She laughed and reached the
door as he stuttered:

'You know, I actually couldn't say if – I mean, there's nothing definite –'

'Just say when,' she said. 'All you got to do is to tell me when.'

She had hardly disappeared before Poll and Lil came in. They too had
stripped down to the bust and Poll had an unlighted cigarette dangling
from her lips. They had decided to work a new one on Mr Charlton.

'Hullo, duckie,' they said and Poll took the cigarette from her lips, broke
it in half, and gave one half to Lil. 'Last one, dear. Not unless Charley can
help us out. Haven't got a gasper, duckie, I suppose?'

Mr Charlton, who smoked moderately at the best of times, had recently given it up altogether because he was scared of cancer.

'Afraid not. Don't smoke now –'

'Came out without a bean this morning,' Poll explained. 'Too early for the damn Post Office. Else we'd have got the kids' allowances.'

'How many baskets?' Mr Charlton said.

'Three dozen.' Poll lit her cigarette and then gave Lil a light, both of them exhaling smoke in desperate relief. 'Gawd, it's hot out in that field. You want a drag every two minutes to keep you going at all. Don't suppose you could lend us five bob so's Lil can nip down to the shop on her bike, can you? Pay you back first thing tomorrow.'

Mr Charlton wrote desperately in the book while the two bare-chested women watched him, though he did not know it, like two brown, hungry, calculating old dogs watching a bone. There probably wasn't much meat on Mr Charlton; they'd better get it off while they could.

'Five bob, duckie. Gawd, it's hot out in that field. Two women fainted. Did you hear about that, duckie? Two women fainted.'

'Work it orf as dead horse,' Lil started to say.

Touched, nervous, and swayed against his better judgement, Mr Charlton was just thinking of lending Poll and Lil the five bob to be worked off as dead horse when he heard, from the field, a sudden pandemonium of yelling and shrieking.

He followed Poll and Lil to the door of the tent. Thirty yards from the tent a ring of semi-naked vultures were shrieking and flapping in the sun. 'Somebody's at it. Somebody's catching a packet,' Poll said and Mr Charlton caught a glimpse, somewhere in the vultured circle, of two bare-shouldered girls fighting each other, like wild white cats.

Poll and Lil started running. Mr Charlton started running too. Then, after ten yards or so, he suddenly stopped as if his head had been caught by an invisible trip-wire.

One of the white cats was Pauline Jackson; the other was Mariette. Like cats too they were howling in the unrestricted animal voices that belong to dark roof tops. With alarm Mr Charlton saw streams of blood on the flesh of hands, faces, bare shoulders, and half-bare breasts, and then suddenly realized that this was really the scarlet juice of mashed straw-berries that the girls were viciously rubbing into each other's eyes and throat and hair. The fair horse-tail was like frayed red rope and the neat dark curls of Mariette that he cared for more and more every time he saw them were being torn from her face. Somewhere in the centre of it all the colossal bulk of Ma was shouting; but whether in encouragement, discouragement, or sheer delight he never knew.

Half a minute later he heard the highest shrieking of all. It came from behind him. He turned sharply and saw The Little Two-penn'orth running from the shelter of the wood, waving her tiny arms in excitement. That high-pitched voice of hers was more like a train-whistle than ever.

When she reached him she started bobbing wildly up and down, like a child too small to see over a fence, and Mr Charlton realized that she could not see any part of the cat-and-strawberry horror that by now had him completely spellbound.

'Hold me up, mister!' she shrieked. 'I s'll miss it!'

He took her by the arms and the tiny body rose into the air like a spring.

'Blimey, it's good!' she shrieked. 'It's good!' By now she was actually sitting on Mr Charlton's shoulder, her tiny short legs drumming continually on his chest and her fists in his hair. 'That'll take some getting out in the wash. Git stuck into her, Mariette! It's good! It's good! It's good!'

Mr Charlton didn't think it was good. He was afraid Mariette would get seriously hurt and he felt a little sick at the thought of it. Suddenly he felt constrained to rush in and separate the two combatants, all scarlet now and weeping and half-naked, before they disfigured each other for ever; and he said:

'I've got to stop them. I've got to make them stop it. Anyway, what on earth are they fighting *for?*'

'Gawd Blimey, don't you *know*, mister?' The Little Two-penn'orth shrieked. 'Don't tell me you don't *know!*'

Even when he was riding home that evening in the back of the truck Mr Charlton still could not really believe that he knew. The notion that two girls would fight for him still had him completely stunned.

Everybody had been sternly briefed by Ma, before the truck arrived, not to say a word to Pop. 'Might give her a good leatherin' if he knew,' Ma explained, 'and it's hot enough as it is.'

Everybody agreed; they were all for Mariette. Mr Charlton was all for Mariette too; he felt himself grow continually more proud of her as the truck, driven at Pop's customary jolting speed, rocked homewards through fragrant hedgerows of honeysuckle, the first wild pink roses and may. He kept smiling at her and watching her dark, pretty, red-stained hair. Somebody had lent her a green sweater to wear over her ripped bodice and you could hardly tell, now, that she had been in a fight at all.

In a curious way it was Mr Charlton who felt he had been in a fight. A total lack of all feeling of uncertainty, together with an odd sensation of actual aggression, began to make him feel rather proud of himself too.

'Well, how was the first day, Charley?' Pop said. In the sitting-room Pop had poured out a Dragon's Blood for himself and one for Mr Charlton, who felt he really needed it. He was as hungry as a hunter too. 'How was the first day? Everything go orf all right? Smooth an' all that? No lumbago?'

'No lumbago,' Mr Charlton said. 'Everything smooth as it could be.'

'Perfick,' Pop said.

He drank Dragon's Blood to the day's perfection and called through to the kitchen to Ma:

'How long'll supper be, Ma? I'm turning over.'

'About an hour yet. Roast beef's only just gone in.'

'How'd you get on today, Ma? Good picking?'

'Earned fourteen pound ten,' Ma said.

'Hour yet,' Pop said to Mr Charlton, 'plenty o' time for you to take Mariette for a stroll as far as the river. They'll be cutting the grass in that medder tomorrow.'

Mr Charlton agreed; he had his thoughts very much on the buttercup field.

Just before going outside, however, he remembered that he had a question to ask of Pop. It was the one about tax on the strawberry lark.

'An awful lot of money gets paid out to these people,' he said. 'Strawberries. Cherries. Hops and so on. Take for example all these Cockneys coming down for the hops. Strictly, in law, they ought to pay tax on that.'

'Pay tax?' Pop said. He spoke faintly.

'I mean if the law is to be interpreted in the strict letter –'

'Strick letter my aunt Fanny,' Pop said. 'Dammit if they was taxed they wouldn't come. Then you wouldn't have no strawberries, no cherries, no nothink. No beer!'

The logic of this argument dashed the last of Mr Charlton's reasoning and he went away to find Mariette, who was just coming downstairs, dressed now in the cool green shantung of which he had grown so very fond.

As Mr Charlton and Mariette disappeared across the yard in the evening sun Ma's only complaint, as she watched them from the kitchen window, was that she hadn't got a pair of field-glasses, so that she could watch 'how that young man's getting on with his technique. If he's getting on at all.'

Pop, after pouring two gills of gin into his second Dragon's Blood in order to pep it up a bit, retired to watch television. It had been on for some considerable time, out of natural habit, though no one was watching it, and now there was a programme on the screen about life in central Africa, about wild animals, pygmies, and their strange, baffling customs.

Pop sat back happily in the greenish unreal semi-darkness. He had had a very good day doing a big lark in scrap that showed six hundred per cent with not a very great deal of trouble. He would tell Ma all about it later. Meanwhile he was perfectly content to sit and sip his beer and watch the pygmies, all of whom hopped about the jungle and the village compounds with unconcern, without a stitch on, all the women bare-breasted. There was hardly a programme he liked better than those about strange hot countries, wild animals, and queer tribes, especially those who had never seen civilization.

Out in the buttercup field Mariette and Mr Charlton were lying in the tall brilliant flowers and the even taller feathery grasses. Mariette, so dark and so pretty in her green shantung, was drawing Mr Charlton very gently to her and Mr Charlton was responding with a proud, searching look on his face so that Ma, if she could have been watching him at that moment through binoculars, would have seen that he had gone some way, in certain directions, towards improving his technique.

· 6 ·

When Pop got home the following evening he found Miss Pilchester waiting in the yard.

'Isn't it absolutely ghastly?' Miss Pilchester said.

The evening seemed warmer than ever, but Miss Pilchester was wearing a thick thorn-proof skirt of cabbage green and a cable-stitch woollen cardigan to match. Pop did not ask her what was absolutely ghastly and she did not offer to tell him either.

There was no need. Everything to Edith Pilchester was always absolutely ghastly. She lived alone and kept numbers of laying hens. The hens were absolutely ghastly, and so, even worse, was living alone. It was absolutely impossible to get any help in the house, in the garden, or with the hens. She couldn't afford to run a car because of taxes and the price of petrol and oil and servicing and repairs. She could just afford a solitary hack of her own, but she couldn't afford a groom. It was all absolutely ghastly. Before the war she had kept a little maid in the house, a man in the garden, and a groom-cum-chauffeur-cum-cook who was an absolute treasure in all sorts of ways, including bringing her early morning tea and hot whisky last thing at night in bed. Now all of them had gone and she could hardly afford the whisky. It was absolutely ghastly. Everybody went out to work in the fields at strawberry-picking, cherry-picking, plum-picking, apple-picking, bean-picking, hop-picking, or at the canning-factories in the town, earning mountains more money than they knew what to do with and in any case more than she could pay. It was all absolutely ghastly.

One of the results of everything being so absolutely ghastly was that Miss Pilchester, who was a fortyish, slightly-moustached brunette shaped like a bolster, threw herself into an amazing number of projects with an energy quite ferocious, desperately trying to put the whole ghastly business to rights again. Prowling from committee to committee, charity to charity, bazaar to bazaar, she was like some restless, thirsty lioness seeking prey.

'Hot again, ain't it?' Pop said.

'Absolutely ghastly.'

When Pop suggested that Miss Pilchester should come into the house and have a drink and cool off a bit Miss Pilchester said no thanks, not for the moment, it was absolutely ghastly. She thought they ought to do the field; there wasn't much time left, thanks to that bounder Fortescue letting them down at the last moment and the committee, with the exception of the Brigadier, having been very nearly as bad. The whole thing was simply too ghastly.

Over in the meadow the grass had been cut and baled during the day. Big fragrant cotton-reels of hay lay scattered everywhere between the house and the river. Only a white and yellow fringe of moon-daisy and buttercup remained standing at the edges, pretty as a ruffle under the hedgerows of hawthorn, rising honeysuckle, and wild rose.

'Damn good field, Larkin,' Miss Pilchester said. 'No doubt about that. Just the job.'

She surveyed it with critical, organizing eye, seeing on it a vision of jumps, judges' tents, show-rings, beer-tents, and horses. It was awfully decent of Larkin to do it, she said, otherwise everything would have been an absolute shambles.

'Always like to oblige,' Pop said and laughed in cheerful fashion.

Miss Pilchester laughed too. One of the things she always liked about Larkin was the man's inexhaustible cheerfulness. Friendly chap.

'What about the car-park though?' she said. 'That's always another nightmare.'

'Use the other field,' Pop said. 'Next door. The little 'un. Simple.'

Swallows were flying high above the meadows and the river, swooping in the blue hot sky, and Miss Pilchester might almost have been one of them in the quick, darting glances of gratitude she gave to Pop.

'All yours,' Pop said. 'Come and go just as you like. Any time.'

Another thing Miss Pilchester liked about Pop was the terrific easy generosity of the chap. Good sport. She had once been casually kissed by Pop at a Christmas village social, in some game or other, and the experience, for her at least had been something more than that of two pairs of lips briefly meeting. It gave you the same feeling, she thought, as smelling bruised spring grass, or new-mown hay, for the first time.

'All we want then is a fine day,' Miss Pilchester said. 'If it's wet it'll be absolutely ghastly.'

'Can't control the tap-water I'm afraid,' Pop said and laughed again, at the same time remarking how thirsty he was. 'Might put something in it, though, if you feel like it now. Drop o' gin? Drop o' whisky? Glass o' port?'

Miss Pilchester darted towards Pop another rapid, swallow-like glance of approval, half-affectionate, half-grateful, her eyes so momentarily absorbed in the baldish, perky profile with its dark side-linings that she quite forgot to say that anything was absolutely ghastly.

Back in the yard a van from the bacon factory had just delivered all of Pop's two pigs – he had decided after all that one would be gone almost before you could wink – except the four sides and two hams, which had been left for curing. In the kitchen, Ma, now a white-aproned expansive butcheress, was busy trimming several score pounds of pork and pork-offal; cheerful as ever she stowed it away in the new deep-freeze. As Pop put his head through the kitchen door he was confronted by a blood-stained mountain of legs, loins, heads, chitterlings, and trotters and the sight gave him enormous pleasure. Ma said:

'Dr Leagrave's in the sitting-room. I said you wouldn't be long.'

'Come to see Mariette?'

'No, pipe down, you loony. Nobody knows anything about that. No: just on his way back from the golf-course. Just passing.'

'Thirsty, I expect,' Pop said. 'Still, just the job – we can get him to run the rule over Mister Charlton.'

In the sitting-room Pop introduced Miss Pilchester to Dr Leagrave, who was a heavyish man in his fifties, rather red-necked in a Teutonic sort of way, and completely bald. The doctor, who played a good deal of golf as a pretence of getting exercise and keeping his weight down, though in reality preferring the comforts of the club-house, remarked that it was warmish. Miss Pilchester said it was absolutely ghastly and flopped into an easy chair with the grace of a cow.

Television was on, out of natural habit, and the programme was one of opera, the composer being a man named Wagner, of whom Pop had never heard. Pop gave the screen a cursory, whipping glance – the programmes were never much catch Tuesdays – and wondered if everybody on it had gone stark, staring mad.

It was a relief to turn to drinks and Miss Pilchester:

'Now, Miss Pilchester. Edith.' Miss Pilchester bloomed softly, smiling as Pop called her Edith. 'What shall it be? Drop o' whisky? Drop o' gin? Drop o' Guinness? I can make you a cocktail.'

Miss Pilchester said she thought cocktails were absolutely ghastly. 'No, whisky for me. And soda please.'

Dr Leagrave chose the same. Pop, in brief thought over the cocktail galleon, wondered if he should mix himself a real snorter, such as a

Rolls-Royce or a Chauffeur, but finally decided to have his favourite Dragon's Blood with lime.

'Your day off, doc?' he said.

Dr Leagrave thanked God it was and took his whisky with uncertain but eager hands.

'It must be absolutely ghastly in this heat,' Miss Pilchester said, 'sick-visiting and all that.'

'Not that so much,' the doctor said. 'Trouble is it's a nice fine evening. By now my waiting-room'll be jam-packed as a cinema with Lolla showing.'

Sipping whisky, an astonished Miss Pilchester asked why that should be and got the answer not from Dr Leagrave, but from Pop, himself as quick as a swallow:

'Ain't got nothing better to do. That's why.'

'Hit it plumb on the head,' the doctor said.

'You mean it makes a difference?' Miss Pilchester said, 'what the weather is?'

'More perfick the wevver,' Pop said, 'the more they roll up. You told me that once afore, didn't you, doc?'

The doctor said indeed he had.

'Absolutely ghastly,' Miss Pilchester said.

'Fast becoming a nation of hypochondriacs,' the doctor said, and Pop looked so suddenly startled at yet another word he had never even heard on television that he couldn't speak. That was the second within a few days. 'Pill-takers. Drug-takers.'

'Ghastly.'

'Then there are young doctors,' Dr Leagrave said, now launching on a tried and favourite theme, 'men of not very great experience, who are prescribing a hundred, two hundred, capsules of new and highly expensive drugs to patients who take two and put the rest into the kitchen cupboard.'

'Ghastly.'

With something like venom Dr Leagrave finished his whisky, his seventh since six o'clock, and said it was no wonder the country was on its beam-ends. Miss Pilchester warmly agreed and Pop took away the doctor's empty glass to fill it up again, at the same time glancing at the television screen, unable to make any sense whatever of a single note or gesture coming out of it.

As soon as he had poured the doctor's whisky he decided to switch the sound off. He couldn't bear to switch the picture off in case something should come on, like pygmies or football or chorus girls, which he liked. In consequence the screen became a pallid mime of open-mouthed puppets singing silently.

'By the way, doc,' he said, 'we got a young friend of ours staying here who's bad a-bed and wuss up. Think you could have a look at him?'

'What's wrong?' the doctor said. 'Not another pill-addict, I hope.'

'Lumbago,' Pop said.

'Ghastly,' Miss Pilchester said. 'I get it. I sympathize.'

Pop said he would try to find Mr Charlton and started to go out of the room, remembering as he did so the kitchen piled with pork.

'Nice piece o' pork for you when you go, doc,' he said. 'How about that? You too, Edith. Like chitterlings?' Pop laughed in his infectious, rousing fashion. 'How about a nice piece o' pig's liver and a basin o' chitterlings?'

Miss Pilchester, who had not yet been reduced to eating chitterlings, nevertheless laughed too. Always made you feel happy, that man, she thought. When Pop came back with a rather hesitant but sun-scorched Mr Charlton, red-faced from a second day in the strawberry fields and more ravenously hungry than he had ever been in his life, the doctor was just saying to Edith Pilchester, again with a sort of evangelical, venomous uncertainty:

'This county alone is spending over a million a year on drugs! This one county –'

'Here's our young friend,' Pop said. 'Friend of Mariette's. Mister Charlton. Been very poorly.'

'Well,' the doctor said, 'perhaps we can have a look at you.' He glanced uncertainly round at Miss Pilchester. 'Is there somewhere –'

'Upstairs,' Pop said. 'I'll lead the way.'

Mr Charlton followed Pop and Dr Leagrave upstairs. On the landing Pop paused to whisper confidentially to the doctor that there would be a whole leg of pork if he wanted it; he hadn't very well been able to say it in front of Edith – the doc would understand?

The doctor, swaying a little, said he understood, and Pop opened the first door on the landing without knocking. 'This'll do,' he said. 'Mariette's room.'

Fortunately the room was empty and presently Mr Charlton, stripped to the waist, found himself lying face downwards on Mariette's bed, his sensations very like those he had experienced when the geese had entwined their necks about his legs, when he had worn Mariette's pyjamas and when, in utter ecstasy, he had breathed the fragrance of gardenia for the first time. The hot room was thick and intoxicating with that same deep, torturing fragrance now.

The doctor, who had not bothered to fetch his bag from the car, pressed his fingers gently into Mr Charlton's lumbar region.

'Much pain?'

Mr Charlton confessed that he had no pain whatever. A day in the strawberry fields had in fact improved him so much, both physically and mentally, that he had actually spotted the double twist Poll and Lil were going to work on him almost before they had started.

'Comes and goes? That it?'

'Sort of like that.'

'Suppose you'd like to go on sick benefit for a couple of weeks?'

To the doctor's astonishment Mr Charlton said no, he didn't think so. He was, though he didn't say so, having a wonderful time in the strawberry field. He was earning money. If he went on sick benefit he wouldn't earn any money and he wouldn't have half the fun. He was learning to use his loaf.

'Well,' the doctor said, 'try to keep out of draughts when you're hot.' He laughed briefly, swayed tipsily, and thought of how perhaps it would be possible to snatch another quick one downstairs before he took the leg of pork and went home. 'And avoid lying in wet grasses.'

Some time after the doctor had gone Pop wrapped up two pounds of loin of pork, about a pound of liver, and a pair of pig's trotters and said that, if Edith was ready, he would run her home. Edith Pilchester, charmed with three whiskies, more than she usually had in a week, and enough food to last her until Sunday, was more than ready and completely forgot, for the second time, to say how absolutely ghastly anything was.

'Got a Rolls now,' Pop said.

Miss Pilchester confessed she had seen it in the yard.

'I said to myself it couldn't be yours.'

In the yard, Pop spent some time, with touches of imperial pride, showing Miss Pilchester the Rolls's burnished monograms, the silver vases for flowers, and the speaking tube.

'If you'd like to sit in the back,' he said, 'you can say things down the tube to me. Orders and all that.'

'I don't want to sit in the back,' Miss Pilchester said. 'Not on your life. I want to sit in the front with you.'

As they drove along Pop demonstrated first the town horn, the sweet one, then the country, the snarl. Miss Pilchester enjoyed this but said, 'Not so fast. I don't like driving so fast,' remembering that she lived less than a mile away. Accordingly Pop slowed down, driving with one hand and with the other half-caressing, half-pinching Miss Pilchester's knee. Since she wore only loose lisle stockings this, he found, was not half so delicious an experience as pinching Ma, who wore nylons and very tight ones at that, but to Miss Pilchester it seemed to be a source of palpitating pleasure. She again became like a swallow, darting nervous, rapid glances.

A few minutes later the Rolls drew up at Bonny Banks, Miss Pilchester's cottage, tiny, thatched, and low-pitched, which she had converted out of a fallen down cow-byre in pre-war days, when things were cheap. Creosoted beams and a gimcrack front door studded with what appeared to be rusty horse-shoe nails were designed to give the little loaf-shaped house an appearance of Tudor antiquity or of having come out of a fairy-tale. But in the evening light, after the hot day, its garden ill-kept, the lawn unmown, the paths a flourish of dandelions, the rose-beds pitted with dust-baths made by escaping hens, it looked shabby even by comparison with Pop's paradise.

Miss Pilchester begged Pop over and over again not to look at it. It was simply ghastly, absolutely ghastly.

'You'll come in for a moment though, won't you?'

Pop had always wanted to see the inside of Miss Pilchester's cottage but when he groped his way through the kitchen, which smelt stale from unwashed dishes, and into a living-room as dark and cramped as a bolt-hole, even he was surprised. A flock of sheep might well have passed through the place an hour before. Bits of wool – raw, unwashed sheep's wool – lay everywhere. It was one of Miss Pilchester's hobbies to gather wool from field and hedgerow and on long winter's nights clean, spin, and wind it for making into socks and jumpers, which she dyed in subdued rough shades with lichen.

'Do take a pew if you can find room, won't you?'

It was difficult, if not impossible, to find a pew. Miss Pilchester hastily removed a basin of eggs, a half-finished jumper, two skeins of wool, *The Times*, a sewing-basket, some grey underwear, and an unplucked brown fowl from various chairs.

'Sit you down. I'll have a drink for you in a jiff. Don't mind anything. I'll just find a plate for the pork and then get some glasses.'

Remains of a boiled egg, a cup of cocoa, and a burnt raspberry tart, the left-overs either of breakfast or lunch, or both, lay scattered about the table. Miss Pilchester gathered up egg and cocoa, dropped the shell into the cocoa and then upset the resulting mess into the raspberry tart.

85

Some seconds later she was calling from the kitchen:

'Absolutely ghastly having no help. But nobody does, do they? Only Professor Fane.'

Fane, a professor of physics, with some distinguished degrees, including foreign ones, used the house next door as a week-end cottage only, coming down on Friday evenings to be bullied for three whole days by an ex-naval artificer and his wife, acting as chauffeur and cook, who borrowed the car all day on Sundays to visit other naval men by the sea or watch dirt-track racing on the hills. The professor spent most of the time in a ten-by-six attic under the roof, listening to Bach and Beethoven, while the ex-artificer and his wife used the drawing-room downstairs, watching the television set that the professor had had to install in order to get them to stay in the house at all.

'He's lucky,' Miss Pilchester called. 'I can't get a soul.'

She was looking in various cupboards for a bottle of whisky, which she knew was there. It wasn't there and it was some moments before she found it tucked away behind another pile of underclothes, a basket of clothes pegs, and a vegetable marrow left over from last year.

An inch of whisky lay in the bottom and Miss Pilchester remembered she had not bought another bottle since she had had a cold at Easter, over six weeks before.

She put another inch of tap water into the bottle and then poured the whisky and water into two glasses, and calling, 'Just coming. Sorry I kept you so long,' went out of the kitchen to find Pop glancing at *The Times*, a newspaper he had never heard of before.

'No television?' Pop said.

'Couldn't possibly afford it.'

'Terrible,' Pop said.

With sudden irritation Miss Pilchester remembered some stock exchange figures she had been reading at breakfast and found herself in half a mind to ask Pop what he thought she ought to do with her $3\frac{1}{2}$% War Stock. He seemed so clever about money. He must be. The stock was another government swindle. She had bought it at ninety-six, and now it stood at sixty-seven – that was the way they treated you for being prudent, thrifty, and careful.

It was perfectly true, as someone or other had remarked to her only the other day, that all governments were dishonest.

'Don't you think all governments are dishonest?' she said. She handed Pop the whisky and explained about the shares. 'All they think about is getting out of you the little you've got. What do you think?'

'What do I think?' Pop said. 'I think you want to get it out o' *them* afore they have a chance to get it out o' *you.*'

Miss Pilchester laughed. She said 'Cheers' and, drinking an economical sip of whisky, thanked Pop once again for being so nice about the field.

'Going to pay your Hunt subscription next season? Hope so.'

Pop said of course he was going to pay a subscription; and one for Mariette too.

'Thank the Good God there are a few chaps like you.'

The Hunt, Miss Pilchester said, was going down. Hardly anybody had any time. The Christmas Meet last year had been an absolute rag-tag-and-bobtail. It was simply ghastly.

'Captain Prettyman's retiring as Master next year,' she said and thanked the Good God a second time. 'Never has been any good. Never got hold of the right end of the stick from the beginning.'

She darted Pop another of her rapid, swallow-like glances.

'You're the sort of chap they ought to have. New blood to pep them up.'

Pop could hardly bear it. In an uncertain spasm of ambition he actually had a swift vision of himself as Master of Fox Hounds. It was dazzling. At the present time he paid a subscription but never rode to hounds, though Mariette always did. The incredible idea of his being Master had never once occurred to him.

'Here, steady on, old girl,' he said. 'You'll get me started thinking things.'

Miss Pilchester, remembering the brief interlude when Pop had pressed her knee in the car, laughed as softly as she could.

'Well, that's always nice, isn't it?' she said.

Suddenly Pop did the thing Miss Pilchester feared most: he drained his whisky in a single gulp, smacking his lips with pleasure, as if ready to go. There was no more whisky left, not even a drop to water down, and she experienced a second of panic before he got up from the chair.

'Well, I must push back. Got a few things to do before bedtime.'

'Oh! must you go?'

With uncertainty Miss Pilchester got up too. She had been careful to sit with her back to the little cottage window, but now twilight was falling rapidly enough to make it almost impossible to distinguish the smaller details of her face. Only her eyes were bright as they gave Pop yet another quick, swallow-like dart.

'You've been an absolute lamb,' she said. 'Don't know how –'

She turned suddenly to find herself wrapped in Pop Larkin's arms, being kissed in splendid silence, with something of the effect of a velvet battering ram. This was the way Pop always kissed Ma but Miss Pilchester, for her part, had never experienced anything quite like it. It had on her something of the effect of Pop's cocktail on Mr Charlton: it explored with disquieting fire a few corners of her body that she hardly knew existed before.

When it was over Pop retired a few inches, took breath and said, in almost exactly the tones he always used when mixing drinks at the glittering Spanish galleon:

'How about one more?'

'Please.'

'Perfick,' Pop said.

Five minutes later a palpitating but very happy Miss Pilchester, trebly kissed – one more for luck, Pop had said – came to the gate of the little garden wilderness to wave him goodbye. If it had been possible she would have kissed him goodbye but she knew that even in the gathering May twilight the ex-artificer's wife would be watching from a window. Not that she cared a damn now. She felt dedicated for ever, with abandon, to the generous, passionate Mr Larkin.

'See you soon!' she waved.

'Any time,' Pop said. He laughed merrily. 'Don't do anything I wouldn't do. Keep your hand on your ha'penny.'

The last of Miss Pilchester's darting glances, this one almost of fire, seemed actually to set the Rolls in motion and with a neat, side-long wink he drove away.

At first he drove rather fast and then, suddenly subdued by the immensely incredible notion that he might one day become Master of Fox Hounds, slowed down to a silent crawl. He didn't want anybody to think he was drunk in charge. Two minutes later he passed a policeman on duty. Seeing the Rolls, the policeman saluted. Pop saluted in reply.

He'd have to tell Ma, he thought, about the Master of Fox Hounds lark. No, he wouldn't though. He'd keep that after all; she'd say he was flying too high. What he would tell her, though, was about the inside of Miss Pilchester's house; that terrible, cramped, untidy, woolly, television-less little bolt-hole. Perfickly awful how some people lived, he would tell Ma, perfickly awful.

When he arrived home Ma was sitting outside the kitchen door, enjoying a Guinness and a few potato crisps after her battle with the pork. It was still hot in the semi-darkness, but Pop feared he could hear, in the distance, a few muted notes of thunder.

'Where's Mr Charlton?' he said.

'Been writing letters,' Ma said. 'Just gone off with Mariette to post them.'

'*Writing letters?*'

Another high, incredible mark of credit for Mr Charlton.

'Whatever's he got to write letters for?'

Impossible to understand how anybody could write letters.

'I think he'd been writing to the tax office.'

'Not about us,' Pop said. 'He ain't got nothing to write there about us.'

'Oh! no,' Ma said. Enjoying her Guinness, she was quite unperturbed. 'I think he's gone and extended his sick-leave. That's all. Since he saw the doctor. Going to stay another week or two.'

'Perfick,' Pop said. 'Jolly good.'

Pop, for whom Mr Charlton was rapidly becoming a more and more agreeable figure, quite exceptional in his literacy, went into the house to pour himself a Dragon's Blood. When he came back Ma said:

'Well, did you kiss her?'

'Course I did.'

'I thought you would.' Ma sat with the Guinness balanced on the precipice of her rolling stomach like a little black doll, again completely unperturbed. 'Do her good. Make her sleep all the sweeter. What was it like?'

Pop considered. He remembered how, in the twilight, some portion of Miss Pilchester's moustache had brushed against him.

'A bit like trying to catch a mole', he said, 'in a dark entry.'

Ma dug him sharply in the ribs and started laughing like a jelly. Pop laughed too at his own joke and then stared up at the sky, his attention rapt for some moments by the young, unquenchable summer stars. A few drops of rain fell, as if by a miracle, from a cloudless heaven, and then ceased in a whisper. Laughing made Pop give a sudden belch and far away, across miles of windless fields, somewhere on the dim hills, nature echoed him in a scarcely audible double note of thunder. Ma looked at the stars too and Pop started to tell her, true amazement in his voice, about Miss Pilchester's Tudor bolt-hole and how perfickly awful it was.

'Never credit it, Ma,' he told her. 'Never credit it. Still, what I always say: you don't know, do you, until you get a look inside?'

For a few moments longer they sat in silence, until at last Ma said:

'Well: I'm waiting.'

'What for?'

'Don't you think it's about time you kissed *me*?'

Pop said he supposed it was. He drained his Dragon's Blood and set the empty glass behind his chair. Then he leaned over and clasped in his right hand as much of Ma's vast bosom as he could hold.

'It's coming to something', Ma said, 'when I have to ask you for one. Are you tired?'

Pop demonstrated that he was far from tired by kissing Ma with prolonged velvety artistry. Ma responded by settling back into her chair into a cocoon of silence unbroken except for an occasional exquisite breath of pleasure, exactly like the murmur of a kitten in a doze.

In the far distance new waves of thunder rolled. From the cloudless heaven a few fresh warm drops of rain fell. For some moments they splashed the two faces as lightly as a sigh but Pop and Ma, like the youngest of lovers, did not heed them at all.

· 7 ·

On the day of the pony gymkhana Mr Charlton was up at half past four. The morning was humid, dreamy, and overcast, with low mist on the river. Pop, who had already been up an hour, giving swill to pigs and fodder to the Jersey cow, and was now staunching back the first pangs of hunger with a few slices of bread and Cheddar cheese doused half an inch thick with tomato-ketchup, said he thought 'the wevver looked a little bit thick in the clear' but otherwise, with luck, it ought to be all right by noon.

Mr Charlton breakfasted on two lean pork cutlets, some scrambled eggs cooked by Mariette, fried potatoes, and four halves of tomato.

'In the old days,' said Pop, whose estimation of Mr Charlton rose almost every time he talked to him, especially on occasions like coming down to breakfast at a good time and getting outside a reasonable amount of food, 'my Dad used to tell me that they always had beer for breakfast. Like a glass o' beer?'

Mr Charlton thanked him and said he didn't think he would. Mariette had just made tea.

'Well, I think I will,' Pop said. 'I don't think a lot o' tea is all that good for you.'

Pop, after pouring himself a Dragon's Blood, had much the same breakfast as Mr Charlton, except that there was a lot more of it and that his plate was gay with mustard, ketchup, and two kinds of Worcester sauce. Mariette, who looked pretty and fresh in dark green slacks and a pale yellow shirt blouse, said she was so excited she could hardly eat but nevertheless managed two eggs and bacon, a pint of milk, and four slices of bread.

Ma was not yet down but had sent word that as the day was going to be a long one she was having a lay-in, which meant she would be down by half past six.

Towards the end of breakfast Pop turned to Mr Charlton, who had not been able to keep his eyes off Mariette for more than two seconds since she had come into the kitchen tying up her hair with a thin emerald ribbon, and said:

'Are you two going to feed and water the donkeys? I've got forty thousand jobs to do and Miss Pilchester'll be here by six.'

Mr Charlton said of course they would feed the donkeys and helped himself to a fifth slice of bread and covered it half an inch thick with fresh Jersey butter made by Ma. Pop watched this process with immense admiration, telling himself he had never seen such a change in a man's health as he had witnessed in three weeks in Mr Charlton.

Mr Charlton was still on sick leave.

'Oh! those sweet donkeys,' Mariette said.

The donkeys that she and Mr Charlton were going to feed were not the rest of the Larkin household but four animals Pop had secured for racing. Pop thought that gymkhanas were sometimes inclined to be on the dull side, what he called 'a bit horseface like – so many folks with long faces you can't very often tell the mares from some of the old women' – and that therefore something was needed to enliven the customary round of trotting, riding, leading rein, jumping, bending, and walk, trot, canter, and run.

This was why he had thought of the donkeys and why, later on in the day, he thought of introducing a few private harmless jokes of his own. What these were he was keeping to himself; but he had not forgotten the one about putting a firework under Miss Pilchester.

To his grievous disappointment the committee had turned down his offer of fireworks. It might well be, they had pointed out, that a few ponies would be late leaving the ground and that some fireworks would in any case go off early and the ponies be distressed. Pop saw the reason in this but if there was going to be one firework and only one it was, he was determined, going to be Miss Pilchester's.

'What time is the cocktail party, Pop?' Mr Charlton said.

Pop was delighted that Mr Charlton now called him Pop.

'Ma thinks eight o'clock would be the perfick time.'

'What a day,' Mariette said. 'All this and cocktails too.'

She went on to confess that she had never been to a cocktail party and Pop said:

'Come to that neither have I. Neither has Ma.'

'What do people normally drink at cocktail parties?' Mariette said.

'Cocktails,' Mr Charlton said slyly and before he could move she gave him a swift playful cuff, exactly like that of a dark soft kitten, across the head.

'Not at this one you don't,' Pop said.

Both Mariette and Mr Charlton were too excited to remember that the whole question of what was drunk at cocktail parties had been discussed a week before.

Since Pop had been unable to indulge himself with fireworks he and Ma had decided that there must, if possible, be something in their place. A cocktail party, Pop said, would be the perfick answer. Ma agreed, but said they ought to keep it very select if possible. Not more than thirty people, she thought, at the outside; mostly the committee and their families and of course nice people like the Miss Barnwells and the Luffingtons and the Brigadier. And what about eats?

Neither Pop nor Ma had any idea what you ate at cocktail parties; therefore Mr Charlton was consulted.

'Canapés, vol-au-vents, pistachios, and that sort of thing,' Mr Charlton said.

A lot more marks for Mr Charlton, Pop thought, as once again he heard words he had never even heard on television.

'You mean nuts and things?' Ma said. 'They won't keep anybody alive very long. I'd better cook a ham.'

Pop warmly agreed; the ham was firmly decided upon. Ma could cut plenty of the thinnest white and brown sandwiches, with nice Jersey butter. And what else?

Mariette said she thought small pieces of cold sardine on toast would be nice. 'They're absolutely marvellous hot too,' Mr Charlton said and got himself still more marks by also suggesting small squares of toast with hot Welsh rarebit, chicken sandwiches, and little sausages on sticks.

Most of this, to Pop, seemed rather light, unsatisfying fare.

'We want to give 'em enough,' he said. 'We don't want 'em to think we're starving 'em. What about a leg o' pork?'

To his disappointment Mr Charlton said he rather ruled out the leg of pork.

'All right,' Pop said. 'What about drinks?'

Pop was all for making plenty of Rolls-Royces and that sort of thing, good, strong ones, together with two new ones he had recently tried out from The *Guide to Better Drinking*: Red Bull and Ma Chérie. Red Bull was a blinder. That would curl their hair.

Mr Charlton said he thought it made it so much simpler if you stuck to two, or at the outside, three good drinks: say sherry, port, and gin-and-french. He suggested the port in case the evening was cool.

He got no marks this time. Pop thought it was all about as dull as flippin' ditchwater. With sudden enthusiasm he said:

'What about champagne?'

93

Both Ma and Mariette said they adored champagne. That was a brilliant idea. Something extra nice always happened, Mariette said, when you had champagne, and it seemed to Pop that he saw her exchange with Mr Charlton an intimate glance of secret tenderness that left him baffled and unsatisfied. Couldn't be nothing in the wind?

'Well, champagne it is then!' Pop said. 'Might as well do the thing properly.'

Here Mr Charlton remarked with tact that since not everybody liked champagne it might be just as well to have some other drink in reserve.

'I'll make a few hair-curlers,' Pop said. 'Red Bull – remember that one? – and Ma Chérie.'

Mr Charlton remembered Red Bull. It had rammed him one evening after a hardish day in the strawberry field. It was not inaptly named.

It was half past five before Mr Charlton and Mariette got up at last from breakfast and went across the yard to feed the donkeys. The four little donkeys had been tied up in the stable that Pop had built with his eye on the day when all the family, with the possible exception of Ma, would have a pony or a horse to ride. That would be the day. Two donkeys had been hired by Pop; two had been brought over by their owners the previous night. Three more, it was hoped, were still to come.

As soon as Mariette and himself were in the half-dark stable, among the donkeys, Mr Charlton took her quickly in his arms and kissed her. His arms and hands, as they tenderly touched her face, breasts, and shoulders, were as brown as her own.

Mariette laughed, trembling, and said she'd hardly been able to wait for that one, the first, the loveliest of the day. Mr Charlton, with something like ecstasy, said he hadn't been able to wait either. He could hardly wait for anything. Above all he could hardly wait for the afternoon. 'Nor me,' Mariette said and held her body out to him again.

Quietly, as the second kiss went on, the donkeys stirred about the stable, swishing tails, restless. Hearing them, Mariette partly broke away from Mr Charlton and said with half-laughing mouth:

'I suppose there's a first time for everything. I've never been kissed among donkeys before.'

Quick as a swallow himself, Mr Charlton answered. It was the answer of a man sharpened by three weeks in the strawberry field, living with the Larkins, and using his loaf.

'Wait till the cocktail party,' he said.

*

It was almost half past ten before Miss Pilchester fell bodily out of the taxi she had hired in desperation, four hours late, to bring her to the meadow. Pop, who was helping the Brigadier to string up gay lines of square and triangular flags about and among the tents, stared in stupefaction at a figure that might have been that of a tired and collapsing mountaineer descending from a peak. Miss Pilchester was armed with shooting stick, rolled mackintosh, a leather hold-all containing a spare cardigan, her lunch and a red vacuum flask, an attaché case containing the judging lists, *The Times*, several books, and a basket of pot-eggs. The pot-eggs, evidently brought for use in some pony event or other, rolled about the squatting Miss Pilchester exactly as if, in a sudden over-spasm of broodiness, she had laid them all herself.

It was all absolutely ghastly, but both Pop and the Brigadier were too stupefied to go over and pick up either Miss Pilchester or the eggs; and Pop, for once, was utterly without words. It was the Brigadier who spoke for him.

'Good God, Larkin,' he said, 'Edith must be either tight or egg-bound.'

Five minutes later Miss Pilchester, the great organizer, was at her work. This was all done, as the Brigadier himself pointed out, at a half canter. With indecisive excitement Miss Pilchester rushed from tent to tent, inquiring if someone had seen this, somebody that, had the caterers arrived, and above all wasn't it ghastly?

The caterers had been on the field since seven o'clock; all of them had knocked off for tea. Where, then, was the loudspeaker for announcements? Hadn't that arrived? It had arrived and Miss Pilchester tripped over two lines of its wires. Cancelled entries – were there any cancelled entries? – all entries, she wailed, should have been cancelled by nine o'clock.

It was now, the Brigadier was heard to point out dryly, half past ten.

Where then, Miss Pilchester wanted to know, were the donkeys? Were the donkeys here?

'Some donkeys', the Brigadier was heard to remark, 'have been here all night,' but the remark was lost on Miss Pilchester, who rushed away to inquire if the ladies' conveniences had been installed. 'They are most important,' she said and disappeared into a far tent as if feeling it suddenly necessary to prove it for herself.

At half past eleven the sun broke through, beginning to dry at last the heavy dew on the grass, the trees of the bluebell wood, and the hedgerows. From the completely windless river the last transparent breaths of mist began to rise. A few water-lilies were in bud, heads rising above wet leaves, and they looked like pipes, gently smoking.

It was then discovered that Miss Pilchester had completely forgotten to meet a London train, as she had faithfully promised, at ten forty-five. The train was bringing a judge who had, in counties west of London, a great reputation for judging such things as The Horse of the Year Show. The committee had specially asked for him.

Now Ma came hurrying from the house to say she'd had a bulldog on the phone. 'And *did* he bark. And *oh!* the language.'

'Why the 'ell couldn't he come by car?' Pop said.

'Said he flipping well couldn't afford one under this flipping government.'

'*We must do something!*' Miss Pilchester said. 'It's absolutely ghastly!'

'Mariette and Mr Charlton can fetch him in the station-wagon,' Pop said. 'They've got to collect more champagne anyway. Ma don't think we've got enough.'

'Champagne? What champagne? Who ordered champagne?'

'I did.'

'*Not for this show?*'

'Cocktail party,' Pop said. 'Me and Ma. Instead of the fireworks tonight. You got your invite, didn't you? Mariette and Mr Charlton sent all the invites out.'

The word fireworks dragged Miss Pilchester back to Pop's side like a struggling dog on a lead.

'Now you will promise, won't you, no fireworks?'

'No fireworks,' Pop said.

Miss Pilchester, remembering Pop's delicate investigation of her knee in the Rolls, the velvety battering ram of the kiss that, as Ma had predicted, had made her sleep so much more sweetly, now permitted herself the luxury of a half-smile, the first of her hurried day.

'I know you. Sometimes you're more than naughty.'

Sun twinkled on Pop's eyes, lighting up the pupils in a face that otherwise remained as dead as a dummy.

'Not today though,' Pop said. 'Got to behave today.'

'And promise no fireworks?'

'No fireworks.'

'Not one?'

'Not one,' Pop said and fixed his eyes on the hem of her skirt as she rushed away to attend once again to the matter of the ladies' conveniences, which were not quite what she had hoped they would be. It was a matter of some delicacy.

As she disappeared Pop reminded the Brigadier of how he had said Miss Pilchester was a splendid organizer and all that.

The Brigadier was more than kind: 'Well, in her own sweet way I suppose she is. Fact is, I suppose, she's the only one who can spare the time. Nobody else has the time.'

That was it. Nobody had the time. In the crushing, rushing pressure of modern life nobody, even in the country, had the time.

A few moments later the Brigadier glanced hurriedly at his watch, saw it was after twelve o'clock and said he must rush back for a bite of cold. Pop begged him to come to the beer-tent for a quick snifter before he went but the Brigadier was firm. Nellie would be waiting. He was going to be adamant this time.

Pop, watching him depart with bemused admiration, remembered that word. The Brigadier had one shoe-lace missing and had replaced it with packing string. His hair badly needed cutting at the back, and his shirt collar was, if anything, more frayed than before. But the word adamant shone from him to remind Pop once again of all those wonderful fellers who could use these startling words. He envied them very much.

Going to the beer-tent he found that the bulldog of a judge had arrived and was drinking with two members of the committee, Jack Woodley and Freda O'Connor. The judge was a squat ebullient man in a bowler hat. With Woodley, a ruddy, crude, thick-lipped man who was wearing a yellow waistcoat under his hacking jacket, he kept up a constant braying duet, swaying backwards and forwards waving a pint mug of beer. Woodley was evidently telling smoke-room stories, at the same time gazing with rough interest at the notorious O'Connor bosom, which protruded by several white marble inches above a low yellow sweater. The coarser the stories the more the O'Connor bosom seemed to like them. Like a pair of bellows, its splendid mass pumped air into the hearty organ of her voice, setting the air about her ringing.

All three ignored Pop and he knew why. He and Ma hadn't invited them to the cocktail party. Not caring, he said in a loud voice, 'How's everybody? Fit as fleas?' as he went past them. Nobody answered, but Pop didn't care. He believed in treating everybody alike, fleas or no fleas.

Glass of beer in hand, he found a companion some moments later in Sir George Bluff-Gore, who owned a large red-brick Georgian mansion that was too expensive to keep up. He and his wife somehow pigged it out in a keeper's cottage instead. Bluff-Gore, yellowish, funereal, stiff, and despondent, had the face of a pall bearer cramped by indigestion. He was not the sort of man you could slap on the back to wish him well.

Nevertheless Pop did so.

Bluff-Gore, recoiling with dejection, managed to say that it was nice of

Larkin to invite him and Lady Rose to this cocktail party. They didn't get out much.

'More the merrier,' Pop said and then remembered that the Bluff-Gores had a daughter – Rosemary, he thought her name was – a big puddeny girl with sour eyes and a blonde fringe, whom he had sometimes seen riding at meetings or pony gymkhanas with Mariette. He wondered where she was; he hadn't seen her lately.

'Hope the daughter's coming too?' he said. 'Welcome.'

'Rosemary? Afraid not. Lives in London now.'

'Oh?' Pop said. 'Doing what? Working?'

With increasing gloom Bluff-Gore gazed at the grass of the beer-tent and thought of his only daughter, who had suddenly decided for some utterly unaccountable reason to give up a perfectly sound, happy, normal home to go and paint in Chelsea. It had practically broken her mother's heart; it was utterly unaccountable.

'Gone over to art,' he said.

It was as if he spoke of some old despicable enemy and Pop could only say he hoped it would turn out well.

Drinking again, deciding that art could only be some man or other that Rosemary had run off with, he suddenly switched the subject, charging the unready Bluff-Gore with a startling question.

'When are you going to sell Bluff Court, Sir George?'

Bluff-Gore looked white. For some moments he could find no suitable words with which to tell Pop that he had no intention of selling his house, Bluff Court, even though it was far too large to live in. Bluff Court had sixty rooms, an entire hamlet of barns, dairies, and stables, half a mile of greenhouses and potting sheds and an orangery where, for fifty years, no oranges had grown. You needed a hundred tons of coal to heat it every winter and eighteen gardeners to keep the place tidy and productive in summer. You needed to keep twenty servants to wait on you and another twenty to wait on them. It was dog eat dog. You couldn't get the servants anyway and you couldn't have afforded to pay them if you could.

But to give it up, to sell it, even though you hadn't a bean, was unthinkable. It was a monstrous idea; it simply couldn't be entertained. Among its miles of neglected beeches, elms, and oaks, Bluff Court must and would stand where it did. It might be that one day it would be possible to let it to one of those stockbroker chaps who played at farming, made colossal losses but in the end came out on the right side because they got it out of taxes. Everybody was doing it and it was all perfectly legitimate, they said. It just showed, of course, what the country was coming to. It was grim. No wonder everybody you met was worried stiff. The country was committing suicide. 'What makes you think I have any intention of selling Bluff Court?'

'Well, you don't live in the damn thing,' Pop said, straight as a bird, 'do you? And never will do if you ask me.'

Bluff-Gore indicated with funereal acidity that he was, in fact, not asking him.

'Damn silly,' Pop said. He started to say that it was like having a car you never rode in and then decided on a more illuminating, more contemporary metaphor and said: 'Like having a television set you never look at.'

The illustration was, however, lost on Sir George, who had no television set.

'There are certain aspects other than material', he said, 'that have to be borne in mind.'

Pop said he couldn't think for the life of him what they were, and Bluff-Gore looked at the perky, side-lined face with tolerant irony and an oysterish half-smile.

'You were not thinking of buying the place, by any chance, were you?'

'Course I was.' The gentry were, Pop thought, really half-dopes sometimes. 'What d'ye think I asked you for?'

The oysterish smile widened a little, still ironically tolerant, for the next question.

'And what would you do with it, may I ask?'

'Pull the flippin' thing down.' Pop gave one of his piercing jolly shouts of laughter. 'What else d'ye think?'

'Good God.'

By now Bluff-Gore was whiter than ever. The eyes themselves had become oysters, opaque, sightless jellies, wet with shock, even with a glint of tears.

'Lot o'good scrap there,' Pop said. 'Make you a good offer.'

Bluff-Gore found himself quite incapable of speaking; he could only stare emptily and with increasing dejection at the grass of the beer-tent, as if mourning for some dear, unspoken departed.

'Cash,' Pop said. 'Ready as Freddy – why don't you think it over?'

Laughing again, he made a final expansive swing of his beer-mug, drawing froth, and left the speechless, sightless Bluff-Gore standing dismally alone.

Outside, in the meadow now gay with strung flags of yellow, scarlet, blue, and emerald, the tents and the marquees standing about the new green grass like white haystacks, Pop found the sun now shining brilliantly. Over by the river, well away from the ring, Mariette was having a practice canter. She had changed already into her yellow shirt and jodhpurs and her bare head was like a curly black kitten against the far blue sky. Mr Charlton was in attendance and suddenly Pop remembered the little matter of the baby. He supposed she wouldn't have to ride much longer and he wondered mildly if Mr Charlton knew. He'd forgotten about that.

Suddenly, from far across the meadow, he heard a rousing, familiar sound. It was Ma beating with a wooden spoon on a big jam-saucepan.

It was time to eat. It was hot in the midday sun and there was a scent of bruised grass in the air.

'Perfick,' Pop thought. 'Going to be a stinger. Going to be a wonderful afternoon.'

All afternoon Mr Charlton watched Mariette taking part in the riding and jumping events she had chosen. Once again, as she took her pony faultlessly through the walk, trot, canter, and run, he could hardly believe in that astral delicious figure, yellow, fawn, and black on its bay pony. Impossible almost to believe that it was the girl who had undressed him on the billiard table, scratched the eyes out of Pauline Jackson, and worked with him in the strawberry field. Once again she looked so perfectly aristocratic that she might have been the niece of Lady Planson-Forbes and he had never been so happy in his life as he watched her.

Ma was happy too. Who wouldn't be? All the children were properly dressed for the occasion, wearing riding habits, jodhpurs, and proper riding caps, even though only Mariette and Montgomery were going to ride. Each of them went about sucking enormous pink and yellow ice-creams; and the twins, who took so much after Ma, had large crackling bags of popcorn and potato crisps.

Nor were there any flies on Ma. She was wearing a silk costume in very pale turquoise, with slightly darker perpendicular stripes. She had chosen a rather large dark blue straw hat that shaded her face nicely and, as the milliner had predicted, 'helped to balance her up a bit'. Her shoes were also blue, almost the colour of her hat, and her hair had been permed into stiffish little waves. The only thing that really bothered her was her turquoise rings. They had started to cut into her fingers again. She would have to have them off.

Beside her the Brigadier's sister looked, as she always did, in her beige shantung and pink cloche hat, like a clothes peg with a thimble perched on top of it.

'Not going in for this 'ere ladies' donkey Derby, are you?' Ma said. Her body quivered with resonant, jellying laughter.

An invitation to strip down to the bare bosom could hardly have brought less response from the sister of the Brigadier.

'I think Miss Pilchester's going in,' Ma said. 'Anyway Pop's trying to persuade her to.'

The ladies' donkey Derby was a late, inspired idea of Pop's. He had managed to persuade the committee that they owed it to him in return for the field. He had also found a silver cup. He had once bought it at a sale, thinking it would be nice to stand on the sideboard. It was engraved with the details of an angling competition, but Pop didn't think it mattered all that much.

While Ma wandered about with the children and Mr Charlton watched the various events, listening with pride every time the loudspeakers spoke the name of Miss Mariette Larkin, Pop was spending some time behind the beer-tent, trying to induce Miss Pilchester to ride in the donkey Derby.

'I honestly couldn't. It would be absolutely ghastly.'

'I thought you liked a bit o' fun?'

'I think you are trying to be very naughty.'

Irresistible though Miss Pilchester always found him, she could not help thinking that this afternoon, in the brilliant sun, Pop looked even more so. He was wearing a suit of small, smart brown-and-white checks, an orange-brown tie, and a new brown Edwardian cap. Like Ma, he compared very favourably with other people: with, for instance, the Brigadier, who was wearing a snuff-coloured sports jacket patched at the elbows with brown leather, his washed-out University tie, and a pair of crumpled corduroys the colour of a moulting stoat.

For the second or third time Pop urged Miss Pilchester to be a sport.

'Just one more rider to make up the seven.'

'Who else is riding? I have never even ridden a donkey in my life before.'

'All girls of your age.'

Miss Pilchester darted one of her rapid glances at Pop. The cast of suspicion died in her eye as she saw the brown new cap. How well it suited him.

'What about that time I took you home in the Rolls?'

'What about it?'

'Best kiss I've had for a long time.'

'You make me feel shy!' Miss Pilchester said.

'Beauty,' Pop said. 'Haven't been able to forget it.'

Miss Pilchester hadn't been able to forget it either; she had even wondered if it might ever be repeated.

'I admit it was far from unpleasant, but what has it to do with the donkey Derby?'

Pop started to caress the outer rim of Miss Pilchester's thigh. With upsurgent alarm Miss Pilchester felt an investigating finger press a suspender button.

'People will be looking!'

'Coming to the cocktail party?'

'I think so. Yes, I am.'

'Repeat performance tonight at the cocktail party. Promise.'

'I know those promises. They're like pie-crust!'

At four o'clock Miss Pilchester was ready to ride in the ladies' donkey Derby.

A quarter of an hour before that Montgomery and Mr Charlton had ridden in the men's donkey Derby. Most of the donkeys, including Mr Charlton's, had had to be started with carrots and the race had been won by a pale sagacious animal named Whiskey Johnny, who didn't need any carrots. Mr Charlton had ridden three yards and then fallen off. His mount had instantly bolted, ending up in stirring style far beyond the tea-tent, by the river, where already a few lovers, bored by the events and stimulated by a warm afternoon of entrancing golden air, were embracing in the long grasses by the bank, profitably dreaming out the day in the world of rising fish, wild irises, and expanding water-lily blooms.

When Pop went to collect the animal, which was called Jasmine, he found it staring with detached interest at a soldier and a passionate, well-formed young blonde, both of whom were oblivious, in the grasses, of the presence of watchers. Jasmine, Pop thought, seemed so interested in what was going on that after being led away some paces she turned, pricked up her ears and looked around, rather as if she wanted to come back and see it all again.

After all this Pop selected Jasmine for Miss Pilchester to ride. The animal stood dangerously still at the starting point, in stubborn suspense, while Pop gave earnest ante-post advice to Miss Pilchester, who sat astride.

'Hang on with your knees. Don't let go. Hang on tight. Like grim death.'

Miss Pilchester, already looking like grim death, gave a hasty glance round at the other competitors, dismayed to find them all young, effervescent girls of sixteen or seventeen. She herself felt neither young nor effervescent and the donkey was horribly hairy underneath her calves.

'Don't mind them, Edith. Don't look at them. Look straight ahead – straight as you can go. Hang on like grim death.'

Miss Pilchester became vaguely aware of carrots, in orange arcs, being waved in all directions. A few animals trotted indifferently up the track, between shrieking, cheering rows of spectators. One trotted at incautious speed for thirty yards or so and then, as if inexplicably bored about something, turned and came back. Another sidled to the side of the track and leaned against a post, allowing itself to be stroked by various children, including Victoria and the twins. Two girls fell off, screaming, and there were gay momentary glimpses of black and apricot lingerie.

Jasmine stood fast. 'Git up, old gal!' Pop said, and started to push her. 'Git up there, Jasmine!' Pop put his weight against her rump and heaved. Nothing happened, and it seemed as if Jasmine had sunk her feet into the ground.

It was all absolutely ghastly, Miss Pilchester was just thinking when over the loudspeaker a voice started up an announcement about Anne Fitzgerald, aged three, who had lost her mother. Would Mrs Fitzgerald please –

The loudspeaker gave a few snappy barks. Jasmine cocked her ears and broke through with frenzy the final waving arcs of carrots, leaving Pop on the ground and everybody scattered.

Miss Pilchester, as Pop had so earnestly and correctly advised, hung on firmly and desperately with her knees, just like grim death, and in thirty seconds Jasmine was back at the river, once more staring into the world of grasses, water-lilies, irises, and a soldier's summer love.

Half-dismounting, half-falling, a dishevelled and demoralized Miss Pilchester stood staring too. It was all absolutely and utterly ghastly and it only made things worse when the soldier, disturbed in the middle of his technique, looked up calmly and said:

'Why don't you go away, Ma? Both of you. You *and* your sister.'

· 8 ·

Pop, uncertain as to quite who had been invited to the party and who had not, spent most of the rest of the afternoon hailing odd acquaintances, generously clapping them on the back, and saying: 'See you at eight o'clock. See you at the party.' The result was that by half past eight the billiard-room was a clamorous, fighting mass of fifty or sixty people, one half of whom had never received a formal invitation.

'I never thought we asked this lot,' Ma said. 'Hardly enough stuff to go round –'

'Let 'em all come!' Pop said.

The billiard-room was the perfick place, he thought, for having the party. The billiard table, covered over by trestle table boards and then with a big white cloth, was just the thing for the eats, the champagne, and the glasses. One of the doors led back into the house, in case people wanted to pop upstairs, and the other into the garden, so that those who felt inclined could dodge out and take the air.

Through the thickest fog of smoke Pop had ever seen outside a smoking concert he and Ma, helped by Mariette, Mr Charlton, and Montgomery, served food, poured out champagne, and handed glasses round. Every now and then people collided with each other in the crowded fog and a glass went smashing to the floor. Nobody seemed to care about this and Ma was glad the glasses had been hired from caterers. That was another brilliant idea of Mr Charlton's.

Now and then someone, almost always someone he hardly knew, came up to Pop, squeezed his elbow, and said, 'Damn good party, Larkin, old boy. Going well,' so that Pop felt very pleased. Ma too moved everywhere with genial expansiveness. In the crowd she seemed larger than ever, so that whenever she moved her huge body from one spot to another a large open vacuum was formed.

In one of these spaces, alongside a wall, Pop found the two Miss Barnwells, Effie and Edna, who, to his infinite pain and surprise, had no crumb or glass between them. The Miss Barnwells, who were thinking of applying for National Assistance because times were so bad, were two genteel freckled little ladies, daughters of an Indian civil servant, who had been born in Delhi. Among other things they kept bees and their little yellow faces, crowded with freckles, looked as if they were regularly and thoroughly stung all over.

'Nothing to eat? Nothing to drink?'

Pop could hardly believe it; he was shocked.

'We were just contemplating.'

'Contemplate my foot,' Pop said. 'I'll get you a glass o' champagne.'

'No, no,' they said. 'Nothing at all like that.'

'Terrible,' Pop said. 'Nobody looking after you. I'll get you a sandwich.'

Coming back a moment or two later with a plate of Ma's delicious buttery ham sandwiches, he returned to the painful subject of the Miss Barnwells and their having nothing to drink at all.

'Glass o' beer? Drop o' cider? Glass o' port?'

'No, no. No, thank you. We are quite happy.'

'Have a Ma Chérie.'

The air seemed to light up with infinite twinkling freckles.

'What is a Ma Chérie?'

Ma Chérie was hardly, Pop thought, a drink at all. It was simply sherry, soda, and a dash of something or other, he could never remember quite what. It was nothing like Red Bull or Rolls-Royce or Chauffeur, the good ones.

'Soda with flavouring,' he said.

'That sounds quite nice. Perhaps we might have two of –'

Pop was away, pushing through the foggy crowd to the living-room, where he presently mixed two Ma Chéries, double strength, adding an extra dash of brandy to hold the feeble things together.

'There you are. Knock that back.'

The Miss Barnwells, who hardly ever had much lunch on Saturdays, took their glasses, chewing rapidly, and thanked him. The air danced with freckles. He was, they said, infinitely kind.

'I'll keep 'em topped up,' Pop said.

A moment later a firm gentle hand fixed itself to his elbow and drew him away.

'Mr Larkin, isn't it?'

A tallish lady in a small grey tweed hat with a peacock feather in it smiled at him over a piece of cheese toast and a glass of champagne.

'Lady Bluff-Gore. You remember?'

Pop remembered; they had met occasionally at village Christmas socials.

'Ah, yes,' Pop said. 'Lady Rose.'

'Afraid we don't run across each other very often.'

She smiled again; her ivory teeth were remarkably long and large.

'I hear you made an interesting suggestion to my husband this afternoon.'

'Oh! about the house? That's right. Time it was pulled down.'

'So I heard.'

All afternoon she had been thinking what an interesting suggestion it was to pull the house down. She had so long wanted to pull it down herself.

'Who wants these old places?' Pop said.

Who indeed? she thought. She had so often longed to pull hers down, and all the miles of silly greenhouses, unused stables, and draughty barns. Perhaps if it were pulled down, she thought, they might have a little money in the bank instead of living on overdrafts. Perhaps Rosemary would come back. Perhaps they could really live in comfort for a change.

'Would it be too much to ask what you feel it's worth?'

'Could take a squint at it tomorrow,' Pop said, 'and let you know.'

Nothing like striking the iron while it was hot, Pop thought. That's how he liked to do things. In a couple of hours he could get a rough idea what bricks, tiles, doors, flooring, and hard core he would get out of it. In two shakes he could be on the blower to Freddy Fox and do a deal with Freddy.

'Yes, I'll take a squint at it –'

'Do you suppose – could we talk elsewhere?' she said. Her voice was quiet. 'It's a little public here.'

Elsewhere, at Pop's suggestion, was under the walnut tree. The evening was overcast and humid, with a feeling of coming rain. Cuckoos were still calling across the fields in their late bubbling voices and a few people were wandering among Ma's flower-beds, taking the air.

'You see it wouldn't be at all an easy business to persuade my husband.'

'No?'

'Not at all an easy man.'

Pop didn't doubt it at all.

'All the same I think I might persuade him.'

If he could persuade Miss Pilchester to ride the donkey, Pop thought, it ought to be possible to persuade Bluff-Gore to do a little thing like pulling a mansion down. Nothing to it. Perhaps by much the same process too?

'It's just a thought,' she said, 'but supposing I did?'

'Don't get it,' Pop said.

'Mightn't it be an idea to come to some little arrangement? You and I?'

Women were clever, Pop thought. That showed you how clever women were. All the same under their skins. He snagged on now. Lady Five Per Cent he would call her now.

'I get you,' Pop said.

'Good. Shall I let you know when we might have another little talk?'

Back in the smoky, clamorous fog he discovered the Miss Barnwells gazing at empty glasses. How had they liked the Ma Chérie? Quite delicious, they thought; and he went away to get them more.

In the comparative quiet of the sitting-room, where it was getting dusk, he got the impression that the entire billiard-room would, at any moment, blow up behind him. The place was a whirring dynamo, rapidly running hot.

'And what about me?'

It was Miss Pilchester, furtive against the Spanish galleon. Another one come to collect her interest, Pop supposed.

'Having a nice time?'

'It'll be nicer when you've kept your promise.'

Might as well get it over, Pop thought.

'Lovely party. Such luck with the weather. Best gymkhana we've ever had.'

Pop put down the two Ma Chéries and braced himself. Miss Pilchester simply didn't know how to hold herself for the act of kissing and Pop seized her like a sheaf of corn. There was a momentary bony stir of corsets and Miss Pilchester gave a short palpitating sigh. She had determined, this time, to give everything she'd got.

For all the velvet artistry he put into it Pop could make little impression on lips so well fortified with teeth that he felt they might at any moment crack like walnuts underneath the strain.

'Thanks. That was just what the doctor ordered. Time for one more?'

'Last one,' Pop said. 'Must get back to the party.'

With thrilling silence Miss Pilchester gave everything she'd got for the second time. It was almost too much for Pop, who throughout the kiss was wondering if, after all, he might indulge in a firework or two. Finally Miss Pilchester broke away, gazing wildly up at him.

'And in case I don't get another chance of seeing you alone again, thanks for everything. Marvellous day. All your doing. Simply wouldn't have been anything without you. Best gymkhana we've ever had. And this party. Made me very happy.'

The length of the speech suddenly seemed to take away the rest of her capacity for calm. She gave something like a sob, patted Pop's cheek, and rushed hurriedly away and upstairs, brushing past two women already on their way up. Once more she had forgotten to say how absolutely ghastly everything was.

'You simply must see the polly,' one woman was saying. 'Purple and yellow tiles with big blue hollyhocks coming out the top. And pink nymphs on the bath mirror.'

'Oh! God!' Miss Pilchester said.

Taking the two Ma Chéries back to the Miss Barnwells Pop found them laughing merrily, chewing at their seventh ham sandwich.

'Going positively to drag you away if you'll let me.'

The longest, slimmest, coolest hand Pop had ever touched suddenly came and took him sinuously away from the munching Miss Barnwells, now eagerly sipping their second Ma Chéries.

'They tell me you practically organized this whole bun-fight single-handed.'

A tall aristocratically fair girl, so fair that her hair was almost barley-white, with a figure like a reed and enormous pellucid olive eyes, had Pop so transfixed that, for a moment, he was almost unnerved. He had never seen her, or anyone like her, before.

'The thing positively went like a bomb.'

The cool, long hand still held his own. The large pale eyes, languidly swimming, washed over him an endless stream of softer and softer glances.

'And this party. What a slam.'

Her dress was pure clear primrose, with a long V-neck. She wore long transparent earrings that swung about her long neck like dewy pendulums.

'Going to have a party of my own next week. Say you'll come.'

Pop, who had so far not spoken a word, murmured something about he'd love to, trying at the same time to decide where and when he'd seen this unheralded vision before, deciding finally that he never had.

'Gorgeous party. Do you dance at all?'

'Used to fling 'em up a bit at one time.'

'Scream.'

She laughed on clear bell-like notes.

'My dear. Absolute scream.'

Bewitched, Pop again had nothing to say. A vacuum left by Ma, three or four feet away from him, made him feel quite naked before it filled up again.

'That donkey ride, they tell me, was your idea. Blistering success.'

Pop, with a certain touch of pride, admitted it.

'The seven foolish virgins. Scream. Couldn't stop laughing. Practically needed changing –'

Again she laughed on pure bell-like notes, the dewy earrings dancing.

'Just what it needed. They can be absolute stinkers, gymkhanas, don't you think? Everybody jog-trotting round. Fond mothers biting lips because little Waffles doesn't win the trotting on Pretty Boy. Oh! absolute stinkers.'

She held him captured with moist splendid eyes.

'But you thought of the virgins. That was the stroke. Absolute genius. Absolute scream, the virgins.'

She suddenly gave Pop what he thought was a fleeting sporting wink.

'So few, after all, aren't there?'

To Pop it now began to seem that he might have met, under the sheer primrose sheath, the dancing earrings, the aristocratic voice, and the shining languid eyes, a character something after his own heart and kind.

'But seriously, dear man, what I came to say was this. My name's Angela Snow. Emhurst Valley. We've got one of these pony-trots coming off in August – what say you come over and bring the donkey outfit and make that one go with a bang?'

The word bang made Pop remember something. It was, he thought, the one thing needed to make the day a perfick one.

'Like fireworks?'

'Love 'em. Adore 'em.'

'Stay here,' Pop said, 'while I fetch you a drop more champagne.' He started to struggle through the smoky screen hemming him in on all sides and then remembered something and came back to her. 'Or a cocktail? Rather have a cocktail?'

'Adore one. Just what I need.'

'This way.'

He started to lead the way out to the sitting-room, but half way he was stopped by Mr Charlton and Mariette, who said:

'Pop, Charley has something he'd like to say to you.'

'Not now,' Pop said. 'Busy now.'

'It's terribly important. It's something he's *got* to ask you.'

Mr Charlton looked unexpectedly strained and tense. Must have found out about the baby, Pop supposed. Pity.

'Be back in five minutes,' he said and followed the tall, reedy, primrose figure into the sitting-room.

There, over his Spanish galleon, he asked the dewy, languid girl which she would rather have – Rolls-Royce, Red Bull, or Chauffeur. Red Bull was the blinder, he said.

'Red Bull then, dear,' she said. 'What names they give them nowadays.'
Pop mixed two double Red Bulls and in the falling twilight the elegant
Angela Snow knocked hers back with the coolest speed, like a man.

'One more of these, dear boy, and I'm ready.'

Pop was ready too. Ten minutes later the first firework went off like a
bomb under Ma, who showed hardly any sign of disturbance at all. The
two ladies who had been to investigate Ma's impossible bathroom met a
Roman Candle on the stairs. The tall reedy girl put two jumping crackers
under the Brigadier's sister and another under Sir George Bluff-Gore. Ma
started laughing like a jelly and Pop put a Mighty Atom under the billiard
table where it set the glasses ringing like a xylophone. The two Miss
Barnwells started giggling uncontrollably and said it reminded them of a
pujah in Delhi and Miss Pilchester was heard saying she knew this would
happen and that it was absolutely ghastly and she'd hide under the stairs.
People started running from the smoky house into the garden, where the
tall, languid girl had a big fizzing Catherine Wheel already going on the
walnut tree and was now getting ready to put a Roman Candle as near
as she could without killing him under a man named Jack Farley, who
was a complete slob and had tried to pinch her three times in the tea-tent
early in the afternoon. A few rockets started shooting up from empty
champagne bottles into a sky now summerily dark, cuckoo-less, and
completely canopied with cloud. Pop did what he had so long wanted to
do and put a beauty under Miss Pilchester, who started shrieking she was
burned. Upstairs Primrose, Victoria, and the twins hung out of the bedroom windows shouting, laughing, and eating the day's last ice-cream,
potato crisps, and apple-tart. In the middle of it all Mariette and Mr
Charlton tried once again, with little success, to speak with Pop, who was
running about the flower beds waving a Golden Rain, calling like a Red
Indian, happy as a boy. When finally Pop had thrown the Golden Rain
over a damson tree Mr Charlton said:

'Pop, I want to speak to you. Ma says I can marry Mariette if you'll let
her –'

'Perfick,' Pop said. 'Let her? – course I'll let her.'

The tall, willowy girl was everywhere, selecting victims. The sky was
comet-bright with sprays of silver stars, rockets, and Golden Rain. A
Roman Candle went off with shattering concussion behind the walnut tree
and Mr Charlton begged of Pop:

'Pop, Ma says if you agree will you announce it? She says now's the
perfect time.'

'Perfick it is an' all,' Pop said. 'Never thought of that.'

A quarter of an hour later Pop was standing on a chair outside the billiard-room, announcing to the gathered guests, in the smoky garden, with a touch of imperial pride in his voice, together with a certain sadness, that Mr Charlton was going to marry his daughter Mariette and had everybody got their glasses filled?

'Give you the toast!' he called into the smoky summer air. 'Charley and Mariette.'

As he lifted his glass a stunning explosion split the air, knocking him yards backwards.

'One for his nob!' Mr Charlton shouted.

'What Paddy shot at!' Ma screamed and started choking in helpless laughter.

It was the last devastating Roman Candle of the cool, tall, primrose girl.

'Quite perfect,' she said.

· 9 ·

When it was all over, and even television had closed down, Ma and Pop sat alone in the kitchen, Ma now and then shaking all over as she remembered the donkeys, Miss Pilchester, and the way Pop had been blown flat on his back by the Roman Candle.

'Nothing at all to eat?' Pop inquired.

'Think there's another apple-tart,' Ma said and got up to get it from the fridge. The apple-tart was large and puffy, with white castor sugar sprinkled on its lid of crust. With it Ma brought two plates, a knife and, out of sheer habit, the bottle of ketchup. 'By the way, who was that girl in the yellow dress? She was a spark.'

'Never seen her in me life. Somebody said her father was a judge.'

'Oh?' Ma said. 'Well, I suppose there's a throw-back in every family.'

Pop cut two six-inch slices of pie. He gave one to Ma, and then started to eat the other in his fingers, at the same time ignoring, much to Ma's surprise, the bottle of ketchup.

'Don't you want no ketchup?'

'Gone off ketchup a bit,' Pop said.

'Oh?' Ma said. 'How's that?'

'Makes everything taste the same.'

Ma, who thought this was odd, went on to say what about port?

'Don't say you've gone off port as well.'

'No,' Pop said. 'Just got some more in. Started to order it in two-gallon jars now.'

He got up, found the jar of port under the stairs and poured out two nice big glasses, inquiring at the same time where Mr Charlton and Mariette were?

'Having a quiet few minutes in the sitting-room.'

Pop said it was very nice about Mr Charlton and Mariette and had Mr Charlton found out about the baby?

'She's not going to have a baby now,' Ma said. 'False alarm.'

'Jolly good,' Pop said. 'Perfick.'

Ma sat meditatively fingering her turquoise rings, which seemed to be getting tighter every day, while Pop listened to the sound of the first gentle summery feathers of rain on earth and leaves as it came through the open kitchen door.

'I am though,' Ma said.

Pop looked mildly, though not disagreeably, surprised.

'How did that happen then?'

'*How?* What do you mean, *how?*'

Pop said he meant when did it all date back to?

'That night in the bluebell wood,' Ma said. 'Just before Mister Charlton came. You said you thought there was a wild duck's nest up there and we went to have a look.'

'That night?' Pop said. 'I never even thought –'

'You don't know your own strength,' Ma said. 'Have some more apple-tart. Pass the ketchup.'

Pop cut himself another biggish slice of apple-tart. Ma, he noticed, hadn't quite finished hers. She was always a slow eater. She was still fingering her turquoise rings, as if for some reason she was engaged in thinking, though Pop couldn't imagine what about, unless it was the baby.

The turquoise rings, however, put a thought into his own mind, and he gave a short soft laugh or two, no louder than the summery feathers of rain.

'If this lark goes on much longer,' he said, 'you and me'll have to get married as well.'

Ma said she thought it wouldn't be a bad idea perhaps.

'I've got to have my rings cut off again anyway,' she said. 'We might as well do it then.'

For some moments Pop sat in complete silence, still listening to the rain and wondering about the baby and if Ma wanted a boy and what names they would pick for it when it came.

Ma sat wondering too, mostly about what it would be like to be married. She couldn't imagine at all.

Eventually Pop spoke. 'Thought up any names for it?' he said.

'It?' Ma said. 'I've got a funny feeling it might be twins.'

'Marvellous. Perfick,' Pop said.

Ma, who had in fact thought a very great deal about names, went on to say that if it did turn out to be just a boy, which she hoped it wouldn't, or just a girl, what about Orlando and Rosalind? – out of that play they saw on television the other night? A very nice play.

Pop said he thought they were jolly good names, just the sort of names he liked. And what if it was twins?

'Well,' Ma said, 'I've been thinking. If it's girls I thought of Lucinda and Clorinda. I think they're very nice. Or if it's boys I wouldn't say no to Nelson and Rodney. They were admirals.'

'Not so bad,' Pop said. 'I like Lucinda.'

The rain was falling a little faster now, though still softly, the dampness bringing out of the air the last lingering smell of firework smoke. At one time the house had seemed full of the stench of gunpowder.

'Couldn't very well make it a double wedding, I suppose, could we?' Ma said.

'Might ask Mister Charlton.'

'Why Mister Charlton?'

'He knows about things. Look what he knew about the party.'

Pop had just finished his second slice of apple-pie and was vaguely wondering about a third – there wasn't so much of it left and it was a pity to let it go begging – when Mr Charlton and Mariette came in from the sitting-room. He said how glad he was to see them and how he could congratulate them now it was quieter. He said he and Ma weren't half glad about things and that it didn't seem five minutes since Mister Charlton had arrived.

'How about a glass of port, you two?'

While he was pouring out two more nice big glasses of port he couldn't help thinking how pretty Mariette looked in her black, semi-fitting cocktail dress with its white cuffs, collar, and belt. He hoped all the girls would take after Ma. He thought too how nice it was about Mariette and the baby – just as well to start with a clean sheet about these things.

'Well, cheers,' he said. 'God bless,' and with a sudden affectionate impulse got up and kissed Mariette. 'Couldn't be more perfick.'

Ma, who said she wasn't going to be left out, then got up and kissed both Mariette and Mr Charlton; and then Mr Charlton and Pop shook hands.

'Got a bit of news of our own now,' Pop said. 'Shall we tell them, Ma?'

'You tell them.'

'Well,' Pop said, 'we thought we'd get married too. Ma's going to have another baby.'

Mr Charlton, who only a month before would have been more than startled by this announcement, didn't turn a hair. Nor did Mariette seem unduly perturbed. The only thing that suddenly occurred to Mr Charlton was that this was a time when it was essential, if ever, to use his loaf.

'Now wait a minute,' he said, 'this wants thinking about.'

'There you are, Ma,' Pop said. 'I told you.'

'Why does it want thinking about?' Ma said.

Mr Charlton took a thoughtful sip of port.

'I was thinking of the tax situation,' he said. 'You see, it actually doesn't pay to get married. It actually pays to live in –'

He was about to say 'sin' but abruptly checked himself, too late to prevent Ma, however, from being a little upset.

'Don't use that word,' she said severely. 'I know what you were going to say.'

Mr Charlton apologized and said what he really meant was that if he were them he'd keep the *status quo*. This was the first time Pop had ever heard such astonishing un-English words used under his roof, but it meant more marks for Mr Charlton. Ma, forgetting that she had been very nearly outraged a moment before, could only look on in silent, fervent admiration.

'Quite happy as we are, I suppose, eh, Ma?' Pop said. 'Nothing to worry about?'

Not that she could think of, Ma said.

'All right. Let's go on in the old sweet way.'

Mr Charlton agreed.

'By keeping to the old way,' Mr Charlton said, 'you'll be better off when the time comes.'

'When what time comes?' Pop said. 'For what?'

'To pay your tax,' Mr Charlton said. 'It's bound to catch up some day.'

'That's what you think!' Pop said.

'I'm afraid they'll take notice of the Rolls. They're bound to say –'

'That old thing?' Pop said. 'Never. Took it for a debt!'

Suddenly Pop started laughing as heartily as Ma had done when the girl in the yellow dress had blown him off the chair with the Roman Candle.

Ma laughed piercingly too and said: 'Oh! that reminds me. Are you going back to that office?'

'That's right, Charley,' Pop said. 'Are you ever going back to that lark?'

Mr Charlton, thoughtful again, said he supposed if he didn't go back he'd lose his pension.

The word pension made Pop laugh even more than the idea of the tax lark. 'You mean sit on your backside for forty years and then collect four pounds a week that's worth only two and 'll only buy half as much anyway?' He urged Mr Charlton to use his loaf. Mr Charlton could not help thinking that it was high time he did. 'I tell you what,' Pop said. 'I'll be doing a nice little demolition job very soon. Some very good stuff. Big mansion. What say we pick the best out and build you and Mariette a bungalow in the medder, near the bluebell wood?'

'Oh! wonderful, wonderful, Pop!' Mariette said and, with eyes impulsively dancing, came to kiss his face and lips and hair, so that Mr Charlton knew that there was, really, nothing more to say.

'Well, that's it then,' Pop said. 'Perfick. Now who says one more glass o' port? And then we go to bed.'

He was intensely looking forward to going to bed. It would top it all up to have a cigar and watch Ma get into the transparent nylon nightgown.

'Yes: time to get a little beauty sleep,' Ma said.

Pop poured four more nice big glasses of port, saying at the same time how glad he was about the rain. They could do with the rain. It was just what the cherries, the plums, and the apples wanted now.

'Shall you come cherry-picking too?' Mariette said to Mr Charlton, but in answer he could only look at her olive skin, the dark shining eyes, the kittenish hair, and the firm young breasts with silent fascination.

Some moments later Pop took his glass of port to the kitchen door, staring out at the summer darkness and the rain. Mr Charlton felt an impulse to join him and stood there staring too, thinking of how spring had passed, how quickly the buds of May had gone, and how everything, now, had blossomed into full, high summer.

'Listen,' Pop said. 'Perfick.'

Everybody listened; and in the dark air there was the sound of nightingales.

· A BREATH OF ·
· FRENCH AIR ·

· 1 ·

Little Oscar, Ma Larkin's seventh, to whom she hoped in due course to give a real proper ribbon of names, probably calling him after some famous explorer, admiral, or Roman Emperor, or even the whole lot, lay in his lavish silvery pram in the kitchen, looking remarkably like a very soft, very large apple dumpling that has been slightly over-boiled.

Continual small bubbles of spittle oozed softly like pink juice from his lips and Pop, coming in to breakfast after giving morning swill to the pigs, paused affectionately to wipe them off with a feeder worked all over in royal blue daisies and a bright scarlet picture of Miss Muffet, the big spider, and the curds-and-whey. Ma, who looked if anything six inches wider since having the baby than she had done even while carrying it, had worked the feeder herself. She hadn't all that much time to spare with seven on her hands but she was surprisingly clever with her plump olive fingers that were almost hidden in pearl and turquoise rings.

'Soon be as fat as a Christmas gander,' Pop said, at the same time pausing to give his son-in-law, Mr Charlton, his customary open-handed clout of greeting in the middle of the back. Mr Charlton, who sat patiently looking through his spectacles at *The Times* while waiting for his breakfast, took the salutation without flinching. Nearly a year in the Larkin household had hardened him a lot.

Ma, in bright purple blouse and pink apron and with her dark rich hair still in curling pins, had three pounds of sausages in one frying-pan, several rounds of fried bread and seven or eight rashers of bacon in another and a basket of fresh pink field mushrooms waiting for a saucepan. Just before Pop bent to kiss her full on her handsome mouth and wish her good morning, she dropped half the mushrooms into the saucepan, where they at once started hissing at an intruding lump of butter as big as a tennis ball, cooking fragrantly.

'Mariette not down?' Pop said. 'Kids off to school? Going to be a beautiful day. Perfick. Mushrooms smell good.'

Outside it was raining in drilling summer torrents. Nothing could be seen of the far side of the junk-yard, the woods, and the surrounding meadows in the cloudy, steamy air. Nearer to the house the only visible moving things were a few hens shaking damp brown feathers under a straw hovel, a line of six or seven Chinese geese wandering dopily in and out of a wet jungle of rusty iron and nettles, and a small flock of sparrows bathing with sprinkling wings in muddy pools of water.

This was July, Ma thought, and it was enough to give you the willies. It was a real thick'un, or what she sometimes called bad courting weather. Not that she had any intention of going courting, but it reminded her of times when she had. Wet summer days and evenings frustrated you that bad you felt all bottled up. You couldn't let yourself go at all. The fact that she had let herself go with splendidly fruitful effect over the years didn't occur to her at all. It was just that she hated rain in July.

Pop, irrepressibly optimistic that the day was going to be a beautiful one, inquired again about his eldest daughter, Mariette. She was nearly always up with the lark, out riding or something, and he missed her when she didn't come down. It wasn't like her.

'Not feeling all that good,' Ma said. 'Bit peaky.'

Pop pricked up his ears sharply. Not good? He wondered what it could be? Morning sickness perhaps. He hoped so.

'Oh?' he said. 'Thought she looked a little bit below par yesterday. Anythink I ought to know about?'

Pop gave a sharp, inquiring look at Ma and then a still sharper, even more searching look at Mr Charlton. But neither Ma nor Charley seemed to think it was anything he ought to know about and Ma went on moodily prodding at sizzling mushrooms and Mr Charlton with *The Times*.

'She needs a change,' Ma said. 'Ought to have a holiday. Weather's getting her down.'

'Soon clear up,' Pop said. 'You'll see. Be perfick by midday. Beautiful.'

'Don't you believe it,' Ma said. 'It's one of them Julys. I've seen 'em before. They never get right. By the time you get into August it's like they have in India. What are they called, Charley, them things?'

'Monsoons,' Mr Charlton said.

'That's it.' Ma, with a gesture of unaccustomed impatience, threw four more links of sausage into the frying-pan. 'I don't know as I shan't be screeching for a holiday myself if this lot goes on.'

The sausages hit the frying-pan with the sound of red-hot irons plunging into freezing water and immediately little Oscar began to cry.

Pop rushed at once to pick him up but Ma said breakfast was ready and began to serve the first of the bacon, the sausages, the fried bread, and the mushrooms to Mr Charlton, who was still deep in *The Times*.

'I know what he wants,' Pop said. 'He wants his morning Guinness.'

'Well, he'll have to wait for his Guinness, that's all,' Ma said. 'Like other folks do.'

Oscar cried out plaintively again and Pop asked with some concern if he shouldn't give him a piece of fried bread to be going on with? Ma said 'Not on your nelly' in a voice very near to severity. It wouldn't hurt him to cry for a bit and in any case he'd have to learn to be patient. You had to learn to be patient in this world. Anyway, sometimes.

'He wants his drop o' Guinness,' Pop said. 'I know.'

Mr Charlton, who had heard nothing of this conversation, folded *The Times* into quarter-page size, then suddenly pointed to a picture in it and said that that was a most extraordinary thing.

'What is?' Pop said, 'wanting a drop o' Ma's Guinness?'

Pop laughed uproariously, as if in fact it was.

'How many sausages, Pop?' Ma said. 'Four? Shall I do you a couple of eggs before I sit down?'

Pop said five sausages and he would manage with two eggs.

'What's extraordinary?' Ma said.

'This picture,' Mr Charlton said. 'It's a picture of a little place called St Pierre le Port. I used to go and spend every summer holiday there when I was a boy. My aunt and uncle used to take me.'

'Let's have a look,' Ma said.

'This is the actual view I used to see from my bedroom window. The actual view – here – along the quay.'

'Seaside?'

'On the Atlantic. The sea goes out for miles at low tide and you can paddle on lovely warm sand and there's a funny little train comes from somewhere inland and goes trundling from place to place along the coast.' Mr Charlton had forgotten sausages, bacon, fried bread, and mushrooms, and even the cries of Oscar in a delicious ecstasy of recollection. 'Oh! I hope they haven't done away with that train. I loved that little train. That train *is* France for me.'

Pop, open-mouthed, stopped biting sausage and looked completely startled at the word France, as if it were something he had never heard of before.

'France? You went abroad?' he said. 'For your holidays? Didn't your Pop and Ma want you?'

'I lost them both when I was six,' Mr Charlton said. 'I think I told you.'

At this moment Oscar started to cry again and Ma said she would switch on the radio to soothe him down. She turned the switch and *The Blue Danube* bellowed out at full blast.

'Uncle Arthur and Aunt Edna adored France,' Mr Charlton said. 'I think they loved it even more than England. They went so often in the end you'd have taken them *for* French. Especially Uncle Arthur.'

In a low voice Pop asked Mr Charlton to pass him the mustard. He could think of nothing else to say.

'It brings it all back,' Mr Charlton said, 'that picture in *The Times.*'

Pop, still submerged in disbelief at the astonishing course of the conversation, now became aware of another remarkable thing. Ma was not eating breakfast.

'Ma, you're not having anythink,' he said. 'What's up?'

Ma got up from the breakfast table. Oscar was crying more loudly than ever, undrowned by *The Blue Danube.*

'Not very peckish,' Ma said. 'I think I'll give Oscar his first. Perhaps I'll feel better after that.'

'Hope so. Terrible. What's up with everybody? Everybody looks pale round the gills.'

Without speaking Ma, who did indeed feel pale round the gills, went over to the pram and picked up little Oscar, who belched sharply and stopped crying immediately. Then she kissed him softly in the nape of his neck and sat down again at the table, at the same time undoing her blouse.

All this time Pop had been silently dipping sausage into mustard, staring at his plate, unable to think of a word to say, but now he looked up in time to see Ma extract from her blouse a large expanse of olive bosom twice as large as a full-ripe melon. Into this mass of tender flesh Oscar buried his face and settled down.

'Was it healthy?' Pop said.

'France you mean?' Mr Charlton said. 'Oh, very. The air's wonderful there in Brittany. All hot and sultry. It was awfully cheap too. And marvellous food. Wonderful food.'

'Did you say hot?' Ma said.

'Some summers we'd never see a drop of rain. And the sea – I always remember how blue the sea was. Vivid. Just the colour you see on travel posters.'

'I should like to feel it hot again,' Ma said. 'Like last year. I haven't felt the sun hot on my chest since that day you and Mariette were married in September.'

'Always hot in Britanny,' Mr Charlton said. 'That's my recollection. You can bet on that.'

Oscar pulled at his mother's breast with steadfast sucks of contentment and an occasional rich, startling plop! like that of cork coming out of a bottle. In silence Pop dipped pieces of sausage into mustard and found himself brooding over a remembrance of the day Mariette and Charley had been married.

A very lovely day that had been, as Ma had said: all light and hot sunshine, with a big marquee in the garden and plenty of iced port, cold salmon, and champagne. He would remember for ever Mariette's striking and unconventional dress of yellow silk, so suited to her dark hair, and her bouquet of stephanotis and cherry-red nerines that appeared to have gold-dust sprinkled all over their petals. Everybody was there that day and Mariette's sisters, Zinnia, Petunia, Victoria, and Primrose, were bridesmaids, each in deep cream, with head-dresses of small golden roses and posies of lily-of-the-valley. Ma, like Miss Pilchester and several of their friends, wept openly at the sight of these touching things and even Pop had a tear in his eye.

It was less than a week after Mariette and Charley were back from honeymoon when Pop began to inquire of Ma if anything was happening yet?

Ma said she should think not – everybody wasn't like him.

'You've only got to start eyeing me across a forty-acre field,' she said, 'and I start wondering whether I'm going to have twins or triplets.'

You'd got to give them a chance, she went on, and Pop could only reply that he thought a fortnight was plenty of chance. He murmured something about the question of Charley's technique, of which in view of his great shyness before marriage Ma had entertained considerable doubts, but Ma replied blandly that she thought that if there was anything Charley didn't know by this time Mariette would soon teach him. Pop said he should hope so.

Ever since that time there hadn't been a day when Pop had been increasingly fired with the hope that Ma would soon have some interesting news to tell him. But nothing ever happened and now at last Pop had begun to have considerable doubts about Charley's desire, or even ability, to make him a grandfather. He thought the whole situation was getting everybody down. Ma seemed mopey and was always complaining of the summer rain. Mariette looked decidedly pale too and even seemed, he thought, a shade thinner and lacked that plum-like bloom that even at seventeen had given her such a dark and luscious maturity.

'Got your watch on you, Charley?' Ma said. 'How long's he had on this side?'

Perfick, Perfick!

Mr Charlton looked briefly up from reading *The Times* to glance at his wrist-watch. With unconcern he gave another glance at Oscar, nestling into Ma's bosom like a piglet into the side of a vast pink sow, and said he thought it was about ten minutes.

Deftly Ma released Oscar from her bosom. There was another rich, milky plop! as Oscar let go the cork of her nipple and then a sudden complaining wail of hunger as she slipped her breast back into her blouse.

'Let me get the door open for goodness sake, child,' Ma said.

'Never known anybody like him for his Guinness,' Pop said.

'Oh!' Ma said, 'haven't you?'

A moment later Oscar was buried again in rosy flesh, all contentment, while Ma held him close to her with one hand, trying at the same time to pour herself a cup of tea with the other.

Mr Charlton was quick to see her difficulties and got up at once to pour it for her himself. That was one of the things Ma liked about Charley: these little touches of nice manners. They did you so much good.

After Charley had poured the tea she took two or three sips slowly, as if in contentment or deep thought or both, and then made a sudden pronouncement that set Pop choking.

'I should like to go to France,' she said.

'God Almighty,' Pop said. 'What for?'

Hot mustard stabbed at the back of his throat and set him coughing.

'For a holiday of course,' Ma said. 'I think it would do us all good to get some sun.'

Pop could think of nothing to say. He sat in meditative, flabbergasted silence while Mr Charlton let out a positive crow of delight and approval at what Ma had said.

'Heavens, that would be marvellous,' he said. 'That would be great. That little train again, that beach, that warm sea. Those little sweet grapes and the peaches. That food –'

He was suddenly overcome with an emotional desire to strike Pop in the back and actually did so. It was a thing he had never felt urged to do before, but its effect on Pop was only to stun him into a deeper more confused silence than ever.

'"Come unto these yellow sands and then take hands,"' Charley started quoting, at the same time getting up from the breakfast table. 'I've simply got to tell Mariette.'

Charley was off, Pop thought. That feller Keats again.

'We haven't gone yet,' Ma said.

'I'll call her anyway.'

While Mr Charlton went upstairs to call Mariette, whistling all the way up, and Ma sipped at her tea and little Oscar at his mother, Pop sat thinking. The first stunning surprise of Ma's pronouncement had passed. It now began to occur to him that the situation was not at all unlike that in which Charley, soon after his marriage, had suggested that Pop should give up the *Daily Mirror* as his daily newspaper and start instead to take *The Times*.

At the time that too had seemed a surprising, unthinkable, revolutionary thing to do. Then Pop remembered that quite a number of other people in the village, including Miss Pilchester, the Brigadier, and Sir George Bluff-Gore, all took *The Times* too and if they could do so why not he? Miss Pilchester was as poor as a church mouse; the Brigadier hadn't had a new suit for twenty years and generally wore socks that didn't match; and Sir George Bluff-Gore was so ham-strung with taxes that he couldn't afford to keep the ancestral Gore Court going and had had to sell it to Pop himself for demolition and then go and live in a stable. They were the aristocracy, of course, these people; they were the toffs; but if they could afford *The Times* so could he.

Now he didn't regret taking *The Times* at all. It gave you something, *The Times* did, though he wasn't quite sure what. Ma liked it too, though she still took the *Mirror* herself, otherwise she would never know what was in her stars. Nevertheless she got a big thrill out of the Saturday *Times* advertisements for rich and exotic foods and was always sending away for lists and catalogues. Such things didn't inspire Pop and he still thought there was nothing so good as roast beef and Yorkshire, rice pudding, lamb and mint sauce, and plenty of roast goose and apple sauce on Sundays. He supposed he might have to change some day, though he didn't see why.

Oscar had taken another five minutes of his mother when Ma pulled the cork of her nipple away from him with another gentle plop and turned him over to lie against her shoulder. The result of this was a series of sudden belches, each richer, louder and milkier than the first.

Ma said that that was better and it must be the gin she'd had last night.

Instinctively Oscar renewed his nuzzling for the breast. Ma said she might just as well turn herself into a four-ale bar and be done with it and gave a sudden deep sigh that had in it a certain note of weariness and even despair.

Pop felt suddenly concerned at this sigh and said:

'Ma, don't you really feel well? Tell me, my old duck.'

In reply Ma could only ask him how he would feel if someone had played football inside him for nine months, but it was a question for which Pop could think of no sensible answer and he was both glad and relieved to hear Mariette and Charley coming downstairs.

'As well as turning yourself into a bar three or four times a day. Somehow I think I'm getting too old for this lark.'

Ma, he thought, had never talked like this before. It struck him as being chronic. Too old? Damn it, she was only thirty-six.

'The trouble is this one's like you,' Ma said. 'Never satisfied.'

A moment later Mariette came in, her dark hair still loose from sleep, wearing a green silk dressing-gown and crimson slippers. In a new state of excitement she ran straight to Pop, who had a mouth full of sausage, mushroom and mustard, and started kissing him with a warm fervour that reminded him of Ma when he had first met her at the age of fifteen.

'Oh! wonderful, wonderful Pop. Oh! you're always so wonderful.'

What had he done now? Pop started to say.

'France!' she said. 'I've always wanted to go to France. When do we start? Do we all go?'

'Who said we were going to France?'

'You did, Charley did.' She turned excitedly to Ma, at the same time kissing Oscar on the back of his neck. 'You want to go to France, don't you, Ma?'

'That's what I just told Pop.'

'There you are – everybody wants to go. Oh! for that sun –' Mariette rolled her handsome body to and fro under its dressing-gown, her breasts rising in voluptuous expectation – 'I can't wait for that sun. It's amazing what that sun can do for you. Oh! to feel the heat of that sun.'

Pop listened with keen alertness. Perhaps it was, after all, the sun that she and Charley had been missing?

'Ah! the heat of the sun,' Charley said, '"Fear no more the heat of the sun –"'

Off again, Pop thought. Keats again. Mr Charlton started laughing happily and Mariette again rolled her shoulders ecstatically in her dressing-gown, laughing with him. Oscar made succulent noises at his mother's breast and Ma sipped with relish at her tea, so that suddenly, for some reason, Pop felt rather out in the cold about things. He couldn't get worked up at all.

'Is it right they eat frogs?' he said.

'Of course,' Charley said. 'And absolutely delicious they are too.'

'Good God.'

Pop felt mildly sick.

'Just the legs,' Charley said. 'They're exactly like chicken.'

Involuntarily Pop burst out laughing in his customary ringing fashion.

'Hear that, Ma? Frogs! Just like chicken.'

'They eat snails too,' Ma said, 'don't they?'

'Certainly. *Escargots de Bourgogne*. Wonderful too they are.'

Pop sat stunned over the breakfast table, open-mouthed at the sound of a new, strange language coming from Charley's lips.

'That was French,' Mariette said with both excitement and pride. 'Did you know Charley speaks French?'

'French? Where'd he pick that up?'

'Playing with French children,' Charley said. 'Every holiday.'

Ma said she was greatly relieved.

'That was the only thing that was worrying me,' she said. 'How we'd make ourselves understood.'

'He's going to teach me,' Mariette said. 'Anyway why don't we all learn?'

'Why not?' Charley said. 'I could teach you all a few simple phrases.'

Pop was speechless. Charley boy speaking French, Charley boy quoting Keats and Shakespeare and spending holidays abroad – there was no end to the surprises of his son-in-law.

Pensively Pop helped himself to marmalade and made a tentative suggestion that Charley boy should give him an example of one or two of the simple phrases.

'Certainly,' Charley said. '*Bonjour – Comment ça va, Monsieur Larkin?*'

'Eh?' Pop said.

Ma sat in silent admiration at these few but impressively fluent words, bemusedly rocking little Oscar backwards and forwards at her bosom. Marvelling too, Pop said, his mouth full of marmalade:

'And what the pipe does all that mean?'

'Good morning. How goes it? How are you?'

'I'm damned if I know,' Pop said. 'I'm getting a bit tangled up with this froggy lark.'

Ma started laughing, her body shaking like a vast jelly, so that for a moment little Oscar lost his grip on her. With a deft movement she heaved him back into his place at the bosom and said she could never get her tongue round that lot.

'Nor me neither,' Pop said.

'Oh! it's simple, it's easy,' Charley said. 'Just say it.'

'Me?' Pop said.

'Yes. Go on. Just repeat it. *Bonjour. Comment ça va?* or *comment allez-vous?* if you like. Same thing.'

'One thing at a time,' Pop said, 'as the girl said to the soldier. *Bonjour* – that it?'

'Splendid. *Bonjour. Comment ça va?*'

'*Bonjour. Comment ça va?*' Pop said, grinning now, his perkiness and confidence coming back. 'Any good?'

'Marvellous. You'd have a jolly fine accent in no time.'

Pop, feeling suddenly proud, started preening himself before Ma, languidly stroking his side linings with the back of one hand.

'Having French lessons now, Ma. Eh? What price that?'

Ma was proud too and looked at Pop in gleaming admiration.

'Oh! Pop, you'd pick it up in no time,' Mariette said.

'Always quick to learn,' Ma said. 'Sharp as a packet o' needles. No flies on Pop.'

Pop, increasingly thirsty for knowledge, preened himself again and said what about some more examples, Charley boy?

'*Au revoir,*' Charley said, '*À bientôt.*'

'What's that mean?'

'Goodbye. See you soon.'

'*Au revoir. À bientôt,*' Pop said swiftly. 'Easy. Like water running off a duck's back.'

Charley said again how marvellous it was and how, very soon, in no time at all, Pop could acquire an accent. Mariette actually applauded, so that suddenly there was no holding Pop, who got up smartly from the breakfast table, bowed to Ma and said:

'*Bonjour, madame. Comment ça va? Au revoir! À bientôt!*'

'Jolly fine!' Charley said and Ma started laughing so much that little Oscar lost his grip on the bosom again. Milk flowed down his pink dumpling face as Ma rocked up and down.

'Can you see us, over there, Ma?' Pop said. 'Eating frogs' legs and snails and me talking froggy?'

'Oh! I can't wait!' Mariette said and again her body went through its voluptuous rolling under the dressing-gown. 'I just can't wait. I'll just lie all day in the sun in a bikini.'

'That's what I'd like to take too,' Ma said. 'A bikini. A bit of sun would firm me up.'

The prospect of Ma being firmed up in a bikini fired Pop so madly that he almost shouted at Charley:

'All right, Charley boy, when do we start?'

'Well, the children will be on holiday in August – that's if we're all going.'

'Of course we're all going,' Ma said. 'It'll be education for the lot of us. Like telly is.'

'All right then. I suggest the third week in August. That'll avoid the French national holiday, which is on the fifteenth.'

Charley boy again – knowing everything. Full marks for Charley. 'Perfick!' Pop said. *'À bientôt!'*

Pop, sitting down at table again, poured himself another cup of tea while Mr Charlton marvelled once more how swiftly, fluently, and excellently Pop had acquired himself an accent.

'How do we get there?' Pop said. 'Swim?'

'I suggest we take the Rolls if it's all right with you.'

'Good God,' Pop said. 'Never thought of that.'

'They won't over-charge us, will they?' Ma said, 'if they see the Rolls?'

'I'll get the Beau Rivage to quote everything first,' Charley said. 'Taxes, *taxe de séjour*, service, everything. I think Mr Dupont will be fair – that's if he's still there. But in France it's always as well to fix everything beforehand.'

A great fixer, Charley. A marvellous fellow for figures, discounts, bills, and all that. In the last six months Pop had left him to deal with all paper work, forms, returns, and what Pop called the dodgy stuff. A great help, Charley.

Pop in fact was more than pleased that Charley, after marrying Mariette, had had sense enough to throw up his job at the tax inspector's office to take up more respectable, more sensible employment. It was worse than awful to think of having anybody in the family connected with the tax lark. Wouldn't do at all. Worse than having somebody who'd been doing time.

In recognition of Charley's sensible behaviour Pop had given him and Mariette five hundred laying pullets. That had set them up in the egg lark. It paid pretty well on the whole, the egg lark, if you worked it right. It was another way of getting doh-ray-me out of the government before they had a chance to get it out of you. In less than a year Charley and Mariette had made enough profit to buy themselves another five hundred pullets and were doing very well for themselves, except that Charley would insist on making proper income tax returns about it all, which was a very bad habit to get into, Pop considered, whichever way you looked at it.

As to the house he had promised to build them out of material from Sir George Bluff-Gore's mansion at Gore Court, when he pulled it down, he'd been much too busy on a variety of other larks even to get round to the house's demolition. It would have to wait a bit. Most of his time had been taken up with a big deal about army surplus, the surplus consisting of all sorts of unlikely things like tins of beetroot in vinegar, rat-traps, body belts, brass collar studs, gherkins in mustard, rubber shoe heels, and bottles of caper sauce: the sort of things that nobody else seemed to think that anybody wanted. Pop knew better. There was always somebody who wanted something somewhere. He had to admit the beetroot in vinegar and the gherkins in mustard were turning out a bit sticky though.

But there was no doubt about the change from taxes to eggs suiting Charley all right. Charley had put on a bit of weight and looked brown. He always ate hearty breakfasts and had stopped worrying over his health and whether he was going to wake up every morning with appendicitis or not. He looked in every way a fit, virile young man. All the more puzzling, Pop thought, that he didn't seem to be able to translate it all into the proper channels. He had to admit that Charley had always been a slow starter – but married nearly a year and no children, that was really a bit dodgy. He wouldn't have thought a young healthy couple like them would have found it all that hard.

'Of course,' Charley said now, 'there's the trouble of passports.'

'Trouble?' Mariette said. 'What trouble?'

With as much tact as he could muster, Mr Charlton reminded them all of the delicate and rather difficult situation concerning Pop and Ma.

'Perhaps it would have been better if you'd got married after all,' he said.

'Well, I suppose we still could,' Pop said, but not with apparent enthusiasm. 'But it's a bit of a palaver.'

'I'm willing,' Ma said blandly. 'Always was.'

Mr Charlton pondered briefly on this and finally said he supposed the solution was that all the children could go on Pop's passport, leaving Ma to take hers out in her maiden name, though he was still not quite sure what that was.

Placidly Ma fondled the head of her seventh child against her large cheek, not unduly concerned.

'Well, I suppose if everybody had their rights,' she said, 'I'm still Flo Parker.'

Pop looked painfully startled, almost embarrassed, more at the word rights than anything else, but also as if he were actually being introduced to Ma by name for the first time. It was a bit unnerving, hearing Ma called Flo Parker.

'Oh! well,' Ma said, 'I expect it'll sort itself out in the wash.'

'The froggies are broadminded,' Pop said and laughed uproariously, 'if all I hear is true. Paris and all that lark, eh?'

'Leave it to Charley,' Mariette said. 'He'll arrange everything. Not the clothes though. Ma, I'll need masses. I'll need a million new frocks.'

Ma had now finished giving little Oscar his breakfast. The huge melons of her bosom were back in the folds of her purple blouse.

'Talking about clothes, Pop,' she said, 'I think it would be nice if you took your yachting cap. The one you bought once for that fancy-dress ball.'

That was a jolly good idea, Pop said. Perfick. Just the thing for the froggy seaside.

A moment later Ma was putting little Oscar back into the luscious folds of his pram and Pop was at the door, suddenly remembering there was work to do.

'Must go. Got to see Joe Rawlings about the straw deal at half past nine.' He stood erect and perky, holding the door knob, and then permitted himself the luxury of a bow.

'*Au revoir!* see you *bientôt!*'

'*Au revoir,*' Mr Charlton and Mariette said together, laughing. '*À bientôt! Adieu!*'

At the same time little Oscar made a series of noises compounded of wind, slobber, and his mother's milk, so that Ma said if they weren't all careful they'd have him at it too.

Outside the rain had slackened, almost ceased. Pop drove the Rolls from a junk yard deep in puddles to a road overhung by oak shadow from which dripped great drops of humid July rain.

Half a mile down the road a figure was walking under an umbrella, wearing a military raincoat of the kind once known as a gorblimey and carrying a grey string bag in his hands. It was Pop's old friend the retired Brigadier.

Like Ma, Pop always felt uncommonly sorry for the Brigadier: always so erect and yet so down at heel, with odd socks, patched elbows, darned shirt collars, and that half-lost, under-nourished leathery look about him. But today, under the umbrella, in the tattered raincoat, and carrying the empty string shopping bag, he looked, if anything, more like a walking skeleton than ever.

Reaching him, Pop drew up the Rolls, leaned out of the window and said:

'*Bonjour*, general. *Comment ça va?*'

The Brigadier stopped sharply and looked immensely startled.

'*Très bien, merci*, Larkin,' he said. '*Et vous aussi j'espère?*'

At this Pop looked even more startled than the Brigadier and could think of nothing to say at all except:

'*Au revoir! À bientôt!*'

'Bless my soul, Larkin, you're in a hurry, aren't you?' the Brigadier said. 'What's all this?'

'Started to learn froggy,' Pop said. 'All going to France. For a holiday. Place in Brittany.'

'Entire brood?' the Brigadier said.

'The whole shoot,' Pop said. 'Baby an' all.'

'Cost you a pretty penny, won't it?'

'Who cares?' Pop thundered. 'Ma wants to go. Mariette wants to go. Charley wants to go. Everybody wants to go. What about you? Why don't you come too? More the merrier, general!'

The Brigadier, who found it hard on his meagre pension to afford a day in London every six weeks or so and who couldn't remember the last time he had had a holiday at all, much less one in France, merely stood bemusedly in the rain, involuntarily shaking his head and having no word of any kind to say until Pop, with a burst of expansive exuberance, invited him to hop in.

'No. No thanks. I like the walk. Part of my constitutional.'

'Still raining. Glad to drop you.'

The Brigadier bemusedly thanked him again and said he really rather preferred Shanks if Larkin didn't mind.

'Just what you like best, general,' Pop said breezily. 'How about France though? Do you a power o' good, general. Get some sun on that back of yours.' The general he thought, didn't look half well as he stood there in the rain. No doubt about it, the mackintosh and the rain made him look, if anything, more drawn than ever. 'Find room for a little 'un like you in the Rolls. Return trip won't cost you a penny.'

In a low circumspect voice the Brigadier inquired if Pop really meant he was contemplating taking the Rolls?

'Course,' Pop said. 'Going to fly the damn thing over. New idea. Over there in two ticks of a donkey's tail.'

'Good God,' the Brigadier said. His white moustaches seemed to bristle and the stiff prawns of his eyebrows leapt upward sharply. 'Bless my soul.'

'Got to get out and see life, general!' Pop said suddenly, in a burst of enthusiastic admonishment. 'See how the other half lives. See the world. What about it?'

The Brigadier, who had spent the better part of forty years in places like Delhi, Singapore, Hyderabad, and Hong Kong, had seen all of the world he wanted to see and could only thank Pop a third time in polite, irresolute tones, adding at the same time that he thought the thing was hardly in his line.

'Well, plenty o' time to change your mind, general old boy,' Pop said. 'Get me on the blower if you do. Not going to hop in after all?'

'Thanks all the same, I won't. Only going as far as the shop to get a little mouse-trap.'

Pop said he was sorry to hear that the Brigadier was troubled with mice. Ma hated them.

'Meant the cheese,' the Brigadier explained. He would dearly have loved a cheese of a better, more imaginative kind than mouse-trap, but the budget wouldn't run to it. 'You'll have beautiful cheeses in Brittany. Delectable.'

Pop had never heard of the word delectable. He marvelled silently and then started to push in the car gears.

'Ah! well, can't stop. Must push on. *Au revoir*, general! See you *bientôt!*'

Pop raised his hand in breezy, friendly farewell and the Rolls drove opulently away. The Brigadier, cadaverous, upright, and still both bemused and startled, stood for some time under the umbrella in the lessening rain, forgetting even to say *'Adieu!'* and merely thinking of the delicious, delectable cheeses one could eat in Brittany and listening to the sound of the Rolls hooter, melodious and triumphant as a hunting horn, cutting through the dripping quietness of the meadows, the oak-woods, and the steaming country lanes.

How should he have the mouse-trap? On toast or *au naturel*? Still shaken by the opulence of Pop's entrance, news, and exit, he decided to have it on toast. In that way he could fool himself, perhaps, that it was really *Camembert*.

· 2 ·

When Pop drew up the Rolls outside the Hôtel Beau Rivage at half past six in the evening of the last day of August a gale was raging in from the Atlantic that made even the sturdy blue fishing boats in the most sheltered corners of the little port look like a battered wreckage of half-drowned match-stalks.

Dancing arches of white spray ran up and down the grey quay walls like raging dinosaurs forty feet high. Rain and spray beat at the windows of the little hotel, crashing pebbles on the shutter-boards. A wind as cold as winter ran ceaselessly round the harbour with unbroken shriekings and occasional whistles like those of Mr Charlton's much-loved, long-distant little train.

'For crying out gently, Charley,' Pop said. 'Where's this? Where the pipe have we come to? Lapland?'

With a sudden feeling of low, cold dismay Mr Charlton stared silently at the Beau Rivage. The hotel seemed altogether so much smaller, so much shabbier, so much more dilapidated and inexclusive than he remembered it being in the last summer before the war. It seemed to have shrunk somehow. He had fondly pictured it as large and gay. Now it looked dismal, dark, and pokey. Its style of creosoted Tudor looked incredibly flimsy and insecure and now and then the blistered brown shutters sprang violently on their hooks and seemed, like the rest of the hotel, ready to collapse, disintegrate, and wash away. On the little outside terrace rows of coloured fairy lights, strung necklace fashion between half a dozen plane trees pollarded to the appearance of yellowish skinning skeletons, were swinging wildly about in the wind, one or two of them occasionally crashing on to the concrete below. There was very little Beau about it, Mr Charlton thought, and not much Rivage.

'Well, I suppose we ought to go in,' he said at last and suddenly led the way with an appearance of remarkably enthusiastic alacrity into the hotel, hastily followed by Ma carrying little Oscar, then Primrose and Montgomery submerged under one raincoat, the twins, Victoria and Mariette under one umbrella, and finally Pop carrying two suitcases and a zip canvas bag.

Pop was wearing thin blue linen trousers, a yellow sleeveless shirt, yellow canvas shoes, and his yachting cap in anticipation of a long spell of French hot weather. In the short passage from the car to the hotel he half-rowed, half-paddled through rising lakes of Atlantic rain and spray. Several times he was convinced he was going under. Once he slipped down and one of the suitcases was blown out of his hands and began to wash away along the quayside. He grabbed it, battled on, and a few moments later found himself shipwrecked inside the vestibule of the hotel, where he was at once assailed by a powerful smell of linseed oil, drain-pipes, French cigarettes, and leaking gas. One single electric bulb burned above the reception desk in the gloom of early evening and this was flickering madly up and down.

When Pop was able to get to his feet again he was more than glad to observe that Charley was already in charge of things at the reception desk. Charley, even if he didn't feel it, looked calm, self-possessed, even authoritative. He was speaking in French. Pop liked it when Charley spoke in French. It seemed to ease and resolve the most anxious of situations.

'*Et les passeports, M'sieur?*'

Behind the reception desk a small, bald, paste-coloured man in pince-nez, with grey, hungry cheeks and brown mole-like eyes, spoke to Mr Charlton in a voice of schoolmasterly irritation, as if hoping to catch him out. But in a split second Mr Charlton had everything weighed up. Swiftly the passports were on the desk: Mr and Mrs Charlton's, Pop's with the six children included on it and Ma's in her maiden name of Flo Parker.

'*Et qu'est-ce que vous avez comme bagage?*'

With a commanding, irritated palm the man in pince-nez struck a large desk bell such a resonant blow that little Oscar, startled, began loudly weeping.

Ma, sitting reposedly in one of several decrepit basket chairs, at once decided that the best way of meeting the situation was to give him a little refreshment.

A few moments later an astonished elderly concierge in gumboots, sou'wester, and plastic mackintosh arrived from dark regions somewhere behind the reception desk in time to see little Oscar bury his face in the contented continent of Ma. The hungry-faced man in pince-nez looked astonished too.

Pop then remembered that there was a good deal of baggage in the car, Ma and Mariette having brought three suitcases each, mostly full of beach-wear, swim-wear, and summer dresses, and he followed the concierge into the driving, howling August rain.

Coming back, both shoes full of water, he saw Charley in process of being lectured, as it seemed, by the man in pince-nez. He looked extremely annoyed and seemed to be accusing Charley of some act of irresponsibility. 'What's up?' Pop called.

'He says he wasn't aware that one of the children was so small.'

'Tell him we've only just had him,' Ma said and moved herself as if to expose her bosom to larger, fuller, and more public gaze. 'I'm trying to fatten him up as fast as I can.'

Earnestly, in French, Mr Charlton spent some moments explaining to the cold eyes behind the pince-nez the reasons for little Oscar's immaturity. The man in pince-nez seemed not only unimpressed by this but more irritated than ever and began to snatch various huge brass-lobed keys from their hooks.

'And tell him we want a cup o' tea,' Ma said and moved with squeaks of wicker irritation in her chair. 'I'm dying for one.'

With mounting impatience the man in pince-nez crashed the keys back on their hooks.

'He says –'

'Don't he speak English?' Ma said. 'I'll bet he does or else he wouldn't have understood what I said just now. You speak English, don't you?'

'*Oui, madame.* Yes.'

'All right then, why don't you speak it? Instead of standing there talking a foreign language?'

'*Oui, madame.*'

'We all want a nice cup of tea. Quick. And if you can't make it I soon will.'

'But in twenty minutes you may have dinner, madame.'

'I daresay I may, but that's not tea, is it?'

The man in pince-nez snatched at a telephone, as if about to pour rasping orders into it, and then stopped.

'*Combien de* – how many teas, madame?'

'Everybody,' Ma said. 'All ten of us.'

With piercing but sightless frigidity the man in pince-nez stared at the sight of little Oscar busily engaged in taking refreshment.

'Even the baby, madame?'

'Oh! he'll have gin,' Ma said. 'He likes it better.'

With cold and extravagant restraint the man in pince-nez put the telephone back in its place and walked out, at the same time calling to the concierge. '*Dix-sept, dix-neuf, vingt-quatre, vingt-huit,*' as if these were orders for prisoners going to an execution.

Pop stood looking at his new canvas shoes. They were full of water. It was running out of them in a stream. Water was coursing down his backbone, through his trousers, and out of his shirt and socks.

There was a sudden smell of fried fish in the air and Ma, catching it, said:

'Smells like fish-and-chips for dinner, Pop. Why don't we cancel the tea and have it later? Go down well with the fish.'

An old, pre-marital nervousness seized Mr Charlton.

'I doubt very much if we ought to countermand the order now –'

'Oh! no, don't let's,' Mariette said. 'I'm dying for a cup.'

'Me too,' Ma said. 'All right.'

'Like a nice glass of hot port,' Pop said. 'I know that. With cloves and cinnamon. Like I rigged up last Christmas.'

'Or else a Guinness,' Ma said.

A fusillade of pebbles, sharp as shrapnel, hit the half-closed shutters. A cold blast chiselled at the door-cracks and the smell of fried fish grew stronger. The smell reminded Ma that she was hungry. She said so in a loud voice and Mr Charlton thought it a good moment to draw her attention to various framed certificates, diplomas, and illustrated addresses hanging about the walls, so much evidence of the excellent, even high-class *cuisine* of the Beau Rivage.

'*Diplôme d'Honneur* Strasbourg 1907. Lyon 1912 and 1924. Marseille 1910, '27, and '29. Paris, six times. Dijon, 1932. Chevalier de Taste Vin – *Foire Gastronomique* 1929 –'

'See, Ma?' Pop said. 'Cooking prizes.'

'Anything for this year?' Ma said.

Mr Charlton was saved the necessity of finding an answer to this pertinent question by the arrival of the tea.

The tea was in a huge white metal coffee pot, with thick white coffee cups to drink it from, and the bill was on the tray.

While Mariette sugared and milked the cups Pop, moving like a deep-sea diver who has only just surfaced, dripping water from every thread, picked up the bill and gazed at it.

'How much is two thousand three hundred and fifty francs, Charley boy?'

At this moment Victoria started crying.

'You take her, Mariette,' Ma said. 'You know how she is.'

Whispering consolatory noises, Mariette took Victoria out, and Mr Charlton, trying in the circumstances to be both discreet and casual, said:

'Oh! about two pounds. Just over.'

'*For tea?*' Ma yelled.

For one moment her bosom seemed to rise into air like an outraged, affronted puff-ball.

'I thought you said it was cheap?' Pop said.

'Well, of course, you've got to remember – in France –'

'Here,' Ma said. 'Hold Oscar.'

Mr Charlton found himself suddenly holding Oscar. Oscar, like Pop, was wet. Ma hastily covered up her bosom and bore down on tea and teacups, stunned to impotent silence while Mr Charlton said:

'After all, tea in France is probably a pound a pound. Perhaps twenty-five shillings. I was reading in *The Times* only the other day –'

'And hot milk!' Ma said. 'Feel this! They brought hot milk.'

No one had any time to comment on this outrage before Mariette and Victoria came back, Mariette tightly holding her sister's hand.

'Hot milk, Mariette!' Ma said. 'Two pounds and over for a cuppa tea and they bring hot milk. Hullo, what's the matter with you?'

'Nothing.'

Mariette looked white and shaken.

'Look as if you'd seen a ghost or something. Look as if you'd had the bill and not Pop.'

Mariette's lip was trembling. She was taking long, hard breaths.

'Whatever's the matter?' Ma said.

'I'd rather not talk about it. Just something out there.'

'You can't sit down!' Victoria said. 'You have to stand up!'

'Good God,' Ma said. 'Think of me.'

There was nothing for it but to give Mariette the strongest cup of tea she could pour out. This was several shades paler than straw and looked and tasted like discoloured water flavoured ever so faintly with boiled onions.

After that Ma swished the tea-pot powerfully round and round in an effort to bring strength where it was most needed, saying at the same time:

'It'll be mice next. I know. I smelt 'em when we came in.'

As if in answer to an outrageous signal the man in pince-nez appeared out of a door marked 'Bureau' with the habit of a hungry burrowing mole. He busied himself for some moments behind the desk, sniffing and rattling keys, and then asked Mr Charlton if he had yet filled up the forms.

Mr Charlton had not filled up forms. There were ten of them. He now gave Oscar to Montgomery, took out his fountain pen, and sat down in one of the many decrepit, disintegrating wicker chairs. His hands were damp from Oscar.

As he started on the forms Ma called:

'I bet they haven't got television. Ask him, Charley. Ask him if they got telly.'

Mr Charlton looked up and asked the man in pince-nez, in French, if they'd got television.

'*Pas de télévision.*'

'No telly, Ma, I'm afraid.'

Pop was stunned. For crying out gently.

'Terrible. You'd never believe it,' he said. 'Never believe it, Ma, would you?'

'Well, good thing Montgomery brought the radio,' Ma said. 'Turn it on somebody. Let's have a tune. Should have brought the new Hi-Fi.'

Primrose switched on the portable radio at full blast and dance music roared forth, momentarily louder than the wind, now punctuated by occasional thunder, that ripped like a half hurricane across the port.

Involuntarily startled, the man in pince-nez rang the desk bell, setting Oscar crying again.

'Ask him if there's a bar,' Pop said.

Mr Charlton, who in the confusion was having difficulty in remembering the date of his own birthday, looked up to ask the man in pince-nez if there was a bar.

'*Oui, m'sieur. Par ici.*'

With one thin finger he indicated that the bar lay somewhere in regions beyond the Bureau, in the direction where Mariette and Victoria had found life so inconvenient for their sex.

'Yes: it seems there's a bar.'

'Good egg,' Pop said. 'That's something.' With relief he abandoned the tepid, onioned tea. 'I think I'll buzz round and have a snifter.'

'Not on your nelly!' Ma said. 'Take hold of Oscar. I expect he wants changing. That's why he's roaring again.'

The concierge came back. Pop took over Oscar. It was now so dark that Mr Charlton could hardly see to write the forms. A tremendous crash of thunder broke immediately above the hotel, setting the shutters rattling, the radio crackling, and the single dim light beside the telephone quaking even more like a candle in a wind.

The man in pince-nez spoke suddenly in French, with a slight sense of outrage, as if still offended by Ma's charge about speaking in a foreign language. Mr Charlton translated:

'He says you can go up to your rooms now if you want to.'

'Well, what the merry Ellen does he think we're sitting here waiting for?' Ma said. 'Christmas?'

Oscar had stopped crying. The concierge picked up the remainder of the baggage and the children their things. Mr Charlton said he'd come up soon, since the forms would take him at least another twenty minutes to finish, not that he'd even finish them then, in view of remembering all the birthdays.

'My belly's rattling,' Petunia said. Zinnia said hers was too and they couldn't stand it much longer.

'We won't bother to unpack,' Ma said. She knew Pop was starved. She was getting pretty well starved herself. 'I'll just change Oscar and wash and then we'll all come down.'

Everybody was ready to go upstairs except Ma and Mr Charlton when a fresh and more stupendous crash of thunder occurred. The light above the telephone went completely out, came on, went out, came on, and repeated the process six more times before going out altogether.

In the comparative silence after the thunder a strange new sound crept into the air. It was that of one of the wicker chairs squeaking, like a horde of mice, in protest.

It was the chair containing Ma.

'Here, hold Oscar, somebody,' Pop said. 'Ma's stuck.'

Mariette took Oscar. Pop went over to Ma, solicitous but unsurprised; it had happened before. Ma had always had difficulty in getting her two-yard bulk into the confines of strange furniture and still more difficulty in getting it out again.

'Give us a hand, Charley,' Pop said, 'before she goes under for the third time.'

Pop and Charley started to pull at Ma, who began to laugh with huge jellified ripples. The man in pince-nez looked on with frigid, withdrawn, offended eyes. Pop and Charley pulled at Ma harder than ever, but with no result except to set her laughing with louder shrieks, more fatly.

Presently Ma went strengthless. It became impossible to budge her. Above the telephone the light came on again, illuminating Ma as a collapsing balloon that would never rise.

'Ma, you're not helping,' Pop said. He pleaded for some small coopera-tion. 'If you don't help you'll have to go round with the damn thing stuck on your behind for the rest of your natural.'

Ma laughed more than ever. The vast milky hillock of her bosom, deeply cleft, rose and fell in mighty breaths. Her whole body started to sink lower and lower and suddenly Pop realized that even if she survived, the chair never would.

He started to urge Charley to pull again. In a sudden wrench the two of them pulled Ma to her feet and she stood there for some seconds with the chair attached to her great buttocks like a sort of tender.

Suddenly, with shrieks, she sank back again. Another peal of thunder, more violent than any other, rent the air above the hotel. The man in pince-nez pleaded *'La chaise, madame – je vous prie – la chaise!'* and for the ninth or tenth time the light went out.

When it came on again Ma was on her feet. Behind her the chair was flatter than a door-mat and by the telephone the man in pince-nez had his head in his hands.

'Madame, madame, je vous –' he was saying. In distress the necessary language for the occasion did not come to him for some moments. When it did so his English was sadly broken up: 'Madame, please could – Oh! madame, I ask – I please –'

With incredible swiftness Pop came forward to defend Ma. Irately he strode over to the man in pince-nez and struck the desk a severe blow with his fist, speaking peremptorily and with voluble rapidity.

'Qu'est-ce qu'il y a?' he shouted, 'and *comment ça va* and *comment allez-vous* and *avez-vous bien dormi* and *qu'est-ce que vous avez à manger* and *à bientôt* san fairy ann and all that lark!'

The little man in pince-nez looked as if he'd been hit with a pole-axe. His mouth fell open sharply, but except for a muted gurgle he had nothing to say. A moment later Pop and Ma started to go upstairs, followed by the children, Ma still laughing, Pop glad in his heart of the excellent tuition given by Charley in various French phrases likely to be of use in emergency.

At the foot of the stairs he paused to turn with pride and perkiness to look back.

'Accent all right, Charley boy?'

'Perfick,' Mr Charlton said. 'Absolutely perfick.'

Pop waved a mildly deprecating hand.

'Très bon, you mean, *très bon,'* he said. 'Don't forget we're in France now, Charley-boy. We don't take lessons for nothing, do we? *À bientôt!'*

· 3 ·

Nearly an hour later, when Ma brought the children downstairs for dinner, closely followed by Charley and Mariette, Pop was already sitting moodily in a corner of the *salle à manger*, a room of varnished, ginger-coloured matchboard and glass built like a greenhouse shrouded with yellowing lace-curtains against the westward side of the hotel. Some squares of glass were coloured blue or ruby. A few, broken altogether, had been patched up with squares of treacle-brown paper and it seemed generally that the whole ramshackle structure, battered by the Atlantic storm, might at any moment fall down, disintegrate, and blow away.

Driven by ravenous hunger and thirst to the bar, Pop had found it furnished with a solitary stool, a yard of dusty counter, a dozing grey cat, and a vase of last year's heather. The stool had two legs instead of three and all about the place was that curious pungent odour that Ma had been so quick to notice earlier in the day: as if a drain has been left open or a gas-tap on.

In the *salle à manger*, in contrast to the silent half-darkness of the bar, a noisy, eager battle was being waged by seven or eight French families against the howl of wind and rain, the tossing lace curtains, and more particularly against what appeared to be dishes of large unpleasant pink spiders, in reality *langoustines*. A mad cracking of claws filled the air and one plump Frenchman sat eating, wearing his cap, a large white one: as if for protection against something, perhaps flying claws or bread or rain.

Three feet from Pop's table a harassed French waitress with a marked limp and loose peroxide hair came to operate, every desperate two minutes or so, a large patent wooden-handled bread-slicer about the size of an old-fashioned sewing machine: a cross somewhere between a guillotine and a chaff-cutter.

This instrument made crude groaning noises, like an old tram trying to start. Slices of bread, savagely chopped from yard-long loaves, flew about in all directions, dropping all over the place until harassed waiters and waitresses bore them hurriedly off to eager, waiting guests. These, Pop noticed, at once crammed them ravenously into their mouths and even gluttonously mopped their plates with them.

Presently the rest of the family arrived: Mariette immaculate and perfumed in a beautiful sleeveless low-cut dress of emerald green that made her shoulders and upper breast glow a warm olive colour, Ma in a mauve woollen dress and a royal blue jumper on top to keep out the cold. Ma had plenty of Chanel No. 5 on, still convinced that the hotel smelled not only of mice but a lot of other things besides.

As the family walked in all the French families suddenly stopped eating. The French, Charley had once told Pop, were the *élite* of Europe. Now they stopped ramming bread into their mouths like famished prisoners and gaped at the bare, astral shoulders of Mariette, Ma's great mauve and blue balloon of a body, and the retinue of children behind it.

Most of the older French women, Pop thought, seemed to be wearing discoloured woollen sacks. The younger ones, who were nearly all tallow-coloured, bruise-eyed, and flat-chested, wore jeans. It was hard to tell any of them from boys and in consequence Pop felt more than usually proud of Mariette, who looked so fleshily, elegantly, and provocatively a girl.

Presently the waitress with the limp brought the menu and then with not a moment to spare hopped off to work the bread machine.

'Well, what's to eat, Charley boy?' Pop said, rubbing his hands. 'Something good I hope, old man, I'm starving.'

Mr Charlton consulted the menu with a certain musing, studious air of English calm.

'By the way, Charley,' Pop said, 'what's "eat" in French? Haven't learned any words today.'

It was Pop's honest resolve to learn, if possible, a few new French words every day.

'*Manger,*' Charley said. 'Same word as the thing in the stable – manger.'

Pop sat mute and astounded. Manger – a simple thing like that. Perfickly wonderful. Unbelievable. Manger. He sat back and prepared to listen to Charley reading out the menu with the awe he deserved.

'Well, to begin with there are *langoustines.* They're a kind of small lobster. Speciality of the Atlantic coast. Then there's *saucisson à la mode d'ici* – that's a sort of sausage they do here. *Spécialité de la maison,* I shouldn't wonder. Hot, I expect. Probably awfully good. Then *pigeons à la Gautier* – I expect that's pigeons in some sort of wine sauce. And afterwards fruit and cheese.'

'Sounds jolly *bon,*' Pop said.

Charley said he thought it ought to satisfy and Ma at once started remonstrating with Montgomery, Primrose, Victoria, and the twins about eating so much bread. She said they'd never want their dinners if they went on stuffing bread down.

'What shall we drink?' Charley said.

'Port,' Pop said. He too was stuffing down large quantities of bread, trying to stave off increasing stabs and rumbles of hunger. Ma agreed about the port. It would warm them all up, she said.

'I doubt if they'll have port.'

'Good God,' Pop said. '*What?* I thought you said the Froggies lived on wine?'

'Well, they do. But it's their own. Port isn't. I suggest we drink *vin rosé*. That'll go well with the fish and the pigeon.'

The harassed waitress with the limp, freed momentarily of bread-cutting, arrived a moment later to tell Charley, in French, that there were, after all, no *langoustines*.

'Sorry, no more *langoustines*,' Mr Charlton said. 'They've got *friture* instead.'

'What's *friture?*'

'Fried sardines.'

Ma choked; she felt she wanted to be suddenly and violently sick.

'Oh! fresh ones of course,' Charley said. 'Probably caught this afternoon.'

'In that lot?' Pop said and waved a disbelieving hand in the general direction of the howling, blackening gale that threatened increasingly to blow away the *salle à manger*.

A second later a vast flash of lightning seemed to sizzle down the entire length of roof glass like a celestial diamond-cutter. A Frenchwoman rose hysterically and rushed from the room. The chaff-cutter guillotine attacked yet another loaf with louder and louder groans and a long black burst of thunder struck the hotel to the depth of its foundations.

Alarmed too, the children ate more bread. Pop ate more bread and was in fact still eating bread when the *friture* arrived.

'They're only tiddlers!' the twins said. 'They're only tiddlers!'

'Sardines never grow any bigger,' Charley said, 'otherwise they wouldn't be sardines.'

'About time they did then,' Ma said, peering dubiously at piled scraps of fish, 'that's all.'

'*Bon appétit!*' Mr Charlton said, and proceeded enthusiastically to attack the *friture*.

Pop, turning to the attack too, found himself facing a large plateful of shrivelled dark brown objects which immediately fell to pieces at the touch of a fork. Scorched fragments of fish flew flakily about in all directions. The few crumbs that he was able to capture, impale on his fork and at last transfer to his mouth tasted, he thought, exactly like the unwanted scraps left over at the bottom of a bag of fish-and-chips.

'Shan't get very fat on these,' Ma said.

In a low depressed voice Pop agreed. Ma's great bulk, which filled half the side of one length of the table, now and then quivered in irritation and presently she was eating the *friture* with her fingers, urging the children to do likewise.

The children, in silent despair, ate more bread. Savagely the guillotine bread-cutter worked overtime, drowning conversation. And presently the limping waitress brought the *vin rosé*, which Charley tasted.

'Delicious,' he said with mounting enthusiasm. 'Quite delicious.'

Ma drank too and suddenly felt a quick sharp stream of ice descend to her bowels, cold as charity.

At last the multitudinous remains of the *friture* were taken away, plates piled high with brown wreckage, and Ma said it looked like the feeding of the five thousand. Pop drank deep of *vin rosé*, raised his glass to everybody, and unable to think of very much to say remarked mournfully:

'Well, cheers, everybody. Well, here we are.'

'We certainly are,' Ma said. 'You never spoke a truer word.'

After a short interval the *saucisson à la mode d'ici* arrived. This consisted of a strange object looking like a large pregnant sausage-roll, rather scorched on top. Slight puffs of steam seemed to be issuing from the exhausts at either end.

Ma remarked that at least it was hot and Pop, appetite now whetted to the full by another sharp draught or two of *vin rosé*, prepared to attack the object on his plate by cutting it directly through the middle.

To his complete dismay the force of the cut, meeting hard resistance from the surface of scorched crust, sent the two pieces hurtling in the air. Both fell with a low thud to the floor.

'Don't touch it! Don't touch it!' Ma said. 'Mice everywhere.'

'I'll order another,' Charley said. *'Ma'moiselle!'*

In silent patience Pop waited, but by the time a waitress could be spared from the bondage of bread-cutting the rest of the family had finished the battle with the *saucisson à la mode d'ici*.

With gloom, drinking more *vin rosé* to fortify himself, Pop waited while Charley explained to the waitress the situation about the unfortunate disappearance of his second course.

The waitress seemed dubious, even unimpressed. She simply stared coldly at Pop's empty plate as if knowing perfectly well he had eaten what had been on there and crushingly uttered the single word *'Supplément'*.

'She says if you have another you'll have to pay extra,' Charley said.

'Better order another bottle of *vin rosy* instead, Charley,' Pop said.

Weakly he started to eat more bread. He had, he thought, never eaten so much bread in his life. He no longer wondered why the guillotine worked overtime.

Suddenly thunder roared again, faintly echoed by the rumblings of his own belly, and presently the little man in pince-nez appeared, making his furtive mole-like way from table to table. When he saw the Larkins, however, he stood some distance off, in partly obsequious retreat, an uneasy grimace on his face, his hands held together.

Once he bowed. Mr Charlton bowed too and Ma grinned faintly in reply.

'Nice to see that,' Mr Charlton said. 'Typical French. He's come to see if everything's all right.'

'Why don't we tell him?' Ma said.

'What do we have next?' the twins said. 'What do we have next?'

'Pigeons,' Pop said. The thought of stewed pigeons made his mouth water. In wine sauce too. 'Pigeons.'

'We want baked beans on toast!' the twins said. 'And cocoa.'

'Quiet!' Pop thundered. 'I'll have order.'

A moment later a waitress, arriving with a fourth plate of bread, proceeded to announce to Mr Charlton a fresh and disturbing piece of news. There were, after all, no pigeons.

Pop felt too weak to utter any kind of exclamation about this second, deeper disappointment.

'There's rabbit,' Charley told him, 'instead.'

Instantly Pop recoiled in pale, fastidious horror.

'Not after myxo!' he said. 'No! Charley, I couldn't. I can't touch 'em after myxo!'

Myxomatosis, the scourge of the rabbit tribe, had affected Pop very deeply. No one else in the family had been so moved by the plague and its results. But to Pop the thought of eating rabbits was now as great a nausea as the thought of eating nightingales.

'It started here in France too,' he said. 'The Froggies were the ones who first started it.'

'Have an omelette,' Charley said cheerfully.

'They don't suit him,' Ma said. 'They always give him heartburn.'

Pop could only murmur in a low, dispassionate voice that he had to have something, somehow, soon. Heartburn or no heartburn. Even an omelette.

'A steak then,' Charley said. 'With chips.'

At this Pop cheered up a little, saying that a steak would suit him.

'*Alors, un filet bifteck pour monsieur,*' Charley said, '*avec pommes frites.*'

'Biff-teck! Biff-teck!' the twins started shouting, punching each other, laughing loudly. 'Biff-teck! Biff-you! Biff-you! Biff-teck!'

Pop was too weak to cry 'Quiet!' this time and from a distance the man in pince-nez stared in disapproval at the scene, so that Ma said:

'Sssh! Mr Dupont's looking.'

'That isn't Mr Dupont,' Charley said. 'He's only the manager. Mr Dupont's dead.'

'Die of over-eating?' Ma said.

Pop laughed faintly.

'The hotel is run by a Miss Dupont – Mademoiselle Dupont,' Charley explained. 'But it seems she's away in Brest for the day.'

'When the cat's away,' Ma said.

'Well,' Charley said, 'I wouldn't be at all surprised if that didn't explain a slight lack of liaison.'

Pop, too low in spirits even to admire Charley's turn of phrase, drank deeply of *vin rosé*.

'Better order some more of the juice, Charley old man,' he said. 'Got to keep going somehow.'

'Biff-teck! Biff-teck! Biff-you! Biff-teck!'

'Quiet!' Pop said sharply and from across the *salle à manger* several French mammas looked quickly round at him with full sudden glances, clearly electrified.

Half an hour later he had masticated his way through a bloody piece of beef roughly the shape of a boot's sole, the same thickness, and about as interesting. He ate the chips that accompanied it down to the last frizzled crumb and even dipped his bread in the half-cold blood.

Ma said she hoped he felt better for it but Pop could hardly do more than nod, drinking again of *vin rosé*.

'Don't even have ketchup,' he said, as if this serious gastronomic omission were the final straw.

Soon the twins, Primrose, Victoria, and Montgomery, tired out from the journey, went up to bed and presently Pop began to throw out broad hints that Mariette and Charley ought to be doing likewise.

'It's only nine o'clock,' Mariette said.

'I used to be in bed at nine o'clock at your age,' Pop said.

'Don't tell me,' Ma said.

'We thought there might be dancing,' Charley said, 'somewhere.'

'There's sure to be a night-spot in the town,' Mariette said. 'Something gay.'

With a queer low laugh and a wave of the hand Pop invited the two young people to look and listen at the signs and echoes of the little port's mad, night-time gaiety: the howl of Atlantic wind and rain on the glass roof of the *salle à manger*, the whirling curtains, the crash of spewed foam on the quayside, and the intermittent lightning and cracks of thunder that threatened every few moments to put the lights out.

'Gorblimey, hark at it,' Pop said and once again urged on Charley and Mariette the fact that they would be much better off, in all respects, in bed.

Mr Charlton evidently didn't think so.

'I'd rather like some coffee,' he said.

'Me too,' Mariette said.

Pop agreed that perhaps it wasn't a bad idea at that. At least it would save him from going to bed on a completely empty stomach.

'I expect we can get it in the lounge,' Mr Charlton said.

In the lounge, in flickering semi-darkness, various French couples were furtively drinking coffee, talking and playing whist, *vingt-et-un*, and things of that sort. A few discouraged moths fluttered about and above the howl of wind and rain no other sound could be heard except a sudden metallic clash as someone lost patience and struck a patent coffee filter a severe blow on top in order to encourage the flow.

While waiting for the coffee, which Mr Charlton ordered, Ma sat staring at the moths and wondering what on earth she and the rest of the family were going to do with themselves for a month. It was Pop who had suggested coming for a month. It would give Mariette and Charley more of a chance, he thought.

Presently, after the lights had taken another alarming dip towards absolute darkness, the coffee arrived in four patent filters, once silvered but now worn very brassy at the edges. The top half of the filter was full of water and the lid was too hot to hold.

'What the hell do we do with these?' Pop said.

'The coffee should come through,' Mr Charlton said. 'If not, you strike it. The filter I mean.'

Five minutes later everyone looked inside the filters and found that the water level hadn't dropped a centimetre. This was often the way, Mr Charlton assured them, and went on to explain that the trouble could often be cured by pressure.

'Like this,' he said and pressed the top of the filter firmly with the palm of his hand. 'That ought to do the trick.'

Pop wondered. Whenever he pressed the filter the top of it scalded the palm of his hand. There was never any sign of coffee coming through either.

'They vary,' Mr Charlton explained. 'Mine's coming through quite happily.'

After another five minutes both Ma and Mariette said theirs was coming through quite nicely too. Pop peered several times at the unchanged water-level in his own with a gloom unbroken except by the arrival of a cognac, thoughtfully ordered by Charley when the filters came. The cognac was, by Pop's standards a mere thimbleful, but it was better than nothing at all.

'No luck?' Mr Charlton said and Pop peered for the ninth or tenth time into the top of the filter, to discover once more that the water-level hadn't varied a bit.

'Better give it a tap,' Mr Charlton suggested.

Unaccountably maddened, Pop proceeded to strike the lid of the filter a sudden almighty blow such as he had seen several of the French couples do. The lid at once went leaping vertically into the air and Pop, in an involuntary effort to save it, knocked the bottom of the filter flying, spilling hot water, closely followed by coffee grounds and the cognac, into the upper parts of his trousers.

'Ma,' he said after this, 'I think we'd better go up. I don't know wevver I can last out much longer.'

It wasn't his lucky day, he said as he and Ma went into the bedroom, but Ma instantly and peremptorily shushed him, urging him to be careful and not to wake little Oscar.

'I'm just going along,' she said. 'Don't put the light on. You can see to get undressed without it.'

'Can't see a damn thing,' Pop said.

'Then you must feel,' Ma said. 'That's all.'

Pop was still feeling when, three or four minutes later, Ma came back. He had got as far as taking off his jacket, collar, and tie but had decided to go no further until he got some further guidance from Ma.

'Where is it?' he said.

'Along the corridor and turn left and then down three steps. Mind the steps. The light isn't very good.'

The light certainly wasn't very good and in fact suddenly went out altogether under a fresh clap of thunder, leaving Pop groping helplessly along the unfamiliar walls of the corridor.

When he finally decided to feel his way back he found himself unsure about the bedroom door but fortunately little Oscar turned and murmured in his sleep and Pop, pushing open the door, said:

'Where are you, Ma? Undressed yet?'

Ma said she wasn't undressing that night. It was too risky. She was sleeping in her dressing-gown.

Pop, demoralized, taking off his wet trousers in complete darkness, didn't comment. Life was suddenly a bit too much: no light, no sight of Ma undressing, no telly, no chance of having a cigar and reading *The Times* for half an hour before turning in. This was the end.

'Did you find it?' Ma said.

No, Pop said, he hadn't found it. That was the trouble.

'There must be a doings in the bedroom somewhere,' Ma said. 'You'd better try and find that.'

Pop started to grope about the completely darkened room, knocking against bed, chairs, and chests of drawers, feeling for what Ma had called the doings.

'Sssh!' Ma said. 'You'll wake Oscar. Can't you find it?'

'Don't seem to be nothink nowhere.' Pop was in despair. 'Have to find somewhere soon.'

'You'd better try the window,' Ma said.

Pop, after a few more minutes of groping, managed to find a window. With some difficulty he opened it and then stood there for some time in concentrated silence except for an occasional earnest sigh or two, facing the Atlantic, its wind, and its rain.

During this time he was too busy to speak, so that at last Ma called:

'You all right? You're a long time. What's happening?'

Pop, sad and remote at the window, murmured something about he was having a bit of a battle with the elements. Ma thought this was very funny and started laughing like a jelly, rocking the bed springs, but there was no answering echo from Pop except another earnest sigh or two.

'Are you winning or losing?' Ma called.

'Think it's a draw,' Pop said.

'Fair result I suppose,' Ma said, laughing again.

A moment later Pop brought the long day to a silent close by creeping into bed with Ma, tired and damp but hopeful that little Oscar wouldn't wake too soon for his early morning drop of refreshment.

· 4 ·

Pop rose from an uncheerful breakfast of one *croissant*, one roll of bread, two cups of coffee, and a small pot of redcurrant jelly in very low spirits. This, it seemed to him, was no breakfast for a man and moreover he had slept very badly.

Outside, the day was slightly less violent. The wind had dropped a little, though not completely, and now rain was merely coming down in a mad, unremitting waterfall, a grey curtain obscuring all but the closer reaches of harbour, sea, and sky.

In the small hotel lounge, behind rattling doors, among a cramped forest of decrepit wicker chairs, Mariette and Charley were looking at French fashion magazines; the twins were playing patience with Victoria, and Montgomery and Primrose noughts and crosses. Several French children were running noisily backwards and forwards or were reading and playing too, constantly pursued by the voices of remonstrating mammas calling them by name:

'Hippolyte! Ernestine! Jean-Pierre! Marc-Antoine! Celestine! Fifi!'

Pop thought these names were plain damn silly and moodily congratulated himself that he and Ma, who was still upstairs giving Oscar his breakfast, had given their children sensible solid names like Zinnia and Petunia, Primrose and Montgomery, Victoria, Mariette, and Oscar.

At last he could bear it no longer. He put on his yachting cap and mackintosh and went out into a grey rain that had in it the chill of December, hopeful of somewhere finding himself an honest, solid breakfast.

The entire length of dark grey *pavé* running along the little harbour was as deserted as the deck of an abandoned ship. Down in the harbour itself the black figures of a few fishermen in oilskins were busy tightening the moorings of their blue sardine boats, on the masts of which the furled sails were rolled like copper umbrellas.

In the morning air was a raw saltiness which sharpened the appetite with a sting. Seagulls made continuous mournful cries as they quarrelled above the boats, hungry too. From a café at the end of the promenade came the smell of coffee, bitter, strong, deliciously mocking.

Inside the café Pop found himself to be the only customer. Presently a waiter who looked as if he had been awake all night and was now preparing to sleep all day came and stood beside his table.

'*M'sieu?*'

'Three boiled eggs,' Pop said. 'Soft.'

'*Comment?*'

Thanks to Mr Charlton Pop knew what this meant.

'Soft?' he said. '*S'il vous plaît.*'

'*M'sieu?*'

'Three boiled eggs. Soft,' Pop said.

'*Ex?*'

'*S'il vous plaît,*' Pop said. 'Soft.' He held up three fingers. 'Three. *Trois.* Soft boiled.'

'*Ex?*'

'Yes, old boy,' Pop said. '*Oui.*'

With his forefinger he described what he thought were a few helpful circles in the air and at this, he felt, the waiter seemed to understand. In a sort of ruminating daze he went away, muttering '*Ex*' several times.

Two minutes later he came back to bring Pop a large treble brandy.

'*Ça va?*' he said and Pop could only nod his head in mute, melancholy acquiescence, deeply regretting that among the French words Mr Charlton had taught him there had so far been none relating to drink and food. It was an omission that would have to be remedied pretty soon.

With increasing depression, as yet unrelieved by the brandy, Pop walked back to the hotel. It would be a pretty good idea, he thought, to buy himself a pocket dictionary and he was about to go over and consult Charley on the subject when the man in pince-nez came hurrying forward from behind the reception desk, mole-like, blinking nervously.

'*Bonjour,* Monsieur Larkin. It is possible to speak with you?'

'*Oui,*' Pop said. 'What's up?'

'Please to step one moment into the Bureau.'

Pop followed the man in pince-nez through the door marked 'Bureau'. The door was carefully shut behind him and the little office at once struck him as being markedly untidy, full of dust, and without a breath of air. Piles of dusty brown paper parcels were everywhere stacked on shelves, tables, and even chairs and in one corner stood a high heavy oak desk with a fretted brass grille running round three sides.

Behind this the man in pince-nez perched himself, less like a mole than a little inquisitorial monkey.

'Monsieur Larkin, it is merely a little matter of the passports.'

'I see,' Pop said and then remembered something. 'By the way, what's your name?'

'Mollet.'

'Molly,' Pop said. 'Always nice to know.'

'Monsieur Larkin,' M. Mollet said, 'I am finding some little difficulty in saying which of your passports is which.' He held up a passport for Pop to see. '*Par exemple*, this one. Mr and Mrs Charlton. This is not relating to you and madame?'

No, Pop explained, it wasn't relating to him and madame, but to his daughter and her husband Charley.

'I see. And this one – Sydney Charles Larkin. This is relating to you?'

That was it, Pop said. That was him all right.

'With the six children?'

'With the six children,' Pop said.

'Then what', M. Mollet said, 'is this one relating to? Florence Daisy Parker?'

'That's Ma.'

'*Pardon? Comment?*'

'That's my missus. My wife,' Pop said. 'Ma.'

M. Mollet peered with startled, troubled, inquisitorial eyes above the top of the grille.

'Your wife? A single lady? With another name?'

'That's it,' Pop said. By this time the brandy had made him feel more cheerful, more his perky self. 'Any objections?'

'You are taking a double room in this hotel to share with a single lady while you yourself have six children?'

Pop actually laughed. 'Right first time,' he said.

M. Mollet, again looking as if he'd been pole-axed, took off his pince-nez, hastily wiped them with his handkerchief, and put them on again. When he spoke again it was with an uncertain quiver of the lips, his eyes looking down through the spectacles.

'In this case I regret that I must ask you to leave the hotel.'

'Not on your nelly,' Pop said. His cheerfulness had begun to evaporate. He had a sudden sneaking notion that the Froggies thought he and Ma weren't respectable. He began to wish he'd had another treble brandy. 'Not on your flipping nelly.'

'Nelly? What is that?'

'Rhubarb,' Pop said. 'Don't bother.'

By now his cheerfulness had evaporated completely; suddenly he was feeling hot and bristly.

'If you will leave without complications we will dismiss the matter of the bill. There will be no charge. Not even for the chair that madame – the lady – was destroying yesterday.'

'Destroying!' Pop said. 'Good God, it might have destroyed Ma! It might have injured Ma for life!'

'Please not to shout, Monsieur Larkin. If you will agree to –'

'Agree my aunt Sally,' Pop said. Suddenly, in an inspired flash of anger, he remembered Mademoiselle Dupont. 'Is this Miss Dupont's doing or yours? Where the pipe is she anyway? Is she back?'

'Mademoiselle Dupont is back. I have tried to spare her the unpleasantness –'

'Unpleasantness? Dammit, I thought Froggies were broadminded,' Pop said. 'Paris an' all that lark.'

'This,' M. Mollet said severely, 'is not Paris.'

'Bet your nelly it's not,' Pop said. 'It's brighter in The Bricklayers Arms at home on a foggy Monday.'

'That I do not know about, Monsieur Larkin. I only know –'

'Get Mademoiselle Dupont,' Pop said. 'Go on, get her on the blower, you whelk.' M. Mollet, unaware what a whelk was, stood in a state of restless suspension behind the grille. 'Go on, get her, I want to talk to her.'

'Very well, Monsieur Larkin.'

With no other words M. Mollet extricated himself with dignified stiffness from behind the grille and went out on legs as bent as wires.

It was nearly five minutes before Mademoiselle Dupont came into the Bureau. She seemed, Pop thought, about thirty-eight, rather plump and of medium height, and was wearing a black dress with pure white collar and cuffs: an arrangement that might well have been a considered attempt to make herself look a trifle younger.

'Monsieur Larkin? *Bonjour, m'sieu.*'

She spoke formally, but with nervousness; she played now and then with a large bunch of keys suspended from a chain attached to the belt of her dress.

'*Bonjour.* Good morning. Hope you speak English?' Pop said.

'I speak some English. Yes.'

'Good egg.' Pop felt more cheerful again. He always felt more cheerful in the presence of women anyway. 'Well, I hear you're throwing us out?'

Mademoiselle Dupont, completely embarrassed and transfixed at the sheer directness of this remark, could not speak. She looked unreal. Her skin had that clay-coloured, slightly unhealthy appearance so common in French women, giving them faces like half-cooked dough. Her hair, parted sharply down the middle, was very black and inclined to be greasy. Her eyes seemed, at first, to be black too, but when seen more closely, as Pop discovered later, they were like two thick pieces of glass, carved from an intensely green-black bottle.

'There are times, m'sieu, when one has to exercise a certain discretion.'

Pop, smiling, looked Mademoiselle Dupont straight in the eyes. This was when he first discovered their unusual intensity and the fact that they were really more green than black.

There was a certain intensity about Pop's gaze too, so that Mademoiselle Dupont at once started to play again with her keys.

A moment later Pop put to her a sudden, simple, alarming question:

'If Ma and me don't mind why should you?'

Mademoiselle Dupont had no answer; she did not even begin to move her lips in reply.

'Ma and me ran away when she was sixteen. Eloped. Spent the night at Brighton. She was thinner then. More like you. More your size.' Once again he transfixed Mademoiselle Dupont, looking straight into her eyes with a gaze of exceptionally friendly, perky intensity. 'Same dark hair as you too. Same sort of skin. Lovely.'

Involuntarily Mademoiselle Dupont drew a deep breath. Without being in the least aware of it she selected a single key from her bunch and started pressing it hard into the palm of one hand.

'Telling you my life story already,' Pop said. 'What a lark. Why should I do that?'

For a moment Mademoiselle Dupont appeared to be thinking in French, for she suddenly said:

'*Je ne sais –*'

'I thought you were going to be a bit sticky about me and Ma. I don't know – bit awkward. Were you?'

Mademoiselle Dupont simply didn't know if she was or not. Pop was talking now in his intimate quick-knitted fashion, smiling all the time, and Mademoiselle Dupont stood listening as if partially mesmerized.

'It was so rough last night we thought of going back home anyway,' Pop said. 'Blimey it was rough. Never thought it could be so rough and cold here in France.'

'Oh! but it will improve!' she said. 'It will get better! It isn't always so!'

'Will it? Ah! but when?' Pop said. 'Blimey, look at it now.'

Once again Mademoiselle Dupont, utterly confused, appeared to be thinking partly in French.

'*Dans deux ou trois jours* – two or three days. The storms come and go and then suddenly all is over and then – *le soleil, toujours le soleil* – *toujours, toujours, toujours –'*

'Soleil?'

'Sun – the sun. In French *soleil* –'

Softly Pop said he wished he could speak French like Mademoiselle Dupont and she in turn stood once again as if mesmerized.

'In July it was so hot you could not bear it,' she said. 'You could not bear the heat on the flesh –'

'No? Bet I could,' Pop said and gave Mademoiselle Dupont a look of rapidity so near a wink, that she retreated sharply into herself and began to think in French again.

'Et *l'orage,'* she started saying, '*vous n'avez pas peur pour les enfants?'*

'*Comment?'* Pop said and remarked that Mademoiselle Dupont had got him there, he was afraid.

Mademoiselle Dupont apologized, began to speak in English again and said she hoped the children had not been frightened by the storm?

'Slept like tops,' Pop said. 'Wish Ma and me had.'

'You did not sleep well?'

'Terrible.'

'I am sorry. It was the storm?'

'The beds,' Pop said. 'And that room. We'll have to change that room, Ma and me, if we're going to stay here.'

For the third or fourth time Pop transfixed her with a smile that was at once perky, soft, and full of disquieting penetration, so that Mademoiselle Dupont found herself torn between the question of the unsatisfactory room and its bed and that brief, tormenting scrap of reminiscence about Pop and Ma eloping and how Ma and she had the same creamy skin and the same dark soft hair.

This flash of romantic reminiscence confused her all over again, so that she pressed the key harder than ever into the palm of her hand and said:

'It is *très, très difficile.* I have no more rooms, Monsieur Larkin. Not one more.'

'Couldn't spend another night in that 'orrible room,' Pop said. He thought of his battle with the elements. He hadn't been dry all night. 'And Ma won't, what's more.'

Mademoiselle Dupont, without knowing why, felt suddenly ashamed. She felt inexplicably sorry that there had ever been any thought of ejecting Monsieur Larkin and his family.

'Nothing for it but the beach, I suppose,' Pop said. 'Bit difficult with Oscar, though.'

Mademoiselle Dupont inquired if Pop meant sleeping on the beach and who was Oscar?

'The baby,' Pop said and added that he thought Oscar was a bit young to start night-work.

Mademoiselle Dupont said, in French, how much she agreed. For some inexplicable reason she felt like weeping. She pressed the key harder and harder into the palm of her hand and listened confusedly while Pop inquired if there were other hotels.

'*Mais oui, certainement,*' she said, starting to think in French again, '*mais ils sont tous pleins* – all full. I know. All are full.'

'Like the sky,' Pop said and with a slow wearying hand directed Mademoiselle Dupont's glance through the window, beyond which the relentless Atlantic was stretching with still greyer thickness its imprisoning curtain over port, quayside, and *plage*. 'Fancy sleeping out in that lot. Eh?'

Mademoiselle Dupont found herself confronted by an emotional and physical dilemma: she was overcome by a violent desire to sneeze and at the same time wanted to weep again. She compromised by blowing her nose extremely hard on a very small lace handkerchief, almost masculine fashion, with a note like that from a trombone.

This stentorian call startled Pop into saying:

'Sound as if you've caught your death. Well, this rain'll give the car a wash anyway.'

Outside, in the hotel yard, the Rolls stood with expansive professorial dignity among a shabby crowd of down-at-heel pupils, the muddy family Citroëns, the Peugeots, the Simcas, the Renaults of the hotel's French guests.

'That is your car? The large one?'

Pop confessed that the Rolls-Royce was his and with a wave of modest pride drew Mademoiselle Dupont's attention to the gilt monograms on the doors. These, he assured her, gave the car both class and tone.

'Some duke or other,' he said. 'Some lord. Feller I bought it from wasn't sure.'

At the word lord Mademoiselle Dupont found herself flushing: not from embarrassment or shyness, but from sheer excitement. It was on the tip of her tongue to inquire if Pop was actually an English milord or not but she checked herself in time, content merely to stare down at the monogrammed aristocracy of the Rolls, so distinctive and splendid among the muddy plebeian crowd of family four-seaters parked about it.

Nevertheless she found it impossible to stop herself from supposing that Pop was, perhaps, a milord. She had once before had an English milord, a real aristocrat, to stay in the hotel. All day and even for dinner he had worn mud-coloured corduroy trousers, much patched, a French railway porter's blue blouse, a vivid buttercup yellow neckerchief, and open green sandals. He had a large golden ambrosial moustache and thick, chestnut hair that was obviously not cut very often and curled in his neck like fine wood shavings. Mostly he smoked French workmen's cigarettes and sometimes a short English clay. He also took snuff and invariably blew his nose on a large red handkerchief.

From this Mademoiselle Dupont had come to the conclusion that the English were to some extent eccentric. All the lower classes tried to behave like aristocracy; all the aristocracy tried to behave like workmen. The higher you got in the social scale the worse people dressed. The men, like the milord, dressed in curduroys and baggy jackets and workmen's blouses and had patched elbows and knees and took snuff. The women dressed in thick imperishable sacks called tweeds, flat boat-like shoes, and putty-coloured felt hats; or, if the weather became hot, in drooping canopies of cream shantung that looked like tattered sails on the gaunt masts of ships becalmed.

The English were also very unemotional. They were immensely restrained. They never gave way. The women said 'My deah!' and the men 'Good God' and 'Bad show' and sometimes even 'Damme'. They were bluff, unbelievably reticent, and very stiff. They were not only stiff with strangers but, much worse, they were stiff with each other and this, perhaps, Mademoiselle Dupont thought, explained a lot of things.

It might explain, perhaps, why some of them never got married. It might be that the milords, the true aristocrats, were a law unto themselves. As with the corduroys and clay pipes and snuff, they could set aside the mere conventions of wedlock lightly.

Suddenly she was quite sure in her own mind that Monsieur Larkin was one of these: a milord whose only outward symbol of aristocracy was the Rolls and its flourishing gilded monograms. In no other way could she explain the charm, the ease of manner, the captivating, even impetuous inconsistencies.

'I have been thinking,' she said. 'There is perhaps just one room that possibly you and madame could have.'

'I hope it's got something for emergency,' Pop said, thinking again of his elemental battle the night before.

'Please to come with me.'

With a final sidelong glance at the Rolls – every time she looked at it now it shone like a princess, she thought, among a shabby crowd of kitchen workers – she led Pop out of the Bureau and upstairs.

Once or twice on the way to the second floor – Ma and Pop and the children were all high up on the fourth – she apologized for the lack of an *ascenseur*. She supposed they really ought to have an *ascenseur* one day. On the other hand it was surprising how people got used to being without it and even, in time, learned to run upstairs.

'I haven't caught Ma at it yet,' Pop said.

Following Mademoiselle Dupont upstairs Pop was pleased to make two interesting discoveries: one that her legs, though her black dress was rather long, were very shapely. They were, he thought, not at all a bad-looking pair. From his lower angle on the stairs he discovered also that he could see the hem of her underslip. It was a black lace one.

This, he decided, was a bit of all right. It was perfick. It interested him greatly, his private theory being that all girls who wore black underwear were, in secret, highly passionate.

He set aside these interesting theoretical musings in order to hold open a bedroom door which Mademoiselle Dupont had now unlocked with one of her large bunch of keys.

'Please enter, Monsieur Larkin. Please to come in.'

The room, though not so large as the one he and Ma were occupying two floors above, was prettily furnished and a good deal lighter. It had one large mahogany bed, a huge Breton linen chest, several chairs covered in rose-patterned cretonne, and curtains to match. It also had a basin with running water. It lacked, Pop noticed, that odour of linseed oil, drain-pipes, French cigarettes, and leaking gas that penetrated every other part of the hotel. It seemed instead to be bathed in a strong but delicate air of lily-of-the-valley.

'The room is not large,' Mademoiselle Dupont said. She patted the bed with one hand. 'But the bed is full size.'

That, Pop said, was the spirit, and almost winked again.

'And you see the view is also good.'

She stood at the window, still pressing a single key into the palm of her hand. Pop stood close beside her and looked out on a view of *plage*, sea, sand-dunes, and distant pines. As he did so he couldn't help noticing that Mademoiselle Dupont herself also smelled deeply of lily-of-the-valley.

'Very nice,' Pop said. 'I'm sure Ma would like this room.'

'I hope so,' she said. 'It is my room.'

Pop at once protested that this was far too good of her and under several of his rapid disquieting smiles of thanks Mademoiselle Dupont felt herself flushing again. There was no need to protest, she said, only to accept. The pleasure was entirely hers: and a great pleasure indeed it was. She merely wanted him to be happy, to be comfortable there.

'And you see there is even a little annexe for the baby – in here,' she said, and showed Pop into a sort of box-room, just large enough for little Oscar to sleep in.

Laughing richly, Pop said he was absolutely sure they would be very comfortable in that pleasant room, with that nice bed, with that nice smell of lily-of-the-valley.

'*C'est curieux, c'est extraordinaire,*' she said, starting to think in French again. 'How did you know this?'

Pop drew a deep breath and told her, in a swift flick of description, almost ecstatic, how he had a kind of sixth sense about flowers and their perfumes.

'Acts like a key,' he said. 'Marigolds – I smell marigolds and in a jiff I'm back in Ma's front garden where I first met her. Bluebells – straightaway up in our wood at home. Cinnamon – and it's Christmas. Violets – only got to smell 'em and I'm back in the woods as a kid. The same,' he concluded, 'with your lily-of-the-valley. Never be able to smell it again without thinking of this room.'

Averting her face, watching the distant pines that she had already assured Pop several times were so exquisite in the strong Atlantic sunsets, Mademoiselle Dupont diffidently confessed that they were her favourite flowers, *le muguet*, they were all of spring-time to her, as roses were of summer.

'They suit you,' Pop said and without waiting for comment or answer thanked her again for all her kindness about the room.

It was perfick, he said, he was tremendously grateful, and suddenly, feeling that mere words were not enough, he gave Mademoiselle Dupont an affectionate playful touch, half pinch, half pat, somewhere between the waist and the upper thigh.

Mademoiselle Dupont's reaction to this was to experience a small but exquisite palpitation in the region of her navel. She could find no coherent word either of English or French to say and she confusedly apologized once again about the stairs:

'I am sorry it was so hard for madame – the stairs. But it is old, the hotel. So much needs doing and one does not know what to do.'

Pop, resisting an impulse to pinch Mademoiselle a second time and with more purpose, merely gazed at the rain-sodden landscape and said:

'I know what I'd do.'

'Yes?' Mademoiselle Dupont said. 'What?'

'Pull it down,' Pop said. 'Pull the whole flipping lot down.'

Mademoiselle Dupont, too shocked to speak, turned on him a face in which the mouth had fallen wide open. A moment later she was biting her tongue.

'But it belonged to my father and my grandfather. My family have always owned it.'

'They're dead. It's dead,' Pop said airily. 'No use being sentimental. Comes a time –'

'I know we need an *ascenseur*. We need so much. But the money – here in France everything is so expensive. *C'est formidable.*'

'Always raise the money,' Pop said. 'Only want the ideas.'

Mademoiselle Dupont laughed – Pop thought rather ironically.

'That may be for English milords and people who have Rolls-Royces.'

'When you want anythink bad enough,' Pop said blandly, 'you'll always get it.'

This casual statement of philosophy plunged Mademoiselle Dupont into a fresh silence of embarrassment, in which she played again with the key.

'Well, I'll go and tell Ma,' Pop said, 'she'll be tickled to death, I know.'

His final disquieting perky smile caught Mademoiselle Dupont in a state of unreadiness again, so much so that she actually made several quick brushes at her greasy hair with the tips of her fingers, as if to show how calm and indifferent she was. Her ears, Pop saw, were pale and pretty and faintly flushed at the edges.

'I will see that your things are moved. Please tell madame not to bother. And if there is something –'

'Only the wevver,' Pop said. 'The sun. That's all we want. Sol –'

'*Soleil.*'

'*Soleil,*' Pop said. 'Masculine or feminine?'

'Feminine – no, no, masculine of course. Masculine. How stupid of me.'

'Should have been feminine,' Pop said and gave her a last, brief, quick-knitted smile.

Long after he had gone downstairs Mademoiselle Dupont still stood at the window watching the unrelenting rain, trying with difficulty to re-shape her thoughts on English milords, the strange, unaccountable, eccentric habits of the English, the Rolls-Royce and its monograms, and the way Monsieur Larkin, who seemed so unlike the English of tradition, possessed the secret of a key through the scents of flowers to events and places long-distant, forgotten, and even lost, as for example with lilies-of-the-valley, *les muguets*, her favourite flowers.

· 5 ·

After three days the sun began to shine, though not very much, mostly in fitful bursts, still whitish and watered down. A steady temperate wind blew in from the Atlantic, generally raising clouds of sand and at times bristling saltily. The evenings were like December.

From time to time it was just warm enough for Mariette and Ma to shed wraps and sweaters and lie in bikinis on the little smooth-sanded *plage*. Mariette's figure, in spite of what Pop thought about its slight narrowing down since marriage, was well suited to the bikini. Her breasts were round but firm, girlishly fresh but quite mature. Her waist was delicate and narrow, with hips of pear-shaped line. From behind she appeared to have a beautiful little saddle, to which the lower of the bikini's three scarlet triangles was tied with the slenderest of strings.

Ma was not so lucky. She hadn't been able to get a bikini quite large enough to fit her. They didn't go quite as high as Ma in size. But there was, as she remarked, nothing much to them and she had consequently run up two for herself: one in bright petunia purple, her favourite colour, and the other in brilliant salmon rose.

Primrose, Petunia, Zinnia, and Victoria all wore bikinis too, in shades of royal blue, green, pink, yellow, and pure white which they changed from day to day. Ma wasn't having her children outdone by any Froggy kids, some of whom she noticed had their hair dyed, generally red, blonde, or black, sometimes to match their mother's.

On the whole Ma wasn't much impressed by Froggy women, young or old. The young girls who lay or pranced about the *plage* all looked what Pop called pale about the gills; they were very pasty, like Mademoiselle Dupont, and looked decidedly unwell about the eyes; they either wore no lipstick at all or far too much of it in the palest of puce and parma violet shades.

Their necks always looked surprisingly yellow too, Ma thought, a funny suet sort of colour, and she was certain sure they all slept in their make-up. Their hair looked uncombed and tatty and they seemed generally to wear it long, either untied or in horse tails, but occasionally they wore it crimped up, in curious frontal rolls that achieved the effect of making their foreheads recede or disappear.

And their figures were nothing, Ma thought, absolutely nothing. 'Compared with our Mariette's,' Ma reckoned, 'you'd think they were boys with a few pimples here and there. I thought French girls were supposed to be so chick and all that. Blow me, some of 'em don't even shave where they ought to.'

She felt quite sorry for Pop in this respect. There was hardly anything for him to look at on the *plage*. Even Edith Pilchester had more to call her own, Ma thought, than some of these. Even Mademoiselle Dupont had a certain firmness of chest and lower line. She did at least look neat and tidy, whereas most of the Mammas who sat about in beach chairs or even in the shelter of red and white striped tents, intensely gossiping and knitting, either looked hopelessly overdressed, with two extra cardigans to keep out the temperate westerly wind, or like moulting hawks restlessly awaiting a false move by younger prey.

The young men, on the other hand, were magnificent. Ma had never seen anything like it. All of them seemed to be tall, athletic, bronzed, and lissom. Innumerable protruding knots of muscle stuck brownly out from all over them, accentuating arms, shoulders, chest, and buttocks. Their hair was always perfectly crimped and waved and round their middles they wore nothing but skin-tight pudding bags tied with string.

The young men occupied the beach all day, tirelessly exercising themselves. They leapt in perpendicular fashion in the air, scissoring brown legs. They stood on their heads, did statuesque hand-stands, or pranced about like restless straining race-horses. They played leap-frog or ran about square-chested, like Grecian runners, hair slightly flowing, breasting the wind. They climbed invisible ropes with arms plaited with brown muscle or did long, silent, earnest, dedicatory breathing exercises for the abdomen and chest.

But mostly they played with balls: large, highly-coloured balls, two or three feet in diameter, in segments of scarlet and green, or yellow and violet, so inflated and so light that the Atlantic wind, when it caught them, rolled them swiftly away across acres of bare beach into distances of sea and dune and pine. When this happened they showed new high prowess as athletes, running after the balls in fleeting file or in handsome echelon, Greek-like again, hair flowing, racing the wind.

Mr Charlton, who could see no point in these exercises, was glad merely to relax with Mariette in the sun, reading detective stories or occasionally turning an eye on Mariette, moving her perfect young body over to brown

on the other side, like a young plump chicken on a spit. He felt mostly relaxed and contented, even when sometimes aroused by the voice of Ma:
'Fetch everybody ice-cream, Charley, will you? There's a dear. Big ones. Bring two for everybody. And some nuts.'

One of the few things Ma was agreeably surprised about in France was the fact that they had ice-cream and nuts. She had been afraid they wouldn't. At least that made it a bit more civilized.

Pop too was content. He liked merely to lie in the sun and look at the sky. With his hypersensitive, keenly developed sense of smell he could lie for hours breathing the scent of sea and seaweed, sun-dried rocks and pines, tarry boats and fish being unloaded at the quay. He could translate these things into separate living scenes without opening his eyes at all, just as he could smell lily-of-the-valley in imagination and recapture Mademoiselle Dupont clear and close to him.

Over the past day or two it had struck him that Mademoiselle Dupont had become more and more refreshingly attentive. She laughed whenever he met her on the stairs. Was the food right for Monsieur Larkin? Did Madame and the family like it? Were the children happy? Was there some special dish they would like? Pop hadn't the heart to tell her he thought the food was mostly a terrible mistake and that what he really wanted was rice pudding, stewed plums, and roast beef and Yorkshire. He merely joked:
'Ma says it suits her a treat. She's slimming. Taken off pounds.'

'If there is something special you prefer at any time please to tell me. *Sans supplément*, of course. Please just to say.'

On the fifth morning she called him into the Bureau in order to give him back the passports, apologizing at the same time for keeping them so long. She also said:

'I have been thinking that you might care to take an excursion on the 8th – that is, to Le Folgoët. There is a great *pardon* there that day. It is the greatest and most beautiful *pardon* we have in Finistère.'

'*Pardon?*' Pop had no idea what a *pardon* was but he listened respectfully as Mademoiselle Dupont went on to explain its religious significance and beauty.

'Not much on religion,' he confessed. 'Don't care for dog-collars.'

'Perhaps Madame and the children would care to go,' she said. 'You must please tell me if they do. I can give them all directions.'

Up to that moment, rather absent-mindedly, Mademoiselle Dupont had kept the passports in her hands. Suddenly she remembered them and handed them back to Pop, giving a little nervous laugh at the same time.

Pop grinned quickly as he took the passports and asked to know what had amused her.

It was quite a little thing, Mademoiselle Dupont said, just something that had occurred to her.

'What?' Pop said.

'*Ce sont les passeports,*' she said, starting once again nervously thinking in French. 'It is rather *curieux*. A little bit funny.'

'Oh?' Pop said. 'How's that?'

'It was when I was looking at the passports this morning,' Mademoiselle Dupont said. 'It was *très curieux* – very *curieux* – but it occurred to me that if you are not married you are still a single man?'

She laughed quickly and rather self-consciously and Pop, in his customary rousing fashion, laughed too. That, he confessed, had never occurred to him either.

'Single chap, eh?' he said. 'Well, well.'

That afternoon, when he went back to the *plage* after having a short after-lunch nap with Ma on the bed, he found Mr Charlton in a state of unusual restlessness.

Charley, who had hitherto been fairly content, had made a disturbing discovery. He had rumbled what the business of the big sailing coloured balls was all about. They were all part of a design for the ensnarement, if not seduction, of Mariette.

The young Frenchmen, he had at last discovered, had every wind direction beautifully worked out. In that way they could be sure that the balls would always float towards her, so that every five minutes or so they would find it necessary to invade the precious territory of scarlet bikini and naked flesh and, with voluble apologies, laughter, and much athletic show, recapture them.

Mr Charlton made it clear he didn't care for it at all.

On the morning of the 8th Pop lay alone on the *plage*, basking for the first time in the true heat of the sun. The sky was actually the colour Mr Charlton had so confidently predicted it would be. It hung overhead like a cornflower, brightest blue to the very distant edges of a sea that seemed to have receded across miles of new-bleached sand to the hazy rim of the world.

The extra-sensory impressions that were so lively in him that morning told him that this was perfick. It couldn't possibly be more perfick anywhere, even to go off to a *pardon*, however beautiful, as Ma and all the rest had done. Only Mariette, it seemed, had shown any reluctance to go to the great *pardon* of Le Folgoët, largely on the ground that it would interfere with her scheme for browning her body all over, but Charley had rumbled that. He had shown swift and admirable marital firmness and had, to Pop's great satisfaction, insisted she should go.

So by ten o'clock the Rolls was away, Mariette driving, the boot packed with a large picnic lunch of Mademoiselle Dupont's preparing, together with several bottles of *vin rosé* and bags of peaches, sweet white grapes and pears. The children now liked *vin rosé* as much as ice-cream and much more than orange juice and Ma was very glad. She thought it was very good for them.

As the Rolls drove away she was already busy giving little Oscar a drop of refreshment and with a free hand waving 'Have a good time' to Pop, who called back that he had *The Times* of the day before yesterday and that it wouldn't be long before he went down to read it over a snifter and watch the Breton women dozing in their stiff white hats and the sardine boats bringing in their catches to the quay.

'Perfick,' he kept saying to himself in the sun. 'Perfick. Absolutely perfick.' He could actually feel the early September heat, bristling with its heavy Atlantic salt, burning his chest and thighs and shoulders. 'Perfick. Good as champagne.'

Twenty minutes later he was asleep on his face and woke only just before midday – a time when the *plage* always emptied itself so suddenly and completely of people that it was as if a plague had struck it – to hear an elegant voice saying:

'Hullo, there. *Comment ça va, mon chéri?* How's the beauty sleep, darling? It's me.'

Pop turned and looked up. Above him a hatless vision, in shirt and slacks of a warm pale shade of apricot, was sitting on the sea-wall above the *plage*. Down over the sand dangled the long, languid legs of Angela Snow, his kindred spirit of the summer party of a year before.

Pop was instantly glad of Charley's brief tuition in French and promptly leapt to his feet and said:

'*Très bien, merci! Et vous aussi,* my old firework?'

'Scream,' she said. 'You speak the language!'

'Just enough,' Pop said. 'Count up to ten and ask for vin rosy.'

'Been dying to see someone who's fun and here you are.'

Angela Snow gave a serpentine twist of her body and leapt down to the sand. Her hair had a glorious gold-white sheen on it and she gave the impression of having chosen the slacks and shirt not to match it but to heighten it and make it shine more brilliantly. Her pretty feet were bare except for flat yellow sandals that simply slipped on, Chinese fashion, without a tie.

When she sat down her long legs curled themselves loosely underneath her. Her clear olive eyes seemed even larger than Pop remembered them and she seemed to embrace him with them as she asked him all about himself, how he came to be there, in this hole, and all that.

'Holiday,' Pop said.

'Not alone?' Her usually languid voice was quick, even eager.

Pop at once explained about the family and how everyone else had gone to the great *pardon* at Le Folgoët.

'Iris too,' she said. 'My sister. Terribly religious, Iris. Got the most God-awful relidge, Iris has.'

Smiling to the uttermost edges of her large pellucid olive eyes she asked Pop, in turn, if he was very relidge.

Pop said he wasn't, very.

'No particular brand, you mean?'

Pop confessed he had nŏ particular brand. He supposed if it came to a definition he would say that being alive was his relidge – that and earth and woods and flowers and nightingales and all that sort of lark and enjoying it and not preventing other people doing so.

'Wouldn't do for Iris,' Angela Snow said. 'Couldn't have that, darling. Couldn't sell her that. She's an Ill-fare Stater. The iller you fare the gooder you are.'

Pop shook his head. Family throw-back? he suggested.

'Got to lacerate yourself, according to Iris. Beds of nails. Fakir stuff.'

'Sack-cloth and ashes?' Pop suggested.

'Dish-cloth and wet-breeches,' Angela Snow said, 'that's Iris. A positive wetter. Even says damp prayers. Sobs away half the time.'

Not much of a chum on holiday, Pop suggested. Why did she come?

'My idea,' Angela Snow said. 'Thought I might find some arresting Breton fisherman to bed her down with. Sort of cure. Don't know of an arresting somebody, *chéri*, do you?'

Pop said he didn't and laughed. He much enjoyed being called darling and *chéri* by Angela Snow.

'And how,' she said, 'are the virgins?'

Throwing back her head Angela Snow laughed with all the rippling limpidity of a carillon about the virgins. She'd never forgotten the virgins. Seven of them and so foolish, riding on the donkeys at Pop's Derby in the summer gymkhana a year before. Almost needed changing still, she confessed, every time she thought of them. Dear virgins.

'Iris is one,' she said. 'The dears do make such hard work of it.'

'This place is full of 'em,' Pop said.

'You don't say?'

Pop referred her to the boyish female skinnies, largely unwashed, who disported themselves listlessly about the *plage*. Ma and he had discussed them thoroughly. Terrible little show-offs, they thought, with nothing to show. And French girls supposed to be so chick an' all. And fast. Even young Montgomery was bored.

'Terribly strict country still,' Angela Snow said. 'Big mother is watching you and all that.'

'Nothing for the Froggy boys to do but make eyes at Mariette.'

'Can't blame 'em,' she said. 'She's inherited all her father's virtues.'

Virtues? Pop laughed and said he didn't think he'd got very many of them.

'No?' Angela Snow said and gave him a smile of luscious simplicity.

Free to look about him again, Pop saw that the *plage* had miraculously emptied itself, as always, at the stroke of noon. In five minutes every *salle à manger* in the place would be full of ravenous masticators. The *potage cultivateur* would be on, stemming the first pangs of the *pensionnaires*. Everywhere the bread-slicers would be working overtime.

Suddenly overcome by a sharp recollection that if you weren't there on time you fell behind in the noon race for nourishment and never really caught up again, Pop half got to his feet and said:

'Suppose I ought to get back to the Beau Rivage. Before the troughs are empty.'

'Any good?' she asked, 'the Beau Rivage?'

Pop was obliged to confess he thought it terrible.

'Bad grub?'

That was the worst part of it, Pop said. He yearned for a good drop of –

'Complain, Sweetie, complain.'

Pop confessed that he hadn't the heart to complain to Mademoiselle Dupont. She probably did her best.

'You must, darling. It's the only way. I'm the great complainer of all time. The great table-banger. And who's this Dupont?'

Pop explained about Mademoiselle Dupont while Angela Snow listened with detachment, unsympathetically.

'All too obviously another one,' she said. 'Like Iris. Plain as a pike-staff, sweetie.'

Pop's insides were light with hunger. Sleep and the bristling air of morning had made him feel empty and fragile as a husk.

'Invite me to lunch one day,' she said, 'and I'll give a demonstration of the arch-complainer.'

What about lunch today? Pop said. He couldn't go on much longer.

'Only place in this hole is Pierre's,' Angela Snow said. 'Out there, towards the forest. About ten minutes, if you don't mind walking.'

Pop said he hoped his legs would carry him. Angela Snow laughed in reply, again in her high, infectious rippling fashion, and actually took Pop's arm in her soft, slender fingers.

'I'll see you don't fall by the wayside, chum. Lean on me, *chéri*.'

Thus fortified, Pop bore up remarkably well until they reached Pierre's, which stood in a clearing where forest and sand joined at the deep central cup of the bay. All his hypersensitive impressions, heightened still further by the growing heat of sun, baking sand, seaweed, and pines, were now fused together in wild galloping pangs of hunger.

Pierre's appeared to be a shack built of bits of bamboo, pine boughs, and old orange boxes. It looked, Pop thought, remarkably like an abandoned coal-shed.

Outside it a few tables without cloths, apparently knocked up out of driftwood, were sheltered by the same number of blue and white umbrellas. Charcoal was smoking away slowly under an iron grid built above bricks. A sign stuck on a pole said *Toilette* and pointed to a flimsy arrangement of almost transparent sacks slung up behind a tree.

Angela Snow and Pop sat down at a table and Angela Snow said this was the greatest place for food you ever came across. The only problem was whether Pierre would like you. If he didn't he wouldn't serve you. He liked to pick his customers.

'Mad on me,' she said.

'Hullo, lousy,' Pierre said. 'Why bloddy hell you turn up?' and then stood over the table to slop into thick glasses two large *camparis* which nobody had ordered.

Angela Snow shook back her sumptuous golden hair and with her slow drawling voice and luscious smile gave back as good as she got.

'How now, brown sow?' she said. 'This is my friend Mr Larkin. Mr Larkin – Pierre. Mr Larkin keeps pigs – he'll understand you.'

Pop actually half rose to shake hands but relapsed at once when Pierre said:

'Hope you enjoy yourself. What you want to eat? I know. Don't say. Rossbiff, eh?'

This was exactly what Pop did want and his juices at once started flowing madly in anticipation.

'Well, you won't get, see? Today you get *moules, châteaubriant*, and the best *brie* your English bloody nose ever stank of and like it.'

'Scream,' Angela Snow said. 'Killing.'

She laughed again in her high ringing fashion and Pierre gave a grin part sugary, part lascivious, his thick lips opening to reveal a row of blackened teeth punctuated in the centre by a positive door-knob of gold. The rest of his sun-burnt body, which Pop thought was almost as wide as Ma's, suffered from these same unclean extravagances. His blue-striped sweat shirt seemed to have been dipped in candle-grease. His uncut black hair could have been knotted in his neck. Glimpses of a belly both hairy and sweaty appeared from time to time between the bottom edge of his shirt and the tops of his trousers, which were held up by some sort of bell-rope, bright scarlet and hung with gilded tassels.

'And what wine you want?'

'Vin rosy,' Pop said.

'Rosy, rosy, rosy,' Pierre said. 'Well, we don't have rosy, rosy, rosy. Here you bloody well have what you get and like it.'

'Mad,' Angela Snow said. 'Killing me.'

Pop thought it would kill him too and was openly relieved when Pierre went away, dragging one foot, like a pot-bellied crab crawling across the sand.

'Going to bring Iris here one day,' Angela Snow said. 'Pierre's the type for her. Half an hour with him and she'd never be the same again.'

Pop was positive she wouldn't be.

'Fun, isn't it?' Angela Snow said. 'Don't you think so? Awful fun. And the food celestial.'

Pop was busy drinking *campari* for the first time and decided he didn't like it.

'These are the only places,' Angela Snow said. 'Real France. All the atmosphere. Piquant somehow – delish.'

Scooping up his mussels and thinking, like Ma, that he wasn't going to get very fat on this lark, Pop watched Pierre grilling the *châteaubriant* over a glowing bed of charcoal. Now and then Pierre scratched his long black hair or the hairs on his chest and sometimes he spat over the grill into the sand.

Watching him, Pop was reminded of Charley's opinion that the French were the *élite* of Europe. France was the place. Everything so cultured.

'Two bloody steaks for two bloddy English. *Bon appétit*.'

A certain belching contempt filled the glowing autumn air. This, however, was merely yet another signal for Angela Snow to break into fresh peals of laughter and say what awful fun it was.

'A change from the deadly Dupont and all that anyway, darling,' she said.

It certainly was, Pop said, and then turned with intense relish to tackle the *châteaubriant* and its accompanying *pommes frites*. After a struggle of five minutes or so it struck him that the meat was, perhaps, a piece of dog. The charred rectangle, when cut, was icy blue inside and exuded large quantities of blood. This, like the *pommes frites*, was stone cold. The inner sinews of the meat itself, so tenaciously bound to each other that nothing could separate them, were stone cold too.

'Terribly naughty of me,' Angela Snow said. 'You'd have liked mustard, wouldn't you?'

Pop still struggling, said it didn't matter. Nevertheless Angela Snow said she'd ask for it, and it turned out to be English when it came.

'Suppose it's *très snob*, wouldn't you think perhaps?' she said. 'English mustard?'

Pop, masticating hard at bits of dog, supposed it was. *Très snob* – rather good expression, he thought. He must tell Ma.

'How about some cheese? Or fruit perhaps?'

Pop, who was feeling a little less light, but not much, said he fancied both.

For the next half hour it was delicious to sit in the open air, on the edge of the pines, and eat cheese, peel big yellow peaches, and suck grapes; and also, Pop thought, to watch newly arrived customers struggling with their rectangles of charred dog.

Now and then Pierre, ruder and louder as he warmed up to his work, poured brandy over the *châteaubriants* and set them alight. Dramatic flames shot into the air, making the customers look keener than ever in anticipation. Pop enjoyed watching this and made Angela Snow laugh ringingly by saying that he supposed this was the way you made hot dog.

'And coffee. What will you have with your coffee?'

Pop said he fancied a Rolls-Royce.

'One of your blinders?'

Pop said it was; though Red Bull was stronger.

'You think Pierre can mix it?'

'Easy,' Pop said. 'Half vermouth, quarter whisky, quarter gin, dash of orange bitters.'

'That'll suit me too,' she said.

'Better make 'em doubles,' Pop said. 'Easier somehow.'

Pierre seemed unexpectedly impressed by the privilege of mixing strange and special drinks and momentarily dropped all rudeness to become softly, almost obsequiously polite: probably, Pop thought, because it was another case of *très snob*.

Out in the bay the copper sails of departing fishing boats lit up the blue cornflower of sky with such intensity in the sunlight that they too were triangles of fire. All illumination too, Angela Snow's hair seemed to shine more beautifully when broken pine shadow crossed it and left it free again as the sun moved over the sand.

Soon the double Rolls-Royces had made Pop feel more like himself and he responded with an involuntary belch and a robust 'Perfick!' when Angela Snow suggested a short siesta in the dunes.

'I'll get the bill,' he said.

'No, no,' she said. 'My party.'

'Not on your nelly,' Pop said.

'Darling, that's not nice. I asked you.'

'I'm paying,' Pop said with all his charm. 'You think I don't know my technique? Rhubarb.'

When the bill came Pop looked at it and suddenly felt cold. There were so many items and figures that he could neither disentangle them nor add them up. His eye merely grasped at a few painful essentials and blinked the rest.

The portions of charred dog had each cost 1,200 francs; the *moules marinières* 700 francs; the cheese 500 francs; the double Rolls-Royces each 1,400 francs, making a final total, with tax on top of service and supplement on top of tax, of 11,650 francs.

As he fumbled to pay this, a last alarming item caught his eye.

'What's *couvert*?' he said. 'What the blazes is *couvert*? We never had *couvert*.'

Angela Snow laughed in her most celestial fashion.

'That,' she explained to him, 'was just the breathing charge.'

Pop, who was never one to be unduly miserable over the cost of pleasure, thought this was very funny and was still laughing loudly about it when they reached the dunes. He must tell Ma that one: the *très snob* lark and the breathing charge. Jolly good, both of them.

He was still more delighted when Angela Snow's first act on reaching the sand dunes was to cast off her shirt and drop her apricot slacks and stand before him in a yellow bikini so sparsely cut that nothing really separated her from pure golden nakedness.

'My God, this is good,' she said and lay flat on her back in a nest of sand. 'This is good. Where are you?'

Pop didn't know quite where he was. He felt more than slightly lost and dazzled.

'Come and lie down with me, *chéri*. Come on.'

This invitation was delivered with such bewitching languor that Pop was at her side, half in a dream, before he really knew it. Almost at once she closed her eyes. The deep olive lids, shutting out the large pellucid eyes that were always so warm and embracing, seemed now to offer him the further invitation to take in the whole pattern of her long slender body: the slim beautiful legs and arms, the sloping shoulders and the tiny perfectly scooped salt-cellars below the neck, the small but upright breasts, and the navel reposing centrally below them like, Pop thought, a perfick little winkle shell.

As if knowing quite well that he was taking his fill of these things, and with some pleasure, she let her eyes remain closed for fully two minutes before opening them again.

Then she smiled: still a languid smile but also rather fixed.

'Suppose you know I'm madly in love with you?'

Pop confessed he didn't know. It was news.

'Outrageously. All-consuming,' she said. 'Night and day.'

'Jolly good,' Pop said. 'Perfick.'

'Not on your nelly,' she said. 'It's hell.'

A recurrent lick or two of fire from the Rolls-Royce raced about Pop's veins and caused him to say that this was crazy.

'Right first time,' she said. 'Crazy. Mad. Mad as those hares.'

For crying out gently, Pop thought. That was bad. By the way, had she ever seen those hares?

'No,' she said. 'Tell me.'

Watching those pellucid olive eyes that now seemed to have added a look of mystery to their largeness, Pop told her about the hares: the strange wild gambollings that you would see in March, the leaping, dancing business of spring courtship.

'Fascinating,' she said. 'That would be a thrill.'

'Bit mysterious,' Pop said. 'All that tearing about and dancing.'

'Not more than us,' she said. 'What do we dance for? I mean all that stuff in Freud.'

What, she asked, did he feel about Freud?

'Never touch it,' Pop said.

'Scream,' she said. 'I love you.'

She laughed so much at this that it was fully a minute before she was calm again and said:

'Here's me madly in love with you ever since that virgin-firework lark and you've never even kissed me.'

This was a state of affairs, Pop said, that could be remedied with no delay at all.

A second later he was lying at her side, kissing her for the first time. He had always been a great believer in first times, his theory being that there might never be another, especially where women were concerned, and now, with velvet artistry, one hand softly under her small left breast, he made the kiss last for ten minutes or more.

This experience left even Angela Snow slightly light-headed. She seemed to come round, already slightly tipsy after the wine, as if after a deep, passionate faint. Her large eyes blinked slowly, in a dream, and there might even have been a tear of emotion in them as she smiled.

He must save one of those for Iris sometime, she said in a languid attempt at light-heartedness, and what a lucky creature his wife was.

It was essential to keep all those things, Pop thought, on a light-hearted level. Else it wouldn't be fair to Ma. This now seemed the critical moment with Angela Snow and he laughed resoundingly.

'What's funny?' she said.

'Well,' Pop said, 'if everybody had their right I haven't got a wife.'

'Joke.'

It certainly was a bit of a lark, Pop said, when you thought of it. Him and Ma not married. And Ma on a separate passport an' all. Did Angela mean she'd never heard?

'Not a peep,' she said. She'd concluded from the offspring alone that all was well.

'Must get it done some day,' Pop said. 'No good. You know we've had another since I saw you?'

Unsurprised, Angela Snow held him in a gaze fully recovered from its first emotional storm and said with languor:

'Good show. Means you're still agile, virile, and fertile.'

Pop said he hoped so and was so amused and even slightly flattered that he granted her the indulgence of a second kiss, holding her right breast this time, again with prolonged tenderness.

Passion and fervour left their mark on Angela Snow even more deeply than before and as she came round a second time she again felt it necessary to check emotion with yet another touch of flippancy.

'Don't know which I liked best. The one from the married man I had first, or the single one I had second.'

'Mademoiselle Dupont knows I'm not married too. Rumbled it from the passports.'

'Oh! she does, does she?'

And once again she gave him a smile of luscious, penetrative simplicity.

They lay on the dunes, watching the sun across the bay and occasional triangles of sail-fire cut across the blue horizon, for the rest of the afternoon. As time went on her almost naked body grew warmer and warmer in the sun. The sand of the dunes became quite hot to the touch as the sun swung westwards and most of the time Pop couldn't help thinking what a beautiful place it would be for Mariette and Charley to try out sometime. It might encourage them a bit.

At last, when it was time to go, Angela Snow said:

'See you soon, poppet. Don't let it be long. The nerves won't stand it.'

'Come and have lunch at the hotel one day,' Pop said. 'Ma'd love to see you.'

'Even the hotel,' she said. 'Anywhere. But don't let it be long.'

Finally, with a long quiet sigh, she drew on her slacks and Pop said goodbye to what he thought, with pleasure but detachment, was the nicest body he had ever seen since he first met Ma.

That night, as he sat in bed reading *The Times* and smoking his late cigar, he broke off several times from reading to tell Ma about Angela Snow, the terrible lunch, the bill, the *très snob* lark, and the breathing charge.

Ma said she was very pleased about Angela Snow; it had made his afternoon.

'Get round to kissing her?'

Pop confessed that he had but Ma, huge and restful in transparent nightgown after a day that had been a strange mixture of religion and fair, French fish-and-chips and saints, remained quietly unperturbed.

'Says she's in love with me.'

'That pleased you, I'll bet. Nice girl. I like her. Bit of a card.'

For the third or fourth time that evening Pop remarked that he was thirsty. He expected it was the mussels. All shell-fish made him thirsty.

'Well, go down and get a drink,' Ma said. 'Bring me one too.'

Pop said this was a good idea and got out of bed to put on a silk dressing-gown vividly embroidered in green and purple with vast Asiatic dragons, a last minute holiday present from Ma, remembering something else as he did so:

'Ma, you remember that lot of pickled cucumbers, gherkins or whatever they were I had left over from that army surplus deal? The one I made nearly six thousand out of?'

'The ones you got stored in the top barn?' Ma said. 'I know.'

Pop chuckled ripely.

'Hocked 'em all to one of the fishing boat skippers this afternoon after Angela had gone,' he said. 'Seems they're just what they want to pep up their diet with. Terrible monotonous diet they have, these Froggy fishermen. Potatoes and fish all boiled up together. Saw 'em doing it. And gallons of wine.'

'Hope you'll get paid.'

'Coming over to pick 'em up himself and pay me,' Pop said. 'Puts in to Shoreham sometimes. What do you want – champagne?'

'Just what I could do with,' Ma said.

Pop, going downstairs, found Mademoiselle Dupont going over her books in the Bureau. She got up to greet him in her customary nervous fashion, fearing another complaint, but Pop at once put her at rest by explaining about the champagne.

'And what mark of champagne do you prefer, Monsieur Larkin?'

The best champagne Pop could ever recall drinking was something called Bollinger '29 at a big Hunt Ball at home, just before the war.

He mentioned this but Mademoiselle Dupont shook her head. 'In all France I do not think you could now find one bottle of Bollinger '29. All is past of that year.'

'Pity,' Pop said.

'But I have Bollinger '34. That too is good.'

That, Pop said, would do him all right.

Later he insisted on carrying it upstairs himself: ice-bucket and bottle and glasses on a tray. As he did so Mademoiselle Dupont stood in her habitual position at the foot of the stairs and watched him in soft admiration, dreamily thinking.

Day by day it was becoming increasingly clear to her that Monsieur Larkin was a milord. Only a milord could smoke such expensive cigars in bed at night and ask for Bollinger '29. Only a milord could walk the quayside with such an elegant lady as she had seen him pass the hotel with that afternoon: so golden and aristocratic in her elegant apricot slacks.

At the turn of the stairs Pop turned, cocked his head to one side, and looked back.

'*Bonsoir, Mademoiselle, dormez bien,*' he said nippily. 'Sleep well.'

'*Bonsoir,*' she said. 'Sleep well, milord.'

Pop thought that this milord lark just about took the biscuit and he told Ma all about it as he uncorked the champagne in the bedroom.

'Called me my lord, Ma,' he said. 'What price that?'

Ma, who sat up in bed popping Chanel No. 5 down her bosom, thought it was a scream.

'Lord Larkin,' she said. 'Sounds all right, though. Not half bad. I think it sounds perfick, don't you?'

Pop said he certainly did and, laughing softly, poured out the champagne. In fact it was more than perfick.

'I think it's jolly *très snob*, Ma,' he said, 'don't you? Very *très snob*.'

· 6 ·

Pop began to watch events on the *plage* with growing uneasiness, if not dismay. Things were not going well at all. It was clear as daylight that Mariette and Charley were right off hooks.

Periodically he talked to Ma about it, but Ma seemed quite indifferent, beautifully unperturbed. With great placidity she sat all day watching the sea, the French mammas, the leaping young gods, the tatty little French girls, and the fishing boats putting out to sea. She knitted, read magazines, sun-bathed, and gave little Oscar the refreshment he needed, serenely unconcerned.

'What's Mariette sulking for?' Pop wanted to know. 'Dammit, she hardly speaks to Charley nowadays.'

Ma made the astonishing suggestion that it was probably lack of variety.

'Variety?' Pop said. This was beyond him. 'Variety in what?'

'Before she was married she never had less than two or three running after her,' Ma said. 'Now she's only got Charley.'

Pop, who had never looked at it in this way, had nothing to say and Ma went on:

'What do you think I let you run around with Angela Snow and old Edith Pilchester for?'

Pop said blandly he hadn't the foggiest.

'Variety,' Ma said serenely. 'Variety.'

Pop still couldn't understand why Mariette should always seem to be sulking. At this rate he and Ma would be fifty before they had any grand-children: a terrible thing. Why were them two always off hooks? Did Ma think that it was possibly some defect in Charley's technique? And if so should he have a quiet word with Charley on the matter?

'Don't you do no such thing,' Ma said. 'I've had a word already.'

'With Charley?'

'No: with Mariette.'

Setting aside the notion that perhaps the whole matter was bound up in some curious feminine secret, Pop said:

'Give her any ideas?'

'Yes,' Ma said. 'I did. I told her to start flirting.'

Pop whistled. Even he was stunned with surprise.

Ma said she didn't see that there was anything to be surprised about. Even the twins and Primrose flirted. Even Victoria had started. Didn't Pop use his optics nowadays? Hadn't he seen Zinnia and Petunia making eyes at those two little black-eyed French boys who wore such funny little pinafores? They were at it all day. They had them in a tizzy.

'Flirting's good for people,' Ma said. 'It's like a tonic. You ought to know.'

Pop laughed and asked Ma if she'd thought of going in for a little herself.

'I might,' she said. 'Only it's a bit difficult with Oscar.'

Pop was pleased at this and asked Ma if she thought a little drop of flirting now and then would do Charley any harm?

'Flirting with who?' Ma, who was sitting placidly on the sand, huge pale legs outstretched, indicated with a contemptuous wave of her heavily ringed fingers the pallid creatures who populated the *plage* on every side. 'With this tatty lot? I pity him.'

Pop said he was thinking more of somebody like Angela Snow. She could teach him a thing or two.

'You should know,' she said. 'He's not her type, though. Not like you are.'

'She's got a sister,' Pop said. 'Very religious.'

'Give the poor chap a chance,' she said. 'I'm trying to make it easy for him. Not –'

She broke off and looked at her wrist-watch. It was ten o'clock: time to give Oscar a drop of refreshment. With a slight sigh she picked him up from where he had been lying with some of her own reposeful placidity on a large clean napkin and then dropped one side of her magenta bikini top and produced a handsome expanse of bosom like a full-blown milky balloon. Into this Oscar buried himself with eager rapidity while Ma went on:

'Oh, talking about flirting and all that, I think we're going to have trouble with our Primrose.'

Primrose was eleven: even Pop, very faintly surprised, thought that was a bit dodgy.

'Trouble? How?'

'In love. Bad.'

Pop said he'd go to Jericho. In love? How was that?

'How?' Ma said. 'What do you mean, how? Naturally, that's how. Developing early, that's how. Like I did.'

Ah! well, Pop said, that was different. That was the right spirit. Nothing like starting young. Who was it? Not some French boy?

'Two,' Ma said.

Pop, laughing good-naturedly, remarked that he supposed there was safety in numbers, to which Ma firmly shook her head.

'That's just it. Can't sleep at night. She's trying to give one of 'em up and can't decide which one it's got to be.'

'Thought you said it was a good thing?' Pop said.

'Said what was a good thing?'

Pop, feeling himself to be rather sharp, laughed again.

'Variety.'

Instead of laughing in reply Ma regarded him with something like severity over the top of little Oscar's bald dumpling of a head.

'Sometimes I'm surprised at you, Sid Larkin,' she said. It was always a bit of a bad sign when she called him Sid Larkin. 'It's a very tricky age. You'll have to be careful what you say to her.'

'Me?' Pop said. 'Haven't said a word.'

Ma, deftly shifting little Oscar from one side of her bosom to the other, looked at him for some seconds before answering, this time with a glance more mysterious than severe, so that he was almost afraid she was going to call him Sid Larkin again. That would have been a bit much. She only did it once or twice a year – so's he'd know it really meant something when she did.

'No,' she said darkly, 'you haven't. But you will.'

'Oh?' he said. 'When?'

'When the time comes,' Ma said blandly, 'when the time comes.'

Ma had him properly guessing now. He couldn't rumble her at all. There was something behind that Sid Larkin touch, he thought, and he was still trying to fathom what it was when Ma, in her habitually unruffled way, abruptly changed the subject by saying:

'Going back to Charley. I think a walk would do him more good. He sits on this beach too long. He's moping. Take him down to the harbour and have a drink with one of your fishermen friends. Didn't you say you had another deal cooking?'

That was right, Pop said. He had. He'd got the Froggy skipper interested in a hundred cases of that tinned gherkins in vinegar that he hadn't been able to hock to anybody else up to now. It would show about three hundred per cent if it came off. Nothing very big: but it would help to keep the pot boiling.

'Good idea,' he said.

He put one finger into his mouth and with a sudden piercing whistle, shrill as diamond on glass, startled the entire *plage* into thinking a train was coming. Mr Charlton, who was idly picking up shells and trying not to notice the antics of the god-like young Frenchmen prancing all about him, recognized the sign at once and came strolling over.

'Put your top hat on, Charley old man,' Pop said. 'I'm taking you down to the harbour for a wet. Fit?'

Charley said he was fit and called a few words of explanation to Mariette, who had discarded her bikini for a remarkable strapless sun suit in brilliant cinnamon with a boned front that uplifted and enlarged her bust to a sumptuous and thrilling degree.

The balls would be floating over any moment now, Charley thought, and he wondered suddenly if he had the courage to leave her there. She looked maddeningly beautiful, as she always did when sulky. Today she was all steamy voluptuousness, lying there languidly pouting in the warm morning sun, and he actually called:

'You're really absolutely sure you don't mind if I go?'

Mariette made no sign. It was Ma who shook her head. Pop was, after all, right about Charley's technique. There really were some serious gaps in it. He really ought to use his loaf sometimes.

'Darling!' he called.

'Yes?' Mariette said.

'You honestly don't mind?'

'Have a good time. Don't get drunk,' she said.

Probably not a bad idea, Pop mused as he and Charley walked along the harbour walls, watching the Breton fishing crews brewing buckets of fish and potatoes into one big steaming stew and loading red wine on to the decks by the dozen crates. It gave Pop great pleasure to watch all this and to gaze at the many furled copper umbrellas bright in the mid-morning sun above the crowded blue hulls.

'Don't see old Brisson about,' he said. 'Anyway we'll have a snifter at the Chat Noir. He'll be along.'

As he and Charley chose a pavement table at the café on the harbour's edge, Pop got the sudden idea that the occasion was one when they might try something a little special. It was too early for wine. It made him sleepy. And he was fed up with the eternal Dubonnet, Pernod, and Cinzano. What did Charley think about a real drink? Red Bull or something of that sort?

'First class idea, Pop,' Mr Charlton said. 'Absolutely first class.'

Pop, slightly astonished at the strenuous vehemence of Charley's tone, gave him a sharp glance of inquiry which he didn't bother to answer.

Charley was feeling a private need for a strong pick-me-up. It depressed him increasingly each time he thought of the young French gods, their stupid great balls, and Mariette sunning herself in her sumptuous cinnamon.

'Rattling good idea,' he said. 'I've been waiting for somebody to ask me that one.'

As Pop was about to call '*Garçon!*' and begin an explanation as to how to mix the Red Bulls he saw Captain Brisson arrive. Pop always called him Captain. Huge, florid, and purple, he looked very much like a large bulldog with heart disease.

Charley, having been introduced, suddenly took off his spectacles and started polishing them madly. Pop, unaware of what made him do this, called to the waiter and at the same time started to explain to the Captain about the Red Bulls and did he want one?

'Plizz, what name? Red Bull, you say?'

'Red Bull. It's a self-propeller!' Mr Charlton said. 'A blinder!'

'Plizz?'

The Captain, like Pop, looked positively startled at the sudden vehemence of the small Englishman who, momentarily without his spectacles, looked so harmless, odd, and short-sighted.

'My son-in-law,' Pop said, as if this explained everything.

Mr Charlton rammed his spectacles back on his nose and in rapid French explained the composition of the cocktail that, only a year before, had knocked him flat. He was stronger now. He could take a dozen.

'Good,' Captain Brisson said, presently tasting the Red Bull, which Charley had had the forethought to order double. 'Good. I like. Good at sea.'

Searching stabs of raw alcohol inspired Charley to fresh, almost rapturous enthusiasm for the virtues of the cocktail.

'Propel the whole ruddy boat,' he said. 'Nothing like it. Absolute blinder. *Santé.*'

'*Santé,*' Captain Brisson said.

'Cheers!' Pop said. '*Santé.*'

'Cheers,' the Captain said.

'*Santé,*' Charley said. 'Down the hatch.'

He already thought, as Pop and Captain Brisson sat discussing the question of sliced gherkins in vinegar, that he felt a great deal better. Pop was feeling pleased with himself too. The Captain had made a very reasonable offer for the hundred cases and the deal was now completed except for the formality of a little paper.

Since Pop was incapable of writing his name and the Captain incapable of writing English it devolved on Mr Charlton to draw up a sort of invoice, agreeing price and quantity. For some reason he chose to do this in pencil. He couldn't think why, since he had a perfectly good pen in his pocket, except perhaps that the pencil needed sharpening and that the short rapid strokes of his penknife gave him the same nervous outlet for his emotions as the mad polishing of his spectacles.

'I am content,' the Captain said. His signature and Pop's cross, binding nobody and nothing at all, were added to Mr Charlton's document, which the Frenchman kept. Pop never kept records. It was all in his head. 'I sank you.'

After this the Captain and Pop shook hands. Then Pop knocked his Red Bull straight back, declaring that the proceedings called for another drink to which Charley added a kind of vehement amen.

'You bet!' he said.

'Plizz,' the Captain said. 'I like to pay.'

'Rhubarb!' Charley said. 'This one's on me!'

After the second Red Bull, he began to feel that the contemptuous memory of the young French gods and their stupid idiotic balls and still stupider prancings no longer disturbed him quite so much. He started to see the harbour through a viscous, rosy cloud.

Now and then he sharpened the pencil madly again and then, after a third Red Bull, actually started to sharpen it at the other end. About this time Captain Brisson said he ought to be going back to his boat and Pop said they ought to be going too.

'Rhubarb!' Charley said loudly. 'Hell's bells. We only just got here.'

'Please excuse,' the Captain said.

'Rhubarb!' Charley said again. 'I thought the French were drinkers.'

The Captain again protested that he had to get back to his ship and Pop said very well, that was all right, and he hoped he'd see him soon. Perhaps in England?

'In England, yes,' the Captain said. 'I come soon. When teeth are ready.'

'What teeth?' Charley snapped.

Without embarrassment and with a certain touch of pride the captain slipped from his mouth what he explained to Pop and Charley were his temporary set of dentures. The new ones, he assured them, would be ready in a month or so: in England.

'National Elf lark,' Pop reminded Charley.

'My mate,' the Captain said, 'he have new wooden leg. Also it is true you can have cognac sometimes? *Oui?*'

'There's the National Elf lark for you, Charley old man,' Pop said. 'Free for all. Even the Froggies. Wooden legs an' all.'

'Rhubarb to the National Health lark!' said Charley aggressively, 'and double rhubarb to the Froggies!'

As if detecting in this a certain note of ill-concealed hostility Captain Brisson, whose face had now broken out in a rash of red and purple blotches, shook hands all over again with Pop and Charley, at the same time forgetting to put his teeth back. It was only when he had gone some yards along the quayside that he remembered the omission and slapped them back into his mouth with a blow so sharp that it knocked him off keel, making him stagger.

Soon after he had disappeared Pop was about to say for a second time that he and Charley ought to be going too when he saw across the street a figure waving to him with a white and chocolate scarf.

He did not need to hear the fluted call of 'Darling!' that followed it to know that this was Angela Snow. She was dressed in trim pure white shorts and a coffee coloured linen blouse and white open sandals in which her bare painted toe-nails glistened like rows of cherries. With her was a girl in a pea-green cable-stitch sweater and a skirt of indeterminate colour that might have once been mustard. Much washing had turned it to an unpleasant shade of mongrel ochre, rather like that of a mangel-wurzel.

'This', said Angela Snow, 'is my sister. Iris.'

Pop and Charley rose to shake hands, Charley unsteadily.

'Good. Splendid,' Charley said. 'Just in time for a snifter.'

'Darlings!' Angela Snow said. 'My tongue's hanging out.'

Iris said nothing but 'Howdedo'. She was a solid, shortish blonde of rising thirty with a skin as hard as marble and more or less the colour of an acid drop. Her eyes were almost lashless; the complete absence of eyebrows made her face actually seem broader than it was, as well as giving it a look of completely bloodless astonishment. Her hair was cut in a roughish home-made bob and she had small white ankle socks of exactly the kind that French girls wear.

Charley demanded of the two girls what would it be and presently Angela Snow was drinking Pernod and her sister a small bottle of Perrier with ice. Charley and Pop decided at the same time that this was as good a moment as any to have a fourth Red Bull and while this was being mixed Pop reminded Angela Snow of her luncheon promise and when was she coming?

'Whenever you say, dear boy. At the given moment I shall be there.'

'Tomorrow?'

'Tomorrow, darling, as ever is. Bless you.'

'And your sister,' Pop said, giving Iris a rich perky look that would have melted Mademoiselle Dupont to tears but that had on Angela Snow's sister only the effect of heightening her appearance of bloodless surprise, 'would she care to join us too?'

'I'm sure she'd adore to.'

'Impossible,' Iris said. 'I go to Guimiliau to see the Calvary and then the ossuary at –'

The word ossuary startled Pop so much that he gave a sort of frog-croak into his Red Bull, which had just arrived. He had as sharp an ear as ever for strange new words but this one had him floored.

'What', he said, 'is an ossuary? Sounds *très snob.*'

'Bone-house,' Angela Snow said.

'Same to you,' Pop said.

'Scream!' she said and everyone, with the solid exception of Iris, roared with laughter.

Even before the arrival of the fourth Red Bull Charley was feeling great. The bit about the ossuary served merely to put him into louder, cheerier, more pugnacious mood.

'Rhubarb!' he said to Iris Snow. 'Of course you can come. It's *langoustine* day tomorrow. Have them every Thursday. Don't you adore *langoustines?*'

Iris, who thought eating had much in common with the other deadly sins and consequently existed mostly on dry toast, cheese biscuits, and anchovy paste, had no word of answer.

'You see she visits somewhere different every day,' Angela Snow said in explanation. 'Ah! the calvaries and the crosses, the dolmens and the menhirs, the *allées couvertes* and the tumuli – Iris has to see them all.'

Pop sat open-mouthed before what he thought was the oddest female he had ever seen in his life but was saved from pondering over her too long by a sudden, almost pugnacious question from Charley.

'And how', he demanded of Iris, 'do you travel, Miss Snow? By car or what?'

Iris permitted herself the astonishing luxury of uttering fifty-six words all at once, speaking with measured solemnity.

'I think walking is the only true and right way of seeing these things. Walking leads to contemplation, contemplation to mood, and mood to meditation, so that when you get there you are one with the place you're visiting. So I walk to all the nearest ones and go to all the distant ones by train.'

'By train?' Charley said. 'What train? Not by any chance that *little* train?'

'Of course. What else? Whenever and as often as its –'

'My God!' Charley gave a positive shout of delighted triumph and gazed at Iris Snow with alcoholic rapture, as to a kindred spirit. 'She knows my little train! Hear that, Pop? She knows my little train!'

Pop, who thought something must have got into Charley – he'd start spouting Shakespeare or that feller Keats any moment now, he thought – could only stare at Angela Snow, who gave him a split-second sporting wink, without the trace of a smile, in reply. He was too astonished even to wink back again.

'That train,' Charley kept saying. 'That little train. You remember, Pop, how that was the first thing that brought it all back again?'

Brought all what back again? Pop wanted to know.

'Me. This. Everything. All that time. All those years. The whole ruddy shooting match.'

No doubt about it, Pop thought, Charley was as drunk as a newt. Pickled. Something had got into him. It reminded him of the time he had first met him and how Mariette had had to lend him pyjamas and put him to bed. There was the same raving, rhapsodic light in his eyes.

'Chuffing away over the heather!' Charley said. He had started to wave his arms about in ecstatic recollection. 'Chuffing away for miles. I remember once – where was it? St Pol de Léon – no, not there. Somewhere else. No. Has St Pol de Léon two cathedrals?'

Without knowing it, and for no sane reason at all, Charley had begun to sharpen his pencil again.

'You might almost say it has,' Iris Snow said. 'There's the cathedral itself, and then of course there's the *Chapelle du Creizker*. Much, much more magnificent.'

'It was there!' Charley said with a rhapsodic jolt in his voice. 'It was there!'

What was? Pop wanted to know.

'Charley's got a spider on the end of his nose,' said Angela Snow, who loved practical jokes and who was dying to get the subject changed, since relics, saints, and pardons were her sister's food and drink, day and night. 'I can see it dangling.'

Charley did nothing about the supposed teasing spider except to snatch vaguely at the air immediately in front of him and then start stirring his Red Bull madly with his pencil, as if it were a cup of tea.

'First time I ever really saw the world,' he said. 'Consciously, I mean. Consciously. From that tower you can see –'

'Seventy other towers,' Iris said. 'Of course on a clear day.'

'Never forget,' Charley said. 'God, you talk about "a wild surmise – silent upon a peak in Darien" –'

'Charley's off,' Pop said. 'More Shakespeare.'

'Keats!' Charley shouted. 'Keats!'

'Same thing,' Pop said.

'Whenever I go there again,' Iris Snow said, 'I shall think of you.'

'Do,' Charley said, 'do,' and started to sharpen his pencil madly again. 'Think of me!'

Suddenly he was on top of the tower again, on top of the world. Everything was splendidly revelatory and wonderful. His insides felt rich with Red Bull. His veins were a jumble of wires that sang like harp-strings. He heard himself order a fifth Red Bull in a voice that echoed inside his head as a cry might have done through one of the sepulchral *allées couvertes* that Iris found so fascinating.

Drinking it, he was aware that his intestines were on fire and he suddenly gave a belch of rude immoderation.

Magnifique, he kept telling Iris Snow. *Magnifique*. Rhubarb! And he didn't care a damn for any of the bastards. Did she?

Whether it had anything to do with this robustly repeated inquiry he never knew but suddenly he came to a vague realization that neither Angela Snow nor her sister were there any longer.

'Where have the Snows gone?' he said. 'Melted?' Jolly good joke, he thought. *Magnifique*. 'Snows all melted?'

Some time later he was dimly aware of walking back to the *plage* with Pop, still madly sharpening his pencil and still saying he didn't care a damn for the bastards, whoever they were.

'All Froggies are alike,' he was saying as they reached the *plage*. 'Eh, Pop? No guts. No Red Bull. No red blood. Eh? Can't take it, eh?'

Without waiting for an answer he made a sudden spasmodic leap on to the sand, landing midway between Ma, who was giving further refreshment to Oscar, and Mariette who, sumptuous in fiery cinnamon in the noon sun, was flirting madly with a muscular Frenchman bronzed as evenly all over as if every inch of colour had been painted on.

Charley at once uttered a queer cry, half in warning, half in anger, and rushed across the sand, seawards, as if about to drown himself. The *plage*, it seemed to him, was full of balls. They were floating everywhere, maddening him as they had never done before.

Suddenly he started charging hither and thither with the violence of a demented buffalo. He was attacking balls everywhere as if they were monsters, stabbing at them with his open pen-knife, making them burst.

One of several loud reports startled a French woman into a scream and another startled Ma in the act of giving Oscar the other side. One ball as vivid a shade of mustard as Iris Snow's skirt had once been was floating in the water. Charley charged it with a dive, leaving it swimming on the surface of the waves like a deflated and forgotten tooth-bag.

Pop, who didn't know what to make of it all, stared blankly at Charley giving the death blow to a big pink and purple ball that went up with a crack like a Roman Candle, merely thinking that perhaps they'd better lay off Red Bulls for a bit, in case Charley got violent sometime. They didn't suit everybody, especially on an empty stomach.

Less than a minute later he was shaken out of this complacency by the sight of Charley rushing back with puffing frenzy across the sand, every ball now triumphantly punctured, to where Mariette, luxuriously lying on her back under the gaze of an admiring Frenchman who stood with hands on his knees, was testing the truth of Ma's shrewd observations on variety.

In full flight, Charley kicked the startled Frenchman twice up the backside. He was, however, less startled than Pop, who suddenly heard Charley, as he lugged an astonished Mariette to her feet, ripping out the challenging words:

'And tomorrow you'll come on the little train! Hear that? You'll come with me on the little train!'

In bed that night, in the quiet of darkness, Pop was still trying to work out this violent episode for himself.

'So that', he said, 'was what all the hoo-ha was about. That little train. Don't get it, Ma. Do you?'

Ma said of course she got it. It was as plain as a pikestaff.

'How? Don't get it,' he said.

'Charley wanted to go on the little train and Mariette didn't. That's all.'

Lot of fuss for nothing Pop thought. All over a little thing like that. All over a train.

'Not at all,' Ma said. 'It's always the little things. That train means a lot to Charley.'

Pop said he thought it seemed like it too.

'It's connected with something in him,' Ma said. 'In his childhood.'

'Never!' Pop said. 'Really?' For crying out gently.

'It stands for something he's lost. Or else something he's never had. Not sure which.'

Pop said he shouldn't think so either. Charley would have to take more water with it, that was all.

'It's psychology,' Ma said. 'You hear a lot about it on telly.'

Wonderful thing, Pop remarked, telly. He missed it on holiday. It learnt you something all the time. Every day. Ma said she agreed. She missed the *Mirror* too. Without it she never knew what her stars foretold and that made it awkward somehow.

At last, lying under the lee of Ma's huge mountain of a body, Pop found himself going back over the day and in the course of doing so remembered something else he thought remarkable.

'Heard a word today, though, Ma,' he said, 'I've never even heard on telly yet. And I'll bet you never have either.'

Oh, and what word was that? Ma wanted to know.

'Ossuary.'

And whatever in the world did that mean?

'Bone-house to you,' Pop told her.

'Do you mind?' Ma said and kicked him hard under the bedclothes. 'Whatever next? You'll have the twins picking it up in no time.'

'Sorry, Ma,' Pop said. '*Dormez bien*. Sleep well.'

'Sleep well, my foot,' Ma said and gave her handsome head a swift twist on the pillow, so that she was lying full face to him. 'What makes you think I'm all that tired?'

Pop said he couldn't think and immediately set to work to demonstrate that he wasn't all that tired either.

· 7 ·

But it was always Ma, in her unruffled way, who shrewdly remembered the best and most important things and it was she who, next morning after breakfast, called Pop's attention to an event a week ahead.

'You know', she said, 'what it is next Thursday?'

Pop didn't; except that they were going home.

'That's Friday,' Ma said. 'Thursday the 29th I mean.'

Pop said he couldn't think what the twenty-ninth meant at all; he only knew that the month at St Pierre le Port seemed to have gone like the wind. He could hardly believe that soon they were going home.

'Mariette and Charley,' Ma said. 'Their wedding anniversary.'

'Completely forgot,' Pop said.

'Forgot, my foot,' Ma said slyly. 'The trouble is you don't get much practice with wedding anniversaries, do you?'

Pop confessed that this was quite true but nevertheless suggested darkly that he and Ma made up for it in other ways.

'Good thing too,' Ma said. 'Anyway, I thought we ought to give them a party.'

Perfick idea, Pop said. Jolly fine idea. Perfick. *Très snob.*

'I thought we could ask Angela Snow and her sister and perhaps Mademoiselle Dupont. How does that strike you?'

Pop said that nothing could have struck him better. It was just the job. Mariette would be thrilled too.

'By the way,' Ma said, 'what's Angela Snow's sister like? If she's anything like her we'll have a high old party.'

She wasn't, Pop said.

'Oh?' Ma said. 'What's she like then?'

Pop found it difficult to say. He could find no handy word to describe Iris Snow with any sort of accuracy. He thought hard for some moments and then said:

'All I know is she wears false boosies and she's very pale.'

What a shame, Ma said. She was very sorry about that. She always pitied girls who had to wear those things. Good boosies were a girl's crowning glory, as you could see from all the advertisements there were about them everywhere nowadays.

Pop heartily agreed and invited Ma to consider our Mariette for instance, which in turn made him remark that he was glad to see that she and Charley were well on hooks again.

'Like love-birds,' Ma said. 'We must give them a good time on Thursday. The tops.'

Best party they could think up, Pop said. What did Ma suggest?

'Well,' Ma said, 'I tell you what I thought. I thought that as we've got Angela Snow coming to lunch today we'd discuss it all then. We can get Mademoiselle Dupont in over coffee and all talk about what we're going to eat and drink and so on. Have a proper laid-out menu and the table decorated and all that. How's that strike you?'

Again Pop thought it struck him very well. They could get all the wines ordered too and he would try to think up some special sort of cocktail. The expense could be damned; the gherkins and the cucumber in vinegar lark would take care of that.

'Good,' Ma said. 'Now perhaps we'll get some real food.'

At lunch, before Mademoiselle Dupont joined them for coffee, a small but quite unprecedented incident took place: in Pop's experience anyway. The day was coolish, with a touch of that bristling westerly wind that could blow fine sand into every corner and crevice like chaff from a thresher. Even Angela Snow had put on a thick red sweater and Pop noticed that in spite of it she shuddered as she first sat down.

'Let's give the vin rosy a rest, shall we, Ma?' Pop said. 'Have something a bit more warming today.'

Just what she felt like, Ma said. Pop must choose a good one.

'Sky's the limit,' Pop said, and with infinite charm turned to Angela Snow and suggested that she should make the choice.

The customary Thursday *langoustines* not having arrived because the sea had been too rough it presently turned out that for lunch there was *potage du jour* and *omelette au fromage* followed by *côtes de porc grillées* with *haricots verts*.

'In that case burgundy,' Angela Snow said.

'A good one, mind, the real McCoy,' Pop said. 'No half larks. The best.'

Angela Snow said she thought in that case that the Chambolle Musigny '47 couldn't be bettered.

'Fire away,' Pop said. 'Make it two bottles.'

A waitress finally brought the wine in a basket cradle. A lot of dust covered the bottle and this, to Pop, was a sure sign of something good. The waitress then pulled the cork and poured out a little of the wine for Pop to taste but Pop was quick to say:

'No, no. Angela. Angela must taste it.'

She did.

'Corked,' she said firmly. 'No doubt about it. Must go back.'

A curious suspended hush settled on the table, broken only after some seconds by Primrose asking in a piping voice:

'What's corked, Pop?'

Pop didn't know; he hadn't the remotest idea what corked was. Obviously this wine lark was a bit dodgy, he thought, and privately decided he must go into it a bit more closely. There were things he didn't know.

'Of course it can happen any time, anywhere,' Angela Snow said. 'It's nobody's fault. It's one of those things.'

Pop said he was relieved to hear it and was on the verge of saying that 'corked' might not be a bad word to describe Iris Snow when he thought better of it and decided not to, in case Ma should somehow misunderstand.

The direct result of all this was that when coffee was brought Mademoiselle Dupont came to the table in more than usually nervous, apologetic mood. She apologized several times for the unfortunate incident of the Chambolle Musigny. Aware though she was of the ease with which it could happen at any time, anywhere, even to the best of wines, she would nevertheless have rather cut off her right hand than it should happen to milord Larkin and his family.

At the word milord Angela Snow was astounded into a silence from which she hadn't recovered by the time Ma was suggesting to an equally astonished Mademoiselle Dupont that the party wouldn't be complete if the children didn't have custard and jelly for afters.

Meanwhile the coffee filters had to be attacked. Pop always dealt with his, though never very successfully, by giving it a number of smart hostile slaps with the flat of his hand. Mostly these produced no visible result whatever. Charley's method was more simple. He merely pressed the top down hard and invariably spilt what coffee there was all over the place.

On the other hand Mademoiselle Dupont seemed lucky enough to be blessed with a special sort of filter, for while everyone else was struggling messily to coax a few black drops of liquid into the cups she was sipping away with alacrity, trying to calm her nerves.

'First, to decide how many people.'

Ma counted up the heads.

'Not counting Oscar and I think he's a bit young, don't you?' she said, 'I think there'll be a round dozen. That includes you', she said to

Angela Snow, 'and your sister. And,' she said to Mademoiselle Dupont, 'you too.'

Mademoiselle Dupont's pale olive face at once started flushing. She was most flattered, most honoured, but really it couldn't be. Her French and English began to mix themselves hopelessly, as always at times when she was excessively nervous, and she could only blurt out that it was *très difficile, impossible*, quite *impossible*. There would be so much *travail* and Alphonse would need much watching.

'Who's Alphonse?' Pop said.

'He is the *chef*. He is not an easy man.'

Drinks, Ma thought. She knew. Nearly all cooks drank. Like fishes, too, though perhaps you couldn't blame them.

'Alphonse will be looked after,' said Pop, who had by now abandoned the struggle with the coffee filter and had lit up one of his best Havanas. 'The main thing is the grub. Kids,' he said to Charley and Mariette, 'what do you fancy to start with?'

Mariette said she's been trying to think but it was Mr Charlton, always so bang on the target in these things, who made the happy suggestion that he thought they ought to begin with *melon au porto*.

'With that', he pointed out, 'you eat and get a drink at the same time.'

It was cordially agreed by everyone, especially Pop, that *melon au porto* sounded marvellous. Mademoiselle Dupont thought so too, saying several times over that she thought she could get the lovely, small *charentais* melons, which were the best, if she tried hard.

'And then may I suggest *filets de sole aux truffes?*'

'Troof, troof!' the twins started saying. 'Troof! Troof!'

'Quiet!' Pop thundered and the twins stopped as if throttled.

'How do you feel about that, Mariette?' Ma said. 'Wouldn't rather have lobster?'

'How is the *filet de sole* composed?' Charley said.

The rather grand word 'composed' seemed to flatter Mademoiselle Dupont so greatly that she started to describe the contents of the dish with both verve and tenderness.

'*Vin blanc*, white wine, butter, *les truffes*, and *quelques autres choses très délicieuses –*'

'Sounds just the job,' Pop said. 'Chips with it?'

Mademoiselle Dupont recoiled from the suggestion of chips with silence, not really understanding exactly what it meant. The milord was a comic man sometimes.

Eventually everyone agreed that the *filet de sole aux truffes* didn't sound too bad at all, though Pop was privately disappointed that there was no further mention of chips. You always had chips with fish. What was wrong?

'And now as to meat? Or should it possibly be chicken? Or perhaps some other bird?'

Suddenly, while everyone was trying to concentrate on the problems of this, the main course, Victoria bit Zinnia sharply on the ear. Nobody took much notice of this except Petunia, who threw at Victoria a piece of *omelette au fromage* she hadn't been able to eat because it tasted of soapsuds. In a second all three girls were crying and Ma was saying seriously, as if there wasn't a ghost of sound to be heard:

'I as good as told you so.'

'Quiet!' Pop thundered for the second time in ten minutes and there was instant silence at the table, so that Ma remarked with pride, as she so often did, that Pop had them at a word.

The effect of this was to impress Mademoiselle Dupont tremendously. The English milord was obviously a most masterful person. A man clearly born to command. You could tell these born, masterful, commanding aristocrats fifty kilometres away.

This was the season for *perdrix*, she was saying suddenly. There were now beautiful young *perdrix*. What was the English word? – partridge? Shouldn't they therefore select partridge? – *perdrix*, perhaps, *à la mode d'ici?*

It suddenly occurred to Pop that he had heard these ominous words somewhere before. They struck a faint and unpleasant chord in his mind. And in a flash he remembered the pregnant sausage-rolls with steam coming out of their ends.

Partridges – no – he said, he didn't think so. No *à la mode d'ici*.

'If it's all right with Charley and Mariette,' he said, 'I know what I want and what I should like to have.'

'Go on. Say it,' Ma said. 'I know.'

'Roast beef and Yorkshire.'

'Biff! Biff!' the twins started saying but this time a single look was enough to silence them.

'Can't wait,' Charley said.

'Lovely!' Mariette said. 'Couldn't be anything better. Oh! Pop, you always have the sweetest ideas.'

Pop, feeling rather flattered by this, gave one of his perkiest, richest smiles at Mademoiselle Dupont, who responded confusedly by saying:

'*Rosbif* of course. That we can arrange. But what else was this you said? This Jorkshire?'

Pop started to explain that this was, in his opinion, a pudding that had no equal. It was about the best in the world.

'I see,' Mademoiselle Dupont said. 'It is merely a question of whether Alphonse can make it. I doubt it very much.'

'Then Ma can make it for him,' Pop said.

Mademoiselle Dupont professed to be instantly and completely horrified. It was quite out of the question. It was unthinkable that a stranger should go into the kitchen, still less teach Alphonse how to make strange dishes. It would only offend him. He was at the best of times a temperamental man and sometimes, after drink, ran about with carving knives.

'Fetch Alphonse,' Pop said. 'I daresay he wouldn't say no to a brandy. I want one too.'

Mademoiselle Dupont now fluffed over her coffee, which she had allowed to get quite cold. Alphonse also, she recalled, but not aloud, had a mistress in Morlaix and two in Brest. He visited the three of them in rotation and they too sometimes had strange effects on his stability.

Alphonse, duly called in from the kitchen, didn't say no to a brandy. He was a man of stocky proportions, inclined to be portly, with very black hair parted down the middle with millimetrical exactitude and polished with a great deal of violet brilliantine. His eyes were protuberant but handsome and in the space of three seconds from first entering the *salle à manger* he managed to give Ma, Angela Snow, and Mariette the quickest, most comprehensive once-over.

Since Alphonse spoke no English it was left to Mr Charlton, translating instructions from Ma, to explain the composition of what Mademoiselle Dupont called the *pouding à la Jorkshire*. These instructions, though simple in the extreme, were listened to by Alphonse with aloofness, not to say contempt, while he drank in the visionary beauty of Angela Snow, who had for a long time sat in a state of bemusement, not saying a word.

Suddenly Alphonse became unexpectedly voluble and first Mademoiselle Dupont and then Mr Charlton translated his words for Ma.

'He says if you will write it down on paper it shall be made as you wish. And is it the same as for *crêpes?*'

'Pancakes,' Mr Charlton explained.

'Exactly the same,' Ma said. 'Couldn't be more right.'

'*Ça va bien,*' Pop said. '*Merci beaucoup, Alphonse.*'

Alphonse said '*Merci, monsieur*' and immediately became suddenly voluble again. This time it was to offer the suggestion that the beef should be the *contre filet,* which Mademoiselle Dupont applauded as being absolutely right, quite excellent.

'And now what about afters?' Ma said.

'Ah!' Pop said smartly, picking it up in a flash. '*Les après.*'

Alphonse looked witheringly about him for a second or two and then held a short conversation with Mademoiselle Dupont, who said:

'Alphonse is suggesting either *crêpes Suzette* for dessert or *bombe surprise.*'

It was at this moment that Angela Snow came out of her half dream to hear Ma insisting on jelly and custard for the children and to find herself being shamelessly and mentally undressed by Alphonse's over-large handsome eyes.

'I think myself the *crêpes Suzette,*' she said, staring straight through Alphonse. 'They'll keep him busier at the time.'

'That about settles it then,' Ma said.

'No it don't though,' Pop said. 'What about the cake? Got to have a cake. Midnight, champagne, and all that lark.'

'Oh! Pop, lovely!' Mariette said and suddenly ran round the table in one of her moments of spontaneous delight to kiss Pop with luscious gratitude. 'Cake *and* champagne – it's like being married all over again!'

'Second honeymoon, Charley, second honeymoon,' Pop said, hoping the cheerful pointed words wouldn't be lost on him. 'Second honeymoon.'

Charley, using his loaf, looked as if he understood. Then Mademoiselle Dupont said Alphonse would be most honoured to make the cake. And if there were any other things, any other thoughts – suddenly a great sense of excitement ran through her, as if the party were really her own, and she ended by half-running out of the *salle à manger* into the Bureau in another fluff, repeating half in French, half in English, a few uncertain sentences which nobody could understand.

For another half hour, while Charley, Mariette, and the children went to the *plage* and Pop for a gentle snooze on the bed, Ma and Angela Snow sat outside on the terrace, drinking coffee. By this time the sun had appeared but the air was quite autumnal. Already at the end of the terrace a few leaves of the plane trees pollarded to give shade in hot weather were turning yellow and even falling to the ground. The bead-like strings of coloured lights, shattered by storm and still unrepaired, gave the trees an air of premature shabbiness that was like a small herald of winter. It was all too true, as Mademoiselle Dupont had remarked to Ma only that morning after breakfast, that the season was coming to its end. The guests were departing. Soon the hotel would be empty. The French had no taste for the sea when October began and in another week or two the little *plage* would be wrapped away for winter.

Presently Angela Snow was saying how much she was looking forward to the party and what a lot you missed by not being married: the anniversaries and that sort of thing.

'Suppose you do,' Ma said. She'd never really thought of it.

'I'll have to settle down myself I suppose one of these days,' Angela Snow said.

'Oh?' Ma said. 'Why?'

She didn't mind a scrap everyone knowing that she and Pop weren't married – most took it for granted they were and anyway it looked the same, even if it wasn't – and she remained quite unperturbed and unsurprised when Angela Snow, who liked to be frank in everything, said in an off-hand way:

'Don't you ever think of marrying Pop?'

Ma threw back her dark handsome head and roared with laughter.

'What?' she said, 'and give him a chance to leave me?'

'Scream,' Angela Snow said. 'Suppose he might at that.'

'Off like a hare.'

Angela laughed so much over her filtered half-cold coffee that she spilt most of it into the saucer. It was undrinkable anyway: as she had long since discovered filtered coffee always was. But she nevertheless supposed the French would always cling to it, just as the Scots did to herring and oatmeal.

'Well, must go,' she said. 'Must see what the adventurous Iris has been up to. Let me know if ever he does.'

Ma laughed in her friendliest fashion.

'Who? Pop? I'll send you a wire. That'll give you a bit of a start on Mademoiselle Dupont.'

'Oh! is she in the hunt too?'

Ma said she was afraid so. She'd be in a whale of a tizzy by the time that party was over.

'And not the only one.'

Graceful and elegant, Angela Snow stooped to kiss Ma a sporting goodbye, telling her at the same time to give Pop her best love, which Ma warmly promised to do, with knobs of brass and tinkling cymbals, as Pop himself was so fond of saying sometimes.

'God bless,' Angela said. 'Have to fix a hair-do somehow before that party. For two pins I'd have my blasted face lifted as well.'

'Where to?' Ma said, laughing again. 'You keep it as it is. Pop'd never forgive you.'

Angela Snow went back into the hotel on the pretext of telephoning a hairdresser but in reality on the offchance of running into Pop as he came downstairs. But the lounge, the reception desk, and the stairs were all deserted and she suddenly realized with unpleasantness that she might run into Alphonse instead. She didn't care for Alphonse. The process of being mentally undressed by strange men had never amused her. Nor, for some reason, did she like men who parted their hair down the middle. But now and then she couldn't help wondering what the virginal Iris would make of those too large, too handsome eyes.

'Did Mademoiselle wish for something please?'

It was Mademoiselle Dupont who came at length to the door of the Bureau and called the words. In reply Angela Snow said she was wondering about a hairdresser and was there one she could go to in the town?

'There is nothing exciting here. Nothing *soigné*. One must go to Morlaix or Brest.'

'Oh? Then I might go to Brest.'

'Phillippe: that is the name.'

'Phillippe,' Angela Snow said. 'Do you go there?'

'I regret not often. I can't afford it.'

'No? Not even for the party?'

Mademoiselle Dupont, who had been torn all day by the question of whether to have a hair-do or a new corset for the party and had almost decided on the corset, could only gaze in silence at Angela Snow's exquisitely smooth aristocratic yellow hair and wish that her own were like it, so that such difficult dilemmas and choices never arose.

'Got to make the party a success you know,' Angela Snow said.

'I think that Milord Larkin', Mademoiselle Dupont said rather loftily, 'will see to that. He has the *flair*.'

Drawn up sharply by the second mention of the word milord that day, Angela Snow had no time to make any sort of comment before Mademoiselle Dupont fluffed again and said:

'I am right in thinking that? Yes? He is a milord?'

'Down to the ankles,' Angela Snow said. 'And like every Englishman he's sure his home is his castle.'

At the mention of the word castle Mademoiselle Dupont was unable to speak. A castle – a *château*. There was something overpowering, *très formidable*, about the word castle.

'You must ask him to tell you about it,' Angela Snow said.

'I will ask that,' Mademoiselle Dupont said quietly.

After Angela Snow had departed Mademoiselle Dupont went upstairs. In her room she took off her dress, as she did every afternoon, and lay down on the bed. Like Angela Snow she had hoped for the chance of running into Pop on the stairs but nothing had happened and she lay for an hour alone and in silence, thinking largely of milord Larkin, the castle, and how altogether surprising the English were, but also of the entrancements of marriage and a lot of other things. She remembered the occasion when Pop had caressed her, brief and idle though it had been, with a warm swift hand, and how he would for ever remember her bedroom when he caught the scent of *les muguets*.

At the end of it she decided there was nothing for it but to have her hair dressed at Phillippe's and buy the new corset too. After all, she thought in typical French fashion, the bill for the party would be a big one and she would be able to afford it out of that.

She would have her hair done in that Empire style that was now so fashionable and that she knew would give her the illusion of height she needed so much. The corset must be a black one, trimmed with lace in parma violet at top and bottom, and every time she thought of it she started trembling.

· 8 ·

The evening of the party was warm and sultry, only the softest westerly wind ruffling the sea into small white pleats on the sand along the *plage*. Dinner, Mademoiselle Dupont had suggested, should be at eight-thirty. This would give the only two French families remaining in the hotel time to finish their food in comfort before retiring to the lounge. She had herself superintended the laying of the one long table, decorating it with bright orange dahlias, dark red rose petals strewn about the cloth, and sprays of asparagus fern.

Pop, who entranced everybody by appearing in a biscuit-coloured light-weight suit and a yellow silk bow-tie with large cranberry spots on it and a handkerchief to match, spent most of the time between six and seven mixing punch in the bar, tasting it frequently to see if it was any good at all. He finally decided it was a bit of a snorter.

He had seen the recipe for punch in some magazine Ma had bought. It was known as Colonel Bramley's Punch and you could have it either hot or cold, Pop deciding that since the evening was so sultry he would make it cold. Plenty of ice was the form.

The main ingredients were rum, white wine, Curaçao, lemon, and sugar, but after the first mixing Pop decided that the flavour of rum was, if anything, rather too prominent. Not everybody liked rum. He added brandy. This brought out a certain heaviness in the mixture. It needed sharpening up a bit. He tried a tumbler of Kirsch for this and decided that it was exactly the right thing for giving the punch a subtler but at the same time more brittle tone. When the ice was added just before seven o'clock, when everybody was expected to arrive, he casually decided that another bottle of white wine and a second dash of brandy wouldn't do anybody any harm at all and these were added together with large slices of fresh orange and a scattering of cocktail cherries, which had the effect of making the whole thing look pretty, amusing, partyish, and at the same time quite innocuous.

Although Ma, Mariette, Charley, and the children came downstairs after seven o'clock and gathered in the bar, from which Mademoiselle

Dupont had actually removed last year's heather and replaced it by bowls of dark purple asters, there was no sign of Angela Snow and her sister until a quarter to eight or of Mademoiselle Dupont until nearly forty minutes later.

Meanwhile the children drank Coca-cola and orange juice and the four grown-ups sampled the punch. Sometimes Ma allowed the children to sample the punch too and also sneak a slice of orange or a cherry out of it with their fingers so that they could have an extra suck.

'Good pick-me-up on a wash-day this, Pop,' she said. Just what she wanted. 'Wondered why you'd been so quiet since six o'clock.'

Ma was wearing a low-cut dress in deep purple, much the colour of the asters, with a narrow mink stole. She was drenched in a new perfume called 'Kick' and was wearing a pearl and diamanté comb in one side of her hair and three handsome rows of pearls round her neck. Mariette was wearing a dress of stunning low-cut simplicity in burgundy velvet, effective in its sheer richness but also because there was so little of it, and a necklace of garnet and diamond that Pop had bought her in Brest for the anniversary.

Now and then Pop decided that the punch was going down rather too fast and added another harmless dash of rum, a little Kirsch, or a glass of brandy.

By a quarter to eight, when Angela and Iris Snow arrived, the character of the mixture had changed completely, though Pop, by adding orange and cherries again, kept it looking much the same. Ma thought that, if anything, it was much nicer now.

'Very more-ish,' she said and settled down to a fifth glass of it. 'And so cool.'

As soon as Angela Snow and her sister arrived Pop remarked how warm the evening was and was quick to press them to a cooling glass.

'Ingredients?' Angela Snow said as she tasted it. 'I think it's another of your blinders.'

Cheers, she went on to say, if it was. If not there was plenty of time.

'Women's magazine recipe. Practically teetotal,' Pop explained. 'It's actually the coolth that makes it what it is.'

Iris Snow, who liked Pop's word coolth, sipped happily.

Their lateness in arrival was, she explained, entirely due to her. She had been to see a calvary at St Thégonnec and had missed the train. She smiled with unusual readiness and apologized. Her hair looked less home-cut than usual, Pop thought, and the dark coffee-brown frock she was wearing, apart from the fact that in the haste of dressing she had evidently had some difficulty in balancing the two protuberances underneath it, so that one was much lower than the other, suited her quite well and was modestly attractive.

But it was Angela Snow's dress that had everyone wide-eyed in admiration. Pop thought it a corker. If she had a stitch on underneath it he would be more than surprised. The embroidered purity of its line, somehow accentuated by her long drop ear-rings, was even more fetching than its colour, a pale turquoise, and the fact that it fitted like a skin.

About eight o'clock M. Mollet crept in, mole-like as ever, as if out of hiding. He had been sent to say that Mademoiselle Dupont wouldn't be long; she had been delayed by complications of the kitchen.

She had in fact been delayed by complications of the new corset. It was rather tight and the zip was awkward. Twice she had run down for one of the chambermaids to come and help zip her up but they were all giving a hand in the kitchen and it was M. Mollet who at last came up to her room, to face the unparalleled embarrassment of finding Mademoiselle Dupont less than half-dressed, with a figure white as marble under a shining sheath of pure black and purple frills.

The experience left him not knowing whether he was going this way or that. It was then crowned by the sudden vision of the tall English girl in long ear-rings and pure turquoise and the disturbing fact that though she was fully dressed she actually seemed to have far fewer clothes on than Mademoiselle Dupont had in her bedroom. A cosmic explosion could hardly have shaken him more. A kind of low sea-sickness rocked through him and Pop gave him a glass of punch, which he accepted in a nervous daze, confident only, as Mademoiselle Dupont already was, that things in the hotel had never been quite like this before and never would be again.

Nobody took much notice of the self-effacing little figure in black coat and pin-stripe trousers and presently he crept out again, head held timidly down, so that he accidentally knocked against Pop, who was ladling out a third glass of punch for Charley.

'*Quel twirp*,' Pop said and there was laughter from everybody except Angela Snow, who suddenly realized that, for some unaccountable reason, she felt intensely sorry for the little reception clerk, who spent all his days burrowing between desk and bureau, for ever like a mole.

It was twenty-five minutes past eight before Mademoiselle Dupont entered the bar. This was a strange experience in itself, since she could recall no one having had a drink there since Liberation Day. In traditional French fashion she was wearing all black, with long pearl-drop ear-rings to give the illusion of that extra height she needed. Tonight she looked

A Breath of French Air

positively *chic* and was enveloped in a strong sensational cloud of lily-of-the-valley.

Pop, whose progress in French had been quite marked – always so quick to pick everything up, as Ma said – went straight over to her, clasped her by both hands and said:

'*Mademoiselle! Enchantay!*' as if he had been doing it all his life.

'Delayed in the kitchen, my foot,' Angela Snow thought and realized suddenly that she was madly, unreasonably jealous. It was quite unlike her.

'Fascinating tie,' she said and went over to finger Pop's large yellow and cranberry butterfly that made him look so dashing. 'French?'

'English,' Pop said.

'Has that air,' she said. 'The Froggies simply couldn't do it, dear boy.'

The word 'Froggies' made Mademoiselle Dupont bristle. She had begun the evening with nervous apprehension anyway, the complications of the kitchen being so great and those of the corset hardly less so. She felt all too conscious of the corset. She was sure it would make her itch before the night was gone.

'Drink up,' Pop said. 'Everybody have one more for the wagon train.'

Mademoiselle Dupont, sipping punch, deliberately turned her back on Angela Snow and asked to be told what this cool, charming liquid was.

'In *anglais*, punch,' Pop said.

'*Ah! le punch.*'

'*Spécialité de la maison Larkin*,' Pop said. 'Larkin Special. Goes down well, eh? *Très bon, n'est-ce pas?*'

'*Extraordinaire. Excellent*,' Mademoiselle Dupont said and then remembered how, in books about England, one always read of gentlemen drinking *le punch*. It was like tea and fog: it was part of the true English scene. Everyone knew, of course, that England was perpetually shrouded in fog, that the sun hardly ever shone there and that no one ever, or hardly ever, drank anything but tea. But now she had recalled *le punch*. Undoubtedly it was an aristocratic thing.

She now suggested that they might, at any time, go in to dinner. Pop, ladling out the last glasses of punch and sending a final tumblerful to Alphonse in the kitchen, cordially agreed.

'Feeling quite peckish,' he said and hoped everyone else was.

The evening had begun well, he thought, and most people were laughing as they left the bar and went into the *salle à manger*. Everyone seemed properly warmed up, companionable, and happy.

Even Iris Snow, who had eaten nothing but two cream crackers since twelve o'clock midday, felt like a canary.

After the cooling punch the softer, warmer touch of *melon au porto* was like a velvety caress. Everyone agreed that that had been very well-chosen. Full marks. Absolutely. Even the twins mopped it up in no time, asking what it was called.

'There it is on the menu,' Charley said. 'You can read it. *Melon au porto.* Melon with port wine.'

The menu cards had been specially printed in gold and Mademoiselle herself had also ordered little decorations of gold doves to be added at each corner. She had searched for a long time for some suitable symbol of marital love and had finally decided that doves were it.

'Porto! Porto! old mother Shorto! Diddlum dorto!' the twins started shouting, and a smiling Pop, for once, had no word of reprimand.

A light white wine of the Loire, a little dry, accompanied the sole. It was colder, if anything, than the punch had been. Charley said he thought they married very well together and Pop said Charley should know. Ma remarked that she thought the sole was the best bit of fish she'd had in France and Mademoiselle Dupont beamed. Pop was sorry about the chips, though, and was on the verge of saying so when he changed his mind and said:

'In front of snails anyway. Anybody want to change and have snails? Don't all speak at once. Twins? Snails?'

'You're a snail!' the twins said. 'You're a silly old snail! Snail, snail, put out your horn –'

Pop, with happy restraint, merely smiled and Mademoiselle Dupont, who had always known how correct, undemonstrative, and reserved the English were, couldn't help thinking that their children, at table, sometimes enjoyed the strangest latitude.

Under these pleasantries and the cold white wine of the Loire, Iris Snow began to feel more and more like a singing bird. Now and then she became conscious of one of her protuberances slipping a little under her brown dress and she gave it a bit of a hitch.

Angela Snow began to wonder if she'd got a flea or something and gave her occasional looks of disapproval. She'd caught a flea once before at one of those wretched *pardons*. You never knew.

'And what's next? What's coming next?' Pop said, rubbing his hands. Things were going with a bang. 'The *rosbif.* Yes? No? I sink so – yes!'

The roast beef was presently wheeled in on a sort of large, ancient perambulator. It reposed there under a kind of silver shed. This had not been used for thirty years or so and, like the coffee filters, had gone rather brassy at the edges.

The wheeler-in was Alphonse, complete with white hat, white choker, a gravy spoon of about quart measure, and a carving knife two inches wide. His too large, too handsome eyes darted rapidly about the room like jets, catching Iris Snow in the act of doing a twitch. This he interpreted as a sign of secret recognition and took good note of it as he turned up the spirit flame that sprang out of the bowels of the perambulator to keep the beef warm.

Presently Alphonse was carving the *rosbif* with pride among rising steam and sizzling gravy. Every red slice came off with a lofty, dandyish flourish. The *pouding à la Jorkshire* was helped to the plates with a touch of fire and almost reverent extravagance – typical froggy, Pop thought.

Ma was given the first helping, Alphonse standing over her in a suspended bow to ask, in French, if madame would taste and pronounce judgement on the *pouding* please?

Mademoiselle Dupont translated this request with bilingual flutterings and Ma took a good mouthful of Yorkshire. Everyone waited in silence while she slipped it down. It wasn't half as good as she knocked up herself of a Sunday morning, she decided, but wasn't bad really and she said, in a strong English accent:

'*Très bon.* Very nice indeed. *Très bon.* Nice.' Ma speared a second piece of Yorkshire on the end of her fork and held it across the table to Pop. 'Better pass your judgement too, Pop, hadn't you?'

Pop, who was feeling in the mood to praise anything, even *saucisson à la mode d'ici*, accepted the pudding nippily and tasted it with a loud elastic smack of his lips. A moment later, searching for a word to describe what Alphonse had created, he was fired by a moment of happy inspiration, remembering a word the Brigadier had used.

'Delectable!' he said. 'Absolutely delectable. Hot stuff. *Formidable!*'

As if at a signal, Alphonse started to leap up and down, spontaneously brandishing the carving knife, at the same time darting flaming glances at Iris Snow, who twitched her bosom again in reply.

A moment later she was astounded to see Alphonse start careering round the table, waving the knife with sweeps of expert extravagance, as if he contemplated chasing her. A sudden transcendent thrill went through her, moving her strangely. It was all a dream. In imagination she suddenly saw herself being pursued by Alphonse over miles of Breton heather, among wild rocks, towards the sea, finally hiding herself from the dark penetrative pursuing eyes in some far-distant *allée couverte*, among secret tumuli.

Mademoiselle Dupont was horrified. After a single second of relief that with the approval of the *pouding à la Jorkshire* the second of the night's ordeals was over, the first having been with the corset, she was now faced with the fact that Alphonse was about to have one of his temperamental fits. Something, as Pop remarked so often of Charley, must have got into him, and she could only think it was the large glass of *le punch* and two equally large *cognacs* that Pop had had sent into the kitchen for the purpose of encouraging him. It was too *terrible*, too *effrayant*, for words.

Ma, on the other hand, starting laughing like a drain. The children started shrieking too, especially Victoria, who was easily liable to accidents if she pitched her voice too high. Iris Snow was laughing loudly herself, uncertain what to do about the second transcendent thrill that went through her at an even faster, more ecstatically piercing pace than the first, making her quiver from throat to toe. All she could do was to giggle wildly whenever Alphonse brandished the knife, each time having a strange spasmodic recurrence of her dream.

Suddenly, after Alphonse had run round the table three or four times, the flame under the meat perambulator leapt up and then went out with an unseemly plop that sounded not at all unlike a belch. As if at a second signal Alphonse stopped running. Breathing hard, he abandoned the carving knife in order to relight the flame and in another second, as the glow sprang from beneath the brassy meat cover, Iris Snow experienced a third transcending rush of emotion that took her far beyond rocks and tumuli and even the roast beef and Yorkshire that everyone was now enjoying happily.

'I sank you, ladish and jentlemens,' Alphonse said. He had learned these few words of English off by heart from the second cook, who had once worked in Whitechapel. 'Blast and damn, *merci mesdames et messieurs*, blast and damn, sank you! *Vive les Anglais! Vive le Jorkshire!*'

At this he suddenly took off his tall chef's hat, raised it, bowed politely, and backed out of the *salle à manger*, giving a final dark undressing glance at Iris Snow, who was trying hard to conceal her emotion by hastily sliding Yorkshire pudding into her mouth. She was not very successful, though she had to admit to herself that she had tasted nothing like the rich red beef and its delicious melting pudding for years.

Rich food, even more than the unaccustomed punch, the port, the white wine, and the Chambolle Musigny that accompanied the beef, was now having a strange and unprecedented effect on her. Its stimulus was most marked where she might least have expected it. She was beginning to feel queer thumpings in the bosom, with sudden longings for air.

Her head on the other hand seemed quite light and clear. Her mind retained all its sane, rippling canary-like quality. She was sure she had been perfectly lucid as Alphonse constantly regarded her with those immense, buttery eyes. Alphonse, on the other hand, thought otherwise and had noted over and over again how often she twitched at him. It was very interesting, that twitch.

'I knew the French'd never do the custard and jelly properly,' Ma said in a whisper to Angela Snow, who was sitting between her and Pop. 'The custard's like billstickers' paste.'

Angela Snow said she thought the French didn't really know custard: as custard, that was.

'Then it's about time they did,' Ma said, with something like severity.

She was in fact merely tasting the jelly and custard for the children's sake while actually waiting for *crêpes Suzette* to come on.

It was past eleven o'clock when Alphonse arrived back from the kitchen to make the business of the *crêpes Suzette* a sacrifice of joy. That was the best part of the evening, Ma thought. So did the children, who sprang out of their chairs every time a pan of golden flame went up and shrieked that it was just like fireworks.

'Ought to have the lights out,' Ma suggested. 'Look very pretty.'

When the lights were put out the flares of flaming liqueurs danced about the darkened *salle à manger*. The bright leaping light gave to the front of Angela Snow's skin-tight dress a remarkable effect of transformation. Her body looked no longer blue but silver and it would have been almost too much for Mademoiselle Dupont to bear if Pop, who was sitting next to her, hadn't thought it as good a moment as any to caress her thigh.

After that the dinner never seemed quite the same to her again. She gradually lost all hope of concentration. From that moment she never knew whether it was the fourth bottle of Chambolle Musigny they were drinking, or the fifth or what it was. In contrast to Iris Snow she had begun to feel quite light-headed and there was still champagne to come.

It came at twelve o'clock, together with the cake that Alphonse had made. Alphonse, more buttery-eyed than ever, bore the cake into the *salle à manger* himself and set it down, with pride and a flourish, before Mariette and Charley.

Perfick, Perfick!

The cake was iced in bright soapy pink, with a single large red candle on it, and on top of it were the words imprinted circularwise, in red:

HAPPY BIRDSDAY ANNIVERSAIRE AND GOOD LOOK

When she read these words Ma felt very touched and then everyone toasted Mariette and Charley in champagne. Even M. Mollet had crept out of hiding again, mole-like and shy, to take part in the toasting, staring with filmy eyes at the blue vision of Angela Snow that had troubled him so much, and so increasingly, ever since he had first seen it at eight o'clock.

All through the toasting, Pop stood with swelling paternal pride, watching Mariette. No doubt about it, she was sumptuous: even more beautiful, he thought, than Ma had once been. Charley boy was lucky all right and Pop could only hope that he would, in the shortest possible time, show his appreciation of the fact in the right and proper way. Pop couldn't help thinking too of the day, perhaps, not all that far ahead, when Primrose, Victoria, and the twins would begin to develop too on those same impressive, luscious lines. Perhaps by that time Mariette and even Montgomery would be having children and – who knows? – him and Ma following suit again. He was all set for that. That would be the day.

As if in answer to his thoughts, as the hotel's old brassy gramophone started playing for dancing, he heard a soft voice say:

'Wouldn't you dance with me, Pop? I'd love to have the first dance with you.'

It was Primrose. There was an indefinable half-sad smile on her face, the sadness heightened by the fact that she had, Pop thought, put just the faintest touch of lipstick on and had crimped her dark hair down over her forehead in a curious little fringe, in the way the French girls did.

Course he would dance, he told her, and she at once held up her slim sun-brown arms, again with a touch of sadness, the fingers rather drooping.

'Thought you wouldn't ask me,' she said sadly as he swung her away to the tune of an old favourite, *La Vie en Rose*, 'I've been hoping you would.'

Pop said he was sorry and also that it hadn't struck him that he'd been expected to ask his own daughter to dance. Laughing merrily, he said he reckoned she ought to have asked him.

'Oh! no,' she said and again the voice was full of her plaintive sadness, 'I couldn't do that. Pop, it just shows how much you know.'

Oh! and what about? Pop asked her.

'Women.'

It was some seconds before Pop recovered from this withering blow.

When he finally did so he suddenly thought it diplomatic to side-step a second one – in case one should be coming – by neatly changing the subject with a ripple of a laugh.

'Well, home tomorrow. Old home sweet home.'

Primrose, unsmiling, wasn't deceived a bit and showed it by looking him full in the face, her dark soft eyes full of sad disapprobation.

'Why do you have to sound so glad about it?'

Glad? Pop said. Glad? Why not? It was nice to go on holiday but it was nicer still to go home. Everybody said so.

'Everybody?' she said. 'Who's everybody? What do they know?'

Pop, unable to think of a sensible answer to this crushing question, found himself looking down at his daughter's bright yellow dress. He was surprised to find it cut rather wide and low at the neck, where she was wearing a double row of pearls. He was even more surprised to discover that the body underneath it was no longer quite that of a little girl, and that she had beautiful little salt cellars, very like Angela Snow's, just at the base of her olive neck, where the pearls were.

'Don't you want to go home?' he said.

He was up against it now all right, he thought. He remembered what Ma had said. He'd got a handful now.

'No, Pop,' she said. 'That's it. I didn't sleep a wink all last night for thinking about it. Nor the night before. Nor the night before that.'

Pop, in his airy way, said for crying out gently whatever was it that had done that to her? For the life of him he couldn't imagine.

'Pop,' she said and again she looked up at him, this time no longer with sadness but with a glance so swift that it had swung away again before he could catch it, leaving him looking down at nothing but the dark oval of her hair. She had very pretty hair and it curled fluffily in the nape of her neck, just like Ma's did. 'I want to ask you something.'

Ask on, Pop said. Fire away. Money, he supposed.

'Pop,' she said and her voice was sad again, with something like low passion in it, 'do I *have* to go home? *Must* I go home?'

Didn't mean to tell him she wanted to stay here, in France, did she? Pop said. All on her lonesome? All by herself?

'Not by myself,' she said. 'I won't be alone.'

It wouldn't be much fun in the hotel, he reminded her. The season was practically over.

'I'll have someone to stay with,' she said.

Before answering Pop permitted himself the luxury of humming a few bars of *La Vie en Rose*. Very good song, *La Vie en Rose*. Good thing

Mademoiselle Dupont had fished out some of these old favourites. They got you.

'Oh?' he said. 'Who?'

'My boy-friend.'

For once unsurprised, Pop was back as quick as a bird, laughing.

'Thought you had two?' he said.

Pained dark eyes held him for a sharp second or two, but whether in renewed sadness or sheer scorn for his brief burst of laughter and the little he understood about women he simply never knew.

'I've given one up,' she said. 'I had to. I had to make the decision.'

Though he'd always held that there was safety in numbers, Pop hummed what he thought were a few consolatory, approving murmurs, mostly mere wordless echoes from *La Vie en Rose*, but somehow they didn't seem to impress her. She was silent for once, unconsoled.

'What's this one's name?' he said.

'Marc-Antoine.'

Typical Froggy, Pop thought. Very fancy.

'And how old's he?'

'A year older than me. Twelve.'

'H'm,' Pop said, heavily, quite unlike himself. 'H'm.'

A second later he found himself looking down at her, but she at once looked away.

'He says I can go and live with him,' she said.

'Eh?' Pop said. He spoke faintly. Good grief, bit early wasn't it? He knew from experience that Ma had been well forward and all that for her age, but dammit. After all, there were limits –

'I mean with his parents. His father keeps a confectioner's shop. A *pâtisserie*. I could – Oh please, Pop' – suddenly he couldn't help thinking that the voice was uncannily, disturbingly like that of the loveliest and most insinuating of all his daughters, Mariette – 'please, Pop, couldn't I? Please?'

Pop, giving what he thought was a sagacious wag of the head, a gesture meant to be taken seriously, said simply:

'You'd better ask your Ma.'

Primrose, who like Mariette wasn't her father's daughter for nothing, was back as quick as a swallow.

'I asked her. She said I was to ask you.'

Cornered, Pop took refuge in a few further light bars of *La Vie en Rose*, but he knew that that lark couldn't go on much longer. There was a crisis about somewhere.

'Well, I don't know,' he said, his voice heavy again. What the devil could he say? He simply didn't know. He could only wonder, in an unprofound moment, what Ma would say? Perhaps Ma didn't know either? 'Well, I don't know –'

Profounder instincts than his own kept Primrose silent. She hadn't even another pleading, imploring please to offer and he knew he was in a spot.

'This wants thinking about,' he told her in another heavy but not very deep excursion – dammit, what was all that psychology lark that Ma talked about? Didn't that come in somewhere? With something like a flurry of desperation, utterly unusual in him, he made an effort to sum up the kernel of the matter in a single phrase and came out with half a dozen words of brave simplicity that struck even him as being not quite what was wanted: 'Long way from home, you know.'

A second later she withered him with a glance both needle-like and wretched. Really downright wretched. He expected any moment to see big, sorrowful tears welling from her eyes. That would be the end. That would get him. Dammit, he was slap in the middle of it now all right.

'It's all very well for you,' she said. Somebody had turned the record over or put on another one and now the gramophone was playing a tune he didn't know at all, but which Primrose did – a heart-twister of yearning southern sorrow called *Anima Core*. 'You're grown up. You've forgotten about things –'

Pop started to assure her that there were some things he hadn't forgotten about yet, but she said peremptorily:

'You'd like to part us, I expect.'

'Well, I –'

'Don't you ever hear that bit Charley's always quoting?' she said. 'It's his favourite bit. "*Love is not love that alters when it alteration finds,*" – we have it at school too sometimes.'

Pop was silent. That feller Keats again. Charley-boy all over. He had to hand it to Charley. Terrific influence on the family that chap had been. No doubt about it.

Gloom hung over him like a cloud and he was profoundly wishing he knew a bit more about psychology, if not Keats, when a cheerful languid voice hailed him and said:

'Why the dark deep furrowed brow, dear boy? The *crêpes Suzette* not settling or what? or shouldn't a girl ask? Cheer up, chum.'

It was Angela Snow, dancing past him with Montgomery, and Pop, suddenly restored to his perky, normal self again, laughed back in typical rousing fashion.

'Only Juliet here,' he said, stroking Primrose's soft dark hair – dammit, he wasn't sure he wasn't very nearly quoting Keats or Shakespeare or somebody himself now, '– wants to stay in France with her Romeo.'

'And rightly so,' Angela Snow said. 'Got the right idea. You're going to let her, of course, aren't you? I'll kick you if you don't.'

'Course,' Pop said. 'Course. Got to start sometime.'

'Sensible man,' she said. 'Anyway I'll be here for a while yet. I'll do a chaperone.'

Unstartled by a word only vaguely familiar to him, Pop watched the turquoise, willowy vision float away and then found himself, a moment later, looking down at a pair of dark eyes brimming over, as he had feared they would be, with tears – except that they were now clear, bright tears of joy.

'Oh! Pop,' was all Primrose could say. 'Oh! Pop. Marc-Antoine will be thrilled.'

French blood in the family now, Pop thought. Blimey, what next?

'It's just like *The Sugar Plum Fairy*,' Primrose said softly, her olive lids quite closed. 'I never imagined –'

'Like *who?*' Pop said.

'Tchaikowsky.'

She was light-headed, Pop thought. Must be. It did that to you when you were young. You went off your grub and got to thinking you were floating about, empty.

He now hadn't the vaguest idea what his daughter, with eyes still lusciously closed, was talking about and he decided it could only be another of them larks they learnt you nowadays at school. And again, as if sensing his thoughts, she said:

'It's about the little girl who goes to bed after a Christmas party and can't sleep and then comes downstairs and watches *The Sugar Plum Fairy* dance and all that. Just like this. Haven't you ever heard of it?'

Pop had to confess he hadn't. Bit out of his range, like that feller Keats and the rest of 'em. Nevertheless he was fascinated, as always, by the hint of an excursion into new upper worlds and asked her what else they learnt them nowadays at school? You never knew.

'Oh! biology,' she said. 'Sex and all that.'

For crying out gently, he thought. No wonder Ma had said she was developing early. It didn't surprise him, considering the help they got. Again, for the second or third time, he didn't know what to say and was saved the necessity of attempting any comment by another airy remark from Primrose, delivered this time with dark eyes fully open, roundly staring up at him, beautifully glistening.

'They don't teach them sex in French schools though,' she said.

'Oh?' Pop said, 'don't they? Well, well. Too bad.' He laughed in his customary rousing fashion. He'd had an idea for a long time the Froggies were a backward lot. Even in sex. How did she know they didn't teach it?

'Because I asked Marc-Antoine,' she said. 'He was awfully surprised we had it.'

Didn't wonder at it, Pop thought. Didn't wonder at all.

'Anyway he was very interested and that's how we started to get to know each other better.'

He must tell Ma all this. Ma would certainly have to hear all about this lark, Pop was thinking. At the same time he was wondering if another glass of champagne wouldn't do him all the good in the world, when suddenly the music stopped.

In the short ensuing silence he saw Ma talking to one of the French chambermaids. He guessed little Oscar was awake and was quite certain of it a moment later when he heard Ma say she'd be up in a minute to soothe him down and that if punch, white wine, red wine, champagne, and *crêpe Suzette* wouldn't do the trick nothing would.

With an involuntary rush of paternal affection he turned to pat Primrose on the head and was astonished to find that he stood with empty arms. A voice low with emotion thanked him with a few happy whispered syllables for the dance and everything. He stood without a coherent thought he could offer in answer, trying hazily to disentangle all that stuff about Sugar Plum Fairies, Tchaikowsky, sex, biology, and what they learnt you nowadays in school, so bemused that he probably wouldn't have heard the next record, which was that old favourite *Night and Day* if it hadn't been that a curious thing occurred.

As Iris Snow heard the opening bars of the music something suspiciously like a sob sprang from her throat. A moment later she hastily pressed a tiny lace square of handkerchief to her mouth and started rushing from the room.

By one o'clock Pop had danced once each with Mariette, Ma, and Angela Snow and was now having a waltz with Mademoiselle Dupont. Ma warned him several times of the virtues of equal shares.

'Got to treat all of us the same,' she said. 'It's Iris Snow after Mademoiselle Dupont. No favouritism. Don't forget.'

Pop, who was ready to distribute favours everywhere, remarked that

Iris Snow had disappeared somewhere and laughingly supposed she might have gone off to catch the flea.

'What flea?' Ma said.

Pop explained how Angela Snow, who was increasingly irritated by her sister, had jocularly told him about the twitch.

'Not a very nice thing to say,' Ma said. 'Still, don't you catch it though.'

He left her to find Mademoiselle Dupont, who was in excited mood. While she danced she kept breathing harder and harder and as the dance went on she threw back her head, laughing freely, and said she felt like singing.

Rather to Pop's surprise she actually burst into a few bars of song. Her voice came out as a rather pleasant not uncultured contralto and not a bit as if she had adenoids, as French singers often do. Pop then said jovially that he felt like having a bit of a warble himself and on the spur of the moment suggested she should join him in *It Had To Be You* – but she didn't know that masterpiece, a favourite of Pop's youth, and they sang *C'est si bon* instead, she singing the French and he, in a light falsetto, what he could remember of the English words. Soon everyone else was singing too and the bright noise was punctuated by the cracking volley of champagne corks.

Iris Snow could hear them as she stood on the terrace outside, talking to Alphonse, in French, under the plane trees. Every moment she felt more than ever like a wild canary. She had never had so much to drink in her life and in rapid sentences she was telling Alphonse how much she adored his country. France was her mecca. Everything about France was so cultured. There was nowhere in the world like France. She adored it, its people, its art, its manners, its wine, and its food.

From a woman who fed largely on soft-boiled eggs, dry toast, and anchovy paste on biscuits this was said with a remarkable degree of passion, and in the lights of the hotel windows Alphonse kept her held with remorseless charm in the overlarge handsome eyes that were now so like big, shining prunes.

Soon she was aware again of a transcendent rushing thrill, that strange, unsteady thumping in the bosom and the panting desire for air. She longed to rush down to the beach, she said. A few moments later Alphonse guided her unsteadily to the *plage*, where she found it much easier to sit down than stand up and where she suddenly found herself remarking recklessly, for no reason at all, in a voice that seemed not to belong to her, that the night was just like Grecian honey. It was all like new warm honey from the south, she said, and she longed to rush to the sea. A moment later she started to take off her shoes and stockings, going about it so ineptly that Alphonse, without asking, started to give help with the suspenders.

With a protesting shriek of joy she suddenly dashed across the beach to the sea. The little pleated phosphorescent waves were just like milk, she thought, and over in the western sky a great star – Oh! no, a planet, she supposed – was hanging like burnt gold above the sea – oh! so like a wonderful great big gingerbread, she called out crazily, with all the gilt still on!

Alphonse, who hadn't the vaguest idea what she was talking about, pursued her to the edge of the water. By the time he reached it she was already paddling, ecstatically westwards, up to her knees. With the water rising up her legs she suddenly decided to tuck her frock in her knickers, which were the same shade of dull coffee brown as the dress. Seeing this, Alphonse started to take off his shoes and stockings too and roll up the legs of his blue and white striped chef's trousers, which Iris adored.

At this point the sea, as Charley had once explained, was shallow for half a mile from the shore, and Iris was still only up to her knees, thirty yards out, when Alphonse caught up with her. He at once embraced her passionately round the lower middle and started kissing her madly on one ear.

In the middle of this she felt her knees buckle underneath her. In a moment she was up to her armpits, kneeling on sand. Alphonse went under too and in this uncomfortable position, still crying out that the night was like honey and the stars like gilded gingerbread, Iris Snow surrendered gladly to whatever was coming, with low sobs of joy.

Back in the hotel, while Alphonse was also making the interesting discovery that the English could be surprisingly unrestrained, Mademoiselle Dupont was taking advantage of Ma's absence upstairs to invite Pop into the Bureau. There was something of importance she wished to say.

With shining eyes she asked him to accept a small green leather box from her.

'A small thing. A little parting gift for you.'

Opening the box, Pop found inside it a pair of silver cuff-links reposing on a bed of emerald velvet.

'Please to look. There is something –'

Pop took the cuff-links out and, looking more closely, found that Mademoiselle Dupont had had his initials engraved on the faces of the links in the form of a monogram.

'Very nice,' he said. 'Absolutely perfick –'

'It is just a small thing. Just –'

'Wonderful. Very *chic*,' he went on and said he didn't know how to thank her. *'Très snob.'*

Mademoiselle Dupont, without saying so, very much hoped he would thank her by kissing her and in fact he did. The kiss was of a kind she had never experienced before and presently knew that she probably never would do again. Under the long extremely well-directed pressure she several times thought the new corset would give way.

When it was all over she stood looking up at him with unsteady luminous eyes, holding his face in her hands.

'Tomorrow you will be back in England,' she said. 'Tell me about your house in England. Your *château.*'

Oh! it was perfick, Pop said. A paradise. You wouldn't find anything more perfick in the world nowhere, he told her, and then in that glowing hyper-sensory way of his warmed up to the business of describing how the junk-yard was in spring, with cuckoos calling, nightingales going glorious hell for leather night and day in the bluebell wood, water lilies gold and white in the stream, fields glowing with strawberries, meadows rich with buttercups and grasses, and all the rest of the marvellous, mad, mid-summer lark in England.

For some time she listened to all this as she might have listened to some sort of celestial revelation and then decided to ask a question. It was perhaps a rather indelicate question, but she knew that if she didn't ask it now she never would.

'And will you perhaps marry one day?'

Pop patted her playfully on the roundest part of the corset with an especially warm affectionate hand, and laughed loudly. Mademoiselle Dupont had never known hands so warm.

'Shall if somebody asks me.'

'Someone will,' she told him with transfixed, shining eyes. 'I'm sure that someone will.'

Better give her the other half, Pop thought, and set the seal on the evening, the gift and her complete and luminous joy by repeating the kiss at even greater length, under even greater pressure.

'I have decided to reconstruct the hotel,' she said. 'To have an *ascenseur* and water hot and cold in all the bedrooms. It was you who gave me such ideas.'

That was the spirit, Pop said. *Très snob.* Pull 'em down. Start afresh. He wouldn't mind putting a bit of money into it himself if it could be wangled.

'We could be partners?' she said.

'Could be,' Pop said. 'Could be.'

'It is always you,' she said, 'who has such wonderful ideas. Before you came to stay here I had no courage for such changes –'

'Courage my foot,' Pop said and gave the corset a final semi-stroking amorous pat in the roundest part. 'Natural. If you want an apple off the tree go and get the damn thing.'

Still pondering on this remark as if it were some mysterious, mystical text for living, Mademoiselle Dupont went back with Pop to the *salle à manger*, where everyone except Angela Snow and M. Mollet was still dancing.

In an astonished spasm of jealousy Angela Snow watched her come into the room, holding Pop in a kind of aerial embrace of wonder. For a few electrified seconds she experienced an amazing impulse to rush over and smack Mademoiselle Dupont's face as hard as she could.

While she was still trying to resist it something surprising occurred. She suddenly found herself being asked to dance by M. Mollet.

M. Mollet had wanted to ask her to dance all evening but had lacked the courage. Now, shy and flushed, pince-nez sparkling, he began dancing with her in a way she hadn't experienced before. He held her consistently at arm's length, as if afraid of letting the front of his body touch the long sheath-like curves of hers. He was several inches shorter than she was, which meant that he was constantly forced to gaze up at her. In this way she found herself concentrating on his eyes. Behind the glasses the pupils were a peculiar mid-shade of brown, like partly roasted coffee beans. They were sad, mute, appealingly funny little eyes and suddenly she liked them.

After a speechless five minutes she suddenly felt a dreamy and extra-ordinary impulse to kiss M. Mollet bang in the centre of the forehead. Fortunately the music stopped a moment later, waking her.

'And a damn good thing too,' she thought. 'If you'd have kissed him the poor dear would have dropped down dead. Don't be so lethal.'

In a second all her flippancy was back. The jealous creature who had wanted to slap Mademoiselle Dupont's face had disappeared.

Meanwhile, on the far side of the room, in the electric light, the delicate little prisms of Ma's diamanté comb flashed with many colours as Pop paused to joke with her.

'It's time you had another dance with Angela,' she told him. 'Fair's fair.'

It was nearly four o'clock, Pop reminded her. He wanted to sit down with a quiet glass of champagne somewhere. Even he was getting tired.

'Do as I say,' Ma said. 'Have one more dance with her and then get into bed.'

Pop threw back his head and laughed uproariously.

'Ma,' he said, 'I think you'd better say that sentence in some other way, hadn't you?'

Ma shrieked, digging him joyfully in the ribs, realizing what she had said.

A moment later Pop found himself dancing with the same languid, casual, flippant vision who had long since endeared herself to him as a sporting, kindred spirit.

She, as if unable to recover from M. Mollet's technique of dancing at arm's length, let Pop hold her in that way too, looking straight into his happy, perky eyes and giving him a sporting wink or two.

'Well?'

'Well?' Pop said.

'Whale of a party.'

Pop said he thought so too and she said:

'One thing missing, though.'

'Oh?'

'That proposal.'

'From me?'

'From you,' she said. 'Very nearly too late now. I've practically given myself to M. Mollet.'

'Have a heart,' Pop said. 'For crying out gently.'

'Love him. Adore him,' she said. 'He's sweet. Surprised?'

Pop admitted he was very surprised but remarked that there was no accounting for tastes.

'But I do, dear boy,' she said. 'He's so small. And moley. And brown and all that. One wants to hug the wretched man. Don't you fathom?'

Pop said he didn't fathom and told her, much to her surprise, that he thought it was a clear case of psychology. It was something she'd missed somewhere at some time or never had. See?

For answer she drew him nearer and laid her lovely head on his shoulder.

'This I wouldn't have missed for all the world,' she said, 'for all the world, my sweet. For all the world I wouldn't have missed it. It's been absolutely perfick. But then with you it always would be.'

Impulsively she kissed him as she had wanted to kiss M. Mollet, in the centre of the forehead, and an astonished Pop almost recoiled from a display of a technique with which he had been totally unacquainted before.

'That's for keeps,' she said, in a whisper. 'Don't lose it, will you?'

Half an hour later the party was over. Nobody in the hotel was awake except M. Mollet, who had been so shattered by the evening's experiences that he was busy taking aspirin, and Mademoiselle Dupont, who lay full length on her bed in darkness, still in her corset, thinking over and over again of how she would reshape the hotel, put in an *ascenseur* and hot and cold water in all the bedrooms and how, perhaps, she might have a partner; and also of the fogless splendours of an England astonishingly revealed as abounding in strawberries, cuckoos, water-lilies, nightingales, and *pouding à la Jorkshire.*

Outside the hotel nobody was awake either; except Iris Snow, who was walking slowly up and down the *plage*, watching the setting planet that was so like a gingerbread with all the gilt still on, trying to find a pair of lost stockings and all the time singing a happy bare-foot song.

· 9 ·

In the morning Angela Snow woke at eleven o'clock with a headache. She had been a miserable meanie about Mademoiselle Dupont, she thought, and it wasn't like her. She felt very, very cross with herself. And without breakfasting or waking Iris, who hadn't come in till six o'clock, she went down into the town and ordered two dozen roses to be sent to Mademoiselle Dupont in the afternoon. There was nothing she could think of to say as a message and she sent them without a card.

Then she decided to go and say goodbye to the Larkins and then, a moment later, impulsively decided not to after all. Enough, after all, was as good as a feast. It was all over now and she could only send them a silent, sporting blessing, thinking as she did of the long, golden, light-headed afternoon on the dunes, when salt and sun had burned her lips and the blown breath of sea and pines had been strong enough to make her even happier and tipsier than Pop's cocktails and the wine had done.

The result was that when the Rolls finally drew away from the Beau Rivage at half past one only two people besides Mademoiselle Dupont and M. Mollet, furtive as ever, stood on the terrace, under the plane trees, to wave goodbye. Like two silent torch bearers, Primrose and Marc-Antoine stood solemnly holding large pink-and-chocolate ice-creams in bright saffron-coloured cornets, giving the tops of them occasional licks with bright pink tongues. Neither of them uttered a single syllable in farewell and after Pop had been struck once again by the dubious distant prospect of having French blood in the family he couldn't help noticing that Marc-Antoine, who was the colour of suet and wore large shining steel-rimmed spectacles, looked remarkably like a younger, smaller, froggier Mr Charlton. Funny how his daughters attracted the type.

When everything was finally packed and everyone was in the car – Ma quite imperial in the back, with little Oscar in her arms – Pop went up to the steps of the hotel and under the astonished eyes of M. Mollet gave Mademoiselle Dupont a prolonged parting sample of amorous affection that even had the children cheering from the car.

'Here, stand back and let the dog see the rabbit!' Ma called.

'*Au revoir!*' Pop said. 'Goodbye, Mademoiselle,' and at last retreated from her dazed figure with several debonair waves of the hand. '*À bientôt! Au revoir, merci!* So long! Goodbye.'

'Goodbye!' she called. '*Au revoir!* Goodbye! *Adieu!*'

'Goodbye! *Au revoir!*' everyone called. '*Adieu.* Goodbye!'

When Pop got back into the Rolls even Ma had to confess she was surprised at the length and generosity of Pop's prolonged farewell.

'You wouldn't be if you'd seen the bill,' Pop said. 'Dammit, might as well have my money's worth.'

The bill was a blinder. He doubted very much if he'd ever get over the bill. Percentages for this, taxes for that, services for the other. Breathing charges. He doubted if even Charley, that master of figures, would ever be able to sort out all the dodgy squeezes in that bill. It had very nearly skinned him out, he told Ma, very nearly skinned him.

'Think we got enough to get home with?' Ma said.

'Might have to pawn the Rolls,' Pop said serenely. 'Well, so much for the French lark.'

Still, he thought a moment later, it was all over, it was well wurf it, and he gave a final chorus of contrapuntal toots of the horn in debonair farewell as the Rolls moved away.

As soon as the Rolls was out of sight and Pop's cheerful tooting of first the melodious tune of the country horn and then the symphonic brass of the town one had died away Mademoiselle Dupont rushed back into the hotel, determined that no one should detect the tears in her eyes. But when the red roses arrived at two o'clock there was no help for it and she lay for the rest of the afternoon on her bed, weepily watching the roses in their big glass vase and seeing over and over again the pictures Pop had painted for her of his home, his *château*, the lordly paradise, in England. Never again would she say that the English were frigid and reticent or restrained or that they took their pleasures sadly or that fog perpetually covered their land. She knew it to be otherwise.

Meanwhile, as the Rolls drove along the coast, Ma called Pop through the speaking-tube.

'I don't know what you did to Mademoiselle Dupont last night but you got her in a proper tizzy.'

'Nothing,' Pop said airily. 'Nothing. Not a thing.'

'Did you ask her to marry you?'

Pop said he rather thought he had. Hadn't he ought to have done? Ma wasn't offended? After all she'd given him the cuff-links. Had to encourage her a bit.

'Oh! it's not that,' Ma said and started laughing in her customary hearty fashion. 'I was only thinking I hope she don't have to wait as long as I have.'

Pop burst out laughing too. That was one of Ma's good ones. Well, bill or no bill, it had been a pretty good holiday. Done everybody a whale of good, he thought, getting to know how foreigners lived. Especially Mariette and Charley, who both looked in the pink. He'd expect results now.

'I expect you asked Angela too, didn't you?' Ma said down the tube.

'Shouldn't wonder,' Pop said. 'She said summat about it.'

Ma said she wasn't worried about Angela. She was a sport. She could take care of herself. But she didn't want Pop going round putting people in a tizzy and breaking their hearts. You'd got to draw the line somewhere.

Pop agreed, but still when you were in Rome –

'Oh! talking about Rome, there's another thing,' Ma said. 'Have you thought any more about little Oscar's names?'

Pop was quick to confess he hadn't.

'Well, I know you've been busy, but we can't let the poor little mite go about all his life with only one name, can we?' Ma said. 'That would be a nice thing, wouldn't it?'

Terrible, Pop said.

'Well, I've been thinking a lot about it. Are you listening?'

Yes, Pop told her on the tube, he was listening.

'Well,' Ma said, 'I tell you what.'

'Half a minute. We want something good. Something special. No half larks. Something a bit *très snob.*'

'I know that,' Ma said. 'Anyway I've thought what I'd like to call him.'

'Oh?' Pop said. 'What?'

'I thought we'd call him Oscar Livingstone David Larkin.'

Pop was silent for some moments. All his strong paternal instincts came steeping warmly to the surface as he contemplated the proposed trio of names for his son. The names had got to be right, he thought again, no half larks.

Almost immediately he had a qualm about it and called back to Ma down the tube:

'No, Ma. Won't do. Not them. Can't have them.'

'Oh?' Ma said. 'Why not?'

'Makes his initials O.L.D.,' Pop said. 'He'll be called Old Larkin all his life. Can't have that.'

Ma cordially agreed; they couldn't possibly have that; and before she could think of anything else to say Pop called her again on the tube.

'Giving us a bit of trouble, this one,' he said. 'Good job it wasn't twins,' and went on to shoot a sudden, uneasily pertinent question at Charley. 'Twins run in your family, Charley old man?'

Not that he knew of, Charley said.

'Well they do in ours!' Pop said in direct, open challenge, 'you want to watch what you're up to.'

And what did that mean? Ma said. Watch what who was up to?

'Well, you know,' Pop said darkly. 'Somebody or other.'

Mr Charlton treated these exchanges with silence, not only because it was a silence he thought they deserved but also because he couldn't for the life of him think of anything remotely sensible to say.

'What was that you said about Rome, Ma?' Pop said. 'Didn't you say once you wanted to call him after some Roman Emperor?'

'I did an' all,' Ma said. 'But I'm blowed if I can remember which one it was now. Tiberius, I think.'

Back in a flash of scolding breath came Charley:

'Not on your life. Not that one. Not on your nelly.'

'Why not?' Ma said.

'You'd hardly want to call him after a judicial murderer, do you?'

Charley at it again, Pop thought, in silent admiration. Charley away again. Amazing feller. You never knew where Charley was off to next. He certainly used his loaf sometimes.

'I should think not,' Ma said. 'He's got a soft nature, this boy. Wasn't there one called Octavius, though? I remember him on telly once. In a play.'

'You can't possibly call him Octavius,' Charley said. 'He's the seventh, not the eighth.'

'Who is?' Pop said.

'Oscar. Besides Oscar Octavius sounds a bit much, don't you think? Call him Septimus if you want a Roman name.'

'Septimus?' Ma said. 'Why Septimus?'

'Septimus – the seventh. Sept – the same as in French. The same as September. The seventh month.'

Mariette, who occasionally found it necessary to keep Charley in check, he was so clever sometimes, said quickly:

'September isn't the seventh month, lovey. It's the ninth.'

Back in a revelatory flash came Charley again:

'Ah! but it used to be, darling, before the calendar was changed. Just as November used to be the ninth and December the tenth.'

Pop was stunned again to silent admiration. Wonderfully clever feller, Charley. Terrific clever feller. No keeping up with Charley.

'I think Septimus sounds rather nice,' Ma said, kissing Oscar on the ear, 'it suits his nature. You like it, Pop?'

He did, Pop said. It had that rather *très snob* touch about it. What Charley sometimes called the *je ne sais quoi*.

'Not too difficult?' Ma said. 'After all we want to give him names people can say.'

Pop treated this remark with a short soft laugh of scorn. What was the name of that kid at the post office? he wanted to know. Horsa or something, wasn't it? Septimus was no worse than that. Who was Horsa anyway?

'Saxon King,' Charley said blandly. 'Had a brother named Hengist.'

Altogether too taken aback to speak, Pop could only silently congratulate Ma on the swiftness with which she once again made one of her nippy changes of subject.

'What was the name of that other explorer?' Ma said and then started laughing inconsequently, thinking of Charley. It would certainly be a bomb under Charley if Mariette had twins. That would make him use his loaf a bit. They could call them Hengist and Horsa too.

'Who?' Pop said. 'Shackleton?'

'No, before him,' Ma said. 'A foreigner.'

The word foreigner struck a certain discord in Pop, who found himself silent again, thinking hard but at a loss. Again Ma couldn't think of the name she wanted either and it was Charley who at last, as so often before, came to the rescue.

'Columbus. Is that the one you've got in mind?'

Columbus, Ma said. Of course. That was it.

'Oscar Columbus,' Pop repeated several times over. 'That's got class. Oscar Columbus. That's a bit of *très snob*, an' all, Ma. I like that.'

Ma said she liked it too and should they settle on Oscar Septimus Columbus David then?

'Oh! not David,' Mariette said. 'I hate David.'

Pop confessed he too wasn't all that gone on David either and urged Ma to put her thinking cap on. Ma was always the one who had the brain waves. She was a dabster for names.

Less than half a minute later Ma confirmed Pop's faith in her by laughing merrily down the tube and saying she wasn't sure but she thought she'd got it.

'How about Dupont?' she said. 'Oscar Columbus Septimus Dupont Larkin?'

It tickled him to death, Pop said. Dupont – just the job. Perfick. It absolutely tickled him to death. *Très snob.*

'That's that then,' Ma said calmly. 'And if we can't have a wedding when we get home, at least we can have a christening, can't we? Fair enough?'

Fair enough, Pop said. Any excuse for a party.

'And I tell you something else I just thought of,' Ma said.

Oh? Pop wanted to know. What was that?

'I thought we'd ask Mademoiselle Dupont to be godmother,' she said. 'Sort of bring her into the family.'

That was a corker, Pop said. He wondered what Mademoiselle would think of that?

'Blessed if I know,' Ma said. 'You never can tell what these French-women are thinking, I always say,' and then realized why. 'After all I don't suppose you can if you don't know their language, can you?'

A moment later the thought of little Oscar having a French godmother set Pop slapping his knee and roaring with laughter. Joyful noises gurgled down the speaking-tube and the sound of the Rolls's contrapuntal horns rang royally across the rocky slopes of heather, somewhere among which Charley's beloved little train, symbol of travel long ago, seemed to let out a terse and mocking toot in reply.

'Godmother Dupont,' Pop said. 'Well, I'll go to the bone-house. I'll go to the ossuary.'

'Which,' Ma told him blandly but not uncordially, down the tube, 'is just about where you'll end up one of these fine days,' and then, with a sigh, settled serenely back on the Rolls's deep dove-grey cushions, a wide handsome spread of maternal bosom exposed, ready to give Oscar Colum-bus Septimus Dupont Larkin a little drop of the best.

· WHEN THE ·
· GREEN WOODS ·
· LAUGH ·

When the green woods laugh with the voice of joy,
And the dimpling stream runs laughing by;
When the air does laugh with our merry wit,
And the green hill laughs with the noise of it:

BLAKE: *Songs of Innocence*

· 1 ·

After parking the Rolls-Royce between the pig-sties and the muck heap where twenty young turkeys were lazily scratching in the hot mid-morning air Pop Larkin, looking spruce and perky in a biscuit-coloured summer suit, paused to look back across his beloved little valley.

The landscape, though so familiar to him, presented a strange sight. Half way up the far slope, in fiercely brilliant sunlight, two strawberry fields were on fire. Little cockscombs of orange flame were running before a light breeze, consuming yellow alleys of straw. Behind them the fields spread black, smoking slowly with low blue clouds that drifted away to spread across parched meadows all as yellow as the straw itself after months without rain.

'Burning the strawberry fields off,' Pop told Ma as he went into the kitchen. 'That's a new one all right. Never seen that before. Wonder what the idea of that is?'

'Everything'll burn off soon if we don't get rain,' Ma said. 'Me included. As I said to the gentleman who was here this morning.'

Ma was wearing the lightest of sleeveless dresses, sky-blue with a low loose neckline. Her pinafore, tied at the waist, was bright yellow. The dress was almost transparent too, so that Pop could see her pink shoulder-straps showing through, a fact that excited him so much that he gave one of her bare olive-skinned arms a long smooth caress, quite forgetting at the same time to ask what gentleman she was referring to.

'Why I'm cooking on a morning like this I can't think,' Ma said. Her hands were white with flour. Trays of apricot flans, raspberry tarts, and maids-of-honour covered the kitchen table. A smell of roasting lamb rose from the stove. 'I'd be watering my zinnias if I had any sense. Or sitting under a tree somewhere.'

Pop picked up a still warm maid-of-honour and was about to slip it into his mouth when he changed his mind and decided to kiss Ma instead. Ma returned the kiss with instant generosity, her hands touching his face and her mouth partly open and soft, making Pop think hopefully that she might be in one of her primrose-and-bluebell moods. This made him begin to caress the nape of her neck, one of the places where she was most sensitive, but she stopped him by saying:

'You'd better not get yourself worked up. That gentleman'll be back here any minute now. Said he'd be back by half past eleven.'

'What gentleman?'

'This gentleman I told you about. He was here just after ten. Said he wanted to see you urgently.'

Insurance feller, Pop thought. Or fire extinguishers. Something of that breed.

'What'd he look like?'

'Dark suit and a bowler hat and a gold watch-chain,' Ma said. 'And in a big black Rolls. With a chauffeur.'

'Sounds like a brewer,' Pop said, laughing, and started to take off his biscuit-coloured summer jacket. Thinking at the same time that a glass of beer would be a nice idea, he paused to ask Ma if she would like one too.

'Had two already this morning,' Ma said. 'Could face another one though.'

Pop put the maid-of-honour in his mouth and started to move towards the fridge. Ma, who was rolling out broad fresh flannels of dough, looked up suddenly from the pastry board as he came back with two iced bottles of Dragon's Blood and laughed loudly, her enormous bust bouncing.

'You look a fine sketch,' she said. 'Better go and look at yourself in the glass before your visitor arrives.'

Pop, looking into the kitchen mirror, laughed too, seeing his face covered with flour dust where Ma had kissed him.

'Good mind to keep it on,' he said. 'Might frighten this feller away.'

He was, he thought, in no state for visitors; it was far too hot. He also had it in mind to ask Ma if she was in the mood to lie down for a bit after lunch. Mariette and Charley were at market; the rest of the children wouldn't be home till four. There wouldn't be a soul to disturb the peace of the afternoon except little Oscar.

'Well, you'd better make up your mind one way or the other quick,' Ma said, 'because here comes the Rolls now.'

Pop sank his Dragon's Blood quickly and Ma said: 'Better let me get it off,' and lifted the edge of her pinafore to his face, wiping flour dust away. This brought her body near to him again and he seized the chance to whisper warmly:

'Ma, what about a bit of a lie-down after lunch?' He playfully nipped the soft flesh of her thigh. 'Feel like it? Perfick opportunity.'

'Don't get me all excited,' Ma said. 'I won't know where to stop.'

In a mood of turmoil, thinking of nothing but how pleasant it was on hot summer afternoons to lie on the bed with Ma, Pop reluctantly walked into the yard. It was so hot that even the turkeys had given up scratching and were now gathered into a panting brood under an elderberry tree from which black limp inside-out umbrellas of berries were hanging lifelessly. Over in the strawberry fields lines of flame were still darting and running about the smoking straw and from the road the sound of the Rolls-Royce door snapping shut was as sharp as a revolver shot in the sun-charged air.

It was in Pop's mind to dismiss whoever was coming with a light-hearted quip such as 'Not today thank you. Shut the gate,' when he stopped in abrupt surprise.

Ma's visiting gentleman in the dark suit, bowler hat, and gold watch-chain had suddenly turned out to be a woman in a white silk suit covered with the thinnest of perpendicular black pencil-lines and with a small black and white hat to match.

She came across the yard, plumpish, blonde, chalky pink about the face and pretty in a half-simpering rosebud sort of way, with outstretched hands.

'Mrs Jerebohm,' she said. 'How do you do?' She spoke with the slightest of lisps, half laughing. 'You must be Larkin?'

Pop, resenting the absence of what he called a handle to his name no less than the intrusion on his plan for a little privacy with Ma, murmured something about *that* was what he always had been and what could he do for her?

Lisping again, Mrs Jerebohm said, with a hint of rapture:

'Mr Jerebohm simply couldn't wait to see the house for himself. So that's where he's gone and he wants us to meet him there. I hope that dove-tails all right? You know, fits in?' It was not long before Pop was to discover that dove-tailing was one of Mrs Jerebohm's favourite and most repeated expressions. She simply adored things to dove-tail. She simply loved to have things zip-up, buttonhole, click, and otherwise be clipped into neat and unimpeachable order.

'If we like it I hope we'll have it all zipped-up this afternoon,' she said. 'That's the way Mr Jerebohm likes to do business.'

Silent, Pop feigned a sort of ample innocence. What the ruddy hell, he asked himself, was the woman talking about?

'They told us at the inn you wanted to sell and the minute we heard we had a sort of thing about it.'

Inn? Pop could only presume she meant The Hare and Hounds and at the same time couldn't think what that simple pub had to do with her constant lisping raptures. She fixed him now with eyes as blue as forget-me-nots and a quick open smile that showed that two of her front teeth were crossed. That explained the lisping.

'Could we go right away? I mean does that dove-tail and all that? We could go in the Rolls.'

Pop, bemusedly thinking of roast lamb and mint sauce, cold beer, fresh apricot flan, and Ma lying on the bed in nothing but her slip or even less, suddenly felt a spasm of impatience and used the very same expression he had once used to Mr Charlton, in the days when he had been as eager as a hunter to collect taxes.

'You must have come to the wrong house, Madam,' he said. 'Or else I'm off my rocker.'

'Oh! no.' When Mrs Jerebohm flung up her hands with a rapturous lilt, which she did quite often, it had the effect of stretching the white suit across her bust, so that it momentarily seemed to puff up, tightly. It made her, Pop thought, with her smallish blue eyes and crossed teeth, not at all unlike a white eager budgerigar.

'Oh! no,' she said again. 'That doesn't fit. There can't be two people who own Gore Court, can there?'

It had hardly occurred to Pop, quick as ever in reaction, what she was talking about before she fluttered lispingly on:

'You can show us over, can't you? You do want to sell, don't you?'

'Going to pull the whole shoot down one of these days,' Pop said, 'when I get the time.'

Mrs Jerebohm expressed sudden shock with prayerful lifts of her hands, bringing them together just under her chin.

'Oh! but that's awful sacrilege, isn't it? Isn't that awful sacrilege?'

Pop started to say that he didn't know about that but the first words were hardly framed before she went lisping on:

'But we could just see it, perhaps, couldn't we? At the inn they assured us you were keen to sell. You see we're mad to have a place in the country. Absolutely mad. So when we heard –'

'Big place,' Pop said. 'Fifteen bedrooms.'

'That would suit us. That would fit all right. We'd want to have people down. My husband wants shooting parties and all that sort of thing.'

'Ah! he shoots does he?'

'Not yet,' she said, 'but he's going to learn.'

A sharp, searching fragrance of roast lamb drifted across the yard, causing Pop to sniff with uplifted nostrils. Ma, he thought, must be opening the oven door, and with relish he also remembered maids-of-honour, raspberry tarts, and apricot flans. He wondered too how many vegetables Ma was cooking and said:

'Couldn't manage nothing just now, I'm afraid. My dinner's on the table.'

'Oh? Not really?'

'Ma'll be dishing up in ten minutes and she won't have it spoiled.'

'Oh! be an angel.'

The appeal of the small forget-me-not eyes was too direct to resist and Pop answered it with a liquid look of his own, gazing at Mrs Jerebohm with a smoothness that most women would have found irresistibly disturbing. It was like a slow indirect caress.

On Mrs Jerebohm it had the effect of making her retreat a little. She seemed to become momentarily cool. she showed her crossed teeth in an unsmiling gap, much as if she had realized that her fluttering 'Oh! be an angel' had gone too far into realms of familiarity.

'I can wait for you to finish your lunch,' she said. 'I'm perfectly content to wait.'

'Oh! come in and have a bite,' Pop said. 'Ma'll be pleased to death.'

Mrs Jerebohm gave an answer of such incredible frigidity that Pop almost felt himself frozen in the hot July sunshine.

'No thank you. We never eat at midday.'

Pop could find no possible answer to this astounding, unreal statement; it struck him as being nothing but a fabulous lunacy. It couldn't possibly be that there were people who didn't eat at midday. It couldn't possibly be.

'I will wait in the car.'

'Have a wet then. Have a glass o' beer,' Pop said, his voice almost desperate. He was feeling an urgent need for a glass, perhaps two, himself. 'Come and sit down in the cool.'

Mrs Jerebohm, already cool enough as she surveyed the piles of junk lying everywhere across the sun-blistered yard, the now prostrate brood of turkeys and the Rolls-Royce incongruously parked by the muck-heap, merely showed her small crossed teeth again and said:

'Have your dinner, Larkin. I'll be waiting for you.'

Turning abruptly, she went away on short almost prancing steps towards the road. Instinctively Pop gazed for a moment at the retreating figure in its pencilled white skirt. The hips, he thought, were over-large for the rest of the body. As they swung fleshily from side to side they looked in some way haughty and seemed frigidly to admonish him.

Going back into the house he felt something more than thirst to be the strongest of his reactions. The morning had suddenly become unreal. In a half-dream he poured himself a glass of beer, drank part of it and then decided he needed a real blinder of a pick-me-up to restore his sanity.

Ma was busy laying the lunch as he concocted a powerful mixture of gin, whisky, and French vermouth, a liberal dash of bitters and plenty of ice.

'Been gone a long time,' Ma said. 'What did he want after all?'

In a low ruminative voice Pop explained to Ma that his visitor was, after all, a she.

'Wants to buy Gore Court. Wants me to show her and her husband over after dinner.'

'What's she like? No wonder you been gone a long time.'

Pop swirled ice round and round in his glass, moodily gazing at it. He drank deeply of gin, whisky, and vermouth, waited for it to reach his empty stomach and then in tones of complete unreality revealed to Ma the shocking news that he had just met someone who, believe it or not, never ate at midday.

'Can't be right in her mind,' Ma said.

'Fact,' Pop said. 'Invited her in to lunch but that's what she said. Never eats at midday.'

'Why? does she think it common or something?'

Pop said that could be it and drank solidly again. A moment later Ma opened the oven door and took out a sizzling brown leg of lamb surrounded by golden braised potatoes, so that the morning at once woke into new excruciating life, with pangs of hunger leaping through Pop like a pain.

'You hear something new every day,' he said, 'don't you, Ma? Something as shakes you.'

Ma said you certainly did and then suddenly, with no warning at all, popped the leg of lamb back into the oven again.

'You mean she's still waiting out there? She'll faint off or something.'

More than likely, Pop thought. Yes, she was waiting. Depressedly he poured another couple of inches of gin into his glass, hardly hearing Ma say:

'I'd better take her a bite of something out. Glass of milk and a slice of flan or something. She can't sit out there on an empty stomach. She'll go over.'

Less than a minute later Ma was away across the yard on an errand that was less of mercy than one of sheer correction. It simply wasn't right for people to do these things. It was as plain as the moon: if you didn't eat you didn't live. It was criminal. You faded away.

Pop had hardly mixed himself a third pick-me-up before Ma was back again, bearing the offering of apricot flan and milk, now rejected.

'On a very strict diet,' Ma said. 'Trying to get her weight down. Got a proper chart and pills and units and points and all that sort of thing.'

Pop, remembering Mrs Jerebohm's over-rounded thighs, tight in the thin white suit, was suddenly jolted by piercing shrieks from Ma. Her great sixteen-stone body seemed to be laughing from every pore.

'I told her to look at me,' Ma said. 'I think it cheered her up a bit. She was no more than a sylph, I said.'

Pop put the word away in his mind for further reference. Ma took the sizzling leg of lamb from the oven again and a few moments later Pop was deftly carving it into generous pink-brown slices, to which Ma added steaming hillocks of fresh-buttered French beans, two sorts of potatoes, new and braised, mint sauce, and vegetable marrow baked with cheese.

Bent over this feast in attentive reverence, Pop at last paused to drain a glass of beer and look up at Ma and say:

'Ma, what did I pay for Gore Court in the end? I forget now.'

'First it was going to be nine thousand. Then it was seven.'

Pop helped himself to five or six more new potatoes, remarking at the same time how good they were in the long hot summer, and then sat in thought for a moment or so.

'What shall I ask? Ten?'

'Show a nice profit. Might be able to have that swimming pool Mariette keeps talking about if you brought the deal off.'

There was a lot of land there, Pop reminded her. And all those green-houses and stables and asparagus beds. To say nothing of the lake and the cherry orchard. He thought he'd ask twelve.

'Why not fourteen?' Ma said serenely. 'You can always come down.'

Pop said that was true, but was Ma quite sure it wasn't too much?

'Not on your nelly. Look at the paltry bits of land they ask five hundred for nowadays. Don't give it away.'

No chance of that, Pop said. Not if he knew it. No fear.

'Go up a bit if anything,' Ma said. 'No harm in trying. Ask fifteen.'

Pop, ruminating briefly, thought he detected sense in this and finally, with an airy flourish of a hand, said he thought it wouldn't choke him if he asked seventeen.

'Now you're talking,' Ma said. 'Now you're using your loaf.' She laughed suddenly, in her rich, quivering fashion. 'Might be able to have the swimming pool heated now. You know how I hate cold water.'

Less than half an hour later, after eating three slices of flan, half a dozen maids-of-honour, and a raspberry tart or two, at the same time abandoning with reluctance the idea of a nice lie-down with Ma, Pop put on his light summer jacket again and went out to Mrs Jerebohm, leaving Ma at the task of feeding little Oscar, now eighteen months old, with much the same lunch he and Ma had had themselves, except that it was all mashed up and in smaller proportion. Oscar, he proudly noted, was getting as fat as a butter ball.

Out in the road a chauffeur in bottle green cap and uniform held open the door of Mrs Jerebohm's Rolls and Pop stepped into an interior of beige-gold, the upholstery softer than velvet.

'Well, here we are,' Pop said. 'Perfick afternoon.'

'I see you too have a Rolls,' Mrs Jerebohm said.

'Oh! that old crate. That's a laugh.'

Pop, who in reality adored and revered the Rolls with pride and tenderness as if it had been the eighth of his offspring, cheerfully proceeded to tear the car's paltry reputation to pieces.

'Took it for a small debt,' he explained. 'Wouldn't pull pussy. Knocks like a cracked teapot. You'd get more out of a mule and a milk float. Still, the best I can afford. Struggle to make ends meet as it is.'

As the Rolls turned the last bend before the house faded from sight he invited Mrs Jerebohm to look back on his pitiful junk-yard, the paradise from which he scratched the barest of livings – if he had good luck.

'Like my poor old place,' he said. 'Just about had it. Falling apart and I'll never get the time to put it together again.'

'Charming countryside, though,' Mrs Jerebohm said. 'I adore the countryside.'

Pop resisted a powerful impulse to praise the countryside. Nothing in his life, except Ma, brought him nearer to celestial ecstasies than the countryside. Instead he now started to concentrate, with a new warm glow, on fresh enthusiasms.

'Ah! but wait till you see Gore Court. Wait till you see that.'

'I'm absolutely dying to. Absolutely dying. We've seen so many that haven't – you know – sort of dove-tailed, but this one gives me a kind of thing –'

A moment later Mrs Jerebohm took a handkerchief from her white suède handbag, releasing an unrecognizable breath of perfume on which Pop's hypersensitive nostrils at once seized with eager delight.

It was a wonderful perfume she was wearing, he said. Could she tell him what it was?

'Verbena. French. You like it?'

It was perfick, Pop said. It suited her perfickly. It was just her style.

'Thank you.'

She smiled as she spoke, this time with her lips parted a little more, so that the edges of her mouth were crinkled. The effect of this was so surprisingly pleasant after the frigidities in the yard that Pop wondered for a moment whether or not to hold her hand and then decided against it. Even so, he thought, it might not be all that much of a hardship to dove-tail with Mrs Jerebohm one fine day.

He was still pondering on the pleasant implications contained in the word dove-tail when the Rolls rounded a bend by a copse of sweet-chestnut, beyond which were suddenly revealed a mass of baronial turrets taller than the dark torches of surrounding pines.

'There!' Pop said. He spoke with a studied air of triumph, waving a hand. 'There's the house. There's Gore Court for you. What about that, eh? How's that strike you? Better than St Paul's, ain't it, better than St Paul's?'

· 2 ·

Mr Jerebohm, who had stayed the night with Mrs Jerebohm at The Hare and Hounds, had been up that morning with the lark. He was not at all sure what sort of bird a lark was or what it looked like, but he knew very well it was the bird you had to be up with.

Numbers of small brown birds in the many thick trees surrounding the pub, which both he and Mrs Jerebohm called the inn, had chirped him awake as early as half past four. He supposed these might have been larks. On the other hand they might well have been robins. He was a stranger in the country; it was a foreign land to him, distant as Bolivia, unfamiliar as Siam. He simply didn't know. Nor did he know anything distinctive about the trees which stood about the pub with tall lushness, almost black in high summer leaf. A tree was a shape. It had branches, a trunk, and leaves. In spring the leaves appeared; they were green; and in autumn they fell off again.

Grass was to be recognized because it too was green, or generally so. It grew on the floor, most conveniently, and cows grazed at it. Mr Jerebohm recognized a cow. It had horns, teats, and gave milk. If it didn't it was a bull. He also recognized a horse because even in London, where stockbroking absorbed him day and night, you sometimes still saw one drawing a cart. You also saw them on films and television, running races. You also hunted foxes with them, which was what Mr Jerebohm hoped to do as soon as he and Mrs Jerebohm had finally settled on a suitable place in the country.

Finding a suitable place in the country had turned out to be an un-expectedly difficult and tedious business. The notion that you rang up or called on a house-agent, described the kind of residence you wanted – Mr Jerebohm invariably referred to houses as residences and their surround-ings as domains – and bought it immediately was nothing but a myth. This was not in the least surprising, since myths were exactly what house-agents dealt in. They were crooks and liars. Their sole idea was to sell you pups.

Mr Jerebohm was determined not to be sold any pups. Nobody sold him any pups in the world of stockbroking and nobody was going to sell him any in the world of larks and cows. He was, since he was a Londoner, clever enough not to be caught by that sort of thing. People in London were naturally clever. They had to be; it was due to the competition.

On the other hand, everybody knew that people in the country were not clever, simply because there was no need to be. There were enough fields, trees, cows, horses, and all the rest of it to go round. You had ample milk, fresh from the cow. You kept hens and they laid multitudes of eggs. Farmers made butter. As to the people, you smelled innocence in the air. They were naturally simple. The sky, even when rainy, was full of purity. The fields had a sort of ample pastoral virginity about them, unbesmirched by anything, and even the manure heaps had a clean, simple tang that was good to breathe.

The exceptions to all this were house-agents. Two weeks of trailing with Mrs Jerebohm from one to another had made Mr Jerebohm tired and angry. He was now constantly taking pills and powders for the suppression of bouts of dyspepsia brought on by viewing manor-houses which turned out to be matchboxes, farms which were nothing but hen-coops and country residences of character which looked like disused workhouses or mental homes.

He wanted no more of house-agents at any price and for this reason had been more than glad when the barman at The Hare and Hounds had told him that a fellow named Larkin had a very nice house that he was planning to pull down. It was a pity and a shame, the barman said, but there it was. Nobody seemed to want it.

'You're sure it's nice?' Mr Jerebohm said. He had heard that word about houses before; it was the most misused, the most callous, in the language. 'Has it class is what I mean?'

Class was what Mr Jerebohm was looking for and class was precisely what couldn't be found.

'I ought to know,' the barman said. 'My missus goes in to air it twice a week and cleans and dusts it once a fortnight. You could walk in tomorrow. Class? – it's a treat. All in apple-pie order.'

Mr Jerebohm thanked the barman and gave him a shilling. It paid to be generous to the yokels.

'Pinkie,' he said that night as he folded his charcoal city trousers and hung them on the bedroom towel-rail, 'Pinkie, I've got a sort of hunch about this house. A funny kind of premonition. Have you?'

Pinkie was his pet name for Mrs Jerebohm; it suited her much better than Phyllis.

Perfick, Perfick!

Pinkie, who in nothing but panties and brassière was squatting on her haunches in the middle of the bedroom floor, hands on hips, balancing a Bible and a thick telephone directory on her head, going through her slimming exercises, said she thought so too, adding:

'I think I've lost another ounce. I weighed myself today in the ladies' at that hotel where we had lunch. But I can't really tell until we get home and I can take everything off and get on the proper scales.'

Mr Jerebohm, saying good for her, got into bed, propped himself up on the pillows and started to read the *Financial Times*. The night was exceptionally hot and stuffy and in any case he knew from long experience that there was no need yet awhile to think of shutting his eyes. It would take Pinkie the best part of another hour to do her balancing acts with books, stretch her legs, touch her toes, do press-ups, take off her make-up and swallow her pills.

'Good night, Sunbeam,' she said when she got into bed at last. She liked to call him Sunbeam last thing at night; it left a blessed sort of glow in the air. 'Sleep well.' She kissed him lightly on the forehead, barely brushing his skin, anxious about her facial cream. 'I'm mad to see this house. It's so beautiful here. Don't you think it's beautiful?'

Mr Jerebohm wasn't sure whether it was beautiful or not. Hot and restless, he found he couldn't sleep well. It was terribly noisy everywhere. The countryside not only seemed to be full of barking dogs. From the fields came a constant moaning of cattle and whenever he was on the verge of dropping off he was assailed from all sides by low asthmatic bleatings.

Later in the night he had a rough bad dream in which Pinkie lost so much weight that she became a skeleton and he woke in an unpleasant sweat to hear a whole eerie chain of birds hooting at each other from tree to tree. These, he supposed, might well have been owls, though he wouldn't have been at all surprised to hear that they were nightingales.

Whatever they were they kept him awake until dawn, when once again the larks started their maddening chorus in the ivy.

· 3 ·

When Pop Larkin first saw Mr Jerebohm, hatless and coatless in the heat, waiting outside the tall wrought-iron gates by Gore Court, it struck him immediately that his face seemed in some way curiously out of proportion with the rest of his body.

Mr Jerebohm was shortish, squat, and slightly paunchy beneath watch-chain and waistcoat. By contrast his face was rather long. It was greyish in an unhealthy sort of way, with thick loose lips and eyebrows that had in them bright sparks of ginger. He looked, Pop told himself, rather like a bloater on the stale side.

'Afternoon, afternoon,' Pop said. 'Perfick wevver. Hope I haven't kept you waiting? Hope you don't find it too hot?'

Mr Jerebohm, who in sizzling heat had tramped about the domain of Gore Court for the better part of an hour, so that his dark city trousers were now dustily snowy with white darts of seed from thistle and willow-herb, confessed to a slight feeling of weariness. But Pop was cheery:

'Cooler inside the house. Wonderfully cool house, this. Thick walls. I daresay,' he said, 'it's above twenty degrees cooler inside. Had a good wander round?'

Mr Jerebohm confessed that he had wandered but wasn't sure how good it was. He had learned to be craftily cautious about houses. He was going to be very wary. He wasn't going to be sucked in.

'Had to fight my way through a damn forest of weeds,' he said. 'Look at me. How long has the place been in this state of disrepair?'

Pop laughed resoundingly.

'That seed?' he said. 'Blow away in a night. One good west wind and a drop o' rain and it'll melt away. Put up any pheasants?'

When Mr Jerebohm rather depressingly confessed that he hadn't put up a bird of any kind, Pop laughed and said:

'Hiding up in the hot wevver. Place's crawling wiv 'em. Partridges too. And snipe. And woodcock, down by the river. Didn't see the river? I'll take you down there when you had a deck at the house. And the lake? Beautiful trout in the lake. Nice perch too. Didn't see the lake? Didn't get that far? I'll take you down.'

Mrs Jerebohm, following Pop and Mr Jerebohm up the circular stone steps leading to the front of the house from a short avenue of box trees, found herself borne along on a mystical flow of lilting information that might have come from a canary. It was so bright and bewildering that she was inside the house before she knew it, standing at the foot of a great baronial sweep of oaken stairs.

'There's a flight of stairs for you,' Pop said. He waved a demonstratively careless hand. 'Handsome, eh? Like it?'

Mrs Jerebohm, almost in a whisper, went so far as to say that she adored it. If anything clicked, that staircase did.

Cautious as ever by contrast, Mr Jerebohm struck the banisters of the stairs a severe blow with the flat of his hand, as if hoping they would fall down. When nothing happened Pop startled him with a sentence so sharp that it sounded like a rebuke:

'Built like a rock! – wouldn't fall down in a thousand years!'

With hardly a pause for breath Pop enthusiastically invited Mrs Jerebohm to take a good deck at the panelling that went with the stairs. It was linen-fold. Magnificent stuff. Class. There were walls of it. Acres. Talk about fumed oak. Fumed oak wasn't thought of when that was made. You could get ten pounds a square foot for it where it stood. And that was giving it away. And did she see the top of the stairs? The Tudor rose? The Tudor rose was everywhere.

Mrs Jerebohm, speechless, stood partly mesmerized. At the very top of the stairs, lighting a broad panelled landing, a high window set with a design of fleur-de-lis, swans, and bulrushes in stained glass of half a dozen colours threw down such leaves of brilliant light, driven by the strong afternoon sun, that she was temporarily dazzled and had to pick her way from step to step, like a child, in her ascent of the stairs.

A man from Birmingham had offered him a thousand pounds for the window alone, she heard Pop say in a voice that reached her as an unreal echo, like some line from a far distant over-romantic opera, but he had turned it down.

'Class,' Mr Jerebohm was half-admitting to himself. 'Class.'

'How old is the house?' Mrs Jerebohm brought herself to say. Her voice too was like an echo.

Pop said he thought it was Georgian or Tudor or something. Fifteenth century.

Mr Jerebohm, with bloater-like smile, was quick to seize on these transparent contradictions and nudged Pinkie quietly at the elbow as they turned the bend of the stairs. It served to prove his point about how simple the yokels were.

'How many bedrooms did you say?' Mrs Jerebohm unable to keep entrancement out of her voice, almost hiccupped as she framed the question. 'Was it ten?'

Twelve, Pop thought. Might be fifteen. If it was too many they could always shut the top floor away.

'There's a beauty of a room for you!' he said with almost a bark of delight. A huge double door, crowned by a vast oaken pediment, was thrown open to reveal a bedroom half as large as a tennis court. 'Ain't that a beauty? Didn't I tell you it was like St Paul's?'

Mrs Jerebohm, stupefied by sheer size and acreage of panelling, heard three pairs of footsteps echo about her as if in a cave. Above them, at the same time, the chirpy solo voice of Pop was urging her to take a good eyeful of the view from a vast blue and pink window that might have come out of an abbey.

'Drink that in!' he said. 'Take a swig at that!'

Mrs Jerebohm, in half-ecstatic rumination, found herself positively gulping at two acres of thistles, willow-herb and docks among which numbers of black conical cypresses and a half-derelict pergola of roses stuck up in the air like a sad fleet wrecked and abandoned. Beyond them a line of turkey oaks, black too in the blistering perpendicular light of full afternoon, cut off completely whatever view was lurking behind.

'In winter,' Pop started to say with a new, more vibrant lyricism, 'in winter, when the leaves are down, and the light's right, and it's a clear day, in winter, Mrs Jerebohm, you can stand here and see the sea.'

In a rush of disbelief, lyrical too, Mrs Jerebohm several times repeated the words in heavy lisps.

'The sea? – the sea? No? Really? The sea?' she said. 'You mean we can really see the sea?'

'Smoke of ships in the channel,' Pop said impassively, 'coming from all over the world.'

'Oh! Sunbeam,' Mrs Jerebohm said, lisping, 'you hear that? You can actually see ships out there. Ships!'

Mr Jerebohm, impressed though still wary, had no time to make any sort of comment before Pop struck him a resounding but friendly blow in the middle of the back. Mr Jerebohm recoiled uneasily but Pop, totally unaffected, merely told him:

'This is the place where you got to use your loaf, old man. Get your imagination to work. Have a deck down there.'

As Pop waved a careless hand in a quick flexible curve in the direction of the impossible thistles Mr Jerebohm half ducked, as if confident of another approaching blow, but Pop merely urged him, taking a great deep breath:

'Imagine roses down there. Imagine acres of roses. Eh? A couple o' thousand roses.'

Without another word he suddenly flung open a casement in the church-like window, again drawing a long deep breath.

'What price that air, eh? Take a sniff at that. Like medicine. Old man, that's pure concentrated iodine.'

'Iodine?' Mr Jerebohm, incredulous, snapped sharp, bloater-like lips. 'Iodine? What on earth's iodine got to do with it?'

With stiff wariness Mr Jerebohm waited for an answer, determined not to be caught by any cock-and-bull nonsense of that sort.

'Air here's stiff with it,' Pop said. 'Saturated. Due to being practically surrounded by sea.'

To the speechless astonishment of both Mr Jerebohm and Pinkie he proceeded to toss off careless scraps of topography.

'Got to remember this country is almost an island. Didn't know that? Fact. Two-thirds of its boundaries are water. It's an island on an island. Understand me?'

Before Mr Jerebohm could begin to say whether he understood him or not Pop thundered out:

'Nobody hardly ever dies here. People live for ever, same as tortoises. Everything grows 'ell for leather. Cherries, strawberries, hops, apples, pears, corn, sheep. Everything! Not called the Garden of England for nothing, this place. Not called the Garden of England for nothing, old man.'

Suddenly, after Pop had closed the casement with a gesture almost dramatically regretful, Mrs Jerebohm felt quite overpowered, in a faint sort of way, by the projected grandeur of sea-scape, roses, iodine, and heights, and asked diffidently if perhaps she could see the kitchens?

'Certainly!' Promptly Pop started to lead the way downstairs, freely admitting as he did so that the kitchens were perhaps a bit on the large side, though of course that wasn't necessarily a bad thing these days. It gave you a lot more room to put telly in for the maids.

That, Mrs Jerebohm said, reminded her of something. Help. What about help? Could help be got? In London that, of course, was the great problem. Would she be able to get help in the country?

'Sacks of it,' Pop said. 'Bags.' If his conscience pricked him slightly as he recalled the constant eager race of village women to get to the rich pastures of strawberry fields, cherry orchards, and hop gardens and all the rest, where families cleaned up sixty or seventy pounds a week, tax free, he momentarily appeased it by reminding himself that, after all, business was business. A fib or two was legitimate. You had to allow for a fib or two here and there. 'All the help you want. Only a question of paying on the right scale and giving 'em plenty o' telly.'

Lispingly Mrs Jerebohm confessed that she was relieved to hear it. The question had been bothering her. It was the thing on which everything depended.

'Quite,' Pop said blandly. 'Quite.'

A moment later he opened the door to the kitchens. A vast funereal dungeon opened up, half-dark, its windows overgrown with rampant elderberry trees. The air was drugged with mould.

'Something would have to be done with this,' Mr Jerebohm said. 'Not much iodine here.'

Pop, severely ignoring the sarcasm about iodine, freely admitted once again that it was all a bit on the large side but anyway you could always put in a ping-pong table for the maids. Help 'em to keep their figures down. He laughed resoundingly. They got fat and lazy quick enough as it was.

Mr Jerebohm, in turn ignoring the joke, started to retreat with relief from the dankness of the kitchen dungeons, saying:

'You're quite sure about the help? What about chaps for the garden and that sort of thing?'

'Oceans of 'em,' Pop said. 'No trouble at all.'

His conscience, pricking him slightly a second time, forced him to think of farm labourers who ran about in cars or mounted on splendid, glistening, highly expensive motor-bikes and of how his friend the Brigadier couldn't get a boy to clean his shoes, and he wondered, not for the first time, what Ma would say. Ma was strict about the truth. Still, you'd got to allow a fib or two here and there.

'Well, I hope you're right.' Mr Jerebohm told himself he wasn't sold yet. Much experience with house-agents, the liars, cheats, and swindlers, had left him sceptical, cautious, and, as he liked to tell himself, sharp as a fox. 'It's of paramount importance.'

Pop, recoiling slightly from the word paramount as if it meant something shifty, said:

'Well, now, what else?' He too was relieved to escape from the kitchens' dank elder-mould darknesses and he was bound to admit they ponged a bit. 'What about a look at the outside?'

He searched the air for a breath of Mrs Jerebohm's light and exquisite perfume and, as he caught it, made her smile with perceptible pleasure by saying:

'That scent of Mrs Jerebohm's reminds me of Ma's garden. She grows verbena there.'

'You see, we'd plan to do a fair amount of entertaining,' Mr Jerebohm said. 'That's why I spoke about the chaps. Shooting parties and that sort of thing. Lot of people at week-ends.'

'Beautiful shooting country,' Pop said. 'Marvellous. Bags of cover. What about a look at the lake now?'

Mr Jerebohm said yes, he was ready to have a look at the lake if Pinkie was.

'You go,' she said. 'I'd like to wander round the house again.'

As she started to go upstairs Pop, in the moment before departing, called up after her:

'If you change your mind it's straight down from the front of the house. You'll see the path. There's a white gate at the bottom.'

As he skirted the seed-smoking thistle forest with Mr Jerebohm Pop put to him what he thought to be an important question:

'What business you in?'

'Stock Exchange.'

'Plenty o' work?'

'Mustn't grumble.'

'Hot weather affected you at all?' Pop said. 'It's caned a lot of people.'

'Not really.' Mr Jerebohm couldn't help smiling behind his hand. Really the yokels were pretty simple. And when you thought of it how could they be otherwise?

'There's the lake for you,' Pop said. 'Beautiful water-lilies, eh? Always remind me of fried eggs floating about on plates.' The lake, low after months of drought, stretched glassy in the sun. On banks of grey cracked mud flies buzzed in thick black-blue swarms. An odd invisible moorhen or two croaked among fringes of cane-dry reed and out on the central depths great spreads of water-lilies shone motionless in the sun.

Pop picked up a stone, aimed it at a distant clump of reeds and threw it. It might have been a signal. A line of wild duck got up, circled, and headed for the centre of the lake, crying brokenly as they flew.

'Thought so,' Pop said. 'Whole place is lousy with 'em.'

Pheasants? Mr Jerebohm supposed.

'Wild duck.' Dammit, these Londoners were pretty simple when you came to think of it. 'Like wild duck? Ma does 'em with orange sauce. Puts a glass o' red wine in too. I love 'em. Shot so many last winter though I got a bit sick of 'em by the end.'

For a painful moment or two Mr Jerebohm's sharply watering mouth told him he would never, never get tired of wild duck. He longed suddenly and passionately for wild duck with red wine and orange sauce, tired as he was of living on yoghurt, toast fingers, consommé, and undressed salads in order to help Pinkie keep her weight down.

'And all this goes with the house? The lake and everything?' he said. 'What's beyond?'

'Parkland. See the big cedar?'

Mr Jerebohm stared at a tall dark object on the skyline and might as well have been looking at a factory chimney. 'Starts there. Quite a few deer in it still. Used to be a pretty big herd. Like venison?'

God! Mr Jerebohm thought. Venison?

'Ma always does it in a big slow double pan in plenty of butter,' Pop said. 'Nothing else, just fresh butter. We always have red currant jelly with it. The meat fair falls apart. Perfick. I tell you, old man, perfick.'

Mr Jerebohm, who had lunched exceptionally early, in unison with Pinkie, on thin slices of lean ham, butterless rye biscuits and China tea, thought 'God!' again in agony, feeling his stomach perform involuntary sickening acrobatics of hunger. There was something not fair about talk of food sometimes.

'Not sure how the trout are holding up,' Pop said. He'd got to be fair about the trout. No use over-praising the trout. To be perfickly fair the herons fetched them almost as fast as you re-stocked and you never really knew how they were. 'Caught sight of two or three fat ones though, last time I came down. Still, it's cheap to re-stock if you wanted to.'

Mr Jerebohm, staring hard at the lake as if in hope of seeing a fish rise, resisted with great difficulty a powerful and insidious temptation to ask how Ma dealt with trout.

'Same with pheasants,' Pop said. 'You'd have to start thinking of re-stocking soon if you wanted to shoot this autumn.'

'I thought you said the place was stiff with them?'

'Old birds,' Pop said with swiftness, unperturbed. 'Pretty wild too. You want a couple o' hundred young 'uns. It's not too late. They're well advanced this summer. Hot wevver.'

Mr Jerebohm, deeply tormented again by agonies of hunger, suddenly abandoned all thought of foxiness and dizzily saw himself as the proud master of all he surveyed. The whole scene was simply splendid. This, he

thought, was it. Lake, trout, pheasants, park, deer, wild duck, venison –
God, he thought, this must be it.

Rapture left him abruptly a moment later, leaving him rational again.

'What, by the way, are you asking?'

'Going to farm?' Pop said.

The question, short and simple though it was, was an astute one. If Mr
Jerebohm was going to farm he naturally wanted to lose money. Pop knew
most of the dodges and this was the popular one. You made it in the city
and lost it on the land. The countryside had never been so full of ragged-
trousered brokers – what he called the Piccadilly farmers – pouring their
money down the furrows.

'Roughly the idea,' Mr Jerebohm said. 'Pleasure too of course. Mrs J. is
mad keen to have a nice rural domain.'

'I've been asking nineteen thousand.'

That ought to dove-tail it all right, Pop thought. Mr Jerebohm, though
speechless, didn't flinch. A few thistle seeds, borne on the lightest of winds,
floated angel-wise down the bank of the lake, here and there settling on
reeds and water. Mr Jerebohm watched them with eyes that might have
been idle but were sharp enough to see a fish rise in a startled circle, a
moment later, far out among the water-lilies.

'Big 'un there,' Pop said. 'Ever have 'em blue? The trout I mean. We had
'em in France once and Ma got the recipe. You want plenty o' brown
butter. You get 'em fair swimming in brown butter and then they're
perfick.'

Mr Jerebohm disgorged a low, hungry sigh. He felt he couldn't hear
much more of the poetry of eating and wished to God Pinkie would come
and help him out a bit. In vain he looked back in the direction of the house
and then said, snapping:

'I'll give you twelve.' Sentimentality was out. Absolutely out. You had
to be firm from the beginning. The class was there all right but you had
to be firm.

Pop laughed in a certain dry, easy fashion.

'I think it's about time I went home,' he said. 'Ma'll be wondering where
I've got to.'

'Oh? It's a perfectly good offer in my view.'

Pop laughed again, this time more loudly.

'Well, maybe in your view, old man,' he said, 'but that ain't mine, is
it?'

Again Mr Jerebohm wished to God Pinkie would come to help him out
a bit. There were times when he needed Pinkie.

'To be perfectly honest I really ought to consult my wife about it first and then let you know,' he said. 'I don't want to be precipitate.'

'Should think not an' all,' Pop said, at the same time wondering what the hell precipitate meant. It sounded like something catching.

'Shall we start to walk back?' Mr Jerebohm said. The afternoon was really shatteringly hot. Sweat was pouring off him in uncomfortable streams. Where on earth was Pinkie? 'I could give you word by Monday.'

Monday, Pop said, might be too late. The chap from Birmingham was coming down again to look at the window and another chap was after the panelling. You didn't see linen-fold like that every day. It was worth all of fifteen hundred if it was worth a bob and once these demolition rats got to work you wouldn't see the place for dust.

The expression 'demolition rats' disturbed Mr Jerebohm to the core. It was even worse than venison with red currant jelly and wild duck with orange sauce. God Almighty, where on earth was Pinkie? As he followed Pop up the path he again looked towards the house in vain.

With inexpressible relief he heard Pop say, less than a minute later:

'Ain't that your missus standing up there under the trees?' Pop paused to point to a grassy knoll, a hundred yards away, crowned by a ring of big sweet chestnuts. 'Waving her hand.'

'Waving both hands!'

It was clear, Mr Jerebohm thought, that Pinkie was in a state of some excitement: unless, as was possible, she was trying out some new slimming exercise. Both arms were waving madly above her head, the hands waggling like spiders.

'Sunbeam!' she started to call. 'Sunbeam!'

The excited lisping call dragged Mr Jerebohm up the slope of parched grass to the knoll as if he had been attached to Pinkie by a rope. He felt unutterably glad to see her and wondered, twice and aloud, what it could be that so excited her?

'Probably came across some buried treasure,' Pop said. 'They say Cromwell was here. One of his prisoners escaped from a window in the house –'

Mr Jerebohm, utterly uninterested in Cromwell, half ran forward to meet Pinkie, who lisped liltingly in return:

'Come and see what I've found. You wouldn't guess in a thousand years.'

Pop started to follow Mr Jerebohm and his wife through the chestnut trees. Masses of prematurely fallen blossom, in dry pollened tassels, had fallen from the trees and clouds of pungent yellow dust were raised as Mr and Mrs Jerebohm ran.

'There! I discovered it. I just absolutely ran across it. I wasn't thinking of a thing and suddenly it sort of conjured itself out of nowhere. It just sort of dove-tailed –'

A kind of pepper box, in white stone, with a domed roof and a marble seat inside, sat with forlorn elegance among the chestnut trees. Black piles of decaying faggots were propped against one side.

'It's a summer house, isn't it? The sort they built in the eighteenth century?' Pinkie said. 'Didn't they call them follies?'

Folly or not, Pop thought, the chap who built this thing was on my side.

'And the view. You must look at the view.'

Turning, Pop had to admit that the view was pretty stunning. It was better than perfick. The lake, sown with water-lilies and framed with long fingers of reed, could now be seen entire, with park and cedars spread out as mature, calm background. It needed only a herd of deer to run lightly across the cloudless blue horizon to set the last romantic seal on it and send Mrs Jerebohm finally and sedately mad.

'Come and sit inside a minute,' Pinkie said to Mr Jerebohm. 'You'll get the full flavour then.'

Though the shady marble struck with ice-cold shock on Mr Jerebohm's seat Pinkie might have been cased in armour for all she noticed the chill on hers.

'Sunbeam, we've absolutely got to have it. What is he asking?'

'Nineteen thousand.'

'Is it an awful, awful lot?'

'I offered him twelve.'

'Would he split do you suppose?'

'I expect so. I could have a stab.'

Mr Jerebohm knew, in his heart, that whether he had a stab or not it really didn't matter. The folly had finally achieved what roses, panelling, iodine, and sea-scape had failed to do. Whatever doubt remained after trout, venison, duck, and pheasant had done their all-tormenting work had gone for ever.

'Try him with fifteen,' Pinkie said. 'We've got to get it laced up some-how. I couldn't bear –'

A sudden dread of colic made Mr Jerebohm rise quickly from the marble seat, his rump half-frozen. It was a positive relief to get out into the hot, stifling air.

'Well, Larkin, my wife and I have talked it over. I'll give you fifteen.'

'Couldn't do it,' Pop said, speaking with great blandness. 'The demolition rats would give me more than that.'

Mrs Jerebohm recoiled from the expression 'demolition rats' as Mr

Jerebohm himself had done down by the lakeside. It was an expression so nauseating that she actually had a vision of real rats, live and repulsive, gnawing away the stone and marble of her beloved folly, and she pinched Mr Jerebohm sharply on the arm.

'I'll split the difference,' Mr Jerebohm said.

'Fair enough,' Pop said. 'Seventeen thousand.'

Mr Jerebohm had no time to protest against the neatness of Pop's arithmetic before Mrs Jerebohm lisped:

'Oh! Splendid. Splendid. I'm so glad we've got it all sewn up.'

Sewn up it was, an' all, Pop thought. Ma would be pleased. And Mariette. They could have the swimming pool easy now. And probably even heated.

'Well, that's it then, Larkin.' Mr Jerebohm shook Pop not uncordially by the hand. Mrs Jerebohm, smiling with winning, crossed teeth, shook hands too. 'Thank you. I'll tell my solicitors to contact you. Presume you'd like some sort of deposit?'

Wouldn't cause him no pain, Pop said. Couldn't manage cash? he supposed.

Mr Jerebohm said he didn't see why not. There were times when it was better that way. The times being what they were, in fact, it actually suited him.

As the three of them walked back to the house Pop turned to Mrs Jerebohm's tight, white-suited figure and asked if there wasn't perhaps something else she wanted to see? The kitchen garden? The asparagus beds? The greenhouses?

'You could grow some beautiful orchids there.'

Orchids were one touch of poetry too much for Mr Jerebohm, who said rather peremptorily that thanks, there was nothing else they wanted. At the same moment Mrs Jerebohm pointed across the valley, where smoke from the strawberry fields was still drifting across the blue brilliant sky.

'A fire!' she said. 'Isn't that a fire?'

Yes, Pop said, it was a fire and went on to explain how, for the first time in living memory, they were burning off the strawberry fields. The strawberry lark was over for the year. In a couple of weeks harvest would be over too. Everything would be over. It would all be finished months ahead of time, thanks to the marvellous summer, and he offered Pinkie Jerebohm the final crumb of comfort needed to make her day supremely happy.

'The women'll all be coming in from the fields early this year. You'll get all the help you want in the house. Been a perfickly wonderful summer, don't you think, absolutely perfick?'

It certainly had, Mrs Jerebohm said, it certainly had, and with one long ecstatic backward glance at the lake and its lilies she felt her eyes slowly fill with tears of joy.

This, she told herself, was paradise.

That night Pop felt the deal called for a bottle of champagne in bed with Ma and an extra good cigar. As he sat in bed, sipping and puffing and watching Ma brush her hair at the dressing table, he caught pleasant glimpses of her body, vast and soft, under the forget-me-not blue nightgown, thin as gossamer, he had bought her for Christmas.

'Think the kids were pleased about the swimming pool,' he said, 'don't you? I thought the twins would die.'

At the supper table he had been surrounded by children choking with excitement. The twins were half-hysterical. Montgomery, Victoria, and a fast-maturing Primrose – he wasn't sure she wasn't going to be the prettiest of the lot after all – were not much better.

'Didn't think Mariette and Charley sounded all that wild though,' Ma said.

'No?'

'No. After all you promised you'd build 'em a bungalow with the stuff you pulled out of Gore Court. And here they are still living with us.'

'Stuff's too good for a bungalow. You couldn't do it,' Pop said. 'I'll give Mariette a thousand for her birthday next month. They can start on that.'

Well, that was nice and generous, Ma said, and got into bed to sip champagne, her nightgown giving off strong clouds of heliotrope, her new perfume.

'Thundering hot still,' Pop said.

Still, he thought, they mustn't grumble. Been a pretty fair day on the whole. He hadn't expected to get more than ten or eleven for Gore Court at the best, but thanks largely to Ma he'd done much better. Ma was a sharp one really. By the way, he said to her, what about Mariette? Any sign of any increase and all that?

'Not yet,' Ma said. 'Charley's going to have a test.'

'Test? Good God.'

The subject of a test was so embarrassing that Pop felt both relieved and glad when Ma changed the conversation abruptly and said:

'You didn't really tell me what Mrs Jerebohm was like.'

Ma, as always, was pleasantly curious, even eager, to hear more of Pop's female acquaintances.

'Fairish,' Pop said. 'Uses some funny expressions. Dithers a lot. Says things like dove-tail and zip-up and clock and so on. Excitable.'

Ma looked sharply up at him at the word excitable and said she hoped he hadn't been up to any hanky-pankies of any sort?

'No, no,' Pop said. 'Nothing like that.'

Ma said she was very relieved to hear it. Unabashed, Pop asked why?

'Because they're going to be our nearest neighbours,' Ma said. 'That's why. We'll be having them in for drinks and all that. You want to start off on the right foot, don't you?'

Pop, sipping champagne, said he didn't mean excitable in that way. He meant she got sort of emotional about little things. He recalled the tears he had seen in her eyes at the lakeside. She was all excitable about the joys of country life and all that lark.

'Except she thinks eggs grow on trees,' Ma said, 'and cream comes out of a tap.'

Well, it wasn't quite so bad as that, Pop said, but it was a damn cert Mr Jerebohm didn't know a duck from a jackdaw. Typical Piccadilly farmer – every pea-pod was going to cost him a bob and every pheasant a tenner.

'Well, if he don't mind,' Ma said.

Oh! he didn't mind, Pop assured her, it was all part of the game. But what a world, wasn't it? What a world when you had to lose a lot of money so as to make more? What a world, eh?

'Certainly is,' Ma said and went on to say that there were times when she thought we were all half crazy. 'Not sure we haven't forgotten what it's all about sometimes.'

Forgotten what all what was about? Pop wanted to know.

'Oh! you know,' Ma said, 'just being here.'

The sudden conscious reminder that he was alive on a hot summer evening full of stars was enough to recall to Pop something he had meant to ask Ma earlier on.

'Had a good mind to ask you to have a lay-down when I got back this afternoon,' he said, 'but you were watering your zinnias.'

'Well, I'm not watering my zinnias now,' she said, 'am I? You never want to spoil a good mind.'

Pop thought that this, like so much that Ma said, made real sense and presently, after getting out of bed and drawing back the curtains and gazing with his own special sort of rapture at the blazing summer stars, got back into a world of chiffon and heliotrope in order to demonstrate to a silently waiting Ma what a good mind he still had.

· 4 ·

Several weeks later, about five o'clock on a warm October evening Pop, in his shirt sleeves, was sitting comfortably in a deck chair on the south side of the house, a quart glass of beer at his side, occasionally potting with a shot gun at odd pheasants flying over from the Jerebohm domain to roost in the bluebell wood beyond the yard.

It was just the sort of shooting the doctor ordered. You sat in comfort, with a nice supply of beer at hand, and picked off the birds like one o'clock. Perfick sport. Like fishing for trout with worms, he didn't suppose it was the real and proper sporting thing to do, but at the same time he reckoned it was streets in front of tramping over sodden stubbles on rainy winter afternoons, waiting for birds to be beaten out of copses at ten quid a time. The pheasant tasted no different anyway and he was very glad he'd managed to persuade Mr Jerebohm to buy a couple of hundred young ones at precisely the right time. Well fed on corn, the birds had fattened beautifully in the extraordinary warm autumn weather and were now as tender and tasty, he thought, as young love. Now and then you missed a bird because at the critical moment you had the beer up to your lips, but on the whole he couldn't grumble. He'd bagged a brace already.

It was not often that he was alone about the house, but Ma and the children, together with Charley and little Oscar, were still hard at the strawberry lark. It was the first time in living memory that the strawberry lark had extended into September and October. There were years when a few odd pounds ripened in autumn but now, thanks to the long hot summer that seemed as if it would never end, there were whole fields of them. Splendid fruit was being gathered in tons. The burnt fields of July had been fed by August thunder rains and had woken into sudden blossoming, as deserts do. It was the most remarkable lark he'd ever known. Ma and Charley and the kids had been at it for six weeks, making pots of dough.

In the fading evening light he missed a bird that planed over too low and too fast for him and then, a minute later, found himself without beer. For a few minutes he sat debating with himself whether to fetch another bottle or to give up shooting altogether and was finally saved the necessity of making a decision by the sight of two figures crossing the yard.

The sudden arrival of the Brigadier, who dropped in quite often, left him unsurprised. It was the sight of Angela Snow, silky haired and lovely as ever, wearing the dreamiest of thin summer dresses, a shade deeper than pale sherry, that made him leap up from his chair. He hadn't seen her since that tenderest of holiday farewells in France, a year before.

'Lambkin,' she said. 'Darling. Given me up for dead or lost or as a bad lot or what?'

Pop, kissed first on both cheeks and then with a light flowering brush on the lips, was actually at a loss for words.

'I was waffling into town to buy an evening paper,' said the Brigadier, who did a great deal of walking, not from choice but necessity, since he couldn't afford a motor, 'and Angela picked me up in the car. Must say I wasn't sorry either. Been damned hot again.'

The word hot set Pop hurrying to the house for drinks, ice and glasses, which he brought out on a tray vividly scrolled in magenta, orange, and scarlet scenes violently depicting Spanish dancers.

'The Brigadier, poor lamb,' Angela said, 'has been crying on my shoulder.'

The Brigadier, angular, thin, and shabby as ever, the elbows of his alpaca actually looking as if gnawed by mice, coughed several times in embarrassment, quite shy.

'Come, come,' he said. 'Now really.'

'Honest to God,' Angela said. 'And I was the great stupid. I hadn't heard about his sister.'

On a morning in April the Brigadier's sister, going upstairs with a small pile of ironing and suddenly lacking strength to reach the top, had simply sat down on the middle steps and quietly died.

'Nice brace of birds,' the Brigadier said, eager to change the subject. 'Got them in the meadow, I suppose?'

Pop, pouring large whiskies on to hillocks of ice, laughed resoundingly and explained how the birds, flying over from the Jerebohm domain, were on the contrary picked off in comfort, from the deck chair.

'Good God,' the Brigadier said. Shocked, he relapsed after the two words into immediate silence. It was really a bit beyond the pale. By Jove it really was. Even for Larkin.

'And what,' Angela said, 'is the great big hole doing in the garden?' She laughed flutingly, pointing across the garden to where, beyond the flaming yellows and scarlets of Ma's zinnias, a vast earthwork had been thrown up, dry as stone from the heat of summer. 'The grave for the poor wretched birds as they fall?'

'Swimming pool,' Pop explained.

'Good God,' the Brigadier said again. Whisky in hand, he stared incredulously across the garden, prawn-like brows twitching. The apparent vastness of the pool, seemingly half as big as a public bath, shocked him even more than Pop's unsporting habits with pheasants. Coughing, he tried a dry joke of his own. 'Quite sure it's large enough?'

'Got to be big to take Ma,' Pop said.

'Scream,' Angela Snow said. 'And when do you hope to use it?'

'If the wevver's nice, early next spring,' Pop said. 'Going to have it heated.'

The Brigadier did his well-mannered best not to choke over his whisky. Angela Snow laughed in her incomparably musical fashion, on bell-like notes, her pellucid eyes dancing.

'And shall we be invited for a dip?' she said. 'If we're not I shall write you off as a stinker.'

'Course,' Pop said, 'probably have a party to christen it,' and went on to say yes, Ma would have it heated. If it wasn't heated, she said, she'd have to have a mink bathing suit and what about that? The trouble with Ma was that she wasn't all that much of a swimmer and got cold very quickly. She floated mostly and if it was warm she had more fun.

'I heard of a bathing party once,' Angela said, 'where all the bathing suits melted as soon as the chaps jumped in. How about that?'

Perfick idea, Pop said. He'd have to think about that. Eh, General?

A certain shyness, not shock this time, left the Brigadier speechless again and it seemed to Pop that Angela Snow, laughing no longer, looked at him with a touch of pity. He suddenly felt overwhelmingly sorry for the General himself. He had heard stories of a daily help serving him bread and cold bacon for lunch or leaving him to dine alone on cold pies of sausage meat as hard as rocks. He felt a chill of loneliness in the air and made up his mind to give the General the brace of pheasants when he left. He could knock off some more tomorrow.

'Another snifter?'

The invitation cheered the Brigadier considerably, though not nearly so much as Pop's sudden recollection of a dish Ma had made that morning and of which there was some left in the fridge. It was a sort of open cheese tart decorated with thin strips of anchovy. It was equally delicious hot or cold. He'd go and get it.

'Ma got the recipe from Mademoiselle Dupont, in France, on that holiday last year,' he said on coming back from the house with the tart, which Ma had cooked in a baking tin a foot wide. 'By the way, Angela, did you go again this year?'

Pop cut handsome wedges of tart and proceeded to hand them to the Brigadier and Angela, who said:

'Couldn't, dear boy. Had to stay at home and look after Iris.'

Pop said Oh? he was sorry about that. Ill or something?

'Nothing so simple, darling. Married.'

For crying out gently, Pop said. That was a surprise. He hadn't thought she was the type.

'Nor did she. Not until that party of yours at the Beau Rivage. That altered the outlook. She lost a precious possession there.'

Pop laughed. He must remember to tell Ma that. The Brigadier, by contrast, showed no sign of amusement at all, not because he was shocked again but merely because he wasn't listening. Chewing with almost excruciating relish on the wedge of cheese tart he stood bemused, a man lost. Two sandwiches of crab paste at lunch time hadn't shown much staying power.

'What about staying for supper?' Pop said suddenly. 'I daresay Ma'll find a couple o' brace o' pheasants. I shot ten or a dozen last week. Expect there'll be strawberries and cream too. Ma generally brings back a few pounds from the field.'

The Brigadier, silent still, felt he could have wept. A prick or two of moisture actually pained his eyes, in fact, as he gave a low cough or two and finally said, in tones intended as cryptic but polite in refusal:

'Oh! no, no, Larkin. Really mustn't. Thanks all the same. No, no, no.'

'Oh! you're a sweetie,' Angela Snow said and the Brigadier looked perceptibly startled, as if thinking or even hoping for a moment that the remark was meant for him, 'of course we'll stay. I'm absolutely starving anyway. Aren't you, Arthur?'

The Brigadier himself had never looked more startled than Pop did at the sudden mention of the General's Christian name, which he had never heard before.

'Good,' he said. 'Good. Ma'll be tickled to death. Especially when she hears you're starving.'

The Brigadier, who was always starving, had nothing to say. The light was fading rapidly now. The scarlet and yellow of Ma's zinnias were like burning embers dropped from the heart of the sunset, the quiet air still like summer, the sky unfeathered by cloud, the sweet chestnut leaves hardly touched by a single brush stroke of brown or yellow. Perfick evening, he heard Pop say as he poured yet another whisky and offered another wedge of tart – that touch of anchovy was masterly, the Brigadier thought, it started all your juices up – and then, a moment later, he heard the first laughing voices of the Larkin family coming home from the strawberry field.

Half a minute later he was aware of a young vision crossing the yard in the twilight. The dark head and olive skin of Primrose were exactly like those of her mother. For a few seconds it actually hurt him to look at her, taller by several inches than when he had seen her last, growing rapidly, her bust ripening. She seemed to him like a younger, less vivacious Mariette. The dark eyes were shy, big and serious, even a little melancholy, and suddenly his heart started aching.

It was uplifted a moment or two later by Ma, carrying in her arms a little Oscar looking as fat as a young seal. Boisterous as ever, brown from weeks of sun, she breezily invited the Brigadier to have a strawberry. In the twilight the baskets of lush ripe berries looked almost black.

'Not surprised to see you here, General,' Ma said. 'But Angela too! Going to stay for supper, aren't you?'

'Already fixed,' Pop said. 'Already fixed.'

'Lovely to see you,' Angela said. 'Can't think what's come over this man of yours, though. Been behaving like a curate. Never a caress.'

'Wait till he gets you in the swimming pool,' Ma said and, laughing like a jelly, went away to put the pheasants into the oven and little Oscar into bed.

The appearance of Mr Charlton, looking astonishingly healthy and brown as a chestnut, startled the Brigadier even more than that of Primrose had done. Charley had filled out a lot too. He was big, even muscular.

'Look remarkably fit, young man,' the Brigadier said and Pop could only think, gloomily, that appearances could be pretty deceptive. He'd begun to think there must be very grave defects in Charley. It was all of two months since Charley had had his tests and neither he nor Ma had the foggiest notion what the results were. The worst of it was Mariette looked astonishingly healthy too. It was a bad sign.

A few moments later he was shepherding everyone into the house, himself carrying the drinks tray, when the telephone rang. Soon afterwards Ma appeared at the door and called:

'Mariette says it's Mrs Jerebohm, wanting me. Will you talk to her? If I'm to get Oscar down and the meal cooked I can't stand there nattering half the night.'

'Charley,' Pop said, 'tot out. Give Angela and the Brigadier another snifter,' and went into the house to answer the lisping voice of Mrs Jerebohm, who said:

'We'd like it so awfully much if you and Mrs L. could come to dinner one evening soon. Thought perhaps the 26th might be nice. It's a Monday – awfully awkward day, I know, but we're down for a long week-end. Hope it dove-tails with your plans? Know you're always terrifically busy.'

Pop, thanking her, said he was pretty sure it would be all right and if it wasn't he'd ring her back very soon. After he had said this there was a long pause from the other end of the line and he said:

'Hullo. Still there?'

Yes, she said, she was still there.

'Thought you'd gone. Nothing the matter?'

No, she said, nothing was the matter. She giggled briefly. It was just his voice.

'Oh? Well, can't help it,' Pop said, laughing too. 'It's just beginning to break, that's all.'

Mrs Jerebohm giggled again, seemingly as nervous as a puppy.

'No, seriously, it sounds so different. Awfully different, actually. One doesn't connect it with you.'

'Ah! well, sorry about that,' Pop said. 'I'll try to do better next time.'

It was the sort of conversation he forgot as quickly as it was made and after going back into the living-room, where the Brigadier already had a third stiff whisky in his hand, he let it go completely from his mind. He would talk to Ma about the dinner later on, probably in bed, over a final snifter.

Wearing a yellow pinafore, Angela Snow floated gaily from kitchen to living-room, helping Mariette to lay the supper table, talking as she did so in high musical overtones. This, she declared, was her idea of fun. The Brigadier, already feeling the third whisky lifting depression from him like a cloud of dark smoke, watched her going to and fro with eyes looking every moment less and less jaded. The juices of his senses had started waking as sharply as those of his mouth had done over anchovy and cheese, so that he began telling himself over and over again that she was a beautiful, beautiful creature.

Soon the delicious unbearable fragrance of roasting pheasant was filling the house. Every few minutes the Brigadier sniffed openly at it like a dog. It seemed as if a long night, a grey mixture of solitude, sandwich lunches, bone-hard apple pies and cold bacon, was at last breaking and passing him by. He hardly noticed the arrival of a fourth and then a fifth whisky and it was from the remotest ends of a waking dream that he heard Pop calling with ebullient cheerfulness to Mr Charlton:

'Shall we have pink tonight, Charley boy? Why not? Get three or four bottles on the ice quick. Ought to go well with the pheasants, I think, don't you?'

'Darling, if that was champagne you were referring to I shall remain faithful to you for ever,' Angela Snow said. 'I adore the pink. It's absolutely me. Quite my favourite tipple.'

The Brigadier might well have wept again except that now, by some miracle, there was nothing to weep for. Had there ever been? He simply couldn't believe there ever had. He was beginning to feel alive again, terrifically alive. Pink champagne? By God, that took him back a thousand aching years. He was again a crazy subaltern on Indian hill-stations, lean and active as a panther: dances and parties everywhere, polo and pig-sticking, affairs with two married women running at the same time, servants everywhere as plentiful as beetles. He was the gay dog having champagne for breakfast, with a certain madness in the air, and nobody giving a damn.

'Glad to see you're perking up, General,' Ma said as she passed him with two deep glass dishes of strawberries, each containing half a dozen pounds. 'Got your glass topped up?'

'Splendid,' the Brigadier said. 'Splendid. Absolutely splendid.'

'Don't spoil your appetite, though, will you?' she said. 'Supper'll only be ten minutes or so.'

The Brigadier found it suddenly impossible to believe how swiftly the evening had gone. The time had whipped along like prairie fire. He took his watch out of his breast pocket and discovered it to be already eight o'clock. Spoil his appetite? He could have eaten horses.

Ma had cooked two brace of pheasants, together with chipolata saus-ages, thin game chips, potatoes creamed with fresh cream and the first Brussels sprouts with chestnuts. Brimming boats of gravy and bread sauce came to table as Pop started to carve the birds, the breasts of which crumbled under the knife as softly as fresh-baked bread.

'Tot the champagne out, Charley boy,' Pop said. 'And what about you, General? Which part of the bird for you? Leg or bosom?'

The Brigadier immediately confessed to a preference for bosom and a moment later found his eye roving warmly across the table, in the direc-tion of Angela Snow, who met the gaze full-faced and unflushed, though with not quite the elegant composure she always wore. This started his juices flowing again and with a brief peremptory bark he found himself suddenly on his feet, champagne glass waving.

'To our hostess. I give you a blessing, madam. And honour. And glory. And long, long health –'

The unaccustomed extravagance of the Brigadier's words trailed off, unfinished. Everybody rose and drank to Ma. The Brigadier then declared that the pink champagne was terrific and immediately crouched with eager reverence over his plate, the edges of which were only barely visible, a thin embroidered line of white enclosing a whole rich field of game, vegetables, sauce, and gravy.

Somewhere in the middle of a second helping of pheasant he heard Pop recalling his telephone conversation with Mrs Jerebohm.

'Wants us to go to dinner on the 26th,' Pop said. 'I said I thought it was all right.'

'Having staff trouble, I hear,' the Brigadier said.

'Oh?' Ma said. 'The women'll all come back in the winter.'

'Has to do the cooking herself, I understand.'

'Well, that won't hurt her, will it?' Ma said. 'If she likes good food she'll like cooking it. Same as I do.'

'I can only say,' the Brigadier said, gazing solemnly into the winking depths of his glass, 'that if the dinner she gives you is one tenth as delectable as this – no, one thousandth part as delectable – then you will be feeding on manna and the milk of paradise –'

Once again the extravagant words floated away. With them went the piled plates of the first course, carried out by Mariette and Angela Snow, who brought back bowls of strawberries and cream to replace them.

Soon the strawberries lay on the Brigadier's plate like fat fresh red rosebuds, dewed white with sugar. The visionary sherry-coloured figure of Angela Snow came to pour the thickest yellow cream on them, her voluptuous bare forearm brushing his hand. Then as she went away to take her place at the table a sudden spasm of double vision made him see two of her: a pair of tall golden twins of disturbing elegance who actually waved hands at him and said:

'You're doing fine, Brigadier, my sweet. Does my heart good to see you. This afternoon I thought you were for the coal-hole.'

What on earth she meant by the coal-hole he didn't know and cared even less. He only knew he was doing fine. The strawberries were simply magnificent; they came straight from the lap of the gods. Only the gods could send strawberries like that, in October, to be washed down by champagne, and soon he was eating a second dishful, then a third.

'The General's away,' Ma kept saying with cheerful peals of laughter, 'the General's away.'

Then a renewed and stronger bout of double vision made him miscount all the heads at the table. The twins and Victoria were already in bed, leaving eight people eating. But now sometimes he was counting sixteen heads, then eighteen, then twenty, all of them dancing round the table like figures in a chorus. Behind them the television set glimmered a ghastly green and Pop's extravagant glass and chromium cocktail cabinet shimmered up and down like some impossible garish organ at a fair.

It was to these figures that he found himself saying hearty and newly extravagant farewells just after eleven o'clock, the brace of newly shot pheasants in his hand.

The evening had been great, he kept saying, swinging the pheasants about with grand gestures. Absolutely great. Straight from the gods. He kissed Ma several times on both cheeks and clasped Pop and Charley with tremendous fervour by the hand. After this he kissed both Primrose and Mariette, saying with unaccustomed gravity, followed by a sudden belch, that Ma and Pop were a million times blessed.

'A million times. A million times. Ten million times.'

Still swinging the pheasants, he started to climb into Angela Snow's car and then paused to give several pleasurable barks in final farewell.

'By God, Larkin, I must say you know how to live!' he said. 'I'll say that for you. I'll say you damn well know how to live.'

Once again he started to swing the pheasants madly about his head and Pop treated him to a sudden clout of affectionate farewell plumb in the middle of the back. The gesture pitched him violently forward and through the open door of the car, unlocking fresh barks of laughter, in which Ma and Angela Snow joined ringingly.

'Sleep well, General!' Ma called. 'Sleep well!'

'Sleep be damned!' the Brigadier said. He waved a majestic hand from the car window, splendidly reckless, eyebrows martially bristling. 'Shan't sleep a damn wink all night! Shan't go home till morning!'

Pop said that was the spirit and urged him not to do anything he wouldn't do. The Brigadier yelled 'Bingo!', exclaiming loudly that he wanted to kiss Ma again.

'Must kiss Ma!' he said. 'Got to kiss Ma. Never sleep if I don't kiss Ma.'

Pop again said that this was the stuff and urged Ma to come forward and give the Brigadier a real snorter, one of her specials.

Ma immediately did so, fastening her lips full on the Brigadier's mouth with powerful suction. The Brigadier, half suffocated, made a rapid imaginative ascent skyward, unable to breathe.

Then Angela Snow called: 'Here, what about me? What have I done? What about this little girl?' so that Pop, not quite knowing at once whether it was his services that were being called for or those of the Brigadier, simply decided that it must be his own and proceeded to give Angela Snow three minutes of silent and undivided attention on the other side of the car.

Pop, who didn't believe in doing things at any time by halves, felt quite prepared to prolong things even further, but even Angela Snow thought there were limits and finally struggled out of the embrace gasping for air, as if half-drowned.

'One for the road?' Pop said. 'Come on, one more for the road.'

'One more like that and I shall be away. There'll be absolutely no holding me.'

'I'm away already!' the Brigadier said. By God, he was too. He had never known sensations like it. Not, at any rate, for a long time. He was sailing heavenwards on imaginary clouds of bliss. There was no stopping him.

'Got your pecker up all right now, haven't you?' Ma said. 'Not down in the dumps now, are you?'

Not only was his pecker up, the Brigadier thought. Everything else was.

'Goodbye, darlings,' Angela Snow called at last to the Larkins. 'Farewell, my lambs. Bless you both ten thousand times. And the same number of the sweetest thanks.'

The Brigadier, not quite fully conscious, felt himself being driven away into a night voluptuous with stars, the goodbyes still sounding behind him like a peal of bells. Soon afterwards, with a reckless hand, he was grasping Angela Snow somewhere in the region of a smooth upper thigh and to his very great surprise found there was no whisper of protest in answer.

'Must come into the cottage and have a nip of brandy before you go,' he said, 'eh? Let's broach a keg. Bingo?'

'Bingo,' Angela Snow said. 'You have absolutely the sweetest ideas. I'm dying for a nip.'

Angela, still recoiling slightly from the velvet impact of Pop's long-drawn kiss, felt half light-headed herself as she stopped the car at the cottage, got out, and stood for some minutes waiting for the Brigadier to find his latchkey. All the time he was still swinging the pheasants about with careless gestures.

'Got it.' Key in one hand, pheasants in the other, the Brigadier groped gaily to the cottage door. It was a bit tricky here, she heard him explaining as she followed, and heard him trip on a step. 'Got to find the lights. Should be a torch somewhere.'

The door of the little cottage opened straight into the living-room and the Brigadier, unlocking the door, went inside, unsteadily groping.

'Stand still,' he urged her. 'I'll have a light in a couple of jiffs.'

Suddenly he turned and, in the darkness, ran full against her. A powerful recollection of Ma's divinely transcendent kiss bolted through him in such a disturbing wave that a second later he was urgently embracing her.

The sudden force of it made him drop the brace of pheasants and trip. Angela Snow, caught off-guard, tripped too and they both fell over, the Brigadier backwards, across the hearthrug.

Dazed for a moment, he found it impossible to get up. Then he realized, flat on the floor, that he didn't want to get up. He told himself that only a fool would want to get up. The silk of Angela Snow's dress spread across him in a delicious canopy and finally he put up a hand and started touching, then stroking, her bare left shoulder.

It might have been a signal for Angela Snow to get up too but to his delighted surprise she, apparently, didn't want to get up either. This prompted him to start stroking the other shoulder and a second later, in response, he heard her give a series of quiet, thrilling moans.

'Heavenly,' she told him. 'Keep on. Just between the shoulders. That's it. Just there.'

Great God, the Brigadier thought. He stroked rapidly.

'Slower, slower,' she said. 'Slower, please. Round and round. Slowly. That's it. Heavenly.'

A moment later, with sudden abandon, the Brigadier grasped the zip of her dress and pulled it with a single stroke down her back. In response she kissed him full on the mouth, more softly and tenderly than Ma had done but still with the instantaneous effect as of veins of fire lighting up all over his body.

Something about this electrifying sensation made him say, when the kiss was over:

'By Jove, the Larkins know how to do it, don't they? By Jove, they know how.'

'And they're not the only ones.'

The Brigadier, urged on, began to think that nothing could stop him now and presently he was caressing her shoulders again and unhooking the clip of her brassière.

'Round and round,' he heard her murmur. 'That's it. Round and round. Oh! that's heavenly. How did you find my weak spot? And so soon?'

The Brigadier hadn't the faintest notion. He was only aware of the entire evening flowering into madness.

'By Jove, I could lie here all night,' he said. 'I could see the stars out. I don't want to go to bed, do you?'

'Oh! no?' she said. 'Don't you?'

Half way up the stairs the Brigadier, at the end of an evening of revolutionary sensations, none of which he had experienced for a generation, felt yet another one rise up, out of the darkness to greet him.

Without warning five of Pop's whiskies, ten glasses of pink champagne and several large brandies joined their powerful forces. One moment he was grasping at the bare voluptuous shoulders of Angela Snow; the next he was sitting on the stairs, at more or less the same place where his sister had sat herself down and left him in final solitude, and passed out swiftly and quietly, without a sigh.

When he came to himself again he was alone, fully dressed, on the bed. The autumn dawn was just breaking and in the middle of it a huge and spectacular planet was shining, winking white as it rose.

· 5 ·

A week later Ma was sure the long, hot summer was at an end. The nights and mornings, she said, had begun to strike very parky. The last of the strawberries were finished; there was frost in the air. She had begun to feel very cold across her back in bed of a night, so that she was glad to tuck up closer to Pop, and already by day she was sometimes glad to wear two jumpers, one salmon, one violet, instead of none at all.

'Think I'll slip my mink stole on when we go to the Jerebohms tonight,' she said.

And by eight o'clock, when she got out of the Rolls outside the big oak front door of Gore Court, she was very glad she had. A cold, gusty, leaf-ridden wind was beating in from the west. Twigs of turkey oak and branches of conifer were flying everywhere.

'I'm duck-skin all across my back already,' Ma said. 'You feel it worse after a hot summer. I hope it'll be warm inside.'

Pop, who had taken the precaution of having three Red Bulls laced with double tots of gin before coming out, said he hoped so too and pulled the big brass bell-knob at the side of the front door.

A clanging like that of a muffin bell echoed through the house very far away, as if at the end of cavernous corridors. For the space of two or three minutes nobody answered it and presently Pop pulled the bell-knob again. By this time rain was spitting in the wind and Ma said she was freezing to death already. Pop said he wasn't all that hot himself but that was how it was with these enormous houses. The servants always lived half a mile away.

A second or two later the big front door was opened by a girl of nineteen or twenty, blue-eyed and very fair, with her hair done up in the shape of a plaited bread roll. She gave Pop and Ma the slightest suspicion of a curtsey and said 'Good evening. To come in please,' in an accent so strong that Pop, fixing her with a gaze like a limpet, told himself she must be froggy.

Inside the huge baronial entrance hall, lit only by a big brass lamp hanging over the head of the stairs, the air struck cold as a vault. It smelled

266

mouldy too, Ma thought, and a bit mousey into the bargain, rather like that hotel they'd stayed at in Brittany.

'No, I'll keep my stole on,' she said to the girl when she offered to take it, 'thank you.'

'*Bitte,*' the girl said and then corrected herself. 'Please.'

Bitter it would be an' all, Ma thought, if you had to live in this place all winter and couldn't get it no warmer than it was now. She'd get pleurisy in no time.

She thought the drawing-room, huge though it was and with all its treacle-brown panelling about as cheerful as a church vestry, seemed a little better. A fire of birch logs a yard long was sulkily smoking – burning was too definite a word for the thick pink mist gushing out of the silvery pile of wood – in a brick fireplace as large as a cow-stall. The heat that came out of it might possibly have warmed a fly, Ma thought, but not a very big one.

'Ah! Larkin.' Mr Jerebohm, with outstretched hand, advanced from the smoky regions of the fireplace. 'Mrs Larkin.'

Mr Jerebohm, who was wearing a black velvet jacket and a claret-red bow-tie, said of course they both knew Pinkie, who now simpered rather than walked across the drawing-room to lisp 'Good evening' and shake hands. Pinkie was wearing a silk evening dress of an indefinite brown colour, rather like stale milk chocolate. It was sleeveless, off the shoulder and rather low at the bust, so that some inches of a dough-coloured pouchy bosom were revealed.

'It'll be pride that keeps her warm,' Ma thought. 'Nothing else will.'

Pinkie lisped that it was awfully nice to see them and did they know Captain and Mrs Perigo?

Still clinging to him, is she? Ma thought. Thought she'd run off with that feller Fanshawe long ago.

'Evening,' Pop said. 'Think we've met a couple o' times.'

Captain Perigo said 'Really?' in a voice remarkably like the groan of an un-oiled gate, and said he didn't believe they had. In expressing his words his bony jaw, which was much the colour of pumice stone and about as fleshless, unhinged itself with rusty difficulty and then remained emptily open, unable to hinge itself back again.

'Often seen you ride at the point-to-points,' Ma said. 'My daughter Mariette rides a lot there.'

'Really?' Captain Perigo said.

This monosyllabic eagerness of welcome was in direct contrast to Mrs Perigo, who spoke heartily and had eyes like ripe black olives. If Captain

Perigo, from continuous association with horses, looked remarkably like an undernourished hunter himself, Mrs Perigo had all the plushy creaminess of a cow. In tones like those of a deep-blown horn she drawled good evenings, at the same time giving Pop a look of openly inviting greeting, eyes in a deep slow roll.

High society now, Ma thought. There was a certain mannered stiffness in the air quite foreign to her nature and she was glad she'd brought her mink.

'Our summer seems to have left us, don't you think?' Mrs Perigo said.

'Absolutely heavenly. We'll never have another one like it, ever, will we? I mean ever? You been away?'

'Not this year,' Ma said. 'Been too busy strawberry-picking.'

'Really?' Captain Perigo stared at Ma in open-mouthed pain, as if she had been doing time.

The unmistakable chill in the air prompted Pop to think that a large snifter would go down well. A moment later he found himself confronted with a tray held by Mr Jerebohm. On it were three or four pink glasses, each about the size of a thimble.

'Care for sherry?'

Pop thanked Mr Jerebohm, raised a thimble of pale amber liquid and stared at it dubiously, not certain whether to knock it back in one go or husband it for a while. He decided on husbandry. Something told him there might not be another.

'Admiring your mink,' Mrs Jerebohm said to Ma, who was also holding a thimble. 'Hope you don't mind? Quite gorgeous. That lovely new colour.'

'Bought it with the money I made in the strawberry field,' Ma said. 'Put in a lot of extra time this year.'

Pop, overhearing this, was ready to laugh aloud and was only saved from doing so by the sudden languorous approach of Mrs Perigo, who bore down on him with dark still eyes and swinging hips. Pop knew all about Mrs Perigo, who was wearing a tight evening dress of geranium-leaf green that fitted her like a pod, and he was already on his guard.

'You sort of live next door, don't you?' she said.

Sort of, Pop said. Half a mile along the road.

'Never see you around anywhere. How can that be?'

That, Pop said, could only be because she didn't keep her eyes open, a remark that caused her to give him another slow inviting glance, openly ripe and full.

'I will in future though,' she said.

Pop laughed and then was silent. He wasn't going to be drawn by Mrs

Perigo. There were men in every village for a radius of ten miles round who wished with all their hearts they'd never met Corinne Perigo.

'Silly to be so near and never have a peep of anybody,' she said. 'That's the worst of the country though, there's so damn little fun.'

Pop, drinking sherry in sips so minute that he could hardly taste it at all, thought that if any woman had had any fun it was Corinne Perigo, who had in her time run off with a naval commander, a veterinary surgeon, and an agricultural inspector. The naval commander had shot himself and the inspector was in a home. Pop didn't know about the vet, but in the process of her adventures the forbearing Perigo had turned into a monosyllabic horse.

'Heard you say there was no fun in the country.' It was Pinkie Jerebohm, offering a plate of the snippiest of cocktail snippets to Pop and Mrs Perigo. 'Have one of these. And what about your glass?'

What about it? Pop thought and was dismayed to hear Pinkie say as she peered into his glass:

'Oh! you're still all right, I see.'

Pop simply hadn't the heart to say anything and he could only suppose there was so little recognizable difference between a full and an empty thimble that you really couldn't blame her.

'Well,' Mrs Perigo said, 'do *you* think there's any fun?'

'My husband does,' Pinkie lisped. 'He adores it. He thinks the days are so long. Much longer than they are in town, miles longer. Perhaps it's because he's always up with the lark. The only thing is that you can't get help for love nor money. I had to get this Austrian girl in. She can't cook though and even she's been spending her days off in the strawberry fields.'

All would be well, Pop assured her, now that the strawberries, potatoes, and sugar beet were finished. She'd get plenty of help now.

'I profoundly hope so.'

A moment later, over in the fireplace, a heavy gust of wind came down the chimney and erupted in a pungent cloud of birch-smoke, so that Captain Perigo, in the act of trying to get a little warmth into his haunches, seemed visibly to rise up, exposed as on a funeral pyre.

This seemed like a signal for Mrs Jerebohm to muster her chilly guests together, which she did with the simpering of a hen gathering stray chicks.

'Shall we go in? I think we might, don't you? I think all's ready. Shall we? Shall we go in?'

Pop gave his thimble sherry a final despondent glance and then switched his gaze to Ma, who was shivering. Better knock it back, he thought, profoundly glad at the same time that he'd insured himself with three Red Bulls. He didn't care for sherry much at the best of times and he was quite right: it was perfickly obvious there wasn't going to be another.

The dining-room was vast too, with polished oak floors that echoed hollow with every step and a big stone fireplace that sheltered yet another pile of smoking birch. If the air didn't quite take your breath away, Ma thought, it wasn't very much better. It was like a stable in winter-time.

The dining-table looked nice though, she thought. Tall red candles rose from green china bowls filled with scarlet hips and haws. There were rose-pink dinner mats, cut wine glasses, pretty silver salt cellars and butter knives with painted handles, all looking discreet and pleasant under golden candlelight.

Everything looked very *très snob*, Pop thought and only hoped the food would be up to the same standard. He was pretty well starving.

Half a minute later, sitting next to Mrs Perigo, he found himself staring down at a small green glass dish in which reposed a concoction consisting of five prawns, a spoonful of soapy pink sauce, and a sixth prawn hanging over the edge of the glass as if searching for any of its mates that might have fallen overboard. You could have eaten the lot, Pop thought, with two digs of an egg-spoon.

'I hope everybody likes prawn cocktail?' Mrs Jerebohm said. A wind whined and whooped like an owl in the chimney as if giving answer. 'I hope you'll forgive me if I don't join you. I'm not allowed it. I have my yoghurt.'

'Give you gee-up?' Ma said. 'Onions serve me that way too.'

Mrs Jerebohm looked frigid. 'Not exactly. It's my diet. I have to watch it all the time.'

'Ma went on a diet once,' Pop said. 'By the time she'd got the diet down her every morning she was ready for a good square breakfast.'

'Really?' Captain Perigo said. 'I mean to say –'

What Captain Perigo meant to say nobody discovered. Mrs Jerebohm toyed with yoghurt. Pop toyed with a prawn, thinking it tasted more like a bit of last week's cod than anything else he could name. Ma sniffed the chilly air, hoping she might catch a smell of steak or something cooking. She rather fancied steak tonight but she merely felt a sense of denial when she remembered how far away the kitchens were.

Presently Mrs Jerebohm swallowed a pill, washing it down with a glass of cold water, and Mr Jerebohm walked round the table, filling glasses with chilled white wine.

Pop, who had made the prawn cocktail last as long as possible, decided he couldn't put off the end any longer and sucked at the last meagre spoonful just as Mrs Perigo dropped her serviette on the floor.

'Do you mind, Mr Larkin? I've dropped my serviette.'

Pop poked about under the table. The serviette had dropped between Mrs Perigo's not unshapely legs, which were held generously apart. The temptation to caress one of them or even both was a strong one which Pop successfully resisted just in time.

When he finally retrieved the serviette and put it back in her lap he was not surprised to notice that she was eyeing him with a keen but voluptuous sort of disappointment. He wasn't at all sure there didn't seem to be a hint of annoyance there too and with a nippy gesture towards Mr Jerebohm he changed the subject.

'Had many pheasants yet, Mr Jerebohm?'

Mr Jerebohm confessed, with a certain air of annoyance too, that he had, in fact, not had many pheasants. Hardly a damned one.

'Oh?' Pop expressed a most fervent and sympathetic surprise. 'How's that? Thought you had plenty.'

So, confessed Mr Jerebohm, did he. But where did the bounders get to? You could walk all the way to the lake and never see a brace.

'Knocking the stoats off?' Pop said, airily.

What on earth had stoats got to do with it? Mr Jerebohm said.

'And what about jackdaws?' Pop said. 'Eh?' Bigger menace than stoats. 'And magpies?' Bigger menace than jackdaws. 'And hawks?' Bigger menace than the lot. Deadly.

Mr Jerebohm, who didn't know a lark from a sparrow, let alone a magpie from a hawk, sat almost as open-mouthed as Captain Perigo while listening to Pop's fluent recital of the pheasant's countless deadly enemies.

'You mean —?'

'Perfickly obvious,' Pop said. 'Your birds are being taken by summink or other.'

Pop stared hard at Ma as he spoke, but Ma didn't move an eyelash in reply.

'Really?' Captain Perigo said. 'I mean say —'

'No doubt about it,' Pop said. 'You'll have to get among the stoats and things. Won't he, Ma?'

Ma cordially agreed. And the foxes.

'Dammit,' Mr Jerebohm said, 'I thought the hunt took care of the foxes.'

'Half and half,' Pop said. 'The hunt takes care of the foxes and the foxes take care of the hunt.'

'Had a fox fetch a goose the other night,' Ma said. 'Right under our noses.'

'I think we fed 'em too well in the first place,' Mr Jerebohm said. 'They simply didn't want to fly.'

'Never. Got to feed 'em. Got to fatten 'em up a bit,' Pop said. 'After all, what's a pheasant if it's all skin and bone?'

Mr Jerebohm said he simply didn't know; he hadn't even seen one. He hadn't seen a snipe, a deer, a hare, or a damn rabbit either. Had Larkin?

'Caught sight of a few in the distance once or twice,' Pop said. 'Too far off, mostly.'

'Really?' Captain Perigo said.

While all this was going on the blonde Austrian maid had been clearing away the cocktail dishes. She was rather a fresh, pretty little thing, Pop thought, and recalled that he hadn't seen her about the village at all. He must look out a bit more and as she picked up his dish he turned and gave her a short warm smile.

She gave him the hint of a smile in reply and a second later he felt the air between himself and Mrs Perigo positively dry up, parched by a withering glare.

While the girl was out of the room Mrs Jerebohm daintily swallowed another pill and drank another glass of water. Pop tried the white wine, all flavour of which appeared to have been chilled out in some deep and distant tomb.

'What about wild duck then?' Pop said.

As if unprepared to discuss the subject of wild duck Mr Jerebohm went over to the sideboard and started sharpening the carving knife. No, he said rather tersely, he hadn't seen any wild duck either. He doubted in fact if there were any wild duck about the place. If there were they were damn widely scattered.

'They come and go,' Pop said. 'We had a brace last week, didn't we, Ma? Not much on a wild duck, but they're beautiful with orange sauce. Perfick.'

Tortured by the renewed description of Ma's wild duck with orange sauce, Mr Jerebohm found himself faced with the task of dismembering three small larded partridges brought in on a dish by the Austrian maid. They not only looked on the small side but they seemed, he thought, rather crisp. He gave the girl a look of slightly curt reproval and then with sinking heart proceeded to thrust the carving knife hard into the breast of the first partridge.

Under this first prod the bird gave a sharp leap about the dish. A second made it dance sideways, skating in gravy. The knife grated against bone as hard as ebony, setting Ma's teeth on edge, and with depressing insistence Mr Jerebohm attacked it again. This time it skated into the two other birds, one of which leapt completely from the dish and slithered full circle round the sideboard.

After the Austrian maid retrieved it deftly Mrs Jerebohm called, lisping: 'Not for me, dear, you know I mustn't. I have my peanut *pâté*.'

On Mrs Jerebohm's plate there reposed the smallest portion of brown-grey *pâté*, looking not at all unlike a mouse nibbling at a solitary lettuce leaf. A still smaller portion of grated celery, together with one sliced tomato, covered some part of the rest of the plate and for a few moments Mrs Jerebohm stared at it all either as if in disbelief or as if wondering whether something, possibly, could be missing.

Watching her, Ma thought she had the clue.

'Salt?' she said. 'Looking for the salt?'

'Oh! never salt,' Mrs Jerebohm lisped. 'Salt is absolutely fatal.'

Never? Ma said. She hadn't heard.

'*And* pepper. They both put on more weight than bread. Oh! I never, never eat salt. Never, never pepper.'

'Really?' Captain Perigo said. 'I mean say –'

By this time the first of the partridges, tortuously dismembered by Mr Jerebohm, were coming to table, garnished with frozen peas and game potatoes. The birds looked, if possible, more charred than ever and as each meagre portion was set down in the pool of glass and silver and candlelight Ma's customary epitaph 'Shan't get very fat on this' flashed sadly through her mind. No doubt about it: they wouldn't either.

'Absolutely delicious,' Captain Perigo said, uttering his first real original sentence of the evening.

In return Mrs Perigo gave him a look of flat-iron contempt, as if he were not supposed to utter sentences of originality. His jaw, falling open suddenly, expressed a pained acquiescence that showed no sign of receding until he presently found time to pick up slowly, one by one, three or four peas on the end of a fork. Even these remained for some time poised before the empty gap, in air.

'Anyone going hunting on Thursday?' Mr Jerobohm said.

He hadn't hunted much yet. The mid-week meets were awkward and not, it seemed, very well patronized. These days, it appeared, you couldn't get the chaps.

'I'll be there,' Captain Perigo said. The peas had only just gone in when his mouth opened again.

This time there was no answering look of contempt from Corinne Perigo, who merely half-glanced at Pop and said:

'I know I can't. I've got a perm.'

'You going, Larkin?' Mr Jerebohm said.

Pop, rather uncheerfully, said yes, he thought he might. He was struggling with elastic bits of partridge, longing for a cheese-pudding or something, a steak-and-kidney pie or something, to fill him up. Had to take a day off now and then, he said, and he hadn't hunted once this year.

At this point some instinct made him turn and look at Corinne Perigo, who to his considerable surprise was attacking a piece of rubbery breast of partridge with silent fury. The normally soft, sensuous lips were being bitten hard and white and for the life of him he couldn't imagine why.

One thing he hadn't any doubts about, however, was the partridge. He hadn't the heart to ask if the birds had been shot on the estate. Once, as he struggled to get a mouthful of flesh here and there, he saw Mrs Jerebohm smile at him across the table. Half in sympathy rather than anything else he gave her a warm and winning smile in reply.

'Like being in the country?' he said.

'Oh! yes.'

Secretly, in fact, she had begun to hate it. The grounds were still full of thistles and willow-herb. The kitchen garden looked sordid and try as you could you couldn't get help. The locals were independent, rude, and treacherous and it would be late spring before she could have asparagus. Even the Austrian girl, simple and nice as she had been on arrival, had started on the path of rural corruption, thanks largely to the strawberry fields.

'Perfick here,' Pop said. 'Wouldn't change it for nowhere else in the world.'

'Never, never want to live anywhere else?' Corinne Perigo said.

'Never,' Pop said and with such resolute finality that Mrs Perigo's lips finally untightened and broke into a smile.

All through the sweet-course, which consisted of ice-cream crowned with a solitary half of walnut, the westerly gale rose in the chimney. Smoke puthered into the fireplace in thicker and thicker clouds, until at last a light grey fog hung about the room. Ma found herself shivering more and more often and began to wonder how soon she could get home and cook herself some good hot eggs and bacon. She wasn't sure she wouldn't jump into a bath too.

'Shall we find more comfortable chairs?' Mrs Jerebohm said, 'and some coffee?'

Through increasing fog, with hollow footsteps, Mrs Jerebohm and her guests filed back to the drawing-room, where Mr Jerebohm began to dispense minute thimbles of crème-de-menthe and brandy.

The Austrian maid was also there, serving coffee and actually smiling with unexpected pertness at Pop as she said, with her strong accent:

'Sugar? One lump or two?'

'Four,' Pop said and while she was still laughing, went on: 'Are you froggy? From France I mean?'

'I am from Austria.'

'Very nice,' Pop said and was not unastonished, in view of the luscious smile he gave her, to see that she served the four sugar-lumps to him herself, smiling with a separate movement of her lips at each one.

These gestures were not lost on Corinne Perigo, who presently cornered him at a safe distance from the smoking fireplace and said:

'Sorry I won't see you at the hunt, Thursday.'

Pop said he wasn't all that sure he could go. Might not find the time.

'No? I'd go if I could change my perm.'

Pop didn't answer. The hunt really didn't interest him this season. He was very busy and the present crowd were pretty rag-tag-and-bobtail. The country, too thickly wooded, with too many orchards, wasn't really good for hunting either.

Nor did Mrs Perigo interest him very much. Nobody could say he wasn't interested in women; he was ready and willing for them any time you cared to name. But Mrs Perigo wasn't quite his kind. Something about her, more especially the voluptuous glances, irked him. He didn't want to go hunting with her either, one way or the other.

'Well, anyway, even if I can't go,' she said, 'you could drop in for a stirrup-cup in the morning, before you went, couldn't you?'

'Never drink in the mornings.'

'No? Simply can't believe it.'

Captain Perigo drank like nobody's business, starting an hour after breakfast.

'Honest fact,' Pop said, straight-faced as an owl. 'Blood pressure.'

Mrs Perigo gave him another deep, slow smile, this time both disturbing and enigmatic too.

'I suffer from it myself,' she said. 'Sometimes. Depending on circumstances.'

Whatever the circumstances were Pop didn't bother to ask and he was glad to hear Ma's warm, friendly voice inquiring of Mrs Jerebohm:

'Get to know many people since you've been here? Made many friends?'

Mrs Jerebohm was too reticent to point out that her poverty in country friendships was only too well reflected in the number of guests at her dinner table. She had conceived, once, the idea of having eight or ten guests that evening for dinner, or perhaps even a cocktail party, but somehow country people seemed to close themselves up, oyster-like, slow to accept you.

'Not too many,' she confessed. 'I did invite a Miss Pilchester to tea last week, but she didn't even answer my note –'

'Batty,' Mrs Perigo said. 'She probably didn't even open it. Or she wove it into a scarf on her loom.'

Ma, who wouldn't have such remarks at any price, rose to Edith Pilchester's defence swiftly and sharply.

'She's not been well, poor thing. Appendix or something. One of those grumbling ones. The sort you have to put up with because they're not bad enough to have out. I keep telling Pop he'll have to go and massage it for her.'

Ma found her rich loud laugh enveloped in a chilly cloud, out of which Corinne Perigo's voice inquired with slow sarcasm:

'Oh? Does he make a habit of massaging appendices?'

'Oh! he'll massage anything for a lark,' Ma said, laughing in bountiful fashion again. 'He's got a waiting list a mile long.'

The frigidity with which the Jerebohms received this announcement sprang less from shock than confusion, which was not improved by Pop saying, with a fresh laugh, that he'd never massaged an appendix in his life.

'Oh! really?' Captain Perigo said. 'Well, I'm damned.'

'You'll have to come over and have a bite and wet with us one day,' Ma said, 'and meet a few people. We'll get the Brigadier and a few more in one Sunday –'

'That's it,' Pop said. 'We'll knock off three or four geese and Ma'll stuff 'em with sage and onions.'

Painfully in a low voice, Mr Jerebohm said:

'Thank you. We'd be glad to.'

This uncordial acceptance threw another chilling mist over the conversation, which stopped completely for half a minute, until Mrs Jerebohm said:

'I hear you have several children, Mrs Larkin. Your house must be full already.'

'Seven so far,' Ma said. 'Quite a little brood.'

'Little? You mean you'd like to have more?'

'Oh! Pop would,' Ma said. 'There's no holding him back.'

In the cool, smoky drawing-room there was no sound but that of coffee spoons stirring at sugary dregs in cups and a few sharp sniffs from Captain Perigo struggling with some obstruction in his nose.

Almost at once Pop's own nose started to sniff out the increasing chill in the air and he was suddenly half afraid that somebody would soon be asking him and Ma if they were married or not and he turned the conversation smartly.

'Seen any hares at all, Mr Jerebohm?'

Mr Jerebohm confessed stiffly that he hadn't seen any hares. He was about to remark that he thought hares in fact were extinct, like wild duck, deer, pheasant, woodcock, and a lot of other things, but Pop broke cheerfully in with:

'Tell 'em how you do hares, Ma. That French recipe, I mean. The one with burgundy and prunes.' In his sudden enthusiasm for the French way with hares he lifted a hand in air, as if about to strike Mr Jerebohm in warm comradeship in the middle of the back. 'That's a beauty. That'll make your gills laugh.'

The prospect of Mr Jerebohm's gills ever laughing again seemed an utterly remote one. The coffee spoons tinkled emptily again in their cups. Captain Perigo sniffed again and then actually brought out his handkerchief and blew at his nasal obstruction, loudly, with a single trumpet snarl that earned him a fresh look of contempt from Mrs Perigo.

'Play crib?' Pop said with great cheerfulness. 'What about a couple of hands at crib?'

Crib? What was crib? Mr Jerebohm was unfamiliar with crib.

'Card game,' Pop explained. 'Very old card game.'

'Perhaps it's getting a little late for cards,' Mrs Jerebohm started to say and was suddenly saved the necessity of continuing by a violent crash of timber or masonry, or both, somewhere in the region of the back door.

'Getting damn windy,' Captain Perigo said and added that he wasn't sure he liked it.

A moment later the agitated Austrian maid burst into the room to say excitedly that half a tree had fallen on the stable roof and that she was getting very frightened. She wasn't used to such winds. They sounded like the sea.

'Better be going,' Ma said. The sudden opening of the door, bringing a driving draught, had set her shivering again. 'Don't want to get myself steam-rollered under a beech tree. That'd be a jammy mess.'

'Well, be seeing you!' Pop said, as they shook hands all round. 'Thank you, Mrs Jerebohm. Thank you, Mr Jerebohm. Don't get doing anything I wouldn't do.'

Mr Jerebohm received this cheerful advice in further silence. The sound of yet another crashing tree branch startled Pinkie Jerebohm into almost running across the wide baronial hallway with Ma's mink stole and Corinne Perigo's big white sheep-skin jacket, which she clutched closely about her shoulders as she turned to Pop to say:

'Well, don't forget that stirrup-cup. If you can find the time.'

'That's right,' Captain Perigo said. 'Roll up for a noggin at any time.'

After Ma and Pop had driven home under a sky of lashing rain and a falling barrage of autumn boughs, Pop was dismayed to find that television had already closed down and that only Charley and Mariette were still up, studying plans for a bungalow on the kitchen table.

While Ma sipped at a good gin-and-mixed and started to fry eggs and bacon, 'because if I don't eat soon my stomach'll drop out,' Mariette said:

'Ma, we can't quite decide. What do you say? Shall we have one bathroom or two?'

'Oh! two, dear,' Ma said with not the slightest hesitation. 'After all, you might not always want to bath together.' She and Pop quite often did.

For crying out gently, Pop thought. What next? He gave Ma a severe and disapproving look which she, over the frying pan, completely ignored. He didn't go much on that lark. It was almost as bad as having separate bedrooms. He stood a fat chance of becoming a grandfather if Ma was going to start putting obstacles like that in Charley's way.

Over the eggs and bacon, together with a few glasses of port, Ma warmed up, saying several times:

'Thought I'd never get the circulation back in my feet. I think I'm going to have a hot bath even now.'

Pop said good idea. He thought he might hop in with her.

'Well, do,' Ma said cordially. 'Why not?'

Ma always got into the bath first, for the simple reason that she displaced such an enormous amount of water that Pop could gauge the depth better when he followed her. Tonight the water-line came almost up to the top of the bath, so that not much more than Ma's handsome dark head, wide olive shoulders and upper bosom was revealed.

'Well, that was an evening,' Ma said. 'I thought I'd never get warm again.'

'Me too.'

Pop was feeling human now. A bath with Ma was about the cosiest, pleasantest thing in the world.

'I shouldn't have thought you were cold,' Ma said, 'with the steamy way that Mrs Perigo kept looking at you. I hope you didn't get any ideas about her?'

'Not my type,' Pop said. 'She's sour.'

Ma, washing her neck and shoulders with a flannel impregnated with special French soap, said she was very glad to hear it and at the same time asked Pop if he could reach the Schiaparelli bath-oil from where it stood on the stool. She'd like a drop more in.

'I'll have to get a bigger size next time,' she said as she peppered the water with a generous spray of oil, 'I use so much of it.'

'Soap at your end?' Pop said.

'Somewhere. Had it a moment ago.'

With adroit hands Pop started a swift search for the soap, but Ma's body occupied such a large space of water that there was very little area left to search in. His hands kept finding Ma instead, so that presently she was half shrieking:

'Sid! If you do that again you'll have me under. You know what happened last time.'

Once Ma had laughed so much that she slid suddenly under, unable to sit up again until Pop climbed out of the bath and pulled her up.

'Sid! I told you. You'll have me under.'

'Got to find the soap, Ma,' Pop said. Ma, all pink and olive, seemed to him to blossom through hot clouds of perfumed steam. 'Can't very well get clean without the soap.'

'Well, it's not down *there*!'

'No?' Pop said and confessed he was surprised. 'Thought you might be hiding it.'

'What's that against my left foot?' Ma said. 'Is that it? or is it you?'

Slightly disappointed, Pop found the soap beside Ma's left foot, the sole of which he tickled lightly, making her shriek again, so that she slapped him playfully in protest. In return he started splashing her with water, saying at the same time:

'Wonder if Mr and Mrs Jerebohm ever bath together? What do you think, Ma? Doubtful?'

'Never,' Ma said. 'She locks herself in and does exercises. She told me.'

Laughing, Pop said some people never had any fun and started tickling Ma again about the soles of her feet, so that she suddenly wallowed backwards like a huge handsome olive seal, laughing too.

Almost prostrate, she lay for some moments helpless and shrieking, half the global map of her body revealed, until finally with an ecstatic rush of joy, telling himself that this was perfick, Pop stretched out his arms towards the familiar continent of pink hills and olive valleys and fished her up again.

· 6 ·

By ten o'clock on Thursday morning Pop decided that he wouldn't go to the hunt meeting after all. Something big was brewing up in the way of another Army surplus deal and it would take him most of the day to sift the prospects out. Probably show something like five hundred per cent if it came off: anyway, wurf while.

Nevertheless as he drove away from the house in the Rolls he told himself there could be no harm in stopping off at The Hare and Hounds and saying hello to one or two people, just to see what sort of rabble had turned up. The weather had turned very mild again. The first elm leaves were colouring a clear bright yellow and above them the sky was a sharp northern blue, washed clean of any trace of cloud. If anything it was too blue, Pop thought, and as he got out of the Rolls his hypersensitive nostrils instinctively sniffed the morning air for the smell of rain.

Outside the pub hounds were prancing and snuffling about the paddock, tails raised like a collection of pump handles. A few pink coats loped to and fro. Captain Perigo, blue of chin and already slightly watery eyed, was having a whisky outside the bar door, his hard hat sitting well down on his ruby ears. Mr Jerebohm had turned up too and was clearly not used to riding very much. His pose of squatting on his horse, posterior pushed out like a rudder, looked part of a game of leap-frog.

Corinne Perigo had, after all, also turned out and was talking to a man named Bertie Fanshawe, the man whom Ma had mistakenly suspected she had run away with. Perhaps Ma had mixed her up with Freda O'Connor, who also often had a fling. She was a girl of spanking bosom and voice of low husky passion who was now talking to Colonel Arbor, a shortish man who rarely talked much but, like a bronchial horse, merely guffawed in a rusty sort of way. Bertie Fanshawe was beefy. You could have cut his face up into prime red steaks. He guffawed too, but brassily, on coarse trumpet voluntaries all his own.

They were a pretty ripe old lot, Pop thought. The cream of county society, eh? It was a good job, he thought, that Mariette had turned out, neat and beautiful as usual, with Montgomery as escort. He was proud of them both. He was glad too to see the Brigadier, though on foot, the poor devil not being able to afford a second-hand motor car, let alone a nag. It would have been pleasant to see Angela Snow appear too but it was, he feared, too much to expect. She lived too far away.

Then, to his great surprise, he saw, less than a minute later, a jeep-drawn horse-box draw up; and out of the jeep, bright as a quince among a collection of sacked potatoes, Angela Snow.

She was a band-box of a girl if you liked, he thought. She even had the knack of being able to choose a horse that perfickly matched herself. Today she was riding a brilliant burning chestnut, lean and silky of body as she was.

It showed Mr Jerebohm's lean black mare up, Pop thought, as rather a poor old bag of bones: an animal with a decidedly uncharitable look in its eye.

'My sweet.' In a moment or two Angela, unabashed by public gaze, was kissing Pop full on the mouth, to the extreme consternation of the Brigadier, who had not been quite the same man since the passionate upheavals on the hearth-rug, and the unpleasant surprise of Corinne Perigo, who started flashing glances of jagged glass on all sides, blackly. 'Not going to come with us today? Abysmally disappointed.'

Pop, who hadn't seen Angela since the gay evening with the Brigadier, blandly explained that he was only a working man.

'Can't afford the time to go gallivanting. Got to scratch a living somehow. Been up since five as it is.'

'Suppose so. And how's the swimming pool? Coming on?'

Slow, Pop said, slow. They didn't work all that hard these days. The heating apparatus had been held up too.

'You stand there, you croaker, and tell me it's going to be *heated?*'

'Course,' Pop said and laughed in his most friendly, rousing fashion. 'Can't have Ma catching cold.'

'Naturally not. Didn't you murmur something too about having a party to celebrate the opening?'

'In the spring,' Pop said airily. 'In the spring.'

Presently a horn flashed copper in the morning sun, a signal to remind Pop that the hunt would soon be away and that therefore there was precious little time left in which to get outside a snifter.

'Come and have one,' he said. 'We'll get the Brigadier in too.'

He took Angela softly by the arm, steering her through a thickening crowd of people, cars, bicycles, horses, and horse-boxes to the door of The Hare and Hounds, at the same time tapping the Brigadier on the shoulder as he passed him.

'Going to buy you a drink, General old boy,' he said. 'Come on. Angela's here,' and was surprised for the briefest moment not to hear the Brigadier's customary grunt of polite refusal in reply.

Nor had the Brigadier the slightest intention of giving it. A storm of volcanic emotions had swept over him at the mere sight of Angela Snow's lips pressing themselves on Pop's. He knew only too well what that felt like. He could once again feel his hand gyrating on Angela's pulsating naked back. He was overwhelmed by a returning rush of every detail of that stormy session on the hearth-rug. If ever he needed a drink, he thought, it was now.

'First you're coming. Then you're not coming. Fickle man.'

A languorous hand held Pop in check three or four yards from the lounge bar door. It was Corinne Perigo, looking at him in a pretence of friendly calm not confirmed by the fact her nostrils were dilating with unusual quickness.

'Couldn't manage it,' Pop said. 'Business to do.'

'And here am I changing my hair appointment.'

For the life of him Pop couldn't think what that had to do with him and was almost ready to say so when she went on:

'And who's the tall blonde piece? Haven't seen her before.'

'Old flame.'

Pop didn't laugh as he said this, but Mrs Perigo did.

'Old I suppose is right. Still, I see she appeals to the Brigadier too. The poor old thing was having palpitations.'

Pop, suddenly tired of a conversation in which his nearest and dearest friends were being put through a mincer, turned abruptly and went into the bar, leaving a stunned Corinne Perigo standing in lethal silence, alone.

Inside the pub he decided he had a call to pay before joining Angela and the General at the bar. It took him only a couple of minutes to pay it, but meanwhile the Brigadier was glad of even that short respite. It gave him a chance to recall the shattering experience on the hearth-rug.

'Rather an evening we had.'

'Momentous.'

Ever since that time an important gap in his memory had bothered the Brigadier very greatly and with a sudden rush of courage he decided that this was as good a moment as any to fill it in.

'I found myself on the bed,' he said, 'and you not there.'

'A girl has to go home sometime.'

The Brigadier said he knew. But it was the time before she went home he was now referring to.

'You were asleep, darling. Very asleep.'

'And you?'

'I was having that brandy you promised me. I needed it too.'

My God, the Brigadier said, half on fire, had the whole affair had that sort of effect on her?

'Devastating, dear boy.'

The Brigadier, completely on fire now, pitched his voice in a low whispered key, expressing everything in a single cryptic but palpitating sentence.

'Folly to repeat it?'

'What do you think?' Angela said and gave him a long, languid smile.

The Brigadier was saved the necessity of answering this enigmatical question by the breezy entrance of Pop, who floated up to the bar, called the barmaid his little Jenny Wren, ordered himself a double Johnnie Walker and urged Angela and the Brigadier to knock theirs back and quick. The hunt would soon be moving away.

'Wish you were coming,' Angela said. 'Both of you.'

'I'm afraid,' the Brigadier said, 'my hunting days are over.'

'Oh?' she said and laughed on high, belling notes. 'Must have been rather something when you were in full cry.'

The Brigadier felt suddenly half way to heaven again. A late peacock butterfly, roused by the warmth of autumn sun, fluttered at the bar window, danced among the bottles and flew across the room. The Brigadier watched it settle and cling delicately, wing-eyes brilliant, to the edges of a curtain. Nobody could have felt more like a peacock than himself at that moment and it was in a dream that he heard the barmaid say:

'Sounds as if they're moving off, sir. Yes, they are.'

'One for the road,' Pop said and pulled a roll of fivers from his pocket about the size of a pint mug. 'Double for the General. Large Madeira for Miss Snow. Another double for me.'

Already horses were moving off outside. Cars were starting up. A couple of pink coats flashed by. The peacock flew again and Pop said:

'Madeira. Don't think I ever tasted it. Any good?'

'Sweet. And warm without being sordid.'

The Brigadier laughed, alternately watching the butterfly and the edges of Angela Snow's extremely fine smooth hair. The two of them were so beautiful that it positively hurt him to look at them and as he sipped his whisky he wished to God his hunting days weren't over. But, dammit, it was no use, they were; he was past pretending; and he knew the best he would get for the rest of the day would be the far cry of hounds and that queer tugging bleat of a horn being blown across bright autumn fields.

'Well, cheers,' Pop said. 'Down the hatch. Have a wonderful day. Even if you don't kill nothing, I mean.'

It was soon after three o'clock in the afternoon that Mr Jerebohm, with growing discomfort, decided that he was far from having a wonderful day. He thought it was developing, on the contrary, into a hellishly unpleasant day. Unlike the Brigadier, he was beginning to wish his hunting days were over. As rain began to fall, at first in mere biting spits, then in a steady chilling downpour, he even started to wish they had never begun.

It wasn't merely that the countryside, under teeming rain, looked and felt more uncharitable with every step he took. The hunt wasn't running very true to form either.

He knew perfectly well what a hunt ought to look like. He had seen it so often in old prints, on Christmas cards and in advertisements for whisky. It was gay; it positively bounced with cheerful life. Against charming rural backgrounds of woodland and pasture, in winter weather always crisp and beautiful, riders and hounds galloped at full invigorated stretch, all together, well-drilled as an army, in pursuit of a small red animal framed against the far blue sky. The pink coats were as bright as hollyberries at Christmas-time and the laughing tails of the hounds as happy as children at play.

But today there was nothing cheerful or well-drilled or invigorating about it. Not only was the rain becoming colder, drearier, and heavier every moment; there was something very wrong with his horse. He had bought it under the impression that it was a hunter; he had paid what he thought was a stiffish price for it; he liked its colour.

Pinkie liked its colour too; she even thought it handsome. There had even been a time, a day or two since, when Mr Jerebohm had thought it handsome too, but now he could have cheerfully hit it with a shovel.

All day the animal had behaved like an engine without steam; it continually lacked the power to pull itself off dead centre. After desultory canters of thirty or forty yards or so it would suddenly draw up, give a congested cough in its throat and then release breath in hollow bursts of pain. Afterwards it stood for some time staring with cautious eyes at the dripping hedgerows, autumn woods, and bare, sloppy stubbles before, with amazing instinct, turning for home.

It had been, in fact, turning for home all day. Three times during the morning Mr Jerebohm had been blisteringly cursed with words such as

'If you can't keep up bloody well keep out of the way!' From time to time he found himself several hundred yards, even half a mile, behind the pack. He was continually losing hounds behind distant woods, where they wailed like lost souls, mocking him. Several times he got off and walked. It seemed quicker that way.

By half past three in the afternoon he knew, with miserable certainty, that he was lost. Pack and riders were nowhere to be seen. It was raining more and more fiercely on a driving wind and his horse held its blowing frame like a sieve to the rain. Mr Jerebohm, in fact, felt like a sieve himself. The rain was driving large holes through his face, chest, legs, shoulders, and buttocks, and the wind, colder every moment, followed the rain.

A growing conviction that the countryside was one big, evilly devised swindle started to come over him as he turned his horse to the west, the direction where he thought home lay. The supposed pastoral nature of it was a ghastly myth. The deer, pheasant, wild duck, hares, and snipe were all a myth too. The fox itself was a myth. There was no such animal. It was extinct, like the dodo. People rode to hounds merely in the hope of seeing the resurrected ghost of one.

Soaked to his chest, he crossed an unfamiliar piece of country that seemed like a barren land, a heath with neither hedgerows nor fences, roads, nor telegraph wires. Occasionally Pop Larkin cantered over it with Mariette; it was open and quiet and Pop thought it perfick. Groups of pine covered the farthest slopes. Young birches, yellow with late autumn now, had sown themselves among brown acres of bracken. In summer cotton grass blew like snow among pink and purple heather.

Travelling across it on his breathless horse, Mr Jerebohm merely thought it harsh and uncivilized. It was another part of the great country swindle. It was wild, miserable, and shelterless. Oh! for a hot bath, he kept thinking, God, for a hot bath.

On a road at last, under the civilized protection of telegraph wires, he heard a car coming up behind him in the rain. A second later his horse reared, gave a skyward flip and threw him. He landed heavily on a grass verge that, though soft and sodden with rain, felt as hard as a cliff of rock.

It was Pop Larkin who ran forward, hailed him, got him to his feet and tried to comfort him with the words:

'Lucky you fell on grass, Mr Jerebohm. Might have been a bit hard if you'd gone the other way. Had a good day?'

Dispirited and shaken, Mr Jerebohm merely groaned.

'Better come in to my place and have a drink,' Pop said. 'It's only just down the road. I'll mix you an Old King Cole.'

What the hell, Mr Jerebohm asked himself and then Pop, was an Old King Cole?

'New drink I found the other day,' Pop said. 'Mostly rum. It'll put fire into you.'

Mr Jerebohm groaned again. He didn't want fire put into him. In terrible pain, he was sure his back was split in two. He was convinced his kidneys were ruptured and that his spleen was not where it ought to be. Trying to limp back to his horse he felt one leg give a crack underneath him and could have sworn that it was broken.

In sympathy Pop said: 'Tell you what. You drive the Rolls back. It's perfickly easy – gears are as smooth as butter. I'll ride the horse.'

Mr Jerebohm, too far gone in agony to argue with this or any other solution, merely dragged his creaking body into the Rolls and let Pop recapture the horse, which reared again in ugly fashion as he did so.

'See you in five minutes,' Pop said. 'Ma's there.'

He seized the bridle and looked the horse firmly in the face. Not only was it an uncharitable animal to look at, he thought, it was downright ugly. It wanted teaching a sharp lesson. It needed a damn good clout and he promptly gave it one, so that the horse, enormously surprised, at once calmed down.

'Nothing but a bag o' horse meat,' Pop said. 'D'ye hear me?'

At the house he found Mr Jerebohm standing in front of the kitchen fire, a glass of rum in his hand, steaming gently. Ma had also given him a good big wedge of cheese and bacon tart, on which he was now chewing slowly but with silent gratitude. Ma had been deeply sympathetic about the fall. She thought she didn't like the look of him all that much and she was just saying, as Pop came in:

'You look a bit peaky, Mr Jerebohm. It's shaken you up. Why don't you sit down?'

Mr Jerebohm knew he couldn't sit down. He felt that if he did sit down he would never get up again. His bones would lock.

'Shall I telephone the doctor?' Ma said. 'I think I ought.'

In low murmurs Mr Jerebohm said no, he didn't think so; he merely wanted to go home.

'Get outside that one,' Pop said, looking into Mr Jerebohm's glass, 'and I'll mix you another.'

Gratefully Mr Jerebohm got outside the remainder of his Old King Cole. He was steaming more noticeably every moment. His riding boots were half full of water. His ribs ached every time he drew breath and only Pop's large rum cocktail, mixed double as usual to save time, gave him any sort of comfort.

It was the warm rum too that started his brain slowly working again and presently caused him to remember something. It was probably just one more example of the big country swindle, he thought, but he would soon find out.

'Most grateful to you, Larkin,' he said. 'By the way, I've got a bone to pick with you.'

'Pick away,' Pop said. 'Perfickly all right.'

'Didn't you tell me when I bought Gore Court,' Mr Jerebohm said, 'that there was a boat on the lake?'

'Perfickly true,' Pop said, laughing. 'But it ain't there now.'

'Oh? So you know? Then where is it?'

'In my boathouse,' Pop said. 'Just before you took over the house Montgomery found a gang of kids throwing bricks at it, so we rowed it up the lake, carried it over the sluice-gates and brought it up the river. It's safer under cover. I meant to have told you.'

Mr Jerebohm listened in silence, but nevertheless didn't want to seem ungrateful. The rum was marvellously comforting.

'I'll row it back in the spring,' Pop said. 'I daresay Montgomery'll give it a coat of varnish in the meantime.'

Overwhelmed with kindness, Mr Jerebohm could still find nothing to say. Nor, for another moment or two, had he any words to answer another remark of Pop's, who presently disappeared into the pantry and came out holding a brace of pheasants.

'Little present for you,' he said. 'Knocked 'em off in the medder last Monday afternoon. They'll want hanging a couple o' days.'

Searching for words, Mr Jerebohm felt he could have wept. 'Wonderfully kind,' was all he managed to mutter. 'Very, very kind.'

'Make a nice change from pills and diets,' Ma said, 'won't they? I don't hold with all those pills. The world takes too many pills by half.'

It damn well did too, Mr Jerebohm thought, it damn well did too.

Blessed with pheasants and rum and Pop's final injunction 'to clout the bounder if he plays up again,' he managed to ride slowly home in the dying light of an afternoon across which, at last, the rain was slackening.

There was even a break of light in the west and as he rode past The Hare and Hounds, with the pheasants slung across the saddle, he could distinctly see the faces of Corinne Perigo and Bertie Fanshawe as they cantered slowly past him.

'Good night!' they called and he said 'Good night' in reply, having just enough strength to raise a hand in courtesy to his hat.

'By God,' Bertie Fanshawe said to Mrs Perigo, 'they shoot 'em from horseback now, do they?' The unexpected vision of a man riding home from a fox-hunt with a brace of pheasants slung across his horse was altogether too much to bear. Dammit, it wasn't the thing. 'Next thing you know we'll be having electric hounds and mechanical horses or some damn lark.'

Mr Jerebohm, if he could have heard, might well have thought it a good idea, especially about the horses. As it was he merely limped on towards home, silently aching from boots to collar, wind-stung eyes on the sky.

Unfamiliar though he was with the passage and change of country seasons he knew perfectly well that it was winter that now stared at him out of a cold watery sunset, and that it looked, if possible, even more uncharitable than the rain, his horse, and the darkening countryside.

· 7 ·

Walking slowly along the lakeside on a shimmering afternoon in late April, the warmest so far of the year, Pinkie Jerebohm saw in the middle distance across the water a floating object, pale primrose in colour, to which for some moments she was unable to give a name.

After staring at it steadfastly for some time, just as incapable as Mr Jerebohm of detecting the difference between one bird and another, she finally decided that it must be, of all things, a yellow swan. She had always supposed that swans were white, but perhaps they turned yellow in the mating season or something of that sort. You never knew with nature.

A few moments later, to her intense surprise, the yellow swan started waving a hand. A sudden impulse made her wave in reply and it took her only a few seconds longer to realize that whatever changes of colour nature might effect in swans at spring-time it worked no such miracles on Pop Larkin.

Pop, gay in a yellow sports shirt, hatless, and fully ready to greet the first fresh burst of spring, was rowing Mr Jerebohm's promised boat, gay itself with new golden varnish, across the middle of the lake. The day was absolutely perfick for the job, as he had told himself over and over again that morning. It couldn't possibly have been more perfick: cuckoos calling everywhere, the sky quivering with larks, the woods rich with blackbird song, his favourite of all except the nightingale's. Even the wood-doves were talking softly away on those wooing notes that were the first true voice of summer.

'Afternoon, Mrs Jerebohm!' Pop's voice was quick as a leaping fish as it crossed the water. 'Perfick day. Decided I'd bring the Queen Mary back. Sorry to have been so long.'

It was most kind of him, Pinkie lisped as she watched him ship oars and let the boat drift into the bank. But there really hadn't been that much of a hurry. You couldn't say it had been much like boating weather, could you?

'Perfickly true,' Pop said. 'It is today, though. You'll have to get Mr Jerebohm to give you a trip round the lake before dark.'

Mr Jerebohm wasn't at home, Pinkie said. Moreover she wasn't at all sure that he rowed.

'Pity,' Pop said. 'Very nice little boat.' With a neat half-wink he invited Mrs Jerebohm to give the fresh-varnished boat the once-over. Montgomery, he thought, had done a very good job on her. 'Even had the carpet-sweeper on the cushions.' The cushions, a bright plum-purple with lemon pipings, looked very gay and spring-like too.

'Like me to give you a trip?' Pop said. Perky as a terrier, he skipped from boat to bank, where he tied the painter to a tree-root, laughing freely. 'Beautiful afternoon for it – might never get another one like it for weeks.'

Pinkie Jerebohm, who was dressed in a close-fitting lavender jersey suit that only succeeded in showing how fruitless all her fond hard work at slimming had been, said that she had, as a matter of fact, actually started out to look for primroses.

'Come to the right place,' Pop said and with an extensive sweep of a hand enthusiastically indicated the woods that came down to the very edge of the shimmering lake at its farthest end. 'Woods are full of 'em. Crowded. Fick as fick. You can even smell 'em as you go by. Hop in. I'll take you over.'

Mrs Jerebohm hesitated. She wasn't at all sure about hopping in. She had Corinne Perigo coming in to tea at four o'clock and what time was it now?

Impressively Pop's wrist-watch flashed gold in the sun. 'Only three o'clock,' he said. 'Bags o' time.'

For another apprehensive second or two Mrs Jerebohm hesitated. Among other things was the boat safe? It didn't leak or anything of that kind? She couldn't swim. She was, in fact, terrified of water.

'Pity,' Pop said. 'I mean about the swimming. Oh! the boat's perfickly safe.' After a succession of unobtrusively quick glances at Pinkie's figure, he decided that, slimming or no slimming, she wasn't at all bad in the right places and would probably look quite passable in a bathing costume. 'Thought you might like to come over and use our swimming pool when we get it open next month. Lovely pool. All blue tiles.'

Mrs Jerebohm thanked him for thinking of her, but said that it wasn't all that much fun, was it, if you couldn't swim?

'Ma can't swim,' Pop said, 'but she has fun all right. Trust Ma. Come over one afternoon and I'll learn you. In a couple o' days I'll have you going.'

Well, Pinkie said, she didn't know about that. Though she didn't say so there were, after all, limits. There were certain proprieties. Mr Jerebohm wasn't often home in the afternoons and he mightn't think it quite nice if his wife took swimming lessons with Larkin when he wasn't there.

'Good for your figure,' Pop said, with some enthusiasm and several more rapid glances at it. 'Not that it's not good now.'

An unusual flutter sprang through Pinkie Jerebohm. Some seconds later, almost without knowing it, she was accepting Pop's offer of a hand and in a fraction of a minute afterwards she was in the boat, facing Pop, who began rowing her away.

'But you *will* keep an eye on the time, won't you?' she said. 'What I mean is – I mean I must absolutely dove-tail in with Corinne. I simply mustn't keep her waiting.'

Damn Corinne, Pop thought, determined not to spoil a perfick afternoon worrying about Corinne, who several times during the winter had put his back up in no uncertain way. At the Hunt Ball, at two o'clock in the morning, she had cornered him in a half-lit draughty corridor on the pretext of getting him to take out a subscription to a new country club about to be started up by Bertie Fanshawe. In reality it was merely an excuse to start pawing his neck. On an evening in January she had somehow winkled him out of the bar of The Hare and Hounds on the pretext that her car wouldn't start. On that occasion, without ceremony, she began pawing him all over and then turned like a snake, actually hissing, when he told her to stop it and quick. 'You need a good belting,' he told her on a third occasion, when she telephoned twice in one evening to invite him over for a drink because the Captain was away. That, she told Pop with savage sweetness, was exactly what she hoped he was going to give her. She wouldn't rest, in fact, until he did.

She'll rest a devil of a long time, Pop thought and a second later put Corinne Perigo completely from his mind by asking Pinkie Jerebohm if she could smell the primroses yet? In his own hypersensitive way he had already caught the lightest breath of them across the water.

'No,' she said and in fact the boat was already drifting in to the far bank, where young hazel and sweet chestnut and a few high, gold-flowered oaks came down to the water's edge, before she actually detected the first scent of them floating on the lightest of airs.

'Wonderful scent,' Pop said. 'Fancy there's a few bluebells there too.' He drew deep breaths, with selective sharpness. Yes, you could smell the bluebells too. 'Get 'em?'

Pinkie Jerebohm, helped out of the boat by Pop's two outstretched hands, had to confess that she couldn't get them. It was all too elusive for her. It was wholly impossible to separate one scent from another, especially when she scarcely knew which was which, and suddenly at the woodland's edge she was deeply aware again of an uncommonly nervous flutter darting through her, leaving her slightly uncertain at the knees.

For the rest of the afternoon, at irregular intervals, she kept experiencing that same sensation without ever being able to decide what caused it. Crowds of white anemones and primroses covered the whole floor of the wood with endless drifts of the softest unwinking white and yellow stars. The tops of the trees were gold-green belfries of bud pouring down birdsong in tireless peals. From across the lake cuckoos called continually, belllike too, the notes taken up, transformed, and repeated in the wooing moan of doves that Pop adored so much.

Pinkie, bending among primroses, sometimes even kneeling among them on patches of big dry papery chestnut leaves, gradually felt intoxicated and absorbed to a point where time no longer mattered. Nor did Pop remind her. It was pretty nearly perfick by the lakeside on such a day. It was his idea of heaven. The only thing that could perhaps have made it more perfick still, he thought, was the chance of having a short, gentle squeeze with Pinkie.

He wondered how she'd take it? Just the same as Edith Pilchester did? he wondered, and then suddenly found he couldn't be sure. They were rather *très snob*, the Jerebohms. She might go sour.

Still, a casual brush among the primroses, accidental or otherwise, would soon tell him. Couldn't do no harm. It wasn't every girl, after all, who got the chance of being stroked in the middle of a primrose wood on a hot April afternoon.

Several times afterwards he found himself watching the bending, rounded figure of Pinkie, plumpish and smoothly tight in its lavender jersey suit in spite of all her slimming, and told himself that the time had surely come when a little bit of dove-tailing might be fun.

Each time she suddenly straightened up and walked away. Each time, too, he told himself he couldn't be absolutely sure about her. Something about the big bunches of primroses that she had gathered and now held in front of her as she walked gave her an odd look of innocence that he couldn't quite get over.

All this time he himself had been gathering violets, mostly fat white ones, but also a score or two of the dark purple kind. Every now and then he buried his nostrils in them, draining them of scent. All the nerves of the spring afternoon seemed to vibrate tautly as he smelled the flowers and once he felt impelled to call out:

'Beautiful, ain't it? Nowhere like the country.'

Pinkie, who was now gathering separate bunches of white anemones, said she agreed, though in fact the winter hadn't taught her so. The winter had been a trial, hard to bear. That was largely because Mr Jerebohm still insisted on living in Gore Court not because it was pleasant, convenient, or in any way desirable but merely as a means of losing money. Mr Jerebohm in fact was now raising pigs. Palatial sties had sprung up everywhere and Mr Jerebohm found a certain satisfaction in feeding the animals on pigswill made of gold. Pinkie, who didn't understand the reasoning behind making money on the Stock Exchange and giving it to pigs to eat in the country, couldn't help feeling she would have preferred a maisonette on the front at Brighton, where she could occasionally parade in her best hat, gossip over morning coffee, and gaze at the sea.

Here there was hardly anyone to gossip with except Corinne Perigo. The natives, she thought, were uncommonly hostile. They kept themselves steadfastly to themselves. Friendliness seemed no part of their nature. The Austrian maid had left two weeks ago in a huff and now, with the arrival of spring, all the women of the village were planting potatoes, hoeing strawberries or doing strange jobs in hop-fields. She knew now that she couldn't get any help for months and suddenly as she thought of it for the fiftieth time that week she gave a long, uncertain sigh.

Pop, hearing it from some distance off, came over to her bending figure, carrying his bunch of white and purple violets like an offering.

'Surely not sighing on an afternoon like this?' he said. 'Too perfick by half for that. Smell the violets.'

Laughing, he thrust the violets up to Pinkie Jerebohm's face and for a delicious second or two she dreamed over them, drinking scent. Broken sunlight fell like a light veil on her face, which was not unpretty in its simpering way, and on her two hands, clasping almost more primroses and anemones than they could safely hold.

This, Pop told himself, might be just the moment for a trial run. Perhaps he should try her under the chin first and see what happened? But suddenly Pinkie, from being almost completely unbalanced one moment in scent and sun and flowers, darted out of herself with a lisping exclamation:

'Oh! you know it's really awfully awfully sweet of you to bring me over here. I do appreciate it. Spending so much of your valuable time –'

Pop, still locked in indecision, uncertain whether to brush her lightly under the chin or go in for a proper squeeze where there'd be no mistaking what it meant, hadn't a second longer in which to make up his mind before she almost threw up her flower-crowded hands in the air.

'Time! But whatever time is it, pray? We must have been here half an hour or more.'

Pop, laughing, flashed a look at his watch and said:

'More like hour and a half. It's nearly half past four.'

'Oh! my goodness. Corinne will be frantic!'

To Pop's intense surprise Pinkie broke into running, actually dropping flowers as she scurried under the trees to the water-side. He followed her on light springy steps, hoping she might possibly slip and fall in a harmless sort of way so that he could have the pleasure of picking her up but to his disappointment she made the boat without a trip or stumble.

A moment later he was there too, catching her lightly by the soft upper flesh of her arm as he helped her into the boat. To his further surprise a couple of extra velvety squeezes had no effect at all on Pinkie, who seemed utterly oblivious not only of Pop but of everything else as she half-stumbled into the boat and flopped rather heavily down on the plum and yellow cushions.

'Don't rock the boat,' Pop said.

'Whatever can I have been thinking about? An hour and a half! Whatever *was* I thinking?'

Pop, taking up the oars and quietly starting to row the boat out into the lake, where silver shoals of small fry were leaping up like little fountains in the sun, noticed that Pinkie in her haste and distraction hadn't had a moment in which to put her dress straight. Her lavender skirt had ridden up well above her knees.

Charmed and slightly excited by the unexpected vision of Pinkie's rather plump silky legs, Pop found himself paying less and less attention to her lisping self-chastisement as he rowed her across the lake in the sun. Except that he damned once or twice the irritating and oppressive entry of Corinne Perigo into the conversation he was enjoying himself very much, both actually and in anticipation. Pinkie, he decided, wasn't half a bad shape after all. Her legs were quite pretty and he could see an awful lot of them.

'I'll never, never forgive myself. It really is a granny knot, isn't it? Inviting people to tea and then just not being there. Oh! I *am* a careless fool.'

'You'll be at the house in ten minutes,' Pop said, full of airy comfort. 'Women are always late anyway.'

'That remark doesn't help,' Pinkie said. The social strain, keeping her at full stretch, almost made her voice break. 'You don't see any sign of Corinne, I suppose?'

No, Pop said and told himself that he was damned if he wanted to. There was something crude about that woman. After all, as Ma often said, you had to have a bit of finesse about you.

The boat was still thirty yards from the opposite bank when Pinkie, hands full of flowers, sat forward on her cushions with all the appearance of a frog ready to leap.

'You wouldn't mind awfully if I absolutely made a dash for it, would you?'

Not much time now, Pop thought. The golden afternoon was slipping away. His chances were disappearing as rapidly and surely as the boat was drifting through shoals of unfurling water-lily pads into the bank.

'Sit still,' Pop said. 'Don't stand up.' Pinkie had actually, in her anxiety, tried to stand up in the boat. 'Wait till I tie her up. You don't want a wet tail, do you?'

Utterly oblivious of her risen skirt, Pinkie sat on the very edge of the cushion, an inch or so of bare thigh revealed above her stockings.

Now or never, Pop told himself. 'Don't move until I say,' he warned her. 'It's a bit deep just here.'

Momentarily calmed by sensible advice, Pinkie sat precariously still on her cushion while Pop, yellow shirt fluttering, nipped on to the bank and pulled the boat in.

'Hold hard till I tell you!'

A second offering of sensible advice was completely lost on Pinkie, who suddenly leapt up, staggered forward to the bank and into the unready arms of Pop, who still had the boat's rope in his hands. Staggered too, Pop dropped the rope, felt Pinkie begin to slip down the grassy slope towards the lake and managed to catch her firmly with both arms, just in time.

'Neat bit o' rescue work,' Pop thought and in a moment had Pinkie in a swift and uncompromising embrace, at the same time caressing her with one hand some inches below the back waistline.

For some moments a light but intoxicating perfume of half-crushed violets, primroses, and anemones filled the air and Pinkie, almost breathless, gasped as she caught at it. At the same time her lisping mouth half opened in what Pop thought was a gesture of encouragement. Stimulated, he gave the roundest part of one thigh an extra nip of affection and was on the point of kissing her full on the lips when, to his pained surprise, she started screaming madly.

He hadn't ever heard anyone, he thought, scream quite so loud. You could surely hear it a mile away. On high, full-throated notes Pinkie lifted her face to the sky and for nearly half a minute wailed wordlessly, at the same time dropping every flower she held.

'Better try to comfort her a bit I suppose,' Pop thought and was just wondering how to start this delicate operation when he saw a new figure running towards him along the lakeside.

It was Corinne Perigo, advancing in a hatless charge.

'Wherever have you been? Whatever has happened?'

Pinkie Jerebohm, white-faced, standing in a pool of stricken flowers, allowed herself a moment of deathly silence before answering in a whisper: 'This man has just tried to violate me.'

Pop had hardly grasped the words before Corinne Perigo gave him a venomous, curdling look.

'You absolute swine,' she said. 'You absolute swine.'

Pop, for once, was at a loss for an effective reply. No one had ever called him that before. It was rather much, he thought. A moment later he was startled to hear Corinne Perigo's voice again, now speaking in tones of even colder venom.

'Have him charged, Pinkie. Put him in court. Let the police deal with him. The swine. It's high time. I'll be a witness for you.'

As a weeping, flowerless Pinkie was led away along the lakeside Pop found himself staring with mild disconsolation at the lake, dismayed to find that the boat, which he hadn't had time to tie up, was drifting away.

One way or another, it was a bad end to a perfick afternoon.

'Not sure you haven't gone and torn it this time, Sid,' he told himself. 'Not sure you haven't gone and torn it now.'

· 8 ·

On that same shimmering April afternoon Edith Pilchester, succumbing at last to the grumbling appendix that had been troubling her for weeks, went into hospital to have it out. When Ma heard of this nearly a week later she was not only full of sympathy for the wool-gathering Edith, always so lonely, but at once urged that Pop must pay her a visit as soon as possible, at the same time taking something nice with him to cheer the poor thing up.

'You'd be worth a dozen boxes o' pills to her. She'd be up and about in no time.'

Pop agreed and presently, on a showery April evening full of thrush song, took Edith Pilchester two bottles of port, a basket of fresh peaches, pears, grapes, and apricots, a box of milk chocolates, a large bunch of deep yellow freesias and several slices of cold breast of turkey. All spring came flowing richly into Edith's room on the strong fragrance of freesias and Edith, pale and meagre, wept.

This, Pop said, they couldn't have; it wouldn't do at all; and immediately sat down on the bed and held her hand. This warm and unexpected gesture merely had the effect of making Edith weep afresh, not quietly now but in a loud, spinsterish blubber, so that soon, when a nurse came in to fuss with a chart, there was cold severity in the air.

'And what,' she said, 'have you been doing to my patient?'

'Making love to her,' Pop said, quick as a jackdaw. 'Like a sample?'

'That will do. I must ask you not –'

'See what he's brought me!' Edith Pilchester sobbed. 'Freesias. Wine. Gold, frankincense, and myrrh –'

The effect of this outburst was so touching that the nurse suddenly felt like weeping too and hastily remembered she had something to do in another ward.

When Pop now suggested that Edith should dry her eyes and have a grape or something she said no, no, no thank you, she couldn't touch a thing.

'Have a drink then,' Pop said and immediately poured out half a tumbler of red port, advising Edith to get it down her at once, so as to warm the vital parts.

Edith, taking the port in one quivering hand and dabbing her eyes on the corner of her flannelette nightgown with the other, apologized several times, begging that Pop wouldn't think her too silly, and said it wasn't merely that the gifts had overwhelmed her. It was a combination of things.

'Oh?' Pop said. 'For instance what?'

'I heard the most awful news about you. It was absolutely ghastly.'

Awful news? Pop, cheerful as ever, couldn't think what that could be.

'This awful woman. This Mrs Jerebohm. They tell me you're actually being prosecuted.'

Pop laughed with a bucolic sort of bark that actually reached the young nurse in another ward.

'Oh! that,' Pop said. 'That's a real lark, that is.'

'But *did* you – I mean *is* there any truth in it?'

'Course,' Pop said. 'Case comes up in two weeks' time.'

'Ghastly,' Edith said. 'Absolutely ghastly.'

Pop, treating the matter with renewed levity, wondered if Edith would mind all that much if he joined her in a glass of port? With bird-like joy, tears drying now, Edith begged him to do so, adding:

'But what *is* it all about? What *are* you supposed to have done?'

Pop, still sitting on the bed, adroitly poured himself a glass of port.

'Pinched her bottom. She was getting out of a rowing boat.'

Edith, half way between tears and laughter, could only give a frog-like croak in answer, silently wishing it might have been her. No such opportunities had come her way for some time, not even at Christmas.

'But aren't you at all *concerned*? You don't seem to be worried about it one little *bit*.'

Pop, she thought, seemed to be taking life in a spirit of jollier, livelier levity than ever. Incorrigible, remarkable man.

'I'll worry when the time comes,' Pop said. It was a major part of his rather loosely made philosophy to cross bridges when he came to them. 'After all, anything might happen before then.'

It might indeed, Edith thought. It might indeed.

'I only hope,' she said, 'you've got a good solicitor?'

Pop, purporting to be utterly unconcerned, gave her one of his sudden smoothly mischievous glances that had the immediate effect of making her toes tingle sharply at the bottom of the bed.

'Going to conduct the case myself,' he said. He laughed rousingly, winking. 'Counsel for the defence – that's me.'

Edith, sipping port, didn't know whether to be alarmed or delighted.

'But do you know *how?* I *mean –*'

'Seen it all on telly!' Pop assured her blandly. 'Court cases nearly every night of the week on telly.'

'But how you *dare!* I should *die.*'

'Well, I shan't. Going to enjoy myself that day. Drink up.'

Edith drank up, raising her glass to Pop at the same time.

'I can only wish you all possible success,' she said, looking Pop straight in the face with a refreshed swallow-like glance, eyes glowing. 'Oh! I *know* it will be. I *feel* it. I've got that sort of *thing* about it.'

Whole thing would go like a bomb, Pop said. Would she be well enough to be there? He hoped so.

'I shall be there if it *kills* me. And so will all your friends. We'll absolutely *band* together.'

Such fervent promises of support had Pop chuckling again. With charm he started lightly urging Edith to peel herself a grape or a peach or something. In reply Edith had to confess, as she gulped down deep rich breaths of freesia perfume, that she was really altogether too nervous to eat anything for the moment.

Something, she said, biting her lips, had just come to her.

'Oh?' Pop said and looked at her bitten lips with concern, wondering if perhaps she had had a sudden post-operative twinge.

'I've just thought that if it could be of any help at all I'd cheerfully appear as a witness,' she said. 'I mean as to character or something –'

Or something? Pop thought. Good old Edith. Very nice of Edith. But he wasn't sure about that something.

'Haven't quite got the case worked out yet,' he said. 'Haven't got the order of battle ready.'

Edith, who was sure it was going to be absolute battle royal when it came, suddenly felt herself go unreasonably coy. She shrank perceptibly into her nightgown, feeling her toes tingle sharply again at the bottom of the bed.

'By the way, what *are* you charged with? I've asked myself over and over again.'

'Indecent assault or summat,' Pop said. 'It's all in the summons.'

The word indecent immediately seemed to whirr and flash about the room like a dragon-fly on a hot afternoon, making Edith flush in her throat. She knew perfectly well now that all night long she would lie awake and wonder about what could possibly have happened in that rowing boat.

'I never have liked that Mrs Jerebohm,' she said. 'Such people don't belong in the country.'

Oh! old Pinkie wasn't bad, Pop said. You could hardly blame Pinkie. It was Corinne Perigo that was the snake in the grass.

'That woman!' Edith said. 'I could kill her!'

The magisterial vehemence of this remark made her suddenly flop back on the pillows, surprised, flushed, and weakened. Pop had to confess to himself that he was surprised too. It was very strong stuff for Edith. Probably the drink had got into her, like it sometimes did into Charley.

'It's women like her who bring disgrace on our sex,' she said. 'They make you – oh! I don't know *what* they make you –!'

Edith, completely crimson in the face now, broke off helplessly, impotent to express another thought. Pop, slightly alarmed that she might start up a temperature or have a relapse of some sort, urged her to take it easy, at the same time holding her hand.

'Easy,' he urged her softly. 'Easy. Easy.'

Easiness came to Edith Pilchester in the form of a long quiet thrill. The last deep sigh before sleep could never have quietened her more effectively than that single repeated word or the clasping of Pop's hands.

'Got to trot along now,' Pop told her some time later. 'Come and see you again soon.'

Light cold April showers were falling on the window. The cloud that dropped them was slate-dark, bringing on an early twilight in which the freesias, the peaches, and the apricots all glowed a curious, almost phosphorescent orange.

In a low voice, though not tired, Edith several times thanked Pop for coming. He would be very much in her thoughts, she said. Very much. Never, in fact, out of them.

Pop, who had made up his mind to treat her to a goodnight kiss, then remembered something himself.

'Forgot to tell you about our swimming pool. Going to have a party when we open it next month. What about a donkey race in the water? Eh? Men and girls?' He laughed with his customary carelessness. 'That's if they don't put me inside.'

'Inside?' Her mind vibrated madly with alarm. 'You don't mean prison?'

He meant prison, Pop said. Well, why not? It was warm. It was free. He believed they even had telly there too nowadays.

'Awful man,' she said. 'I believe you're really trying to frighten me.'

'Not on your nelly,' Pop said and a second later, pressing her back on the pillows, gave her a faultless dream of a kiss that couldn't have acted more like a sedative, so much so that when the nurse came back, twenty minutes later, she found Edith peacefully sleeping, the half-drunk glass of port still in her hands.

'Visitor for you,' Ma said, when Pop reached home half an hour later. 'And I'll bet you'll never guess who.'

Pop could guess all right; he knew.

'Sergeant Buzz-whiskers.'

Sergeant Wilson, that was. He was the policeman who had originally served the summons. Hated doing it to Sid, he confessed, but there it was. Duty.

'Well, it's not the sergeant,' Ma said. 'That's caught you.'

It had caught him too, Pop said, and after two or three guesses decided he might as well go into the sitting-room and see for himself while mixing a decent pick-me-up at the same time.

He had hardly decided on this before a small figure, not unlike Pop but twenty years older, nipped into the kitchen. He looked very much like an artful grey terrier who had spent a lifetime gnawing an infinite number of bones, a practice that had knocked several of his front teeth out. His bony yellow forehead had a perceptible hollow in the centre of it. If by some chance this had been filled with a third eye it could hardly have increased the strong magnifying qualities of the rest of his face. The lively little grey eyes were telescopic lenses, picking up every detail. The ears were bulbous earphones, tuned to every breath.

'Uncle Perce!' Pop said. 'Haven't seen you since Mariette's wedding day.'

Uncle Perce, in a voice no less diamond-sharp than his eyes and ears, said Perce it was and shook Pop's hand with a restless rat-trap of wiry fingers.

'Calls for a drink, this,' Pop said and had just started to mix a couple of Red Bulls when his son-in-law Mr Charlton came in. After an evening hanging curtains with Mariette at the new bungalow in the meadow Charley was thirsty too. So, Ma said, was she. Pop consequently found himself mixing about a pint of Red Bull, well-iced, to which Ma added an offering of fresh cheese-straws and a bottle of Worcester sauce.

'Well, what's it all about, Perce?'

'Hear you're in trouble, Sid boy.'

A combination of owl and fox gave Uncle Perce's half-toothless mouth a remarkably impressive twist.

'Oh! that,' Pop said.

'They were chewing it over at The Hare and Hounds when I dropped in on my way over,' Uncle Perce said. 'First I'd heard on it. Why didn't you tell me?'

'Nothing to tell,' Pop said, bland as ever. 'Nothing to it.'

One lid of Uncle Perce's searching eyes dropped like a trap.

'Allus come to Perce when the flag's down,' he said. 'You know that.'

'Who was nattering at the pub?' Ma said, carefully sprinkling Worcester sauce on a length of cheese straw. 'Anybody you know?'

Uncle Perce cast a pair of artful eyes on Ma and said:

'Some I did and some I didn't.'

'Oh?' Ma said. 'Who didn't you?'

'There was a piece there,' Uncle Perce said, 'calling herself Mrs Perigo.'

Ma's bosom, in outrage, was suddenly swollen like a pouter pigeon.

'Don't talk about her! That woman's got no finesse,' she said, pronouncing the word finesse to rhyme with highness. 'She's the one who started it all.'

Uncle Perce went through the startling act of closing both eyes, as if actually thinking, thus looking more artful than ever.

'I've seen that piece somewhere before,' he said. 'And it won't be long afore I remember where.'

'Sooner I forget her the better,' Pop said. 'Drink up, Perce. You're slow.'

'I'm thinking,' Uncle Perce said, drinking up. 'I'm always a bit slow when I'm thinking.'

'What about you, Charley boy?' Pop said. 'Room for another?'

Charley was readily agreeing that he had room for another when Pop suddenly remembered something. He hadn't set eyes on Charley all day, not since breakfast. Had Charley been egg-hunting or something?

'No, as a matter of fact,' Mr Charlton said, 'I've spent a good deal of the day at the public library.'

'God Almighty,' Pop said, almost exploding over the glass and chromium expanse of the cocktail cabinet. 'Anythink wrong?'

It alarmed him to think that Charley and Mariette might be off hooks again. He could think of no other reasonable excuse for a man spending all day at the public library.

'Better get outside that one quick,' he said, handing Charley a large second Red Bull. 'That'll put you right. You look a bit dicky.'

Mr Charlton, looking both calm and healthy, said that there was in fact nothing wrong with him at all. He had merely been doing a little legal research.

In fresh amazement Pop asked Ma if she'd finished with the Worcester sauce for a moment. Ma said she had and passed the bottle, into which Pop dipped a fresh cheese straw. There was no fathoming Charley boy sometimes. Legal research?

'I thought I might get a few tips for you,' Mr Charlton said. 'For the case, I mean.'

Pop, supremely confident that he didn't need any tips, merely laughed in easy fashion, and went on to say that it was very nice of Charley, but –

'You see,' Mr Charlton said, 'it isn't as if you'd done this sort of thing before.'

Pop cheerfully admitted as much, but after all he'd seen it often enough on telly.

'Yes,' Mr Charlton said, 'but you've never been in court –'

'Should think not,' Ma said. 'The idea.'

'Might have been a couple o' times if it hadn't been for me,' Uncle Perce said. 'Remember that time –'

'We don't want to hear it!' Ma said. 'Do you mind?'

Uncle Perce, artfulness momentarily crushed out of him by the second peremptory rising of Ma's pouter bosom, hadn't a syllable to say in answer and merely stared into his glass, thinking.

'The essence of this case,' Mr Charlton said, in a sudden flush of words so professionally assured that Pop wondered if he oughtn't to let Charley boy do the defending after all, 'seems to me this. The case of the prosecution must rest almost entirely on corroborative evidence. Corroborative evidence there must be, otherwise Mrs Jerebohm, as I see it, can stand there until the cows come home.'

What the pipe was corroborative evidence? Pop wanted to know. A bruise or something? Where he'd pinched her?

'That'll have worn off a bit by now,' Ma said, huge body bouncing with laughter.

'Corroborative evidence,' Mr Charlton said, 'is evidence from some person or persons able to substantiate the accusation Mrs Jerebohm is making against you. In other words did anyone else see what happened? For instance Mrs Perigo?'

'She was there all right,' Pop said, 'shrieking at the top of her voice. Calling me an absolute swine.'

'No finesse, that woman,' Ma said. 'No finesse whatever.'

'I shall remember where I've seen that piece in a minute,' Uncle Perce said. 'I shall remember all right.'

'As I see it,' Mr Charlton said in another rush of supremely calm assurance, 'you need call only two witnesses. Mrs Jerebohm and Mrs Perigo, of whom Mrs Perigo is the most important. Alternatively you can elect to go into the box yourself and speak on your own behalf. That, however, I wouldn't advise.'

Temporarily startled, Pop recovered enough to remind himself, as so often before, what a marvellous feller Charley was. You had to hand it to Charley sometimes.

At this point Uncle Perce, dropping an artful eyelid, suggested he might come as a witness too. How about that?

'Why?' Ma said and to this rather cryptic challenge Uncle Perce had no answer except to look immensely thoughtful again.

A moment later a cry from upstairs reminded Ma that little Oscar was awake and with her own calm assurance she left the kitchen to see what she could do for the baby, licking her fingers clean of Worcester sauce as she went, half-wondering if a bit of sauce on a cheese-straw wouldn't help to soothe him down. She hoped Pop wouldn't be put inside. She really did. It would make it rather awkward in many ways.

'Well, I must go too,' Mr Charlton said, 'or Mariette'll be wondering where I am.'

'That's it,' Pop said, terrifically cheerful, 'off to bed.'

'Do you mind?' Mr Charlton said. The April evening, its showers finished, still glowed faintly golden outside. 'I haven't had supper. It's hardly bed-time yet.'

'Then it ought to be,' Pop said smartly and wished Mr Charlton a very good night, with pleasant dreams and all that lark, hoping the urgent hint wouldn't be lost on him.

Alone in the kitchen with an increasingly thoughtful Uncle Perce, Pop suggested another snifter and didn't Perce think the Worcester sauce went well with the straws? Idea of Ma's. Uncle Perce agreed and got outside another snifter in very fast time. This encouraged Pop to mix a fourth and for the next half hour or so they sat drinking in steady contentment, one or other of them occasionally dipping a straw into the bottle of sauce.

Finally Uncle Perce said he ought to be getting back and Pop said he would run him home in the Rolls. Perce, who was boots and odd-job man at a hotel called The Three Swans five or six miles away, had walked over for the exercise but confessed he didn't feel like walking back. The snifters made him sleepy.

In the Rolls he fell into a sudden doze and it was only when the car stopped at the end of the journey that he abruptly sat up, sharply awake, and said with all the old compelling artfulness:

'Sid, I just remembered who that piece is. She's no more Mrs Perigo than I'm the Duke o' Wellington. You're going to want me as a witness after all.'

Driving the Rolls back into the yard, in darkness, Pop couldn't help feeling, on the whole, rather pleased with himself. What with Charley's legal research and all that lark, and now Uncle Perce, things were looking rather more rosy.

These pleasant reflections were shattered, almost as soon as he was out of the car, by a voice.

'Hullo there,' Corinne Perigo said.

'The gate's over there,' Pop said, hardly bothering to look at the hatless, mackintoshed figure leaning against the front wing of the Rolls. 'Or there's a short cut over the fields. It's quicker.'

'Suppose we take the short cut? What I've got to say won't take long.'

'Tell it to the marines.'

'Look, let's not be silly,' she said, 'shall we? Why be silly?'

'Speak for yourself,' Pop said. 'I'm off to have my supper.'

'Listen,' she said. 'Supposing I said I thought the whole thing was a ghastly mistake?'

'Suppose you said the stars were potato crisps?'

'All I wanted to say was this.' Her voice was low and languid in the darkness. 'If you and I could come to terms I might –'

'Terms?'

'Well, an arrangement. Just you and me. Strictly *entre nous* and all that.' Pop heard the dry rustle of the mackintosh as she suddenly swung away from the car and came closer in the darkness. 'After all, what quarrel have we?'

Pop, thinking that so stupid a question didn't require an answer, started to walk away.

'No quarrel at all. All you've got to do is to give me the signal and I think I can persuade Pinkie to call the dogs off.'

'Signal?' Pop paused, half way across the yard. Dogs off? 'What signal?'

'Come back and I'll show you.'

'Good night,' Pop said.

Again he heard the dry rustle of the mackintosh in the darkness.

'After all, it's only a question of pride with her. I don't believe she really wants to go on with it. After all, who does? Nobody really does, do they?'

'You'd be surprised,' Pop said and a moment later left her standing there, a ruffled bundle alone under the April stars.

· 9 ·

Although the regular Friday Petty Sessions at the Police Court in Fordington opened at half past ten it was nearly half past twelve before Pop heard a police constable calling his name.

By that time he was feeling decidedly peckish and couldn't help wishing he'd nipped across the road to The Market Arms for a glass of beer and a piece of pork pie or a couple of sandwiches. The court had taken what he thought was a damn long two hours to deal with three straightforward drunks, a speeding motorist, a dustman accused of stealing twenty-three boxes of cigars, and a barrel of a woman, arrayed in a man's cheese-cutter cap, who had hit her next-door neighbour over the head with a coal bucket.

'Call Sidney Charles Larkin.'

Pop, who was wearing a natty black and white check suit with hacking style jacket and a yellow tie, at once stepped briskly forward, said 'That's me!' and stood in the well of the court facing the magistrates' plain mahogany dais at the far end.

That morning five magistrates were sitting and a pretty ripe old lot they looked too, Pop thought. Sir George Bluff-Gore, the chairman, in a dead black suit and plain grey tie, looked more like a dyspeptic pall-bearer than ever and regarded Pop with a cheerless oyster eye. On his left sat a Miss Cathcart, a tall, mannish, peg-like woman wearing pince-nez, a thorn-proof suit of nettle-green and a matching hat with a pheasant's feather stuck in the side. Miss Cathcart shared a house with a tiny nervous brown sparrow of a companion named Emily, whom she unmercifully bullied night and day, at the same time devoting much of her time to moral welfare.

On Sir George's right sat Major Sprague, a maroon-faced comatose bull of a man with staring eyes who appeared to be continually searching for something to ram his head against. A Mrs Puffington, a miniature over-neat lady with a shining mother-of-pearl face, sat tucked under the broad flanks of the bull rather like a new-born calf sheltering from the morning's stinging wind. The fifth magistrate was a round soapy bubble of pink flesh named Portman Jones, a retired local preacher, bald as an egg, who quavered at the very end of the bench with an air of impending doom, rather like a pirate's victim quaking at the plank's end.

Pop, already damn certain he wasn't going to get much change out of that crew, presently heard the Clerk of the Court, a tallish man in a charcoal-grey suit, reading out the charge against him.

'Sidney Charles Larkin, you are hereby charged that on the twenty-third day of April of 1959, at Gore Court, you unlawfully and indecently did assault a certain female, namely Phyllis Monica Jerebohm.'

The clerk then proceeded to point out to Pop that he had the choice either of being tried by a jury or of having the case summarily dealt with, to which Pop replied promptly that he would have it dealt with there and then.

'Very well. Do you plead guilty or not guilty?'

'Not guilty o' course. What do *you* think?'

'Never mind the of course. Nor what I think. Are you represented in court?'

'Course I am,' Pop said and waved an airy hand to the little public gallery at the back of the court, where Ma was sitting with Mr Charlton, Mariette, Edith Pilchester, the Brigadier, Angela Snow, and the landlord of The Hare and Hounds. If they weren't representing him nobody was.

'What I mean is this – are you represented by a solicitor?'

'Yes,' Pop said. 'Me.'

'Do you mean by that that you are conducting your own defence?'

'I am.'

'You are quite sure?'

'Sure?' Pop said. 'Course I'm sure.' Moses, for crying out gently.

'Very well.' As the clerk, with a withering look, turned his back on Pop, a solicitor named Barlow bobbed stiffly up and down again in front of Pop like a small tarred cork and said: 'I appear for the prosecution.'

'Defendant conducting his own case?' mumbled Sir George Bluff-Gore.

'Yes, sir.'

'Very well. Proceed.'

A moment later Mr Barlow rose and, in a matter-of-fact tone of voice, proceeded:

'The facts in this case are very simple, sir, and are as follows. On the afternoon of April the twenty-third last Mrs Phyllis Monica Jerebohm, who resides with her husband at Gore Court, was walking alone by the lake in the grounds of the mansion. It was a fine warm afternoon and it was her intention to gather primroses. As she walked along the lake she observed the defendant rowing towards her in a boat –'

Pop, bored already, found himself going off into a dream. He felt ravenous already and wondered what Ma had for lunch today. At any moment his belly would rattle emptily.

It actually did rattle, and quite audibly, a minute or two later, so that Mr Barlow, in the act of finishing his recital of the facts, glared sharply at Pop as if accusing him of manufacturing a deliberately insulting noise.

'I will now call Phyllis Monica Jerebohm,' he said.

'Phyllis Monica Jerebohm!' called a police constable in the passage outside and in the space of a few seconds Pinkie, clearly unable to see very straight, was up in the witness box, grasping the book in her gloved right hand and already starting to read the words of the oath in rapid, nervously simpering scales.

'Remove your glove, please.'

More nervous than ever, Pinkie removed her right glove, keeping the other one on.

Pop, who knew as well as anybody what had happened by the lake, wasn't worried very much by the questions put by the prosecution to Pinkie, who all the time stood clasping the front of the box with both hands, on one of which she still wore a white glove while holding its pair in the other.

The only time he had occasion to feel in the slightest degree apprehensive was when she was asked if, at any time that afternoon, she had been afraid, and she said Yes, she had been afraid. He hadn't thought of that. She did in fact drop her glove on the floor of the witness box as she answered the question and when she rose again after stooping to pick it up her face was grey.

'Were you in fact more than afraid?'

'I was.'

'Were your reactions in fact those of any decent, respectable woman face to face, alone, with unexpected and undesirable interference from a molesting interloper? – or, for all you knew, an attacker?'

Before Mrs Jerebohm could answer Ma's voice rang out sternly from the back of the court.

'I beg your pardon!' she said. 'I beg your pardon.'

'Silence!' called a policeman and at the same time another policeman heaved himself towards the public gallery.

'Silence my foot,' Ma said.

'Silence in court!'

'Whoever is interrupting from the public gallery will have to be removed,' Sir George Bluff-Gore said, 'if this continues.'

'Come and do it,' Ma said, well under her breath this time, 'it'll need three of you and a crane.'

Sir George, who knew quite well who was interrupting from the gallery but was reluctant to do anything serious about it, simply coughed several times in an important sort of way and said 'Proceed', which Pop presently did by rising to put his first question to Pinkie.

'Mrs Jerebohm –'

He paused abruptly and rather lengthily. You had to stand back and let the dog see the rabbit – that was how they did it on telly. He knew. He'd seen it scores of times. It kept the witness on the hop.

'Mrs Jerebohm,' he said, 'I want to ask you a very simple question. Can you swim?'

The question startled not only the court but Mrs Jerebohm, who almost dropped her glove a second time, and in the public gallery Ma started choking.

'No. I can't.'

'Are you afraid of water, Mrs Jerebohm? I mean,' Pop explained, 'the sort you fall into?'

Several people at the back of the court started laughing, with the result that a police constable shouted 'Silence!' and still another policeman moved on cautious feet towards the gallery.

'I suppose I am.'

'Either you are or you aren't,' Pop said blandly. 'No supposing. In fact I put it to you, Mrs Jerebohm, that you are terrified of water?'

'I wouldn't say exactly terrified.'

Pop, smiling in his cool, perky fashion, wondered if Mrs Jerebohm would mind casting her mind back to the afternoon in question? Weren't almost her first words to him on that day 'I can't swim. I am simply terrified of water'?

'They may have been.'

'Mrs Jerebohm, do you feel you are lucky to be alive today?'

'I suppose we all do,' Pinkie said, her gloved hand clutching hard at the edge of the box. 'It's only natural.'

'Never mind about all of us,' Pop said. 'Do you?'

Pinkie, who had already been more than surprised by several of Pop's questions and couldn't for the life of her see the point of this one, almost inaudibly murmured 'Yes' and then was still more startled to hear Pop say:

'Have you any idea, Mrs Jerebohm, how deep the lake is?'

Mrs Jerebohm, growing more nervous every moment, confessed that she had no idea at all.

'If I told you it was fifteen feet in places, even twenty,' Pop said, 'would it upset you?'

'It possibly would.'

'Give you bit of a turn like?'

Pinkie simply stared straight in front of her, in silence. No answer was forthcoming and none was necessary. She was clearly having a bit of a turn already.

'Now, Mrs Jerebohm, do you recall that when I rowed you into the bank that afternoon – that's where the lake's fifteen feet deep by the way – I warned you on no account to move until I got the boat moored?'

'You may have done. I was in a great hurry.'

'To go where?' Pop said. 'To the bottom of the drink? Because, strike me, that's where you would have gone if I hadn't grabbed hold of you when I did.'

Pinkie, more pallid than ever, looked suddenly sick.

'I disagree,' she said, after a moment or so, in a remote voice that she hoped sounded dignified, if not calm. 'I could well have looked after myself.'

'Not on your nelly!' Pop said.

'What was that strange expression?' Sir George Bluff-Gore mumbled. 'I didn't catch that.'

'It's an expression,' the clerk said, 'in the current vernacular.'

'I beg your pardon?' Pop said. He had no intention of being insulted and put so much severity into his voice that the clerk, biting his lip, seemed to recoil visibly.

'Just two more questions,' Pop said. 'What did you do after the alleged attack?'

'I screamed.'

'Why,' Pop said, 'didn't you attack me?'

'Because you were holding both my hands.'

Pop gave the swiftest, perkiest of smiles at the same time only wishing he could telegraph it to Ma and his friends in the gallery.

'So now,' he said, 'I've got three hands, have I?' He held up his hands for all the court to see. 'One to pinch you with and two to hold you with.' Pinkie's face had suddenly gone from extreme grey pallor to boiling crimson. 'Adam and Eve and Pinch Me, eh? Thank you very much, Mrs Jerebohm.'

After the pale and shaking Pinkie the next witness, Mrs Perigo, looked icy, almost arrogant, by contrast. She was wearing a tailor-made tweed suit in a sort of dull rhubarb shade and a close-fitting hat to match.

The questions he wished to put to her, Mr Barlow said, were very simple in themselves but, nevertheless, very important. First, did she see the attack? Secondly, was the nature of it as described by Mrs Jerebohm herself? And thirdly was the reaction of Mrs Jerebohm that of a lady in a state of most alarming and acute distress?

To all three questions Mrs Perigo answered yes, merely adding to the last of her answers that Pinkie was hysterical. This, Pop knew, was the corroborative evidence stuff that Charley had briefed him about and he listened eagerly as the solicitor for the prosecution went on:

'One more question. Did the defendant at any time offer, in your presence, any sort of expression of regret or apology for his action?'

'No.'

'None whatever?'

'None whatever. He merely laughed.'

'He merely laughed, you say. Thank you.'

This, Pop knew, was the tricky part of the business and when he finally rose to question Mrs Perigo he stared her straight in the face and opened with a question like a bullet, not bothering to pause for emphasis, as he had done with Pinkie.

'You are Corinne Lancaster Perigo?'

'I am.'

'You're quite sure?'

'Naturally.'

Nothing could have been more haughty than the word naturally and at the back of the court Ma felt her blood starting to boil.

'Absolutely certain?'

'Of course I'm absolutely certain!'

When the fury of the words had died down a bit, Pop went on:

'You say you saw the alleged attack?'

'Certainly.'

'Can you tell the court from what distance?'

'Several yards.'

'Can you tell the court how many yards is several?'

'Oh! three or four. Half a dozen.'

Pop, pulling himself erect, wagged his finger at Mrs Perigo with accusing severity.

'I suggest to you, Madam,' he said, 'that if you had a neck as long as a giraffe's and a fifty-foot extension ladder and a three-inch telescope you couldn't have seen pussy from where you were.'

'Indeed I could. And did.'

Ma, in a fury of her own now, could bear it no longer.

'Wheel her out!' she called.

'Remove that person from the court at once.'

'All right,' Ma said. 'Don't touch me. I'm going. I'll be over at The Market Hotel, Sid. I'll see if they've got some decent steaks for lunch. I forgot to ring the butcher.'

'Good egg!' Pop said. 'See if they've got some smoked salmon too.'

'Right!'

While Ma was being removed from the court, as large as ever but more dignified, the clerk rose stiffly to ask with great acidity if Pop had quite finished with his personal catering arrangements? If so, could the court proceed?

'No more questions,' Pop said.

Mrs Perigo, haughtier and colder than ever, withdrew from the witness box, sweeping across the well of the court on a positive breeze of perfume, leaving the solicitor for the prosecution to rise and say: 'That is the case for the prosecution.'

'Do you wish to call any more witnesses, Larkin?' the clerk said.

'I do,' Pop said. 'Uncle Perce.'

'What was that?' Sir George Bluff-Gore said. 'Uncle who?'

'Call Percival Jethro Larkin!'

Quick as a fox, Uncle Perce nipped into court and was already half way through a toothless recitation of the oath before the book had actually been handed up to him.

'Morning, Sid. Cold for the time o' the year.'

'The witness will refrain from making observations,' the clerk said. 'Either about the inclemency of the weather or any other matter.'

'Yessir. Sharp 'un this morning, though.'

'Quiet!'

Uncle Perce was instantly and obediently quiet, though not for long.

'Well, I wouldn't be anybody else, would I?' he said in answer to Pop's question as to whether he was in fact Percival Jethro Larkin?

'And do you at the present time live at The Three Swans hotel at Wealdhurst?'

'That's me.'

'Where you are employed as handyman and boots?'

'That's me.'

313

'The witness will answer the questions either in the negative or the affirmative,' the clerk said. 'And not by observation.'

'Yessir.'

Pop, before addressing Uncle Perce, again made one of those timely and dramatic pauses he had so often seen enacted, and with such effect, on television.

'I want you to glance round the court. Take your time. Have a good long look.'

'Yessir. Sid, I mean.'

Uncle Perce took an all-embracing, owl-like stare round the court, at the same time picking one of his few good teeth with a finger-nail.

'Do you see in court,' Pop said, 'anyone known to you as Mrs Perigo?'

'No, that I don't.'

'Quite sure?'

'Sure as I like a nip o' rum on a cold morning.'

'Take a good look at the lady in the dark red costume who sits over there.'

'Her with the red bag on her head?'

That was the one, Pop said. Did he know her as Mrs Perigo? No, Uncle Perce said, he'd be blowed if he did.

'Quite sure?'

'Sure as I like a –'

'Answer yes or no!' the clerk said.

'Yessir.'

'Very well. You don't know her as Mrs Perigo,' Pop said. 'But you do know her?'

'Oh! yes, I know her.'

'Mr Larkin,' the clerk interrupted. 'Can you tell us what all this is designed to show? Where is it meant to lead us?'

'To the truth!' Pop thundered.

'Very well. Proceed.'

'Now,' Pop said, 'can you tell the court when you last saw the lady?'

'About three weeks ago.'

'And can you say,' Pop said, 'where you saw her?'

'In bed.' Uncle Perce spoke with smart emphasis, almost with a snap of his jaws.

'Alone?'

'With a gent.'

Several people in the gallery broke into spontaneous laughter but the various policemen, the clerk, and Sir George Bluff-Gore seemed momentarily mesmerized and offered no word of reprimand. Nor was there any word from Corinne Perigo, who was now as grey and tense as Pinkie still was.

'You say you saw the lady in bed. Can you tell us where this was?'

'At The Three Swans o' course. I took their early morning tea up. One of the maids'd got bronchitis and we were short-handed at the time.'

Pop permitted himself a smile. He was really starting to enjoy himself. The court lark was a drop o' good after all.

'But the lady, you say, is not Mrs Perigo?'

'No. Her name's Lancaster. Mrs George Lancaster.'

A sensational tremor seemed to go through the court and Sir George Bluff-Gore sat forward on the bench by more than a foot, eager for every word.

'Are you quite sure the name is Lancaster?'

'Course I am. I had another dekko at the visitors' register yesterday.'

Pop waved an airy, modestly expansive hand.

'So the lady describing herself in this court, on oath, as Mrs Perigo, did in fact register herself at the hotel as Mrs Lancaster?'

'That's a fact,' Uncle Perce said. 'Yessir.'

'Which amounts to this, does it not' – Pop, television-taught, paused for emphasis again, convinced that this was the right time, if ever, to let the dog see the rabbit – 'that either at the hotel or in this court the lady has been telling a lie?'

'You're right, Sid!' Uncle Perce said. 'And a thundering big 'un too if you ask me.'

'Bingo!' the Brigadier said softly and gave a smile of winning triumph at Angela Snow, who returned it affectionately.

Ten seconds later Pinkie Jerebohm suddenly fell forward in a bumping faint. Corinne Perigo, chalk-faced, rushed from the court as if scalded. Two policemen lifted Pinkie bodily and carried her out through a door, closely followed by a buxom policewoman carrying her handbag and flapping a big white handkerchief. The clerk scratched among his papers rather like a black and white hen searching for a mislaid egg and Sir George Bluff-Gore conferred for some moments with his magisterial colleagues, all of whom looked suddenly like hens too, heads slightly to one side, clucking under their breaths.

From somewhere at the back of the public gallery Mr Jerebohm, breathing like a train on a difficult gradient, pushed with flapping arms past ushers, policemen, solicitors, and clerks and finally disappeared in the direction where Pinkie had gone. In the confusion everybody seemed to have forgotten Pop, who stood not unconfused himself in the well of the court, and it was not until Sir George rapped sharply on the bench in front of him that order was restored. Then a policeman shouted 'Silence!' and Sir George said:

'Mr Barlow, do you feel in the circumstances that you can carry this case any further?'

'No sir,' Barlow said. 'In the circumstances I do not.'

'Very well. The defendant is discharged.'

'You may go,' a police sergeant said to Pop, who went without delay, finding himself two minutes later in the bar of The Market Hotel, where Ma, Mariette, Charley, Montgomery, Miss Pilchester, Angela Snow, the Brigadier, and the landlord of The Hare and Hounds were all waiting, glasses in hands, ready to give him a chorus of acclamation.

'Everybody's staying to lunch here,' Ma said, giving him her own personal greeting in the form of a kiss laid on his lips like a cushion. 'I've got it all fixed. Smoked salmon and steaks for the lot.'

'Well done, Larkin,' the Brigadier said. 'Damn good staff work.'

'Sweet man,' Angela Snow said, kissing him lightly on both cheeks. 'Blistering success. Had 'em cold from the word go.'

'Don't they call it purgatory?' Ma said, laughing splendidly over a Guinness, 'or is it perjury? I never know. By the way, where's Uncle Perce?'

To her almost stupefied surprise Uncle Perce came in a moment later with the old enemy, Mr Barlow, who immediately came up and shook Pop by the hand, told him he had done well, in fact, very well, and what were he and his good lady going to have?

Ma, remembering the word attacker, thought for a moment she'd a good mind to sue him for defamation of character and then abruptly changed her mind and said 'A large Johnnie Walker' instead. That would learn him.

'Yes, you did well, Larkin,' Mr Barlow said. 'Congratulations.'

'Oh?' Ma said. 'You didn't help much, did you?'

'All in the day's work,' Mr Barlow said. 'All got to live.'

'I couldn't bear it,' Edith Pilchester said. 'It was absolutely terrible. Every minute was ghastly.'

'Uncle Perce is the one we got to thank,' Pop said, gratefully accepting a quart of light ale from Mr Barlow, at the same time catching him a fraternal blow in the ribs with his free elbow. 'Thirsty work, our job, eh?'

Mr Barlow laughed, proving to be as human as anyone else after all, and Uncle Perce, finding a brief moment when he could lift his face from his own quart glass of ale, laughed too and said:

'I told you I'd remember that piece, didn't I, Sid? I knew I'd remember. I can see her now in that bed. She'd got a black lace nightgown on – that's what brought it back to me.'

'Don't talk about that woman,' Ma said. 'Don't spoil the party. I always said she'd got no finesse.'

'Well, cheers,' Angela Snow said, her voice more than ever cool and languid. 'It only goes to show.'

Show what? Ma wanted to know.

'The truth,' Angela Snow said, 'of the old Chinese proverb.'

What proverb was that? Pop wanted to know and a second later heard Angela Snow, to the accompaniment of golden peals of laughter, telling him the answer.

'If you're going to be raped,' she said, 'you might as well relax and enjoy it while you can.'

· 10 ·

It was not until a warm Saturday evening in early June that Angela Snow, in a pure white swim-suit gleaming as a snail-shell, dived with cool grace from the springboard of the Larkin swimming pool and swam the whole length of the bath under water before finally surfacing and turning on her back to float motionlessly in the sun.

'Pool's christened!' Pop shouted. 'Everybody in!'

Soon everybody was in the water, which shone clear and blue as turquoise. The Brigadier, spidery of leg, his middle covered by what looked like a discarded length of faded pink face flannel, duck-paddled to and fro in the shallow end, where Ma, in a bright magenta bikini that seemed to sit on her body like an arrangement of well-inflated balloons, was playfully teaching little Oscar a gentle stroke or two. Little Oscar, fat as a balloon himself and wearing a startling costume of blue and yellow stripes, wasn't very interested in strokes and spent most of his time bobbing out of the water to lick at an ice-cream, a melting super-bumper in thick layers of chocolate and raspberry.

At the deep end of the pool the twins, together with Victoria, Primrose, Mr Charlton, and Montgomery, were either diving off the board or the edge of the pool. Primrose, grave and bewitching in a bikini of emerald green, sometimes sat on the edge for long periods in a dream, staring mostly at Mr Charlton. She wasn't at all sure she wasn't in love with Mr Charlton, who in turn thought she was growing more and more like Mariette every time he looked at her. Mariette was in the house, occupied with the final touches of preparation to ham and fresh salmon sandwiches, prawn *vol-au-vents*, sausage rolls, asparagus tips, cheese tarts, salads, and things of that sort. She was being helped in the kitchen by a more than usually shy, fussy, and indeterminate Edith Pilchester, who was trying without success to summon enough courage to change into a swim-suit, a royal blue one, which she'd bought specially for the day. She hadn't worn a swim-suit for years.

'You see I'm not all that frightfully good a swimmer,' she was explaining, 'and somehow –'

'Ma isn't either,' Mariette said. 'What's it matter? Go up and change in the bathroom. Pop won't like it if you don't try the pool.'

'You don't think he'll take offence?'

'Not offence exactly,' Mariette said. 'But you know how Pop is. He adores people to enjoy themselves. He's been waiting a long time for today.'

'I know. I absolutely long to. It's just that I –'

It was just that she was so dreadfully shy about that sort of thing, she persisted in explaining several times. She wasn't used to it. She supposed she was getting too old for it or something, she said, and it was not until Mariette finally made the suggestion that what she needed was a little Dutch courage to stimulate her that she allowed herself the luxury of a whisky and said she'd have a stab at it after all.

In the pool, in an evening growing more and more embalmed every moment, the air a pure light gold, Pop was enjoying himself by giving imitations of a porpoise or riding little Oscar on his shoulder. Sometimes he dived under Ma, brushing her body playfully on the way up or down.

The Brigadier, watching this sportive play and listening to the steam-valve of Ma's laughter shrieking into air every time Pop touched her, couldn't help wishing he had the courage to try something of the kind on Angela Snow, but a queer sort of diffidence had come over him too. Every time he watched her white cool figure cutting the water or diving from the board in the evening sunshine he knew he could have done with a little Dutch courage himself.

All this put him into a day-dream of his own and when he finally came out of it some time later it was to see with relief that Pop, in his customary fashion, was handing round drinks on a tray.

'Drink, General? Everybody enjoying themselves? Help yourself. Eats are coming in a moment. Everybody here? Where's Edith? I don't see Edith nowhere.'

'She was in the house helping Mariette a few minutes ago,' Ma said.

'Time she was here,' Pop said. He liked his guests on the spot; he liked a party to go with a bang. You couldn't have people missing when the party was just warming up. 'The grub'll all be gone if she don't soon get here.'

'You'd better go and find her, hadn't you?' Ma said. 'If you don't want her to starve.'

Pop, agreeing that this was something like the right idea, went into the house, deciding to renew the trayful of drinks at the same time.

'Help yourself to another before I go, General,' he said. The Brigadier didn't hesitate and then, with a drink in either hand, padded on thin white legs to the far side of the pool, where Angela Snow sat gazing at a half-empty glass, softly splashing her long legs in the water.

A palpitating remembrance of all that had happened on the hearth-rug swept through the Brigadier as he sat down beside her and she said:

'Hullo, my lamb. Thought you were never coming to talk to me. Afraid you'd jilted me.'

She was hardly his to jilt, the Brigadier thought. He only wished to God she were. A twinge of loneliness nipped him and then was gone for a moment, banished by the sudden pleasant realization that he was sitting only a bare inch or two from her smooth long limbs.

'How are you, my sweet?' she said. 'You look sort of pensive to me.'

The Brigadier, with a rumbled bark of heartiness that didn't deceive her at all, said that he was actually in fact splendid. Absolutely splendid.

'Sweetie, you're in a dream.'

'Oh?' The Brigadier was greatly startled. 'Really?'

'I've been watching you.'

The sentence was of such direct simplicity that the Brigadier, momentarily unnerved, said:

'Your glass is half empty. Have some of mine – allow me? May I?'

With a hand on the verge of trembling he poured a generous part of his second glass into hers and then added the remainder to what was left of his first. As he did so she felt an inexplicable twinge of her own, a sudden bristling at the nape of her neck, that caught her unprepared. She remembered then how the Brigadier had surprisingly found her weak spot in the darkness and she started wondering what she would do about it if he found it a second time.

'Well, cheers, honey,' she said. She lifted her glass to him, turning on him her pellucid, almost over-large olive eyes. 'Nice, sharing your drink with me. That's made my day.'

The Brigadier, for the first time, found himself looking straight into her eyes. He hadn't realized before how remarkably sympathetic they were. It struck him that they were like wide, warm pools. They held him closely, with a great stillness, and he couldn't get away.

'It's rather made my day too,' he said and to his infinite astonishment she started running one of her fingers along the back of his hand.

Meanwhile, in the house, Pop had searched both kitchen and living-room for Edith Pilchester without success. Mariette had vanished into the garden too and he was about to follow her with a second tray of drinks when an alarming sound, like that of a battering ram, brought him to the base of the stairs.

Edith, in shy haste, bathing cap in hand, had slithered down the full flight of stairs and now lay, a vision of royal blue and purest white, prostrate on her back.

'Oh! I do feel a ghastly fool.'

'All right?' Pop said. 'Not hurt?'

Edith, in her bathing suit, relieved of the encumbrances of tweed, corset, and heavy woollens, was suddenly revealed as having a figure of modestly good proportions. Her legs were smooth and hairless. She had very white, sloping shoulders.

'No, absolutely all right. Absolutely.'

Eager not to miss anything, Pop hastily set down the tray of drinks and helped her to her feet. Edith, clumsy as ever, half jumped, half rolled from the stairs, to find herself a moment later in Pop's arms, held in a palpitating squeeze.

'How's your operation today?' Pop whispered and held her so uncompromisingly close that Edith, who had never been so unashamedly near to anything male in her life, had hardly breath enough left to say:

'I won't put you in court. You know that don't you?'

'Wouldn't stand a chance if you did,' Pop said, laughing. 'No corroborative evidence. One more?'

'One more. Please.'

Pop kissed her for the last time and a moment or two later, with a final spirited slap from him, she was in the garden, flushed and feeling almost naked as she half-walked, half-ran to the pool.

Pop, following with the drinks, met Primrose coming into the house, graver than usual and with only half a sentence to offer him in answer to his 'Not going to bed? Party's only just begun.'

'Just going to the wood for a walk,' she said dreamily, 'and –'

From her visit to the wood she came back, half an hour later, carrying a bunch of butterfly orchids, like palest green wax insects, which for some reason she gave to Angela Snow, who said 'Sweet. Thanks, my pet,' and then tucked them into the bust of her bathing costume.

The intoxicating, almost too sweet breath of them rose at Angela's throat. The little swarm of greenish flower wings seemed at the same time to give fresh lightness to her splendid bare skin, so that the Brigadier, who had never seen anything remotely like it in his life, suddenly realized that even the most arid moments had magical impulses, the power to bloom sensationally.

He wanted suddenly, in a wild moment, to ask her to marry him, but he either daren't or couldn't frame the words. Instead he started to murmur something about whether she could cook or not, then suddenly felt it was all too obvious and said instead:

'Perhaps you'd come and have dinner with me one night, I mean?'

'Adore it.'

'Which night would suit you?'

'Oh! any night, honey,' she said, saying the words as if she were making a personal sacrifice for him alone.

He could hardly suppress his joy and in a lyrical moment thought of how he would give her scampi, asparagus, and veal cutlets or something of that kind. You could get them all, even the scampi, at the village shop nowadays. It was part of the rural revolution. He would try to cook all the meal himself. He would do his damnedest to make it nice for her.

All of a sudden the tranquillity of the evening was heightened by the sound of church bells. Across the meadows the pealing changes, in practices ready for Sunday, came in waves of crystal clearness, pursued by their own echoes.

'Do you go to church?' she said.

'Very occasionally.'

'Would you come to church with me tomorrow morning?' she said, 'if I came and fetched you? And then come to lunch with us? I've always wanted my father to meet you.'

Almost before his stuttered 'Yes, most kind of you, delighted,' was out of his mouth an ebullient Pop had arrived, loudly uttering reproaches about empty glasses.

'This won't do, General. This won't do. Refills all round, come on!' he said and then to his utter surprise saw that Angela Snow had actually laid two finger-tips on the back of one of the General's hands.

Back with Ma, who was sitting on the edge of the pool holding little Oscar on one enormous knee and a Guinness on the other, Pop confessed that you could knock him down with a feather. It was perfickly stunning. Angela and the General were sitting holding hands.

'Why shouldn't they?' Ma said. 'Perhaps he's going to ask her to marry him. Lucky girl.'

Pop, ignoring whatever slight reproach about matrimony there might have been in Ma's voice, said 'Good egg!' and shouldn't he go over and give 'em a bit of encouragement or something like that?'

'Something like what?' Ma said.

'I dunno,' Pop said. 'Like champagne.'

'Give us a chance,' Ma said. 'I'm still on Guinness,' and turned to give a sip to little Oscar, who in fact took several sips and then solemnly wiped his mouth with the back of his hand.

'Let's leave the champagne till it gets dark,' Ma said. 'Why don't you get some fun and games organized? I thought you said we were going to have races?'

Pop, leaving Ma to carry on with the business of filling up glasses, suddenly became more acutely aware of the sound of bells. For some reason they always reminded him of Christmas. They made him think of snow on holly, musical chairs, Paul Jones, and Postman's Knock. They inspired him to fun. And suddenly in a brilliant burst of enthusiasm he was laughing in his most rousing fashion and shouting:

'Everybody in the pool! Going to have Blind Man's Buff in the pool!'

Ma laughed rousingly too. That was a good one. Trust Pop to think of that.

'Who's going to start it?'

Pop was tempted to say Edith, but suddenly realized that he'd better do it himself, so as to hot it up from the start.

'I will,' he said. 'Come on, everybody in. Kids an' all. Angela, Edith. All in. General, where are you?'

Presently everybody was in the pool except, it seemed, Mariette. Somehow this evening Mariette was always missing. Where was Mariette?

'She's gone to fetch Oscar a woollie,' Ma said. 'She'll be back.'

Presently Pop was in the pool, eyes bandaged, playing Blind Man. With one corner of the handkerchief ever so slightly raised he could easily tell the difference between Edith, Ma, and Angela and so knew which of them to chase at the right time. Not that he could miss Ma very well; she took up such an expanse of the pool. Several times Edith shrieked, stumbled in escape and wildly went under but there was a time when he grabbed lusciously at what he thought was Angela Snow, only to find that it was Mr Charlton.

When it was finally Mr Charlton's turn to be Blind Man it was Primrose who allowed herself to get caught. Mr Charlton was exactly the right type for her, she had decided. He was her dream. In the wood she had actually shed a tear or two and now to be caught by Mr Charlton made her confusedly happy. In her joyful confusion, when it was her turn, she immediately caught the Brigadier, who then wandered about the central parts of the pool like a searching spider, desperately hoping it would be Angela he touched. His singular misfortune at running several times into the large bulk of Ma finally made her so sorry for him that suddenly she pushed him flat into Angela's arms and for a suspended second or two he remained there, until Pop shouted in lyrical encouragement:

'Kiss her, man! Kiss her!'

To everybody's astonishment the Brigadier actually did, still with the handkerchief over his eyes, standing in water up to his armpits, half as if at a baptism, half as if embalmed.

The whole thing, so unexpected, made Ma laugh so much that she had to go and rest at the side of the pool. While she was there, choking afresh at the sight of Mr Charlton passing and finally torpedoing Edith Pilchester at the deep end, Pop joined her and said:

'Charley boy's getting fresh tonight. Mariette'll have to watch out. By the way, where is she all this time?'

'I expect she's gone to have a lay-down.'

'Good God. Lay down? What she want to lay down for?'

'She's just resting.'

'Resting? What's she want to rest for? It's only eight o'clock.'

'The doctor says she's got to,' Ma said blandly. 'Anyway for the first month or two.'

In a positive whirlwind of joy Pop raced twice round the pool before finally jumping in, feet first, at the deep end. As he landed almost on top of Edith Pilchester, blindfolded now, he told himself in a shout that he hoped it would be a girl. Another Mariette. No, he didn't. He hoped it would be twins. He hoped in fact that all his family would one day have twins. He hoped that if Angela and the General ever got married they too would have twins. He hoped even Edith Pilchester would have twins. Why not? He wanted them all, every one of them, to have a life of double richness.

In a second whirl of excitement he grabbed Ma from the side of the pool and ducked her four times in rapid succession, at the same time shouting to Charley:

'Get the champagne, Charley boy. Pink and red! Plenty of ice. It's your night, Charley boy.'

With a thump on the back that almost broke Mr Charlton in two he urged Charley boy on his fruitful way to the house and then found himself standing, some moments later, in a sort of delirium of suspense, on the diving board.

For some seconds longer he stood there gazing down at the blue water and all the faces of the people he loved. Across the golden evening the peal of church bells, together with the song of a late blackbird or two and in the near woods a bubbling call of pigeons drifted in on a high chorus of midsummer sounds that exhilarated him like laughter. This was life, he told himself. This was how it ought to be.

A moment later, laughing too, he dived. The evening air flowed past him like silk and from across the meadows came the scent of drying hay.

·OH! TO BE IN·
·ENGLAND·

This book is dedicated to

Stephen
Jeremy
Andrew
Beverley
and
Emma

· 1 ·

As Pop Larkin loaded the last pieces of junk into his newly-painted yellow-and-scarlet pick-up all the essence of the fine June morning seemed to pour down like dreamy honey from thick boughs of oak-flower, gold-green against a sky of purest blue, unblemished except for a few floating white doves of cloud. It was a morning when he felt it was good to be alive; you could fairly hear the grass growing. All the air was brilliant with bird song and farther up the road, on a little rise, a field thick with buttercups shone brighter than a bank of sovereigns.

'Well, I think that's the lot, Lady Violet. Quite sure you're satisfied?'

'Oh! absolutely, Mr Larkin. Absolutely –'

'Because now's the time to say if you ain't. I want to be fair.'

'Oh! you've been more than fair, Mr Larkin. More than fair, I assure you. The offer I had from two men from London was far, far less.'

'Never trust blokes from London,' Pop said, quite sternly. 'Never trust Londoners. Not at no price.'

Lady Violet stood with a kind of hungry frailty in the sunshine, rather like a small brownish moth wearing gold-rimmed spectacles. Soft wisps of sepia whiskers grew about her face, giving it a curious downy charm.

Pop took a cigar from his breast pocket and started to pierce the end of it with the gold-plated cutter Ma had given him for Christmas. Sometimes he used it to pick his teeth with too, but Ma really didn't like the habit very much. It was a bit primitive, she thought.

'Well, I'll just run over the lot again,' Pop said, 'just to see I've got everything. One bassinet –'

'Oh! I was wheeled about in that bassinet. So was my sister. I tipped her out of it on many occasions.'

'One butter churn –'

'I used to help turn the handle in the dairy. Every Wednesday and Saturday. I can hear the flop-flop now.'

'One hip-bath. One foot-bath –'

'I think they're sweet, don't you? Especially the foot-bath, with the pink

329

roses. They're Regency, you know. I suppose nobody ever uses them today?'

'Put flowers into 'em,' Pop said. The Regency wash-basin, the two Regency ewers and the three Regency chamber pots all had pink roses on them too. 'Two bedsteads and a knife cleaner. One secretaire and two oak chests. Two stags' heads and one pike in glass case. Two shields and four battle-axes –'

'And of course the two suits of armour. I must say I think it was wonderfully noble of you to take the suits of armour. I never thought you would.'

Pop, blandly waving the still unlit cigar, warmly assured her that he was very glad to have the suits of armour. They were the prize pieces of the lot: just what he'd been looking for.

'You don't think you'll have difficulty in finding a customer for them?'

'Customer?' Pop said. 'Customer? I got one already. Me.'

The two suits of armour were going to stand in the passage at home, one each side of the sitting-room door. Pop had the picture of them already quite clear in his mind. The two shields and the four battle-axes were to hang each side of them. He might even fit the vizors up with lights, he thought, or if they were too big for the passage they could stand outside the front door, on sentry, sort of. Wherever they stood they'd certainly give some tone.

'Well, I think that's the lot. Oh! the buggy, of course. I'll have to make a special trip to fetch the buggy. I'll have to have my son Montgomery come and give me a hand with that.'

'The dear buggy. I've ridden in it so often.'

'Tell you what. Me and Ma'll come and fetch you out for a ride in it one Sunday. Now if you're perfickly satisfied I'll settle up with you.'

Pop stuck the unlit cigar into his mouth and then produced from his inside pocket a roll of five-pound notes as thick as a fair-sized bible.

'Oh! you must come in and have a glass of sherry before you go. Or port. I've got one or the other. I'm not sure which. Do, please.'

Lady Violet turned and led the way into the cramped spaces of a wooden bungalow surrounded by unkempt beds of purple lupins, pink and white peonies and a few early roses. It didn't seem to Pop much larger than a decent dog kennel and as he went inside he found himself suddenly overcome by an irremediable sadness.

It was the same feeling he got sometimes when he was talking to his old friend the Brigadier. It hurt him to see the top people coming down so low. He could remember without difficulty the time when Lady Violet and her family had lived in a big black-and-white half-timbered house with a moat round it and great splendid stables and farm-barns as dignified as old cathedrals. He supposed change was inevitable but there were times when he didn't hold with it being so drastic, especially here in England.

'I won't be a minute with the sherry. And do you prefer a cheesy biscuit or a ginger nut?'

Pop confessed he preferred the ginger nut; he was a sweet-toothed man. While waiting for the sherry to arrive he stared about him. There was a great shabbiness in the air. The dust that lay everywhere on furniture, mantelpiece and carpet was, like Lady Violet's soft brown whiskers, thick as down on moth wings. Horse hair sprouted from the arms and seats of chairs. A dish of primroses, now brown dried emblems of an already distant April, stood on a window sill, forgotten. A few rings of apple-peel, yellow and shrivelled, lay scattered about the hearth, above which a large barn owl in a mahogany case stared out with big saucer eyes, for ever spiritlessly searching. Pop felt sure the floor was rotting underneath him. The air was full of a church-like odour of decay and he longed to light his cigar.

'It was sherry after all. And there are the ginger nuts.' Lady Violet handed Pop the smallest possible thimble of sweet sherry and he helped himself to a ginger nut. 'Good health to you.'

Pop thanked her and said 'Cheers, Lady Violet, and down the hatch,' and could have sworn at the same time that there was dust on the ginger nut too. He felt he wouldn't get very steamed up on the sherry either and for a few painful moments he longed not only for the luxury of his cigar but for a pint of Dragon's Blood or a decent cocktail. During the past week he'd invented a pretty good new one consisting of two parts vodka to three of rye whisky with a dash of rum and Kirsch to warm up the flavour. He'd christened it Moon-Rocket and he thought on the whole it went down pretty well.

'Mind if I light my cigar? Wouldn't offend you?'

'Oh! dear, no. Of course not. Please do. I adore the smell of cigars.'

Suddenly full of mischievous entreaty, Pop gave a scarcely perceptible wink, his eyelid swift as a dragonfly, and made the suggestion that perhaps Lady Violet might even care for one herself? Did she indulge? – he meant on the quiet like?

Lady Violet gave the merest echo of a giggle and her small eyes dithered in tremulous response behind her glasses.

'Well, I don't really. But I do confess that I once took several teeny-weeny puffs of one of my father's.'

331

'Like it?'

'I'm ashamed to say that I did. Rather much.'

Pop gave his first good real laugh of the day and started to light his cigar, feeling better already. He didn't often get the willies about junk – it was just impersonal stuff, most times – but the sight of a leaking wood-shed half-filled with the suits of armour, the old buggy, the butter churn and even the chamber pots had got him under the skin somehow. It was like seeing another bit of England go.

He puffed richly, filling the little room with smoke, and then, full of mischief, winked again, this time broadly.

'Have a draw, Lady Violet. Go on.'

Lady Violet, at the mere suggestion of having a draw, flushed quite deeply. It was as if she had been caught out in some awful act of impropriety.

'Mr Larkin, you're quite outrageous –'

'Course I am. What of it? You said you liked 'em. Go on, have a draw. A little bit of what you fancy –'

'I was only sixteen when I did it before.'

'Don't look much older now.' Lady Violet, who was on the verge of becoming seventy-five, felt flattered into a sudden spasm of mischief of her own and made an impetuous grab at the cigar.

'All right. You dared me to. I always loved a dare.'

'Have a good old drag,' Pop said. 'Do you all the good in the world.'

Lady Violet, powerfully tempted for one moment to take Pop at his word, finally decided on prudence and merely puffed discreetly.

'Quite delicious.'

'Glad you like it. I thought you would. Best Havana.'

'Thank you very much. You'd better have it back now. You've tempted me quite enough.'

Pop, laughing again with all his customary ringing heartiness, said he liked tempting girls, at the same time resisting a strong temptation to pat her playfully.

'No, keep it. Have another go while I count the money out. What did I say for the lot? – sixty-five quid? Call it seventy. The jerries alone are worth another fiver. Ma'll be tickled to death with 'em – ring-a-ring-a-roses, eh?'

Lady Violet, still puffing gently, smiled down at the thick wedge of notes from which Pop was counting out her money.

'I heard someone say the other day that they're actually coming back into fashion again.'

'Never been out as far as Ma's concerned! Well, there you are then, seventy quid. Better count it to see if it's right.'

'I don't think I need to, Mr Larkin. I trust you implicitly.'

'Just as well somebody does. Well, I must be on the trot. Thank you for everything. Like to keep the cigar?'

'Oh! certainly not. I wouldn't dream of such a thing.'

'Course you would. Keep it. Plenty more at home.'

'I must say it's absolutely delicious. It's absolutely made my day.'

'Perfick,' Pop said. 'Perfick. That's what I like to hear.'

Lady Violet tottered gently as far as the front door of the bungalow to say goodbye to him, the cigar still alight in her hand. The frailty of the downy face, with its air of groping hunger, seemed for fully half a minute to disappear. The small eyes were now quite brilliant behind the gold rims of her spectacles. Framed against the gimcrack door she looked positively alight with life and there was something almost jaunty about the way she waved the cigar.

'Goodbye!' Pop said. 'Thanks again. Be over for the buggy tomorrow.'

'Goodbye, Mr Larkin – Oh! no, not tomorrow. I've just remembered. I have to entertain my niece and nephew tomorrow. They're coming to stay for Whitsun.'

'Not to worry,' Pop said. 'Make it the day after.'

'Splendid. Thank you again for all you've done. Goodbye.'

Cigarless but happy himself, Pop drove slowly home through narrow lanes thick with green-white kex, each head like stiff fragile lace, and by woods of bluebells heavy with the deep eternal perfume that never failed to set all his senses quivering.

It had been a very good morning. It was good to be alive, better still to be alive in England. He chuckled to himself several times about the armour and also wondered what Ma would say to the ring-a-ring-a-roses.

He couldn't help thinking they'd look very nice with hyacinths in them for Christmas.

· 2 ·

After quenching his thirst with a steady quart of shandy at The Hare and Hounds Pop arrived home in the expectation of finding Ma in the kitchen, surrounded as always by dishes, saucepans and piles of food. His eager mating call of 'Hullo, hullo, where's my old sunflower?' remained, however, unanswered; and it was some minutes before he discovered her in the garden, where she had set up easel, canvas, paint box and camp stool and was busy painting a picture of Mariette in the nude. She seemed fatter and rounder than ever, sitting on the tiny camp stool.

When she saw Pop crossing the garden Mariette deftly but with otherwise no great concern, covered her resplendent and now maternal nakedness with the *Daily Mirror*, which in turn linked up with the only garment she was wearing, a pair of transparent purple briefs with lace edges. Having given birth two months before to a boy who, at Ma's suggestion, had been named John Marlborough Churchill Blenheim Charlton, she was now anxious to coax her figure back to its normal splendid proportions and to get it, if possible, brown all over. The result was that Ma was now doing a different picture of her almost every other day, either from the front, the back or the sides, according to which part of her was most in the need of being sun-tanned. Mr Charlton found the canvases of intense and palpitating interest, so much so that he had had two of them, one a full-blooded frontal view, the other a horizontal back view of Mariette lying among buttercups, framed.

'Hullo, hullo,' Pop said. 'Art class? Very nice too. How's it coming on?'

Looking over Ma's shoulder he surveyed, with something more than paternal pride, the stunning contours of Mariette's upper figure as seen by Ma. It was six months since Ma had taken up painting, largely because practically everyone else, from Churchill downwards, had taken it up too. She was surprisingly good at it, everyone thought. She had also read the great man's little book on the subject and as well as being inspired to name the new baby after him had also taken his advice to revel in paint as a physical luxury.

'Bit blue, ain't they, Ma?'

Greatly though he admired Ma's newly revealed talents, there were times when he thought she might be going a bit too modern. The splendour of Mariette's upper contours looked, he thought, not only as blue as cornflowers but also a bit lop-sided somehow, but he supposed it all depended on how you looked at them. The artist's eye and all that.

'Well, they're no bluer than you'll be if you don't soon make yourself scarce so's I can get another look at them. Go and get yourself a drink, do. I can't very well see through the *Daily Mirror*, can I?'

Pop cordially agreed, at the same time blandly suggesting that he himself had no objection if Mariette wanted to take the *Daily Mirror* away. What did it matter? It was all one to him. It was all in the family.

'By the way,' Mariette said, 'there's some letters for you. One of them with a foreign stamp on.'

'That's it,' Ma said, 'go and read your letters. And bring us both a decent cold drink when you come back. It's hot out here in the sun.'

Making a final survey of Mariette's shining blue breasts Pop suddenly announced that he had a good mind to take up the painting lark himself. He knew Mr Charlton was thinking of taking it up too.

'You should,' Ma said. 'It's a wonderful thing. It's so soothing. There's nothing like it for passing the time.'

A second later an electrifying thought occurred to Pop: none other than that if he took up painting it might be possible to get somebody like Angela Snow to sit for him as a model. In the never-never, of course. Did Ma think she would?

Ma, with complete unconcern, said she didn't see why not. Pop should ask her.

'Daresay she'd love to be painted by you. By the way, how did you get on with Lady Violet? She's no oil painting, poor thing.'

'Perfick,' Pop said. 'Got two suits of armour and two sets of shields and battle-axes. Thought they'd look nice in the passage. Oh! and a present for you.'

'That's nice,' Ma said, as if suits of armour, shields and battle-axes were no more unusual than apples, oranges and pears. 'Give me a kiss.'

Pop promptly kissed Ma full on the lips, not with his usual protracted and burning intensity but rather as if casually taking a little light refreshment.

'Still think they're a bit too blue, Ma.'

'Well, they're going to be pinked up a bit in a minute if you'll make yourself scarce so I can get on with it. Go and get the drinks, do.'

While Pop had gone into the house to fetch both drinks and letters Ma proceeded to touch in a few pink lights on the upper edges of Mariette's breasts, remarking at the same time:

'Suits of armour, eh? Going baronial and all that. Next thing you know we'll be having a butler.'

Five minutes later Pop came back from the house carrying a tray of drinks and his letters in one hand and one of the three Regency chamber pots in the other. Ma started shaking and laughing like a ripe jelly and Mariette in turn was so overcome with cascades of laughter that for a moment she forgot all about the *Daily Mirror*, with the result that Pop had a brief and satisfying glimpse of his eldest daughter as Nature had made her. It merely served to convince him that Ma was altogether wrong about the blue, though he didn't like to say so.

Ma now surveyed the rose-ringed chamber pot with tearful eyes.

'What am I supposed to do with that?' she said.

Pop remarked blandly that he thought hyacinths would look nice in it for Christmas, or tulips or something. There were three of them. They were very old. Regency.

'Well, they'll come in handy for something, that's certain,' Ma said and broke once again into rich, ripe laughter.

'They're all the fashion now,' Pop said, 'these Regency things.'

'Now you've gone and put me off,' Ma said and proceeded to lay her brushes and palette down on her paint box, afterwards wiping her hands on a piece of rag. 'I'll carry on after lunch. You'd better run and put your dress on, dear. And see if little Oscar's awake and if he is bring him down.'

Pop had made a jugful of his new Moon-Rocket, double strength as usual, with plenty of ice, and he now gave it a final merry stir or two with a spoon. Its strength was such that it might well have reeked as he poured it out into large cut-glass tumblers, each holding nearly half a pint, but Ma merely said as she sipped at hers:

'Lovely. Just what I wanted. Delicious. One of the best you've ever thought of.'

Pop treated these compliments with airy modesty. It was nothing. One thing he was certain of, though – there was a bit more to it than Lady Violet's sherry.

'Ah! yes, tell me some more about Lady Violet,' Ma said. 'What else did you buy?'

Pop told her about the buggy and Ma said that was nice too. He also told her about the bassinet and Ma said they were all the rage for putting flowers into nowadays. Then he told her about the little room, the dust, the dusty ginger nuts, the dead primroses and the staring owl. He knew they would haunt him for a long time.

Finally he told her about the cigar and how he thought it had made her happy. He didn't expect Ma to laugh about it and he was really glad when she said, half-reproachfully:

'What did you do that for? You've probably gone and made the poor thing bad by this time.'

'She went at it as if it was Christmas pud and turkey,' Pop said. 'Like a meal. I half wish I hadn't done it now.'

He drank deeply at his Moon-Rocket and then filled up the two glasses again.

'Think she'd be offended if I took a bit of grub round when Montgomery and me go to fetch the buggy the day after tomorrow? She looks as if half a puff of wind would blow her away.'

'We've got that big ham in cut,' Ma said. 'And I'm making *Quiche Lorraine* and sausage rolls tomorrow. I'll make a bit of a basket up. By the way, who's your foreign letter from?'

Pop, laughing, his sadness about the morning receding now, said he was damned if he knew. He didn't know anybody in foreign parts. Not a soul.

'Well, open it and see.'

'I'll just mix another jugful first,' Pop said. 'When the ice starts melting it waters it down a lot. Hullo, here comes Charley with Blenheim.'

Mr Charlton now appeared from the direction of the house, carrying his baby son in one hand and a large glass of lager beer in the other. Pop delighted in calling his grandson Blenheim; it was such a nice round apple of a name.

'Well, how's Charley boy? And how's my little apple?'

Pop at once started to treat his grandson as if he were a pink rubber ball that had to be frequently bounced about a bit, but Ma instantly made loud noises of remonstration and said the child was only just awake and did Pop want salt water in his drinks or what?

'Give him to me,' she said and Mr Charlton's little son instantly disappeared like a rosy fledgeling into the vast bolster of her bosom, nuzzling eagerly against her. 'And you needn't go in there, young man, either. There's nothing there for you.'

Mr Charlton now found himself staring down at the rose-ringed chamber pot, which Ma had placed by her camp stool.

'Oh! you might well look,' Ma said, laughing ripely again. 'That's Pop's present to me. And there's two more.'

Accustomed as he was to living in the Larkin household, Mr Charlton was now never surprised by anything, even by the newest kind of present Pop had decided to give to Ma. He had already seen the pick-up heavily laden with its morning load of junk and even the suits of armour hadn't raised in him the slightest ripple of surprise. He remembered a day when Pop had bought a church organ, fifty-odd pews, about the same number of hassocks, a brass lectern and a pulpit.

He now merely took a calm swig of his beer and gazed with enraptured admiration at Ma's blue interpretation of his wife's bust and then heard Pop say:

'This letter's all in Dutch. Or German or summat. Here, Charley boy, you'd better look at this.'

Mr Charlton took the letter, which was in a neat slanting hand, and looked at it.

'French,' he said, 'not Dutch.'

'It's all Dutch to me,' Pop said. 'Who the pipe's it from?'

Mr Charlton indulged in a short flutter of laughter.

'It seems to be from your old friend,' he said. 'Mademoiselle Dupont.'

'Well, I'll go to Jericho,' Pop said.

'Love letters from France now, eh?' Ma said laughing again. 'What perfume is it soaked in?'

'Well, translate,' Mariette said. 'Let's hear. We're all waiting.'

Mariette had returned from the house less than a minute before, but without little Oscar, who was still asleep. She was now wearing a light purple blouse and rather tight pale green shorts, against which her bare limbs shone like brown butter.

'Well, she first of all presents all her dearest felicitations to the whole Larkin family, from Milord Larkin down to little Oscar. Scarcely a day passes but what she thinks of them and of England. She thinks especially of the milord and the Rolls-Royce with the monograms and also the nightingales. She says the nightingales arouse in her an impassioned nostalgia –'

'Good God,' Pop said, 'sounds like some form of asthma.'

'She is bewitched – no, perhaps enchanted is the better word – by the thought – no, the desire, the constant desire – to come to England. The desire, she says, has lately become irresistible and would it any way incommode the Larkin family if she could come soon? Ah! yes, she goes on – for the special occasion –'

'Special occasion?' Ma said. 'What special occasion?'

Mr Charlton folded up the letter and said in his mild way that he'd be damned. It wasn't often that he was damned but this was one time when he clearly was and he now reminded Ma that they all seemed to have forgotten something.

'After all you did ask her to be godmother to little Oscar. I wrote to her myself. And after all one of his names is Dupont.'

'All right,' Ma said in the blandest possible way, 'what about it?'

'She wants to come for the christening.'

'Christening?' Pop said, exactly as if this were some strange, outlandish tribal rite of which he had heard only very recently. 'Christening? We never said nothing about no christening, Ma, did we?'

'Not that I can think of.'

'Well, if Ma says we didn't, we didn't, and that's that. What's he got to be christened for?'

'Well it *is* customary,' Mr Charlton said, with an irony so faint that it was utterly lost on Pop. 'Well, in most families anyway. It *is* done.'

'Never?'

'Certainly Mariette and I are going to have Blenheim done.'

'Never?' Pop seemed astounded, even pained, by this startling announcement. 'Never had none of ours done, did we, Ma?'

'My God,' Mr Charlton said. 'Not one?'

Mr Charlton for once felt shocked. It was heathenish. It simply wasn't the thing. It had been hard enough for him to get used to the fact that Ma and Pop weren't married and that in painful consequence all the seven children, including his own wife, had been born out of wedlock, but this new discovery was too much.

'But why?' he said. 'Why?'

'Got plenty else to do, hadn't we, Ma?' Pop said and swiftly gave her one of his bolder winks which she returned just as swiftly with a handsome and deliberately seductive smile. 'Eh?'

'Busy as bees,' Ma said. 'I had four in five years once, with the twins.'

'Really never had the time,' Pop said.

Crushingly defeated by this blank, simple statement of historic fact Mr Charlton could only sip at his beer resignedly, saying that anyway even if it was too late to do anything about Montgomery, Mariette, Zinnia, Petunia, Primrose and Victoria they could at least have Oscar and little Blenheim done. That was if Ma and Pop had no objection?

'Oh! no objection at all,' Ma said. 'Any excuse for a party.'

This remark not only made her laugh again but reminded her that it was getting on for lunch time. Pop had better start carving the ham while she put on the potatoes. And if Mariette wanted to help she'd find three melons cut ready on the kitchen table. They were French and a bit expensive but that was all the more reason for having a drop of port in them. There was no sense in buying expensive melons if you were going to be measly about them, was there?

Pop agreed and said in that case they might just as well have port to drink anyway and urged Mr Charlton to go and put a bottle on ice right away. Mr Charlton, quiet now, went into the house, followed by Ma carrying little Blenheim and Pop carrying the chamber pot, which he now and then struck sharply with his knuckles, so that it gave out a ringing, almost clarion sound.

'Good quality,' he said, 'this 'ere Regency stuff.'

Over large plates of the tenderest ham, princely in flavour – Pop had raised the pig himself – together with new potatoes richly buttered and freckled with fresh parsley, Mr Charlton presently opened a discussion on the question of godparents for the two babies and the eventual date of the christening.

'We shall have to consult the Rev. Spink,' he said, 'and fix a day.'

'Oh! old Frog-face,' Pop said. 'Gawd A'mighty.'

The prospect of the christening, especially by the Reverend Frog-face, began to please him less and less. The Reverend Frog-face struck him as a damned old humbug. Very tall, elderly, cadaverous, onion-skinned and altogether of half-perished appearance, Spink rode aloofly about the village on a bicycle of antique design that had a strange net-work saddle rather like a sagging tennis racquet left out in the rain. Half-intoxicated with popery, Spink intoned Sunday services in Latin, which no one could understand even when they could hear it, which was seldom, with the result that most Sundays there were rather more people in the choir than in the congregation.

A conviction that it was just as good to worship the Lord of creation in a wood of bluebells as in an atmosphere stale with incense and the odour of spent candles had long since struck Pop as being a right and sensible one and now he felt plunged in gloom.

'What about asking Edith Pilchester to be one of the godparents for your little Blenheim?' Ma said. 'That would be a good idea, wouldn't it?'

Mr Charlton said firmly that he couldn't agree. He hated to say it, but Edith was too old. The essence of the thing was that a godparent should be young. Comparatively so, anyway.

'Got anybody in mind?' Ma said.

'Well, as a matter of fact we've already asked Angela Snow.'

Pop instantly perked up as if pricked by a hot pin.

'What did she say?'

'Oh! she was delighted.'

340

'You never told us,' Pop said. 'You don't suppose she'd act for little Oscar too, do you?'

'It's entirely up to her,' Mr Charlton said. 'If she feels up to the responsibility.'

'I'll ring her up tonight!'

With the gloom on his horizon suddenly largely dispelled, Pop watched with great relish the first strawberries of the year come to the table. They were fat, shining as if enamelled and half-drenched in cream.

Their summeriness suddenly excited all his thoughts about Angela. It would be good to sort of have her in the family. She was still as sensationally beautiful as ever and he couldn't help thinking that it was, after all, a good thing she hadn't married the Brigadier. It was the sensible thing; now they were just good friends. The Brigadier had rightly decided that he was too old for her and it didn't seem right, as Pop had often remarked to Ma, to cramp her style.

'Well, I must be off,' he said, after a third plate of strawberries and another glass or two of port. 'I think I know where I can lay hands on a nice little piebald for the buggy.'

'Buggy?' Mariette said. 'What buggy?'

'Pop's bought a nice little buggy from Lady Violet this morning,' Ma said.

'I thought it would be nice for Oscar and little Blenheim to have rides in,' Pop explained. 'Round and round the meadow, so they wouldn't get run over.'

'Oh! Pop,' Mariette said, 'you still think of the nicest things,' and suddenly gave him one of those full-mouthed generous kisses that always reminded him so powerfully of Ma in the prime of her youth.

Out in the garden, in the hot sun, a combination of the rich calling of birds, the smell of earth warmed and grass juicily rising and finally the sight of Ma's canvas, stool and easel inspired him to remember Mariette posing in the never-never and also the idea that he too, perhaps, might yet take up the painting lark.

That, he thought, would be the day.

· 3 ·

Two days later the morning was so beautiful, drenched with all the full essence of summer, that Pop decided to walk the piebald pony over to Lady Violet's bungalow himself, leaving Montgomery to feed turkeys, hens, guinea fowl, pigs, geese, cats and anything else that might need nourishment about the junk-yard. It was only a mile away.

He felt wonderfully calm and at peace with the world. He thought the pony was very pretty with its cocoa and cream markings and the idea had already occurred to him that he ought to try and lay his hands on a couple of silver bells for the harness, one to be engraved Oscar and the other Blenheim, so that there would be a smart old jingling as pony and buggy jogged along. The children were going to call the pony Blossom and the only thing that worried him at all was whether it would be man enough to draw Ma, if and when the occasion arose.

He was surprised, at the bungalow, to see a thinnish, straight-haired woman of forty or so on her hands and knees in the middle of the garden path, armed with an ancient pair of scissors, prising up weeds. Her face, yellowish in colour, looked very like a deflated chamois leather bag. Her stony eyes were depressingly neutral in colour and they seemed to jump, as if frightened, when he greeted her.

'Morning. Beautiful morning. Lady Violet in?'

'I'm awfully afraid she isn't up yet. She isn't feeling very well.' She darted nervous glances towards the bungalow. 'I'll call my husband.'

She at once fluttered desperately back up the garden path, to be met on the threshold of the bungalow by an ebullient man, beer-faced and with a walnut-brown, well-kept moustache, dressed in a thick red flannel shirt, a yellow tie and green linen trousers.

'For Jesus Christ's sake, woman, why must you always run? Don't run everywhere! I've told you a million times.'

'There's a gentleman – a man –'

'All right, all right. He won't *eat* you, will he?'

The man advanced heavily down the garden path, periodically grooming his moustache with elaborate strokes of his hand.

'Morning, morning,' Pop said. 'Larkin's the name. Nice morning.'

'I'm Captain Broadbent. What can I do for you?'

Pop explained about the buggy. The Captain's voice was coarse. His manner was florid and set Pop on edge. The too-often repeated habit of grooming the too-handsome moustache not only irritated him but even made him, a rare thing for him, slightly ill-tempered.

'Ah! you're the johnny who buys junk. I've heard of you.'

Pop so highly resented being called a johnny that he found himself, with amazement, resisting an unusual and powerful impulse to knock the Captain down. His good nature saved him, however, and he merely walked away.

The Captain followed. Pop untied the piebald where he had left him by the garden fence. The Captain gave the pony a brief look of undisguised contempt and said something about the untutored animal not getting very far in the Derby, laughing at the same time. Pop decided to ignore the joke and walked across to the wood-shed, where the buggy stood.

'You're never going to ride about in that damned contraption, are you? It's murder.'

Pop, in silence, started to back the piebald into the buggy shafts and the Captain laughed again.

'Well, I suppose it's one way of amusing yourself in this bloody awful countryside. God, what a hole. How anybody possibly sticks it out I'm damned if I know.'

'We manage somehow.'

Having heard his beloved countryside befouled Pop felt that he was ready for anything and started, again in silence, to buckle up the harness.

'Even the one and only pub's a bloody mausoleum. At nine o'clock last night there was one cock-eyed yokel in there with the twitch and two fat old trouts who never said a word. What do you do with all the women round here? Lock the poor bitches up in purdah?'

'Oh! there's a tidy bit o' talent about if you know where to look for it.'

'Is there indeed? Tell me where?'

Pop, not answering and not really wanting to listen either, stood dreamily buckling the harness, silently dwelling on the attractions of Ma, Mariette, Primrose and the rest of his daughters. He thought also of Angela Snow, whom he had tried to telephone the previous evening about the christening, but without success. The idea of the christening, largely because of Angela, no longer depressed him. All seemed to be going well. Mademoiselle Dupont had already been written to and Ma and Mariette were already up in London, buying Blenheim's christening robe. It seemed as if the date would be the last Sunday in July and it would be a good excuse, as Ma said, for a party.

'I'll lay you a fiver to a boiled egg that if you held a beauty-contest here there wouldn't be a piece of tender meat among the lot. They breed 'em coarse here, like the cattle.'

From a sudden pained recollection of the stony-eyed woman weeding the garden path Pop's mind abruptly leapt, in a moment of inspired vision, to a thought of someone else. Unable to explain why, he was suddenly thinking of a girl named Jasmine Brown. He had been introduced to Miss Brown in a beer-tent at a point-to-point meeting at Easter and had talked to her for a few convulsive moments before someone had whisked her away.

Miss Brown was unforgettable. In her own particular way she out-rivalled Angela Snow. Whereas Angela was all golden, languid and as smooth as honey, Miss Brown was a very dark, smouldering, big-built girl who had matured at twenty into the full-blown mould of a woman ten years older. She was the sort of girl who in a most sensational way radiated heat while remaining, apparently, surprisingly cool herself. She had managed to get him, in Ma's words, properly on the boil.

This inspiring recollection, following so close on the depressing remembrance of the Captain's wife fearfully scraping up weeds, made him first thoughtful and then, in a quiet way, good-humoured again.

'Sorry you don't think much of our girls. You ought to come over to my place sometime.'

The Captain preened his moustache with superior strokes from the back of his right hand.

'Why? You keep a harem or something?'

Pop laughed, stooping down at the same time to buckle the pony's belly-band.

'Well, it looks a bit like that some Sunday afternoons with all of 'em prancing in and out of the swimming pool.'

'Ah! you've fallen for the new status symbol.'

Pop said he didn't know about status symbol. He'd got the pool for swimming in. For fun.

'Junk trade must be flourishing.'

Well, it was fair, Pop admitted, striving hard not to lose his temper again. It was fair.

Suddenly he remembered something else. Ma had decided at the last moment that it really wasn't very nice to send Lady Violet a gift of ham and sausage rolls. It might seem to imply that a titled lady couldn't afford

food or was starving or about to go on National Assistance or something
of that lark. She thought it would be more tactful to send a bottle of her
own cherry brandy. It was very powerful stuff, the cherry brandy.

'I'm sorry to hear Lady Violet ain't all that grand,' Pop said. He privately
hoped it wasn't the cigar. Perhaps it was a bit rash, after all, the cigar.
Still – 'I've got a little present for her. I just remembered.'

Before tying up the pony he had put the bottle of cherry brandy under
the seat of the buggy and he now leaned over to fetch it out.

'By Jove, a bottle, eh? What's this, what's this?'

'Cherry brandy. Morella. Ma's special. Seven years in bottle.'

'By God, this'll make the day.'

'And when I say brandy I mean brandy. None of your muck. Napoleon
V.S.O.P.'

The Captain, for a moment shedding arrogance, seemed to become
positively friendly. In an unguarded moment he actually addressed Pop
as 'old boy'.

'Ma does peach and apricot too,' Pop said. 'You know where my place
is? Drop in and have a nip sometime.'

Was this an invitation? the Captain wanted to know.

Pop, who tried to find some good in everybody, even the worst of
stinkers, outsiders and the rest, said in his customary expansive fashion
that of course it was.

'Drop in next Sunday afternoon and have a swim. We'll have a party
going by about three.'

'Sounds damn' tempting. Harem and all?'

Pop laughed, at the same time reflectively stroking the pony's mane,
and said he'd do his best to find a few good hand-picked ones and then
added, in his blandest fashion:

'Course, I know you're not narrow-minded or anything. Man of the
world and all that. But don't be surprised if you see one or two of 'em
running round in the never-never.'

'The girls? Good God.'

Airily Pop explained about Ma and the painting lark and anyhow the
Captain must know how it was these days. Everybody free and easy and
all that. Nobody capable of being shocked by nothing no more.

He didn't know about that, the Captain had to confess. There were after
all limits. He suddenly seemed rather stiff, poised somewhere between
pained surprise and curiosity. For a few seconds he positively scrubbed his
moustache with a hand so nervously eager to demonstrate a dignified
superiority that it was almost priggish.

'Well, I shall have to see how I'm fixed. Very kind of you and all that, Larkin –'

'Here, dammit,' Pop said, 'if I'm going to all the trouble to hand-pick 'em for you and when I tell 'em you'll be there –' the Captain fell to preening his moustache with a now gentler hand – 'you twig what I mean? And after all they'll all be nice girls. Five of 'em my daughters. Just a family party with a few more thrown in. There's be some pretty good snifters too.'

At the thought of snifters the Captain became suddenly amiable again. Well, he expected he'd be there all right. He'd got to relieve the bloody tedium somehow. He glanced with significance towards the bungalow and Pop, silent again, seemed once again to see the fragile figure of Lady Violet and the fearful hunted figure of the wife fumbling among the weeds.

'About three on Sunday then. Perfick! Let's hope it's a good sweltering hot day. Some of the girls are trying to get brown all over.'

A moment later he was in the buggy, waving an abrupt farewell and driving away. The pony trotted well, he thought; it seemed quite at home in the buggy. It seemed as aware as any human being of the bright pristine beauty of the summer morning and now and then gave an excited snorting sniff with its nostrils, as if drinking at the scent of bluebells, growing grass and may.

Pop breathed hard at them too. The air was cleaner now. The only blemish on the face of the morning was the picture of the Captain's wife among her weeds and somehow he couldn't get that yellow, fearful, fumbling figure out of his mind.

· 4 ·

Late that evening, after admiring for the eighth or ninth time since supper the suits of armour, the shields and the battle-axes in the passage – there was no doubt that they gave the place terrific tone, terrific – Pop called Angela Snow on the telephone. Her voice, drawling, aristocratic and bewitching as ever, reproached him in tones of languid honey.

'I hate you, sweetie. I don't love you any more. You abandon me for weeks on end.'

Laughing, Pop was quick to assure her with a honeyed affection of his own that she was, on the contrary, for ever in his thoughts.

'In, yes,' she said, 'and out again. You must want something badly, sweetie, or you'd never ring me.'

Pop blandly confessed that he did indeed want something. In fact, two things.

'Greedy wretch. What's the first?'

When Pop explained about the christening she made purring noises at the other end of the line, assuring him of her undying devotion to himself, Ma and little Oscar. She was even ready, she declared, to be godmother to all his children if need arose and Pop was on the point of saying that it might well do at that when she said:

'Well, and what was the other?'

The other, Pop said, wasn't so easy. It was about a girl.

'You cad. You serpent. You stinking traitor.'

'I just wondered if you knew her, that's all.'

'If I do I shall promptly wring her neck. And yours into the bargain, sweetie.'

'Well, if it's like that,' Pop said, 'I'd better hang up, hadn't I?'

'You do and I'll never forgive you. Who is this Venus you're after? Won't I do instead?'

'Her name's Jasmine Brown. Know her? I met her –'

'Dearest Jasmine. Of course I know her. We graduated through virginity together.'

These remarks were exactly the sort of thing that endeared Angela

347

Snow very deeply to Pop. She was his sort all right, he told himself, laughing with quiet satisfaction. It might even be, he hoped, that Jasmine Brown was his sort too.

'Are you still there, sweetie?' Angela Snow said. 'You make me very suspicious. What do you want with Jasmine?'

'I just wondered if you'd like to bring her over for a swim on Sunday.'

'What a piffling excuse. You make me more suspicious than ever. She's blisteringly attractive, this girl. As if you didn't know.'

'No, honest,' Pop said. 'I'm just trying to make up a good party. Got to get some good scenery, after all. There's a feller named Broadbent coming along. Captain Broadbent –'

'Oh! my God, not that one.'

'So you know him too?'

'Met him once at a party, sweetie. Which was quite enough.'

'Stinker?' Pop said.

'The great self-styled ladykiller of all time, I gather.'

Pop laughed loudly, so that the sound crackled joyously in Angela Snow's ear, making her say:

'I'm still awfully suspicious, sweetie. I can't help thinking you're up to something. You're not by any chance thinking of sacrificing Jasmine and me on the Broadbent altar, are you?'

'Good Gawd, no,' Pop said.

'I'm profoundly glad to hear it, sweetie. We're sporting girls, but not that sporting. I gather he's already been thrown out of every club and hunt in the county.'

Pop positively barked with delight into the telephone.

'It was somethink like that,' he said, 'that I'd got in mind.'

'You don't mean it? Charming. Absolutely charming.'

Pop didn't say a word for another moment or two. He didn't want to do anything indelicate, he thought, and he found his next sentence for once rather a difficult one to phrase.

'Is she the real sport?' he said. 'Jasmine, I mean?'

'My dear, she's the most uninhibited creature on God's earth.'

'Unin – what?'

Pop, continually eager though he was to broaden his education by television and such means, now and then still came up against another long word that had him floored.

'I mean she's like me only more so. She's the sort of girl who goes to a shop to try on a new dress, sheds all and doesn't bother to pull the cubicle curtains.'

This delicious picture of the wholly uninhibited Miss Brown set Pop chuckling warmly. This was the stuff, absolutely perfick, he was about to tell her when she said:

'The nice thing is that she's got brains too. Just give her a bare hint of what's expected of her and she'll –'

'Bare it might be an' all,' Pop said darkly, chuckling again. 'Anyway bring her to lunch. I'll get Ma to do a turkey. I've got a new lot o' sparkling red burgundy – I'll get it nice and cold. Must go now. Ma's gone up to bed already. Goodbye. Bless you. Love.'

'Farewell, dear man. Fondest love. We'll be there.'

When Pop finally went upstairs ten minutes later it was to find Ma still sitting at her dressing table, brushing her thick dark hair with a silver brush half as big as a tennis racquet and wearing a bright magenta nightgown so short in style that it merely covered little more than the top half of her huge cushion body like a parasol.

'Been having a long chin-wag with somebody, haven't you?' she said. 'Who was it?'

'Angela. Been inviting her and one of her girl friends over for a swim on Sunday. Girl named Jasmine Brown.'

'Nice one?'

Pop, laughing richly, proceeded to explain to Ma about Miss Brown's entire lack of inhibition, careful at the same time not to use the exact word in case Ma shouldn't be any more familiar with it than he was.

'Sounds just your type,' Ma said, laughing too.

Pop said he hoped so; he was looking forward to it a lot.

'Very glad to hear it,' Ma said. 'You've been a bit quiet lately. I'd almost begun to think you'd gone off the boil.'

Pop freely admitted he'd been quiet but not by any means off the boil: not on your nelly.

'Something your mind?' Ma said. 'You'd better get it off your chest if there is.'

Pop said as a matter of fact there was and proceeded to tell her about Lady Violet's niece, Mrs Broadbent, and how he hadn't been able to get that crushed, haunted, groping figure out of his mind all day.

'She looked as if she'd been horse-whipped,' he said.

'Who by?'

Pop, standing at the foot of the bed, taking off his collar and tie, explained about the Captain, his distasteful contempt for local ladies, his arrogance about Pop's beloved countryside and how, it seemed, he was the self-styled ladykiller of all time.

349

'Sounds *most* attractive. What did you tell him?'

'I invited him for a swim on Sunday.'

'Well, that's a fine thing. Are you mad? Do you want the pool contaminated or something?'

'No, no. I just thought he ought to meet a few real ladies, that's all. Like Angela and Jasmine Brown.'

'Oh! it's like that, is it?'

Pop, laughing, said it was, or somethink of that sort. Ma, who had now finished brushing her hair, started drenching her great bosom with Chanel No. 5, shaking it from what seemed to be a quart-sized bottle. As she did so she thought of Angela Snow. What had she said, Ma wondered about the idea of being godmother?

'Thrilled to bits.'

'That was nice of her. That reminds me – the parson telephoned. He'll be round tomorrow evening to fix up about the christening.'

'Frog-face, eh?'

No, Ma said, it wasn't Frog-face. It was a young man – a locum or whatever it was they called them. Frog-face was away sick – having an operation for gallstones or something nasty.

Pop said he was sorry to hear that and wondered if he ought not to take some sort of nourishment, preferably liquid, in to the patient? A bottle of vodka, perhaps? It might dissolve the stones.

'They say they do dissolve them nowadays,' Ma said. 'Anyway he won't be well enough for the christening, that's sure.'

'We'll make a marvellous do of it, that day, Ma. We'll really light up.'

'I should think so too,' Ma said. 'After all we've never had a christening in the family before.'

The following evening a young man of earnest demeanour, pale ginger-haired hands, scrubby, carroty hair and a voice that ended all its hesitant sentences with an almost musical squeak, like that of dry leather, sat in a state of stupefied bewilderment in the sitting-room, utterly unable to reconcile Pop's chromium galleon of a cocktail cabinet with the baronial armour regaling the passage outside or the luscious graces of Primrose and Mariette with the bucolic comradeship of Pop, who frequently called him 'Mr Candy, old man' and had, in response to a mild request for 'just a little whisky please', given him three quarters of a tumblerful, neat except for a couple of cubes of ice and the merest teaspoon of water.

Mariette and Primrose having been introduced as 'two of my daughters, not the ones to be christened, though' and Primrose more especially as 'the intellectual one of the family, sort of. Likes poetry', Mr Candy sat in a state of twitching suspense, enmeshed as a fly in a spider web by the rapturous beauty of Primrose, now, at fourteen, as fully developed as a woman of twenty and every bit as well aware of it too. Her dark eyes dwelt on Mr Candy with open insistence, bringing his face out in a repeated tepid blush.

After Pop had apologized for the absence of Mr Charlton, who had gone out to take a trial run in a second-hand Jaguar that Pop had just taken over in a deal, Mr Candy said:

'Oh! I'm sorry I shall miss him. He of course is the father of the two children who are to be christened?'

'Oh! no,' Pop said. 'He's the father of one and I'm the father of the other.'

'I see. Son and grandson. Rather unique.'

'You can't say "rather unique",' Primrose said, gazing at Mr Candy with almost fervent remonstration. 'It's either unique or it isn't.'

Mr Candy, the hairs on whose head and hands actually seemed to redden even deeper as the blood rushed to his skin, admitted that of course you couldn't. It was silly of him. He ought to have known better.

'Clever girl, our Primrose,' Pop said. 'You can't get over Primrose.'

Mr Candy, acutely embarrassed, started fumbling in his inside jacket pocket for pen and paper. As he did so his dog collar went slightly askew, cutting against his Adam's apple, which stuck out prominently from his rather scraggy neck. This caused Ma to think that perhaps he was another one of those who didn't get enough to eat and inquired with earnest solicitude if he wouldn't like a piece of pork pie?

'Oh! no, no, no. Thanks all the same. I really wouldn't.'

'Well, I would,' Pop said, 'Good idea.'

'I'll get it,' Primrose said.

'And bring the ketchup,' Pop said.

Before Primrose came back with a pork pie a quarter cut, a bottle of tomato ketchup and several knives and plates the Rev. Candy said:

'And now may I have the names of the two children? I always like to make sure of the spellings and so on.'

'Well,' Ma said, 'Oscar – that's ours – is going to be called Oscar Columbus Septimus Dupont Larkin.'

Mr Candy, who seriously thought for one painful moment that he must be having his leg pulled, flushed deeply again and seized on the word Septimus, inquiring:

'Septimus. The seventh? You have seven children?'

'Think so,' Ma said, laughing richly. 'Lose count a bit sometimes. What with little Blenheim and everything.'

'Blenheim?' Mr Candy said. 'Blenheim?'

'Oh! he's the other one,' Ma said. 'Mariette's baby. He's going to be called John Churchill Marlborough Blenheim Charlton.'

'Great Heavens.'

'Something wrong?' Ma inquired.

It was nothing, Mr Candy said, so embarrassed again that he actually answered Pop's enthusiastic 'Have a piece of pie, old man? Very good. Ma's own make', with an unexpected yes, after all, he thought he would.

Primrose cut the pie with her own hands, placing a big wedge of it on a plate, with a knife, in front of Mr Candy, at the same time inquiring if he wouldn't like ketchup? Mr Candy, who was desperately trying to write down the names of Mariette's baby correctly and in correct order, said he didn't think he would and took a strong gulp of whisky.

Pop, who was dipping his own piece of pie with great relish into a large red pool of ketchup, then remarked that Ma had painted a very nice picture of Blenheim and Mariette the other day. Perhaps Mr Candy would like to see it?

Mr Candy said he would. 'It seems everyone is taking up painting nowadays. My mother paints. Mostly flowers.'

'Go and fetch the picture, Primrose,' Ma said, 'there's a dear. It's on the top of the fridge.'

Two minutes later Mr Candy, abruptly pausing in the act of putting a piece of pork pie into his mouth, found himself gazing at a picture of Mariette entirely in the nude except for a narrow glimpse of the purple briefs. The baby was asleep slightly to the side of one splendid breast. Ma had been for some time very exercised about the purple briefs, not knowing whether to paint them in or not, in case they might not be understood. Now she thought they looked very nice – and art, she had read somewhere, had to be honest if it was to be anything at all – especially against Mariette's skin, which she had on this occasion painted the deep gold colour of a ripe pumpkin.

'Think it's anything like her, Mr Candy?' Pop inquired with a sort of brisk innocence.

Mr Candy, unacquainted as he was with the sitter, or at least those parts of her so boldly depicted by Ma, was simply crushed to silence, redder than ever. A trembling cube of pork-pie jelly stuck to his open lips, faltered there for a few moments and then went bouncing down his black clerical front, from which Mr Candy at last retrieved it with fumbling fingers.

'Well, anyway, Ma, I'll tell you this,' Pop said, 'I like 'em better now you've done 'em that gold colour instead of blue.'

Well, they did look more real, certainly, Ma admitted.

'You're getting better at it, that's what it is, Ma. More experienced,' Pop said. 'I tell you what – you ought to do a big family group one of these days.'

Mr Candy was saved from any further discussion of this interesting possibility by the sudden entry of the twins, Zinnia and Petunia, each wearing bright scarlet bathing wraps and sucking iced lollies of a sort of pistachio green shade. Ma, having introduced them by name to Mr Candy, then introduced Mr Candy in turn as the gentleman who was going to christen Oscar and little Blenheim.

Simultaneously the twins demanded in shrill voices to know why they couldn't be christened too? They hadn't ever been done, had they?

Profoundly shocked, a piece of pork pie poised at his lips, Mr Candy said he most fervently hoped so.

'Surely, Mrs Larkin?'

'Afraid not,' Ma said.

'Great Heavens, what an extraordinary omission.'

In tones of velvet wonder Primrose now inquired what about her?

'Good Lord,' she said, giving Mr Candy the most provocative of luscious looks, 'haven't I been christened either? I can't wait!'

Mr Candy, held by the precocious, luscious eyes, felt he couldn't wait either. He desperately wanted to flee. It would have been merciful if he could have hidden himself somewhere. For a moment he half-choked on a chunk of pork pie and Ma said:

'You look a bit pale, Mr Candy. Feeling all right?'

'Perfectly. Only it's rather an odd circumstance to find a whole family of seven that hasn't received baptismal rites.'

'Suppose it is,' Ma admitted, 'but you see Pop and me were too busy at the time getting on with other things.'

'Oh! couldn't we all be done together?' Primrose said. 'We could, Mr Candy, couldn't we? There's no age-limit, is there?'

Unfortunately not, Mr Candy wanted to say but couldn't bring himself even remotely to the point of saying it. In a daze, the sudden victim of open feminine entreaty, he could only say:

'One can receive the baptism at any time.'

'Marvellous,' Primrose said. 'Absolutely marvellous. Let's all be done together.'

'Cheaper by the dozen, I suppose?' Pop said. 'Drop more whisky, Mr Candy?'

'No, no, no. Really not, thank you.'

'Go on, old man. Drink up. You'll need it. After all you've got a lot more work on your hands than you bargained for, haven't you?'

He had indeed, Mr Candy thought, he had indeed. If one could call it that.

Silent again, he watched Pop replenish his already generous measure of whisky, Pop at the same time inquiring if Mr Candy couldn't find room for the other bit of pork pie? Mr Candy protested, though not very strongly, that he couldn't and was pained and astonished a moment later to hear the seductive voice of Primrose entreating:

'Go on, Mr Candy, share it with me. Half and half. You and I share.'

With unresisting eyes Mr Candy wretchedly watched her cut the remains of the pork pie in half and then with a deliberately over-delicate gesture put the larger portion on his plate. The moment was one of such intimacy that for the next few seconds he was mesmerized into thinking that she and Mariette, so alike in their dark beauty, had become interchanged. The golden bust seemed to mature into palpitating reality before his eyes.

'I love pork pie, don't you?' she said, in tones also golden, so that she might actually have been inviting him to accept some rare physical favour.

There was no doubt that people were right when they said girls grew up fast these days, Mr Candy thought. They certainly did; they were women before they started, he told himself, and for one awful moment had a vision of himself in church, painfully enacting the ritual of baptism for one beautiful Larkin after another.

'Oh! I'm absolutely thrilled,' Primrose said. 'I can't wait for that Sunday. We'll all have new dresses, won't we, Ma?'

'Course,' Ma said. 'You don't think we're going to turn out in sack-cloth and ashes do you?'

Pop was also moved to express his thrill and pride. He was blowed if it wouldn't be quite something to see his whole brood being sprinkled at one go, little Blenheim an' all.

Fortified by a further gulp of whisky Mr Candy was impelled to remind Pop that the occasion was one of great solemnity.

'Course,' Pop said. 'Course. Pardon me.'

'If you don't mind my saying so your attitude ought to be one of "better late than never".'

'We'll see it doesn't happen again,' Ma said.

Pop couldn't help wondering what Ma meant by that exactly. You could take it two ways.

'Well, shall we settle on the day?' Mr Candy said. He felt again that it was time to go. The over-generous measure of whisky was putting a slight slur on his speech and the already warm June evening seemed to be growing rapidly more and more stifling. 'You did suggest the third Sunday in July?'

'That's right,' Ma said.

'And there will be how many for baptism? Seven?'

'Eight,' Ma said. 'Three boys and five girls.'

The Lord give him strength and patience, Mr Candy felt himself silently entreating.

'Eight,' Pop said. 'That's set me back a shillin' or two.'

Mr Candy pointed out that there was, on the contrary, no charge for the service. But of course a contribution –

'Leave that to me,' Pop said in his most generous fashion, 'leave that to me. Nice to know there's a few things left that are free.'

'Yes, isn't it?' Primrose said, again looking Mr Candy straight in the eyes.

Mr Candy felt he could bear no more; this was the signal for departure. He started to get to his feet, succeeded in rising seven or eight inches or so and then fell back again. The act of sitting down in the chair, far from being awkward or embarrassing, was pleasurable. He actually gave a short chuckle.

'Perhaps Mr Candy would like a lift home?' Ma said.

'Be a bit difficult,' Pop said, 'unless I take him in the pick-up. The Rolls has got a flat tyre and Charley ain't back yet.'

'I could take him in the buggy,' Primrose said.

'No, no,' Mr Candy said. 'I shall walk across the meadows, the way I came.'

'Riding in the buggy's absolutely marvellous,' Primrose said. 'We've only just got it.'

'I don't think I've ever ridden in a buggy.'

'No? It's an absolutely wonderful sensation. Quite different from a car. You feel sort of on air.'

'You do?' Mr Candy said and started to get up again, this time succeeding in standing fully erect, so that Pop said:

'You let our Primrose drive you home, Mr Candy. She handles the piebald like a real dabster. All my kids are good with horses.'

'That's right,' Ma said. There was something quite attractive about young parsons, she thought, in a moley sort of way. Perhaps it was the collar being wrong way round. 'Well, off you go. Then you can get back before you need the lamps.'

355

Ten minutes later Mr Candy was sitting in the buggy wrapped in a midsummer dream. Primrose said she would drive by the back lanes; it was quieter that way; there was hardly any traffic. Already Pop had fixed the silver bells to the harness and as the buggy jogged along, not very fast, the delicate jingle of them leapt to the height of the thick hornbeams and hawthorns arching across the road and then came as delicately prancing back again.

'Wonderful sensation. Like it?'

'I do, I do.'

'It must have been wonderful in the old days.'

'What must?'

'This. Riding about like this. Not racing everywhere. You can take everything in so much better.'

Mr Candy, now slightly recovering from the effects of the whisky but still in a pleasant daze, agreed. The little piebald slowed to a walk and Primrose said:

'You notice that? That's a trick of his. He's very artful. It's to get me to stop on the side of the road and let him graze.'

'Is it indeed?' Mr Candy said. 'Is it?'

'Clever as a monkey, this pony,' Primrose said and a few moments later drew the buggy into the shadow of a big Spanish chestnut, by a gateway. 'You simply let him graze for a few moments and then he's all right again.'

The pony grazed; an occasional solitary tinkle of bell broke on the calm and pellucid air. Many birds were still singing, deepening rather than breaking the silence, and the scent of may was clotted and intoxicating everywhere.

'I'm thrilled that you're going to christen me.'

Primrose spoke in a whisper and Mr Candy sat silent, unable to think of a suitable reply.

'I mean I'm thrilled it's you and not anyone else.'

'Really? Me? Why me?'

'Because you're you and no one else.'

Mr Candy started to feel uncomfortable to the point of trembling. His hands felt hot and clammy. In confusion he started to say something about the act of christening being something into which no hint of personality could or should enter and she said:

'I know all about that. But it'll be different with you. I know.'

All of a sudden Primrose appeared to be holding up her face to be kissed. Mr Candy, recoiling, didn't know whether to resist this in outspoken refusal or clerical reprimand, but Primrose saved him the trouble by putting her soft, moist, partly opened lips on his.

Mr Candy felt himself reel in complete astonishment and then become inert, his lips hard and flat. After about half a minute of this Primrose disengaged herself from the unequal struggle and said:

'You don't encourage people very much, do you?' and in the artless innocence of the question it might well have been Ma speaking.

'I don't think it's proper that I should.'

'Proper, why proper? We're all alone, aren't we?'

'Well, even if I thought it proper I don't think your mother would quite approve.'

'No?' The single word, so palpably innocent as to imply almost nothing at all, was followed by a hint of mischief. 'Perhaps you'd rather talk about poetry or something like that?'

Mr Candy didn't particularly want to talk about poetry either and was about to say so when she gave him a lustrous glance of inquiry and said, her voice very soft:

'Do you know Donne?'

Mr Candy was sorry, but he didn't know a thing about Donne.

'He was a parson like you,' she said. 'You mean you don't know that marvellous, marvellous poem of his that begins *"I wonder by my troth what thou and I did till we loved"*?'

Mr Candy didn't know about that either and excused his ignorance by pointing out that he'd spent a good part of the last three or four years helping out in a parish in the East End of London where, on the whole, he didn't think Donne would cut much ice.'

'In the East End? Doing what?'

'Oh! welfare work. Youth clubs and that sort of thing. Rather toughish sometimes. One had to learn to take care of oneself.'

'I'm sorry you don't know about Donne,' she said. 'He puts it all so gorgeously.' She turned and sat full face to him, dark eyes absolutely still, and gave him another glance of such lustrous and captivating quality that he felt the muscles of his throat contracting sharply. 'There's another one that starts *"Dear love, for nothing less than thee would I have broke this happy dream."* Don't you know that?'

Mr Candy confessed he was absolutely ignorant of that one too.

'Rather like us, sitting here, don't you think? I mean I feel in a dream too and don't want anything to break it.'

It was utter madness, Mr Candy suddenly thought, wildly. It had got to be broken. Here he was, sinking under the seductive power of a girl of

357

fourteen and letting himself go under. It was illegal anyway. It was full of ghastly possibilities. It was like being tempted with ripe fruit. Clearly, like all the rest of the family, she hadn't the shadow of an inhibition in her whole being. You could fairly hear her thinking with the pores of her skin.

'I think I really should go –'

'Oh! don't go. Why? You're not afraid of being alone with me here, are you?'

Oh! no, it wasn't that he was afraid –

'What then?'

Well, it was just that there were – well, to put it frankly, certain limits beyond which – well, you couldn't be involved.

'Oh! are there?'

'Of course there are.'

'Well, it doesn't worry me. I'm doing the involving.'

With irresistible fingers she touched his face. Every pore in Mr Candy's own skin responded in a protest that was also, against all his better nature, as physically pleasurable as the eating of ripe fruit. There was a faint but detectable scent of honey on her lips and a moment later her arms were completely round him and she was giving him a kiss of such protracted, accomplished and passionate nature that he fell back flat against the cushions of the buggy, her young body pressing full against him.

Oh! God, Oh! God, was all Mr Candy could think. He was sunk; he was in for it now. And how in the name of all the saints was he ever going to get through that awful, awful Sunday?

· 5 ·

Over-smartly dressed in a light blue suit, sugar-pink shirt, blue and white tie and white buckskin shoes, a dandified curl in both his moustache and hair, Captain Broadbent arrived at the Larkin house about half past three on the following Sunday afternoon. The weather, as Pop had hoped it would be, was hot and the junk-yard a dozy dormitory of prostrate pigs, soporific geese, hens, turkeys and guinea-fowl all resting in the shade of ruined bits of machinery, elder trees and haystacks. Pop's yellow-and-black Rolls-Royce stood under a corrugated hovel and the new Jaguar, a discreet dove-grey, in the shade of a willow tree whose gently turning leaves provided almost the only movement in the summer air.

Outside the front door of the house, to Captain Broadbent's astonishment, stood the two suits of armour, each now nursing a battle-axe in its arms. Ma had decided after all that the inside passage was slightly cramped for them, especially after she had run sharply into them in the twilight one evening. She thought that if anything they looked even more classy outside than in and Pop was inclined to agree with her, especially at night, when he was able to switch on the red, yellow and blue fairy lights inside the vizors.

Walking round to the back of the house, Captain Broadbent presently found himself facing a scene that merely served to increase the contemptuous astonishment already aroused by junk, armour and general farmyard menagerie. People simply didn't live like this; it just wasn't done. The big swimming pool, its depth a brilliant turquoise blue, was almost indecent in its ostentation, a blown-up status symbol if ever there was one. The screaming of many children reminded him of one of those awful day trips to the seaside. More astonishing than anything else, perhaps, was the fact that Pop, in anticipation of Mademoiselle Dupont's visit from France, had already run up the tricolor on one side of the top diving board with the Union Jack on the other. Ma had badly wanted to fly the Royal Standard too, but Montgomery had pointed out that you couldn't do that unless the Queen was in residence, which wasn't likely to be yet. Ma, a fervent royalist, said more was the pity.

Half way along one side of the pool Ma, in a bright canary yellow bathing costume, gave the impression of a large well-filled balloon that had ever so gently descended from space and was now resting on the tiniest of camp stools. She was painting on a really large canvas today, trying to embrace the entire pool, tricolor, Union Jack, gambolling figures and all.

On the opposite side of the pool was erected a piece of apparatus the like of which Captain Broadbent couldn't ever remember seeing before. It beat the band, he told himself, for sheer vulgarity. He supposed the thing was some sort of portable drink-wagon or bar. The entire affair was made of bamboo, with a roof of palm thatch and designs of coconut and pineapple scratched about it in dark poker-work, so that the whole had a marked Polynesian effect. It was set about with glasses of all colours, emerald, vermilion, purple, amber and blue, together with corkscrews, bottle-openers as big as horse-shoes and scores of bottles and siphons of different kinds. It looked like something out of some beastly opera, Captain Broadbent thought.

He was just on the point of turning his back on this second and even louder symbol of status when Pop, with splendid warmth, hailed him from behind the bar, shaking a vast silver cocktail shaker as his signal of welcome.

'Ah! there you are, Colonel. Didn't think you'd been able to find us. Perfick day, Colonel, eh?'

More by instinct than design Pop was always inclined to promote a military man if he could. In return Captain Broadbent seemed to preen himself at this sudden rise in rank and at once went through the ritual of brushing his moustache with an extravagant sweep of his hand.

'Afternoon, Larkin. Not too early, I trust?'

'Just right, Colonel. Perfick. Come and meet the family. Ma!' he yelled across the pool, 'Colonel Broadbent's just arrived. Colonel, this is Ma. Recently taken up the painting lark. Mostly goes in for the nude.'

'Afternoon, Colonel,' Ma shouted. 'Sweatin' hot, isn't it?'

The Captain, in the middle of the stiffest of bows, slightly recoiled at this description of the day and Pop at once proceeded to introduce the rest of his family.

'Zinnia, Petunia, Montgomery, Victoria – where's Victoria? Oh! that's her, in the red bikini, floating. And Primrose – that's Primrose, just taking the umbrella to Ma. Ma's finding it a bit too hot I fancy. Hope she won't get one of her turns.'

Ma sometimes had turns when it was over-hot and it was a bit of a job sometimes to get her round. Rum generally helped, though.

'And this is my eldest, Mariette. Mrs Charlton. I think Mr Charlton must be having a lay-down indoors somewhere. Unless he's larking about somewhere with the girls.'

As he said this Pop gave the Captain the most indiscreet and knowing of winks, as if the two of them shared some very saucy secret. The Captain hardly knew what to do in return. The young goddess in her dark green bikini, swinging her body along the far side of the pool, a black umbrella twirling over one shoulder, had already unnerved him, so much so that he was totally unprepared to deal with the vision of a three-parts naked Mariette, now turning over on her back on a bright blue foam mattress, her breasts every bit as eloquent as her dark eyes as she raised them to the sun.

'Hullo, Colonel,' she said softly, smiling. 'You chose a good day to come,' and it was almost as if she had conferred the promotion on him herself, so that he felt he would surrender his rise in rank only with extreme reluctance, if he surrendered it at all.

'Snifter, Colonel? What'll it be?'

'Something soft and cold, I think, if –'

'Just mixing a new one up,' Pop said. 'Moon-Rocket. Pretty harmless. Mostly ice – dash o' vodka and all that, for flavour. Care to try it? It's a good quencher.'

The Captain, still unnerved and slightly aloof, said he would and Pop made athletic manoeuvres with the cocktail shaker.

'What price our little paradise, Colonel, eh?'

The Captain remained mute; he could put no price on the little paradise at all.

'Well, here we are, Colonel. Try that for size.'

Pop now handed the Captain a tall, silver-rimmed glass that seemed to contain about a pint of amber liquid topped by a sprig of mint, a slice of orange and a cherry. The glass was beautifully frosted and the Captain raised it to his lips at first with caution, then decided it seemed aromatically pleasant and drank deep.

Some twenty seconds later he found himself going through the alarming experience of supposing that he had been electrocuted somewhere in the pit of his stomach. He choked, fighting vainly to regain both equilibrium and breath.

'It's got somethink, Colonel, hasn't it?' Pop said. 'Drink up! Cheers!'

Pop proceeded to lower the level of his own glass by several inches and immediately made as if to fill both glasses up again. The Captain, who was by now convinced that his eyeballs were standing an inch or so out of the top of his head, managed to put his hand over the rim of his glass, at the same time entreating Pop in a much weakened voice to be steady.

Pop, smacking his lips, assured the Captain that this was one of the best he had ever invented. Ma adored it too.

'Ma!' he shouted across the pool, at the same time lifting the cocktail shaker. 'How about you?'

'Please.'

A few minutes later the Captain was assailed by a new vision. It was that of Angela Snow appearing from the direction of the house, tall, elegant and languid as ever, and suddenly he suffered yet another alarming experience: that of supposing she had nothing on. In a moment he remembered Pop's jovial warning to him not to be surprised if he saw some of the girls running round in the never-never and he could only suppose this was some new evidence of vulgarity. Then, as Angela came nearer, he saw that the illusion of nakedness was actually caused by the briefest of bikinis, in colour almost exactly that of her light golden skin. He felt much relieved.

Then as she came nearer still he recognized that he had met her somewhere before: perhaps once or twice at a party. He vaguely recalled that her father was a judge or something of that sort. Anyway she came from the right bloodstock and he couldn't for the life of him think what a well-connected girl like her was doing with this vulgar crowd. He wasn't against democracy and mixing with average chaps and all that but by God there were things which shook you.

'Want you to meet Miss Snow, Colonel. Angela. Very old friend of ours.'

'Colonel?' Angela turned on the Captain the most bewitching and languid of smiles. 'You were Captain the last time we met. Promoted, eh?'

'Well, I –'

The Captain brushed his moustache, reluctant to deny his sudden rise in rank and Angela said:

'Well, congratulations.'

'Well, actually –'

'Calls for a drink, don't it?' Pop said. 'Angela? What about it? One of my specials?'

'Gorgeous idea.'

The Captain was confused. He preened his moustache with an elliptical sort of sweep, haughtily. He felt uncomfortable and hot. Perhaps, he thought, it was time to get changed? A dip might cool him down.

'Perhaps I might get into some cooler togs, Larkin. Where could I change?'

'In the house,' Pop said. 'I'll come and show you.'

'Jasmine's there,' Angela said and gave Pop a slow, soft, secret wink of her own. 'She'll show the Colonel where.'

'Drink up before you go,' Pop urged the Captain, 'I'll have another ready when you get back,' and the Captain, bracing himself, drank as if at a poison cup.

In a rather shrill voice Ma then called across the pool:

'Why didn't you bring your wife over, Colonel, on a lovely day like this?'

'She doesn't care greatly for the social life, I'm afraid.'

'Oh! don't she? Pity. Wouldn't like me to ring her up and get her over for a cuppa tea, I suppose?'

'I fancy not. She never really stirs out much.'

Once again Pop, as he listened, saw in his mind the image of the fearful, fumbling figure scraping at its weeds.

A moment later little Oscar, chasing a large red-and-blue ball, stumbled awkwardly, fell on his face and lay prostrate, bawling loudly. This was a signal for everyone else to shriek with abandoned laughter, so that the whole afternoon suddenly seemed to explode violently about Captain Broadbent's ears. The din was perfectly maddening and suddenly the Captain, again brushing his moustache, fled from it with what he thought was a certain critical dignity.

The echo of children's caterwauling was still ringing in his ears when he stepped over the Larkin threshold. He supposed he would have to change and get into that filthy pool with all those filthy kids but for a few uncertain moments he found it hard to lower himself to do so. That filthy drink of Larkin's together with the thought of his accidental rise in rank didn't help much either and for a few moments longer he struggled desperately with the idea of whether or not to abandon everything and run.

Two words were enough to extract him from his dilemma and they were spoken so softly that for a moment he was not only uncertain as to where they came from but if they were real at all.

'Hullo there.'

Another feminine vision, this time so stunning as to be almost frightening, stood halfway up the stairs. Like something carved out of flawless cream marble, every limb splendidly unblemished, the tall Jasmine Brown leaned voluptuously on the banisters, saved from sheer nakedness only by a trifling arrangement of taut pale-green triangles. Even two of these were not enough to cover fully her two deeply assertive breasts, so that the glorious flesh of them stood out half-exposed, in vibrant splendour.

'I'm Jasmine Brown.'

'Oh! yes, they told me – they said something about – you know, you'd show me where to change.'

The Captain moved as if to go up the stairs but to his great consternation Jasmine Brown at that moment decided to sit down plumb in the middle of them, barring his way with legs curved in such a way that, in trying hastily to look away, he gave an undignified stumble and fell up a step or two.

Jasmine Brown laughed softly, in a voice of alarmingly seductive quietness.

'Steady now. You've been having one of those Larkin specials. I know.'

'No, no. I beg your pardon – forgot to introduce myself. Colonel – Captain Broadbent.'

'Colonel or Captain?' she said, in a voice of beautifully modulated inquiry, low and innocent, so that he found it impossible to look her in the face and found himself once again completely mesmerized by her legs, which she had now elegantly drawn up together.

'Colonel,' he half-muttered under his breath, his own voice now so low that it was doubtful if she heard.

'Glorious, those drinks of his.'

'Made me damned hot, if that's anything. I'm dying to get into something cooler.'

'Cool? You look marvellously cool. That's a wonderful suit of yours. I love that colour.'

'Really?'

The Captain, leaning with one hand on the banisters, preened his moustache with the other.

'Stunning. And that shirt and tie. All looks splendidly cool.'

The Captain, though greatly flattered, made as if to advance another step or two upstairs but Jasmine Brown made no sign of moving to help him except to run her hands slowly up and down her legs with a sibilant whisper that was hardly audible even in the profound quietness of the summer afternoon.

'You look so awkward standing there. Why don't you sit down a minute? Come on.' She patted the stair just below her calves. 'Sit.'

'I really ought to go and change –'

'Oh! sit down. There's oceans of time.'

'I suppose so, but – well, one ought to play ball and all that. Not that I particularly want to swim –'

'No. Why not?'

'Damn bedlam out there. It's like some ruddy awful circus. You can't hear yourself think.'

'And who,' she said, again in that voice of lilting innocence, 'wants to think on an afternoon like this? Not this girl, I'll tell you. Come on, sit down.'

The Captain, who had held out firmly until this moment, now sat down on the stairs, only to find in the very same moment that she had slipped her body down one step nearer his.

In this increasingly intimate situation, not knowing what else to say, he bluffed:

'I don't mind telling you I damn nearly ran just now.'

'Not from me I hope?'

'No, no, of course not. From that rabble –'

'If all I hear about you is true the last things you run from are women.'

'Oh? Oh?' he said with a hint of dark inquiry. 'Who's been telling you this?'

'Oh! friends.'

'Friends, eh? Men or women?'

'Both. I understand you make all the men blisteringly jealous and all the women, well –'

Bathed in intoxicating waves of flattery, the Captain could only murmur something about so that's what they said, did they? Well, he supposed he'd had his moments –

'I'll bet you have. And still will, I hope.'

With an increasing uneasiness the Captain found himself caught full in Jasmine Brown's deep, dark stare. Her large black eyes, liquid and hypnotic, held him relentlessly imprisoned for fully half a minute until in desperation he suddenly released himself and lowered his own eyes, only to find himself facing, a mere fifteen inches away, the full glory of her breasts, which seemed to rise and fall in invitation.

'You know, I honestly ought to go and change –'

'Don't change. I love you in that suit. I really do. Stay here.'

The Captain again preened his moustache but nevertheless felt bound to point out that Larkin would be wondering where the hell he'd got to and after all there were the ethics of the damn thing. He, the Captain, was after all a guest.

'Oh! the Larkins never worry about things like that. Guests can do what they like here. Disappear to the woods. Play hide and seek. Sit on stairs. Any old thing. It's all free and easy. You know of course that they're not married?'

'Good God.'

'And that none of their children have ever been christened? A great scream, that – they're going to have them all done next month. Wholesale.'

'Are they, by Jove?'

This stupefied reaction expressed not only the Captain's affront at the extraordinary habits of the Larkins but his own rising embarrassment at yet another move of her body. Her warm naked shoulder actually brushed against him as she tossed back her dark hair, no less glorious than the rest of her, so that he actually averted his face.

'I love sitting on stairs and talking, don't you?' she said.

The Captain, suddenly overheated again, felt he would have given anything for a breath of air. It was getting pretty stifling. With discomfort he fidgeted on the stairs but all the encouragement she gave him was another long, bewitching stare, accompanied by the prettiest and most lustrous of smiles, her lips gently pursing and slightly pouting.

'You know, I honestly think you're trying to escape from me,' she said, 'aren't you?'

'Oh! no, no, no.'

'Tired of my company.'

'Oh! no, no, no. Dear no.'

'Go if you want to. Hate to hold anybody against their will. Hate to. Especially you. With everybody after you.'

'It's just that I find it a bit hot – I mean, there's no air –'

'Let's find somewhere cooler then. Shall we? The woods?'

The Captain hesitated about the woods. He sensed in the woods a trap far worse than the stairs. With what he hoped was an offhand gesture he swept a hand across his moustache and opened his mouth to say something even more trivial than usual when she said:

'I know. I've got the nicest, coolest idea. The river. What about the river?'

'You mean swimming?'

'No, a boat. The Larkins have a boat. In fact, two. Do you row?'

Proud of this unexpected chance to reveal another side of himself, the Captain confessed that in fact he rowed rather well. But would Larkin mind?

'Oh! Lord, no. He got the boat all ready to take me himself before lunch but Ma called us in to eat. Oh! he won't mind our taking the boat.' She laughed with a beautiful deep contralto. 'He'll just be jealous of you.'

'Will he, by Jove?'

Across the meadow lying between junk-yard and river Jasmine Brown walked deep in buttercups, her half-naked breasts thrust forward like those of some stately figurehead, her bare feet bright yellow with pollen. Once she started running and the rear view of her, its curves firmly marked and yet quivering, was of so sensational a substance that the Captain actually halted in his stride. It was only when she suddenly stopped, turned and held out both arms to him as if he were the only person in the world that he was prompted to move again.

'Come on! Race you, Colonel, race you!'

In puffing pursuit, the Captain caught her up at the boat-house, where Pop's new golden row-boat lay side by side with its sister status symbol, the motor-boat, both resplendent with purple and yellow cushions.

Stripping off his jacket, the Captain told himself that this was really where he came in. He could really show some prowess now. With a strong arm he held the boat steady while Jasmine Brown climbed in. Her body, if sensational on the stairs, was now positively volcanic in its unsparing beauty as she lay full length, every curve and contour tautly revealed, on the brilliant cushions.

The Captain got into the boat too and rowed out into a stream just wide enough at that point to take his oars. The surface of the river, broken here and there by small islands of water lilies just coming into flower, was sometimes rippled by the gentlest breath of air. Now and then a leaf of yellow flag-iris twisted on the banks. A swallow or two occasionally came low over the stream, piercing the air with voices of needling excitement, but these, except for the level slip of the oars, were the only sounds.

By Jove, this, the Captain let it be known, was rather good.

'Absolute heaven.' Jasmine Brown, cool but radiating that same sensational heat of which Pop had taken such good notice, stared up at him with eyes that seemed to fill with a deep entrancement of wonder. 'You row beautifully.'

The Captain was sure that he did.

'After all I used to stroke –'

'Stroke?'

The single word seemed to be caress, flattery and invitation all in one. She raised her arms and clasped them together behind a head almost too beautiful in its frame of black hair. This gesture too seemed to be open invitation but the Captain made no sign of accepting it, and merely made steady progress with the oars. Like a cat snuggling down to half-sleep she then nestled even lower into the cushions, the soft underparts of her arms quivering, and held him with blissful, predatory, drowsy eyes.

'Come on. Do I have to drag you down here? You bring a girl out in a boat and then do absolutely nothing about it.'

The Captain, though half-terrified, could resist no longer. With nervous hands he shipped oars, stood up precariously and then half-sat, half-knelt on the cushions beside her.

The boat rocked. At the same moment Jasmine Brown seized him in an embrace as fierce and all-enfolding as that of a lioness overcoming its prey. Her splendid frame encompassed him completely. The boat rocked again and the Captain, half-suffocated, uttered a stifled shout. Her lips smothered his own with a passion so well simulated that he actually found himself struggling against it and then the boat rocked a third time, this time with violence, dangerously.

A moment later the Captain, flamboyant as a tailor's dummy, flopped helplessly overboard and Jasmine Brown fell with him, shrieking with splendid laughter.

Ma's casual suggestion about telephoning the Captain's wife for tea had made Pop curiously uneasy, almost upset. He was haunted yet again by the unhappy, grovelling figure among its weeds. In moments of anything like unhappiness he always confided in Ma and now he walked round the pool to where, in her unruffled way, she was busy at her canvas under the black umbrella.

'Ma, you said summat about asking Mrs Broadbent over to tea. Why don't we? I got an idea that woman don't very often get off the hook.'

Nice idea, Ma thought. Pop had better go and get her on the blower.

'They're not on the blower. It would mean I'd have to fetch her. Think I should? It makes me miserable to –'

Certainly, Ma thought. She understood his feelings perfectly. He had so often described that moment or two of wretchedness on the path.

'Take her out of herself a bit. You go and I'll lay a bit of quiet tea in the sitting-room. She'll very likely find it a bit noisy out here with all the kids shouting and rushing around. By the way, where's Jasmine? Haven't seen her lately.'

He hadn't the faintest, Pop said.

'Funny,' Ma said, 'that you shouldn't know after the way you've had her in your inside pocket all day.'

To this Pop could conjure no sort of answer and merely walked airily away, his habitual jauntiness back, whistling.

Some time later Mrs Broadbent, astonishingly rescued from the all-embalming boredom of Sunday afternoon, sat in the sitting-room nibbling like a mouse released from a dark box at cucumber sandwiches, chocolate biscuits and Ma's delightful maids-of-honour. An infinite shyness kept her silent for the greater part of the time. Now and then Pop, in his customary way, made springy, jovial attempts to enliven the proceedings but he noticed that she never laughed at all.

Her shy nibblings reminded him greatly of the two little Barnwell sisters, Effie and Edna, who also sometimes came to tea, their little elderly yellow faces so crowded with freckles that they looked perpetually as if stung by bees. But in their case hunger, so richly satisfied as it always was in the Larkin household, made them chatter brightly and even inspired in them, at times, fits of immoderate giggles. It was the same with Edith Pilchester; food and drink went rapidly to her head, making her tipsy with happiness and even, as Pop had often noted, a little bit sexy. He expected it was really some urge in all of them, as he frequently told Ma, that hadn't yet been satisfied.

But in Mrs Broadbent, he was sure, there was neither sex nor laughter; he doubted even if there was life apart from the mere mechanics of movement; and he was just about to reach the point of half-wishing that he'd let well alone and hadn't invited the poor woman over at all when Ma, looking out of the window, suddenly leapt up and very nearly dropped her tea-cup on the floor.

'Good Gawd Almighty,' she said, 'whatever in the name of Beelzebub has happened to the Colonel?'

Pop got casually to his feet with an air of indifferent surprise, as if the incident were, to him, totally unexpected.

'Got caught in a thunderstorm or somethink.'

The erstwhile flamboyant figure of the Captain, now dragging itself across the yard, looked like that of a ship-wrecked mariner washed up on some blighted shore.

Mrs Broadbent got slowly to her feet too and stared out of the window. She stared for perhaps some fifteen seconds or so before the room was filled with the strangest of sounds, her loud uncontrolled cascades of laughter. It was as if she had been rocked to near-hysteria by an explosion of sudden joy.

Fearful of some explosion in himself, Pop slid out of the room, to be met at the front door by Angela Snow who slipped her cool aristocratic hand in one of his.

'We didn't fail you?'

'Think everythink went perfick.'

'Good. Absolutely splendid. Well, that's one christening over, dear man. And without benefit of clergy.'

Pop laughed, kissing her with mischievous lightness on one ear, in silent thanks.

'By the way, Jasmine and I tossed up for it.'

'Did?'

'Yes: I won. But I put her in first. Hadn't you better go and find her?'

'Where do you think she is?'

'I rather fancy she's in the boat-house,' Angela Snow said, in that lovely drawling way of hers, 'waiting for a little thank-you.'

That night, sitting in bed, smoking his late cigar and watching Ma at the dressing-table, brushing her hair, Pop suddenly made a remark of casual profundity.

'Ma, I've been thinking.'

'Now steady.'

'No, serious. I mean about people, men and women.'

That was a tall one, Ma said. If he got started with that he'd be stuck with it all night. There was no end to that one.

'They're funny,' Pop said. 'People, I mean.'

Not, he hastened to assure her, people like him and Ma. Or even Angela or Jasmine. Not normal people. No, the others: some of 'em anyway. The Colonel for instance. And Mrs Broadbent.

'How do you work that one out, Ma?'

Ma said she was blessed if she knew.

'Me, neither. You'd want Solomon on that one. By the way what did you think of Jasmine?'

'Girl after my own heart.'

'Good. Thought you'd like her. Well made, too, don't you think?'

'You should know. You were in the boat-house long enough with her before lunch today.'

'That was a sort of briefing, Ma, sort of dummy run,' Pop proceeded to explain blandly, with all his customary frankness. 'After all I'd got to get the idea into her head somehow.'

Dummy run? Ma wanted to know what on earth he was talking about. Dummy run? Idea? What idea?

'The Colonel's christening.'

Pop, laughing, started to explain about the Colonel and how Jasmine and Angela had tossed up for the privilege of performing the ceremony.

'Well, praise God from whom all blessings flow,' Ma said and burst out into one of her own uncontrollable fits of jellified laughter.

'Really, on the whole,' Pop said airily, 'I think it went orf perfick.'

Laughter, especially at night, always put Ma into the warmest and most magnanimous of moods and now she suddenly turned on him with a slow, engaging smile and said:

'You know something, Sid Larkin?'

'No, Ma. What?'

'I believe if I'd have married you,' Ma said, 'you'd have committed bigamy long ago.'

'More than likely,' Pop said with great cheerfulness, 'more than likely.'

· 6 ·

On a damp dull afternoon in mid-July – it was what Ma was accustomed
to call a wet day and no rain, or alternatively bad courting weather – Pop
drove the Rolls-Royce out of the junk-yard and, though using the contrapuntal horn with care and frequency, almost ran into the figure of his
old friend the Brigadier, walking dreamily in the mizzle on the road
outside. The open black umbrella he was carrying over his shoulder might
well have been borrowed from a scarecrow. One of his shoelaces, a brown
one as opposed to its fellow, which was black, was undone and flapping
muddily about its canvas shoe. His once-cream trousers hung sack-like
about his spindly legs, the behind showing a patch of some thicker
material that might possibly have come from a bed quilt. It had a distinctly
raised pattern of flowers on it and, though once white, was now worn to
a sort of pied grey. But the Brigadier's crowning sartorial features were
new to Pop and made even him start with surprise. The first was a pale
pink rowing blazer, of a sort of crushed raspberry shade, with a white and
black silk badge on the pocket, and the second a small and very ancient
rowing cap in a rather deeper shade.

'What cheer, General!' Pop said, laughing with most friendly robust-
ness, 'must look where you're going, else we'll be having cold mincemeat
for supper.'

Pop's choice of cold mincemeat as opposed to hot struck the Brigadier as a singularly apt one, if rather macabre, and woke on his face
the driest of smiles. He readily confessed he'd been day-dreaming and Pop
said:

'Well, hop in, General. It's no day for walking.'

The Brigadier coughed abruptly and thanked Larkin all the same but
said he really preferred the exercise. It helped him, among other things,
to let off steam.

'About what? Summat bothering you?'

'It's that damned common market all the time. I frequently feel my blood
boil.'

'Don't like it much, eh?'

'I call it a damned unholy alliance. Damned unholy, I tell you. Always loathed the French anyway.'

In reply Pop barked out a loud and cordial ''Ear 'ear!', the immediate result of which was that the Brigadier snapped down the umbrella, opened the Rolls's monogrammed front door and got inside the car.

'Changed my mind after all.' He struck Pop a sharp genial blow on the knee. 'Man after my own heart, Larkin. Man after my own heart. Where are you bound?'

Down to the coast, Pop told him. He'd got to see a man about a little deal in cats' meat. And while he was there he'd got to get Ma a pint of whelks and winkles. Did the General care for whelks or winkles?

'Not awfully, I'm afraid.'

'Ma adores 'em. Well, anyway, come for the ride. I was thinking of picking up Edith and giving her a spin. Just for company. I get the pip without company.'

'Ah! the Pilch, eh? Haven't seen her for a long time.'

Pop laughed with great vigour, at the same time letting in the clutch, so that the Rolls moved smoothly away. It always made him laugh when the General, in his drier moods, called Edith Pilchester the Pilch, though he could never tell him why. He would have to get Ma to explain to him what a pilch was one day. He didn't suppose the General knew.

'Doesn't she know you're calling? She'll probably be spinning wool or something. Or deeply engaged in making mead.'

Pop, laughing again, said if he knew Edith she'd come even if she'd broken both legs.

'The last time I saw her she was in a state of some excitement about a yellow flower she was growing,' the Brigadier said. 'Going to make woad with it, she fancied. That blue stuff, you remember, that the Ancient Britons painted their bodies with.'

'Good Gawd.'

A fantastic vision of Edith Pilchester, unclothed and painted blue, floated before Pop's eyes, leaving him otherwise speechless. You never knew what women were going to be up to next. It bowled you flat.

'Cats' meat?' the Brigadier said suddenly. 'I wasn't aware you were in the meat trade.'

Tinned, Pop explained. Big call for it nowadays. West Indians ate most of it. It was cheaper than the butcher's.

'Good grief,' the Brigadier said, feeling very faintly sick. 'What will one hear of next?'

Five minutes later Pop was poking his head round the back door of Edith

Pilchester's low-pitched thatched cottage, Bonny Banks, even more gim-crack in its pseudo antiquity than Lady Violet's bungalow, and calling was anybody at home? Something like an alarmed sigh instantly answered him from one of the tiny bedroom windows, from which the head of Edith Pilchester popped out like a jack-in-the-box a moment later, her shoulders hastily covered with a shawl of her own knitting and dyeing. This was of rather an indeterminate toad-like hue and once again Pop was for a moment or two utterly silenced by the thought of what Edith might possibly look like if dipped blue all over.

'Oh! my goodness, Mr Larkin, you caught me unawares! My dear! –'

'Thought you might like to come for a trip in the Rolls. Going as far as the sea.'

'Oh! but – my dear, I'm simply not ready – it's absolutely ghastly –'

'No hurry, Edith. I can wait. I got the General with me. I'll go and talk to him.'

'Oh! will you? I'll just slip something on – I'll be down the *instant* I'm ready.' Miss Pilchester disappeared swiftly from the window, only to come back a moment later to ask with piping fervour: '*Will* I need an umbrella? *Will* I, do you think?'

'No,' Pop said, with that bland innocence of his that might have concealed anything, winking at the same time. 'I'll keep you dry.'

'Awful man.' A sort of indrawn giggle fell from her lips and Pop found himself momentarily transfixed with a toothy, dedicated smile. 'You *do* put meanings into –'

An interval of a bare five or six minutes was enough to bring Edith Pilchester stumbling from the cottage in partly dishevelled haste. The slight mizzling rain had ceased by now and a burst of light wind seemed to catch her half way down the garden path and fairly blow her into the Rolls, the front door of which the Brigadier was holding open for her with a combination of his best military and rowing *politesse*. He actually raised the rowing cap as she half-crawled, half-fell into the car, giving her at the same time a dry, charming smile and saying cryptically:

'Dear lady. I trust I see you well?'

In tones of loud and hearty excitement Miss Pilchester, who had for-gotten to close the door, confessed that she literally didn't know. It was all such a *thrill*, so absolutely *unexpected*. Had she been an *age*? If only she'd been able to collect her thoughts a little better, she thought wildly, she might even have been a teeny bit longer, so that perhaps Pop might have been forced to search for her, and then – Well, it was terrifically nice of him to come anyway.

'I'll just shut the door, Edith. Otherwise we'll be having you in the cold mincemeat lark too.'

'Extraordinary thought!'

Pop, leaning across her and lightly brushing against the cabbage-green suit of hairy sack-like material she was wearing, closed the quiet, heavy door of the Rolls. This sudden physical contact with him at a moment so early and unprepared sent a half rapturous quiver through her body, to be followed a second or two later by an almost cataclysmic palpitation as Pop deftly and with an accuracy born of long practice pressed one of her right suspender buttons. Heaven, she would dream of this, she knew, for days.

'All right, General? Don't mind sitting at the back? Have a doss-down if you feel like it.'

'Wouldn't dream of it. Feel as lively as a cricket.'

'Perfick. We'll get crackin' then.'

As the Rolls moved regally and smoothly away Edith Pilchester felt lively as a cricket too. Another five minutes and she'd have been off to the post-office and she'd have missed it all. The thought was too absolutely ghastly.

On the luxurious dove-grey seat at the back the Brigadier started to say something and then realized that, hermetically sealed off as he was by the car's glass division, his voice couldn't be heard with anything like precision in the front. At this instant Pop barked down the speaking-tube:

'Use the tube, General, old man. Use the tube.'

Hanging on to a yellow silk cord with one hand and taking up the speaking tube with the other the Brigadier gave several dry, gruff coughs and then said:

'Larkin, my dear fellow, it was in my mind to ask you something.'

'Subscription or summat?'

'No. Merely that rumour has it that some character or other nearly got drowned at your place the other day.'

'Oh! that.' Pop laughed with crackling delight into the tube. 'Just a bit o' sport, that's all.'

'Not serious then?'

'Well it was for *him*. The rest of us had a good giggle out of it.'

'It was that ghastly man, Broadbent,' Miss Pilchester said, with loud, sudden and positively tigerish ferocity. 'Damn him. I sometimes feel like braining him myself. The brute terrorizes that little wife of his so that she's forgotten what talking is. He's made her into a crazy mute. He doesn't need

375

drowning. It's too good for him. He needs the fiery furnace. Slowly, the snob.'

The unexpected savagery of this outburst had Pop temporarily speechless. With his mouth wide open he simply couldn't think of a word to say. A rapid glance at Edith revealed that in indignation she had gone a remarkable bluish shade, so that for a moment Pop was half convinced she had been dipping herself in that Ancient Briton stuff, woad or whatever it was. He'd never heard a burst from Edith like it. It was what Ma would have called real primitive.

'Do I hear Edith sitting in judgement on somebody?'

'You do, an' all, General. Shook me to the nellies.'

'Indeed?' The Brigadier was about to express himself as unfamiliar with this particular expression when Edith, in a fresh but by no means as ferocious a burst, declared ah! but they didn't know her. There was a real positive demon inside her that was terrible, absolutely ghastly and terrible, when it got roused.

'Now and then I can't help it. It just pops out.'

'Good Gawd,' Pop said and heard the Brigadier, from the luxury of the back seat, echo the words as if in a soft amen.

'Moreover, he threatens to sue you.'

'Me?' Pop said, his customary laughing self again. 'Nothing to do wiv me. He just went on the river with a piece of crumpet.'

'A piece of what?' the Brigadier said.

'Crumpet. There she is,' Pop said, 'that's her,' and having taken a picture of Jasmine Brown from his inside pocket pushed back the glass division and handed it to the Brigadier.

In stupefied silence the Brigadier gazed for several minutes at the sensational lines of Jasmine Brown reclining in a white bikini against a dark rock by the sea. It was almost too much for his elderly frame to bear and he was momentarily sad in heart when Pop unthinkingly declared down the speaking tube:

'Friend of Angela's. Job to know which is more perfick, eh?'

In silence the Brigadier handed the picture back to Pop, who in turn handed it to Edith, who also had nothing to say. Something told her that it wasn't for nothing that Pop carried this gripping picture of all-but-naked flesh about with him and it actually seemed for a moment as if the demon in her snorted its indignation at her folly and Pop's own particular brand of faithlessness but at that strategic moment Pop elected to run a caressive hand across her middle thigh, so that her tremulous veins ran with forgiving and ecstatic light again.

Two minutes later Pop was bringing the Rolls to an unexpected halt
outside a small wayside whitewashed pub called The Lamb and Flag. In the
grass paddock behind the pub, between rows of dark elms, a little roundabout, a coconut shy, a pair of swings, a dart stall and a shooting gallery
lit up with yellow, scarlet, green and blue the damp, dull July afternoon.

'Strike me if I don't think it's my old pal Fruity,' Pop said. 'Old Fruity
Pears.'

'How's the swings and roundabouts? How's the fair lark, Fruity?'

'If it ain't me ole china Sid. If it ain't me ole china.'

The fragile monkey-faced figure in charge of the coconut shy, dressed
in black trousers, a cream polo-necked sweater and a small old-fashioned
black bowler, needed only a towel slung over his shoulder to be a second
out of some fairground boxing ring. His toothless mouth shot open like a
trap. His eyes, completely colourless, watered suddenly with surprise,
disbelief and pleasure. His scrawny, yellow fingers gripped Pop's hand like
eager talons.

'Must be ten year. Must be ten year.'

His voice was cracked. Pop, pump-handling with friendly vigour, asked
again how the fair lark was, the swings and roundabouts and all that and
then, taking a swift look about him, knew there wasn't much need for an
answer. Four children on the roundabout, where the fat little figure of Mrs
Fruity was turning the handle, and two youths with heavy side-burns and
stiff crew cuts, in black sweaters, drain-pipe jeans and winkle-pickers,
made up the entire custom of the afternoon. There wasn't even any music
coming from the roundabout, which went round and round in silent
procession, cockerels following little racing cars, peacocks after buses, like
a ghostly quaking wheel.

'Finished. Busted. Thinking of turning it in. Can't compete with telly.
Some days we don't take half a quid.'

Another little bit of old England gone, Pop thought, and in an immense
effort to be cheerful slapped the fragile Fruity on the back, a blow which
made him quiver like a straw in the wind, and then introduced his friends
Miss Pilchester and the Brigadier.

Fruity, gazing at the pinkly arrayed figure of the Brigadier, said something like 'Strewth!' under his breath and silently wondered if he hadn't
better start up a freak tent again, with two-headed dogs and a bearded
lady, like the one he'd had twenty years ago. He'd never seen anybody
quite like the Brigadier before.

'Well, we'll have to see if we can't boost the till up a bit, shan't we?

What'll it be, General? Roundabouts, coconuts, swings or what? Don't have no music on the roundabout, Fruity. How's that?'

'The old organ's busted and I can't git it mended. Couldn't afford it even if I could.'

'Edith, what about you? Try the lot? Go on the swings with me? What'll you start with?'

'I should absolutely adore to knock a coconut.'

'Coconuts it is an' all then. Give us five bobs' worth o' balls, Fruity old man.'

Over at the swings the two youths in winkle-pickers were larking with the boats, swinging them at crazy angles. One boat splintered against an upright and Fruity paused at the business of handing out coconut balls to yell creakily for them to stop it and merely got a gesture of two stiff obscene fingers in reply.

'They was 'ere one day afore,' Fruity said. 'It was them what busted the old organ up. Didn't like the tunes it played. Not new enough, they said.'

'Ignore 'em,' Pop said. 'Only thing to do. Edith, your first throw.'

'The old organ cost me fifty quid when I bought it. Hi! cut that out, you young bastards! I tell you stop it, the pair of you!'

Laughing, the winkle-pickers crashed the boats again.

'Throw, Edith. Ignore 'em. Take no notice.'

With surprising force and inaccuracy Miss Pilchester hurled wooden balls at the coconuts. The Brigadier started throwing too, with no success at all and so vigorously at one attempt that his pink cap dropped off. Fruity picked it up for him, and staring at it with greater disbelief than ever, laid it on the crate of balls.

Pop also started throwing, with a mixture of athletic flourish and abandon, twice striking a coconut with such force that Edith Pilchester shrieked 'Splendid!' at top voice. Playfully, when the coconut didn't fall, Pop accused Fruity of having 'em stuck on with glue or summat and Fruity looked pained, more monkey-like than ever, and said he never went in for that sort of thing and Pop ought to know him better.

The balls were expended rapidly and Edith Pilchester cried with a sort of rapturous lack of hope that it was absolutely ghastly and that she'd never get one and it was the one thing she absolutely must have.

Pop started to call for another five bobs' worth of balls but his voice was smothered by a shattering crack of wood against wood from the direction of the swings as a boat, upended, twisted from its hooks and fell.

The alarm sent three children scurrying from the roundabouts. Fruity, his monkey face grey with rage, started running too. Pop held him back.

The Brigadier thought it prudent to pick up his umbrella and started to say something about 'Hadn't they better close ranks?' when the two winkle-pickers, suddenly tired of the swing-boats as of a broken toy, started sidling across the paddock.

'Keep throwing, Edith. Ignore 'em. You'll get one yet.'

Something in Edith Pilchester's normally rather loose and ungainly frame seemed to tighten up. She limbered herself to throw and did so with such accuracy that she actually struck a coconut fair and square. For a few seconds it wobbled but failed to fall and she cried out again in typical anguish that it was absolutely ghastly.

The winkle-pickers were now at the shooting gallery. The taller of the two, who sported a thin red boot-lace tie, picked up a rifle and started loading it. Fruity yelled again and over at the roundabout Mrs Fruity hustled the remaining children away.

'Put that bloody gun down! Put it down and git orf, I tell you. Put the bloody thing down!'

The winkle-picker with red boot-lace turned and with arrogant calm pointed the gun straight at Fruity. The horror of seeing a loaded gun pointed at someone so outraged every military instinct left alive in the Brigadier that he ripped out sternly, shaking his umbrella:

'By God, don't be a damn fool! Never point a gun, you idiot!'

The tallest winkle-picker slung the gun over his shoulder, holding it by the barrel. Together the two of them sidled over to the coconuts.

'Everybody's got big mouths round here. What's all the shouting for? Everybody shouts.'

Pop turned his back and threw two balls with calm and accuracy at the coconuts.

'Keep throwing, Edith. We'll get one yet.'

'So the lady wants a coconut, does she?'

The Brigadier was pale. He thought the situation sticky. It mightn't be so bad for himself and Pop but he feared for Edith and said:

'Now look here, you fellows –'

'Belt up, Tweedledum.'

'Now, one moment –'

'So the lady wants a coconut, does she? So the lady shall have a coconut. Give the lady a coconut.'

Nobody moved.

'I said give the lady a coconut, grandad. You 'eard.'

Again nobody moved and again something seemed to tighten up in Edith Pilchester.

'All right, if grandad won't give the lady a coconut somebody else'll 'ave to.' In two lazy strides the taller winkle-picker was over by the pile of coconuts. He picked one up. He spun it in the air, turned and thrust it into Edith Pilchester's hands. 'In fact two coconuts. The lady shall 'ave two coconuts.'

He picked up another, put that into Edith Pilchester's hands too and said:

'Everybody 'appy now? We want everybody to be 'appy. Everybody 'appy? No, grandad don't look very 'appy. Why you not 'appy, grandad?'

'You leave my bloody gear alone!'

'Nobody's not touching no gear. Nobody's not touching nothing. Not touching nothing, are we, Jed?'

Jed said no, nobody wasn't touching nothing.

'I ought to bust your clock in!' Fruity said, 'you ignorant bastard.'

'You called me that once already, grandad, but not no more.'

The butt of the rifle made a short swinging stab through the air. It struck the left side of Fruity's monkey face just behind the ear. Without a cry he made an almost trance-like fall over the pile of coconuts, pouring blood.

Pop, not often enraged, turned with fury, only to find the shorter of the two winkle-pickers, Jed, pointing an open razor straight at the pit of his stomach.

'Go on, stick it in. I'll just bleed shandy.'

'No funny business. Back over there. Go on, back.'

The razor made sinister bright passes at the air and Pop backed seven or eight paces away from the coconut shy. Nobody said a word and the dull damp afternoon seemed curiously dead until suddenly a cataclysmic fury broke out in the form of the demon rising out of Edith Pilchester.

With an accuracy born of pure rage she hurled a coconut. It struck the shorter winkle-picker dead in the small of the back. His surprise was not merely infinite. It paralysed him where he stood. His fingers stiffened open with shock and he dropped the razor.

Pop, stooping to pick it up, was confronted by the extraordinary spectacle of Edith Pilchester running amok or going berserk or whatever it was they called it. He'd never seen anything like it. The demon was in full cry. A second coconut struck the shorter winkle-picker in precisely the same place as the first. The thud of it sickened the air and he crumpled slowly to his knees with a sort of gulping tender sigh.

A moment later Edith Pilchester started madly hurling coconut balls in all directions. Pop, having now picked up the razor and turning just in time to see the red-tie winkle-picker in sharp retreat, found himself in a shower of wooden rain. Balls were falling wildly all about him and one, straight as an arrow, hit him full in the left eye, as plumb as could be.

Half-blind but undaunted he tore after the retreating winkle-picker. He caught him by the top scruff of his crew cut with one hand and with the nimblest of gestures slit the razor through the thin leather belt with the other. The slow resulting fall of the trousers half way to his knees brought from Edith Pilchester a low howl, which in turn rose to a scream and finally to a great burst of demoniac laughter.

The Brigadier, helping Mrs Fruity to staunch Fruity's blood with a handkerchief, paused to utter cryptic congratulations.

'Well played, Edith, good show. Stout fellow, Larkin.'

Edith, coming out of a sort of mad trance, could only stare at Pop's face and howl again. My dear, how in heaven's name had she come to do anything so absolutely ghastly? Pop, in turn, felt momentarily a bit cockeyed and started to walk round in odd circles. The eye was going to be a beauty.

It was enough to make you die laughing, though, in a way, he thought. He'd never seen anything like it. It was almost worth a shiner to see Edith like that. It really made you wonder what was inside people and suddenly he actually began laughing and said:

'Well, we've had the winkle-pickers but somehow I don't think Ma'll get her whelks and winkles now. We'd better get old Fruity to a doctor.'

Back at home, Ma looked with remarkably dispassionate interest at the eye, now darkening beautifully, and asked what happened to the other fellow?

'It was a woman.'

'Oh? Well, I'm always telling you how you'll end up.'

Pop proceeded to explain, with an almost light brevity, that it had, in fact, been Edith.

'Oh? Went too far for once?'

'No. Nothing like that. She hit me with a coconut ball.'

At this Ma laughed so much that she couldn't get her breath for several minutes and had to be thumped hard on the back by Pop, just as if she'd swallowed a fish-bone. For a time Pop seriously thought she was going to have one of her turns.

When she had calmed herself again and dried her eyes Pop apologized about the whelks and winkles but said that after all he and Edith and the Brigadier had really been very busy with other things. Ma said it didn't matter a bit: she'd make do with a drop of champagne and smoked salmon instead.

*

381

Coming home the following evening from visiting Fruity in hospital, where he had taken him a few modest comforts such as grapes, strawberries, cherries, half a pound of tobacco, a bottle of whisky and a tin of butterballs, Pop kissed Ma in prolonged and passionate greeting, as if he hadn't seen her for a month or so, and then said, laughing, that he had a big surprise for her. Could she guess what?

'How many guesses?'

'Three.'

'Well, I'll start with women.'

Rather to Ma's surprise – though she never really experienced any very deep or protracted surprise at anything Pop said or did – Pop said no, it wasn't wimmin.

'Funny. By the way your eye's come up lovely.' There was something peculiarly funny about the eye; she very nearly collapsed every time she looked at it. 'Hurt much? Shall I put a bit more steak on it?'

No, it was a waste of good steak, Pop thought. Next guess?

'Not been drowning anybody again?'

Pop said no and what was more he'd never drowned anybody anyway.

'Charley says it was a good job too. He says it's what's called being an accessory before the fact.'

'Never? Accessory, what's that? Blimey. One more guess.'

Ma, laughing warmly, said she hoped it hadn't got anything to do with any more Regency pots? and Pop said no, it wasn't that either.

'Well, go on then. You'd better make a clean breast of it straight away.'

Pop, who by this time had lit up one of his Havanas, blew exquisite smoke, looking exceptionally pleased with himself. He looked what Ma called extra cockatooish, almost like he sometimes did just before he got half-whistled, so that she could only guess he must have brought off some very nice deal.

'No, as a matter of fact, Ma,' he said, 'I just bought a fair.'

'Oh! really? A fair? What sort? Roundabouts and that?'

'Swings, coconut shy, shooting gallery, one roundabout and a dart stall.'

'Oh! really?' Ma said. 'Sounds very nice. Where'd you pick that up?'

Pop went on to explain about Fruity: how the telly and all that had pretty nigh ruined Fruity and how, what with one thing and another, getting old and teddy boys playing him up and now the blow on the conk, he felt he couldn't carry on. Had to sell out.

'Felt I had to make it up to him somehow. Might never have happened if me and Edith and the General hadn't been there. After all it practically all started with Edith and her coconuts. By the way the doctor says if Fruity hadn't been wearing his bowler he'd have been in Kingdom Come.'

'Makes you sick.'

'Edith's looking a bit pale round the gills an' all too today. Says she can't understand it. Can't think what got into her. I told her it was the Ancient Briton coming out in her.'

Oh? Ma said, unperturbed by this inconsequential reference to the distant Britannic past, how did he account for that then?

'Sort of throw-back,' Pop said. 'She's been making woad or something. The General told me.'

Woad? Ma said. Something to drink wasn't it?

'No, that's mead,' Pop said. 'This woad stuff was what the Ancient Britons painted their bodies with. She's going to dye wool with it. Blue, it is.'

Really, Ma said. Still, they did funny things in those days, though she supposed it wasn't all that different, when you came to think of it, from rubbing yourself with sun-tan lotion and all that.

'Suppose not,' Pop said.

'By the way, who do you think you're going to sell this fair to?'

Pop, looking mildly pained at this question, said:

'Sell it, Ma? Sell it?'

'Course. Got to hock it to somebody, haven't you?'

'Not going to hock it, Ma. No fear. Going to keep it. For myself. For the kids. For us.'

'Us? Bit on the big side, don't you think?'

Pop's voice immediately took on that special tone of velvet fervour he reserved for more eloquent soliloquies on his beloved countryside, its nightingales and blackbirds, bluebells and primroses, hay-time and high summer; and above all his beloved England.

It was, he went on to explain to Ma, – the fair, he was talking about – a little bit of old England. He wanted to save it for himself. Very like, in a few years, you wouldn't see no more fairs, like Fruity's, in little paddocks, behind little pubs. They would all be gone, like harvest home and may-poles and all that. The telly would have killed 'em all like it killed every-thing. Pop was getting tired of telly. They were all going boss-eyed, watching telly. What was on tonight anyway?

Ma said she thought there was nothing on worth watching at all. It was all a load of rubbish, like old Monty talking about winning the battle of Agincourt.

'Got the wrong battle, haven't you, Ma?' After all they'd got to be fair to old Monty. They'd named a son after him.

'Well, they're all the same,' Ma said. 'Battles. Not a pin to choose between 'em. They make you tired.'

'Going back to the fair,' Pop said. 'It might sound sentimental and all that to some folks. But that's how it is. That's how I feel.'

'Where are you going to put it anyway?'

In the paddock, he told her. He was going to have the old busted organ repaired too, so that they could have a bit of gay music. He'd already asked Fruity what sort of tunes the old thing played and Fruity remembered there was *Waiting For the Robert E. Lee*, *Lily of Laguna* and several others, including that waltz, *Gold and Silver*. Did Ma remember that waltz? They'd danced to it a good few times in the old days.

'And I'll tell you what else I thought.'

'Yes?' Ma said. 'What was that?'

'I thought we'd open it for the christening. I thought it would be just the job for the christening.'

Nicest idea he'd had yet, Ma said. Like Mariette often said, he really did have the nicest ideas sometimes. The fair would make it a real good day. Oh! and that reminded her of something. Was he aware that the christening was only ten days away and what had he done, if anything, about thinking up a nice present each for the two godmothers? Of course she hadn't much experience of christenings but she thought it would be nice. She thought it was probably the done thing.

'Present? Such as what?'

'Something personal, I should think. Nice set of underclothes. Nice nightie. A nice nightie's never in the way.'

Pop started to roar with laughter and Ma said:

'Never mind. You know what I mean. And there's another thing. Don't forget you've got to go and meet Mademoiselle Dupont off the boat.'

Pop said he hadn't forgotten; he had, in fact, given a lot of thought to that.

'Serious, I hope?' Ma said. 'She's come a long way and we want to make a good impression. After all it's her first visit to England and we don't want her to go away with any wrong ideas. Even if she is French.'

Pop cordially agreed. They most certainly didn't. They had to make a good impression and, as he got up to stroll in the garden and finish his cigar and listen for a few moments to a late nightingale pouring song on the cool summer air, he assured Ma that they most certainly would.

'After all, Froggies are human, I suppose, Ma. In a way.'

· 7 ·

Mademoiselle Dupont stood in the sunshine on the deck of the cross-channel steamer and gazed at the cream-white cliffs of Dover, crowned by their gigantic grey brooding lion of a castle, with a mixture of strange and conflicting emotions. Normally a person of a temperament tautly if not highly strung, she had experienced all day an apprehension verging on fear, a happiness at times very near to sickness and a sense of wondering expectancy so irrational that several times she had desperately wished she could turn and go back to France again. After all it wasn't every day that you went to stay in the house of an English milord.

Deeply binding these feelings into a strong physical tension was a sense of almost primitive suspicion. Not a suspicion of anything or anybody in particular: merely a deep-rooted, peasant-blooded suspicion of being abroad, in a strange new country. For this reason she had put all her money into a suède leather belt which she had buckled under her corsets, had taken half a dozen aspirins against the dreaded likelihood of *mal de mer* and the paralysing excitements of travelling in general and had put on two sets of underclothes and two thick woollen jumpers against England's notorious, crippling, even killing dampness. A deep superstition that she would be inevitably accosted by strange men or have her pockets picked had also made her put on dark glasses; by some illogical process of thought she felt she wouldn't be seen so easily that way. The result of all this was that her stomach, even though the sea was soft and calm, seemed to have risen to the level of her too tightly corseted bust and was full of an astringent, contracting bile.

These insurances against fate and the half-dread of England's shores were, however, small against the greater precaution she had taken with luggage. Five suitcases and a giant blue-and-green plaid hold-all contained among other things twenty dresses, six jumpers, eight nightdresses, a great assortment of lingerie and stockings, several pairs of heavy woollen bed socks, several scarves, three overcoats, two mackintoshes, seven hats and four bottles of cough cure.

It was her unshakeable conviction that the social and domestic life in the house of an English milord would inevitably take her in a bewildering, paralysing grip. Every eventuality, from cocktail parties to dinners, tennis parties to race-meetings, tea parties to gymkhanas, not to speak of the christening itself, had had to be covered. And she had, she thought, covered them all.

After the boat had docked she found herself a porter, who wanted to know if she would be travelling by car or by train.

'By car,' she told him. 'And it will be a Rolls-Royce.'

'Very good, lady. Meet you outside the station.'

The porter's words merely served as yet another cause for misgiving. She suddenly experienced the fear that Milord Larkin wouldn't be there to meet her. Something would have gone wrong. She would find herself deserted, her day in ruins.

Things were even worse when a customs officer took a not unsuspicious view of a Frenchwoman with five large suitcases and an even larger hold-all and it was nearly half an hour before she found herself outside the station, hot and flustered in her overweight woollens, looking for the Rolls.

To her intensely emotional relief it was there. She nearly wept. Pop too was there and with him someone who, dressed as he was in a pink jacket and small pink peaked cap, she could only think was some kind of old retainer, a footman or something of that sort.

'Ah! bon jour, Mademoiselle!' Pop, advancing cheerily into waves of lily-of-the-valley perfume, kissed her with gallantry on both cheeks, having been strictly warned by Ma not to kiss her on the lips in public, as this would undoubtedly upset her. Kissing on the lips in public wasn't, she understood, quite the thing in France. Nor was he to call her froggy. 'Comment allez-vous? Had a good journey? Nice crossing?'

'Merveilleux, Monsieur Larkin,' she said, pronouncing Larkin in the French way and oh! how good it was to see him.

'This is the General,' Pop said, with another show of gallantry. 'And, General, this is Mademoiselle Dupont.'

The Brigadier, bowing with a certain military stiffness, expressed himself as delighted to meet her and held open the back door of the Rolls. The shining monograms seemed positively to wink in the sun. And odd though the elderly retainer's uniform was – she almost supposed it was some medieval survival or something of that sort – Mademoiselle Dupont nevertheless felt a wave of flattery that completely calmed the last of her fears until she suddenly remembered something.

'Quelle horreur, mes bagages! Where is my baggage?'

'All is well, dear lady,' the Brigadier said. 'All in the boot. All taken care of.'

With a final gulp of relief she sat back on the Rolls's luxurious cushions and the Brigadier, with a certain air of old-world circumspection, closed the door.

Pop decided that this was a good moment to have a mint-humbug. Ma didn't like smoking in the Rolls; it made it smell like a four-ale bar. Nevertheless Pop often felt he had to have something to chew on while driving and mint-humbugs were the answer.

'Mint-humbug, General?'

The Brigadier courteously declined the offer of a mint-humbug, at which Pop said:

'Perhaps Mademoiselle Dupont would like one. Mind asking her?'

The mint-humbugs were large, rather like big gold-striped snails, and sticky. Mademoiselle Dupont, when offered one by the elderly pink-uniformed retainer, could only think it strange. Perhaps it was some old English custom which it would have been discourteous to refuse?

When she had put the mint-humbug into her mouth, where it clashed with some awkwardness against the top plate of her false teeth, the Brigadier got into the front seat of the Rolls with Pop, who now made instant use of the speaking-tube.

'Well, Mademoiselle Dupont, this is England!' he called to her, as if this astonishing truth were in danger of being overlooked or something.

Mademoiselle Dupont, now completely tongue-tied by the mint-humbug, could only utter some unintelligible mumble in reply.

'Well, sit yourself back and make yourself comfortable now,' Pop called. 'We'll be home in half an hour.'

Ma, supremely anxious to make the best of impressions, had placed dark red and bright yellow roses in the silver flower vases at the back of the Rolls and these, rich and beautifully scented, gave an air of great aristocracy to the interior, almost a sense of royalty.

England, here urban, there pastoral, here downland, there a forest of television aerials, glided in its odd and entrancing mixture of scenes and styles past the windows of the Rolls. Every bit as anxious as Ma was to make the best of impressions, Pop now and then threw casual and concise information into the speaking-tube.

'See that hill? Used to be called Caesar's camp. Now turns out it was probably your bloke, William the Conqueror. Very old church just coming up. And a pub. Very old as well. The Saracen's Head. Something to do with the wars of the Roses.'

'The Holy Wars,' the Brigadier reminded him. 'The Crusades.'

Pop said he was very sorry. His mistake. Holy wars. Crusades. Very old anyway. He was supremely anxious to stress the fact that everything was very old and now inquired if Mademoiselle Dupont was familiar with the word pub? Pubs were a great feature of the land; Pop didn't know what they'd do without 'em.

Mademoiselle Dupont, rather despondently engaged in unequal struggle with the mint-humbug, which among other things was now making her perspire stickily, could only slobber, offering no word in reply, so that Pop confided to the Brigadier that he thought she'd gone deaf or something since he last saw her.

'More probably extreme shyness.'

'Could be. She's a bit the nervous type.'

'By no means unattractive.'

You were telling him, Pop said and promptly recalled not unpassionate moments in bedrooms at the Hôtel Beau Rivage which Mademoiselle Dupont kept at Saint Pierre le Port in Brittany, at the same time inviting the Brigadier to admire the cuff-links she had given him as a farewell present a few summers before.

'Bit in love with me. Had a job to hold her back once or twice.'

To this modest confession the Brigadier offered no comment and Pop said:

'Got her a present too. For the christening. Set of underwear. Ma thought it would be the thing. Black. Sort you can see through.'

'Not in danger of being misinterpreted?'

Pop said he didn't think so; she was old enough to know what was what by now.

Mademoiselle Dupont, who had now been able satisfactorily to disengage herself from the mint-humbug, which she had popped into her handkerchief and thence into her handbag, thought England looked remarkably pretty as she gazed from the windows of the Rolls. Oats were turning to a beautiful pinkish yellow in some fields; in others wheat bore on it a kind of bloom, almost blue, that heralded full ripening, and everywhere along the hedgerows wild roses and honeysuckle were in full, abundant bloom. She wasn't disappointed.

What she was really looking for, however, were the great houses. She had conjured up in her mind, over and over again, a picture of an English house such as that milord Larkin might live in. Rejecting the idea of moats, drawbridges, turreted walls and battlements as being perhaps almost too much to expect, she nevertheless knew it would be old, probably in that style of black-and-white timbering she had often seen in travel magazines, with tall, fine chimneys and black oak doors, and certainly full of calm, peace and dignity.

A few moments later the Rolls went past exactly such a house and all the thrill of long pent-up expectancy shot through her, actually making her cry out with emotion and excitement.

'Ah! that house! – ah! how really most beautiful!'

'Very old,' Pop assured her. 'Manor house. Very like Elizabethan.'

'*Ah! manoir. La Reine Elizabeth.*'

This, this was it, she thought; this was what she had come for.

'Home in about five minutes,' Pop called down the speaking-tube.

'Sounds extraordinarily excited all of a sudden,' the Brigadier said. 'Still, the Gallic temperament, I suppose. Odd how very different they are from us, especially when you think how much of their blood really runs in ours.'

'Well, foreign, ain't they?' Pop said, as if this explained, even if it didn't condone, all sins.

'By the way,' the Brigadier said, 'what time is the christening on Sunday?'

'Twelve o'clock. Midday. Afterwards you're all coming to lunch – you, Angela, Jasmine, Edith, Mademoiselle Dupont, the Rev. Candy, the lot. Going to have a marquee. Ma's going to lay it out with stacks of cold stuff. Plenty of champagne – three colours, ordinary, pink and red – and barrels o' beer and cider. And then when that lot's gone we'll open the fair. Got the old organ fixed – plays some very nice old tunes.'

'Clearly going to be quite an event.'

'It is an' all. First time me and Ma have had a wholesale christening anyway, I'll tell you. And probably the last. Still, you never know.'

A few minutes later Pop drew up the Rolls in the Larkin yard, riotously sounding first the town horn and then the country one to announce his arrival, the continuous contrapuntal clamour disturbing geese, turkeys, hens, guinea-fowl, pigs, ponies and all the rest and finally bringing Ma, Primrose and Victoria running from the house in greeting.

In the back of the Rolls Mademoiselle Dupont passed from a temporary state of paralysis into a dark bad dream. Her vision of calm antiquity, of dignity distilled from the aristocratic wine of centuries, disappeared under a mad, ruinous mess of muck-heaps, rusty iron, old oil drums, decaying tractors, nettles, haystacks, crumbling hovels and all the rest of Pop's perfick paradise. An earthquake could hardly have shattered her more; and as she finally bestirred herself, shocked and actually trembling, and saw the old pink-coated retainer holding open the door of the Rolls for her

– no, he couldn't possibly be an old retainer, after all, she thought, he could only be a member of some strange exclusive English club – she was desperately near to tears.

So much so that she hardly heard Pop's stentorian announcement of 'Well, 'ere we are!' and in confused desperation dived into her handbag for her handkerchief, which she pressed nervously to her face so that for the space of about a second the mint-humbug was stuck there.

A moment later it fell off and as if at this signal one of the twins switched on a gramophone at the open sitting-room window, where it blared out *La Marseillaise*, while the other switched on the lights in the suits of armour, so that the two vizored heads grinned out in blue, red and yellow welcome, convincing Mademoiselle Dupont that she was the centre of some awful, garish, medieval nightmare.

· 8 ·

While Mademoiselle Dupont, overwhelmed by the day's too-powerful emotions, retired to her room and there sobbed inconsolably into her pillow, Ma proceeded to remonstrate rather severely with Pop, particularly in the matter of the mint-humbug, actually calling him Sidney Larkin several times, which he was fully aware was the greatest expression of reprimand she could muster.

'If I thought you'd been larking about with the poor dear and upsetting her, Sidney Larkin, I wouldn't half give you what for with the chill off. I might even keep you *rationed* –'

'Good Gawd, Ma, steady. I never done a thing –'

'Well, I believe you. Thousands wouldn't. All I can say is you'll have to make it up to her. She's started off with a very bad impression and that was the last thing I wanted. You'll have to be very, very nice to her.'

'Yes, but –'

'Never mind yes, but. You go and be nice to her. Taken her present up yet? No? Well then, go and take it up. And then ask her to come down for a champagne cocktail. No Red Bulls or Moon-Rockets or that lark tonight. She wants her nerves calming. And you've got to keep sober too.'

'Good Gawd, Ma, have a bit of heart. You sound as if you'd got the pip.'

Shortly afterwards Pop proceeded to marshal all his forces of diplomatic gallantry. He found the set of lingerie, which Ma had wrapped in a box with mauve and silver paper round it and a big broad yellow ribbon, and took it upstairs. For a few moments he considered getting Primrose, whose French was pretty fair, to write some few well-chosen words of French greeting on a card, but Primrose was in the bathroom, shampooing her hair in readiness for Sunday, and he decided to give the idea the go-by.

'Mademoiselle Dupont?' With quite uncharacteristic discretion Pop tapped very gently on her bedroom door. 'Mademoiselle Dupont? May I come in?'

There was no answer.

'Mademoiselle? Have a word with you?'

Presently he heard her footsteps coming across the bedroom floor and the key turning in the lock. Then the door opened and a singularly depressed-looking Mademoiselle Dupont stood before him, eyes crimson and downcast. She had clearly been copiously weeping.

'Bear up now, bear up!' Pop said with the tenderest sort of cheerfulness. 'Mustn't turn the milk sour. Worse things happen at sea.'

Mademoiselle Dupont, who couldn't for the life of her understand what the sea had to do with her own particular distress, said nothing. Her lips merely trembled.

'*Pour vous,*' Pop said, holding out the gay silver, mauve and yellow parcel, '*avec amour.*'

'*Pas pour moi? Non?*'

'*Oui, oui.* Little present. From me. Sort of welcome to England.'

Pop, who was nowhere near as bi-lingual as Mademoiselle Dupont, now decided to give French the go-by too. It was a lot of fag really and he'd only get himself all tangled up. He was however astute enough to remember a French gesture and with something like courtliness he bent and kissed her hand. This was entirely the wrong thing to have done, as it turned out, because she instantly started weeping again, not very loudly, but with very low, heartfelt sobs.

Pop, half afraid that Ma would hear and start giving him the old salt and vinegar again, led her into the bedroom and shut the door. He had already decided that comfort had better take a physical form, with as few words as possible. With this in mind he put his arm round her waist and squeezed her several times, the pressure positive but not urgent – very far from the sort of thing that, in Ma's words, would bring her to the boil.

Eventually she sat on the bed, with the parcel on her knees, and started muttering muted words of apology and how it was all so strange. She supposed she had become ridiculously over-excited. Pop didn't say a word but merely continued with the physical treatment, which presently began to have some success, so that she actually dried her eyes and prepared to undo the parcel.

'You should not do this. I am very foolish. I do not deserve such things.'

'Well, open it anyway,' Pop said and was on the point of adding some quip about trying it on for size when he remembered Ma's strict injunctions and merely said:

'It's from me. A present for the christening.'

By no means tranquil yet, Mademoiselle Dupont untied the yellow ribbon with fingers that now and then jumped electrically. They jumped even more when she finally had the parcel open and picked out from among white layers of tissue paper a black bra, a black slip and a pair of black briefs so scanty and transparent that they might have been for the sole purpose of revealing more than they covered.

It was a moment of such transcendent and palpitating intimacy and altogether so utterly unexpected that she was completely speechless and went very red. It was also a moment that Pop could resist no longer, warnings from Ma or not, and he said, in the lowest and most engaging of whispers:

'Just about your size, eh?'

'Monsieur Larkin!'

In answer Pop kissed her with considerable pressure on her left ear, with the result that one of the long pearl drop earrings that she always wore to give her shortish figure the illusion of greater height fell off and slipped down the front of her dress, inside the bosom. Pop, though on the verge of executing some instantaneous rescue act, decided it was perhaps rather early days after all and instead merely invited her, in his best free and easy fashion, to stand up and shake the bag.

She stood up and shook herself several times, but without success. The tightness of her corset and the fact that she had been too *distraite* to take off her money belt stopped the earring on its journey, though not before the slide of the earring against her body had produced in her a strange, beautifully irritant sensation, so that she actually began laughing, with a real touch of merriment, and for the first time.

'No luck? Got lost on the way,' Pop said and wondered where.

She laughed again and slowly, in this way, became soothed and mollified. The nightmare of the afternoon receded. England seemed not so bad after all. Kindness and generosity were in the air.

She duly thanked Pop several times for the gift he had made and said she would try never to be so foolish again. In turn Pop led her to the bedroom window and showed her the second of the day's great surprises. There was, as it turned out, still a third to come but now, as she gazed down at the roundabout, the swings, the coconut shies, the dart stall and the big white marquee already erected in the paddock beyond the junkyard, she actually cried out with disbelief and delight. The English were a strange, strange people. One could only think that they were, in the nicest degree, mad. They wore strange pink coats and caps. They had fairs in their back gardens and suits of armour on their doorsteps. They were beyond all understanding.

'Notice the French flag?' Pop said.

Pop had caused a second tricolor to be run up on the marquee.

'*Ah! le tricolore!*'

'For you,' Pop said. 'In honour of you.'

Then suddenly some of her mystification cleared.

'Ah! it is a sort of *pardon*. Yes?'

No, Pop told her, it wasn't a *pardon*. It was just for the christening. He'd bought the fair specially.

She again marvelled at this, with another loud 'Ah!' and Pop said:

'Might as well make a proper do of it. After all there's a lot o' people to be christened.'

This was again beyond her understanding and everything now seemed stranger still.

When they finally went downstairs it was to find that the Rev. Candy had arrived. Mr Candy, who was in a state of bewilderment as great as that of Mademoiselle Dupont, perhaps greater, had called to acquaint himself with the Sunday order of battle. He hadn't been sleeping very well. The moon had been coming to its full. Night after night, restless-eyed, his mind jumping about like a kangaroo, he had grappled with the problem of the christening. It wasn't merely that there were so many people to be christened. It wasn't merely that he was certain he would forget more than half those long fanciful strings of Larkin names. It was the awful intimate familiarity of the thing. It was the discomforting nature of the Larkin beauty. It was having to baptize a schoolgirl who was practically, in body as well as intent, a grown woman. It was that dreadful moment when he would have to touch her head with water and she would torment him with those too dark, too luscious eyes.

'Mr Candy, this is Mademoiselle Dupont. From France. Going to be little Oscar's godmother. That's one of his names. Dupont.'

The Rev. Candy and Mademoiselle Dupont shook hands, each nervous. Mr Candy, his timidity now accentuated into further complexity by the unexpected presence of a strange Frenchwoman, then sat down at the table, where he had already spread out several sheets of black paper. Ma was sitting at the table too and now, after sympathetically inviting Mademoiselle Dupont to take an easy chair and at the same time giving Pop an old-fashioned look or two, as if suspicious that he hadn't been behaving very well, said:

'Pop, you get the champagne while me and Mr Candy work these names out.' She laughed broadly, shaking like a jelly. 'We don't want little Oscar christened Primrose or Victoria called Blenheim if it comes to that. Sometimes I half forget what some of 'em are called myself.'

Pop laughed too and said he was blowed if he didn't too, sometimes, and went to find the champagne, asking as he went:

'Red champagne, Ma, or ordinary?'

'Oh! ordinary,' Ma said. 'We had red last night.'

The mere mention of Primrose's name brought on the Rev. Candy a further attack of the acutest apprehension. But at least it was a relief that she wasn't there. He thanked heaven, at any rate, for that blessing. Nor was Mariette and he could only pray, tonight, that he wouldn't be called upon to give an opinion of her figure as seen in all its naked wonder by Ma.

'Now Mrs Larkin, in what order would you like the christening to be? I mean the babies first or –?'

Oh! it was all one to her, Ma said.

'Well, may I suggest we start with the babies, since the ceremony is bound to be rather protracted.'

All right, Ma said, they'd better start with Blenheim.

'And what are his full names to be?'

'John Marlborough Churchill Blenheim Charlton,' Ma said.

The Rev. Candy wrote this down with slow and dutiful care and put the figure one against it.

'And then Oscar. It is Oscar, isn't it?'

'Yes. Oscar Columbus Septimus Dupont Larkin.'

'Ah! Septimus the seventh. I must say you've shown the most extraordinary imagination in choosing your children's names.'

'Oh?' Ma said. 'It's not everybody who's got it.'

'I once knew a man named Decius. The tenth.'

'Get away with you,' Ma said. 'You'll be putting ideas into my head.'

Deep in further embarrassment the Rev. Candy wrote hard again, eventually pausing to say:

'And who next?'

Ma said she thought it ought to be the twins next. They were always as full of mischief as a pair of magpies and it'd be better to get 'em out of the way. They were fair devils sometimes. She wouldn't put anything past 'em – even in church.

Oh! Lord, Mr Candy thought. Great Heaven.

Pop now came back into the room with a tray of champagne cocktails, all jewelled with bubbles and invitingly golden, with half moons of orange floating about in them, and proceeded to offer them to Mademoiselle Dupont, Ma and Mr Candy.

Ma took hers with a vast sigh of satisfaction, as if she hadn't had a glass of anything for a month or more and an eager 'Ah! just what I wanted' and Mademoiselle Dupont hers with a certain restrained finesse, the little

395

finger of her right hand delicately extended. Amazement at the nature, content and doings of the Larkin house danced in her mind as quickly and effervescently as the bubbles rising in the glasses and she merely uttered a low bi-lingual phrase of thanks.

To Pop's infinite astonishment the Rev. Candy, on the other hand, refused the cocktail. Pop felt less hurt than concerned at this extraordinary behaviour and said:

'No? Sure? Not feeling dicky or anything?'

Mr Candy said No, it wasn't that he was feeling dicky or anything. It was merely – he was too shy to confess that he dreaded not being able to keep a clear head – it was simply that he wanted to be sure of getting all the names down correctly. Perhaps he might have a *soupçon* later?

Pop, who hadn't the faintest notion what a *soupçon* was, uttered a hearty 'Course, course,' and said he'd be mixing a new lot up in a minute or two.

'And the twins?' the Rev. Candy said. 'Might I now have the names of the twins?'

Ma took a deep gulp of champagne and said Oh! the twins were fairly easy. They almost had the same names.

'One's Zinnia June Florence Nightingale and the other's Petunia June Florence Nightingale.'

As he wrote down these names the Rev. Candy was struck by another awful thought. The twins were dreadfully, dangerously alike; they were like two eggs; he would never tell them apart.

'I wonder,' he said, 'will they be differently dressed? Or perhaps they have some distinguishing mark I could note? A mole or something?'

'Well,' Ma said, giving one of her deeper, fruitier chuckles, 'Zinnia's got a mole, but not where you'd be likely to see it in church.'

'Could they wear, perhaps, different dresses? Or different coloured hair ribbons?'

Ma said she thought hair ribbons. What about a scarlet one for Zinnia and a purple one for Petunia? Same colour as the flowers.

The Rev. Candy said he thought this would do and carefully wrote the colours down, at the same time saying to Ma that he profoundly hoped they wouldn't – he was going to say 'try anything on' – but hastily added the words 'make any confusion' instead.

'They'd better not,' Ma said, 'or I'll warm their bottoms. And in church too, if I have to.'

'That I fancy, is four,' the Rev. Candy said. 'Exactly how many more have we?'

'Four,' Ma said. 'We're half-way.'

'Like dipping a flock o' sheep,' Pop said. 'Eh?'

It was indeed, Mr Candy thought, and could only hope and trust that the Lord would make him a good shepherd.

Ma then proceeded to give him the full names of Montgomery and Mariette and while all this was going on Mademoiselle Dupont listened in a growing trance of disbelief and wonder. Half hypnotized as she was already by the vastness of the Larkin television set, the lavish and even grotesque nature of Pop's cocktail cabinet, all glass and chromium, in the form of a galleon, she now found herself facing the even more grotesque fact that, apparently, none of the considerable concourse of Larkins had ever received the blessing of holy baptism. This incredible and shocking fact had her, as Pop might have said, on the floor. It revived in her the strong belief that there was something outlandish about England – some-thing, well – the *mot juste* escaped her and she merely sipped champagne in silent reflection, at a loss even for a silent word.

'And who is next?' the Rev. Candy said.

'Me. I mean I'm next now but I don't want to be then. I'd like to be last. Somebody's got to be last and Victoria doesn't want to be.'

Mr Candy loked up to see that the vision he dreaded, that of Primrose, had suddenly entered the room. He quailed silently. The already too beautiful black hair, freshly shampooed and brushed, glowed deeply, with dark blue lights in it. Every separate hair seemed to vibrate; the entire mass of it was a thick and tremulous wave. It might have been washed in the juice of elderberries and anointed with oil of roses. There was a strong seductive fragrance in the air.

'Well, I suppose that's all right,' Ma said. 'Somebody's got to provide the finishing touch.'

That, the Rev. Candy thought, was what he feared and he was now dismayed to see Primrose sit down at the table, directly opposite him. He looked down hard at his papers and quailed once again at the precocious, womanly air of the girl in front of him. She was wearing a shortish mauve dressing-gown, quite open at the neck, and he could have sworn that she was wearing little, if anything, underneath it. The soft, sallow skin of her neck curved away into a taut bust uplifted and enlarged by the particular way she folded her arms underneath it. She ran her tongue over her lips, moistening them slightly, and fixed him with dark, still eyes.

'You don't mind if I'm last, Mr Candy, do you?'

'Oh! no, no, no, no, no.'

'You really don't?'

'No, no. Of course not. Of course.'

'I'm so glad.'

There was no other escape from this disquieting piece of temptation, apart from running like a hare, except to ask, as Mr Candy now did, in one of his squeakier moments:

'And may I – I – please – have your names?'

'I've got one more than all the rest,' Primrose said.

Oh! Lord, Mr Candy thought, it simply wasn't fair.

'Born bang in the middle o' spring,' Pop explained. 'Drop o' champagne now, Mr Candy? Beautiful spring too, it was an' all. Rich. Busted out all of a sudden. Everythink was sort of in calf all at once.'

Something in the Rev. Candy surrendered. He confessed weakly that he would indeed like a drop of champagne. The vision of the world in calf, in all its reproductive splendour, was too much. The champagne cocktail was like liquid manna to his soul.

'And what, please, are your names?'

As Primrose said each of her names in reply the exact expression in her eyes seemed to change by an infinitesimal fraction, but Mr Candy's own eyes were downcast, so that he was mercifully saved the sight of these variations on a seductive theme.

'Primrose, Violet, Anemone, Iris, Magnolia, Narcissa.'

At the name Narcissa Mr Candy was compelled to look up; and the open face of the purest white narcissus could hardly have faced him across the table with greater innocence. He quailed yet again before the sheer candour of its charm.

'Narcissa? Or Narcissus?'

'Narcissa.'

'Prettier than the "us" at the end, don't you think?' Ma said.

'Oh! much, much.'

'I think so,' Ma said and then proceeded to put to Mr Candy a devastating theory of her own. 'I always say she's like *all* her names. Primrose one minute, Violet the next, Narcissa the next – you can see it all in her eyes. She's several people in one, our Primrose. Of course I don't suppose you see it, but I do.'

Involuntarily Mr Candy looked up, only to be confronted not by the quick chameleon-like beauty of Primrose's eyes but by a fractional glimpse of her bare upper breast, firm and cool as a shell. It unnerved him even more than her eyes' flowery variations.

'I'm sorry, Mr Candy,' Ma suddenly said. 'Would you like something to eat? Bloater paste sandwich or something? Don't think we've got any smoked salmon left today.'

Mr Candy recoiled at the thought of a bloater paste sandwich. 'Thank you, but –'

'*Gentleman's Relish*, then?'

The sound of the words *Gentleman's Relish* in Mr Candy's ears was like nectar. It was an irresistible delight; he went for it bald headed.

'Well, if you really have it –'

'Course,' Ma said. 'We always have it. Never without it.'

'I'm afraid I can't afford it very often.'

'Good. I'll get some made up –'

'No,' Primrose said and there was something sinuous, not at all flower-like, in the way she slipped sideways out of her chair and got up from the table. 'Sit still. I'll get it. You've still got Victoria to do.'

Victoria, though really named after a plum, was blessed with other names that were queen-like. Ma was very much given to queens, especi-ally those, like Marie Antoinette, she could feel sorry for. Accordingly Victoria had also been named Adelaide, another unhappy one, Anne – after the queen who had had eighteen children without any of them surviving, a fact that tore something dreadful at Ma's heartstrings – and Cleopatra. Perhaps because of this burden Victoria was the quietish one of the family. She ate well and all that, as Ma said, but from time to time she was inclined, as Pop said, to go cluck, like hens did.

'Well,' Pop said, 'got the wholesale order wrote out? *En gross*, eh, Mademoiselle Dupont?'

'May I ask a question?' Mademoiselle Dupont said. 'Would the curé perhaps explain my part? I am not to be godmother to *all* the children?'

'Blimey no,' Pop said.

Mr Candy allayed Mademoiselle Dupont's fears by saying that there was nothing to worry about; it was all very simple; and only wished his own could be so easily tranquillized.

On the contrary, several minutes later, they were greatly stimulated, again by the entry of Primrose, carrying a dish of *Gentleman's Relish* sandwiches, nicely decorated by lettuce leaves and tomatoes. Mr Candy felt his mouth water; the evening perhaps hadn't turned out so badly after all. He seized one of the proffered sandwiches with alacrity and started munching, only to discover that in her absence Primrose had changed from her dressing gown into a canary yellow jumper and a green skirt. The jumper seemed at least a size and a half too small for her and produced an effect even more electrifying than the dressing-gown, so that he munched in tremulous preoccupation.

'What's all this going to cost me?' Pop suddenly said. He liked to be fair and square and above board in these matters. 'Fair old whack I suppose?'

'Oh! as I told you before, if you remember, there is no charge for baptism, Mr Larkin. Of course, if you'd like to make a small contribution to funds for –'

'Course, I remember now. Quid a head be all right?' Pop said with that bird-like swiftness so greatly characteristic of him. 'Make it ten,' and suddenly tugged from his pocket a roll of fivers far fatter than a polony sausage, peeling off two.

Mr Candy was overwhelmed. It was too much. The desperations of the earlier evening didn't merely disperse; they left in their place a warm, compensatory glow. It was a joy, almost an exulting one, to be blessed with a generosity so free and open-handed.

A moment later he was crushed again, this time by Ma, who said:

'What I did feel, though, Mr Candy, was this. There's such a big lot of us and it's such a piece-work order for you and all that I wondered if you wouldn't accept a little present from me?'

'Oh! my dear Mrs Larkin, there absolutely isn't any need –'

'It's just a little thing,' Ma said. 'One of my pictures.'

The Rev. Candy felt himself go very cold and very flaky all over, like a lizard. It was a subject he devoutly hoped would never come up again. With something like despair he fairly charged into a *Gentleman's Relish* sandwich, only to find himself on the verge of half-choking as Ma said:

'It's one I've done of Primrose. She posed specially.'

Posed? Mr Candy heard himself asking silently. Posed? The word had a dreadful significance. He could only remember Mariette.

'Mrs Larkin, you really needn't –'

'Oh! I hope you'll like it,' Ma said. 'Everybody seems to think it's a very good likeness.' Mr Candy quailed silently. He knew those likenesses. They could explode in your face, he thought, and once again felt himself go very cold and very flaky all over. 'There's a few points I don't like myself. Couldn't quite get the eyes. You know? Anyway, fetch it down, Primrose. It's in our bedroom.'

For the next few minutes Mr Candy wolfed at sandwiches of *Gentleman's Relish* as if they had something medicinal or antidotal about them. He accepted with neither a flicker nor syllable of protest another glass of champagne. He heard himself asking Mademoiselle Dupont in a voice distant and flaky too if she already knew England and heard her echo his own thoughts, rather enigmatically:

'I think there is much that is difficult to know in England.'

Mr Candy thought so too. He could now hear the footsteps of Primrose coming downstairs. They beat with doom at his heart. And then, a few moments later, she was in the room, carrying the picture and Ma was saying:

'Put it somewhere where there's a good light on it, dear. It wants a good light on it.'

Mr Candy actually shut his eyes and saw a vision, before opening them again, of the naked glories of Mariette as seen by Ma. A moment later he found himself looking at a picture of Primrose, in a green jumper and a black skirt, sitting in a chair and modestly holding a small basket of primroses painted in from memory by Ma.

The shock was so great that he felt his body go stiff. A portion of *Gentleman's Relish* sandwich fell from his fingers. He was suddenly aware of the floor coming up to meet him. He felt colder than ever and a moment later fell forward, as through a black tunnel, on his face, dropping at the feet of Mademoiselle Dupont, who cried '*Quelle horreur!*' and spilled a slow stream of champagne on his face in a final surprising act of baptism, while Ma wondered aloud but imperturbably whatever could have come over him all of a sudden.

· 9 ·

Ma woke in the night, disturbed by a strange feeling that someone or something was prowling about in the yard outside. She could hear nothing as definite as footsteps and might have let the whole thing slip from her mind as something no more serious than a wakeful turkey if it hadn't been that suddenly she was sure that she heard the clatter of an empty oil drum turning over.

She gave Pop a quick nudge with her elbow in the middle of the back and Pop, who often confessed to having nightmares in which old ladies were chasing him with equally old umbrellas, groaned.

'You awake, Pop?'

Pop said no, he didn't think he was.

'Well, you'd better be. Unless I'm very much mistaken there's somebody prowling about in the yard.'

Pop sleepily wondered who that could be at this time of night and Ma said, rather sharply:

'Poachers, I shouldn't wonder.'

Unperturbed and still more than half asleep Pop wondered aloud who might be poaching and, if so, what?

'Plenty to poach, I should think,' Ma said. 'Geese, turkeys, chickens. Suits of armour –'

'Good Gawd.'

The thought of losing two of his proudest and most treasured possessions made Pop suddenly sit up with an alacrity that surprised even Ma.

'Nobody'd do a thing like that,' he said, 'would they?'

'Oh! wouldn't they?' Ma said. 'They'll nick anything these days. I was reading in the papers only the other day how a gang nicked two great lions from a park. Stone ones, I mean. They weighed a ton apiece or something. You'd better get up and have a peep.'

Pop agreed and got out of bed, stark naked. The experience of sleeping without a stitch of clothing on was one that, in summer, he greatly enjoyed. It compared very favourably with swimming in the never-never, an experience he also enjoyed, quite often, early on summer mornings.

At the bedroom window he half pulled back the curtains and stood looking out. A faint rim of daylight hung over the woods to the east and in the half-light he could just make out the colour of the trees.

'See anything?' Ma said and Pop replied that as far as he could tell everything was as quiet as a church, a remark that by some odd association of ideas reminded Ma of Mademoiselle Dupont.

'You don't suppose it's Mademoiselle by any chance, do you?' she said. 'Sleep-walking or something like that? You never know with these foreigners.'

Pop agreed. Could be. Foreign blood an' all that.

'She's the highly emotional type all right,' Ma said. 'She looked restless all evening, I thought.'

At this remark Pop chuckled deeply.

'Might be out looking for a bit o' stray,' he said.

'Never you mind about looking for a bit o' stray,' Ma said, with quite unusual asperity. 'You go down and have a look-see before somebody nicks your suits of armour.'

Pop said he certainly would and turned as if to move to the door.

'Well, not like that, I hope,' Ma said. 'The least you can do is put your trousers on. You don't want to give the poor dear the fright of her life, do you? That would put the tin-lid on it.'

Pop accordingly put on trousers, shirt, socks and slippers and, before going downstairs told Ma that he somehow didn't think he'd be all that long. It wouldn't surprise him in the least if it wasn't just one of the turkeys. They sometimes got restless too just as dawn was breaking.

'And if it *is* her,' Ma told him firmly, in a final word of warning, 'just remember what I said. Behave. No larking about. It might be misunderstood.'

Pop, after giving the most solemn of promises on this particular matter, went downstairs and into the yard. A few light pools of mist lay over the river and the meadows. Thick white dew, shining as rain, covered the grass. A few birds were stirring and one of his young cockerels, in a comic broken voice, started crowing in a barn.

After being greatly relieved to find that his much-treasured suits of armour were still safely in their places he started strolling about the yard. Everything seemed quiet and normal, he thought, and then suddenly one of his geese started cackling stridently. Instantly every one of his hyper-sensitive nerves were alert and every instinct warned him that he wasn't alone in the yard.

Somehow he was uncannily sure, also, that he wasn't going to bump into a wandering Mademoiselle Dupont, sleep-walking at dawn. Ma sometimes used the word kipperish to mean something extra fishy and that was how it felt to him now. It felt in fact more than kipperish and the thought made him stop and pick up the broken handle of a hoe that someone had discarded on a muck-heap.

Some few seconds later he heard the sound that Ma had heard: the distinct clatter of an empty oil drum turning over. It seemed to come from the direction of the hovel where the Rolls was kept and he started walking there.

But less than thirty paces further on he suddenly stopped, convinced that out of the corner of his eye he had seen the flap of a black leather jacket sleeve behind a corner of the barn where his fowls roosted.

He half-walked, half-ran round the side of the barn and suddenly found himself face to face with a girl. She was standing flat against the side of the barn, both hands behind her back. She seemed, he thought, about eighteen or nineteen and was wearing, besides the black leather jacket, tight dark red jeans. Her figure was as flat-chested as a boy's and her face, without a trace of make-up, was a kind of dirty putty colour that threw up into garish relief the big piled-up bee-hive of her hair, the dyed strands of it coarse as string and something of the colour of trampled yellow straw.

'So girls have started poaching now.'

Her lips were thin and colourless and she kept them shut.

'What is it? – chickens, eggs or what?'

He noticed she didn't look at him; instead she kept her eyes on the handle of the hoe.

'What are you up to in my yard?'

'Nothing.'

'Anybody else with you?'

'You got eyes.'

'Don't cheek me. I might warm your backside.'

'You and who else?'

'Don't cheek me.'

She curled her lip.

'Well, you got the big stick. What are you waiting for?'

'What's that you got behind your back?'

'Nothing.'

'Show me.'

She slightly lifted her eyes. They were a cold neutral colour, a sort of rat's tail grey. Otherwise she didn't move and Pop said:

'Show me. Quick.'

'Oh! belt up.'

'What's a kid like you doing out this time o' night?'

'Night? Thought it was day.'

'I said what are you doing in my yard?'

'Well, not chasing an old cock like you, that's for sure.'

'And I said what have you got behind your back?'

'And I said belt up. You put bloody years on me.'

Pop started with anger and moved to grab her arms. She squirmed with steely agility, ducked and slid along the wall. He moved to grab her again but she used the wall of the barn like a spring-board and leapt clear away from him by yards. A second later she was racing round the corner of the barn and just as she disappeared Pop saw, for the second time that month, the flash of an open razor.

Some time later he stood so seriously in thought in the bedroom that Ma was moved to ask if he'd seen a ghost or something?

'No.'

'Who was it then?'

'A kid. A girl.'

Ma gave a short laugh and said it was coming to something, wasn't it? Secret meetings at night now, eh? Kidnapping? Pretty?

'Got a razor.'

Oh? Ma inquired. Sort of protecting her honour or something?

'That was summat she never had. The low-down dirty little crawl.'

It wasn't often Pop talked in this vehement way and Ma was perturbed. It was a nice howdedo when girls with razors prowled round your back-yard at night. Next thing they wouldn't even be safe in bed. How did Pop account for a thing like that?

'Search me. It's the way they're dragged up nowadays. Some of 'em, anyway.'

It was almost full daylight by now and Pop still stood by the window, deep in thought, looking out on the yard, so that presently Ma was prompted to ask him whether or not he was coming back to bed, careful not to frame the question as if it were a direct invitation in case he might not feel in the mood.

Very much to her surprise he didn't. In an absent, preoccupied sort of voice he told her:

'No. Don't think so. I think I'll go and look for mushrooms. It looks like a good mushroom morning to me,' finally adding as an almost melancholy after-thought: 'Well, Ma, we might not have had the kids christened, but at least they growed up a sight better than that dirty little crawl.'

By the time he reached the meadow all trace of mist had cleared. The sun was coming up quickly from behind shoals of fish-shaped clouds, all deep rose except for upper fins of gold. The awnings of the shuttered stalls and roundabouts were damp with the night's dew and he paused for a moment or two to look at them. There was something a trifle sad about a fair by daytime and the sight on this particular morning did nothing to lift his melancholy.

He was still wondering unsuccessfully what a mere kid of a girl could be doing in his yard in the half-dark of the morning with a razor – he felt in some curious way as if he had been cheated, almost betrayed about something – when he became aware of a figure running after him. It was Primrose.

'Ma said you'd gone mushrooming, so I thought I'd come too. Think there'll be any?'

'Caught sight of a few in the distance yesterday but hadn't time to get 'em. You're up early. Restless or something?'

'Couldn't sleep.'

'Summat disturb you?' He was curious to know if she'd heard anything in the night and felt for a moment half-inclined to tell her about the incident of the razor and then decided not to. The whole thing was like a dirty secret. He wouldn't tell another soul.

'Just thoughts.'

Oh! it was like that, was it? he thought to himself and didn't say a word.

'Where was it you saw them yesterday?' she said.

'Over there on the far side o' the medder. Near that big hawthorn.'

Suddenly she stopped and started to take off her shoes and stockings. It was better than getting them soaked with dew, she said. Like Mariette's, her legs were golden brown, almost the same colour and with much the same smooth shine on them as a ripe acorn. She was growing in beauty every day; you could feel maturity possessing her.

When they walked on again her eyes were quick – quick as his own, he thought, perhaps quicker – and it was she who saw the first mushrooms, like a clutch of five white eggs in a patch of longish grass beyond a big straddling hawthorn half-pitched over by some winter gale.

She ran forward to gather them and he followed with a basket. It never failed to excite him to see the first pure whiteness of a new-grown mushroom and the tender salmon of the under-gills when you turned it over. Like the sight of the very first primrose, it made all his veins run faster.

'Beauties,' he said. 'Beauties.'

Her responses were exactly like his own, except that, whereas he walked about the field, she ran. The mushrooms were rather few and far between – the season was a bit early, yet – and now and then he found himself tricked by a scrap of sheep's wool, a daisy or a piece of stray paper showing white in the dewy distances.

'This is blowing the cobwebs away,' she said, when they met again. 'I was feeling all frowsy and fuzzy.'

It wasn't doing him any harm either, he thought, and he'd got perhaps a bigger need than she had for a little morning freshness. He didn't suppose anyway that it was anything very serious that had kept her from sleeping and he was half on the point of asking what in fact had kept her awake when she said, in a remarkably secretive sort of way:

'Pop?'

Yes, he said, what was it?

'Know what kept me awake?'

Pop said in his most off-hand way that he hadn't the foggiest.

'Thinking.'

She'd said that before, he reminded her. What had she been thinking about?

'Mr Candy.'

What, he said, made her think about Mr Candy?

'I think I'm in love with him.'

'You *think?*' Pop said and was about to remind her that love was something you couldn't be in two minds about – it either got you by the short hairs or not at all – when she gave him the most melting of glances and said:

'In fact I know I am. I really know.'

Wasn't Mr Candy perhaps a bit old for her? Pop wanted to know, a question to which she replied with an equally direct one of her own:

'How old were you when you fell in love with Ma?'

Oh! about fourteen, Pop supposed.

'You see.'

Exactly how old was Mr Candy anyway? Pop asked her.

'Twenty-four. But age doesn't matter. Age is nothing.'

There was something in that, Pop thought, and stooped to pick two of the most perfick mushrooms he had ever seen: two round sunken shells just moist with dew. The fate of Primrose in the matter of Mr Candy didn't surprise him very much; as he had quite often remarked before it was an extraordinary thing how his daughters, or at least two of them, were inclined to go for the timid type rather than the muscular, he-man sort.

'Does Mr Candy disturb you?' she suddenly said.

Not in any particular way he could think of, Pop said.

'He disturbs me.'

Got under her skin, did he? He knew that feeling all right. Angela Snow gave it to him sometimes.

'No, it isn't that,' she said. 'I just feel there's a lot we don't know about him. I feel he's a bit mysterious.'

That hadn't struck him at all, Pop said. Mr Candy mysterious? How?

'Can't really explain. But he used to work in a parish in the East End of London and he's a bit cagey about it. All rather strange, I think.'

Pop suddenly laughed and made the pronouncement that you could hardly expect anything else with parsons. They were a rum lot. Comical, he thought.

'Oh! Mr Candy's not comical. I don't think so, anyway. I think there's a side to him none of us have ever seen yet. It'll come out one day.'

That was what you called feminine tuition or summat, Pop supposed. Women were clever, really, the way they saw through you. No foxing 'em. What other side of Mr Candy could possibly be revealed? he wondered. All he saw was a timid young man as nervous of girls and company in general as a new-born pup. Nothing hidden, nothing mysterious about him at all.

'I think we've just about cleared the field,' he said. He thought the mushrooms in the basket probably weighed less than a pound but they were clean and fresh and would make a couple of good breakfasts. 'Shall we go back? Feet cold?'

'Oh! no. Lovely. Washed in dew. Better than a bath.'

Washed in dew, Pop thought. That just about described it. He suddenly drew in large exquisite breaths of morning air and looked down with paternal fondness at the young pretty brown feet walking through the wet summer grass. In return Primrose looked up at him and smiled slowly, with a slight hint of indulgence, as if she saw through him too.

The smile dispelled the last of his uneasiness of mind. As they walked the rest of the distance to the house he felt more and more as if washed in dew himself and that the incident in the night might never have happened.

Pop normally ate two breakfasts, one a mere snack designed temporarily to stave off the first morning pangs at about six o'clock, the second, his proper breakfast, at somewhere between eight and half past; but today the incident of the girl with the razor and then that of Primrose and the mushrooms had caused him, surprisingly, to skip the first completely. Still more surprisingly he found himself not over-hungry at eight o'clock and was content to toy with a mere half dozen rashers of bacon and a plate of mushrooms.

While he was eating these Mr Charlton arrived in the kitchen and Pop greeted him with a 'Morning, Charley boy' which, rather low in tone, lacked much of his customary clarion sprightliness.

Mr Charlton, at Pop's instigation, had lately taken up the pheasant-chick lark and it was turning out to be a very paying game. You got a very nice price for the chicks, which by the time they were full grown and roaming the autumn stubbles would cost the shooters not less than a tenner a time. It all seemed sheer folly to Pop, who couldn't blame the gypsies for frequently poaching half of them with gin-soaked raisins.

'Morning, Pop,' Mr Charlton said. 'You sound a trifle under the weather.'

'I fancy he is too,' Ma said.

'Haven't let the police-court get on your mind, have you?'

'Good Gawd, the police-court! It's Friday. Ma, I forgot every word about it. It's the day Edith and the General and me have to go and give evidence. Gawd strike me pink, I forgot.'

At the recollections of the police-court Pop's spirits seemed suddenly to drop again. The prospect of wasting half a summer day kicking his heels in court simply appalled him.

'Gawd, Charley boy, I got a million things to do. Any idea how long they might keep us there?'

'I'd deal with 'em in five minutes, the hooligans,' Ma said, 'if I had my way. And no half larks. I'd cut their livers and lights out. Cold.'

'It all depends,' Mr Charlton said.

'On what?' Pop said.

With precise and expert smoothness Mr Charlton at once proceeded to explain, while Pop listened marvelling, open-mouthed, that it all depended on which type of offence had been committed. In all probability the two accused would plead not guilty, reserve their defence and elect to be tried by jury at the Assizes or Quarter Sessions.

'Good Gawd.'

'There are in fact three types of offence of this nature,' Mr Charlton airily went on to explain. 'Under *The Offences Against The Person Act* 1861, *Section* 18 and again *Sections* 20 *and* 47 –'

Pop felt himself recoil under the sheer brilliant weight of Mr Charlton's expert words. You certainly had to hand it to Charley. He wondered where he got it from. There were no flies of any kind on Charley boy.

'My impression,' Mr Charlton said, 'is that they will be committed to the next quarter sessions or assizes, where you'll have to give evidence. The whole thing, I should say, will come under *Section* 18 of the Act, for which in fact these jokers can get imprisonment for life.'

'Never?'

'Good egg!' Ma said. 'And a good horse-whipping too.'

'In any case, you shouldn't be there very long today. By the way, which car are you taking? The Jag or the Rolls?'

Pop said he thought the Rolls; Edith was so fond of it. Why did Charley ask?

'I'll wash it over for you if you like,' Mr Charlton said. 'I've got nothing much to do.'

'Very nice of you, Charley boy. Very nice of you. Just once over lightly.'

'Finish your breakfast in peace. I'll get on with it right away,' Mr Charlton said and went out into the yard.

Less than five minutes later he was back again, more than slightly agitated, to inform an astonished Pop that he somehow didn't think he'd be going to court in either the Jag or the Rolls after all.

'Why?' Pop said. 'How's that then?'

'You'll be needing ten new tyres for a start. Every one's been slashed. With a razor I should say.'

Ma instantly gave a loud, irreverent snort and said it fair made you want to spit.

'Your poaching little crawl in the night,' she said. 'Want me to come along as body-guard? Unless I'm very much mistaken you'll be needing a bit of protection one of these fine days.'

'The Rolls!' was all Pop could say. 'The Rolls! To do a thing like that to the Rolls!'

Pop was back home for a late lunch, having stopped on the way to fortify himself, the Brigadier and Edith Pilchester with several large and much-needed brandies at The Hare and Hounds.

'Well,' Ma said, 'tell me about it. What happened? Put 'em away for a good long spell?'

No, Pop proceeded to explain, it was just exactly like Charley boy had said — you really had to hand it to Charley — they were both remanded on bail to appear at the next Assizes.

'Looked about as arrogant as a pair o' Nazis. I thought one of 'em'd spit in the Clerk o' the Court's eye.'

'Disgusting.'

'How did poor old Edith take it?'

Pop said he thought Edith was really frightened; he was worried about Edith, living in that cottage of hers all alone.

'Tell her about the girl and the razor?'

Pop confessed that he hadn't; he was honestly afraid to, in case it might make her more frightened still.

'But you'll have to tell the police?'

'Going back there this afternoon.'

Ma then proceeded to ask about the Brigadier. How had the Brigadier shaped up to it all?

'Well,' Pop said, 'it was rather funny in a way, about the General. He turned up sort of all dressed up and on parade. Best suit, rolled umbrella, gold watch-chain and bowler hat. Looked ready to defend the Right and the Faith and all that.'

Here Pop paused to give a sprightly and passable imitation of the Brigadier defending the Right and the Faith with his rolled umbrella. It failed, surprisingly, to make Ma laugh.

'Not that he'd stand much chance with them birds. They'd cut their own grandmother up for cats' meat.'

For a moment Ma seemed about to utter a typical expression of disgust but instead she grew unexpectedly pensive. Though she couldn't yet bring herself to confess it to Pop, she too was frightened. One day everything in the garden was lovely; the next there was poison in the air.

At that moment Pop, intuitively sensing that she was ill-at-ease, put a consolatory arm round her enormous waist and asked if she wouldn't join him in a Red Bull, his favourite cocktail?

'I will an' all,' she said. 'And you can mix it up good and strong and quadruple into the bargain. I need it bad.'

'Not worried, Ma?'

To this Ma had no answer to give until Pop had put into her hands the largest Red Bull even she had ever seen – Pop remarked that it was a real pepper-upper – when she said:

'I don't mind telling you I am. What's more, if this goes on you'll have to start keeping your shot-gun by your bedside.'

Pop, after gravely taking a good, deep gulp of Red Bull, slowly shook his head.

'Can't do that, Ma.'

What did he mean? Ma wanted to know. Couldn't do what?

'What you said. I already asked Charley boy about it. Can't take up fire-arms to use against jokers like these breaking in at night. Mustn't use no more force than is reasonable. Charley says so. And Charley knows.'

Ma, in great disgust, took an almost savage swig at her Red Bull.

'What are we supposed to resist 'em with, then? Spoons?'

Pop rather gloomily confessed he didn't know. But that, according to Charley boy, was how it was.

'What are we all coming to?' Ma suddenly demanded to know in a positive flame of passion fed by yet another furious swig at the Red Bull. 'Where in the name of all the saints are we supposed to be? England? I sometimes begin to doubt it.'

Pop had half begun to doubt it himself and was presently further shattered by Ma thrusting an empty glass into his hands.

'Here, give me a refill, do. A good big one an' all. My faith needs a bit of restoring today.'

· 10 ·

On Sunday morning, while the Larkins were unconcernedly breakfasting on their customary fried eggs, bacon, sausages, mushrooms, tomatoes and fried bread, with much ketchup, Mademoiselle Dupont stayed late in bed, sipping weak tea, which she regarded more as a medicine than anything, and munching on dry toast and honey. Though the duty lying before her was really a light one she still viewed it with alarm and a tension springing from nerves frayed from the dismaying experiences of two days before.

Ma and Pop had held brief court on these alarms and tensions, in bed, the night before.

'Bundle of nerves, you can see that,' Ma said. 'Hardly eats anything either. Jumpy as a kitten.'

Pop agreed, but nevertheless, recalling the Brigadier's trenchant words on the subject, had a simple explanation. Foreign blood.

'Suppose so,' Ma said. 'You've been behaving yourself, though, Sid Larkin, I hope, haven't you?'

'Not kissed her yet,' Pop said, as if this interesting experience might have provided a solution to Mademoiselle Dupont's emotional crisis. 'Suppose I ought?'

Ma said she thought it would be a far better idea if he drove Mademoiselle to church in the buggy. It would be a more tranquillizing experience than the Rolls.

'Might make Edith jealous,' Pop said.

'You and your women,' Ma said. 'Why don't you start a harem?'

'Strength's a very fine thing,' Pop said and Ma, laughing with spontaneous splendour, gave him an affectionate wallop in the back.

Mr Candy was another very bad case of nerves, she went on to say. She sometimes didn't know what to make of Mr Candy. She could only suppose it was living alone and all that. Not having anybody to share things with.

'By the way,' Pop said. 'Primrose's in love with him.'

'Oh! really?' Ma said. 'Not surprised.'

'And she was telling me too how he used to work in an East End parish in London,' Pop said. 'Very like that accounts for something.'

Ma said she shouldn't wonder. It was more than likely. London was no good to anybody. It was good enough to unmoralize you. Give her the country any day.

'Talking about unmoralizing,' she went on, 'is it next week you have to go and give evidence at the Assizes about them two hooligans?'

'No, the next.'

'Pity. I must say I'll be glad when it's over.'

Mademoiselle Dupont, rising at last between eleven and half past, found herself facing the first problem of the day. It was whether to wear Pop's tantalizing gift of black lingerie or to settle for something more modest and substantial? The experience of wearing so intimately personal a gift would hardly make for serenity, yet the least she felt she could do was to wear it, so to speak, in honour of the day.

At last she put the garments on, only to find herself quivering so much that she immediately took them off again, replacing them with plainer and more honest things, the lower of which she secured, in case of possible accident, with two enormous safety pins.

She then took four aspirins, finished putting on her plain black dress with white sleeve and collar pipings, her black and white hat and her white gloves. Finally she crossed herself several times, said a short prayer and bathed her forehead in eau-de-cologne.

Going downstairs at twenty minutes to twelve, she found most of the Larkins ready. Ma was wearing a dress of mauve chiffon, with a large picture hat decorated all over with violets and pink daisies. Pop was in a remarkably subdued suit of clerical grey, with a large red clove carnation in the buttonhole. The christening lark had got to be treated with a bit of seriousness, he had finally decided, whatever goings-on might happen later, when grub and totting out and all that started.

The twins, all in white except for the distinguishing scarlet and purple ribbons in their hair, seemed to Mademoiselle Dupont like a pair of little angels. They reminded her so much of the young girls one saw in those lovely confirmatory processions back home in Brittany. The sweetest, most angelic things.

'Well, it's going uphill for twelve,' Ma said. 'Where's Primrose? Everybody's ready except Primrose.'

'Still making up,' Victoria said.

Victoria was in palest blue, a colour that gave her a certain visionary serenity.

'Better nip up and tell her to hurry,' Ma said. 'Oh! do be quiet, little Oscar. You'll drown the living daylights out of us.'

Little Oscar was sitting in a chair at the table, which he was loudly and vigorously banging with one of Ma's wooden spoons. He was wearing a light cream tussore suit which threw up into shining relief his fat red moon of a face, which seemed almost beery in its healthiness.

'Oh! go to Mademoiselle Dupont for a minute, do.' Ma instantly plonked the well-stuffed shape of Oscar into Mademoiselle Dupont's unready arms, so that she almost staggered as she clasped him with a sudden rush of Gallic affection to her deep firm bosom. 'Go to your godmother.'

'*Ah! mon chéri! Chéri —tchook, tchook, tchook!*'

'Nice an' warm in 'ere!' little Oscar said, using one of his favourite expressions.

Presently, with Primrose still nowhere to be seen, Mr Charlton, Mariette and little Blenheim arrived. Mr Charlton too was wearing a charcoal grey suit with a dark red rose in his buttonhole and to Ma's infinite astonishment was carrying a black bowler and a black rolled umbrella. Altogether Ma thought he looked so posh that she half-wished Pop had sported a bowler too. She'd a good mind to buy him one for Christmas – perhaps one in green or brown.

Mademoiselle Dupont gazed at Mr Charlton with inexpressible rapture. He, at any rate, with his *melon*, his *sang-froid* and his umbrella, epitomized the England of her dreams. Here at last was the true, real Englishman.

Mariette, who looked a model of sheer allurement in a white silk suit and a white birthday cake of a hat with many buttercup flowers springing up all over it, suddenly said:

'Personally I think we ought to get started. Mr Candy'll be having an accident or something if we keep him waiting.'

'Quite right,' Pop said. 'Time's getting on. Charley boy, you take the Rolls and load up. I'll bring Mademoiselle Dupont and Primrose in the buggy. Where is that gal? Snifter afore you go, Charley?'

'No snifters!' Ma said with a firmness almost unparalleled at that particular time of Sunday morning, when she and Pop would normally have been sharing snifters by the dozen, 'we don't want the church to pong like a four-ale bar.'

With the newly tyred Rolls moving sweetly out of the yard and little Oscar waving his wooden spoon out of the back window Pop found himself presently caught between the dual temptation of the cocktail cabinet and Mademoiselle Dupont. He couldn't quite decide whether to give Mademoiselle Dupont a couple of rapid nerve-soothers or to mix himself a quick Red Bull in spite of Ma.

He was saved from the necessity of making this excruciating decision by the serene arrival, at ten minutes past twelve, of Primrose. Her make-up, though by no means obtrusive, had taken her well over an hour and now had the effect of making her look all of nineteen. Her dress, quite low at the neck and very short-sleeved, was exactly of the right primrose colour to match her name. The belt round her waist was broad and in emerald green and gave her a high up-lifted bust. Her gloves were of the same colour as her hat and threw into relief the deep sallow colour of her arms. Her hat was the merest spider's web of green lace and looked as if it had dropped on to her rich black hair with the morning dew.

Even Pop was stunned. He vaguely murmured something about 'Ready?' and had neither the heart nor will to scold her for lateness. He'd always said she'd be the *belle* of the family; he wasn't sure she wasn't even lovelier than Mariette. She even approached his vision of an earlier Ma, splendid in her own precocious maturity.

Impressed too, Mademoiselle Dupont gave an enchanted sigh and two minutes later the three of them were driving away in the buggy, to a jingle of bells, into a morning from which the muggy vapours of July were at last lifting, to let the sun come through.

The Rev. Candy had not merely had one accident that morning, but several. First he had cut himself an uncountable number of times while shaving, so that for a time he had gone about with bits of white cotton-wool sticking out all over his face, rather like a tattered Christmas party snowman. Then out of sheer anxiety he had mistaken the time and arrived at the church at a quarter to eleven instead of a quarter to twelve. There was no morning service, so that for an hour he had been obliged to sit alone in the vestry, until finally deciding to make himself a cup of instant coffee, which through impossible nervousness he promptly spilled down the front of his trousers.

When he finally emerged from the vestry he got the immediate impression that there were far more people gathered about the christening font, on which a number of candles were burning, than he or the Rev. Spinks ever saw at a service.

Nor, he thought, had he ever been confronted with quite such an array of beauty. To the collective allurements of the Larkin family were now added the ravishments of Jasmine Brown and Angela Snow. Like a cool but hardly blessed pair of sirens, one brunette, one blonde, they stood together, radiating a strange compulsive sort of calm. Miss Pilchester was also there, wearing a rather outdated purple pork-pie of a hat, which Ma slowly recognized as one she had long since sent to a jumble sale.

'Good morning to you all,' the Rev. Candy said. His voice was low though not appreciably nervous. He was determined to keep an iron hand on himself, come what might. 'Well, I think we might commence if everyone is here.'

'Just waiting for Mr Larkin and Primrose and Mademoiselle Dupont,' said Ma, who was jogging little Oscar gently up and down. 'I thought I heard the buggy draw up just now.'

This unexpected delay in the programme caused Mr Candy to draw a hard breath and go cold and flaky again. He shifted his book of service from hand to hand and tugged nervously at his vestments.

A moment or two later the three late-comers entered the church. Instantly a kind of disquieting radiance fell on the scene. Primrose might have been a flame burning her way down the nave and Mr Candy, as she gave him the most direct of smiles, felt himself quail as he had never quailed before.

For some inexplicable reason he took refuge in humour. A solemn joke sprang from his lips before he could stop it.

'Has everyone his or her little book giving the form of service? And is everyone now familiar with the batting order?'

Conscious as they all were of being in church, nobody laughed, and in the succeeding hush Mr Candy felt abysmally ashamed.

'Little Blenheim's first,' Ma said.

'Who is to be the god-parent of this child?'

Angela Snow said she was and succeeded, as she stepped forward a pace, in looking ravishingly demure.

'Oscar Larkin is next, I believe. Who is the godparent of this child?'

'I. Mademoiselle Dupont.'

'Step this way, please.'

Angela Snow, Mademoiselle Dupont and the Rev. Candy retired some distance from the font and went for some moments into solemn conclave. In the resulting hush the only sounds that could be heard were the shrillings of swallows and sparrows above the roof outside and an occasional cough from the Brigadier, who had discreetly taken up a strategic guard position some distance down the nave.

The service presently began. Little Blenheim, being not only very tiny but also fast asleep, presented no difficulty and lay sweetly swaddled and oblivious in Mr Candy's arms while Mr Candy poured unnecessarily large quantities of water over the back of his minute bald head, so that Ma was quite disgusted and said under her breath:

'Here, don't drown the child in the drink, for goodness' sake.'

417

Mercifully Mr Candy didn't drown little Blenheim in the drink but gave him back to Mariette and then turned his attention to little Oscar. Little Oscar, not by any means all that little now, was a great weight in his arms. Mr Candy could hardly hold him. Oscar was also very restless and with his red cherubic face looked not at all unlike a slightly inebriated piglet struggling about.

'I baptize this child Oscar Columbus Septimus Dupont,' Mr Candy said, hoping to heaven that he had the names right and at the same time slopping more unnecessarily large quantities of water over Oscar's head.

Almost immediately afterwards Oscar, who had insisted on bringing Ma's wooden spoon to church with him – and why not? Ma said, if it would keep the child pacified – struck Mr Candy a severe blow on the top of the head with it. Mr Candy recoiled in pain.

The twins instantly giggled and even Mademoiselle Dupont could hardly suppress a laugh. Little Oscar actually laughed too, in the form of a delighted crow, and Ma whispered under her breath:

'Oscar! Remember where you are.'

In reply Oscar, having greatly enjoyed the experience of striking Mr Candy once, now proceeded to strike him a second time, but rather more severely. Mr Candy instinctively ducked and the sound of the wooden spoon cracking down on his skull was distinctly hollow.

'Nice an' warm in 'ere!' Oscar said.

'Here, give him back to me,' Ma said and Mr Candy promptly did so, with undisguised relief and a faint smile that seemed to indicate that he was quite used to this sort of thing.

Instantly Oscar, rudely deprived of the pleasure of using Mr Candy's head as a drum, burst loudly into tears, with the result that Ma had hastily to take him out of church, where she promptly pacified him with a large Bath bun she had thoughtfully popped into her handbag in case of such an emergency. Little Oscar dried up at once. There was nothing like a bit of grub, Ma thought, for stopping that sort of nonsense.

Confused by the unexpected attack on him, Mr Candy now discovered that he had forgotten the batting order and began searching in his trousers' pocket for the little book in which he'd written it down, only to discover that the book was sliding slowly down his trousers' leg. The hole in his pocket was one he had been meaning to mend for a month or more.

The result of this was that he called Montgomery next and Montgomery, being covered in adolescent masculine shyness as opposed to the serene aplomb of the girls, hastily stepped forward, only too glad to get the ordeal over. He was shortly followed by Mariette, who treated the occasion with such grace and dignity, together with complete detachment, that Mr Charlton felt a great lump of pride rise in his throat.

Pop, on the other hand, thought Mr Candy was holding Mariette's head far too near the candles. He didn't want to see any of his kids go up in smoke and him having to act as fireman or anythink of that lark, and he was almost constrained to tell Mr Candy as much when to his relief he saw Mariette walking back to Mr Charlton. At one point in the service he couldn't help thinking there was a dickens of a lot of water slopping about but perhaps it was just as well after all.

During all this Primrose kept her eyes firmly fixed on Mr Candy, who was deeply and hopelessly conscious of it all the time. The beautiful dark stare had him in a celestial vice. There was no escaping it and even when he stooped down to pick up the little book containing the batting order he could feel its silent penetration at the back of his head.

Some knowledge of the batting order was now essential because of the twins. That simply had to be right and Mr Candy hastily refreshed his memory about their names and ribbon colours. Zinnia would be wearing the red ribbon and Petunia the purple.

The twins now stepped meekly forward and, white and innocent as milk, stood by the font. You couldn't tell them apart. They might have been two identical cherubs cut in stone.

'Let us see,' Mr Candy said to Petunia, 'you are Petunia, with the purple ribbon.'

'No,' Petunia said. 'I'm Zinnia.'

'But you're wearing the purple ribbon.'

'I know. But we changed.'

'Zinnia is supposed to be wearing scarlet. Isn't that right?'

'Yes,' Zinnia said, 'but Petunia hates purple.'

'So Zinnia is now wearing purple and Petunia scarlet?'

'That's right,' they said almost together, 'would you like us to change back again?'

Suddenly, to his horror, Mr Candy found himself in what Ma would have called a terrible two-and-eight. He simply didn't know where he was. Desperately he recalled Ma's words about the mischief-loving nature of the twins and just as desperately looked round for some help and succour from Ma. But Ma was still outside, feeding Bath bun to little Oscar, and Mr Candy could only turn his extreme desperation on the twins.

'Now you are quite sure about this? You wouldn't want me to give you the wrong names, would you?'

'Would it matter?'

'Of course it would matter.'

'Well, I think we changed ribbons three times, but I'm not sure,' Petunia said. 'We had a bit of a tiff. Because I don't like purple.'

'*You* don't like purple – Oh! my Heaven, this is awfully awkward,' Mr Candy said and with fresh desperation turned to Pop. 'Mr Larkin, can you tell me which girl is which? I must be sure.'

'Search me, old man,' Pop said, 'they're more alike some days than others. Ma's the one what knows. You'll have to get Ma.'

'I'll fetch her,' Mariette said.

Still fixing Mr Candy with that dark, celestial stare of hers, Primrose said in a slow soft voice:

'Zinnia has a mole. You'd know if you found that.'

Mr Candy's already carroty hair seemed suddenly to turn several deeper shades of ginger. Nervously he jerked his vestments about, so that the candle flames waved.

'What's all this?' Ma said.

'We've run into some difficulty, Mrs Larkin,' Mr Candy said. 'Can you please tell me which twin is which?'

'That's Petunia,' Ma said promptly, pointing to Zinnia, 'and that's Zinnia,' she said, pointing to Petunia. 'That's right, isn't it?'

The twins, who hitherto had been straight-faced, now merely smirked.

'Are you two wearing the right ribbons?' Ma said.

'They say they changed,' Mr Candy started to say, only to be promptly interrupted by Ma, who now had doubts of her own and said she'd be blowed if she was certain after all.

'Nothing for it but to have a look,' she said, seizing the twin she thought was Zinnia by the head and hastily taking her behind the red vestry curtains.

While this was going on Primrose gave Mr Candy a slow smile of sheer honey, which he involuntarily half-returned and which she repeated, infinitely more slowly, when Ma came back and said:

'Sorry, Mr Candy. This is Petunia. I'll warm their bottoms when I get them home.'

The twins, once again indivisible in heavenly, milky innocence, didn't turn a hair and merely waited for the blessing of baptism in patient silence, as if wondering what all the fuss was about.

After these nervous difficulties the task of christening Victoria Adelaide Anne Cleopatra would have been an infinitely simple one if it hadn't been for the flame that was Primrose. Somehow Mr Candy knew he was going to burn his fingers there. Feeling very flaky and very cold all over again, he could only pray silently for a quick and merciful delivery.

Then when Primrose at last came forward to the font, her green-gloved hands lightly clasped in front of her, he discovered to his immense surprise that she did so with a modesty almost touching. The smile had gone from her face. Her large dark eyes were solemn. He suddenly felt that the two of them were alone in the church and that her beauty might have been that of a bride.

Finally as she raised and then lowered her head over the font, he touched her for the first time and as the holy water dropped on her forehead he said:

'I baptize you Primrose, Violet, Anemone, Iris, Magnolia, Narcissus.'

'Narcissa,' she whispered, 'you silly.'

He was too confused to grasp whether the words were of reproval or affection, but when he had finally corrected himself and she had lifted her head again she gave him the benefit of the most forgiving and disarming of smiles. And this, accompanied as it was by the embarrassingly distinct sound of low sobbing from Mademoiselle Dupont, unnerved him so much that he actually knocked one of the candles over and only just saved it from dropping into holy water.

Twenty minutes later he was standing in the marquee with Pop, who was clapping him on the back with extreme jollity and saying:

'Very well done, old man. Very enjoyable. You umpired well. Very good umpire. Calls for a drink, eh?'

Mr Candy could only think it called for several drinks.

'What'll it be, old man, eh? Whisky, gin, rum, brandy, champagne?'

Mr Candy said if it was all the same to Pop he'd prefer a small whisky.

Pop turned smartly away and came back a fraction of a minute later with two and a half inches of whisky in a tumbler and a glass of champagne for himself. The marquee was now filling rapidly with people; dresses and beauty floated everywhere. There was a smell of food and bruised grass and with pride Pop urged Mr Candy to cast his peepers on a vast board laden with cold turkey, duck, chicken, ham, tongue, salmon, green seas of water-cress and salad, scores of bottles and many red-and-snowy dishes of strawberries and cream.

'Very proud day, this,' Pop said, raising his glass, 'for me and Ma. Thanks, old man.'

Mr Candy raised his glass too and drank and then found himself some few moments later alone in the world for the second time that morning with Primrose, who greeted him with words that fell on him like a sweet and final benediction.

'Thank you,' she said, holding him with that slow dark smile of hers, 'you did it so beautifully.'

'Thank you, Narcissa,' he said, also with a smile, and knew that for the first time in several weeks he was happy.

·11·

By mid afternoon the sun was shining brilliantly from a sky broken by occasional high white sails of cloud. A clear candescent light lay everywhere and Ma, her easel set up-in the shade of the walnut tree, was busy sketching in the gay scene of marquee, flags, roundabout, swings and all, determined to preserve it for what she sometimes called prosperity.

Miss Pilchester, with the twins, was strenuously hurling balls at coconuts; Mademoiselle Dupont had retired to her room ostensibly to sleep but in reality to shed a few quiet, happy tears. Montgomery was working the roundabout for a dozen children or more, among them little Oscar who, inseparable from his wooden spoon, was banging the head of the cockerel he was riding even more fiercely than he had banged that of Mr Candy. Pop and Mr Candy, in shirt sleeves, were in the kitchen with Angela Snow, Primrose and Jasmine Brown, all washing up, Pop now and then pausing to pay caressive attention to Angela and Jasmine and occasionally warmly urging Mr Candy to follow suit. Mr Candy, however, was firm in refusal. He had, he thought, had quite enough emotional exercise for one day.

As Pop was drying the last of the dishes he suddenly put to Mr Candy, in his quick swallow-like way, one of those inconsequential questions of his:

'Anybody poor in the village nowadays, Mr Candy? I mean real poor. Poor and hungry.'

Mr Candy, caught unawares, pondered briefly before answering, and then said no, he honestly didn't think so. Times had changed.

'Telling me,' Pop said. He recalled the days when the village shop had little to offer but candles, tea, paraffin, lard and cuts of rough old bacon. Now every Tom, Dick and Harry rolled up for scampi, smoked salmon and fancy larks of that sort.

'Why do you ask?' Mr Candy said.

'Plenty of cold turkey left,' Pop said, recalling that Ma had cooked four big ones, 'and I was just wondering if you could think of anybody who'd like a chunk or two.'

Mr Candy, who couldn't help thinking that he wouldn't mind a chunk or two himself, said:

'There's old Mrs Francis. She lives alone. I fancy she doesn't often see such luxuries.'

'Good egg,' Pop said. There were the little Miss Barnwells too, Effie and Edna; he often fancied that they lived, as Ma said, on bread-and-scrat. Perhaps Mr Candy wouldn't mind taking them some too?

'Gladly. Gladly.'

'Then let's go over and do a bit of disjointing. Don't go away, girls. Be back in no time.'

'We're going to put our swim-suits on,' Jasmine said.

'Why bother?' Pop said blandly, at the same time running a strategic hand over the fuller, rounder parts of the girl, certain that she had little if anything on underneath her thin silk dress. 'Anybody want unzipping?'

On this flippant note he and Mr Candy walked across to the marquee, merely pausing for a silent second or two on the way to admire Miss Pilchester, who was winding and unwinding with an almost masculine ferocity as she hurled frequent balls at coconuts. It was all very gay, all very perfick, Pop thought. He loved especially the laughter of kids from the roundabout and the way the organ tunes – the old *Gold and Silver* waltz, Ma's favourite, was the one playing at the moment – fairly danced on the air. You couldn't hardly find anythink more perfick, or more peaceful, nowhere.

In the marquee Pop started to disjoint, with his fingers, the three quarter remains of a twelve-pound turkey, frequently popping morsels of stuffing into his mouth and also genially suggesting that Mr Candy should help himself at the beer keg if he had a mind.

Mr Candy, though grateful, said no, he'd rather not. A few glasses of champagne had made him very thirsty. What he'd honestly really like was a glass of water.

'Good God,' Pop said. 'Water?' It didn't seem possible. Was Mr Candy feeling dicky?

'No. Merely thirsty. It's the champagne.'

'That's what Ma always says. Just a good excuse for drinking more, I always say.'

There was, as it turned out, no water but Mr Candy found a jug of lemonade and poured himself a glass of that.

With this in his hands he stood watching Pop doing deft work with the turkey when suddenly, out of the corner of his eye, he was aware of two figures standing at the door of the tent, each in black sweater, stove-pipe trousers and winkle-pickers, the taller of the two also wearing a red shoe-string necktie.

'I think you have visitors, Mr Larkin,' he said.

Pop turned sharply, paused in the act of halving a turkey leg and merely said:

'Ah! the big brave boys.'

Mr Candy slowly set his glass of lemonade on the table.

'Look who's here, Jed. Palsy-walsy Larkin and parson's nose. Lemonade boy.'

'What do you two want?' Pop said. 'Buzz. I'm busy.'

'Nobody don't mean nothing unfriendly, do they Jed? We just 'eard you 'ad a party.'

No, Jed said, nobody didn't mean nothing unfriendly. How could they, with parson's nose here?

'No, not with clergy-wergy about. Wouldn't be nice. Not with clergy-wergy pudden an' pie.'

Mr Candy didn't move at all as the two men advanced across the tent and Pop merely picked up another leg of turkey.

'Nothing a bit unfriendly. Only wanted to make a little social call. By the way, palsy-walsy, where's the old trout?'

'Yeh, where's the old trout? The old coconut trout, we mean. Got to 'ave a word with 'er, see? Got to trim 'er nails a bit, see?'

'Ah! get lost,' Pop said. The sudden mention of Edith Pilchester made him fearful and he crooked an angry elbow. 'Go and drown yourself. Quick.'

'Now, now. Now, now. Temper. And where's Tweedledum? We got to 'ave a word with Tweedledum too, see? Old pink-cap, we mean, see?'

'Yeh, got to 'ave a word with everybody, see? Old mother coconut, pink-cap and palsy-walsy. The lot. On account of we don't want no trouble in court, see? Don't want to 'ave nobody saying nothing they don't mean, like, see?'

Pop, trembling now with anger, shook a turkey leg in the air like a threatening club.

'Now I give you jokers just ten seconds –'

'Don't you wave no bony-wony at me, palsy-walsy boy. Else I might make pretty patterns on your kiss-woz, see?'

Pop saw Jed whip a hand inside his inside jacket pocket but before he himself could move Mr Candy stepped forward.

'I suggest you go,' he said, 'unless you want me as a further unfriendly witness.'

''Ark who's talking! 'Ark who's unfriendly. Old parson's nose. old clergy-wergy.'

'I merely –'

'Keep your big mouth shut, clergy-wergy. Belt up.'

'Unless you want me to shut it for you,' Jed said. 'What say?'

'Oh! you shut it,' Mr Candy said with great politeness. 'It's so much easier.'

'I bloody well will an' all!'

A second later Jed aimed a cruncher at Mr Candy's jaw but Mr Candy, with an alacrity so smart that Pop had never been more surprised in his life, ducked smartly and was astonishingly revealed ready for instant action as a southpaw.

'Cut him to bacon-rind, Jed!'

'Your move,' Mr Candy said. 'Come on.'

Jed came on, two fisted, and a moment later Pop had the second surprise of his life. Mr Candy suddenly had a half-nelson on Jed so well locked that any moment Pop expected to hear the crack of a bone.

'Shall I break it?' Mr Candy said. 'Won't take a second.'

Jed started to yell in vicious pain.

'Knock him off! Knock him off!'

'Call your whippet off,' Mr Candy said. 'Or I'll break it.'

'God, you parson bastard!'

In answer Mr Candy put another ounce or two of pressure on the half-nelson. Jed screamed in wild agony.

'You're not even chicken,' Mr Candy said. 'You're just the white of the egg.'

'Let me go! Let me go!'

To Pop's infinite astonishment Mr Candy let him go.

'Now scramble,' he said. 'Scramble. Pronto. Or next time I'll break it. I'll break both of them.'

Only a moment or two later Mr Candy and Pop were alone in the tent, Pop so astounded that for once in his life he was completely speechless. He simply couldn't think of a thing to say. He even went so far as to do another utterly unprecedented thing by picking up Mr Candy's glass of lemonade and taking a long, sharp swig at it. By God, he'd go to Jericho. He'd ruddy well go to Jericho.

'Did a fair bit of it at one time,' Mr Candy said. 'Had to. At the club. I broke a bone once. Nasty sound. I thought perhaps I might have been a little out of practice.'

At this moment Pop, still utterly speechless, could think only of the sharer of all his secrets, Ma. He simply had to tell Ma. He simply had to! and with a sort of hunting cry he rushed from the marquee, leaving Mr Candy in a mood of what seemed to be quiet reflection, helping himself at the beer-keg.

Ma, rather to Pop's surprise, was no longer at her easel and he could only guess that she'd gone upstairs for a lay-down. He profoundly hoped so anyway. In that case he could kill two birds with one stone.

He went upstairs and, so excited by events that all thought even of Jasmine Brown had gone from his mind, hastily opened the bedroom door, poked his head in and said:

'Ma, my little old sunflower. You there?'

Ma was there, tucked up in bed, a bottle of aspirins and a glass of water standing on the table at the bedside. Pop stood greatly astonished. He could think of only one good reason why Ma should come to bed on a Sunday afternoon and it had nothing to do with aspirins.

'All right, my old sunflower? Not feeling dicky?'

Ma, he couldn't help thinking, looked a tiny bit pale round the gills.

'Just tired.'

'Long day. Too much excitement. Upset you to tan the twins too, I expect?'

'Didn't tan them after all. Hadn't the heart.'

Ma sounded sort of limp, Pop thought, and urgently asked if he couldn't get her a drop of something – brandy, port, rum or perhaps a cocktail?

Ma shook her head and refused without a word, so that Pop was compelled to ask if she'd had one of her turns?

'No. Nothing like that,' Ma said. 'I probably shouldn't have started painting. But I wanted to get it down as a sort of memento.'

Pop suddenly sat down on the bed, all prepared to tell Ma about the exciting revelation of the new athletic Mr Candy and how the hooligans had been routed but Ma merely said:

'Don't bump about, Pop. Please.'

Pop was now quite certain that Ma must be feeling a bit dodgy and said:

'Sorry, Ma. What I came up to tell you about was something terrific that just happened in the marquee. Perfickly terrific. Mr Candy –'

'Not now. Later.'

Pop felt greatly mystified, even rebuffed. What made it worse was that the idea of killing two birds with one stone clearly wasn't on any more. It was all a bit worrying and suddenly he leaned over Ma, kissed her very lightly on the forehead and said:

427

'Sure I can't get you a drop of somethink, Ma?'

'No, thanks. Just leave me.'

This, Pop thought, was a bit serious. Ma was obviously more than off colour. She wasn't often like this he said, was she?

'Well, I have been once or twice.'

'Oh?' Pop said. 'How's that, then? Whatever's the matter, Ma?'

Ma turned in the bed. Her dark eyes were soft and sleepy.

'Oh! it's nothing very much,' she said, 'but somehow I don't think it'll be very long before we have another christening.'

· A LITTLE OF ·
· WHAT YOU FANCY ·

· 1 ·

Most mornings, especially in spring and summer, when the liquid chorus of dawn bird song often roused him as early as four o'clock, Pop Larkin was awake some time before Ma, a circumstance that afforded him the silent pleasure of drinking in the sight of her warm dark head cradled in tranquillity on the pillow and even, sometimes, if the night had been exceptionally warm, of gazing on the olive amplitude of her expansive bust, its naked slumbering curves swelling and slipping from the lace fringe of her flowery chiffon nightgown.

While Ma still slept Pop almost invariably went downstairs in his pyjamas and brewed a pot of strong fresh tea. The exceptions to this occurred on the very warmest of summer mornings, when Pop was inspired to think that Ma, perhaps, would prefer champagne. Ma was exceptionally fond of champagne, more especially before breakfast.

On some occasions Pop was moved to go even further than mere champagne and concoct a cool but potent mixture of about equal parts of brandy and champagne, preferably pink, with a dash of angostura bitters and a slice of orange. This was the perfick stiffener to start the day on. In particular the pinkness seemed always to have a highly stimulating effect on Ma and as he came back upstairs with bottles, glasses and orange, the glasses already frostily sugared, Pop always hoped that Ma, perhaps, would be in the mood.

Very often Ma was.

'Drop o' champagne, Ma?' On a humid morning in early July the voices of wood pigeons liquidly calling to each other across the meadows had, in Pop's ears, a sultry, sensual sound. 'Plain or cocktail?'

'Better make it a cocktail while you're about it.'

'Cocktail it is then. Have it now or afterwards?'

Ma, well-knowing what afterwards implied, responded by a great voluptuous upheaval of laughter, huge sleep-soft breasts half-escaping from her nightgown.

'Better make it a sandwich, hadn't we?'

'Perfick.' Pop liked the idea of the sandwich. 'Which part in the middle?'

'I think,' Ma said serenely, already drawing her nightgown over the dark mass of her handsome ruffled hair, 'we'd better see how we get on.'

Pop now laughed too and said he didn't see why they shouldn't get on pretty well as usual, though it was thirsty work. Was she sure she wouldn't have a drop first, as a sort of pipe-opener?

Ma, responding with a dreamy sigh, her body now stretched out in full nakedness, the bed-clothes thrown back, said well, no, she didn't think so. He'd got her too excited about the other now. She was nicely in the mood.

Pop, declaring with typical gusto that he was very glad to hear it, prepared to enfold himself in the warm, olive continent of Ma when she suddenly interrupted him and asked if he hadn't better lock the door?

'Else we'll have those two monkeys in. Oscar's got eyes all over the back of his head and Phyllida isn't much better.'

Phyllida, Ma's eighth, who had already been christened in perfectly orthodox fashion Phyllida Cleopatra Boadicea Nightingale had turned out, greatly to Pop's surprise, to be blessed with singularly bright red hair, a fact that Pop was utterly unable to square with the fact that both he and Ma were very dark, until Mr Charlton, his son-in-law, knowledgeable in so many matters, explained that it was all to do with the laws of genetics.

'Good Gawd Almighty,' Pop said, 'what next? What the pipe is genetics? Summat to do with the National Elf lark I'll bet.'

Not at all, Mr Charlton assured him. It was just that dark-haired parents quite frequently produced red-haired children.

'Just fancy that,' Ma said. 'We'll soon be having blackbirds with red breasts I shouldn't wonder. Or else donkeys giving milk.'

Donkeys, Mr Charlton assured her in his most knowledgeable fashion, did give milk; and even Ma was silenced.

Anyway, as she was frequently fond of saying, there was no doubt that Phyllida was the pick of the entire Larkin bunch, not at all unlike a perky bright-eyed robin herself, her soft smooth hair rich as purest copper. Quick as lightning too.

Pop having locked the bedroom door, he now paused to listen once again for a moment to the voices of pigeons exchanging sultry greetings across the meadows and then slipped back into bed with Ma, who received him with a deep soundless embrace, her half-opened lips pressed against his. Such was the powerful effect of this union that Pop, conferring the tenderest of caresses on the brown-pink crests of Ma's ample bosom, had no word to say either for the next half hour or so.

It was Ma who spoke first. 'Nice and satisfactory,' she said.

This brief understatement in fact concealed the most affectionate of compliments. That was the nice thing about Pop, she always told herself. He knew his technique all right; very good technique.

'Now for the champers,' Pop said.

'Won't say you didn't earn it,' Ma said and presently sat up in bed, still naked, ready to receive the further blessing of the first cocktail of the day.

'Goes down a treat,' Pop said with a fruity smack of his lips. 'Perfick start.'

'Anything particular on today?'

'Nothing much. Army surplus job. About five hundred walkie-talkie sets. Should show about three hundred per cent.'

'Ought to keep the wolf from the door.'

Pop said it certainly ought and, observing that Ma's glass was already almost empty, reached for the champagne bottle in readiness to top her up. This he did with such typical generosity that he filled the glass to overflowing, the champagne spilling down on Ma's left bosom. Instantly recognizing this as an interesting opportunity for further drinking Pop bent down and proceeded to taste the twin delights of wine and breast, causing Ma to struggle with playful delight, thus spilling more champagne.

'Whatever will you think of next?' Ma said, as if Pop hadn't never thought of it before. 'You must be in your hot-blood or something.'

Pop said he shouldn't wonder if he wasn't and proceeded yet again to taste the twin pleasures of Ma and champagne, so that Ma shook all over with rich gusts of laughter, finally remarking:

'You'd better get it out of your system, hadn't you? Else we'll be here all day.'

'Why not? Perfick idea.'

Ma said she could think of worse.

Pop suddenly felt a great new rush of ardour, his heart racing. This sudden rapidity of its beating seemed for a moment to echo the trilling sweetness of wren song from the garden outside. Then the rippling of it became, for a moment, shot with pain. Pop found himself pausing, then actually gasping, for breath.

Ma, now filled with fresh ardour herself, watched the pause without misgiving, concerned only to ask what was holding him up? She'd had an idea he was going to give her an encore.

The pain having passed as rapidly as it had shot through him, Pop replied in his habitually warm and robust tones that he certainly was. He was all for encores. It was rather like drinking champagne. The first glass, though always nice, was only a sort of pipe-opener. It was the second glass that really got you going.

Voluptuously, at this moment, Ma rolled over in bed, her wide and splendid figure half-smothering Pop, who received her breasts in his two hands rather like a hungry man receiving the gift of two round, warm, fresh-baked loaves of bread. From this new and unexpected point of vantage Ma, he thought, looked more inviting and sumptuous than ever.

Ma, at the same time, found herself wondering about Pop's technique. There was, she told herself, no question of it standing the strain. She merely wondered what form it would take. The slow, quick, slow? or what she sometimes called the old-fashioned waltz time? You never knew with Pop. He wasn't merely a man of technical excellence. He went in for a lot of variation.

A moment later Pop, instead of proceeding to demonstrate some fresh variation of technique by physical means, actually started a brief discourse. This was inspired by something he had read somewhere in a magazine. It was all about these two people, he explained to Ma, who didn't get on very well – in bed, that was. They'd sort of kept to the orthodox form of service, Pop explained, laughing richly, for years. Didn't work, though.

How did he mean? Ma said, utterly confounded that such a condition could befall any mortal man and woman. It didn't *work?*

'Well, *he* worked,' Pop said. 'But she was sort of unemployed.'

Ma let out a rich shriek, quivering all over like a vast jelly. 'You mean she was on the dole?' Ma said, 'or on strike?'

Oh! no, Pop explained, nothing like that. She wanted work. Eager for it. But somehow –

'Technique wrong.'

Bit like that, Pop said. How did Ma know?

'Been in the business long enough, haven't I?' Ma said and again gave a shriek of laughter, causing the most disturbing of tremulous movements from her breasts down to the very soles of her feet, which she suddenly began to rub caressingly against Pop's calves. 'I ought to by now.'

'What made you do that?' Pop suddenly said.

'Do what?'

'With your feet. Smoothing me up and down like that.'

Ma said she didn't know. She hadn't the vaguest. She supposed it was some sort of instinct. Why?

Telepathic was the word that sprang instantly to Pop's mind, telepathic being one of those words he had picked up from the informative Mr Charlton, his son-in-law. Ma, in other words, he suddenly realized, was reading his mind.

It was what this woman did, he explained.

'Did what?' Ma said. She didn't get it.

Pop went on to explain that it was about the discovery of a new technique. Well, very old technique really. It was all to do with the time when we were apes and all that and feet were as important as hands and suddenly this woman had discovered it. It was to do with foot-worship or summat. Mr Charlton had told him all about it. He'd discussed it with him.

'Never?' Ma said, amazed.

'Fact,' Pop said. 'After years of being on the dole, sort of, this woman had suddenly discovered that by using her feet she'd struck it rich. Two minutes with the soles of her feet and she'd got herself into a tizz like hot rum and brandy. No stopping her. She was on the boil all night long.'

'The things they get hold of in these magazines,' Ma said. 'It makes you wonder.'

'Ended in divorce.'

'Never?' Ma said. That beat the band.

'Beat Fred, that's what it was.'

'Fred? Who's Fred?'

Fred was the husband, Pop explained. Had to drop out. Couldn't stand the pace.

'Well, the fast so-and-so,' Ma said. 'Don't they have a name for that sort? Lesbians? – no, not Lesbians. That's having butter no side of the bread. Well, it doesn't matter, anyway. The things some women do to get hold of what they were after – really I don't know.'

'Lovely grub, though.'

'I should say so. I'd better keep my feet to myself in future.'

Another peal of laughter, rich and healthy, shook both Ma and the bed. All this time Ma had been allowing the warm continent of her body further and further to envelop Pop, whose only evident sign of resistance was an occasional languid attempt to push Ma's breasts away – merely, in fact, so that he could see them better. All this, gentle and modified as it was, was thirsty work nevertheless, and he was on the point of suggesting that Ma, being in the better position, should pour another glass of champagne, when he abruptly realized that Ma was caressing him slowly up and down with the naked soles of her feet.

An instant and totally unheralded nervous spasm shot through him, both exquisite and excruciating. It was a sensation he had never remotely experienced before, even in the long fruitful years of union with Ma. It was at once a pain and a joy. It ravaged his heart, his chest, his stomach and then ran rapidly and hotly down to the soles of his own feet. He was soon nervously hot all over, his heart painfully racing.

'Here, steady Ma, you'll have me on the boil next.'

And what else, Ma said, did he think she was up to?

Ma, murmuring in dreamy tones something about it was always nicest, second time round, was now in a state of total ecstacy herself. Her compulsive possession of Pop was so absolute that Pop, straining with every nerve and pulse of blood to meet her demands, was suddenly assailed by the idea, at once both joyful and slightly alarming, that if they didn't put the brakes on they might well be in for another pair of twins.

Less than a minute later Ma did, fact, put the brakes on.

'Lovely,' was her next word. 'Lovely. You remember that drink you made once? Peaches and champagne and a bit of maraschino. Like that. Just like that. Lovely.'

Pop, to his slight concern and dismay, suddenly discovered himself to be unusually tired. He lay back on the pillows, panting. Ma was still spread across him, eyes dreamily half-closed, still locked in the ravishing peace of utter satisfaction.

Now and then she also gave a great sigh of pleasure in recollection, rather as if drinking a draught of one of Pop's more memorable liquid confections. These expressions of ecstacy, far from arousing any sort of response in Pop, seemed to leave him cool, so that presently Ma was prompted to remove one bosom some inches away from its resting place on Pop's neck and remark.

'Don't want me now, do you? I know.'

Pop murmured that he didn't know about that. They'd had two innings already, he reminded her, and it still wasn't seven o'clock.

'What's time got to do with it?' Ma said. There was a note in her voice of the very slightest injury. 'You feeling weak all of a sudden or something?'

Oh! nothing like that, Pop declared. He felt sort of languid like, that's all. After all, you'd got to re-charge the batteries.

'Better re-charge them with a drop o' champers then,' Ma said and proceeded to reach out of bed for bottle and glasses. 'Don't want you losing grip.'

At this suggestion, faint thought it was, that he was losing grip, Pop felt a little affronted. Him losing grip? That was a bit off, he told Ma.

Ma, not speaking, serenely poured champagne. As she sipped at it there was a glint in her eye that was like a distilled reflection of the bubbles sparkling at the glass's brim. It was more than evident, Pop told himself, that she was in one of her primrose-and-bluebell moods.

Then, as he made the first movement to lift his head from the pillow in order to drink from his own champagne, he became aware again of a curious lassitude. At the same time his chest seemed to ache again. He heaved himself slowly upright, panting a little, and sipped with such slow relief at the champagne that Ma was actually moved to tease him gently, telling him she hoped he wasn't getting past it?

'You won't get very far with your girl friend at this rate,' she said.

Which girl friend? Pop wanted to know. He had so many.

'Angela Snow,' Ma said, blandly. 'I heard you fixing it up with her on the phone the other night. Something about a four-poster bed you'd found for her or something.'

'She asked me if I ever saw one to nab it for her. She wants it for her new flat.'

'Very good excuse. New flat, eh? I wonder what it's like in a four-poster? Four times as good, I expect.'

Ma's joke fell on unresponsive ears. Normally the thought of Angela Snow, that willowy, languid and highly persuasive creature, excited him more than considerably but now the thought of her evoked no response in him either. He merely released a great sigh, totally unlike Ma's deep purr of pleasure in recollection, and in doing so let champagne dribble over the rim of his glass and then down his chin and chest. Ma laughingly reproved him for this, saying he'd need his bib on next if he didn't watch it.

'That'll be the day,' she said, laughing in great jelly-like heaves, in her best primrose-and-bluebell fashion, 'making love with your bib on.'

Again the joke fell on an unresponsive Pop. He merely felt weak, he told himself, and yet was too weak to say so.

'I'll have to give you over to Edith Pilchester for a rest cure,' Ma said, again in teasing fashion. 'I saw her collecting a big bag of lambs' wool the other day. That'll be nice and soft to lay your head on.'

The thought of laying his head down side by side with the spinsterish Miss Pilchester would normally have had Pop in a fit, but now this joke too merely produced in him a vague solemnity.

'Champagne's a bit weak this morning, isn't it?' Ma said, taking a deep draught of it as a sort of test. 'Didn't put too much brandy in, I'd say.'

'Drained the bottle.'

'Nice thing. Only half rations now. We're getting down to something now, I must say. Starvation level.'

Pop managed to say there was another bottle downstairs. He'd go and get it. Heavily he tried, without success, to rise.

With gentle mockery Ma invited him not to strain himself, then promptly got out of bed herself and stood for a moment or two by the window, stark naked, looking out at the garden below, remarking that it was really the week for roses. All the roses were in bloom. Whether viewed from back or front Ma looked not at all unlike an enormous full-blown rose herself, creamy and summery, her bosoms full to bursting.

'Shan't be a tick,' she said. 'Don't overdo it while I'm gone,' and then left the room without benefit either of wrap or nightgown.

It was not uncustomary for Ma to nip downstairs in the early morning without a stitch to cover her vast form and the circumstances held no surprise for Pop. When once reminded that the children might see her Ma had merely remarked with her customary serenity that they'd got to know sometime hadn't they? When further reminded that she might run into the postman she merely retorted blandly:

'Well, I shall have to shut my eyes then, shan't I?'

During Ma's absence, brief as she had promised it would be, Pop became aware that his unnatural spell of lassitude had become an ache, and the ache, every twenty seconds or so, a pain. He was actually lying back on the pillows, holding his chest in the region of his heart, when Ma came back into the bedroom, bearing a bottle of her favourite brandy, Remy Martin.

Something about the incongruous sight of her completely naked and carrying the full bottle of cognac abruptly induced in Pop a notion that Ma was on the verge of being ready for a third innings. Normally on warm early summer mornings this would have been perfick. Now he could only view the prospect with a faint and uncharacteristic dismay.

'Still there then?' Ma said. 'You want to take more brandy with it, that's your trouble.'

Laughing fleshily, Ma proceeded to pour generous measures of Remy Martin into both Pop's champagne and her own. That ought to pep up his ego, as Mr Charlton often said. Ma rather liked the word ego. When she had first heard it she'd thought it was something rather rude. But now she understood, though it really meant the same thing as she'd thought it referred to in the first place.

'Oh! by the way the papers have come and I looked up your stars.'

Ma was a great believer in the stars and what they had to say. Very important, the stars. Pop had been born under Taurus, the bull, which was good. It was strong and lucky. According to the signs it made for a potency well expressed by *Red Bull*, an explosive cocktail of Pop's own invention. It was what made Pop what he was.

Today, however, he told himself that he couldn't care less, either about Taurus, the bull, or the stars.

'Know what they say?' Ma said, meaning the stars. '"A personal relationship will bear fruit early but discretion may have to be exercised as the day goes on. A business project may cast a shadow."' Ma drank deeply at her brandy and champagne, at the same time slightly raising her glass, as if actually toasting the stars' prophecies.

Pop merely smiled, wanly.

'I like that bit about bearing fruit,' Ma said. 'I think I've borne enough fruit already. Still, while the tree's there it might just as well bear another crop now and then.'

In a sidling, languorous movement Ma started to approach the bed, a brandy-deep glow in her dark brown eyes, her big breasts swinging with lazy invitation. This, Pop suddenly told himself, wasn't merely one of those primrose-and-bluebell moods. It was one of those blinders she went in for now and then. He was in for the third innings any moment now.

'Think I'll get dressed now, Ma,' he said. 'Got a fairish way to go. Got to be there by half past ten.'

What was his hurry? Ma wanted to know. It was summer. It was beautiful. It was warm. All the roses were in bloom. It was there to enjoy, wasn't it? Well then, why not enjoy it? This morning she felt like roaming round all day with nothing on, ripening like a fruit herself in the sun. Tomorrow – you never knew – she might be glad of her lamb's-wool knickers.

All this was so much a reflection and echo of Pop's own philosophy – *carpe diem*, Mr Charlton called it in the infinite wisdom for which he was noted – that normally Pop would have laughed in boisterous agreement and clasped himself to Ma's ample bosom in simmering response.

But now he felt himself locked again in that curious, half painful languor that he couldn't explain and said:

'Think I'll have the papers up in bed for a few minutes, Ma. Look at the race-card. There's a filly up at Pontefract I fancy. Thought I'd put a tenner on its nose. I'll put one on for you too if you like.'

Ma, however, was not to be bought off. Nor was she to be foxed by talk of race-cards. She knew perfectly well what it was behind it all. He wanted to lounge there like some Eastern potentate and watch her dressing.

It was idle, on Pop's part, to pretend that he didn't like to see Ma dressing. On the contrary it was a source of unfailing interest. It was a process of infinite, indeed passionate delight.

Ma had devised two methods of getting dressed. The first consisted of her getting out of bed in her nightgown, which she then proceeded to use as a sort of protective tent. Under this tent she then executed a series of movements, some strenuous, some serpentine, some agitated, a few of positive anguish. Having finished them at last – a performance never either easy or brief – Ma at last emerged completely encased in shining purple corset, knickers of much amplitude and a bra of the expanse and depth of a pair of barrage balloons. That she was still not fully dressed merely added acutely to Pop's enjoyment. The fact that fringes of certain of the more interesting areas of her body were still not totally hidden served to fill him with a curiosity as great as if he had never seen them before. It was a moment of intense frustration when Ma finally covered it all with her slip.

Ma's second method was to emerge from bed as she was now, stark naked, and proceed to go into conflict with her most serious adversary, the corset. This was a process not unlike that of trying to press a melon into an eggcup. In Ma's case there were, however, four melons: two in front, and two, rather larger, though not all that much, behind.

The chief of Ma's early difficulties was not merely to get the rear melons inside the corset, but both of them in, if possible, at the same time. As if counterbalanced by some delicate principle, however, one melon would invariably insist on going in before the other, leaving its fellow exposed. When finally the second melon was induced to slip in the first instantly slipped out. The balance having been partially restored by Ma fighting with all her strength at the purple corset there arrived a moment, miraculous and stupendously fascinating to Pop's eyes, when Ma seemed suddenly to have developed a second bosom at the back of herself, but lower down and even more expansive than the front one provided by nature. At last, under the impulse of a great sigh rising through a slow crescendo to a positive groan, this phenomenon finally disappeared, silkily and firmly encased in shining purple, itself a balloon inflated to bursting point.

This more serious part of the struggle over, there remained only the comparatively minor excursion with the bosom. Even here, however, the principle of counterbalance came again into play, so that as fast as one bosom slipped into its cup one side the other slipped out of the other. Whenever this happened Pop was reminded of one of those little weather houses in which a male figure pops out to forecast rain and a female to forecast fine, a thought that often caused him to call out from the bed, much to Ma's pretended disgust:

'Left titty out first this morning, Ma. Going to rain before the day's gone.'

This morning, however, Pop watched Ma proceed through her dressing battle with neither excitement nor comment. The pain across his chest now and then seemed to harden. Each time this happened it grew more stubborn, lasted longer and was more difficult to move.

Ma having at last finished battle with the purple corset, the melons safely encased, both back and front, she now stood in her slip, gazing at Pop from the foot of the bed, inquiring if something wasn't the matter with him this morning? Pop, not daring to confess that there was, replied that he didn't think so and why?

'Must be something wrong with my figure,' Ma said in a tone of slight affront, her figure being, even when firmly corseted, all of two yards wide. 'Don't seem to get much response this morning anyway.'

Pop said No? He'd been taking it all in all right. Not to worry.

Taking it all in all right, her foot, Ma told him. He hadn't even noticed the right boosie had popped out first this morning, meaning it was going to be a fine day. She didn't know what he was coming to. Next thing she knew he'd be asking for his breakfast in bed.

Breakfast? He wasn't all that hungry, Pop said, his voice distant, even a little feeble. At the same time a new ache shot through his chest, causing him sharply to catch and then hold his breath.

Ma, slightly concerned now, told herself that it was bad enough Pop not noticing which boosie had popped out first this morning, even allowing for a natural slackening of interest after passion had been spent, but the confession that he wasn't hungry was a truly alarming one.

'Have some more champers,' she said and was about to proceed to fill Pop's glass when she discovered that he had hardly touched it since she had filled it last. 'Here, drink up. Can't think what's got into you.'

Another sharp attack of pain caused Pop to confess that he didn't feel all that great, to which Ma replied blandly that she expected it was wind, most likely. Or lack of food.

Lack of food, in the Larkin household at any rate, was a highly serious matter. It might lead to all sorts of things. Now what would Pop have? she said, her voice richly cheerful. The usual? Porridge, bacon and eggs, sausage, fried bread, potatoes, tomatoes, the lot? She wasn't sure, but she thought she even had a few kidneys too.

The mere mention of kidneys afflicted Pop with a curious nausea in his throat. He suddenly wanted to be sick, but at the same time knew he couldn't be. The nausea slipped from his throat to his chest, to be joined there by a new stab of pain. Involuntarily he clutched his chest, gasping, and for the first time Ma was visibly alarmed. Even so she couldn't for the life of her think what could possibly be the matter with him and in solution to the problem could only offer the thought that perhaps they'd overdone it a bit that second time. It has been a bit hot and strong, perhaps, after all.

Pop, for once unable to find comment on the unthinkable and astonishing suggestion that making love to Ma might have serious after-effects, sought comfort in champagne. A slow sip or two of it presently caused him to belch mildly. Ma, relieved to hear it, commented that that was better and urged him to have another good burp or two.

A second rising wave of wind stuck in the lower part of Pop's throat, then receded and became part of his general pain. He could suddenly neither belch nor swallow. He found himself fighting for breath. Involuntarily he clutched at his chest, a gesture that made Ma perfectly sure that the cause of all was undoubtedly going it a bit too strong on an empty stomach. No doubt about it.

'Ma,' Pop tried to say and for the first time in his life discovered that he was utterly unable to say the word. His mouth was suddenly dry and rigid. It seemed to him too that somebody was ramming a crowbar through the upper part of his chest. It was being driven, iron and relentless, clean through his heart.

In his moment of agony he sank back on the pillows, face suddenly white, vision clouded, forehead coldly drenched with sweat. Desperately his eyes searched to focus Ma at the foot of the bed and discovered for an awful moment or two that she wasn't there. A white blank wall had replaced her: a terrible nothingness.

The thought of a world without Ma suddenly brought Pop to the verge of the ghastly conviction that he was dying. He was fighting not merely for breath but for life. Through the insistent pain of all this there shot through him the even more agonizing thought that his last two acts on earth might have been to drink champagne and make love to Ma. He had a sudden desire to cry.

Then he abruptly realized that the blank wall at the foot of the bed was a sheet. Ma was behind it. She was holding it. He could just see the tips of her fingers. She was drawing the sheet over him, gently. A second awful thought that this was death, this was what they did to you, covering you with a sheet, drove him down into a dark silent well of despair.

His pain was now so excruciating that he had lost all capacity and will to fight it. The sheet enveloped him, his face for a moment covered. Then he was vaguely aware of it being lifted from his face. Ma's own face appeared beyond it, faintly smiling but somehow pained too. She spoke; but what it was she said he never knew.

Then Ma wasn't there again. Vaguely he heard voices. They seemed to reach him from the end of a long, echoing corridor. They were the voices of children. Then Ma's voice was among them too, proclaiming silence, breathlessly. The house. suddenly tomb-like, merely served for some moments as a sounding board for the voices of birds in the garden outside, the shrill sweetness of a wren, the rising broken moan of a pigeon. He listened to them too as if they might have been the last sounds he would hear on earth. Then the singing of wrens and the liquid moan of pigeons stopped completely. They too might have been dead.

He lay for a long time alone. His fight with pain had now reversed itself. The pain was fighting him. The bar of iron had driven so far into his heart that he was transfixed immovably to the bed. Everything about him was darkness. Everything beyond the darkness was silent.

After what seemed hours he was dimly aware of not being alone any more. Ma was with him again. Her solitary but amazingly diminished figure stood vaguely at the bottom of the bed. Then it multiplied into three and he realized that his beloved Mariette and Mr Charlton, both in dressing-gowns, were also with her. A searing conviction that he was seeing them too for the last time overcame him so greatly that tears ran bitterly into his eyes a second time. Quite strengthless, he let them flow, so that Ma and Mariette and Mr Charlton dissolved away.

Ma, with a damp towel, gently wiped both his sweat and tears away. The effect of this act was momentarily to clear his vision. He then became aware that it was Mr Charlton, Charley boy, who had, as so often in the past, provided the unexpected. Once so dim and impracticable, Mr Charlton now had a way, a positive genius, for rising to crises with realism. Now he appeared suddenly as a figure possessed with coolness, much resource and calm.

'I'm going to take your temperature, Pop,' Mr Charlton said. 'Dr O'Connor will be here in a quarter of an hour. Lie flat. I'm going to take away one pillow.'

The cool practical nature of Mr Charlton's words did something to restore Pop's faith in living. He was aware of desperately wanting to live. He told himself he had to live, not merely for his own sake but for Ma's sake especially and all the rest of them.

The thermometer seemed to be stuck for hours under his tongue. Mr

Charlton, with an air almost professional, was also taking his pulse. Pop, still in insufferable pain, felt him take the thermometer away.

Now he became aware of the smell of eau-de-cologne. Mariette was bending over him, gently assuaging his forehead. He was at once assailed by an inconsolable conviction that he was seeing her, always so like a younger, more shapely edition of Ma, for the last time. He tried to touch her hands, only to discover that they had no response to his. And then, to complete his inconsolable depression, he was aware that Ma was no longer in the room.

'Where's Ma?' he managed to say. 'I need Ma.'

'She's downstairs, waiting for Dr O'Connor.'

And then Dr O'Connor was in the room. Dr O'Connor was thinnish, young, his hair inclined to sandiness, his long hands freckled. His Irish voice seemed to express a certain sardonic amusement at the situation in which Pop found himself.

'Now what's all this, Mr Larkin? Been overdoing it a bit, eh?'

Pop, facing death, fighting with hopelessly diminishing strength the pain that drove deeper and deeper across his heart, actually managed the faintest of smiles.

It was marvellous how the news got round, he started to say and then saw the brief flash of a hypodermic syringe in the air and felt the prick of its needle in his upper arm.

Then he was there no longer.

· 2 ·

Long, long later – he never knew how long it was – Pop came back to consciousness: to a strange, confused, familiar yet unfamiliar world of living. It seemed to him that he had died and had somehow come back, mysteriously, from death.

His first key to this world was vision. At first he merely saw shapes. After some time the shapes became people. He saw Ma, Mariette, Mr Charlton, another of his daughters, Primrose, and Dr O'Connor. Then he saw another, elderly figure, with a stethoscope hung about his neck. This, he slowly realized, was a second doctor. This doctor surveyed him with eyes of grey calm, from behind gold-rimmed spectacles, with a gaze slightly professional, though also vaguely cheerful.

Pop felt not at all uncheerful himself. He felt rested, calm, relieved of pain.

'This,' Dr O'Connor said, 'is Mr Millington. Mr Millington is a consultant.'

Mr Millington, now advancing closer to the bed, smiled with further cheerfulness.

'We are going to do,' he said, 'a small job of work on you, Mr Larkin. Lie absolutely still. No talking.'

Between them Dr O'Connor and Mr Millington produced a piece of apparatus sprouting many antennae. These antennae were presently attached to various parts of Pop's body, so that he looked very like a prostrate spider with many legs. He became aware of much pressing of buttons and repeated clickings. A long sheet of graph paper then ran from the apparatus: recording, as Mr Millington remarked, what the body had to say.

To Pop there suddenly seemed something curiously comic about this length of paper. It was a great joke to think that, having come back from the dead, he had been reincarnated, as it were, as a printing machine. Irrepressible as ever, he was prompted to remark on this, asking how the racing results were coming through and if he'd won anything on that filly at Pontefract in the two-thirty?

445

The joke caused, unfortunately, intense dismay.

'I am afraid you have now ruined,' Mr Millington said, 'the whole middle portion of the record.'

Pop made a low apology, which received from Dr O'Connor, in turn, a rather severe injunction for him to keep absolutely quiet. No talking. Absolutely still.

For a second time Pop became aware of much pressing of buttons and many clickings. The sheet of graph paper ran off at great length until at last removed and stopped by Mr Millington, who gave one end of it to Dr O'Connor while holding the other himself.

'We are now going,' Mr Millington said, 'to have a little natter about you. Take it easy. Relax completely until we come back again.'

Dr O'Connor and Mr Millington disappeared. For a few moments Pop lay in suspense, his senses pierced by a single sound of whose intense sweetness he realized he had never been wholly aware before: the trilling voice of a wren in the garden outside. For so tiny and frail a creature its voice seemed suddenly to have an amazing power and Pop listened to it in wonder and fascination. It was his first experience of illness magnifying trivialities.

'Cardiograph.' It was the voice of Mr Charlton, explaining the apparatus. 'Recording what the heart does.' Truly, Pop thought, Charley boy was a wonder. Cardiograph – that unfailing mine of Charley's information had done it again.

Pop, feeling rather like a recalcitrant schoolboy who had already ruined one experiment and was afraid of spoiling another, said nothing, merely permitting himself the faintest of smiles. From far across the room came an answering one from Ma, so subdued and unlike her that it might have come from some old static photograph.

'The heart has suffered some damage.' Mr Millington and Dr O'Connor were back in the room. Mr Millington was speaking. 'It will mean complete rest for several weeks. Lying completely flat. No pillows at first. Perhaps one after a week or two. Then another. Goodbye now, I'll come back and see you in a week. Take care of yourself. Good men are scarce.'

Mr Millington waved a cheerful farewell hand and was gone. Dr O'Connor meanwhile was busy writing what appeared to be various prescriptions. Then he came to the bedside in order to take Pop's pulse. He too looked not uncheerful.

It was perhaps this slight air of cheerfulness, whether forced or not, that now caused Ma to come out with what Pop thought was an excellent and timely suggestion.

'Don't you think it would do him good to have a nice large brandy now, Doctor?'

'Not on any account.'

'I always thought brandy was good for the heart?'

'Not on any account, Mrs Larkin.'

Ma, stunned by the severity of the denial of her proposal to give Pop the very thing that would do him most good, quite apart from the fact that it was the thing he most wanted, let out a very severe pronouncement of her own.

'Whatever next? He loves brandy. He thrives on brandy. It peps him up no end.'

'Pepping him up, Mrs Larkin, is exactly what we do not want to do.'

Well, she would go to the bone-house, Ma said, using one of those expressions that had become part of the family vocabulary ever since she and Pop had taken the family to France for a holiday and had visited an ossuary. Whatever were things coming to? No brandy, her foot.

At the mention of the word bone-house Dr O'Connor gave Mr Charlton a silently significant look as though suggesting – as Mr Charlton afterwards confessed he actually had – that that was exactly where Pop was on his way to if they weren't all very careful.

'Very well, then' Ma said, 'a small brandy.'

'Not even a small brandy. Not on any account.'

'Good God.' Ma looked highly affronted, if not actually insulted, as if her idea of what was best for Pop was being doubted. 'Whoever heard of a drop of brandy hurting anybody? Besides he must be famished. He hasn't had a morsel of anything inside him for twelve hours. We don't want him starving, do we?'

Lack of food was, in Ma's opinion, a very serious matter. The mere thought of starvation was a catastrophe.

'He needs a good square meal,' she said, 'that's all. A beefsteak-and-kidney pud and a bottle of Beaujolais'll put him right in no time.'

Dr O'Connor, appearing to wave aside the suggestion of beefsteak-and-kidney pud and Beaujolais as if it were something subversive, was in fact signalling to Mr Charlton, Mariette and Primrose to leave the room.

When they had done so he turned to Pop and Ma less in the manner of a doctor than a person about to intone, Ma thought, a final benediction. They hadn't quite come to that yet, she thought, and Dr O'Connor needn't start thinking they had. She felt highly aggrieved. The restorative powers of her steak-and-kidney pud had, it seemed to her, been called into question and she didn't like it. It was as bad as doubting her virtue.

Dr O'Connor now proceeded to repeat the injunction that for the next week or two Pop must lie on his back, pillowless, with as little excitement as possible: and then said:

'Now, as to diet.'

'I'll feed him up well,' Ma said, 'don't you worry about that.'

'As to diet. And I mean diet.'

'I know what he likes and what he doesn't like. Good solid rich food and plenty of it. Where d'ye think he'd be today if I hadn't seen he got it all these years?'

'He might not be here.'

'Well,' Ma said, again very affronted, 'there's two ways of looking at that.'

Dr O'Connor said indeed there was and again assumed his benedictory attitude.

'I'm talking about diet, Mrs Larkin. About *not* eating. I am giving you advice as your doctor. Mr Larkin must have no sugar, no butter, no animal fats, very few carbohydrates, no stimulants –'

Good God, Ma said, did he mind? Life wouldn't be worth living.

'No alcohol –'

At the mention of the word alcohol Pop made an involuntary movement to lift his head sharply from the bed in protest, found himself too weak to manage it and fell back, pale as if cudgelled.

'No alcohol?' Ma said. 'No *drink*, you mean?'

'No drink.'

'What's it poison then, now?'

'Tantamount to that.'

Tantamount – another of those big words again, Pop thought. He certainly needed Mr Charlton here.

'I don't know about tantamount,' Ma said. 'The point is how much can he have?'

'None. None at all. Nothing. None whatever.'

'*You mean he's got to be T.T.?*'

'Precisely.'

'Good God, you must be joking.'

'I am not joking.'

'You're having me on, then. Been at it all his life and it's never done him no harm yet.'

Gravely Dr O'Connor assured Ma that he was neither having her on nor joking.

'No alcohol,' he repeated. 'Absolutely no alcohol.'

'But how long *for?*'

'The foreseeable future.'

'And how long might that be for God Almighty's sake?'

'For ever. Perhaps for ever.'

If Pop had felt faint and strengthless before these words, he now felt utterly crushed and condemned. He had a feeling of being dragged to the scaffold.

'Teetotal!' Ma said. 'It's a libel. He'll never live it down.'

He never would at that, Pop thought. There was never a truer word.

'He'll never be able to hold his head up again,' Ma said. 'Whatever will people think? What's he going to say when anybody asks him to have one?'

' "No." '

'You'll have to strap him down,' Ma said. 'You'll have to put the handcuffs on.'

There was now a sudden silence. In the course of it Pop grew very tired. The rims of his eyes started to quiver. The figures of Ma and Dr O'Connor danced, became glazed and finally, in a renewed wave of semi-consciousness, drifted away, taking with them the ever fainter and fainter trilling sweetness of the voice of the wren in the garden beyond.

Downstairs, in the kitchen, Dr O'Connor held a short conference at which Ma, Mariette, Primrose, Mr Charlton, little Oscar and bright redheaded Phyllida Cleopatra Boadicea Nightingale were the listeners. Its tone was so ominous that towards the end of it Phyllida Cleopatra Boadicea Nightingale burst into tears. Little Oscar burst into tears immediately afterwards and then Ma cried too.

It was left once again to the incalculable Mr Charlton to provide comfort by being practical, resourceful and calm.

'I'll take the children off and go and get the prescriptions,' he said. 'There seems to be one here for you, Ma, too.'

· 3 ·

Down in the village, in her gimcrack little cottage, Bonny Banks, a converted cow-byre that always looked like a crumbling piece of fairy-tale stage scenery that was about to fall apart at any moment, Edith Pilchester had just finished a late breakfast of oatmeal bread, margarine, sardines, cocoa, rose-hip jelly and a cold fried egg left over from her previous night's supper, when she heard the church clock strike eleven.

She had in fact been up since five o'clock, but it was a morning in which everything, more even than usually, had gone wrong. She had not only lost time but all count of it. She seemed to have done a thousand things and yet done nothing. She still had a thousand more to do and it was absolutely ghastly.

The great trouble was that this month, July, was undoubtedly the busiest, maddest of the whole year. During the six hours since waking she had already spun large quantities of sheep wool, made a dozen pots of lemon curd for the Church bazaar, pulled half a hundredweight of rhubarb and gathered a skip of elderberry flowers, both to make into wine, and had done half an hour of *gros-point* on the cushion she was making for a sale of work being held in aid of some society for unmarried mothers, of whom, in Miss Pilchester's view, there had recently been, in spite of all you read and heard in papers and on radio, a distressing increase. She sometimes wondered how girls found time for these things; she never did.

She had also written several letters and now, having finished her breakfast without clearing the kitchen table, which was still littered with the remains of last night's supper things, the pots of lemon curd and piles of elderflower and rhubarb, realized that she had run out of stamps and would have to walk as far as the village post office to get some.

It was noon before she was finally ready to go. The day, though warm, had a certain promise of thunder about it. The air was drenched with that moist, intoxicating summer richness that was a pleasant though enervating compound of hay, roses, elderflower, pinks, meadowsweet and even a touch of the odour of the first Spanish chestnut bloom. It was what her dear friend Mr Larkin might well have called 'perfick'. In consequence she had not only put on a thin cotton summer dress, an affair of washed-out pink design which looked as if run up hastily out of old curtains, but she was also prudently armed with an umbrella in case it came on to rain and a tattered oatmeal sweater of her own spinning and knitting in case it turned cold. With the English weather you never knew.

As she went out of the garden, closing the gate behind her, she was surprised to see her next-door neighbour, Professor Fane, clipping his privet hedge along the road. She at once said a polite though distant and frigid 'good morning', to which the Professor promptly replied 'good afternoon'. This however in no way surprised her, since the Professor was, in her opinion, quite batty. As Miss Pilchester was equally batty in the eyes of the Professor little was lost on either side.

Apart from his obvious madness the Professor was also, in Miss Pilchester's view, one of those people, a foreigner, who used the country as a mere convenience. He did not belong. His cottage was a mere weekend bolt-hole for escape from London and the exhausting routine of teaching physics to long-haired and unwashed students who apparently spent more time marching with banners of protest than at lectures. The Professor was undoubtedly, as Miss Pilchester had long suspected, a Communist. He was also a sort of blue-bottle fly. He buzzed in and out of the countryside as and when it suited him, a nuisance, impermanent, contributing nothing. Such people didn't, in her view, belong to the countryside. They were nothing more than fleeting parasites.

Not surprisingly, therefore, she looked on the Professor with both suspicion and contempt. It had not always been so. At his first arrival she had been civil enough to send him, as a gift of welcome, a small basket of red currants and a pot of blackberry jelly. These had been returned with a note of acid brevity, explaining that the Professor was on a diet, which appeared mainly to consist, Miss Pilchester discovered, of yoghurt, rye bread and Vichy water. Such poisons as red currants and blackberry jelly were not for him.

Thereafter the Professor and Miss Pilchester scarcely exchanged a word. The Professor regarded Miss Pilchester as a lamentable case of inverted nymphomania, a phrase of his own, whereas Miss Pilchester thought the Professor not only as being a Communist, itself bad enough in all conscience, but also a bilious bladder of lard. Apart from occasionally passing the time of day with her, and then always sarcastically, his only other communication with her was to write impersonal letters of complaint about her bonfires, which he called 'your incautious but calculated conflagrations', a phrase Miss Pilchester thought highly contradictory even if it meant anything at all, which she doubted.

On one occasion, fired by a double whisky followed by parsnip wine, she had thrown over the fence, like a verbal hand grenade, the phrase 'red egg-head!' to which the Professor responded by setting his garden water sprinkler in such a way that the west wind blew spray all over her washing. This made her so angry that she seriously considered whether it would be possible to mix strychnine – you could get it legitimately for killing moles, she discovered – with lemon curd without detection, and send him a pot, but in time her fury calmed and she merely accepted the Professor as one of those evils that, in the mysterious dispensation of the Almighty, were sent to try ordinary decent people like her.

Slightly tired, perhaps, on that moist and thundery morning that was presently to become catastrophic, though she did not at that moment know it, Miss Pilchester felt her feathers decidedly ruffle up as the Professor replied to her 'good morning' with his 'good afternoon'.

'Morning,' she informed him.

'Afternoon. If I'm not mistaken.'

'As you habitually are.'

'Indeed? Unless my hearing is defective the church clock has struck twelve. Afternoon it therefore is.'

'I never go by the church clock. It's always fast.'

The Professor, giving a sharp snip with his hedge-clippers, murmured something about *tempus fugit*. The bandying about of Latin tags was always, to Miss Pilchester, a source of annoyance and she instantly surprised herself, in a moment of temper, by tartly retorting:

'All right. Have it your own way. *Chacun à son goût.*'

The Professor laughed, low and despicably as Miss Pilchester thought, and said something about the marvels that women's emancipation had wrought. He had no idea that French had penetrated so deep into the countryside.

This remark brought their conversation, the longest so far between them, to such a point of imminent conflict that it seemed suddenly likely to develop into a combat between hedge-clippers and umbrella. Miss Pilchester in fact actually lifted the umbrella and was only saved from bringing it down on the Professor's head by the wail of an ambulance siren coming up the road.

As the melancholy wail increased and the ambulance finally tore past them, travelling very fast, Miss Pilchester remarked:

'Another accident, I expect. Another poor innocent laid low, I shouldn't wonder.'

'There are few innocents left,' the Professor said. 'And no poor.'

Miss Pilchester, able to stand it no longer, gave a positive snort, together with a savage swirl of the umbrella, and stalked away. As she swept into the road the Professor delivered what he himself would undoubtedly have called his Parthian shot and called:

'French you may speak. But in this country we still drive on the left of the road.'

To her dismay Miss Pilchester abruptly realized that she was wandering, half-blind with anger, somewhere to the right-centre of the road. She wasn't looking where she was going at all. It was truly awful. It was absolutely ghastly.

It was all the fault of that wretched foreigner, that Communist, that cynic, she told herself over and over again as she tramped her way up to the post office, half-exhausted by anger, so that now and then she felt compelled to pause and draw in savage breath. The countryside could well do without such people, it really could. Suddenly the delicious, sweet, intoxicating air of summer felt tainted.

What a contrast, she told herself, with her friend Mr Larkin. Mr Larkin was himself like summer: eternally intoxicating, always sweet, always perfickly delicious. The only thing was that, like the precious days of summer themselves, he appeared so rarely. It seemed weeks since she had seen him last. Now and then she had seen him float serenely past her cottage in the splendour of his shining monogrammic Rolls, once with a brief wave of his hand, once with a few symphonic chords, both high and low, on the horn, and once with a gesture of such meaningful airiness that she was unable to sleep that night and kept telling herself that unless she was grievously mistaken the gesture was, in fact, a blown kiss.

The precious nature of such rare displays of distant affection from Mr Larkin couldn't lightly be dismissed, still less forgotten. She still treasured beyond all expression the original palpitating rapture of the first kiss he had ever given her in the cottage and still more of that other time, after the gymkhana, when Pop had seized her like a sheaf of corn and had passionately urged her with that luscious compulsion of his to give everything she'd got and she had tried so hard to do so, even though knowing it wouldn't possibly be half enough.

Ever since that time she had longed, over and over again, to give all she'd got. She'd give it any time. Sometimes, in fact, she gave it in the last moments before sleep, metaphorically wrapped in Pop's arms, murmuring to herself, as in an intoxicated lullaby, that it was perfick, absolutely perfick, and urging Pop, if possible, to do it again.

As she went into the post office, which was also the village shop, Miss Pilchester found herself as usual in a state of tart wonder at the revolution that had, over the past few years, taken place there.

Where once the counter had held little but a block of margarine, a red wedge of mouse-trap cheese, a few pock-marked apples and a cube of sweet, cheap dates, it was now bright with tempting delicacies, French, Italian, Spanish and even Indian and Chinese, from Bisque d'Homard to canneloni and chop suey. In another corner of the shop stood a vast deep freeze cabinet stuffed with smoked salmon, *escargots de Bourgogne*, scampi, smoked trout, petit pois, smoked cod's roe, smoked eel, salami and sausage of every kind, palm hearts and ice creams great and small, bright-coloured as the flags of the United Nations. On the shelves above stood regiments of tins containing mangoes, paw-paws, lychees, *fraises des bois* and exotics of every kind.

In front of her a fat young woman further rotund in pregnancy, with four children sucking green-and-pink ice-lollies of such magnitude that they were actually washing in them, as in frothy soap, was filling baskets with mangoes, fresh Italian peaches, Bisque d'Homard, scampi, Emmenthaler, Brie and Stilton cheese, packets of spaghetti Bolognese and smoked salmon, at the same time complaining in rough, loud country accents hadn't they got no Rocquefort this week then? It was coming to summat now when you couldn't get no Rocquefort. She didn't know what her husband would say. There wouldn't half be a carry-on. Last week he very nearly hit her with the poker because they never had no *escargots*. She didn't know what things were coming to.

Miss Pilchester, silently and tartly wondering why on earth it wasn't caviare that had caused the incident of the poker – after all the Russians, the Communists, practically regarded it as a staple diet – then had to wait nearly five minutes at the post office counter while the woman drew a vast sum in children's allowances and complained again, as she counted up a fat wad of notes, about the absence of a particular brand of cigars her husband was more than partial to.

'He don't 'alf raise 'ell if he don't 'ave 'is cigars, I tell you. Raises bloody 'ell, 'e does an' all. Ain't you got no chianti again this week then? That'll make 'is blood boil I tell you.'

Finally Miss Pilchester was able to buy six fourpenny stamps, a quarter of tea, a small tin of baked beans, a quarter of mouse-trap cheese and a packet of potato crisps: the limit she could afford. At the mention of potato crisps one of the children started shouting that he wanted potato crisps too, at which the mother promptly belted him across the ear, demanding to know if he thought she was bleedin' made of money?

Trying hard to look the other way, Miss Pilchester then asked the girl behind the counter how much that would be and got the astonishing reply:

'One pound sixteen and fourpence, Miss Pilchester, please.'

Miss Pilchester stood aghast. She knew that prices had risen pretty steeply these last few years; she was fully aware of the social revolution in which, among the working classes, so-called, smoked salmon and Rocquefort had replaced margarine and mouse-trap, but this was, she thought, altogether a bit too much.

'Haven't you,' she said, 'made some slight mistake?'

'Oh! my goodness, Oh! dear, Oh! Miss Pilchester, I'm terribly sorry.'

She should think so, Miss Pilchester told herself. It was yet another example of the futilities of modern education. Nowadays people couldn't even add up.

'I make it, unless I'm much mistaken, nine-and-three.'

'So it is, Miss Pilchester. I'm sorry. I'm terribly sorry. I'm all of a tizzy this morning. I'm all of a heap.'

Some of these words were drowned by the howling of the small boy who, having been belted about the ear once, was now being belted twice, this time with a packet of crisps. Either as an act of appeasement or example his brother and sisters were being belted too and were responding by tearing open the packets of crisps like ravenous wolves who had had nothing to eat for several days.

'Now bleedin' be quiet or else I'll give you summat to remember next time. If you don't shut your gob you won't have no scampi.'

In the confusion of din caused by belting, howling and the crackling of crisps Miss Pilchester started to ask the girl behind the counter why she could possibly be all of a heap when the girl promptly burst into tears.

What on earth was the matter? Miss Pilchester wanted to know. All of a sudden the place was Bedlam.

'Haven't you heard?' the girl said. With painful difficulty she sucked back her sobs. 'I mean – it's so awful.'

'So awful about what?'

'Mr Larkin.'

'Mr Larkin? What about Mr Larkin?'

The girl now broke into louder weeping, causing the children who had been belted to bawl even louder still.

'They say Mr Larkin's dead. Mr Larkin's dead.'

In the confusion of weeping, gossip and crackling of crisps over the next few indeterminable minutes Miss Pilchester stood like a pillar of salt. Vaguely she heard the young woman far gone in pregnancy say Oh! yes, it was right: knocked down by a bus, to which an elderly man drawing his weekly pension promptly corrected her by saying No, a stroke. It was gospel. A stroke. About eight or nine o'clock that morning, he understood. Very sudden. Out like a light.

In a slight pause among all the confusion the voice of the eldest child, having finished bawling, suddenly piped up with the irrefutable truth that 'Ah! well, we all have to go some time,' a remark which caused Miss Pilchester to recover her own voice. A moment later the pillar of salt melted and her voice with it. In that moment too Miss Pilchester remembered the ambulance going past her door.

'Oh! no, it can't be. Oh! no – God wouldn't do it. God would never do a thing like that –'

In the act of frantically clutching her head with both hands she dropped tea, beans, crisps and mouse-trap on the floor and then blindly rushed from the shop.

Totally unaware for the next few minutes of where she was or where she was going, her only really conscious impression was being alone. The village street was utterly deserted. The whole place was like something stricken, itself dead, with not a soul in sight.

Too stunned to cry, she desperately longed for someone, even a stranger, to talk to. The emptiness of the street seemed to mock her. She then observed, coming out of the shade of a big chestnut tree overhanging a wheelwright's yard just beyond the church, a horse.

It was a big, handsome chestnut, coat gleaming in the midday sun, and something about it seemed suddenly of great comfort. One could talk to a horse. One could even confide in a horse. One could even, failing all else, weep with a horse. She knew. Long ago, when times had been better, she had had a horse, a mere hack it was true, but in both body and spirit she and the horse had been one. But those days were far off – now she had no horse. The dividends on her gilt-edged – mocking term – pitiful enough as they were, kept constantly falling, and horses were no longer a possible part of her world.

She then saw that the horse was being ridden by a woman. Horse and woman were, she then saw, well married, the big shining flanks of the animal being handsomely repeated in the round thighs, round buttocks and even rounder bosom of Freda O'Connor, who was dressed in jodhpurs, bright yellow sweater and a crimson scarf on her head.

Freda O'Connor, breasts protruding over the neck of the horse, as Pop Larkin had once observed, like headlamps, was notorious as a woman of shifting affections. During the week she lived with a retired naval commander; at weekends she had matters of great interest to discuss with a horse-dealer two villages away. Out hunting, she had a propensity to disappear into coppices after invisible foxes, closely followed by a former guards officer who was using his gratuity to grow mushrooms that nobody apparently wanted to buy. When new foxes appeared in the village, preferably in the shape of sporting or other military men, she was out hunting for them. The lines of the marriage service, 'to have and to hold', had not, as Pop's friend the Brigadier had once caustically observed, been precisely written for her. A lot of men had had her. Few had held her for long.

'Morning. Damn nice morning.'

Freda O'Connor's voice, as if she had long modelled it on her regiments of men, was loud and brassy.

A bitter thought in the mind of Miss Pilchester, who liked neither Freda O'Connor nor the men with whom she consorted, reminded her that nice though the morning might be it was also damned.

'Corn looks well. Early harvest I shouldn't wonder. See the show-jumping on TV last night?'

No, Miss Pilchester had seen no show-jumping on TV, purely because, as she put it, she had no machine. Nor could there be any harvest, she thought, now that Pop was dead.

'You've heard the awful news, I expect?'

No, Freda O'Connor hadn't heard the awful news. What awful news?

'Pop – Mr Larkin – is dead.'

'God. Holy catfish. You don't say.'

Miss Pilchester was silent, merely staring at the bright eyes of the horse, soft and oily as it seemed to her with comfort, at the same time ignoring the big yellow figure of Freda O'Connor swelling like a brassy statue above it.

'What happened? Accident?'

There appeared to be, Miss Pilchester said, conflicting reports. Some said a car. Some said a stroke.

'And some say elbow-lifting, I shouldn't wonder.'

Miss Pilchester icily begged her pardon?

'Bit excessive with the old bottle, I mean. Get me?'

Miss Pilchester said No, she didn't get her and added, in a voice frozen now to flat, level bitterness, that there were, after all, excesses and excesses. Or didn't Freda O'Connor know?

The oblique, insensitive reference to Pop's drinking habits enraged her so much that she was a hundred yards away from Freda O'Connor, striding past the old wheelwright's yard and then the church, before she was fully conscious again. When her mind finally began working once more she could think of only one thing. Like Pop himself, she needed a drink. She needed a long, stiff, powerful whisky.

Somewhere between the church and The Hare and Hounds a sudden pang of conscience arrested her. Perhaps, after all, she ought to go into the church instead: there to pray, if only words could be found, for Pop's departed soul. Thus stricken, she stood for fully a minute in the middle of the road, struggling with her conscience and its problem until she decided after all that whisky, rather than prayer, was perhaps the more appropriate medium with which to send the soul of Pop on its last, long journey.

Inside The Hare and Hounds she found herself still so possessed by the struggle with conscience and mournful thoughts of Pop that in the abysmal agony of trying to grapple with them she actually found herself talking in his language.

'Give me a snifter. God, a big one too. God. Whisky.'

It was of course awful to speak of the Almighty in such terms, in the same breath as whisky, but the occasion, she felt, was hellish enough to demand it. It was hellish enough for anything. It wasn't merely absolutely ghastly. It was sheer absolute, nightmare hell.

Mr Foreman, the landlord, was himself serving at the bar, his only other customers being a farm labourer apparently half-talking to himself over a pint of beer, his jacket covered with sprigs of boughs and leaves from a hedge he had been clipping, and a retired butcher who, himself red and beefy of face, with small jolly blue eyes, looked not at all unlike a prize piece of beef cattle fattened and ready for market.

'Don't often see you in here of a morning, Miss Pilchester,' the landlord said. 'What'll it be? Black and White? Johnny Walker?'

'Hell. Anything. The stronger the better. And double please.'

Knocking back a good half of the whisky with a speed not unworthy of Pop himself getting outside one of his special Red Bull cocktails, Miss Pilchester gave a great sorrowful gasp and muttered in a voice slightly incoherent something about she might well be seen there all day and every day from now on – God, how she'd needed that – the snifter, she meant, the stiffener.

This slightly wild demeanour of Miss Pilchester's drew from the land-lord, who was used enough to seeing people go out of the pub drunk but not to come into it in the same condition, the question as to whether she was all right? Was something the matter?

Draining the whisky, growing slightly incoherent but not enough to prevent herself ordering another, Miss Pilchester gave the astounding reply that the roof had fallen in and God shouldn't have let it. It was hell. It was absolutely ghastly.

The reference to roof, God, hell and the ghastliness all in one breath left the landlord with a growing suspicion that Miss Pilchester had already been at the bottle somewhere. That was largely the trouble with women in the country. Frustrated and lonely, they got at it in secret and then didn't know when to stop. If he knew the form, which from long ex-perience he did, Miss Pilchester would at any moment start weeping.

Which, at the arrival of her second whisky, Miss Pilchester promptly did.

'Now, now, what's it all about?' the landlord said and thought it a not inappropriate moment to shift the burden of responsibility to his missus and then remembered that she had gone into town, shopping. 'It can't be as bad as all that, surely.'

Bad? Not bad? Not hell, when a great, good man like Pop Larkin had gone? Wrested from them, struck down.

'Larkin? Pop? You don't mean? –'

Yes, she meant, Miss Pilchester said. She was sobbing openly now. Some said it was a stroke, some a car. She had seen an ambulance. The details didn't matter. All that mattered was the going, the fact of it –

'Might be just a rumour.' The landlord made consolatory gestures as he mopped up spots of moisture, that might well have been Miss Pil-chester's tears, from the bar. 'You know villages. Rumour fair gallops round.'

No, no. Rumour she was sure it wasn't. Rumour it couldn't be. She felt it in her bones. Her heart. 'The Lord giveth,' she suddenly said, starting in further incoherence to make consolatory gestures herself, 'and the Lord taketh away' – but there were plenty of others he could have taken, she declared with vehement sorrow, other than Pop. She could name them too, she thought, thinking of Freda O'Connor and her horsey, whoring crowd.

'I could name them. I know them. They should have been cast out of the Temple long ago.'

This further mystifying excursion into vehemence, accompanied by

459

strange accusations about the Temple, utterly convinced the landlord that Miss Pilchester had undoubtedly been at the bottle all right somewhere, but not in time enough to prevent the butcher from coming up to the bar and ordering her another whisky, at the same time offering the consolatory but sensible suggestion that wouldn't it be a good idea to telephone somebody and find out if it was true? The butcher knew old Pop Larkin wasn't one to give in lightly.

'Give in? You don't give in when somebody knocks you flat with a car. You're in Kingdom Come. The Lord hath taketh.'

'Best to telephone.' The butcher offered her the third consolatory whisky. Miss Pilchester grabbed at it eagerly but vaguely, hardly seeing it through her tears. 'It'll set your mind at rest.'

Miss Pilchester waved her glass about; as if, apparently, ready to strike the butcher with it. At rest? *Rest?* The word was a hollow, absolutely ghastly, mockery.

'I'll ask my Jackie. He'll know.'

The voice of the labouring hedge-clipper had a certain sepulchral quality. It seemed to Miss Pilchester to come from afar off, from some region of outer darkness.

'Jackie? Who's Jackie? How would he know?'

'Jackie allus knows.'

To the mysteries of accusation, expulsion from the Temple and whether or not Miss Pilchester had been at the bottle all morning was now added the mystery of Jackie.

It took Miss Pilchester some moments longer to solve it and when she finally did so it was with a mixture of repugnance and disbelief. The labouring hedge-cutter had been talking not to himself but to a jackdaw, darkly nestling between his jacket and waistcoat as he sat at the end of the bar.

'This is my Jackie. Allus take 'im wimme.'

At once Miss Pilchester was sure that the bird was one of ill omen. Jackdaws – or was it crows? – or ravens perhaps? – she had read about them all somewhere. They were all birds of ill omen. In united blackness, without doubt, they foreshadowed misfortune, catastrophe and death.

At the very thought of it she started to feel physically, positively ill. In an equal spasm of depressive gloom she knocked back the butcher's whisky and in return, hardly knowing what she was doing, invited him to have another with her, an invitation to which the butcher readily and solemnly assented.

'Talk to 'im all day long,' the hedge-cutter said. 'Talks sense too. Talks a damn sight more sense than some I could name.'

In loud agreement Miss Pilchester banged her glass down on the bar. 'That I will second! That I will drink to!'

'This 'ere bird,' the hedge-cutter said, 'talks more sense in three croaks than you'll hear in Parliament in a month o' bloody wet Mondays.'

'That I will second!' Again Miss Pilchester banged her glass, this time a fourth whisky, on to the bar. 'That I will certainly drink to!'

The jackdaw now gave a loud, harsh croak, cocking his head out of the hedge-cutter's waistcoat, saucily making his presence felt.

''e 'eard you, Miss. Wants a drink.'

Drink? Drink? Miss Pilchester again waved her glass about. Did jackdaws, for heaven's sake, drink?

'Gin,' the hedge-cutter said. 'Makes 'im talk more. Drop o' gin and 'e'll talk till the cows come home.'

Then, Miss Pilchester said, give the bird gin! A large gin. Let the bird talk for goodness' sake.

'Says the Lord's Prayer sometimes.'

'Didn't I hear him,' the butcher said, 'say the 23rd Psalm once, too?'

'You did, Bill, that you did.'

'Masterpiece of a bird,' the butcher said, eyeing the jackdaw over the top of his whisky. Miss Pilchester, scarcely able to focus by this time, eyed it too.

'Two gins,' the hedge-cutter said, 'and 'e'll recite the whole of bloody Genesis.'

At these words Miss Pilchester suddenly realized that the jackdaw hadn't even got its gin. Peremptorily she banged the bar again and demanded that gin be brought. A double gin at that.

'Now Miss Pilchester –' the landlord started to say.

'Bring the poor thing its gin! Great God Almighty, we all need a drink some time, don't we? I'll say we do. You wouldn't deny the bird a drink, would you? You're here to serve drink, aren't you? Then give the bird its drink. The poor wretched ceature may be shot down at any time. Cut down in its prime. Give it its gin for goodness' sake. I'm paying, aren't I?'

There being some show of reluctance on the part of the landlord to give the jackdaw its gin, Miss Pilchester now made further loud noises of remonstration, at the same time fumbling for her purse in her shopping bag. Eventually a double gin was pushed along the bar to the hedge-cutter who, while Miss Pilchester fumbled in her purse, lifted the gin to the beak of the jackdaw, making at the same time moist sucking noises, earnestly trying to beguile the bird into at least the pretence of consuming alcohol, even if it didn't want to.

'Not very dry this morning,' he was moved finally to observe. 'Perhaps don't like this pertickler sort. Very fussy sometimes. Very dainty.'

As if the gin was in fact not of the pertickler brand to suit the jackdaw's palate, the hedge-cutter was moved to taste it for himself, finally pronouncing it to be quite all right, very good in fact, nothing wrong with it at all. A second pretence of offering gin to the bird having had the same result the hedge-cutter took a second swig, pronouncing it to be in fact, rather better than before.'

'What about the Lord's Prayer?' the butcher said.

'Give 'im time. Give 'im time. Got to 'ave 'is tot.'

The hedge-cutter having chosen to take the jackdaw's tot for him, the next thing Miss Pilchester heard was the first low muttered notes of the Lord's Prayer, croaked out as through a veil of muslin. Unable to see through her watering eyes whether in fact it was the beak of the jackdaw or the lips of the hedge-cutter reciting the familiar, sacred words, Miss Pilchester felt deeply moved, feeling more ill now than ever, cruelly on the verge of new floods of emotion.

After a time she became aware that the recital of the Lord's Prayer had stopped. This moved her still further. The bar, it seemed, was very still and she in turn couldn't see very straight.

'What about the rest?' she said, gropingly.

'Doesn't he know the rest?'

The hedge-cutter, having got as far as 'which art in Heaven', said no, he didn't think he did, he wasn't in much of a Lord's Prayer mood.

'Try the 23rd if you like,' he said.

Miss Pilchester, now past the moment of caring or knowing whether it was the Lord's Prayer or the 23rd Psalm that she wanted the bird to recite, actually heard, a few moments later, the first gentle croaking syllables of 'The Lord is my Shepherd' and had got as far as 'He maketh me to lie down' when she herself proceeded suddenly to lie down, not in green pastures, but on the floor, and very heavily, with a very loud bang, of the saloon bar of The Hare and Hounds.

At the sound of her falling the jackdaw gave a short, funereal croak. The hedge-cutter downed the last of the gin. The landlord went to the back of the bar and shouted down the open hatch of the cellar to the cellarman below:

'You there, Alf? Better bring the wheelbarter.'

Ten minutes later the hedge-cutter and the butcher were wheeling Miss

Pilchester home in the barrow, the jackdaw perched on one handle, through a lane summery with the cream of cow-parsley and meadow-sweet, rich with wild rose and honeysuckle, beyond which flocks of sheep were safely grazing in green pastures.

Women were funny, the hedge-cutter said and the jackdaw, with another funereal croak, might have been in agreement. Didn't take much to upset 'em.

· 4 ·

At regular intervals throughout the rest of the day Pop, as in a spider-web of his own making, emerged for a few vague inches towards the fragile outer threads of full consciousness and then drew darkly back again.

Free of pain, tranquillized, he was only faintly aware of Ma occasionally coming to administer pills and tuck in the bed sheets, of occasional comforting glances from two of his daughters Primrose and Mariette, and for a longer period of some mysterious manoeuvres, at first barely understood, by Mr Charlton.

Remarkable feller, Mr Charlton. He seemed to be weaving a web of his own. With skill and stealth he unwound a complex of wires round, under and behind the bed. These were finally attached to the bed-post, giving the impression that Mr Charlton had himself turned doctor and was about to conduct his own researches into the state of Pop's damaged heart.

'Inter-comm.' Mr Charlton at last explained. 'Press the button and Ma'll hear you in the kitchen. Just press the button – anything you want –'

Miraculous bit of work, Pop told himself. Trust Charley boy to think of a thing like that. He smiled faintly at Charley in gratitude and then withdrew again into his web of unconsciousness.

Downstairs, in the kitchen, Ma was deeply immersed in manoeuvres of her own, in culinary exercises on a gigantic scale. The many pills and tablets Mr Charlton had brought back for Pop, red, white, blue, green and even brightest yellow, were no doubt as necessary as she hoped they would be effective but what Pop clearly needed was, in her own view, nourishment. And plenty of it.

To this end she was making steak-and-kidney pie, apple-and-apricot flan, dough cake, plum cake and caraway cake, the last a special favourite of Pop's, maids-of-honour, curd tarts, strawberry and raspberry mousse, both from fresh fruit, cheese straws, shortcakes and coconut ice. She had pondered for some time on whether or not to cook a turkey and with it a plum pudding left over from Christmas but had finally decided against these as being on the heavy side until Pop gets his strength back.

She was in no possible doubt that Pop would get his strength back, and quickly; you couldn't keep a man like Pop down for long. What chiefly troubled her was the possible cause, or causes, of Pop's sudden and distressing decline in the first place. Once or twice, casting her mind back to the events of the early morning, she told herself that perhaps it might conceivably have been something to do with doing too much on an empty stomach.

It was hardly likely, though. He had, after all, done it often enough before. It had never set him back at all in the past. It was quite unthinkable that it could do him any possible harm. On the contrary Ma thought of it rather as something in the nature of a hobby. Nor, she reasoned, could it possibly have anything to do with the early consumption of champagne, still less of brandy. They were, after all, like making love to Ma, everyday features of Pop's life, the very bone and marrow, as it were, of his entire existence.

If she was troubled at all by these things – and she was troubled by one thing especially – she scarcely showed an outward sign of it. Vast, placid, hands and bosom flowing over the pastry board, Ma characteristically told herself that it was no use moaning about these things. Moaning would get her nowhere; nor weeping. She had had her little weep; it had done her good; and that was that.

What really troubled her, and very often, were those words of Dr O'Connor, ominous and incredible, about 'the foreseeable future – for ever, perhaps for ever'. The mere suggestion that Pop might have to forgo the pleasures of alcohol for some brief period was in itself outrageous enough; but the notion that it might be for the foreseeable future, perhaps for ever, was plain purgatory.

Pop would never endure. If anything was calculated to set him back at all that was it. A good stiff brandy, of which she and Mariette had already had several during the course of the day, would in her opinion work wonders in no time. There was nothing like spirits, as she often remarked, to keep your spirits up; nothing like a little of what you fancied to do you good. She would have to have a serious word with Dr O'Connor about the matter.

The house was very quiet. Scarcely a sound came from the warm, flower-drenched garden outside. Heat quivered in shimmering pulses across the meadows where hay lay about both in frothy rows and pale green bales ready for carting. On the kitchen table, among all the paraphernalia of cooking, stood a vase of honeysuckle, freshly gathered and waiting to be taken up to Pop's room, and the heavy fragrance of it, exquisitely intoxicating, was strong enough to rise above the smell of cooking.

Mariette, a tower of wonderful strength all morning, had now gone home, taking the youngest children, Oscar and Phyllida, with her. Mr Charlton and Montgomery had gone off in an attempt to complete the deal in walkie-talkies that Pop had missed. The twins, Zinnia and Petunia, were now away at boarding school, an exclusive and expensive establishment at which they consorted with at least one princess of the realm, together with another half dozen from foreign parts. Victoria was at a finishing school at Château d'Oeux, in Switzerland. All costing a shilling or two, Pop was the first to admit, but wurf while, very wurf while. His children deserved the best. You had only to consider Mr Charlton to see what education would do.

All this left Ma alone with Primrose. The development of Primrose into a creature both physically celestial and alluring, even more devastatingly so than Mariette, was something to astonish even the habitual tranquil attitude of Ma towards matters of sex, a word she herself never used, preferring to call it 'letting Nature take its course'. Nature had in fact several times so taken its course with Primrose, so aptly named, that Ma had been mildly disturbed by several false alarms, until Primrose had told Ma not to worry, the Pill was taking care of that.

When Ma told Pop about Primrose and the Pill he wasn't sure that he was exactly overjoyed. He was all for letting Nature take its course too. When Ma pointed out blandly that consumption of the Pill allowed Nature to take its course even more freely and enjoyably than before Pop was forced to admit that this was so. He only hoped Ma wasn't taking the Pill too.

'Do you mind?' Ma said. 'I haven't come to that. I've got on very well without it so far.'

Pop said he should think so too. His motto being the more the merrier, he wasn't at all sure he approved of this Pill lark. There was something a bit immoral about it, sort of. Very thing for girls like Edith Pilchester though, he said, in his customary rousing jocular fashion, to which Ma offered a slightly stern reproof:

'Have a heart. Poor Edith. She drew the curtains a long time ago.'

In the warm July afternoon Primrose was dressed – if the word was not inappropriate – in an almost transparent yellow blouse with small red spots on it and the briefest of mini-skirts in delicate green. The blouse was remarkable for being less of a blouse than a piece of loose material tied across her breasts, revealing six or seven inches of bare midriff and navel below and an even wider expanse of naked flesh above. The mini-skirt contained hardly less material and from under it her legs swept in brown, ravishing curves. Ma guessed that she was wearing neither stockings nor tights and also rather suspected she was not wearing panties either. You could hardly blame her though, Ma told herself as she glanced at the rich curves of Primrose's firm high breasts protruding over the open blouse: the afternoon was hot enough for anything.

Ma, having now finished making the last of her curd tarts and maids-of-honour, was on the point of taking the vase of honeysuckle up to Pop in case he was awake and would like a cup of tea, when she suddenly heard the front door bell ring. The front door bell was in fact a whole concerto of rings, rather like a combination of a Venetian carillon, 'The Bluebells of Scotland' and the chimes of an ice-cream van.

'That'll be the doctor back again,' she said. 'I'll go.'

'Sit still. You've been rushing about enough as it is. I'll get it.'

Primrose sidled sinuously rather than walked from the kitchen to the front door and then came back, some moments later, with a visitor.

It was the Reverend Candy.

Mr Candy appeared, at first sight, to have suffered the grievous blow of some recent catastrophe. He was pale. There was even a certain trembling clutching of his hands about his neck, rather like that of a nervous hen scratching at its feathers. It at once occurred to Ma that all this was the probable natural reaction to the news of Pop's illness and she promptly got up from the table to make a cup of tea.

The catastrophe that had overtaken Mr Candy was, in fact, Primrose. He hadn't seen Primrose for some considerable time. Nor had he actually gone out of his way to do so. There was no need. The vision of her, ripe in prematurely rich development, honeyed, seductive, even exotic, with the beautiful dark stare that always had him swooningly trapped in a vice, was almost always in his mind. It scarcely ever left him. Nor did all the other moments of being with her, including that moment of near-disaster when he had christened her Narcissus instead of Narcissa, had sprinkled holy water on that most luscious and yet disturbingly innocent of foreheads and had received her half-seductive, half-forgiving smile in return.

Now the sight of her in the miniest of mini-skirts, blouse unbuttoned, the upper rims of her breasts white as washed seashells against the sun-brown of her neck and legs and face, was too much. It turned him cold and flaky.

'I must apologize for not having – that is, I only just heard – just after lunch. Then there were all sorts of rumours – I trust that –'

'Heart,' Ma said. 'Sit you down. I'm just going to make a cup of tea.'

'I'll make it,' Primrose said. 'You haven't been still all afternoon.'

'No, I can do it,' Ma said. 'You sit down and amuse Mr Candy.'

The words, Mr Candy told himself, were scarcely well chosen. Amuse! – he could have thought of better. Mesmerize would have been one of them. Who could be anything else, faced with those melting, honeyed black eyes, the shell-like breasts and that most compulsively seductive, miniest of skirts.

'Yes, do sit down, Mr Candy,' Primrose said in the creamiest of voices. 'Hot, isn't it? You look a bit tired.'

Mr Candy was indeed tired. Far from being hot, however, he felt himself turn colder, flakier than ever.

In confusion he began to say that he was relieved to hear that it was only heart, then realized that relieved was hardly the right word either. It was in fact hard, even impossible, to think straight. What he actually meant was that he had heard of an accident – a car – of Mr Larkin – well, gravely injured. He trusted all was not too serious?

'Sleeping like a lamb,' Ma said. 'They knocked him out after it happened. Very good thing.'

'I'm so relieved. So relieved.'

Ma, after buttering a heap of fresh scones, began to pour tea.

'Sugar? One lump or two?' Primrose said to Mr Candy. 'Cream? You like it in first or last?'

Dear God, Mr Candy thought. Heaven help me. Really the use of words like cream ought not to be allowed. Ever. Not from those lips, anyway. Cream: the word was torture.

'Apricot jam, lemon curd or quince jelly?' Ma said.

'I adore quince jelly,' Mr Candy said, relieved beyond measure to be able to concern himself with the comparatively innocent virtues of quince jelly, a pot of which Ma now passed to him, at the same time apologizing:

'Excuse the pot. We're a bit bottom-uppards today, what with Pop and all that.'

'Oh! please don't apologize. Quince jelly is splendid at any time. I adore it. Pot or no pot.'

Something about this remark made Primrose laugh, her voice low and deep with what seemed deliberate allurement, so that Mr Candy sought desperately to escape from it by delivering a totally unexpected sentence:

'Not that one can't have too much of it, like anything else. Someone once said – I rather think it was Coleridge – that one can't live for ever on quince jelly.'

468

'I don't see why not,' Ma said. 'Mine's always pretty good.'

'Oh! I didn't mean that,' Mr Candy said. 'Don't misinterpret me. It's excellent. More than excellent.'

It was now Primrose's turn, to Mr Candy's intense embarrassment, to produce an unexpected question of her own.

'Didn't the Greeks – or was it the Romans – use it as an aphrodisiac?'

Dear God, Mr Candy thought again and could find no word to say.

'What's aphrodisiac?' Ma said. 'Sounds like an insecticide or something,' and laughed in her customary ripe, bouncing fleshy fashion. 'Or else a rude word.'

'You never needed it,' Primrose said, giving Mr Candy one of those long, sideways, serpentine glances that seemed to coil about him, enthralling his very flesh. 'Some people never do.'

Desperately Mr Candy sought to extricate himself from the torture of this moment by saying:

'There was, in fact, a curious rumour going about – oh! I don't mean about Mr Larkin – quite apart from that. I had to verify it three times before I found it was true.'

'Never believe rumours,' Ma said. 'They got it about once that Pop had run off with Angela Snow. Piffle.'

'Well this, though I say it as shouldn't, as they say, is gospel. It concerns –'

'Come on,' Primrose said, 'I love scandal.'

'Scandal I suppose you could call it, too.'

'Come on, let's have a bite then,' Ma said.

'Well it seems – and I've got three unimpeachable sources of information – that Edith Pilchester went into The Hare and Hounds and got tiddly. Helplessly, hopelessly tiddly. Sozzled. Stoned, as I believe they call it nowadays.'

Ma started laughing again like a jelly, unable to draw breath through her great wobbling frame except in a series of loud gigantic wheezes.

'And had to be taken home in a wheelbarrow.'

Ma fell about, helpless. She couldn't contain herself. She half-wept into her tea.

'Whatever did Edith want to go and do a thing like that for?'

Mr Candy paused, glad of the momentary chance of being distracted from Primrose, who was laughing too but in a very different way from Ma. Her laughter had a liquid, seductive, dangerous sound.

'Well, it appears – it would seem that she'd been very upset by – she heard a rumour – just a rumour of course – about –' Here Mr Candy paused again, searching for the appropriate, least embarrassing word – 'about Mr Larkin's demise.'

'Oh! really? Do you mind?' Ma said. 'He's certainly not suffering from that.'

Desisting suddenly from laughter, she gave Mr Candy a stern, reproving sort of look, at the same time handing him the choice of a plate of shortcake or lemon curd tarts. Mr Candy accepted shortcake, of which he was very fond, and in politeness offered the plate to Primrose. She thanked him with one of those smouldering, bewitching looks of hers that always turned him cold and flaky and said no, she'd rather have a slice of the caraway.

Demise, Primrose now explained, meant that Miss Pilchester had heard that Pop was dead.

Ma said Really? Whatever next? The things people got about. If some of them didn't keep their traps shut she'd have to iron them out. Gossipy lot – she expected some of them would like to see him dead.

These unchristian remarks, so unlike Ma, briefly shocked Mr Candy, who hastily sucked at crumbs of sugar from the shortcake and didn't know what to say. Perhaps one could excuse such outbursts at such a time of tension.

Then Ma, never one to be put out of her stride for long, started laughing uncontrollably again, the great wheezes for breath once more turning to tears.

'In a wheelbarrow. For crying out loud. In a wheelbarrow – Oh! my lord. I remember once they brought my old Dad home in a wheelbarrow, but I thought that sort of thing had gone out of fashion.'

The laughter having at last calmed down through a series of hilarious sobs until her body merely heaved in huge ponderous breaths, so that she looked not unlike a porpoise about to give birth, Ma finally got up from the table and said she would really have to go up and tell Pop all about Edith and the wheelbarrow. She really would. That would set him up all right. It would do him more good than all the pills in the world.

Taking the little vase of honeysuckle with her – it was Pop's favourite flower, one that always gave him ideas, as he put it, and would make the bedroom smell nice – she left the kitchen and went upstairs, pausing only to remark from the door:

'If the colour television set arrives tell them to wait while I give the all clear.' One of Ma's first acts after the trouble with Pop's heart was to ring up a radio dealer for a colour television set. It was the least she could do. Pop could have it in the bedroom and it would cheer him up. 'Help yourself to anything you want, Mr Candy.'

Mr Candy, far from helping himself to anything he wanted, sat in a sort of trance, left all alone with Primrose, a circumstance that never failed to cause him the acutest embarrassment. This hot afternoon the embarrassment seemed to have properties almost lethal. He hardly knew which way to look. He positively snatched at a second piece of shortcake, biting into it desperately.

By contrast Primrose was eating her slice of caraway cake very slowly, with an absent air. Both sunburnt arms crooked on the table, she held the caraway gently against her lips and now and then took soft exploratory bites at it, rather like a drowsy butterfly at the petals of a flower. From Mr Candy's point of view this looked like a deliberate essay in seduction, in every way devised to torture and beguile and defeat all sensible resistance on his part.

But to Primrose the situation was in fact entirely the opposite. It was Mr Candy who was seductive. It was that shyness of his, that sort of she didn't quite know what. It was the paleness and the quiet. There were times when it really sent her. She would have to do something about it, seriously, one day.

From one of these dreamy, absent bites at the slice of caraway cake a crumb fell. Like a stone lightly dislodged from a cliff-top it fell gently down the slope of Primrose's chest, at last coming to rest midway at the exposed curves of bosom. It lay there like a magnet, transfixing Mr Candy's gaze with utter torture. He had always been commanded, as a child, not to drop crumbs down himself. He had been severely scolded if he did so, and now the sight of the caraway crumb lodged in the ivory cleft of Primrose's bosom filled him with guilt remembered – so painfully remembered that he felt an intense compulsion to tell her about the crumb or pick it off with his own fingers.

He was saved from the necessity of doing either of these things by Primrose suddenly and sharply leaning back in the chair, again reduced to some moments of laughter by a remembrance of her own – the picture of Edith Pilchester taken home in the wheelbarrow.

This new recumbent attitude of Primrose's was worse than anything that had gone before. It served to bring her naked midriff, and its navel, into fullest view. Magnetized to a degree hitherto unconceived, Mr Candy now dropped crumbs down himself too and gave unsteady gulps at his tea. The sight of this fresh display of nervousness or whatever it was, that sort of she didn't know what, set Primrose gently laughing again and her midriff quivered sinuously and softly, all pulsating fleshy tenderness.

At the same time her mini-skirt was drawn up almost to its fullest extent, so that Mr Candy was suddenly assailed by the same convictions that had occurred to Ma, only in her case by no means seriously: namely that Primrose was wearing nothing whatever underneath. Primrose was in fact wearing something underneath, brief though it was, and a sudden sight of it, a mere pink triangle, had a more palpitating effect on Mr Candy than if she had been wearing nothing at all.

Before he had recovered from this shattering moment a second crumb fell, this time in the form of a caraway seed. In one of the ripples of Primrose's laughter it was shaken free from the slice of cake and fell downwards towards her navel. This unnerving sight drove Mr Candy to a point of silent excruciation. He was momentarily paralysed. Torn between an almost frantic desire to remove the caraway seed or to do something about the mini-skirt he did neither. He merely sat transfixed, hopelessly mesmerized, instead, by the navel and the caraway seed.

His silent stare at the bare midriff for fully half a minute finally drew a remark from Primrose.

'Penny for your thoughts.'

A millionaire couldn't have bought Mr Candy's thoughts at that moment. In silent, wild surmise he had just found, he thought, the exact simile for the navel. It was exactly, he told himself, like a soft young raspberry. That was exactly it; and in another moment he was aware of the taste of raspberries on his lips, and his mouth watered.

He was distractedly wondering what might possibly happen next, and had almost decided that nothing more devastating possibly could, when Ma came back into the room.

'Another cup, you two?' Ma said. 'You haven't been sitting there letting it get cold, have you?'

Mr Candy told himself they certainly hadn't been sitting there letting it get cold, far from it; and there was little doubt that his cup was full, almost, to overflowing. Nevertheless he thanked Ma, then said he would have another cup of tea.

'I'll pour it,' Primrose said. 'Mr Candy likes the cream in first.'

Cream! – This household, Mr Candy thought, dear God, this household; and was on the verge of doubting if he would ever have the courage to visit it again when his practical self reminded him that he hadn't asked after Mr Larkin. How was Mr Larkin?

'Well, I know what Pop would say,' Ma said. 'Bad a-bed and wuss up. But there's an improvement. He's had a good long sleep. I don't think he still quite knows where he is but he loved the honeysuckle.'

'Is there something I could do? Could I possibly go up?'

'No visitors today,' Ma said. 'Got to be kept absolutely quiet today. He's doped anyway. He'd hardly know you.'

Feeling slightly doped himself, Mr Candy watched Ma pick up the teapot and then, after urging Mr Candy to have a slice of caraway cake, he'd hardly eaten a thing, said she thought she'd make a fresh pot for Pop and take up a cup to the bedroom.

Mr Candy replied with thanks that he'd really had quite enough. The word crumb, he told himself, was a meal in itself. He would never forget that crumb, or that caraway seed.

'Did you tell Pop about Edith?' Primrose finally wanted to know.

Ma confessed she hadn't. On second thoughts she'd decided it might be too much for him. It might, she said, laughing again but no longer so boisterously, give him another turn. It would keep, the bit about Edith, it would keep.

'Yes, indeed. Might act as a sort of therapy in good time,' Mr Candy said and Ma gave him another stern sort of look, half as if he had suggested something rude.

'How is he really, Ma?' Primrose said. Primrose, perhaps of all the children, with the possible exception of Mariette, was closest to Pop. There was much of Pop in her, Ma often thought. There was that something – you couldn't say what it was but it was sort of rich and warm and it got at you. It was like something catching. The sudden shocking business of Pop's heart had very much upset her. 'When does the doctor come again?'

'Before surgery. About half past five.'

It now suddenly and instinctively occurred to Ma that Primrose's question was one of real anxiety. Rapidly she changed the subject by running a hand over Primrose's smooth brown bare shoulder and with disarming innocence asking Mr Candy a question:

'Getting nice an' brown, isn't she, Mr Candy? Pretty well the same all over.'

Mr Candy, having seen pretty well all over by now, was unable to think of a word to say in answer.

'I tell you what,' Ma said. 'I was going to get some flowers for Pop's bedroom but by the time I've taken him a cup of tea and shaken his bed a bit the doctor'll be here and I won't get time. Why don't you two go?'

'Oh! let's do that. Shall we, Mr Candy?' Primrose spoke with that warm allure that was part of her inheritance from Pop and that always sent Mr Candy cold and flaky. 'Shall we?'

Hesitating, trying hard to think of some valid excuse for refusal but able to recall nothing but a meeting of the Parochial Church Council, more than three hours away – Great Heavens, Miss Pilchester was supposed to be on it too, and what on earth would people say? – he was saved from further trial by Ma, now back to her usual, outwardly buoyant self, saying: 'That's it, you two go along. Get some nice things with plenty of scent. You know how Pop loves perfume. Carnations and lilies and roses and all that sort of thing. Plenty of scent.'

'Come on, Mr Candy,' Primrose said. 'I'll cut and you hold.'

Cut and hold – Oh! the profundity of simple words, Mr Candy thought and prepared to follow the glorious, brown mini-skirted legs of Primrose into the garden, shining in shimmering July sunlight.

The heat of the sun had scarcely touched his face, however, before he was arrested by the voice of Ma, calling from the kitchen door.

'Here, take a basket. You can get some raspberries too while you're at it,' she was saying, and Mr Candy could have fainted.

· 5 ·

Three mornings later Pop woke to see a clear limpid blue sky shining beyond the windows. Somebody, he could only suppose Ma, had already drawn back the curtains and now brilliant early sunlight was streaming strongly into the bedroom. Lying flat on his back, without pillows, he had a slightly upward view of the summer sky and against it, at the edge of the open window, a single rose-leaf, new, pink-copper in colour and slightly curled, not unlike a curved sea-shell half-transparent in the sun.

He watched this single leaf for some long time. Soon he saw it not as a shell but a map, a small leaf-island crossed by a central river, with many little tributaries and a host of even tinier streams. At the edges of it the brightness of sun, clear gold, created an illusion of delicate little waves breaking on the leaf-shore; and the sky the further illusion that the sea itself was spread far beyond it, an expanse blue as chicory flower, and marvellously calm. This leaf-island and its surrounding summer sea he saw as something not merely wonderful; it was a miracle. It was yet another experience that illness incredibly magnifies the most trivial of things.

His long preoccupation with the marvel and loveliness of this single simple rose-leaf also created in him the strongest feeling of suspense. He might have been poised in space, a leaf himself, breathlessly held in air. He took several long, deep breaths: he felt unbearably glad to be alive.

All this was rather like a man savouring the marvels of a dry crust at a table laden with a bountiful and luscious feast. His bedroom seemed to be a combination of green house, wine-shop and fruit stall. Flowers – carnations, roses, gladioli, even nosegays of meadowsweet, wild grasses and willowherb – stood fragrantly about in vases everywhere; the sun gleamed on the necks of champagne bottles as on crusty golden candles; a pyramid of fruit, a glowing cornucopia of pineapple, peaches, pears, white and black grapes and apples stood on top of his new colour television set, a note on it from Angela Snow saying in words as languid and liquid as her own voice: 'Wanted to send you something madly in character: mangoes, persimmons, paw-paw, passion fruit and all that – but those

475

scabs in London wouldn't play. Get well soon, dearest man. Fondest thoughts, Thirsting to see you soon. P.S. Your pining Jasmine joins me in profoundest embrace and all that.'

The cheering comfort of those words, together with the mental vision of the willowy and honeyed Angela and the magnificent sculptured flesh of her friend Jasmine Brown, of whom Pop had memories that didn't now bear dwelling upon, had served to raise his spirits, though not in the manner that Ma sometimes referred to as 'the old pepper and mustard'. He still felt fragile; the recollection of moments of velvet flirtation with both girls didn't merely seem impossible: it made him continually wonder how he'd stood up to it at all. You needed a bit of strength for that sort of thing; and strength, he often felt as he lay there pillowless and prostrate, was something that seemed to have left him for ever.

And not merely strength; but gaiety too. It was a very solemn Pop who lay there finding solace of amazingly restorative depth in a mere rose-leaf. He hadn't even been able to raise much of a smile at Ma's story, jubilantly told, of Edith Pilchester being taken home, 'laying-down drunk', as Ma said, in a wheelbarrow. It didn't somehow seem very funny; on the contrary it struck him as rather sad. It belonged to the ghastly fact, as Edith herself would have put it, that he was never going to be able to drink again, perhaps never to taste the twin delights of Ma and champagne in bed, still less the surreptitious delights of girls like Jasmine Brown in the boat-house. His heart would clearly never stand the strain. It was, in Edith's words again, 'absolutely ghastly'.

It was, in fact, far worse; it was funereal. There were even depressive moments when he thought it was the death knell – no more champers, no more brandy, no more cigars, no more stiffeners in the shape of his favourite cocktails, Rolls-Royce and Red Bull, no more Ma and all that, no more nothing. You might just as well get ready, he told himself, to tuck down under the daisies. It was the bone-house. It was as good as all over.

He was suddenly shocked out of these melancholy reflections by a staggering vision entering the room, accompanied by an equally shattering sound. The vision was that of a pure white, starchy, over-blown administering angel. The sound was like that of the crackling of a vast packet of potato crisps.

'Good morning, Mr Larkin, good morning. And how do we find ourselves this morning?'

Pop was about to reply automatically that he was fit as a flea, then realized that he wasn't and furthermore that the words wouldn't have been very well received even if he was.

'I am Nurse Soper. I have come to relieve your wife for a few days. The strain was proving rather much for her.'

Pop lay speechless. This was less because he could think of nothing reasonable to say than because he was trying to drink in the magisterial figure of Nurse Soper, now shaking a thermometer and preparing to plunge it into his mouth. The presence of the thermometer having finally removed all idea of speech completely, Pop merely gazed at the vast starchiness of his nurse with wonder, awe and disbelief.

Nurse Soper appeared to be a figure composed on the one hand of one of those marble attendant angels you saw in churchyards and on the other of a heavyweight boxer who had forgotten to shave for a day or two. A thickish area of dark moustache on her upper lip seemed to have sown fresh progeny, in the shape of a ring of little tufty beards, on her chin. Her nose, like that of a boxer, was broad and slightly flattened. A further area of dark moustache had sprouted from that too. Her hair, or as much of it as Pop could see from under the stiff-starched helmet of her nurse's cap, was naturally grey in colour but had recently been dyed an unpleasant shade of yellow, so that it looked rather like the coat of a moulting vixen.

As if these things were not hard enough to bear her voice sounded like the engine of a car that had run out of oil and was about to seize up. Pop was briefly disposed to think that her big end had gone.

Having taken Pop's temperature, Nurse Soper grunted, though whether in approval or disapproval of the reading Pop found it impossible to tell, then lit a cigarette. The fact that smoking was yet another of the pleasures of life Pop was having to forgo, perhaps for ever, the cloud of cigarette smoke she now blew into the summer morning air served to irritate him even more than the words which followed.

'And now, Mr Larkin, do we wish the bottle?'

Something about the offensive commanding nature of this sentence served not merely to irritate Pop still further; it suddenly and unexpectedly inspired him to a breath of mischief.

'Yes, good egg. I'll try the champers.'

'No champagne, Mr Larkin. As you well know. No alcohol.'

'Brandy then.'

'No alcohol. Nor was it that kind of bottle to which I was referring.'

Nurse Soper glared. Her eyes were like ice-grey screwdrivers. They were, Pop was beginning to think, not quite human. It was clearly obvious, too, he decided, that she and him were already off hooks.

'Well, Mr Larkin, do we wish the bottle or not?'

Pop was now amazingly inspired to a second flicker of mischief and said:

'I always use the Throne.'

'You mean you have been getting out of bed? That is very, very naughty. Who authorized *that*? That is extremely naughty.'

'Very comfortable, the Throne.'

The Throne, which stood by his bedside, was in fact most comfortable. It had been sent for Pop's use from the village by the two Miss Barnwells, the genteel freckled little ladies, daughters of a retired Indian Civil Servant, who found times under the all-sheltering roof of the Welfare State more than a little hard and were now classed, sadly, as Distressed Gentlefolk. The commode, Victorian, with cabriole legs, in smoothest walnut and covered with ruby velvet, had seen much service East of Suez, and inside was inscribed with the words 'The Royal Universal'.

'There will be no more using the Throne, as you call it, while I'm here. Let's get that quite clear. Now do we wish the bottle or not?'

'Very nearly breaking my neck,' Pop said.

'Then we'd better have it quick, hadn't we? Before a mistake is made.'

With the bottle under the sheets, Pop proceeded to spend a few quiet contemplative minutes while Nurse Soper went along to the bathroom.

Pop was still urgently concerned with the business in hand when to his great relief Ma appeared. She looked tired, apologetic and generally not quite up to the mark, he thought.

'What the pipe, Ma?' he said. 'What did we have to have her for? Old Soapy?'

Ma proceeded to explain, in tones unaccountably subdued for her, that she was sorry but the whole thing had begun to get her down. It was fifty yards from the kitchen to the bedroom, up and down, which Mr Charlton had worked out was as something like two miles upstairs and downstairs a day. It was like training for the Olympics.

Clever fellow, Charley boy. Very strong on mathematics. But why her? Why the Soapy?

'Had to get somebody quick,' Ma said. 'Dr O'Connor insisted. She was the best we could get.'

Pop silently reflected that if this was the best what in the name of all that was holy could the worst be like? It had already been at the back of his mind that, in a day or two, if all went well, Ma and he could be having a quiet, secretive snifter up in the bedroom and nobody the wiser. Now clearly, that was out. The bedroom was more than ever a prison. With the Soapy in charge, the wardress, he was chained hand and foot. There was no escape. He was sunk in gloom.

'The doctor said we had to do it,' Ma said. 'If we didn't I might crack up and then where would we be?'

Where indeed? Pop thought and had no answer to this depressing question except 'up the ruddy creek' when Nurse Soper was back, carrying wash-bowl, sponge, soap, towels and a bottle of eau-de-cologne.

'I understand that Mr Larkin has been getting out of bed, Mrs Larkin. That is strictly forbidden. Is it understood? Strictly and absolutely taboo.'

'He said he felt well enough, so I let him.'

'There could be nothing more dangerous. This business is very much an affair of snakes-and-ladders. You are up one day and down the next. One minute you are at the top of the ladder, the next you are at the tail of the snake.'

Pop, not being very fond in any case of snakes-and-ladders, took the whole comparison of himself with that game as yet further proof that things were getting very dicy. With gloom he surrendered the bottle to Nurse Soper, who promptly held it up to the light for critical scrutiny, as if perhaps it were a light Hock or some special vintage. The vintage having been finally passed as apparently satisfactory she then stalked out of the room with it, to return some moments later with the bottle empty.

'Now we must have our bath. Thank you, Mrs Larkin.'

This signal for Ma's dismissal depressed Pop yet further. He was only partially restored by hearing Ma ask from the door:

'Like a cup o' tea? I've got the kettle on.'

'In half an hour,' Nurse Soper said. 'Not before.'

'And put a drop o' cream in, Ma,' Pop said and for the first time Ma could have sworn he actually gave the minutest of winks at her. 'You know, from that Scotch cow.'

'Now, shall I shave you before we bath or afterwards?' Nurse Soper said, standing above Pop rather like an eager executioner.

'Might as well get my throat cut first,' Pop said and stared, his brief moment of mischief destroyed, at the rose-leaf by the window. Even that, in his gloom seemed to fascinate him no longer.

The last vestige of shaving soap having been wiped by Nurse Soper from his chin, Pop just managed to resist an impulse, rising from his old self, to say that it might not now be a bad idea if *he* shaved *her*, when she started to take his pyjama jacket off, then cover the sponge with soap and then begin to wash him down.

As she leaned closer over him, stern and stony-faced, Pop felt he now knew what it was like to be face to face with one of those distorted gargoyles that you saw glaring and pouting down from above the buttresses of churches. He told himself that he'd never given Edith Pil-chester better than a 300–1 chance in a beauty contest, but the Soapy was far down already, in his estimation, among the also-rans. The strenuous diligence of her scrubbing gave him the painful impression that his chest was being scoured by sandpaper: and on purpose at that.

Having washed and dried him, as Pop put it, upstairs, she put back his pyjama jacket and then proceeded to take off his pyjama trousers in readiness to wash him downstairs. The possible direction of the rest of the programme began to fascinate Pop no end. He awaited it with much expectation, even eagerness. It would be a bit of a lark, he couldn't help thinking, when she reached the point of no return, sort of.

Point of no return: he must tell Ma that. He betted she'd heard it called a lot of things but never that. The idea made him, for a brief moment or two, feel quite his old self again. Perhaps a bit of the old buck would work on Soapy if he tried? After all, he reasoned, she must be human under-neath, even if it was a long way under.

Anyway, he'd see what the point of no return did for her. According to which way the cat jumped he might get a thick ear or perhaps, on the other hand, persuade her to share a mid-morning snifter or something of that sort. Who knew?

Meanwhile Nurse Soper was busy as a bee in Pop's downstairs field. With diligent energy she scrubbed his calves and feet, minutely ferreting between his toes, and then worked upwards to his thighs. All this time she never spoke a word and it couldn't help crossing Pop's mind that the silence might be one of anticipation. Was it a possible idea that the point of no return might get her in a tizz? You couldn't tell. Interesting thought, though.

At last, after she had scrupulously dried him from feet to thighs, it suddenly seemed to Pop that some sort of skirmish was about to start in the middle. Was the point of no return about to be reached? He found himself not at all unfascinated by the prospect. Might as well be at the ready in case of attack, he told himself, and was on the point of considering a few tactics when he found himself with a wet sponge in his hands.

'Perhaps,' Nurse Soper said, 'you would care to finish off the rest yourself?'

Finish what off? Pop thought and then wondered briefly what might happen if he said no, he wouldn't. She could hardly disregard the call of duty. Perhaps a bit of what Mr Charlton would have called shrewd compromise might be a good tactic after all, he decided, and was prompted, with a slight sign to confess that now he felt a bit tired.

A Little of What You Fancy

'Surely not too tired to deal with a little thing like that?'

Little thing like what? Pop thought. Did she mind? There were two ways of looking at that. Another bit he'd have to tell Ma, he thought. That would cheer her up.

'Come along, Mr Larkin. We haven't got all day. I've work to do.'

So, apparently, had he, Pop thought, and said:

'Do-it-yourself lark, now, is it? I thought that was your job?'

'Now come along, Mr Larkin. Don't tell me you're incapable –'

Incapable? Pop thought. That was coming the old acid a bit, wasn't it? For crying out gently – incapable, eh? Well not yet, he hoped.

'I'm afraid I can't stand here all day, Mr Larkin. Are you going to do the rest yourself or are you going to leave it as it is?'

Going to leave it as it was, Pop said. After all it had been there a good long time.

'I don't *think* I care,' Nurse Soper said, 'for innuendo.'

Nor did he, Pop said with a remarkable flash of his old sharpness. It always gave him wind.

At this point Nurse Soper stalked from the room. The battle was won and lost, whichever way you cared to look at it, and Pop was left to deal with the point of no return alone.

The rest of the day passed miserably. It was a day, largely, of refusal and denial. No, Mr Larkin could not have sugar in his tea; nor butter on his bread. Sugar and animal fats were utterly and absolutely out. No, Mr Larkin could not have a slice of pineapple; the fruit was too acid. As lunchtime drew near Pop detected in himself the return of a slight peckishness and said he rather fancied one of Ma's cheese-puddings and a slice of treacle tart. The result was two dry cream cracker biscuits, three lettuce leaves and a plate of orange jelly.

At each bestowal of these munificent offerings Nurse Soper grew more than ever like a stony gargoyle: ruling not merely with a rod of iron but with one of sharpened steel and a whip too. Even the already infrequent visits of Ma were now much constricted and timed, as it seemed, by stop watch.

'Time we went, Mrs Larkin, time we went.'

During one of these brief and precious conclaves together Pop confessed to Ma that he was going downhill fast. He couldn't stand it much longer. With unaccustomed asperity Ma agreed, then declared she had no doubt where the trouble lay.

'Never had the pleasure, that's what. Never had the pleasure. It makes all that difference.'

You bet your life it did. Pop said and wretchedly wondered if he would ever again have the pleasure himself either.

Down in the kitchen, at last, towards early evening, the crisis between Ma and Nurse Soper became precisely that of two wrestlers standing face to face, ready for a final deciding bout. Ma's temper, which she had tried to keep down all day, was now truly up, so that she viewed Nurse Soper with a certain robust and radiant scorn, ready to put a half-Nelson on her.

Periodically, throughout the day, Nurse Soper had recited, as from Holy Writ, the text not merely for the day but, it appeared, for all and every day.

'Mr Larkin is my patient and as long as he is my patient he will do as and what I say and how and when I say it.'

Ma, fortified by a second large brandy and half in a mind to take one up to Pop and chance the consequences, was at last able to bear the sanctimonious creed no longer.

'And I'll have you know he's my husband and if he's going to die I'll see he dies happy.'

'Your husband is not going to die.'

'No? I'm glad you think so. From where I stand he's gone downhill since morning.'

'Your husband is in no danger.'

'Not while you're about. That's for certain.'

Which, Nurse Soper said with level acidity, was a most uncalled-for remark.

'Well, you call for it any time and you can have it. Wrapped up. With pink ribbon.'

Nurse Soper snorted. There was a certain vulgarity in the house, she told herself, that was hardly describable in civilized terms. She had already noted the three television sets, including the colour one; the Rolls-Royce and the Jaguar; a vast new cocktail cabinet in the shape of a Venetian gondola, complete with gondolier holding a long champagne swizzle-stick and lamps that actually lit up when you lifted the ice-box lid; the incredible suits of armour, also illuminated, now accompanied by two figures of black boy slaves holding torches; an electric organ which apparently nobody ever played – it hadn't at first occurred to Ma that it could be a possible joke when she had first declared her intention of giving Pop an electric organ for Christmas – and an entirely new bar set up in the style of a French *bistro*, with gay French posters on the walls and sawdust on the floor, just to remind the family of the time, both happy and otherwise, they had once spent across the channel, seeking a breath of French air.

It was all, in Nurse Soper's eyes, of an incredible, stupefying vulgarity.

She had in her time worked for the nobility, the diplomatic service, the racing set, even the theatre: but never once, never, for anything quite like this. She supposed it was true that money would buy anything – with one exception: manners.

Hereabouts, in order to preserve sanity if not calm, Ma proceeded to pour herself a third, very handsome brandy. This, with that churchy, gargoyle look of hers, Nurse Soper viewed with stone-cold eye. That was clearly another thing about this house: alcohol had taken charge.

The thought moved her to reflect, aloud, that she wondered if half a bottle of brandy by half past five in the evening was exactly wise?

'I never consider the wise,' Ma said, 'only the why-for. Perhaps if you'd seen your husband as good as dying before your own eyes you'd take a nip or two yourself.'

'Nip? I only hope you know what it's doing to your liver.'

'I haven't been in to see,' Ma said. 'But it hasn't complained yet.'

'Complain it undoubtedly will. One day. With cirrhosis.'

'Who's he when he's at home? It's nothing to what I'll complain with if –'

At this moment, before Ma could finish what was clearly about to be, in wrestling terms, a fall, the outraged Nurse Soper looked sharply at her watch, muttered 'Pills', actually seemed to take wings, and departed.

Ma sat at the table alone, partly in fury, partly near to tears, and swigged hard at her brandy. She was half a mind, she told herself, to phone everybody up and have a party. Everybody: Angela Snow, Jasmine, the Brigadier, even the Miss Barnwells and Edith Pilchester. She'd rope the whole family in too. They'd have a real old beat-up. It was the only thing to save her from going completely stark, staring crackers.

She was about to telephone Mariette and Mr Charlton to see if they too thought it a good idea when there was a loud and repeated buzzing at the receiving end of Pop's inter-comm.

Ma rushed swiftly upstairs. Pop, it was clear, was in sudden need of her. On the landing outside his bedroom she almost crashed into Nurse Soper – the two vast figures once again meeting as in the opening hold of a bout of wrestling – carrying a large vase of scarlet gladioli. On the floor of the landing other vases stood about: roses, carnations, even the jug of wild flowers gathered by Phyllida and little Oscar.

From the bedroom the voice of a strangely rejuvenated Pop was shouting:

'You meddling virgin old tit, what the ruddy blue hell are you doing with my flowers? Bring 'em back for Christ's sake – quick, afore I bend your arse across the bed. Can you hear me, you old vinegar tits? Bring 'em back!'

Dashing into the bedroom, Ma was astounded to see Pop actually sitting bolt upright in bed, shaking with such righteous fury that she was actually pleased rather than alarmed, as she knew she ought to have been. The fortification by brandy had done its work on her and she was glad.

'Don't let her take my flowers, Ma. Don't let her take 'em. For Gawd's sake.'

Once again, now in the bedroom, Ma and Nurse Soper stood facing each other braced in the very act of physical sparring.

'Bring his flowers back,' Ma said. 'He wants 'em. He needs 'em.'

'I shall do no such thing. It is customary in nursing to remove flowers from bedrooms and wards at night.'

Customary, her foot, Ma said.

'Bum!' Pop said very loudly from the bed.

'Why?' Ma said. 'Why?'

Nurse Soper proceeded to explain that it was all to do with oxygen being taken up by the plants and carbon dioxide being given off at night and so on when Pop shouted 'Bum!' again from his bed, louder than ever.

Icily, a vase of orchids poised archly in her hand, Nurse Soper inquired if that offensive remark was intended for her?

'Yes!' Pop shouted. 'You old fat arse.'

'His flowers are his life,' Ma said. 'He loves 'em under the electric. That's when he has all the pleasure –'

'Very well,' Nurse Soper said, 'it is entirely up to you whether you wish to defer Mr Larkin's progress or not.'

'He'll progress!' Ma said, 'as soon as we get some stale air cleared out!'

Nurse Soper banged down the vase of orchids on the table by the colour television set with such force that the screen actually shook and the delicate pink and cream lips of the orchids trembled.

'In that case,' she said, 'my services are clearly no longer required.'

With totally unexpected vehemence Pop declared that they never were and never had been; and then further informed her, with a flash of the old jocularity that if it didn't quite have Ma in a fit at least woke her to the refreshing fact that he must be on the mend, that she ought to have been a nun.

'Never want none, never give none and never had none!'

Nurse Soper, with immense cold dignity, swept from the room.

A moment later Ma found herself in Pop's arms. Apart from the pure physical sublimity of the moment Pop was acutely aware of another pleasure. With his sharp, hypersensitive gift of smell he suddenly detected that Ma, languished in his arms, smelled unusually nice.

Ma agreed. 'Want some?'

Pop said he thought he could do it a little justice.

'Double?' Ma said.

'Treble,' Pop said and Ma, unbalanced, began laughing so much that she finally fell off the bed with an elephantine crash and for a long time couldn't get up again.

· 6 ·

By next morning Nurse Soper had departed, though not without leaving behind her a warning ghost: namely that the business of the heart was like snakes-and-ladders. One day you were up; before you knew it you were down.

That morning Pop was very down.

Even Ma was forced to admit that the set-to with the Soapy had set him back a peg or two. He was down at the tail of the snake. It was very serious. For this she partly blamed herself, partly the brandy. She was used enough to the brandy, but she didn't often lose her temper. Her extreme affability led her to take people much as they were; her motto was live and let live.

'He will *have* to have a nurse,' Dr O'Connor informed her. 'There's no questioning that. It's absolutely essential.'

'Not another Soapy,' Ma begged. 'Not another old bag. That'd finish him off good and proper.'

'Well, we must see what can be done.'

Dr O'Connor had appeared at eight o'clock, in response to Ma's agitated call that Pop was in a state, as she put it, of God-awful pain. The searing crow-bar had again driven its torturing stab through his chest. He lay grey, gasping, fighting a deeper, vaster agony than the first that had struck him a week before. As he lay there, struggling, open-mouthed, eyes dilated, it struck Ma that he looked exactly like a mouse caught, still alive, in a trap.

While Dr O'Connor was giving him a pain injection the telephone rang. Ma went to answer it and heard the voice of Angela Snow.

Angela had rung up every day, regularly, with fondest felicitations, to inquire of Pop. In those sinuous tones of hers from which it was difficult to keep a certain seductiveness even when inquiring about the sick she always wanted to know how that sweetest pet of a man was? Had they taken the handcuffs off the dear thing yet? – a reference to the fact that Pop had been compulsively driven out, rather like a John the Baptist, into a teetotal wilderness. She simply couldn't bear the wretched thought of it. It was hideous. It had her on her knees.

Ma, in a state of totally uncharacteristic agitation as she answered the telephone, mumbled in answer to Angela's usual seductive inquiry about her dear lamb that Pop was all right, well no he wasn't really, he was a bit down this morning, and finished by murmuring confusedly something about that woman, that old bag.

Angela at once pricked up her ears and said what was that she heard? Woman? Some floosie tampering with his hormones she shouldn't wonder.

Ma didn't comment on this. She knew all about hormones. They were the things that interfered with sex.

Not that she and Pop ever discussed things like that. They never in fact ever used the word sex. They enjoyed a bit of indulgence and all that now and then but that was what it was for, wasn't it? Not to talk about. As a result they tended instinctively to turn away from the word and its all too frequent use in newsprint, on television and on radio. After all there was sex and sex. It was one thing to hear and read about it, and even see it, on television; it was quite another matter what you did in your own home. She and Pop knew that it was all right without bandying a lot of words about it in public. There was an awful lot of bare bosoms and people in bed together naked and a lot of squirming about and biting and all that and there were times, watching television, when she didn't think it was very nice. It struck her as being sort of immoral.

Calming a little, Ma proceeded to explain to Angela Snow that it wasn't some floosie but a nurse she was referring to. The old bag had gone but not before the damage had been done. Now they had got to get another and God knew where.

'*The Angela Snow Distressed Chaps Aid Service Speaking,*' Angela promptly informed Ma, much to Ma's astonishment, in tones both dulcet and dryly mocking. '*You have the worst crises, we solve 'em.*'

'Come again?' Ma said.

'Leave all with me. I know a virginity graduate with First Class Honours who runs a sort of Sainted Aunt thing – gets your smoked salmon for you and your Pill and sees grannie across London and knows where all the nicest tarts live and acts as general dogsbody for anything from trial marriage to baby-sitting for a crocodile. Fabulous gal. What you haven't got she'll see you soon have.'

Ma, being in her present state of distress not quite able to grasp all this, merely murmured did that mean she could get a nurse for Pop and if so how soon?

'*Toute suite*, darling. She'd even get you a dirty-weekend with the Foreign Secretary if that's what you wanted.'

'That'll be the day,' Ma said, knowing who the Foreign Secretary was and added, rather ambiguously: 'How soon can you let me know?'

'I'm practically on the hot line to the dear gal now. I'll get her out of bed if necessary and if I can find the bed. She has a slight propensity towards nocturnal wander-lust at times.'

Ma was slightly stupefied by such language; but by and large, thought she got what it meant.

'I'll buzz you back,' Angela said. 'Not to fret. Meantime give the dear man my fondest and tell him yes. I couldn't come and hold the frail hand for a time I suppose? I long to see him, the pet. It's been an age. I'm an-hungered and a-thirst.'

Ma thanked Angela very much but said she was sorry: the doctor still said no visitors.

'No? Not even the dear Edith?'

The conversation with Angela was such that Ma now actually laughed. Edith? – she must remember to tell her about Edith some day. Not now though. There wasn't time. That was a laugh all right. That would bring her on.

Angela now laughed too, so that it was as if a whole carillon were in full peal at the other end of the line. She didn't want bringing on, however, she informed Ma. She wanted holding back.

'Bye,' she said at last. '*The Distressed Chaps Service* will be back. Meanwhile fondest salutations and all that. *Avec* knobs. Bless.'

Pop, deeply drugged again, slept through the morning. The day was one of those wrapped in soft, mizzling humidity, when minutest myriad drops of night rain still clung glistening to every leaf and blade and branch, undispersed by sun. Mistily, like pearled head-dresses, spiders' webs had been woven everywhere, so that Ma, rather as Pop had done, felt herself enmeshed in a strange sort of muslin drowsiness as she again engaged in a heavy session of cooking in the kitchen, always listening for a buzz on Pop's inter-comm., never quite sure whether silence from it was bad news or not.

It was just after ten o'clock when the telephone rang. Again it was Angela Snow.

'Hullo, darling. *Distressed Chaps* again. Sorry to have been an age. I always thought Fridays was her Cypriot night, but she's switched, it seems. Found her with a Korean eventually. In Windsor of all places. However, all is well. All fixed.'

Ma felt so relieved that for one desperate moment she thought of brandy again and then swiftly rejected it and told herself to be sensible.

'I only hope she's not like the last. Can't do with another like her.'

'Sweet child, I'm told. Level-headed, strong sensible shoes type, unfussy and competent. How's that?'

Ma indicated that she heard it with relief. She was glad and grateful.

'Trust my girl friend. She may go in for sport but she's got the business head all right. You want it, she'll get it. Anything more I can do for you, darling? How is the dear lamb anyway?'

Ma, saying that there was nothing more, thanked Angela again and said that Pop was sleeping.

'Splendid. Bless him. Oh! her name's Trevelyan. The nurse, I mean, I think she's colonial or something.'

Colonial? Ma said. She hoped that didn't mean she was black? She didn't mind lending Pop out a bit to most types, even to Angela and the luscious Jasmine Brown, but she wasn't sure about these coloured bits. She well remembered Pop watching some African tribe on television with all the girls dancing about with bare titties and all that and how the effect on him had been something chronic. No, she was a bit against black bosoms now she thought of it.

'Oh! no. White. Australian, I think. And she'll arrive bang on the dot at twelve o'clock. By train. Can you meet? If not, darling I'll be glad to cope.'

Ma, again thanking Angela, said that she thought Mariette could well meet the train.

'Splendid. Anything more I can send the dear man? I'm still trying to get those mangoes and passion-fruit but those swabs in London still won't play. Disappointing. I thought the passion-fruit would be much in his line.'

Ma confessed she didn't think Pop had much time for passion just now, as things were.

'Devastating thought. Jolly unfair. Like a nightingale going off song or something. "Thou wast not born for –" Good God, what am I on about? It's jolly unfair, anyway. Shouldn't happen. Well, if you need *The Distressed Chaps* again you know where I am. Farewell for now. Kiss the slumbering forehead for me. Farewell, darling, farewell.'

Behind the smooth, honeyed tongue of Angela Snow there lay something very human, warm and practical. It was much after Ma's own heart. In consequence she was able to go through the rest of the humid, mizzling morning, enmeshed in its bright spider webs, with faith restored.

She was further comforted, about half past eleven, by the unexpected arrival of the Reverend Candy, accompanied by Primrose, still wearing the briefest of mini-skirts, this time in brilliant turquoise. The Reverend Candy had been picking raspberries again. Primrose was carrying two vegetable marrows, young and pale cream, one under each arm, in a position that the Reverend Candy found more than slightly disturbing.

'Oh! hullo,' Ma said. 'I didn't know you two were here. When did you creep in?'

'You were on the phone when Mr Candy arrived.'

Well, it was very nice to see Mr Candy, Ma said. Mr Candy had discarded all clerical gear for the morning and was dressed in a surprisingly ochre-yellow open-necked shirt and pale blue trousers. And how was Mr Candy?

Mr Candy responded with a positively spring-like enthusiasm that he was well, very well indeed, in the pink. He was only sorry that he understood the same couldn't be said for Mr Larkin.

'Have a cheese-straw,' Ma said. 'Oh! he's having a nice long sleep. It'll do him the world of good. And he's got a new nurse coming.'

Mr Candy helped himself to several of Ma's cheese-straws, still warm from the oven. Primrose said she would get the raspberries ready for lunch. What else were they having?

'Well, I've got a roast leg of pork with stuffing, braised onions, new potatoes and carrots, baked potatoes and broad beans and we can have the marrow with cheese sauce too if you like.'

To Ma's way of thinking there was no sense in going hungry even in times of extreme crisis. You'd got to keep your strength up. You'd got to eat. Didn't Mr Candy agree?

Mr Candy agreed with the utmost cordiality. He already felt in torture. The very smell of roasting pork and stuffing was itself enough to drive one crazy. He could actually hear the pork and its crackling sizzling in the oven and the echo of this most delicious of sounds seemed to go hissing through his insides like some exquisite set of variations played on fragile strings.

By this time the rain, never more than a lightly clinging mist, had cleared, leaving a sky gently breaking into sun.

'Who's this new nurse?' Primrose said. 'I hope she's better than the old bar of soap.'

Ma, now peeling and cutting the two young vegetable marrows into shapes less disturbing to Mr Candy, said that Angela Snow had managed to get hold of her. Ma understood she was a nice, solid, level-headed, sensible sort of girl and no nonsense about her.

'That sounds about right,' Primrose said. 'We can't have Pop boiling over any more. He needs peace and quiet from now on.'

And peace and quiet, Ma said, was what he was going to get.

Presently, tortured still further by the fragrance of roast pork and stuffing, Mr Candy started to say that he thought he really ought to be going. It was the better part of valour, he told himself, or something. Ma, however, cut him very short, and rather severely. Go, her foot. How was all the roast pork going to get eaten up if Mr Candy didn't do his bit? No, no, she said, she wouldn't have Mr Candy going. There was more than enough for everybody, she assured him. Gracious, they'd got to eat, hadn't they? she demanded of him in slightly indignant accents, as if it were some sort of crime not to.

Though protesting diligently, Mr Candy in fact needed no second asking and thanked Ma in terms of generosity that he could only hope matched her own. He secretly confided to himself that he couldn't have borne that torture much longer. It would certainly have had him down.

'Well,' Ma said, 'that settles that. You and Primrose can lay the table. There'll be five of us for lunch. That includes Mariette and the new nurse, Little Oscar and Phyllida have gone off to the seaside with the postman's wife and her two. How about a snifter all round?'

Mr Candy murmured 'excellent' and, modest as always said he would settle for a glass of sherry. Ma, remembering the near disasters of brandy, thought she possibly ought to draw her horns in a bit and helped herself to a gin-and-tonic very nearly large enough to wash in. Primrose declared she wouldn't have anything; it was alcohol that put the weight on, a statement that made Ma look quite concerned. She didn't believe in losing weight. Very bad thing. It wasn't long since that Pop, watching her dress one morning and observing that the rotundities of her figure didn't seem quite so jolly as usual, inquired with some anxiety if Ma was slimming or something, a remark which made Ma shiningly indignant. Did he mind? Slimming, her foot. She liked her figure as it was and was going to keep it that way. It was all hers, wasn't it? All 55–55–55 of it.

The train evidently being slightly late, it was one o'clock before Mariette's car was heard drawing up outside the house.

'Now for it,' Primrose said.

'She'd better be good,' Ma said, 'else it'll be marching orders.'

Some few moments later Ma, Primrose and the Reverend Candy appeared to have been suddenly shattered by some dire explosion. Mr Candy actually felt the onset of an acute paralysis and even Ma, for fully half a minute, had no word.

'This is Sister Trevelyan,' Mariette said. 'Sorry we're a bit late. The train was held up.'

'Hullo,' Sister Trevelyan said with only the very slightest of Australian accents in her low warm voice.

'Hullo,' Ma said too. Even she, never at a loss for a word, could find no other to say.

Sister Trevelyan was rather less like a girl than a big, smooth, handsome chestnut mare. Her gleaming hair was neither auburn nor blonde. Her eyes were two black olives, glistening with melting brilliance. The sensational curve of her splendid shoulders was only matched by the further splendours of a superlative bust. Her legs were long, brown and athletic. Bronzed, magnificent in carriage, smooth as a deer in movement, she had altogether the look of some prize and lovely animal entered in a show.

Even Ma, who was ever ready to make her daughters odds-on favourites in any beauty contest you cared to name, was fully prepared to admit, even if not aloud, that in Sister Trevelyan you had a right starter and one with a bit of pedigree. Nothing virginal about it either, she told herself, having a quick eye in these matters.

'Like a drink?' she managed to say at last. 'Sherry, gin, whisky, bitter lemon –'

'Brandy,' Sister Trevelyan said, 'if there is.'

There certainly was, Ma said, mightily pleased. Girl after her own heart.

'Cheers,' Sister Trevelyan said, raising a glass containing the largest brandy she had ever been privileged to see. 'Not supposed to drink on duty, but I'm not quite on duty yet, I suppose. How is my patient?'

'Sleeping,' Ma said, 'like a dormouse.'

'Should I take a peep at him?'

No, no, Ma said. Lunch first. They must all have lunch first. She was all ready to dish up.

'Shall we have wine, Ma?' Primrose said. 'And if so, what?'

Of course they were going to have wine, Ma said, with no little indignation. They always did, didn't they? The idea of not having wine was on the verge of shocking. And what sort? Better have a choice, she thought: drop o' red and a drop o' white. She thought the Beaujolais and the Liebfraumilch. Pop always had a choice. It was only good manners.

'Mr Candy'll get the corks out, won't you, Mr Candy?' Primrose said and then, finding him almost sightlessly transfixed by the vision of Sister Trevelyan, gave him a look of a certain critical severity. 'Corks, corks – the wine – draw the corks –'

'Oh! yes, yes, of course,' Mr Candy said and as if to excuse his dilatory lapse added, at once drawn into a state of fresh hypnosis by the incredible

figure of Sister Trevelyan, something about a day without wine being like
a day without sunshine.

It was now Ma's turn to look at him with some severity. Shrewdly
detecting his eye positively dithering over Sister Trevelyan, she wondered
if there wasn't something behind that last remark?

As if the stunning surprise of Sister Trevelyan wasn't enough, Ma
produced another as they all sat down to lunch.

'Pork or pheasant, Mr Candy? or both? I popped a couple of pheasants
in too just in case,' though in case of what Ma didn't say. 'Remembered
I'd got 'em out of the deep-freeze last night. Have both if you like. Or start
with pheasant?'

To be caught between the succulent tortures of both pork and pheasant
was exactly like being caught between the torturing beauty of Primrose
on one hand and the new nurse on the other. Mr Candy, for some
moments, simply didn't know where he was.

'Really, honestly I don't know. It's an awfully difficult choice. I really
don't mind – both or one –'

Rather tartly Primrose suddenly urged him to keep his mind on his
work, which Mr Candy at once proceeded rather guiltily to do.

Ma, who was carving while Mariette poured the wine, chopped a
pheasant in two and put a half on Mr Candy's plate, together with a vast
slice of pork and crackling, adding that he could come again as soon as
he'd got outside of that lot.

'Wine, Ma?' Mariette said. 'Red or white?'

Ma said no thanks, she didn't think she'd have wine. She'd have a
Guinness instead. She needed building up.

Having now served Sister Trevelyan with exactly the same portions as
Mr Candy, Ma proceeded deftly to carve for herself and the girls, giving
herself the knuckle end of the pork, her favourite bit. Her Guinness having
now been brought in by Primrose, who suddenly seemed a bit aloof-like,
Ma thought, for some reason, if not even toffee-nosed, Ma raised her glass
to Sister Trevelyan and said:

'Well, cheers and welcome,' and added that she hoped the pheasants
were tender. They ought to be: they were both females.

The explanation behind all this was that Mr Charlton and Montgomery,
Ma's eldest son, had now gone into the pheasant lark. This was another
of Pop's ideas and a very good lark it had turned out to be. Pop had
shrewdly noticed that England was rapidly becoming populated with a
new kind of country gent. These invaded the countryside, if they didn't
live there already, with one avowed intention: namely that of shooting

pheasants. The fact that you could buy a pheasant for twenty-five bob at the poulterer's, and ready plucked, was no sort of deterrent; it was far more fun to shoot them on freezing winter days, in miserable discomfort, at ten quid a time. As all the pheasants were near-tame when let loose in the autumn they constantly flew so low when driven from copse and hedge-row that the shooters not only massacred them without mercy but all too frequently shot each other as well.

As for Pop, he vastly preferred to sit in his own garden in comfort and shoot whatever of his neighbours' stray birds happened to fly over. This sensible habit finally inspired him to reason that because so many birds were shot an even greater number were needed to replace them, since the population of shooters was already increasing every year, in spite of a growing tendency on their part to kill each other off. It was the old law of supply and demand again, Pop told himself. You couldn't go wrong.

So now Montgomery and Mr Charlton were in the pheasant lark: the raising of eggs and poults, a business that to Pop's native wisdom made a great deal of sense. This new passion for having a place in the country had brought so many mugs out of hiding that even Pop, sometimes, thought it wasn't quite fair. It was daylight robbery. It was cruel to take their money.

'And what's your other name?' Ma said to Sister Trevelyan. 'We can't call you Sister all the time, can we?'

'Vanessa.'

'Oh! lovely name,' Ma said. Oh! she liked that. She really genuinely loved Vanessa.

This friendly genuine enthusiasm of Ma's was not reflected in Primrose, who picked up a piece of crackling in her fingers and snapped at it loudly with her teeth.

'Your first visit over here?' Mr Candy said.

Oh! no, she'd been here before, Sister Trevelyan said. Last year she'd been all over the Continent too. France, Spain, Italy, Germany, Switzerland. She'd really been around.

Silently Mariette betted she had, then exchanged a low, calculated glance with Primrose that was not precisely friendly.

Totally unaware of these feminine exchanges Mr Candy ate and drank his delicious, tortured way through lunch. Not only was the food delectable in every way – the choice between the excellence of pork and that of pheasant could only be described as being between manna and the food of the gods – but the Liebfraumilch, with which he had started the meal, had its virtues too. When Ma finally reminded him that 'he hadn't got no

Burgundy' Mr Candy agreed with almost apologetic alacrity and at once proceeded to sample several glasses of Beaujolais. That was pretty good stuff too, he told himself. More body, more fire. He could fairly feel it singing through his veins.

Body and fire: the words were, perhaps, not inappropriate. Just as he had been tortured and torn between the succulence of pork and pheasant so he continued to be even more enraptured by the opposing bodies and fire of Primrose and Sister Trevelyan. Under the influence of the two wines, it sometimes seemed, the two bodies actually melted together. They were marvellously, celestially fused.

'Vanessa – at least I hope I may call you Vanessa – I haven't got my dog-collar on but I am the parson here – and I was just wondering what denomination you might be?'

'Oh! no denomination,' Sister Trevelyan said and gave a laugh of such honeyed physical richness that even Angela Snow could scarcely have rivalled it. 'I'm what we call in Australia a "oncer". I went once and never again.'

'We must see if we can't convert you.'

And what exactly might that mean? Primrose thought and sharply bit at another piece of crackling like a sniper biting at a bullet.

It finally became clear to Ma that the air was growing more and more electric with tension. The fire was in Mr Candy's eye; you could see it. And the look in those of Primrose wasn't exactly yesterday's ashes either.

It was time to clear the decks and change the subject, she told herself. She didn't want any more truck with tension. She'd had enough of tension with Soapy yesterday.

As she served raspberries, strawberries, meringues, treacle tart and mixed fruit pie, all with cream, she pointedly remarked that she thought the raspberries would only just go round. Somebody had better pick some more this afternoon.

Ten minutes later Primrose, as if more in response to command rather than suggestion, went upstairs to change into what Mr Candy had come to think of as her 'raspberry blouse' and finally came downstairs wearing a garment that seemed composed of nothing more than two children's handkerchiefs, pink and practically transparent, leaving a greater area of midriff than ever exposed.

At the same time Ma had deemed it tactically wise to suggest that it was time for Nurse Trevelyan to go up and see her patient, leaving Mariette to clear the table. She could only hope that Pop was feeling strong.

The afternoon was turning out to be very warm and muggy. It was one of those dog days of July when you felt you needed to find somewhere cool, silent and in the shade, only to sleep.

This was the very thought in the mind of Primrose as she and Mr Candy reached the avenues of raspberry canes, red and fragrant with fruit in the sun.

Here Mr Candy, groping among the canes, his legs deliciously unstable, stretched out a hand in order to steady himself and instead found it grasping Primrose's smooth naked shoulder.

Great God, he thought, how warm the flesh was.

Soon Primrose was inspired to suggest that it was becoming too hot to gather raspberries. It seemed slow work, she thought. It took a long time to fill a basket.

'Ah! well, two for the price of one,' Mr Candy said, *apropos* of nothing much, except possibly the fact that, with benefit of wine, he could now see double. 'Aren't they large too? Marvellous.'

They certainly were, Primrose said, and pressed another huge luscious one to her lips, so that they too seemed to be smeared with the crimson of new-pressed wine.

'That pheasant was pretty marvellous too,' Mr Candy said, by no means for the first time. He would never forget that pheasant: food of the gods. Manna, indeed.

'Talking of pheasants,' Primrose said. 'Have you seen where Montgomery and Charley raise them – I mean the eggs and the chicks? It's in the field beyond the wood.'

'Oh! so that's what they're for, those pens. I often wondered.'

'That's what they're for.'

As he and Primrose started to walk across the meadow the great confliction in Mr Candy's mind was inspired not only by the memory and effect of pheasant and wine but by a recollection that went much further back in time.

It was of the occasion when he had first been passionately kissed by Primrose as a girl of fourteen and she had quoted to him, with an exhilarating earthiness that amounted to sheer, deliberate seduction, Donne's lines 'I wonder by my troth what thou and I did till we loved'.

Ever since that devastating moment, to be followed not long later by others still more devastating when he had been called upon to christen her and the rest of the Larkin brood in a sort of holy package deal, Ma and Pop having overlooked the fact of having the ceremony performed when they were in infancy, he had tried to avoid Primrose, not because he didn't like her – quite the contrary – but because she frightened him cold stiff. Now the crisis of Pop's heart attack had brought them together again.

The trouble with Primrose was that she was not only the most beautiful and earthy of all the earthy Larkins; she was clever too. She found much of herself reflected and expressed in the poets. This found Mr Candy all too often out of his depth, in more ways than one. Some years of curacy in London's East End dock areas had prepared him for many things but not for rural seductresses who disarmed you not by physical means alone but by quoting Herrick and Donne, two gentlemen who didn't, as Mr Candy had once remarked, cut much ice in Stepney.

'It's getting hotter and hotter,' Primrose said. 'Shall we sit down and rest a minute? Can you smell the honeysuckle?'

Before Mr Candy could give any answer about the honeysuckle Primrose was lying down, not sitting, in the shade of the woodside. Rather like a man not too anxious to sit too close to a roaring fire, in case he got roasted, Mr Candy sat down some two yards apart from her, confronted by a wide expanse of naked sun-brown midriff in the centre of which the navel dwelt darkly, ripely pulsating.

Though trying desperately not to look at it too obviously Mr Candy found that frequent recurrences of his double vision merely had the effect of providing him with two navels, as it were, for the price of one. That the price itself had the prospect of being heavy was reflected in a sudden huge sigh, which caused Primrose to inquire of him, with a slow voluptuous look, if he was tired?

'Oh! no, not tired. Not tired at all. It's merely that it's – after all that – you know, the food, the wine – it's all so – so heavenly.'

'The honeysuckle's heavenly too, isn't it?'

Intoxicating was the word for honeysuckle that crossed Mr Candy's mind like a wave of the sublime fragrance itself but he merely murmured: 'Yes, heavenly.'

'Come and lie down.'

Mr Candy presently found himself stretched full length on the grass, less perhaps in obedience to another slow voluptuous look of invitation than in the sheer relief of being able to look up at the purity of the sky above rather than down at the darkness of the navel below.

In its overpowering sultriness the afternoon was hushed. There was no note of birdsong. Mr Candy wondered once or twice about the young pheasants and where were they? and then let such a mundane thought drift down the stream of the afternoon like a light fallen feather.

'There's a line in Blake that I keep thinking of,' Primrose said at last. 'You know Blake?'

Dozily Mr Candy confessed that his acquaintance with Blake was slight, always supposing he had the right Blake – 'England's Green and Pleasant Land' and all that?

'That's him. It isn't all in the poetry, though. The verse. Did you ever read "The Marriage of Heaven and Hell"?'

No, Mr Candy said, he feared he hadn't read 'The Marriage of Heaven and Hell'; and with trepidation he wondered what was coming next.

Primrose soon enlightened him.

'"As the caterpillar chooses the fairest leaves to lay her eggs on, so the priest lays his curse on the fairest joys."'

Mr Candy was silent. Dreamily spoken though the words were, with an intoxication of sound even more soothing than the smell of honeysuckle, he couldn't quite make up his mind whether he was being educated, teased, or merely got at.

'Isn't that beautiful? And true too – as true now as the day it was written.'

'Oh! no, I can't have that,' Mr Candy was spurred to sudden mild indignation. 'I think that's jolly unfair.'

'And how can it be jolly unfair?'

'Because it is. It just is.'

'But how? Just how?'

'Well, in the first place –'

'In the first place, what? The caterpillar chooses the fairest leaves to lay her eggs on, doesn't she?'

'Not always. Sometimes they lay them on nettles.'

'In which case the priest would have to be careful he didn't get stung.'

Mr Candy found himself utterly at a loss to say anything in answer to this. That was the trouble with Primrose – she was so awfully unpredictable. You never knew quite what form she would appear in next. He wasn't at all sure she wasn't like a caterpillar herself, smooth and golden and sinuous, creeping and entwining herself about him, weaving a sort of cocoon. It was the caterpillar that weaved the cocoon, wasn't it? or was it the chrysallis? He didn't really know. He was getting terribly lost.

'I suppose it was actually the next bit that you thought was jolly unfair, wasn't it?'

'The next bit?'

'"So the priest lays his hands on the fairest joys."'

'Curse, you said the first time. Not hand. Curse.'

'No, hand I think it is. "Hand on the fairest joys." '

Mr Candy felt desperately confused. He was sure it was curse; he was sure she was making it all up. It was all deliberate. She was deliberately misquoting. It was all jolly unfair. Curse was what she had said, curse.

Then, just as he was trying to express at least some of these protestations into words, he discovered that she had suddenly abandoned her prostrate position and was sitting up, bending over him, closely.

This was bad enough; but worse followed a moment later. He knew suddenly that she was reading his thoughts. He had always said of her that you could fairly hear her thinking with the pores of her skin, but now she was reading his mind. She had this awfully intuitive thing that was all the more terrifying because it wasn't really conscious.

It wasn't only the mind that was intuitive, either; it was the body too. The body was now very close to him. The upper of the only two garments she was wearing was as flimsy as a pair of butterfly wings. They were fully spread and her two big, firm young breasts, now close to his face, seemed about to fall out of them.

'I know what you were thinking,' she said. 'You were thinking I was a caterpillar.'

'No, no, I wasn't. Really. Never. I never thought of you as a caterpillar.'

'Then what did you think of me as?'

'I don't know – really I never thought –'

'A butterfly?'

There she went again: reading his thoughts.

'I hoped you'd think of me as a butterfly. They're so nice, don't you think, butterflies?'

Yes, yes, Mr Candy agreed. He knew that. He knew about butterflies. They were beautiful, very beautiful.

'And they lay the eggs.'

'Oh! do they? I thought it was the caterpillar. Isn't that what Blake said? The caterpillar – on the fairest flower –'

'Blake was dotty.'

'I thought you said he was wonderful.'

'All wonderful people are dotty. Don't you think so? Genius and all that. Don't you think so?'

Mr Candy was about to say that he thought he'd need notice of that question when he felt Primrose stroking his nose. Her fingers tickled him softly and he lifted his hands to brush her own away. In doing so he caught his own hands against her breasts and in a moment of stuttering confusion said he was sorry.

'Whatever for?'

Mr Candy didn't know whatever for. It was all the fault of Blake. Perhaps he'd better get back to Blake.

'Now is it the butterfly or the caterpillar which –'

'Don't take your hands away. There's nothing there to bite you.'

Great God, that's where she was wrong, Mr Candy thought, that's where she was wrong.

'After all, who brought all this up, anyway?'

Mr Candy, who wasn't aware of having brought anything up, now felt a surge of excitement run through him like a spear. What on earth was she talking about, bringing things up? Here he was, enmeshed in a cocoon of her own making and all this talk of Blake and caterpillars and flowers and eggs and all that and she was trying to blame him, Mr Candy. Trying to make him the guilty party. Whereas it was she who was to blame; it was all her fault. No, it wasn't. It was the fault of the two of them, she and that fellow Blake. It was all a conspiracy.

Her breasts were warm. His hands trembled as he took them in his own.

In that exquisitely unbearable moment Primrose kissed him, but neither too long nor too lusciously but rather as if letting him take the first delicate bite from the outer flesh of a peach. Mr Candy felt all his senses water; and then she said:

'You know something else Blake wrote?'

At that moment, feeling one of her hands free one of his and take it in a long drifting line of exploration down her body until it came to rest on, so to speak, the equatorial line, Mr Candy couldn't have cared less what Blake had written.

'"The road of excess leads to the palace of wisdom."'

Great God, Mr Candy thought, he didn't doubt it. He was, without question, on the road of excess already. Whether it was wise or not he wouldn't know, it was impossible to tell, until later.

'Well,' Primrose said at long last, with a slow sigh, 'that was nice while it lasted.'

Mr Candy, with a great thundering of excess pounding through his blood, fully agreed. He was only sorry it hadn't lasted longer.

'Is there any reason why it couldn't?'

Borne far down on the road of excess Mr Candy found himself overcome by an earthy, delicious sleepiness. He was woken out of it not long later by the near distant voice of a cowman calling his cattle home across a meadow and this earthiest of country sounds woke him at last to a new consciousness of the naked body lying beside him. It seemed to him very, very beautiful.

'From now on,' Primrose at last said, 'for "curse" read "hands".'

'Agreed. Or blessing.'

'Blessing, I think. I'm sorry I fibbed.'

'And is it the caterpillar or the butterfly? –'

Primrose laughed with that deep midsummer laugh of hers.

'Perhaps it's both. Perhaps it's a bit of cross-pollination.'

Mr Candy laughed too. There she went again: thinking through the pores of her skin, going deep to the heart of the matter.

'After all,' she said, laughing again, 'that's what everything's all about, isn't it? Cross-pollination?'

That indeed, as Mr Candy had discovered, was what everything was all about: a sort of sublime, celestial cross-pollination.

Long later, he thought at quite six o'clock, Primrose got up and dressed herself – that is if you could call putting on two garments a process of dressing – and Mr Candy watched her with all the minute and fascinated attention that Pop always gave to Ma on similar if slightly more complicated occasions.

'I'm a bit surprised at you,' Primrose said. 'Where did you learn all that?'

All what? Mr Candy started to say and then, rather airily, as a man recently returned from pleasurable conquest, said he didn't quite know. He could only suppose he'd picked it up as he went along.

At which Primrose laughed her rich midsummer laugh again.

'That's the best way,' she said. 'Next time you'll be able to play it by ear.'

'Certainly not,' Mr Candy said. 'I shall play it the way we played it today.'

· 7 ·

It was soon after five o'clock that same afternoon when Ma, having provided Sister Trevelyan with what she called 'a rough cup', consisting of tea, buttered scones, shortbread, iced buns, plain and plum cake, four sorts of jam, chocolate biscuits and strawberries-and-cream, together with tomato ketchup, in case she might want a little with the iced buns, as the Larkins often did, remarked that she was sorry she'd had to knock it all up rather quick but Dr O'Connor was coming at a quarter past five, before he began surgery.

'In that case I'll go up and see that my patient's fit and ready,' Sister Trevelyan said, 'and got his clean bib and tucker on.'

'I'll come with you.'

Ma, always quick to sum up people in the shortest possible time, had already decided that Sister Trevelyan came, as Pop might have said, from the right stable. She was without doubt a girl after her own heart. She was also more than good on the eye. If out of uniform she looked very much like some splendid gold-brown mare, in uniform she looked more like a statue of one, the lines of her figure sculptured, smooth and polished, purest snow-white marble. The uniform also gave the impression that she was, both in shape and bearing, even more magnificent. There was something little short of sensational in the carving of the bust, something classical about the brilliant gold-auburn helmet of hair.

Some minutes before this Pop had woken at last from a long drugged slumber with that strange uplifting feeling of resurrection that he had experienced before, the wondering sensation of having come back from the dead. Through the divisions of the drawn curtains of his bedroom he could just discern thin swords of gold brilliance tipped with blue. He lay watching them without daring to move, fearful that pain might come back.

Pain didn't come back and he closed his eyes, seeming to float gently in a vacuum. In this state of light suspense he presently heard voices. He then opened his eyes, only to feel that he was now the victim of a great illusion.

It seemed to him that the ghost of Soapy had incredibly come back, much enlarged, whiter, shining, in readiness to haunt him. He instinctively slipped a little lower under the bed clothes. Then Ma said:

'This is Sister Trevelyan, Pop. Our new nurse.'

There was something immensely reassuring about that one word 'our'. Pop lifted an eye over the edge of the sheets. The passing of one illusion left him with another. Soapy had somehow undergone an astonishing, stunning transformation.

The creature into which Soapy had been transformed quietly moved towards him and then actually stretched out a hand.

'Hullo, Mr Larkin. What on earth have *you* been up to?'

Very personal, those words, Pop thought, very intimate: as if he and this amazing creature had known each other closely for a long time. They gave Pop not merely the feeling that an old friend had turned up but that the friend was one full of the warmest affection.

Her hand touched him. It too was warm. Then she actually allowed him to hold it for what seemed a long time. His own hypersensitive touch responded to this so sharply that she in turn responded by squeezing his fingers gently, at the same time giving him a slow soft smile.

This so comforted and brightened Pop that he was briefly moved to joke.

'You the new medicine?'

'I'm the new medicine.'

'Perfick. Three times a day in water?'

'Four times if you don't behave yourself.'

Pop gave her one of those quick looks of his in which there was faintly visible a touch of the old self.

'Behave? My blood pressure's up already.'

'Then,' she said, 'we'd better see about getting it down, hadn't we?'

She gave a light laugh. Her fingers moved to his pulse. While she was busy taking his pulse Pop was able to give brief study to her splendid bust, her olive-black eyes and the gold-auburn fringes of hair creeping in burnished curls from under her cap. These having proved excitingly satisfactory, a great thought crossed his mind.

What price the point of no return now? he thought, the do-it-yourself lark? Inspired by possible answers he told himself that he felt a lot better already. Life was getting interesting again. She had cheered him up no end.

'Where have they been keeping you all this long time?' he said.

'Australia.'

Perfick, Perfick!

'I had an uncle went out there once. Years ago. Good looking feller. Probably chased your mother.'

'Now, now,' Ma said. 'None of that. I told you he'd be cheeky, didn't I, Sister.'

Sister Trevelyan laughed again and astonished Ma by saying she liked cheeky patients. They were inclined to get on. It was the groaners she couldn't do with.

'Well, don't you encourage him too much,' Ma said. 'He'll be running you round like the hens before you know it, trying to make you lay.'

For a few moments Sister Trevelyan lost what little dignity she had and shrieked with laughter. Ma laughed like a drain too and said she really hadn't meant it quite like that, not the laying part anyway.

'I'll bet,' Pop said, looking at Sister Trevelyan's rich sun-brown skin, 'you'd lay nice big brown 'uns if you did.'

'Now, now,' Ma said. 'You've got him cheeky already, Sister. Just you calm down, Sid Larkin. You'll have your blood pressure up a lot more by the time the doctor gets here and then where will you be?'

'Bottom of the snake,' Pop said.

'Perhaps a little wash might be a good thing before the doctor comes,' Sister Trevelyan said. 'Just a freshener.'

Perfick, Pop thought. Just what he was waiting for. He watched the upper half of Sister Trevelyan glide smoothly from the room, wondering at the same time what the bottom half looked like. If it matched the top half there was no doubt she'd be perfick too. Unfortunately, lying on one pillow, he couldn't yet see the bottom half.

While Sister Trevelyan had gone to the bathroom to fetch soap and towels and warm water Ma deemed it a prudent moment to take the opportunity of giving Pop a brief lecture.

'Now none of your hanky-panky larks with this one, Sid Larkin.' It was always a very serious matter when Ma called him Sid Larkin. Sometimes he knew he even had to watch out when she called him 'young man', but Sid Larkin was serious indeed. 'She's a very nice girl and she comes of a very good family. Her father's a very high-up brain surgeon in Melbourne. Don't you start any of your saucy tricks with her. She's not that type.'

Never crossed his mind, Pop said, never even crossed his mind.

'And it better hadn't, either. Besides, there's the ethics.'

Pop didn't quite know what Ma meant by ethics. He only hoped it wasn't something catching.

'What I mean is don't you try one of your Edith Pilchesters on her. You know what I mean.'

Pop murmured something about it being a different technique altogether with Edith and then asked how Edith was? He'd missed his friends: Edith, the Brigadier, Angela, Jasmine and all the rest. None of them had been allowed to see him yet. It was worse than awful. It was even as bad as not drinking.

'Nobody's seen her much since what I told you about. She's sort of been in *purdah*.'

At this Pop gave the strongest, healthiest laugh that had passed his lips since he had been first laid low.

'And whatever is there so funny about that?' Ma said.

'I thought you said in pod, Ma. I thought you said in pod. That'll be the day.'

'Outrageous,' Ma said and then proceeded to laugh twice as heartily as Pop, shaking all over like a jelly.

There was still a trace of laughter on Pop's face as Sister Trevelyan started to wash him. The first few strokes of the sponge were like balm. It was as different from Soapy as wine from vinegar. The only worrying problem was how to keep his eyes shut so that the soap shouldn't get into them and at the same time keep them open enough to allow him as frequently as possible to look at Sister Trevelyan's face, held just above his own.

He didn't suppose she'd be doing a point of no return job this evening, he told himself. That would be something to look forward to tomorrow. But it was all very pleasant, very soothing, very beautiful. To be back from the dead yet again was marvellous enough in itself. To be back and resurrected by a face like that of Sister Trevelyan was little short of a miracle.

'Now is there anything else you'd like me to do for you?'

Normally such a leading question would have inspired Pop to very interesting replies but now, remembering the severity of Ma's injunctions about his behaviour, he merely shook his head, disregarding all possible jocularity about the bottle and said no, thank you and shook his head.

'I thought I heard a car,' Ma said and went from the room, taking off her pinafore designed in bright orange poppies and purple butterflies as she went. 'I expect it's the doctor now.'

'Good boy,' Sister Trevelyan said. 'You look fine.'

With the smile of a goddess she ran her hands smoothly, gently and warmly across Pop's forehead and Pop could have wept.

During the next week or so the arrival of Sister Trevelyan had two main revolutionary effects. To the resurgence of Pop himself – he was now allowed to lie a little less horizontally, propped by one pillow – was added an astonishing revival among his friends. Where no visitors at all had been allowed, dozens now seemed to spring up from everywhere, like mushrooms appearing overnight.

The very first of his visitors was his old friend the Brigadier. Ill-shod in a pair of old white cricket boots tied with brown laces, a cream shantung jacket of which one pocket was entirely missing and the other patched up with what looked suspiciously like an old face flannel, his much-washed University tie, a brown straw hat that looked like a beehive riddled by buckshot and a pair of cream trousers, once long, that had been cut down to just below knee length for coolness in the summer heat, with the edges left frayed, the Brigadier looked seedier, poorer, shabbier, yet somehow more English and aristocratic, than ever.

'Frightfully sorry to hear of all this, Larkin. Damn bad turn of the wheel. Struck down when I heard it. Plunged in gloom.'

Already restored to a certain quickness of eye, Pop told himself that the Brigadier, far from being plunged in gloom, had about him a certain eager perkiness. After sitting for a mere moment or two by the bedside he was continually nipping up to peer out of the window.

Pop couldn't think why. It couldn't be the garden, which under pressure of recent events Ma had to her sorrow been forced to neglect a good deal; nor could it be the junk-yard, the only new addition of any importance to which was a vast collection of army surplus foot-baths, which Pop with his natural aptitude for a good thing hoped to sell to a firm of landscape gardeners for flower urns. You could never tell what they were going to put flowers into next, nowadays, what with chamber-pots and all that, and he thought the baths were perfick, besides being capable of showing a profit of about 700 per cent.

'Splendid new item of scenic detail, Larkin.'

Scenic detail? Pop couldn't think what the pipe the Brigadier was talking about. He could think of no scenic detail.

The shape, the Brigadier would have him know, the shape.

For some moments Pop could think of no shape either.

'Get her by advertisement, stealth, subterfuge, bribery or what?'

It now became suddenly clear to Pop what had been the cause of the Brigadier's constant nipping and bobbing up and down to the window.

'Oh! my nurse. Sister Trevelyan. Angela got hold of her. Australian.'

'I heard rumours. But by God.'

'Very nice girl. Comes of a very good family.'

'Sensational.'

The Brigadier said the word as if taking a draught of some exquisite drink, a fact that caused Pop to ask him if he wouldn't have one? The Brigadier accepted with a muttering show of reluctance which in fact concealed a positively panting eagerness, so that Pop invited him to help himself: it was all on the table beside the television set.

Addressing himself to the vast array of bottles there, the Brigadier inquired if he couldn't knock up a chota peg for Larkin at the same time? When Pop immediately informed him that he was on the wagon, utterly teetotal, perhaps for ever, the Brigadier turned extremely pale.

'Good God.' The Brigadier was aghast. 'Under whose edict is this? Rome? New encyclical or something?'

'Doctor. Two doctors.'

'Catastrophic. Is this yet another of the legion of sufferings under the National Health Service?'

'No, General, this is private. Private practice.' Pop laughed. 'Probably if I'd been on the National Elf lark I could have got it free, by prescription.'

The Brigadier felt a great compulsion to take a deep earnest swig at a large whisky-and-soda. The world was becoming a damn rum place.

'I rarely ask for special dispensation, Larkin, but this might be an occasion.'

Oh! he was getting used to it, Pop said. There were compensations. Silently he thought of his coming back, twice, from the dead, and the rose-leaf by the window.

'Such as the scenic detail? Don't say that field is taboo as well.'

He hadn't had much chance to exercise his talent lately, Pop said and then remembered the occasion when, contrary to Ma's instructions, he had briefly tried to. It had been the occasion of his first bath, some few days ago, with Sister Trevelyan: the old point of no return.

Pop had decided that when the opportunity of the do-it-yourself lark arose he would respectfully decline. He didn't know what the odds against success were but it was wurf a flutter. In due course Sister Trevelyan washed him upstairs with gentle thoroughness and then downstairs with equal efficiency, leaving the way open to the expected invitation of 'would you like to do the rest yourself?' to which Pop replied with a sort of amiable innocence, No, he didn't think he would.

'No?'

'No.'

'And why ever not?'

Pop had long had his answer ready. He was too tired.

This confession drew from Sister Trevelyan the sweetest of smiles and then a short sentence that perfectly matched it.

'Little boys who don't do their homework can't expect to have any privileges, can they?'

After which, without another word, Sister Trevelyan glided from the room with all the grace of a ballet dancer, her head uplifted with the very slightest hint of victorious *hauteur*, an exit which left Pop, for once in his hitherto optimistic and exuberant life, both crushed and speechless.

He was just reviving memories of this infinitely depressing occasion when Sister Trevelyan came into the bedroom, carrying Pop's late morning dose of pills and medicine on a tray, looking if anything more elegant and ravishing than ever, so that Pop's heart gave a dangerous somersault or two.

Nor was this supreme entrance lost on the Brigadier, who at once leapt up and bowed slightly from the waist, almost as if to royalty.

'This is my new nurse, General,' Pop said. 'Sister Trevelyan.'

'Madam,' the Brigadier said and bowed a second time, now rather lower than before, extending his hand and shaking hers, half in the act of kissing it. '*Enchanté*. We have already met.'

To all this Sister Trevelyan responded as if the Brigadier had been some sort of ambassador presenting his credentials. She was already charmed by the Brigadier. He was a bit of the real old, vanishing England, a relic of the old imperial. That was what made England and the English so fascinating: on the one hand you had perfect gentlemen dressed rather like absent-minded tramps and on the other girls with micro skirts up to their navels and somehow it all fitted beautifully together in unparalleled eccentric pattern.

'Excuse me while I give Mr Larkin his pills,' she said.

The Brigadier promptly and graciously made way for her, at the same time seizing the opportunity to pour himself another large whisky-and-soda. This he did without benefit of invitation, having long learnt that in the Larkin household you lived according to the Larkin philosophy, which was 'it's there, ain't it? Help yourself then. That's what it's for.'

Pop having been given a dose of his many pills the Brigadier then turned his attention once more to the seductive sculpture of Sister Trevelyan.

'I hear you're from Australia, Sister.'

'That's right. Melbourne.'

'I would never have guessed it,' the Brigadier said with gallantry, 'from your accent.'

'Well, you see, I'm only half Australian. My mother is English.'

'Splendid. From which part?'

'Worcestershire. She was a Bressingham-Coutts.'

The Brigadier gave a large and astonished gasp, drank deep of his whisky and then gasped again. Suddenly, as in the flashback of an ancient film, he was transported some six thousand miles away, over a space of many years.

'By Jove. Good God.' The Brigadier drank deep again. 'Unless I'm vastly mistaken I once knew a relative of yours. Was her name not Cicely?'

'Surely, my grandmother. Cicely Victoria.'

'Great God. Small world. Damn small world.'

The Brigadier positively preened himself. His veins now running warm with the fires of memory he permitted himself the luxury of recalling that not only had he known Cicely Bressingham-Coutts; he had in fact seduced her. In Simla, on several occasions, in the summer time. The fact that he was seducing another young married woman at the same time had never at any time caused him any excess of guilt, but rather the contrary. Seduction, in those days long before mini-skirts, had been both an art and a military exercise. The doors were well guarded, the defences materially impregnable, or apparently so. There had to be a great deal of subterfuge, deployment of forces, flanking manoeuvres and even ambush. A chap could reckon that surrender achieved under such conditions was indeed a feat of arms. He had reason to know; he had won many a distinguished and rewarding campaign.

'Yes, we met in India. I knew her well. Tolerably well at least. Socially, socially. Charming woman, charming.'

'Was she married then?'

The Brigadier thought it prudent to say that he couldn't remember. Nearly all the women he had seduced while a young officer had been married; it was a great deal more fun, the conquest sweeter.

'I just wondered, that's all,' Sister Trevelyan said, 'only there's always been a sort of scandal about her in the family. We always laugh about it. That was in India too.'

'Oh! India teemed with scandal. The gossips fed on it like termites.'

The sensational possibility that he might well be Sister Trevelyan's grandfather suddenly filled the Brigadier with highly conflicting emotions. He had already toyed with the idea of asking her to his little place one evening for a spot of light supper. He was still confident that age had not entirely extinguished his powers of entertainment. A little salmon trout, if he could get it; and a good light Hock might well work the wonders that had once been worked, on a not dissimilar occasion, with the glorious and uninhibited Angela Snow. He flattered himself that he had not entirely failed on that occasion.

Nevertheless he had to admit that the possibility of blood relationship rather spiked his guns in that direction. That was damn serious. He could hardly start committing – well the unmentionable – at his age. You had to draw the line somewhere – with granddaughters anyway.

Compromise in these matters was perhaps, as always, the safest ploy.

'Perhaps you might care to drop in at my little place for a drink one evening?' he said. 'Very modest, I'm afraid. But I'd be delighted. I've still a good few old photographs of India lying about in albums – we might peep through them. Might well be fun.'

'It might. I'd love to,' Sister Trevelyan said and gave the Brigadier the most alluring of anticipatory smiles.

The old dog, Pop thought, and lay plunged in increasing gloom.

Life, he couldn't help telling himself, was getting worse than awful all the time. It was enough to make a saint swear. No drink, no cigars, the old point of no return lark a complete flop and above all, worst of all, Ma sleeping all the time in a separate bedroom. That took some getting over if you like. That was immoral all right. Most things he'd been able to bear, but Ma in a separate bedroom was just plain criminal. There should be a law against it. Not to wake in the middle of the night and feel Ma beside him, like some vast warm sand-dune, was enough to drive him to drink, except that, damn and blast it, there was no drink he could be driven to.

In the depths of these depressing thoughts he looked up in time to see the Brigadier raising his third large whisky full in the direction of Sister Trevelyan's black glistening eyes as if he was either toasting or celebrating something, though in his gloom Pop couldn't think what.

'Well, don't hog the bar to yourself, General,' he said. 'Remember the workers.'

'Ah! deeply sorry. My apologies. Is she allowed – I mean in the course of duty and all that?'

'Always has a nip about this time,' Pop said miserably. 'Her and Ma. Brandy.'

A light of gaiety, almost mischief, lay in the Brigadier's eye as he poured brandy for Sister Trevelyan. 'Well, cheers, Larkin. Here's to the day.'

Pop couldn't think what day, except perhaps some far distant day, deep in the future, when he might be permitted to become human again. 'I must say I admire you. I mean the resistance to temptation and all that. How on earth you do it I simply don't know.'

'Will power,' Pop said, more miserably than ever. 'Will power.'

'Ah! the day will come,' the Brigadier said with revolting cheerfulness, 'the day will come, won't it, Sister?'

'Not for a good while yet,' Sister Trevelyan said. 'Not unless he wants to poison himself.'

Pop shut his eyes, hardly able to bear any more of it. He then opened them to see Sister Trevelyan draining her glass and to hear her telling the Brigadier that she was afraid his time was up. She had to get Mr Larkin's lunch now.

Lunch? Pop knew what lunch was. Dry toast, calves' foot jelly, stewed prunes and water. It was a wonder he lived through the day.

'Well, farewell, Larkin.' The light in the Brigadier's eye shone still more cheerfully. His voice was rich with the plumminess of good cheer. 'Will report at the same hour tomorrow if the medico permits. Press on.'

Pop, never having felt less like pressing on in his life, waved a wretched and feeble hand in farewell.

The next day the Brigadier was back again, prompt as if taking parade.

But now, on him too, a revolution had been worked. No longer was he dressed in seedy habit, in shabby rags left over, as it were, from some distant and dusty Afghan campaign. Instead he wore a pair of cream flannels that had been pressed with knife-edge creases, a red, white and purple college blazer, an almost new panama hat and a certainly new pair of white tennis shoes. His hair and moustache had been sprucely clipped. Fuzz of long growth had been clipped from his nose and ears. He even smelled, with some pungency, of a combination of eau-de-cologne and a hair cream impregnated with what seemed to be a strong essence of clove carnations.

'Hail, Larkin. How fares the patient?'

The abounding cheerfulness of the Brigadier's presence, spruce and spry, plunged Pop still further into gloom. This was by no means improved when the Brigadier said he hoped Pop didn't mind that he'd brought his swimming trunks too? They were all going for a dip in the pool: Sister Trevelyan, Mariette, Primrose, Ma, and he even believed, the Reverend Candy.

'Your dear Mem Sahib suggested it. She also asked me to stay to lunch. Roast duck and green peas I fancy she said.' God, Pop thought, God. He could only urge the Brigadier not to swim on a full stomach. You never knew what might happen.

The Brigadier was undeterred. They were going to swim before lunch. Then they were going to lunch under the big walnut tree in the garden, where it was cool and quiet, so that they shouldn't disturb Larkin while he had his afternoon siesta. Splendid idea all round, the Brigadier thought.

It was purgatory, Pop said.

'Oh! and I believe there's just a chance that Angela may come. She telephoned but wasn't sure. She's ringing back.'

This additional and unexpected news cheered Pop no more than ever so slightly.

'I only hope she hasn't aged a lot,' was all he could think to say, with an echo of gloom. 'It seems like a ten-year stretch since I set eyes on her last.'

Everything, in fact, had begun to seem like a ten-year stretch. The impression that he was a man serving a long prison sentence for a crime he hadn't committed increased considerably during his meagre lunch of toast, cold turtle soup and prunes, none of which he wanted anyway and after which he fell uneasily to sleep.

In the last few minutes before he dozed away he could hear, very faintly, the sound of voices, among them the shrieks of children, coming from the swimming pool through the open bedroom windows. The afternoon was hot. Normally the tinkle of children's voices about the pool on such a day of high summer would have drawn from him the old habitual comment that it was perfick, absolutely perfick. Now he had no feelings about it. Nothing was perfick now. Nothing was perfick any longer.

When he eventually opened his eyes again it seemed already to be twilight. Then he realized that someone had been into the room to draw the curtains. Waking thus, alone, in the shadowy prison of the bedroom, he found it impossible to resist fresh waves of gloom. The dismal conclusion that life wasn't worth a hatful of crabs, which was one of Ma's expressions for how she felt after a particularly miserable hang-over or something of that sort, grew stronger, unrelieved by an uneasy sleep in which he had seemed to grope down long and interminable corridors, like a purblind mole, seeking some way out.

In this funereal state of mind, rapidly approaching one of self-pity, an emotion he had never experienced in his life before, he told himself not only that he was unwanted but that he didn't want to have anything to do with anybody even if they wanted him. Let them all go to hell; he was there already anyway.

A soft tap on the bedroom door fell on ears that he deliberately made deaf. He didn't want visitors. Damn all visitors. A second and rather louder tap caused him to vent snappy irritation on it with the words 'Well, who is it? If you want to come in, come in. Don't just stand there tapping.'

It sounded like some ruddy woodpecker, he told himself, and further that it was probably that old dog the General back again, still hoping to try his military craft on Sister Trevelyan. Pop knew, he reminded himself miserably, what the General and all the rest of them wanted. It wasn't him; it was Sister Trevelyan they were after.

The door opened. The sight of a figure in a cornflower blue two-piece swim-suit of unparalleled brevity failed to arouse him to any more than a grunt in answer to a question that hadn't even been asked.

'No tea, thanks. No tea.'

'Sweetie, I am not the bearer of tea.'

A pair of light warm lips pressed themselves first on his forehead and then on his lips.

'Darling man. It's me. They tell me you need a night nurse.'

The lips and the voice were those of Angela Snow. He couldn't see her very well in the half gloom of the bedroom and he gazed up at her much as if he were still the purblind mole of his dreams, groping for some way out.

'Shall I draw the curtains? Nice sleep?'

Without waiting for an answer she started to draw the curtains, saying that she'd been up once before to have a peep at him but that he'd been well and truly away. Cruelty to disturb him.

He muttered half to himself that he'd never been asleep. All he had been was a ruddy mole in a dark ruddy tunnel. He'd once known a girl with a mole of a different sort on her right bosom and normally the recurrent memory of it would have caused him to make some nippy joke about it, but now who cared?

'How's my sweet man? Haven't seen you since the Ice Age.'

Ice Age? Pop thought. This was the Ice Age.

Angela came to sit on the edge of the bed. Normally a situation where Angela Snow, covered merely by three cornflower triangles that revealed rather more than concealed the fundamental parts of a figure smoothly brown as an autumn beech leaf, would have had him at the starting gate, like some race-horse steamed up. Now he merely gave her the palest of smiles.

'Ma said to ask if you needed tea or anything. Buzz and she'll bring it up.'

Pop merely shook his head.

'I brought champers. And a box of Havanas. Would you like those instead?'

'Give 'em to the rabbits.'

Angela slightly changed her position on the bed. This smallest of movements so jarred his nerves that he begged her, not with the flippancy that would normally have accompanied the words but with the despondency of a man already half thrown overboard, not to rock the boat.

'We had some of the champers before lunch. It's '59. A girl friend of mine knows a type in Rheims who loads her with the stuff every time she beds down, which is a fair amount of frequency, and not only with him. Amusing creature. When asked if she preferred it sweet, dry or extra dry she simply said demi-sex.'

Pop failed to respond. Angela, granting that the joke might well have been too subtle, went on:

'Ma's duck was marvellous. In fact it all was, as if I didn't know it always is. Besides the champagne – this girl friend gives me a case now and then as a sort of ten per cent for having introduced her to this Rheims joker in the first place – we got outside three bottles of Volnay '53 and ended up happily ever after.'

Pausing for a moment, Angela gave one of those golden provocative laughs of hers that would normally have had Pop more than half way on the boil. This time he merely listened without a simmer.

'By the way, I must say our Mr Candy is a changed man. Of the three bottles I should say he practically killed one on his own. So much so that I asked him if he wasn't giving Unholy Communion, but he didn't seem to think it awfully funny.'

Pop didn't think so either. Mr Candy hadn't been to see him more than once or twice, and then only with formal brevity. He expected it was another one who really came to see Sister Trevelyan. From the General to the Parson they were all at it.

Ignoring, or trying to ignore, the prevailing air of gloom, Angela continued to elaborate and expand her dry jocularity.

'Actually the demi-sex thing isn't so way off the ball it seems. You know the reputation these frogs have got – magnificent bedders and all that – I mean you practically have to take out an injunction every time they look at you – well, it seems with this character it's practically a case of unleavened bread, sort of, most of the time, if you get what I mean? Hence the demi-sex. *Très* disappointing.'

There being no sort of response in Pop to all this Angela now gently took his hand and, as if with casual idleness, held it lightly against her thigh. To hold a hand lightly against the thigh of Angela Snow under any circumstances, let alone in bed, would normally have been a signal to Pop that he was practically in business. Now he could only mournfully tell himself that, like the character in Rheims, he was in the unleavened bread lark. He had a certain sympathy with the feller. If you couldn't make the bread rise it was clearly a pretty poor look-out all round.

'I must say it had no ill-effect,' Angela went on, 'I mean the Volnay and

Mr Candy. After lunch he insisted on taking your Primrose out for a ten mile walk or something. Most athletic. When I pulled his leg and asked him if he was training for the Decathlon he looked a bit peeved and said he hadn't started to read it yet. Thought I meant *The Decameron*.'

What with Decathlon and *Decameron*, Volnay and demi-sex, the look on Pop's face was now becoming one of intensive despondency. Normally he would give Angela as good as he got, in more ways than one, but now his light was less than that of a glow-worm against the sun itself. And more worm than glow, it seemed, at that.

In a further attempt to rouse at least a spark of that interest which normally, Angela Snow had to admit, had her swiftly on the boil too, she now leaned over him, one breast actually brushing the sleeve of his pyjama jacket and murmured Sweetie, wasn't there something she could do for him? He'd only to name it and she was ready to play. Though she didn't openly suggest it, it would have been the easiest possible thing in the world to have slipped into bed with him, even if only for five minutes of demi-sex.

'Play?' The word struck Pop, in his gloom, as being one of doleful irony. He couldn't even play dominoes.

Angela, fully aware that Ma's injunction of 'you go up and have half hour's *tatey-tate* with him' had in it that touch of more serious meaning that Ma had once expressed in the words to Pop: 'Why do you think I let you out to have a bit of fun with Edith and Angela now and then? Variety,' now began to have more serious thoughts herself.

The quick and high degree of intelligence that lay under the languid, golden surface of her wit and patter was one of the things that had first drawn and then endeared her to the Larkin philosophy: namely that life was sweeter, fuller and richer if you went with the stream rather than tore your heart out rowing against it. Ma's apparently casual air of allowing Pop licence to seduce others wasn't a sign of levity; it was naturally wise. And Angela was deeply happy and satisfied now and then, to be part of it.

Nevertheless the *tatey-tate*, she realized now, was going badly. She had had other *tête-à-têtes* with Pop, notably on the hot sand-dunes on the Brittany coast, and there had been nothing demi-sex about them. They had filled her with a sense of deep fruition in which there was no hint of guilt, so that she perfectly understood Ma's licence to permit occasional variety, Ma well knowing that her own love was as solid as the Rock of Gibraltar and as deep as the ocean.

In one last attempt to let light into Pop's deep passages of gloom she started to recount yet another anecdote of her friend in Rheims who, rather like Hamlet, had come to the moment when she needed to ask 'The Pill or not the Pill? that was the question' and had decided, wittily, as Angela put it, that it was of no consequence; but the joke, like the others that had preceded it, fell somewhere far away, like a dismal arrow.

It seemed to Angela, in fact, that Pop had now reached his own special point of no return. He lay enshrouded in a vast frustration. His tunnel had no light at the end of it and none had ever been needed more badly.

'I'm thinking of taking a house or bungalow or something over in Le Touquet for August and September,' she suddenly said. 'You know – gorgeous sun-bathing all day, casino at night, walks in the forest, marvellous picnics on the beach, lovely wine. I thought you and Ma might share. It's big enough for six. I mean as my guests of course. You remember France?'

Pop remembered France: but not, now, with much relish.

'I thought it might be something for you to look forward to.' That, she thought, was the whole core of the matter. Pop must set his sights on something far beyond the confines of the bedroom. 'I might get my chum from Rheims to come and share. She's a great sharer. She's shared more beds than anyone since Catherine the Great. She'll come at the drop of a pillow, so to speak, if I ask.'

Normally such a sketch, brief as it was, suggesting both beauty and licence, would have been enough to prompt Pop to ask, at least, what the girl looked like. But having waited more than a minute for even a hint of inquiry Angela was forced to supply the information herself, doing it with that dry, offhand graphic method of hers that normally had Pop near-mesmerized in admiration.

'She's a sort of super relief map. All curves and contours. A kind of luscious mountain range. Some chaps climb the Alps – a lot prefer exploring her. I'm sure she'd love to lead you over the passes.'

It was all too much for Pop, who silently stared at a bee in one of the bedroom windows, striking its head with senseless futility against the glass. It too was struggling in vain, to get out.

'Would you come?' Angela said. 'I thought about the middle of August. The way you're going you'll be fit for the Decathlon yourself by then.'

The way he was going, Pop thought, he'd be down the drain any day now. Either that or up the ruddy creek.

'Very dark. Almost swarthy, you might say. Of course she's half-French herself and it's probably that that gives her that *je ne sais quoi* touch. I always think she's rather what Cleopatra must have looked like. Serpent in the boosie and all.'

Extravagant though the description of the temptress from Rheims was it failed to produce more than a murmurous grunt from Pop, but whether of approval or indifference Angela didn't stop to think. She made one more try:

'I can have the house from August the fifteenth. If I had a week to get installed, you and Ma could come about the twenty-fifth. How's that? That gives you more than a month to get your sea-legs. Not that you'll need them. We can fly in a quarter of an hour.'

In hollow tones Pop begged her not to make him laugh. Sea-legs? He hadn't even been out of bed yet. Not even to get on the Throne.

'You know, I knew a bomber pilot once,' Angela suddenly said with that skilled propensity of hers to strike off at an unexpected and dazzling tangent. 'He told me that the only thing that kept him from going stark stinking bats on those ghastly night trips over Bremen and the German wilderness generally was fixing his mind on a pub he knew in some village near his station. The Cat & Custard Pot it was called. Cat, custard, cat, custard: that's all he'd think of all the way home. Cat, custard, cat, custard – it was the only thing that stopped him from going utterly round the twist.'

It was only towards the end of this longish attempt to get Pop to set his sights on something pleasant and not too far ahead that she suddenly realized that she was talking to a man with closed eyes. It occurred to her that she might have lulled him to sleep: and then that she had talked too much.

She had sense enough to sit there for another five minutes without a word. It was a spell of silence that touched her very deeply as she looked at his face, apparently in repose but curiously not restful. She couldn't help telling herself that he looked like a balloon, once gay, high-coloured and irrepressibly buoyant, that had become shrunken and deflated. There was a grey pouchiness about the eyes that was negative. It prompted in her the uneasy thought that a man could easily die of things less tangible than a heart attack and that one of them was, in fact – she scouted for a word and then thought: the heart has many – then couldn't remember the rest of the sentence and at last was frightened.

She moved quietly off the bed in readiness to go. The slight movement roused him. The greyish eyes looked up at her half in a daze and half as if begging her not to depart. She decided she must, smiled gently and said:

'Must go. Your nurse'll be up soon. Anything you want?'

'Tell Ma that if anybody else comes visiting today I don't want them.'

'Sorry I stayed so long.'

He gave her the very slightest hint of the old smile. No, it wasn't that;

not her. He was thinking of stinking bores like Captain Perigo, who lived a life based on the Gospel According to Hunting and hardly ever said a word except 'I mean t'say –'; or a man named Fanshawe, who had exhausted most if not all of the local mistresses and had merely made a visit to Pop the excuse to see if Sister Trevelyan, of seductive report, would perhaps make up the deficiency; and a dozen others, even Edith Pilchester's hated Freda O'Connor, who had been one of Fanshawe's mistresses in between being somebody else's and had also made a visit to Pop an excuse for seeing what the nurse's profession had produced by way of possible rivalry. He was sick of them all; he wanted only to be left to himself.

Lightly Angela kissed him. Rarely had a body been held so closely to him with so little cover to it without invoking anything more than the briefest of smiles in response. Even then his eyes had little light in them and she said:

'Think of France. August twenty-fifth. That's your date. Think of that.'

'Right.'

'Say I will.'

'I will.'

'Darling man.' Her smile, superficially gay, almost brought tears to his eyes. 'That makes you married to the thought if not to me.'

She was about to kiss him yet again and this time in final farewell when there was a series of bird-like tappings on the door and into the room came Phyllida and little Oscar.

Each was bearing an untidy, bountiful bunch of wild flowers: clover, meadowsweet, rose-bay willow herb, purple loosestrife, honeysuckle, wild roses, marjoram and even ears of gold-green barley. The gift of his favourite flowers from his two youngest was accompanied by a mixed duologue explaining in touching terms that they had also brought him a frog, but Ma wouldn't let them bring it up to him.

'I thought you were going to bring me mushrooms,' Pop said, a fraction more cheerful now.

They were going to, they brightly explained, again in a jingled duologue, but Primrose and Mr Candy had got there first.

'Primrose and Mr Candy mushrooming, eh?'

'That's what they said they were doing.'

'Get many?'

They really didn't know, little Oscar and Phyllida said. Mr Candy and Primrose had told them to go away. They were lying down and having a rest by the wood.

'Alas! dear Yorick, no mushrooms for breakfast,' Angela said and blew Pop a fond and final kiss of farewell.

Somewhere about that same time Mr Candy had begun yet another pleasant excursion down the road of excess. The air was rich with the scent of honeysuckle, wild clover and the thick odours of Spanish chestnut bloom from the great trees in the wood overhead.

The blissful if slightly exhausting nature of Mr Candy's excursion left him in a state approaching swoon. This in itself was so pleasant that he was hardly prepared for the next move from Primrose, who rather to his surprise and dismay again began to talk of her favourite among poets, Donne.

'Do you know what his greatest poem was? The greatest, the absolute greatest?'

Mr Candy drowsily confessed he didn't.

'It was his last. His very last.'

'Quote,' said Mr Candy, who had long since become resigned to poetry being mixed with love.

Primrose, softly caressing Mr Candy's face with fingers like the wings of an amorous moth, quoted:

'"When thou hast done, thou hast not done. For I have more."'

· 8 ·

Ma was sometimes very critical, indeed scornful, of what she called the *status quo* symbol. She didn't altogether hold with it. There was, in her opinion, far too much of it about nowadays. You never knew what was going to be a *status quo* symbol next. Swimming pools, yachts, electric organs, deep freezes, colour television, washing machines, spin dryers, vintage cars: all these of course had long been in the *status quo* symbol lark. But now people were going in for old steam rollers, old threshing machines, old hansom cabs, brakes and landaus, quite apart from converting old windmills and chapels and warehouses and cow barns into cottages in the country or keeping peacocks, pythons and even crocodiles. The best *status quo* symbol Ma had ever heard about was a swimming pool that had heating and tropical palms all set about it but no water. It made you wonder what was coming next.

And then education and all that: degrees and universities. She wasn't at all sure they weren't *status quo* symbols too. She didn't hold with all this business of students parading and marching about in protest about this, that and the other, carrying banners with slogans, especially when half the slogans were spelt wrong. It just showed you where education could land you if you let it get on top of you.

The fact that Pop hadn't had any education and couldn't even write his name had never worried Ma very much. After all he'd got on very well without it so far. Ma couldn't grumble. She and Pop had three television sets, including the new colour one, a Rolls-Royce, a Jaguar, and an estate car just for running about in, a washing machine, a washing-up machine and a spin drier, a deep freeze that was too big to go into the kitchen and had consequently to stand in one of the out-houses, three ponies for the children to ride, a heated swimming pool, the new French bar, a private cinema which Pop had rigged up in the cellar with nice plush seats and a fridge so that everybody could have ice creams in the intervals while Mr Charlton changed the films, a nice boat and a nice boat-house to put it in, and above all plenty to eat and drink. You couldn't say they lacked for very much and you couldn't say it was the result of education. You really don't need education and writing and all that when you got on with things like Pop did.

Nevertheless she had to admit that there were times when writing helped. For instance she would have liked Pop to write to the Miss Barnwells and thank them for the loan of the Throne. It was only decent and proper, she thought to write to them a little note about it. Unfortunately Pop wouldn't have been up to it anyway at the present time even if he had been able to write and it would therefore have to be Mr Charlton, as usual on these occasions, who'd have to come to the rescue.

This was one of the things that Ma, Mariette, Mr Charlton and Angela Snow discussed as they sat in the kitchen drinking champagne cocktails later on during the evening when Angela Snow had suggested a course of convalescence in Le Touquet as something for Pop to look forward to and when Mr Candy had taken another course in the pleasures of excess in the mushroom field.

'Well, how did he strike you?' was the first question of importance that Ma put to Angela after Charley had mixed the cocktails. 'Pop, I mean.'

Sipping her champagne cocktail and at the same time recalling how little effect her story of her chum in Rheims and the demi-sex had had on Pop, except if anything to increase his gloom, she said she might as well be frank about it: Pop didn't strike her very favourably at all. In fact she thought he was very low.

'I feel he needs something to look forward to. Like a child looking forward to Christmas,' she said.

Then she went on to tell of the house she was renting across the Channel and how she'd like Ma and Pop and anyone else in the family to come and share it for a month, since it was her belief that another breath of French air would do everybody, Pop especially, a power of good.

Ma said it was very generous of Angela and thanked her very much. They would have to see when the time came.

'That's exactly the point,' Angela said. 'We have to fix a time. A date. If we said the twenty-fifth of August or something definite like that he'd have it fixed in his mind and every day he'd be able to feel it was that much nearer.'

Ma agreed. It was very like the children. Only ten more sleeps to Christmas they would say.

'Yes,' Mr Charlton said, 'there's no doubt that there comes a point where the psychological approach is essential.'

At the mere mention of the word psychological Ma gave Mr Charlton an extremely severe look. She didn't altogether hold with this psychology stuff. She wasn't at all sure it wasn't another of those *status quo* symbols. You saw a lot of it on telly. You had situations, for example, where a child had done something terribly wrong, like hitting its grandmother with a poker and nicking her old age pension, and all you did to punish it was this psychology thing, instead of giving it a good belt and telling it to give over or else. It wasn't right. Or if it was an adult person you got him or her lying on a couch and there was a lot of probing into their past sex life and all that: as if that got you anywhere.

She then proceeded to make a remarkable psychological suggestion of her own.

'It's my belief,' she said, 'that he wants something to make him good and angry.'

The utter astonishment caused by this totally unexpected remedy for Pop's gloom and apathy expressed itself in fully a minute of complete silence, which was finally broken by Mariette getting up to fetch another bottle of champagne and saying:

'Oh! no. I don't think that would work. After all, he's only allowed to sit up with his second pillow for half an hour at a time. Anything that made him angry would be enough to finish him completely. His heart would never stand it.'

A profound, far-off look on Mr Charlton's face presently told Ma that he was thinking; and some moments later this proved to be right. Mr Charlton said he wasn't at all sure Ma hadn't got something there.

'Like hair of the dog,' Mr Charlton said.

Hair of the dog was Pop's favourite remedy when you'd had one or two over the eight and there was no doubt, as Mr Charlton well knew and Ma had to admit, that it worked. You were, as Pop often remarked, back on your feet in no time.

'No, no,' Mariette said. 'I can't see it. Look what happened when he got mad with old Nurse Soper. It set him back weeks.'

Mr Charlton disagreed. He didn't think they should underestimate the curative powers of anger, a remark of such profundity that everyone was again stunned to silence for several minutes until Mr Charlton eventually proceeded to reinforce his point by quoting, of all things, the Scriptures.

'After all, the refiners fire and all that,' Mr Charlton said, to Ma's utter stupefaction. '"And he shall purify." In other words fire not only burns and kills. It refines and restores. You follow me?'

Ma didn't. She'd never heard anything like it. Either Charley had been drinking more than she thought he had or else it was education again.

It just showed you where too much of it got you if you didn't watch it.

Angela Snow on the other hand was impressed. She was in fact about to offer a parallel to the hair of the dog theory by adding something about serum and snake-bites when, by a fortunate chance, Primrose and Mr Candy walked in.

'Oh! Hallo,' Ma said. 'Where are they?'

Where were what? Primrose wanted to know.

'The mushrooms. Oscar and Phyllida said you two were mushrooming.'

Mr Candy, who had been too immersed for the past couple of hours in exploring the pleasures of excess to think about mushrooms, looked so embarrassed that he actually blushed and said:

'Oh! they turned out to be toadstools. They're awfully deceiving from a long way off.'

Ma wondered. She had had her suspicions about Primrose and Mr Candy for some time. Her guess was that the Reverend Candy was turning out to be another Mr Charlton. She wondered if he knew his technique? If not, some way would have to be found in learning him.

'Ah! you're just in time, Mr Candy,' Charley said. 'We were discussing Pop and saying he probably needs some treatment other than medicine to get him going again. Ma suggested a spot of anger and I was inclined to agree. I was trying to quote that bit from the Bible about the refiner's fire and He shall purify when you came in, but I couldn't quite remember chapter and verse.'

Mr Candy couldn't remember chapter and verse either. He was however, saved from eventual embarrassment by Primrose, who promptly came up again with Blake.

'"The tigers of wrath,"' she said, '"are wiser than the horses of instruction."'

Good God, Ma thought. Though proved right after all she silently asked herself whatever next? She really didn't know. The things Primrose came out with sometimes. Well, she could only suppose it was education again.

'And which chapter and verse does that come from?' she said.

'"The Marriage of Heaven and Hell,"' Primrose said, leaving Ma still further stupefied. 'Blake. Any champers left? It's thirsty work looking for mushrooms that turn out not to be. We're famished too.'

Mr Candy couldn't help agreeing. He was, to quote the scriptures again, an-hungered and a-thirst. The road of excess certainly took it out of you.

'Get another bottle, Charley,' Ma said, 'and I'll see what's in the fridge.'

As she did so, searching for any pieces of cold pie, cheese tarts, smoked salmon, salami, olives and anything of that sort that might be hanging about, she told herself she didn't know about the tigers of wrath and the horses of instruction, but she had a shrewd idea that a good steak-and-kidney pie and a bottle of Chambolle Musigny were more likely to be the things to put Pop right. She'd been saying so for some time and pretty soon something would have to be done about it.

What with one thing and another it was getting worse than awful. In fact if things went on like this much longer, she told herself, jokingly, she wasn't at all sure that she wouldn't have to get a lodger.

Next morning, about eleven o'clock, Mr Charlton went up to Pop's bedroom with pen and notepaper in order to discuss the letter Ma had long insisted should be sent to the Miss Barnwells in gratitude for the Throne. It was, though neither Pop nor Charley knew it at the time, a momentous occasion.

A straight, steady rain was falling, cooling the air, and now and then Pop could hear the monotonous beat of a thrush cracking a snail on the garden path below his bedroom windows. Something about the dual monotony of falling rain and cracking snail had on him the most dismal, imprisoning effect. He felt more dreary, irritable and despondent than ever. A little earlier Sister Trevelyan, normally a person of the sweetest patience and temper had left him in a slight huff, telling him that if he let his self-pity get any bigger it would stick in his wind-pipe and choke him. The words, not entirely unintentional, caused him to snort after her to shut up and if she wanted a fight she was going the right way about getting one.

The words rather pleased her. They went some way towards proving the interesting theory about the tigers of wrath, which Ma had told her about: so that just before closing the bedroom door she put her beautiful golden-copper head round it and said with a coolness at once maddening and delicious:

'I'll have you know I've fought better men than you. And lost.'

And what the hell was he supposed to make of that? Pop snapped. Lost? Lost what? It was enough to drive a man barmy, which in fact was exactly what, Sister Trevelyan told herself, she was trying to do. She was inclined to agree with Ma after all. Anger, perhaps, was the great healer.

A few minutes later Mr Charlton came in with pen and notepaper, explaining that he'd come to discuss the letter.

'What letter?' Pop's voice was unaccountably sharp.

'To the Miss Barnwells. To thank them for the Throne. Ma told you about it.'

'Never said a word.'

'She spoke about it only yesterday.'

'Did she? Then why the blazes doesn't she write it?'

'For one thing she's had a hard morning. Oscar fell out of a tree and got a bruise on his head as big as a duck egg. Ma started to do some washing and then it rained. And now she's gone off with Mariette to get your new pills.'

'New pills? Why new? They all have the same ruddy effect – depress you like hell. If anybody had any sense they'd get me a treble brandy.'

Mr Charlton, faced with such untypical conduct from Pop, had the forbearance not to argue about brandy.

'The letter won't take long. You just say what you'd like to say and I'll put it down.'

'Well, if you're putting it down you might as well say it.'

'It needs to be personal.'

'Well, why bother about a letter anyway? Can't Ma or somebody ring 'em up?'

'They're not on the telephone. The poor dears can't afford it.'

'Time they could.'

Ignoring the testy brevity of such remarks, Mr Charlton patiently prepared to sketch out with pen and paper what he thought might be an appropriate note of thanks to the Miss Barnwells.

'Dear Miss Barnwells – no, perhaps not. How do you usually address them? Do you know them well enough to call them Effie and Edna?'

Pop, whose custom it was to be on Christian name terms with everybody if possible, merely grunted.

'All right,' Mr Charlton said. 'Let's say "Dear Miss Effie and Miss Edna Barnwell". Then what?'

'Oh! just say thanks for the potty.'

Mr Charlton demurred. Potty, he said with some reticence, was hardly the word.

'Well, what else is it?'

It wasn't exactly a question of the choice of word, Mr Charlton said. It was one of etiquette.

'Oh! they call it that now, do they?'

Mr Charlton, again ignoring such uncharacteristic testiness, now deemed it necessary to stop asking questions and get on with the composition of the letter himself: which he promptly did, finally clearing his throat in readiness to read out the preliminary draft.

'"Dear Miss Effie and Miss Edna: I sincerely hope you won't think it remiss of me not to have thanked you before now for your great kindness during the occasion of my illness. But, as I am sure you will understand, I have had to take things very quietly and have only now begun to feel something like my usual self. Please forgive me therefore for not writing to you before. I do so now with the utmost gratitude for the loan of the commode, which will be returned to you as soon as my doctor deems that I am strong enough to resume normal activities." '

Listening to this, Pop was struck completely speechless. He had always admired Charley boy, but this was masterly. He didn't know how Charley ever thought it up. Masterpiece of a feller.

'Don't think it's a trifle ambiguous,' Mr Charlton said, 'the last bit?'

'Ambig – what?'

' "Resume normal activities." Can be taken in two ways, I mean. Feel a bit ambiguous to you?'

Pop said he'd never felt ambiguous in his life. Bit constipated once or twice, but you got that from laying in bed. On the whole he thought the letter was perfick.

'Even so, I think we'll alter that bit. Let's say "as soon as I am up and about again". Yes, that's better. And I think some little personal touch at the end, don't you?'

Still inclined to testiness, Pop said he didn't think so. It was perfick as it stood.

'What I really meant,' Mr Charlton said, 'was that you should express it in rather more tangible form.'

Tangible form? Pop thought. What the pipe was that?

'I mean like asking them up to visit you? I'm sure they'd love it. They've sent no end of messages of inquiry about you.'

Pop started to mutter about how he'd had enough of visitors and how they tired you out and all that, but Mr Charlton, tersely authoritative all of a sudden, cut him short.

'Oh! I think so. After all there are still certain standards.'

This, the most crushing remark made by anyone since Pop had been in bed, had the immediate effect of silencing him completely.

'Yes: I'll simply say "If at any time you are passing this way I should be delighted if you would drop in and see me. Again with my warmest thanks for your kindness and with very best wishes from Mrs Larkin and myself. Yours sincerely S. C. Larkin." I think that about squares it, doesn't it?'

Pop, still speechless in admiration, thought it squared it good and proper. Unlike Ma, he was stunned by the marvels of education.

*

A Little of What You Fancy

The eventual effect of Mr Charlton's inspired decision to 'express it in more tangible form' was that rather less than a week later, on a soft early August afternoon when already the first combine harvesters were beginning to crawl about barley fields like huge humming scarlet beetles, the two Miss Barnwells put on their best hats, each rather like a little blue upturned basket decorated at the brim with pink daisy chains, and their best frocks, which looked not unlike a combination of chintz curtains in faded rose and cream and nightgowns that had hems of slightly deeper colour tacked on to them either from some impulse of modesty or because they had shrunk in the wash, and set off to accept Mr Larkin's kind invitation to drop in and see him if they were passing that way. They were, also carrying umbrellas in case it came on to rain, the umbrellas of an identical shade of mothy brown, and two little boxes of home-made fudge, one of chocolate and one of coffee.

The Miss Barnwells, if ever they had drawn themselves upright, which they never did, would have stood rather less than four feet seven inches in their stockings. Frail, genteel and seemingly near-sighted, they looked not at all unlike little twin budgerigars, yellow in colour and much freckled: the freckles having apparently been the result of their keeping bees, which appeared to have stung them all over.

The impression that a puff of wind might have blown the two little ladies away was entirely illusory. They were both resolute and tough. Daughters of a retired Indian civil servant they were in reality two little pillars of iron upholding with dignity, pride and a certain patriotic passion the fact that there would always be an England and if ever by some disastrous consequence there wasn't it wouldn't be their fault and it would be over their dead little bodies anyway. England was England; like the sun and the moon it was and always had been and ever more would be so. To think otherwise was blasphemy, sheer, subversive, repellent blasphemy; and they, like some tiny infantry brigade, were going to fight, with their dying breaths, and God being their helper, to keep it that way.

This was one of the reasons they so admired and liked Mr Larkin. Mr Larkin too stood for England: the green and pleasant land of that other side of Blake so often quoted by Primrose in excursions along the road of excess, the meadows, the bluebell woods, the blackbirds, the nightingales, the lanes of hawthorn and primrose and meadowsweet, the cherry orchards, the pubs and the soft, sea-stroked air. These, they would say with their chirpy dying breaths, we have loved; and so would Mr Larkin.

They had in consequence been greatly touched by Pop's letter in relation to the matter of the commode. The commode having so often travelled with them over India's vast, steaming, dusty spaces, they were all too well aware of the comforting and practical nature of its virtues. They had indeed been honoured to lend it for Mr Larkin's use. They too had long christened it The Throne, almost as if partly regarding it as a symbol and a seat of majesty. Long after imperial Caesar had turned to clay, The Throne remained, to them, symbolic of the things that mattered.

That morning they had first taken the precaution of telephoning from the post office, in the name of good manners, to ask Mrs Larkin if a call that afternoon would be convenient or not and had received a typical Ma reply:

'Of course. Drop in about tea-time. I'm baking. Lovely to see you.'

This news, since in their slightly frugal circumstances they lived mostly on tea, cornflakes and bread and honey, more than delighted them. They couldn't help recalling, as it were from long ago, Mr Larkin's splendid party after a donkey Derby and gymkhana, when Pop had plied them with delicious nourishment and one of his patent cocktails, Ma Chérie, mixed double strength to prevent its becoming mere water, a combination consisting of sherry, soda and a dash or two of vodka, whisky or anything else Pop had in mind at the time. It was what he called one of his make-ups. You ordained both strength and mixture according to the needs of the moment. To the Miss Barnwells it had, in their language, been absolutely *pukka*. They would never forget its powerful virtues either.

They were therefore greatly looking forward to the visit to Pop, which was more than could be said for Pop himself. He was regarding it with jaundiced eye. It was true that he didn't dislike the Miss Barnwells; he was on the contrary always much touched by their gentility, the slight pain of their reduced circumstances and by the fruitful energy of their tiny frames, concealing as they did a tireless energy for the pursuit of good works, collecting for good causes, and the defence or welfare of the oppressed, the sick, the needy and, if necessary, the betrayed. Two or three times a year they begged subscriptions of Pop in support of such causes and to these he always gave with simply splendid, almost princely generosity.

He wasn't so sure about the betrayed, though, meaning unmarried mothers, and on one occasion, when the Miss Barnwells had spoken of some organization called The Society for the Protection of Women's Rights, he had suggested that on the contrary they should set one up for The Protection of Women's Wrongs, a remark that caused the little Miss Barnwells to fall about, the air around them seeming to dance with golden freckles.

He was therefore ready to receive them in slightly disgruntled mood. The fact that he had now been able to walk round the bedroom for the third time rather made things worse instead of better. It made him feel tired and foolishly wobbly on his pins.

'Here you are, dear. Two nice ladies to see you.' Ma, almost on the dot of four o'clock, brought the two Miss Barnwells up to Pop's bedroom. 'Would you like them to have tea up here with you or shall they have it downstairs?'

Well, that put him on the spot, Pop thought, but suddenly remembering Mr Charlton's reminder about 'certain standards' said with an almost gallant reticence that he suggested they please themselves. He'd no doubt they didn't want to be bored too long by him.

'Oh! *please*. Up *here*. If we *may*.' Like two little budgerigars who had been taught to repeat certain catch-phrases, the Miss Barnwells had a habit of chirping out the same sentences, word for word, at the very same moment, together. 'Oh! we should *love* it up here.'

Ma having presently retired to get the tea, the Miss Barnwells proceeded to place their boxes of home-made fudge on Pop's bed, at the same time remarking, in brightest unison:

'Oh! it's *nothing*. Just a little *something*. Only we *thought*, didn't we, dear? And how *are* you, Mr Larkin? Everyone's been so *distrait* about you.'

Distrait, had they? Pop thought, seizing on the new word with an alacrity that seemed almost as if he were sort of catching up a bit, mentally anyway. Well, he wasn't bad; taking two steps forward and one back, as the grasshopper said when he fell over the trip wire in the fog.

This remark also caused the little Miss Barnwells to fall about as if they had taken two or three Ma Chéries too many, so that Pop invited them to sit down and take the load off their feet.

In spite of this singular piece of jocularity, Pop looked, in the Miss Barnwells' opinion, acutely pale. They mustn't tire him, they told themselves, and the conversation became, rather like the soft August afternoon, desultory.

After speaking about the weather, Pop's letter and how charming it was, the harvest and how it had already started, the Miss Barnwells slowly ran out of topics of conversation, so that Pop was intensely relieved when Ma came back, bearing tea and its infinite accessories on a large silver tray.

'Tea up,' Ma said and set the gleaming silver tray, with the best Georgian silver tea-pot, sugar basin and milk jug on the table by the television set. 'Want me to pour?'

'Oh! *please*,' the Miss Barnwells said. 'You be mother.'

'Had plenty of practice,' Ma said, wistfully wondering, by no means for the first time, when she was going to get some more.

Tea having been poured and the Miss Barnwells having decided delicately to get started on the salmon-and-cucumber sandwiches, not the least ravishing items of the great array of buns, biscuits, cakes, tarts and so on that the tea-tray bore, Ma suddenly said:

'Oh! I meant to ask you. How's Edith? Haven't heard a peep out of her lately. Not since that – you know – since that business. You know.'

The Miss Barnwells knew.

'Well,' they said in customary unison. 'Well.'

Ma, sipping tea, waited for some elaboration of the word and received it in the form of the information that, in fact, nobody had seen Edith for some long time.

'Gone broody or something?' Pop said.

Well, the Miss Barnwells said, there were rumours.

'Having an affair with that Professor next door I expect,' Pop said, a trifle sourly, so that Ma was forced to administer a reprimand.

'Pop. Do be decent.'

'Well, there are,' the Miss Barnwells said, yet again in unison, 'two schools of thought.'

Blimey, Pop thought. Schools of thought now, eh? Whatever next? Ma wondered too, eager to hear what Edith had been up to. Couldn't be the Professor next door, could it?

'Oh! no, she *hates* him. She *loathes* him. She can't *bear* him.'

Ma was shrewdly silent. She'd heard that kind of thing before. You'd only got to hear a girl say she couldn't stand the sight of some man and before you knew where you were she'd married him.

'Some say she's on holiday. And some,' the Miss Barnwells said, 'say she's in a Home.'

'Probably far better off,' Pop said.

'Well, we did hear she was in *purdah*,' Ma said, at the same time giving Pop a severely warning look in case he came out again with the unfortunate suggestion that Miss Pilchester was in pod, 'but a Home. That don't sound too good.'

'In *purdah* she undoubtedly *was* for some time,' the two Miss Barnwells admitted, 'but we rather discount the *other*. Edith's very independent and anyway the windows of the cottage were open when we came past.'

'Oh! she's all right,' Ma said, with her customary cheerful air of charity, 'it's her jam season.'

With a rapidity astonishing for creatures so small, the Miss Barnwells masticated their way through everything eatable on Ma's tray, accompanying it all with cup after cup of tea, so that Pop actually began to tell himself that if they kept emptying the pot like that much longer there might well be some sudden demand for The Throne. Normally he would have thought little or nothing of making such a suggestion aloud but now there was a certain constraining influence in the air.

'Well, I must give her a tinkle,' Ma said, meaning Edith, and at the same time made the light suggestion, not very well received by Pop, that 'perhaps she'll come and baby-sit for you one night while Sister Trevelyan goes out.'

The subject of Edith having been at least temporarily exhausted Ma said she would clear the tray, and then as she went to pick it up noticed that a single salmon-and-cucumber sandwich, sole relic of the meal, remained.

'Well, we can't let that go begging, can we? Isn't somebody going to eat it up?'

Like two eager birds the Miss Barnwells picked it up, broke it in half and quickly minced it away.

'Well,' they said at last, 'we must be going. We mustn't *tire* you. But there was just one *teeny* thing we wanted to ask you.'

'Ask away,' Pop said, the thought of their departure having induced in him a slight rise in the temperature of cheerfulness. 'Say the word. What is it?'

Well, the Miss Barnwells said, Mr Larkin was always *so* generous, he gave *so* willingly, *always*, for *whatever* they asked.

Pop, ever ready to dig his hand deep for charities, children's outings, old people's parties and anything else that would keep the ball rolling for people who were a bit unfortunate, said if Miss Effie wouldn't mind looking in the top drawer of the dressing table she would find his wallet. What was it this time, anyway?

'Well, it's our Fund.'

Fund? Pop said. What sort of Fund?

The two Miss Barnwells, in all probability for the first time in their lives, suddenly stood up to their full height, all four feet seven inches, like two little soldiers in the act of enlistment for battle.

'Our Fund,' they said, 'for saving England.'

Well, you could have knocked him down with a stone block of wood, Pop said. Saving England? Was someone thinking of pinching it, then?

'Yes,' the Miss Barnwells said, not only with great firmness but with a militancy that rasped on the air like the snap of a rifle bolt being drawn back. 'They most certainly are.'

Pop, sitting up in bed and taking sharp notice of the highly determined look on the faces of the Miss Barnwells, who now looked less like budgerigars than a pair of miniature eagles, begged to be told what he was supposed to make of that remark. The country was a bit big to cart off under somebody's arm, wasn't it?

It was not, the Miss Barnwells sternly informed him, exactly that kind of pinching. It was worse. It was political, nasty and subversive. It was composed of the most wicked subtleties.

It was fortunate that at the very moment when Pop was trying to digest this extraordinary meaty offering of words from the two little ladies that Ma came back into the bedroom, accompanied by the Brigadier, who had been lured to the house by the prospect of seeing the enchanting Sister Trevelyan and was now rudely disappointed to find that it was her day off and she had gone with Mariette and various of the children to the sea. A certain deflated look of grey cheerlessness in his eye at being faced with the beauties of the Miss Barnwells rather than that of the luscious Sister Trevelyan wasn't lost on Pop, who promptly invited him to help himself to a snifter, even though it was still not five o'clock.

'Thanks all the same, Larkin. Hardly over the yard arm, yet, though, is it? –'

Oh! who cares about the yard arm? Pop said. The Brigadier knew Pop's approach in these matters, didn't he? If he wanted a drink for Gawd's sake let him have a drink.

The Brigadier, in his terse military fashion, uttered low thanks again and suffered himself to be tempted to a very large whisky.

'The Miss Barnwells were just telling us about how somebody's going to steal England,' Pop said. 'You heard anythink about that, General?'

The Brigadier coughed brusquely. A certain air of unease, almost guilt, hung about him, rather as if he had been part of a conspiracy and had only just been found out.

Pop, at once suspicious that they were all trying to keep something from him, was more than relieved to hear Ma say:

'Well, it's this Tunnel. This Channel Tunnel, that's all.'

Oh! that was it, was it? Pop said. Well, he wasn't interested in no Tunnel.

'Then,' the Miss Barnwells informed him with the voices of irate eagles, 'you should be!'

Pop was stunned into silence. The Brigadier drank deeply of his whisky.

Ma fidgeted with her hands in an unaccountably nervous way. And finally the Miss Barnwells demanded in pointedly barking voices:

'We are an island, are we not?'

Before Pop had time to admit to the truth of the ancient fact that they were an island indeed the Miss Barnwells rose in full, outraged flight:

'Very well then, do you not wish to remain an island? Do you wish to be swallowed by the Continent? We have been an island for all time, haven't we? Hasn't it served us well? Isn't it our strength, our salvation? Wasn't it that that saved us during the war? The sea is our defence, isn't it? Do you want to see it destroyed?'

Not the least remarkable thing about this resolute outburst was not merely its strength or that it came from creatures so frail and small but that its method of delivery had changed entirely from one of unison, so that now the sentences were delivered by the two sisters alternately, like set speeches long learned by heart.

'Do you wish us to be governed from Rome?' Miss Effie demanded.

'Do you want us to lose sovereignty?' Miss Edna said.

These sudden references to the Common Market had the Brigadier snorting and huffing over his whisky like some horse growing increasingly impatient to gallop. The Common Market, Rome and Papism generally being his most frequent sources of insular outrage he suddenly thundered:

'By God, no. Hell's bells.'

The very word Rome had been known to inflame him, in fact, to public protestation. The Reverend Candy's predecessor in incumbency had been, in the Brigadier's view, a bounder, a theatrical showman, a priestly impresario, a fraud. Given to dressing up in private in sulphur-yellow riding breeches, scarlet waistcoats and purple cloaks and in public in vestments that could only be described as looking like the left over trappings from some impossible Wagnerian pomposity in opera, the fellow had so far goaded the Brigadier as to make him rise in church on one occasion and demand as with military command:

'Are we now to suppose, sir, that the whole service is about to be conducted in Latin?'

As if about to repeat this fierce demand the Brigadier drank deep at his whisky again, went very red in the face, snorted and seemed about to bellow forth when he was stopped in his tracks by an astonishingly quiet pronouncement from Miss Effie, who said:

'During the war Edna and I often faced Hitler. Alone.'

Ma, the Brigadier and Pop waited with equal, silent anticipation for some explanation of this astonishing and compelling statement, which finally came, rather unexpectedly, from Miss Effie, who now took the centre of the stage while Edna, as it were, remained in the wings, more or less as prompter.

'Before the war we had a house on the coast. On fine days you could see France. Sometimes even the clock tower at Calais, couldn't we dear?'

Miss Edna said yes, they could. And with the naked eye.

'Well, there we lived. At peace. Until the war came. And then of course there was talk of invasion and we were forced to close the house and move here, weren't we, dear? The coast was a forbidden area and you were only allowed into it if you had special business or property, weren't you, dear?'

Miss Edna said yes, they were. Once a month. With special passes.

'So,' Miss Effie said, 'down we would go, once a month, and sit in the garden and look across the Channel. Twenty miles away. Didn't we dear?'

Miss Edna said yes indeed, they did. At Hitler.

'We always took our lunch with us, wet or fine. Spam sandwiches and tea mostly, wasn't it, dear?'

Yes, it was, Miss Edna said. But once or twice, especially in that very cold winter of 1941, they took a drop of home-made parsnip too.

'Edith's brew?' Pop asked, suddenly more like his old self, sharp and perky.

'Oh! no. Edith was in the Navy at that time.'

At this Pop was even more stunned than the Brigadier, who gulped afresh at his whisky and said 'Good God. Never? Edith in the Navy?'

'She was a Wren,' Miss Effie said. 'Oh! you mustn't underestimate Edith. She has a medal somewhere.'

Good Gawd, Pop thought. Where? No wonder we won. Edith with a medal? Probably got it for giving all she'd got, he shouldn't wonder.

Following this brief interruption the Miss Barnwells resumed their duologue, now once more speaking in unison, describing how they would sit in their long-deserted garden, their little bit of England, stare across the Channel, drink tea or home-made parsnip, chew on spam sandwiches and curse the invisible figure of Hitler somewhere across the water. There was often an artillery bombardment going on and often a battle in the air and sometimes it was terrific fun. The shells burst awfully near.

'Do you remember that day,' Effie said 'when we were blackberrying and that air-raid warden came by and said we were in danger? You remember, dear?'

Yes, Miss Edna said, she remembered, and they said danger from whom? That twit?

At the recollection of this moment of defiance the Miss Barnwells laughed in a series of merry little giggles, as if it had all been a very great joke, a jolly little pantomime.

'And that's why,' Miss Effie said, 'we are out to save England. What on earth do you think we saved it for then? Not to give away again for the dear Lord's sake, surely.'

'Hear, hear,' the Brigadier said. 'Hear, hear.'

'We are an island,' Miss Edna said, 'and we are determined to keep it that way!'

'Moreover,' Miss Effie said, 'what kind of people, as Churchill said, do they think we are?'

'Hear, hear,' the Brigadier said again. 'Sound the trumpet!'

At this point Ma, who had been remarkably if not indeed suspiciously quiet all this time, was moved to admit that it all reflected her own feelings on the matter very much indeed.

'Of course we don't want to be governed from Rome. Or Berlin. Or Paris. Or by that de Gaulle or Russia. Or that Stalin. Or that Cosy Gin.'

'Cosy Gin?' Pop said and was actually moved to laughter. 'That Russian feller? Very good name for a cocktail.'

When the Brigadier gently reminded Ma that de Gaulle was no longer in office and that Stalin was dead Ma simply snorted. She knew she wasn't very hot on world affairs but did it matter who was dead and who wasn't considering the gang of crooks who ran things?

She wasn't at all sure, she went on to say, if you asked her, that it wasn't all part of that persuasive society you heard so much about nowadays.

'Permissive,' the Brigadier gently corrected her.

Oh? Ma said, singularly unimpressed. You'd got to be persuaded before you could permit, hadn't you? at the same time thinking chance would be a fine thing.

Pop, who had listened to all this with only the one comment on his part, now said that perhaps a few weeks in bed had dimmed him up a bit but he still wasn't sure how they were going to lose England and who was going to pinch it?

Miss Effie, in a sudden blistering moment of fresh militancy, was moved to a pronouncement that had everyone staggered.

'*We* are! *We!* If we aren't careful we shall be *our own executioners.*'

'Indeed we shall,' Miss Edna said. 'Are we going to sit here like a lot of supine, bloodless worms while the entire heritage of this island is sent to the pawnbroker's? I should say not. We were never in pawn to Hitler, damn his soul and may God forgive me for saying so. And I say we'll not be in pawn to the Devil.'

535

'Whether you call him Common Market, Rome, decimal, Channel Tunnel, Europe, Centigrade or whatever,' Miss Effie said, in a burst of insular outrage that even outmatched her sister's.

'Hear, bloody well hear,' said Pop, who was now beginning, he told himself, to see daylight.

The true daylight had, however, not yet dawned. It was in fact this that had kept Ma so uncommonly and suspiciously quiet for so long and it was now Miss Effie, in a further expansion of her case for the Defence of the Realm, who put the matter into words.

'And of course the Road.'

Road? Pop wanted to know. What road was that?

'Well, it's this Road,' Ma said, going on to explain that they'd known about it for some time but that it had been considered that Pop hadn't quite been well enough to be told about it. Now both Dr O'Connor and Sister Trevelyan thought he was fit enough. 'Well, there was this man from the Ministry here about three weeks ago.'

Man from the Ministry? Pop was always highly suspicious of any man from the Ministry. Income tax, he expected. Well, that was no bother. He knew how to deal with fellers from the Income Tax. Two or three of his Red Bull cocktails, mixed double strength, would see them off all right.

'It's the Road to the Tunnel,' Miss Effie now explained.

Tunnel? And what, Pop prayed, had the road to the Tunnel to do with him? The Tunnel would be thirty or forty miles away.

'But the road would come through here,' Miss Edna said.

'Yes, through here,' Ma said and now the reasons for her long quietness were becoming clear at last. 'Bang through the middle of our place. Our garden, Pop. Our yard.'

Pop shot bolt upright in bed: his first agile and vigorous act since thrombosis had struck him down. His teeth were shown in rage. The anger that Ma in her native wisdom had deemed to be a necessary force for cure now filled him with a new and vibrant alertness: proving, as Primrose had predicted, that the tigers of wrath were wiser than the horses of instruction.

At the same time he was speechless. It was something like being crucified and then having a dagger struck through your throat for good measure. The first grey iron pain of his heart attack hadn't pained him more.

It was the recollection of the visit of a Man from the Ministry that finally broke his silence and then in a burst of righteous rage.

'I'll be damned,' he suddenly said, 'if I'll be shoved around by a lot of farts from Whitehall!'

At which Ma gave him one of her sharp looks, this time quite lost on him. He mustn't bandy words like that about. After all there was a time and place for everything.

'Now you see why we've started our Fund,' Miss Effie said.

Miss Edna chirped in agreement.

'Our Cause,' she said. 'Our Great Cause.'

Pop said with righteous irritation that he didn't know about their Cause. It was his Cause too, very much his Cause, wasn't it?

'The part is symptomatic of the whole,' the Brigadier said in a moment of solemn and surprising revelation, as if he had produced the words out of some Bill of Rights or something of that sort. 'Damme, it's riding roughshod.'

This mixture of solemnity and the vernacular completely mystified Ma, who hadn't the remotest idea of what the Brigadier was talking about. Pop wasn't sure either.

'Well, one thing is certain,' Miss Effie said. 'We are going to *fight*.'

'We are indeed going to fight,' Miss Edna said. 'But of course it will need money.'

'Well that's no trouble,' Pop said. 'Ma, get the box out of the wardrobe.'

Ma immediately proceeded to open the wardrobe and produce from it one of those old-fashioned tin travelling trunks once a familiar part of railway life three quarters of a century or more ago. The trunk was actually too heavy for Ma to lift and she begged the Brigadier, if he would, to give her a hand with it.

The trunk having been lifted out on to the bedroom floor, Ma then did an astonishing thing. She appeared, greatly to the surprise of both the Brigadier and the Miss Barnwells, about to undress. This seemed abundantly clear from the way in which she unzipped her blouse from the back, slipped one side of it over and down her left shoulder and then plunged a hand bosomwards, as if searching for some source of irritation there, perhaps in the form of a mosquito or something.

There was in fact no such source of irritation. A momentary vision of an olive chasm between the fair hills of Ma's bosom was accompanied, on Ma's part, by a great sigh as she heaved up a long gold chain with a bunch of keys at the end of it. Among these was the key to the tin trunk. She always kept the keys down there because as she said, it was the last place anybody would think of looking for them and the first place where Pop always did. There was nothing like having security and pleasure provided, so to speak, under one roof. What could be nicer, Pop often asked himself, than having two of the most important things in his life, Ma's bosom and the keys to his money, safe under the same corset?

Having at last freed the key from the encumbrances of blouse, slip, corset and chain, Ma proceeded to unlock the trunk.

The Brigadier gave a great involuntary gasp.

'By Jove, Larkin, damme. Been reading *Treasure Island* or something?'

The comparison was not inapt. The Brigadier hadn't seen so much money, in the raw so to speak, since pay days in the army.

Pop waved a characteristically deprecatory hand.

'Always keep a bit in the house in case,' he said, though in case of what he didn't bother to explain.

'After all you never know when you'll need a bit of loose change do you?' Ma said and gave one of the jolliest, jelliest laughs she had given for a very long time. The fact that she and Pop had half a dozen similar trunks, one in the roof, two in an attic, one in the cellar, one under a pile of straw and a sixth in the most unlikely place of all, locked in the top of an old stone well at the bottom of the garden, was something that this was neither the time nor place to mention.

All this time the Miss Barnwells had had nothing to say. They too, tortured as they were by the ever-increasing need to submit themselves to the indignity of asking for Supplementary Benefit or whatever name the largesse of the Welfare State went under nowadays, had never seen so much money in their lives.

Here, also with more jollity than he had shown for some considerable time, Pop demanded what sort of sub. they had in mind?

'Oh! *anything*. We should be grateful for the *teeniest* thing. Two guineas? Whatever –'

Two guineas her foot, Ma said, a remark that Pop followed up by saying Did they mind? Was that the price they put on his place? His yard? He'd have them know it meant as much to him as Buckingham Palace.

Before the Miss Barnwells could refute an assertion they had never made the door of the bedroom opened and Mr Charlton came in. Mr Charlton and Montgomery had been doing so well at the pheasant lark, among other ventures, that the sight of the trunkful of money had nothing like the stupefying effect on him that it had had on the Miss Barnwells and the Brigadier.

'Counting the coconuts, Mr Larkin, sir?' he merely said.

'Just in time, Charley boy,' Pop said. 'You've heard about this road lark I take it?'

Charley had. He had been part of, indeed the instigator of, the plot to keep it from Pop as long as possible.

'Well, what the pipe are we going to do about it?'

In answer to this question the two Miss Barnwells struck up in shrill, indignant unison.

'Oh! *anything*. *Everything*. We've already got a petition with three hundred signatures. We'll even have one of those protest marches if necessary. Like they have against Nuclear Disarmament and Vietnam and all that. We've even thought of getting Mr Candy to preach a sermon about it.'

It was now the turn of Mr Charlton to raise a deprecatory hand.

'No, no,' he said and the very tone of his voice, calm and authoritative, told Pop that Charley was on the verge of using his loaf. 'All that, I suggest, is out. Nothing is to be gained, I suggest, by the emotional approach.'

Masterpiece of a feller, Charley. Now who else would have thought of a thing like that? Emotional approach.

'This thing,' Charley went on to say, 'must be tackled like a military operation.'

'Hear, hear, Charlton,' the Brigadier said. 'Bingo.'

'But that,' the Miss Barnwells chirped in fearful unison, 'would cost an *awful deal* of money!'

'Well, not short of a few pennies, are we?' Pop said, waving an airy hand towards the bulging tin trunk, beyond which the Brigadier was helping to reinforce himself, as if in early preparation for battle, by pouring another very large whisky.

'Here, while you're pouring out, General,' Ma said, 'why don't we all have a sniff?'

Why not indeed, the Brigadier said and with true military correctness bowed towards the little Miss Barnwells and courteously awaited orders.

Before these could be given – the Miss Barnwells deeming that a gap of a mere hour between tea and alcohol was in some way slightly immoral – Mr Charlton made a further, explanatory pronouncement.

'I said military. What I really meant was legal.'

'But that would cost an even *greater deal* of money!' the Miss Barnwells cried out, quite pained.

'Never mind about that,' Ma said, with that imperturbable kindness of hers. 'What are you going to have? Gin? Whisky? Brandy? Sherry? One of Pop's cocktails?'

At the mention of the word cocktail the two Miss Barnwells instantly recalled that delicious concoction with which Mr Larkin had regaled them that evening, now seemingly so long ago, after the gymkhana. They would never forget that cocktail. Nor its name. Ma Chérie.

'Well, could we, perhaps, have a little – the *teeniest* one of those cocktails? Ma Chérie? Only a *soupçon*, the merest *soupçon*.'

Pop, not bothering to seek translation of the word *soupçon*, merely laughed and said that Ma Chéries were old-fashioned now. He'd cut them out.

He suggested A Blonde Bombshell instead.

If the two ladies were about to protest that this sounded like a drink of some belligerency they were saved from doing so by Pop, who declared it to be a mere summer refresher and said:

'Mix a couple up, Charley boy. You know the form.'

Charley knew the form: two parts vodka, one brandy, one whisky, a dash of angostura and a nip of soda. Normally mixed double strength, these had the power of cure-alls, Pop was fond of saying, but now a wink in the direction of Mr Charlton, busy at the bedroom bar, was enough to indicate that singles would, in this case, be adequate. He could only wish, with some pain, that he were having one himself.

Instead he suddenly had – indicative of the sharp improvement the tigers of wrath had already had on his mind – a great thought.

Legal? He suddenly remembered Angela Snow. Wasn't her father a judge or something?

'Something at the Bar, I believe,' Charley said.

'Then I'll join him,' Pop said. 'What's her number?'

In the early days of his illness Pop had once or twice used the telephone by his bedside, but the very act of lifting the receiver had had such an effect on him that he had found himself at the bottom of the snake in no time, in consequence of which he had been forbidden its use.

'Now, now,' Ma said. 'Don't get excited. You know what happened last time.'

'But if it's going to be a legal do, we want legal advice and a legal bloke don't we?' Pop said. 'Besides, if I know my Angela we might get it free.'

'If you don't know your Angela by this time nobody does,' Ma said darkly. 'And you watch it. What do you mean, free? She might ask you to pay in kind.'

Which she added to herself and not with her customary merriment. Pop was in no position at the moment to do, more was the pity.

'I'll have a word with her,' Charley said. 'It's a possibility. A thought.'

While the little Miss Barnwells supped with delicacy at concoctions powerful enough to bring tears to their eyes and Ma sucked smoothly at

Remy Martin, her favourite brandy, Mr Charlton dialled Angela's number and waited for it to be answered.

'It's ringing now,' he said.

'Let me have it,' Pop said and Ma, greatly to his surprise, took the telephone from Charley and passed it over. Her shrewd native intuitions detected that Pop was on the up and up. She'd been right about the anger.

'Angela.'

At the sound of Pop's voice there came, from the other end of the line, a golden, aristocratic, languid peal of laughter.

'Darling. Sweet man. Made my day.'

And how was Angela? Pop wanted to know.

'Pining. Wilting away. What's more to the point, darling, how are you?'

Mustn't grumble, Pop said. Surviving.

'And what can I do for you, sweetie?'

Pop said he'd rung her to see if she'd do him a favour.

'You mean you're fit enough, darling? I simply can't wait.'

It wasn't that sort of favour, Pop said, worse luck, but he didn't doubt the day would come.

'It will, sweetheart, it will. On those sand-dunes at Le Touquet.'

Well, he didn't know about that, Pop said. His main concern at the moment was that he had a problem on his mind.

'Then you mustn't have, darling. Remove it. Take it off at once.'

Pop said he was trying to do that, which was why he was ringing her. And by the way wasn't her father a judge?

'Q.C., darling. Queen's Counsel. Why?'

Pop proceeded to explain why: all about the Tunnel and the road and the Cause and the Fund and how the road, so they threatened, these Ministry blokes, was coming right bang through the very middle of his place.

'The snotty bastards.'

Pop laughed, quite in his old style, almost uproariously. It was good to be talking to Angela again. She was worth a million doses of medicine. Perhaps the sand-dunes didn't seem all that much in question after all.

Still, it was serious, Pop went on to say. He was up in arms. Everybody was up in arms. It was what Edith would have called absolutely ghastly. It was sort of like treason. Something had to be done about it.

'Of course darling. The stinking slobs. We must slay them. We must put poison down.'

The word 'we' suddenly shone, for Pop, like a good deed in a naughty world. It was the very thing he'd been waiting for.

'Wondered if your father could help? Charley boy thinks we should make it a legal battle. Cut out the emotional approach and all that.'

Pop, using Mr Charlton's very words, suddenly felt grand and militant himself.

'Your voice sounds strong, darling,' Angela Snow suddenly said.

Did it? Pop said, more than a little flattered. Perhaps she'd better watch out for them sand-dunes after all?

Again the peal of golden laughter came ringing from the other end of the line.

'I take it you'd like me to consult with Papa?'

Pop said that was the line of country. And as for the dough-ray-me, not to worry about that. Pop would see to that. Sky was the limit.

'You swab. You dare suggest it. Of course you won't pay.' Again the seductive golden peals poured their music into Pop's ears. 'Oh! yes, on second thoughts you will. Me. In kind.'

Which was exactly what Ma had said, Pop reminded himself, laughing too. Amazing how women's minds worked. Perfickly amazing.

'Well, I'll do your bidding, darling – as if I was ever likely to do otherwise. He'll be home tonight. We'll consult. I expect he'll be free on Sunday. Might we possibly come over and see you then?'

'Course. Come to lunch. Free house on Sundays.'

'Splendid, darling. Look forward to it passionately.'

Dangerous word, Pop thought of saying, dangerous word; but merely said instead:

'Perfick. Perfick.'

'See you Sunday then, sweetheart. Oh! by the way, have you met any of those rats from Whitehall yet? No? Well, let me tell you this, darling. Whoever or wherever they are they might just as well drop dead. Goodbye. Everlasting love.'

So blessed, Pop answered with his own most cheering farewell, feeling infinitely better already. There was something about that girl, he told himself. Her nature was just what the world needed more of.

'Her father's not a judge,' he announced, putting down the telephone. 'He's a Q.C. Queen's Counsel.'

At this announcement, Ma, great Royalist as she was, felt enormously flattered. It was a tremendous honour to feel that she had a Queen's Counsel coming to Sunday lunch. She wasn't quite clear in her mind what a Queen's Counsel was and could only suppose he was a gentleman who went about with the Queen giving her counsel as and when required and perhaps wearing black knee breeches and stockings and carrying a long stick, a sort of 'thy rod and thy staff they comfort me' or something of that sort. Anyway he was bound to be of enormous importance. She wasn't at all sure they oughtn't to roast an ox or something in honour of his coming.

The two little Miss Barnwells having supped their way down to the dregs of their Blonde Bombshells, Mr Charlton, without asking, filled them up again. As if this were not bounty enough Pop said:

'Ma, give the Miss Barnwells a hundred to go on with and if they want more they know where to come to. Got to support this Cause with every penny we've got. Got to beat this ruddy lot somehow.'

With quivering hands the Miss Barnwells accepted Ma's gift of a hundred pound notes tied into a packet with green wool – she always tied the hundreds with green, the fities with blue and the five hundreds with pink – like pilgrims accepting some holy, treasured relic at a shrine.

Dear Mr Larkin. Wonderful Mr Larkin. They simply couldn't believe their good fortune.

'Nothing,' Pop said. 'Nothing. Plenty more where that comes from.'

Like the Brigadier said, they weren't going to be rid roughshod over.

'Hear, hear, Larkin. Bingo. Sound the trumpet,' the Brigadier said and with a kind of eager deference helped himself to another whisky.

'Oh! and if you see Edith,' Pop said, 'rope her in. Must have Edith with the troops. Tell her to come and see me.'

'We will indeed.'

'We will indeed.'

'Haven't seen her for such a long time,' Ma said, renewing her Remy Martin with generosity. 'Tell her if she doesn't soon show her face we'll be forgetting what she looks like.'

'Stout girl, Edith,' the Brigadier said. 'Navy, eh? Medal, damme.'

'And what,' the little Miss Barnwells said, 'about Mr Candy? Shall we put aside the idea of the sermon for the time being?'

Mr Charlton suddenly said he thought so. The law might, in this case, have more power than the pulpit. Even if it costs more.

Though partially stunned by Mr Charlton's display of wisdom Pop laughed, almost in his old ringing fashion.

'Not going to cost us a penny. Like you said, Ma, Angela says I can pay in kind.'

Oh? Ma said, looking at him very darkly. Then she only hoped his credit was good.

'Then we will leave Mr Candy for the moment, shall we?' the Miss Barnwells said. They were still a trifle uncertain as to the wisdom of leaving Mr Candy and the church out of things. Empty though the pews all too often were, the church still had its voice.

'I'll have a word with Mr Candy,' Pop said.

Come to think of it, he hadn't seen much of Mr Candy either lately. He wondered what he'd been up to?

Half an hour later the little Miss Barnwells walked gently home in the cool of the evening, except that it didn't seem cool to them, but amazingly, marvellously beautifully warm, and that they were not walking, but sailing, as it were lightly over water, as over some divine Sea of Galilee.

Wonderful, marvellous Mr Larkin. Their Cause was in great hands. The age of miracles had not yet passed.

· 9 ·

Ever since the morning when she had decided that whisky rather than prayer was the more appropriate medium with which to express farewell to Pop Larkin on his last long journey Miss Pilchester had not merely been in *purdah*, but in a state of shame, guilt, confusion and even despair. Her shame and guilt rose from the fact that she had rejected prayer and come to grief, her confusion from the fact that she had chosen whisky and Pop had recovered. Had prayer lost its efficacy and whisky gained in powers both healing and miraculous? She had asked herself the questions a thousand times; and confusion, despair and *purdah* were her only answers. Whichever way one looked at it, she told herself, it was all absolutely ghastly.

When therefore she heard that Pop had so far recovered as to wish to see her she accepted the invitation the very next afternoon, with both alacrity and a fearful joy.

Pop, who was so far on the way to recovery as to tell himself that he was feeling as strong as a nip of brandy in a pint of water and was eagerly looking forward to the day when it would be the other way round, had spent more than an hour out of bed in the morning, had slept for another on the strictest orders from Sister Trevelyan after lunch and was now sitting out again, alternately watching a race meeting on telly, which bored him, and his beloved junk-yard, which didn't.

The joy to be derived from little things or from things once deemed ordinary and taken for granted had never left him since the day he had first gazed out on the young rose-leaf on his bedroom window. And now the junk-yard, in consequence, looked perfick. Nobody was going to take that from him: not on his nelly. This was his own, his beloved bit of England.

And how perfick it looked, his paradise, he kept telling himself. Pink willow-herb was growing up in forests of tall feathery spires among all the massed junk of barrels, muckheaps, hen coops, wrecked cars, discarded bits of machinery, wire and lumps of old iron, making a beautiful picture. The old iron was specially good. You'd see a lot worse, as Ma often

545

remarked, in some sculpture exhibition in London if some of the photos she saw in the papers were anything to go by.

Miss Pilchester had telephoned to ask if half past four would be a convenient visiting time and had been told by Ma yes and would she stay for tea, which was what she had hoped for. But unexpectedly, about four o'clock, Mr Candy arrived before her.

'Ah! nice to see you, Mr Candy,' Pop said, very cheerful himself, though thinking that Mr Candy, in dog collar, looked sort of formal, nervous and a trifle tired. 'Haven't seen you lately.'

'Well, yes, that's true I'm afraid. I –'

Pop interrupted to say that he expected Mr Candy had had other things on his plate?

'Well, life's been awfully full. I won't exactly say I've been run off my feet – but you know how it is.'

Pop knew how it was. All that christening and marrying and those sermons.

Mr Candy had no comment to make on this. He merely seemed to grow more nervous.

'Well, I just – I just – I felt I ought to sort of drop in and see you. About a little matter –'

Perfick, Pop said. He expected it was the Cause?

Mr Candy, who hadn't thought of the particular matter on his mind as being exactly a cause, but rather an effect, supposed that that was one way of putting it, though he didn't say so.

'Thought as much,' Pop said. 'I talked it over with the Miss Barnwells.'

Mr Candy, hitherto merely nervous, now seemed to become exceedingly flaky and fragile. With difficulty he dabbed sweat from his brow.

'Got very excited about it, the pair of 'em,' Pop said. 'Told people in the village it was a miracle.'

Mr Candy immediately went paler still.

'Said you might be preaching a sermon about it.'

Oh! dear no, Mr Candy said. That was – no, he didn't think that was the appropriate thing at all. It was the most unlikely subject for a sermon.

'No? Anyway, got to give it as much publicity as we can. That's what we all feel.'

Once again Mr Candy, in rather a limp voice, said that he didn't on the whole think the idea a very good one. He murmured something about he thought they were treading on sacred ground.

'Oh?' Pop said. He couldn't see how. What was sacred about it?

Mr Candy had no time to answer this interesting question before there was a tap at the bedroom door and Ma came in preceding Edith Pilchester, whom she announced with the cheerful words:

'Well, here's your girl friend. I'm just off to the village with Mariette. Be back in about an hour. Like a lift, Mr Candy?'

Mr Candy seemed delighted at the opportunity of a lift and the escape it offered and immediately got up to shake hands with Pop and Miss Pilchester, who in contrast to Mr Candy's extreme paleness was rather red in the face.

Ma then said that Sister Trevelyan would be bringing tea up and then, rather to Pop's surprise added:

'Well, I'll leave you two to it. You'd better get into bed.'

Pop, not sure if this was an indirect invitation to have five minutes under the sheets with Edith or not, gave one of his ringing laughs and in his best innocent voice said:

'Why?'

'Because Sister says so. That's why. She says you've sat out long enough for this afternoon.'

Pop dutifully took off his dressing-gown and got back into bed. Ma said goodbye, not to worry, she wouldn't be back for a good hour or more, and then left with Mr Candy, only to reappear a few seconds later to say:

'Oh! by the way, there was a note from Angela by the afternoon post. Her father can't make it on Sunday. Playing golf or something after all. It'll have to be the Sunday after.'

Left alone with Edith and finding the first moments with her somehow rather uneasy, not to say embarrassing – she was still very red in the face and seemed unaccountably nervous – Pop sought to relieve the tension by asking in characteristic fashion if she would take a nip, a snifter or something before tea?

The subject of alcohol being a highly unfortunate one, Miss Pilchester went even redder in the face and rapidly declined the offer, confessing that she'd long since given it up. The memory of that dreadful morning at The Hare and Hounds, though she didn't dare mention it, still lay on her soul like an accusatory, leaden cross. Nor had the sight of Pop after so many weeks made it any easier to bear.

'Well, how have we been?' Pop said, wondering at the same time if there was any need to ask. Edith, though much thinner than before, looked as red as a hen about to lay.

Well, on the whole she was fairly well, Miss Pilchester said, lying without much conviction, knowing that for weeks she had been feeling absolutely ghastly. What was more important, how was Mr Larkin?

'Perfick,' Pop said. 'Perfick. Feeling better every day. Eating well. Sleeping well. Doctor says the heart's mended perfickly.'

For the first time Miss Pilchester smiled, secretly telling herself that she only wished hers had. There were times when she thought it was irrevocably broken. Then to her infinite dismay Pop suddenly said:

'Got a bone to pick with you.'

The prospect of having to pick a bone with Pop was yet a further means of agitation for Miss Pilchester and she tremulously murmured Oh! had he, why?

'Never been to see me.'

'Oh! but I –'

'Nice thing. Lay here thinking about you every day. All the time. And you never come near. Out of sight, out of mind. I know.'

'Oh! but I –'

He had been cut, Pop said, to the quick. It was bad. Terrible. Worse than awful. He couldn't bear it when his best girl friends deserted him.

Miss Pilchester became quite speechless. She didn't at all know what to say. Impossible to acquaint Pop with the awful paradox that she hadn't been to see him first of all because she had heard that he was dead and she had taken to drink instead of prayer as a result of it, and then because of her consequent guilt and shame. The total confession would be altogether too ghastly.

Unaware of this remorseless torture, Pop went on to tease her still further by saying something about fair weather friends and his hour of need and all that and how it had shook him to the – he was about to say 'to the tits' and then rapidly changed it to 'the bottom of his heart'.

In answer to all this Miss Pilchester gave a loud sniff. A moment later Pop knew there was a tear in her eye.

'Now, now, now,' he said. 'This won't do, Edith. Can't have this. Can't have you turning the tap on.'

Miss Pilchester sniffed even more loudly, crying openly now.

'Here, here, come, come,' Pop said. 'Dry them eyes. First time you come to see me and you start tuning. Here, come over here and sit by me a minute.'

Needing no second invitation, Miss Pilchester went over and sat on the bed beside Pop.

Pop took her hand. Even in circumstances so ghastly the very touch of Pop's hand on hers was enough to make her tremble even more, so that without further warning she began sobbing hopelessly. This was an excellent excuse for Pop to take her by the other hand, at which she sobbed even more loudly still.

Ever willing to give comfort when and where it was most needed Pop now took her in his arms, stroked her hair and even gave a consolatory kiss in the region of her left ear. Her response to this was to palpitate, very rapidly, all over. The distressing thought even crossed her mind that Pop was about to ask her to give all she'd got and that unhappily she might not be in a position to do so.

The very same thought, at the very same moment, crossed Pop's mind. Having lately been in the unfortunate position of a man lacking practice it suddenly occurred to him that here was a good opportunity to get some in. A trial run with Edith, taken steady, in low gear sort of, might do no harm and might, into the bargain, do Edith a bit of good.

Pop's first excursion in this matter was to stroke her hair again and then give her a slightly more prolonged kiss under the left ear. His second was to fondle her neck, now so constrained from sobbing that it was as taut as a piece of hose-pipe. His third was an attempt to hold her more closely somewhere in the region of the left bosom.

To his infinite surprise there was no bosom there. This apparently unfortunate oversight on the part of nature was in fact merely the result of her having lost a great deal of weight in *purdah*, a fact that left him so astonished that he found himself, for once, with no other trick to play. This omission was however promptly remedied by Miss Pilchester, who suddenly stopped weeping, gave a great sigh and lay down with him on the bed, greatly comforted, her head on his shoulder.

At this point another immense sigh went through her, causing further spasms of palpitation that went down as far as her feet. This interesting development immediately caused Pop to think that there was, after all, one further trick he could play. No harm in trying, he told himself. After all, practice made perfick.

His execution in this further manoeuvre was however halted by the abrupt arrival of Sister Trevelyan who, seeing her patient in a position of some compromise on the bed with Miss Pilchester, didn't turn a hair. She had already been warned by Ma that she might well find Pop and Edith having what she called 'a bit of custard and jelly' when she took the tea up, but not to worry, she'd been letting Edith get it out of her system for years.

'Carry on Mr Larkin,' Sister Trevelyan said in the serenest of voices, 'nothing like a little therapy.'

So that's what they called it now, did they? Pop thought. Therapy. He'd often wondered what therapy was and always had a vague idea that it was something to do with the study of bones. This was perfickly true as far as Edith was concerned. Plenty of material there.

'Of course I *can* draw the curtains,' Sister Trevelyan said. 'The sun *is* rather bright.'

These words had the effect of bringing Miss Pilchester, briefly sunk into a state of spongy solace on Pop's chest, back into a world of blinding reality. Hopelessly ashamed, she sat bolt upright, almost fell backwards off the bed, then recovered with groping but elated indecision and the sudden information that she was admiring the scenery.

Sister Trevelyan said she was glad to hear it.

'Anything else you'd care for?' she said, most sweetly, setting down the tea-tray. 'I hope you don't mind, but I brought up a pot of the lemon curd you kindly came along with.'

'Oh! no, not at all –'

Edith had come, that afternoon, not only as a visitor but as a bearer of gifts: as it were, almost, offerings of restitution. Besides the pot of lemon curd she had brought jars of damson cheese, green tomato chutney, black-currant jam, a very special white-currant jelly and a bottle of elderflower wine.

'Of course Mr Larkin can't enjoy all you have to offer all at once,' Sister Trevelyan said, again with the sweetest serenity. 'He has got to get his appetite back.'

In further confusion Miss Pilchester could think of nothing to say in answer to this before Sister Trevelyan was ready again with her next light, sweet question.

'Shall I pour? Or will you be mother?' she said. 'Before it gets cold?'

Miss Pilchester, torn between elation and dire confusion, immediately decided it was best to be mother before it got cold.

Sipping sweet strong tea, she gradually recovered composure, even so far as to say, at last:

'You don't really, really think I neglected you, do you?'

Of course he did, of course, Pop said. He was cut to the quick. Left cold on the doorstep.

'But it was all so ghastly. I was absolutely *mortified* when I first heard about it. Absolutely *mortified*.'

Pop told himself he knew the meaning of the word mortified.

'So was I. Prit near.'

'Oh! Mr Larkin, don't talk of it. I can't bear it. I couldn't bear it – not all over again.'

After that, Pop having decided that he'd had enough of therapy for one day and Miss Pilchester having rejected all thought of further solace in Pop's arms, on the bed, the talk turned on what Miss Pilchester had been doing lately, apart from making jams and curds and being in *purdah* and things of that sort.

'As a matter of fact I've been delving into a little local history.'

Oh? Pop said. He hadn't realized she was interested in that sort of thing.

'Oh! yes, it's quite one of my secret passions.'

Secret passions, eh? Pop thought. He'd always suspected it.

'Well not exactly passion. I mean it's one of my pet hobbies. It's all so fascinating. I mean to go *back* in time. To the moon – forward – to Mars – no, that's not for me. But *back* – yes. To think of Caesar and his legionaries camping just up there on the hills. A Roman villa just behind the village. And vineyards perhaps. And the Pilgrims going to Canterbury. I mean we're so absolutely *steeped* in it, aren't we?'

Further marvels of what education could do, Pop thought. He only wished he'd had time for it.

'The Pilgrims especially – I like to think of them coming through here on some spring morning, "When that Aprille with her showers swote –"'

Here Pop was saved the trouble of asking what the pipe Edith was talking about by the unexpected arrival of Phyllida and little Oscar – little Oscar singing a hymn he had learnt at school:

Through all the Changing Gears of Life
Through Hell and Toil and Pain,

a version that struck Pop as not inappropriate to all that had been happening to him for the past several weeks, so that Pop patted the boy with paternal approval on the head and said:

'Hullo, what do you two monkeys want?'

The monkeys had brought him a frog, Phyllida said, and some fish for his supper.

The frog was nestling in a wet hemlock leaf and the fish, two stickle-backs, a very small gudgeon and a dead minnow, in a jar together with a water snail.

Well knowing that Ma didn't approve of such things in the bedroom, they had sneaked up with these precious offerings in her absence. Pop was very touched by the gesture, especially the thought of fish for supper.

'Oh! you are so lucky, having all these many children,' Miss Pilchester said. 'I sometimes wonder how you and Mrs Larkin manage it.'

She did? Pop thought. Perfickly simple, he was about to explain to her, then realized that it was scarcely the time and place, when Miss Pilchester said:

'And where did you get those lovely, lovely fishes from?'

Phyllida and little Oscar said they got the fish out of the little brook behind where the well was and the frog out of the bulrushes. Like Moses. Sweet things, Miss Pilchester said. And what well was that?

Pop proceeded to explain that it wasn't a well exactly. More a sort of spring, coming out of an old stone grotto down at the bottom of the yard, behind the pigsties. The spring came up out of the ground and then overflowed into a brook and then the brook went across the medder into the river proper. Very good water in the spring, very pure. Never failed in the driest summers.

'And cold,' little Oscar said. 'Like ice lollies.'

'And all covered over with moss,' Phyllida said. 'I mean the stones. All covered with moss and old. Very like you are.'

Far from being either insulted or upset by such descriptive candour Miss Pilchester suddenly seemed to experience a moment of revelatory joy. She leapt up from where she had been sitting by the window, spilt tea in her saucer, dropped a cucumber sandwich on the carpet and exclaimed with jubilation:

'Great God, I believe I've uncovered it!'

Had she really? Pop thought. Uncovered what? He couldn't wait to have a look.

'I mean this is *It*. This is the missing link I've been trying to find. This is the *Secret Bit*.'

If he hadn't seen Edith drinking tea with his own eyes, Pop thought, he'd have sworn she'd been at the parsnip or elderberry or somethink like that.

'You see,' she went on, 'on all the old maps there's the teeniest, teeniest cross marked where your house stands and I've always wondered what it meant.'

And what did it mean? Pop wanted to know.

'Well at the moment it's a mere surmise – I'm only guessing – but I *think* this may well have been a resting place for Pilgrims on their way to Canterbury. I mean it might be a Holy Well.'

Well you could have knocked him down with a nine-gallon barrel o' beer, Pop said. Holy? In his yard?

'Consecrated. Hallowed. I mean we may well be on Sacred Ground.'

Ah? Sacred Ground – now, Pop told himself, he knew what Mr Candy had been driving at, and proceeded to tell Edith so too.

'Oh! splendid. It may well be a case of two great minds thinking alike,' she said, laughing with excited gaiety. 'But you know what it *means*, don't you – what it *may* mean?'

Pop said no, he didn't quite, he hardly snagged on.

'It *may* mean – I oniy say *may* – it may well mean – that *if* this is consecrated ground they may never be able to drive that *awful, ghastly* road through here.'

It was now time for Pop himself to give a great sublime sigh of delight. 'Edith I could kiss you. Come over here. I could kiss you.'

With alacrity, needing no second invitation, Miss Pilchester went over to the bed where Pop, with that velvet authority of his, enfolded her in his arms and proceeded to get in a short spell of much-needed practice. Edith, free at last of shame, guilt and the long tortures of *purdah*, responded by giving all she'd got and, she told herself, a bit more.

Truly, as the Miss Barnwells themselves had said, the age of miracles had not yet passed. It was almost as if the frog, the gudgeon, the two sticklebacks and the dead minnow had been turned, like the three loaves and the five little fishes, into a feast for a multitude.

'Edith,' Pop said, 'I never knew history was so important.'

'Oh come on, let's go fishing again,' little Oscar said and went away with Phyllida, singing 'Through All the Changing Gears of Life' again.

'No,' Pop said, 'I never realized history was so important.'

'Ah! but there are far, far more important things than history,' Miss Pilchester said, 'don't you think?' and suffered herself to be kissed again, giving more, and with more palpitation, than she'd ever given before.

Long after she had gone Pop remembered that he'd forgotten to ask her what she'd won her medal for. Surrender, he shouldn't wonder. Then he decided no, it was probably, or ought to have been, for history; and was once again inspired to much thought on the wonders of education.

· 10 ·

There were three reasons why Ma was glad that the visit of Angela Snow's father, the Queen's Counsel, had been postponed.

First of all it gave her more time to go out and buy a new outfit proper to the occasion – after all you couldn't wear just any old thing for the visit of somebody as posh as a Queen's Counsel – then it gave her a chance to give a bit more thought to the food. After rejecting, reluctantly, the thought of a roasted ox as being too difficult in case the weather turned funny one way or the other, she was finally down to a choice between geese, turkey, pheasants and roast pork on the one hand and a baron of beef on the other. She finally decided on the baron of beef: it was after all in the titled class so to speak and not all that far removed from royalty, and it would also, she thought, go a long way.

Her third reason was contained in the hope that Pop would at last be well enough to come downstairs, and perhaps even into the garden, if the weather held, for lunch. She had great hopes of this. Both Dr O'Connor and Sister Trevelyan had promised as much, if he behaved himself, a matter to which Pop was giving serious attention. He was now able to walk about, go to the bathroom himself, bath himself and dress himself. It might well be that, in a day or two, he would walk up and downstairs. Whether the tigers of wrath had done the trick or not Ma didn't know; but steadily and surely Pop was becoming himself again. There was hope, Ma thought, one way or another, of Nature returning to its course.

After much trial Ma finally decided on a dress of oyster satin for the occasion, together with a three quarter length coat of the same material: the whole very subdued for her and looking rather more appropriate to a Royal garden party than Sunday lunch under the Larkin walnut tree. She also had high-heeled shoes to match and a big gold-silver handbag that sparkled so much it looked as if it had accidentally fallen into a sack of sugar.

After a late period of indecision she at last rejected the baron of beef for the good reasons that, at anything up to a hundredweight it would have been too large for the oven and that no butcher could supply one anyway.

Instead she chose two twenty pound turkeys and a whole baked ham. As this would be preceded by a whole smoked salmon she told herself that she didn't think anybody would starve.

The twins being at holiday camp in Devon and Victoria being gone off to Spain in an old London taxi, with three young men, an excursion that Ma thought would learn her, if nothing else did, to look after herself, this left seven of the Larkins and Mr Charlton for lunch, together with the Brigadier, Miss Pilchester, Sister Trevelyan, the Reverend Candy, Angela Snow and her father and finally the two Miss Barnwells. Pop had rightly insisted that the two Miss Barnwells should come since it was, after all, their Cause.

While Ma gave much serious thought to food and clothes Pop, who had been sitting out for increasingly long periods in the garden for the last three days, had given equally serious study to the drinks. As it was a question of entertaining a Queen's Counsel he thought they ought to be plain but posh: no mucking about. Mr Charlton, called in for consultation on the matter, cordially agreed: no fancy stuff. He suggested a vintage champagne with the smoked salmon, Chambolle Musigny for the turkey and a Château Yquem with Ma's many afters, one of which was going to be a Christmas pudding. No Red Bulls, no Rolls-Royces, no Blonde Bombshells or indeed any liquid fireworks of that nature. The whole affair had got to be kept, Mr Charlton said, on a certain plane.

The first person to arrive, to the dismay of Ma, who was hastily knocking up a large steak-and-kidney pie, just in case, was somebody who apparently hadn't been invited. Looking out from the kitchen window Ma observed on the lawn a dandy little gentleman in a smart Oxford blue mohair suit, a claret silk bow-tie with white spots and a jaunty little russet-red trilby hat cocked saucily to one side.

For almost a minute she was convinced that this was the Queen's Counsel himself. She was about to rush upstairs and change quickly into her oyster satin when she astonishingly realized that the dandy little gentleman was none other than the Brigadier who, seeing her gazing from the kitchen window, jauntily doffed his hat to her in the best manner of some Edwardian gallant-about-town.

'Hallo, General,' Ma said, 'didn't recognize you.'

'*Bon jour, madame*,' the Brigadier said, coming to the open kitchen window and, as if the excursion into French wasn't enough, actually kissed her hand.

The next to arrive was Mr Candy, apologetic, hot, thirsty and fearing he was late. He had had to conduct a church service at which the choir had outnumbered the congregation by fifteen to six, one of whom was a baby who had to be baptized, a circumstance that never failed to unnerve Mr Candy in view of the agonizing memory of all that had befallen him in christening Primrose. What with this and that Mr Candy had, as Pop put it, a lot on his plate nowadays.

'A Guinness, please, if you don't mind,' he said in answer to Pop's hearty invitation to a snifter. He needed it. It might, he thought, put his strength back; and Heaven knew when he mightn't need that, too.

The weather, as the Brigadier put it, almost as if he had unaccountably denied all his principles and gone over to the Common Market, was *Comme ci, comme ça*: neither too hot, nor too breezy: a dreamy mixture of rippling sun, white cloud and gentle shade.

The long lunch table having been laid out under the walnut tree, with a second table packed with a vast army of bottles beside it, Mr Charlton presently appeared from the house in a light smart cream suit, carrying corkscrews, bottle openers and ice-buckets as if prepared to deal with the drink situation in the manner of a butler.

Ma had at one time, in fact, seriously thought of having a butler. You could hire them. She expected any Queen's Counsel was bound to have one at home and the very thing she didn't want to do was to let the side down. But Mr Charlton's own counsel had prevailed in this particular matter, and very firmly.

No, no, he said, he thought no butler. It rather smacked of *folie de grandeur*, a remark that had Ma back on her heels, with nothing more to say.

At one o'clock, by which time Mariette and Primrose had taken over in the kitchen – no bikinis and bare midriffs today, Ma had warned them – leaving Ma to nip upstairs and bottle herself up in the oyster satin, there came the second surprising entry of the day.

Ma, looking down from her bedroom window, was suddenly surprised to see in the garden another figure she didn't recognize. At first she guessed it to be one of those Sunday moochers who occasionally turned up at the junk-yard looking for bargains in old chaff-cutters, old cider jars, old brass bedsteads and the sort of mullock people collected nowadays, all part of the *status quo* symbol, but then she wasn't sure.

The man talking with Pop and Angela Snow was dressed in one of those shirts that seemed to have been cut out of old boarding-house wallpaper, an affair of violet, green and pink, a pair of crumpled orange slacks and a pair of open sandals in black and silver. Straight out of Carnaby Street, Ma thought, and could only assume that this was some new boy friend of Angela and that by some unhappy mischance the Queen's Counsel hadn't been able to make it.

Just our luck, she thought, as she went back downstairs, rather crushed at the thought of the oyster satin perhaps having been bought to no purpose and then immediately afterwards telling herself not to worry: the Queen's Counsel would surely be coming along separate, in his own Daimler or Rolls or something, with his own chauffeur.

When she reached the garden and went across the lawn Angela came to meet her with a blissful 'Darling' and a kiss on both cheeks. Sweet to see Ma. How ravishing she looked. Angela adored the outfit. Perfick.

'And this,' she said, turning to the handsome figure in orange slacks and the old boarding-house wallpaper, 'is my father. Sir John Furlington-Snow.'

Ma speechless, could have dropped. As if Queen's Counsel wasn't enough it had to be 'sir' too.

'I never use the Furlington bit myself,' Angela said. 'Too fatuous and fussy for words. But it's important for Papa professionally.'

'Mrs Larkin. How delightful to meet you at long last. I've heard so much about you.'

Ma could have passed out. You could have knocked her down, as Pop had it, with a stone block of wood. She had never heard such a beautiful voice in all her life. Languid, golden, smoothly aristocratic, it was exactly like Angela's except that it was richly, deeply masculine. Ma could only suppose it developed that way from talking to the Queen so much. And that longish, thick gold-grey hair, curling about the ears, and the sort of lamb-chop whiskers: they had the real aristocratic, almost royal, touch about them too.

'Oh! good morning, sir. Very nice to meet you, sir. So glad you could come, sir. Aren't we lucky with the weather, sir?'

'Oh! please don't call him "sir", Ma,' Angela said, 'he hates it.'

'Oh! no, please, Mrs Larkin. Call me Furly. Everybody does.'

'Yes, sir,' Ma said and immediately begged to be excused and fled to the kitchen, red and trembling.

'Well, glass o' champers?' Pop said to Angela's father. 'Plain, pink or cocktail?'

Sir John Furlington-Snow said well, if nobody minded, he'd have a beer.

'Beer it is,' Pop said, hardly concealing his surprise. He himself was on ginger ale. 'This is my son-in-law, Mr Charlton. This is me old friend, the General. And this is the Reverend Candy – here, where's Mr Candy got to? He was here a minute ago.'

Mr Candy, having fortified himself with Guinness, had vanished into the house to find Primrose. With some of his much-needed strength back, he had an urgent question to ask her.

The urgency of the question faded utterly, however, when he found her waiting in the sitting-room, all alone; and, in defiance of Ma's orders, clad in a ravishingly tight micro-skirt of a kind of shot mauve-apricot shade, altogether more disturbing than any bare midriff had ever been.

'Just one little quick one. I thought you were never coming,' she said and then held up her lips and proceeded to give him a kiss of such prolonged and destructive artistry that Mr Candy felt himself fading gradually away into a state, as it were, of intoxicated benediction. He longed, even though against his will, to say Amen, but Primrose was having none of it and had just started a repeat performance when Ma's voice abruptly brought it all to an end.

'Dishing up!'

Mr Candy, feeling not a little dished up himself, wandered into the open air, breathless and thirsty all over again, to find almost everyone now assembled about the long table under the walnut tree. The two little Miss Barnwells were now among the guests and, like little Oscar and Phyllida, were already sitting at table, as always like two eager budgerigars, gazing hungrily on the plates of smoked salmon, waiting to be fed. The only person who hadn't arrived was Miss Pilchester, who was always late, anyway, Ma reflected, and probably thought it was still Saturday or something.

'Am I late? Am I late? It *is* the right day, isn't it? I had one of my hens die in the night and it was absolutely ghastly. I just couldn't leave – you know – until – well, what with the warm weather and I couldn't eat it, could I? I very nearly thought of fetching you, Mr Candy, to conduct the – Oh! am I *awfully, awfully* late?'

Again Ma found herself without a word to say. The reason this time was that Edith too had gone out and bought herself a new dress in honour of the Queen's Counsel. Ma gazed at it enraptured. It was appropriately of royal blue. The skirt was calf length, the neck high, the front covered, like a bandsman's tunic, with large gold frogs. All this did nothing for Miss Pilchester's figure since there was in fact little or no figure to do anything for. Nor could Ma decide whether or not it was meant to be a housecoat, a bath-robe or something left over from Edith's service in the Navy.

Soon, the smoked salmon having rapidly disappeared and a good deal of champagne with it, Mr Charlton and Montgomery having carved and dismembered the turkeys, and Pop having done the honours with the

Chambolle, there was much champing at the table, no less from the little
Miss Barnwells and the Brigadier than from Edith Pilchester who, hugely
enjoying herself on being released at last from *purdah*, kept saying:

'Delicious. Delicious. Now if I kept turkeys and one of *them* had died
what *would* I have done? That *would* have been a dilemma. What *would*
I have done?'

'Sung the whole of the *St Matthew Passion* I shouldn't wonder,' the
Brigadier said tersely and not unexpectedly downed a third glass of
Chambolle Musigny '59. 'Splendid stuff, the Chambolle. Quite delectable.
Of the Divine Order itself.'

Ma had so arranged the table that Angela sat on one side of Pop and
Edith on the other; herself on one side of Angela's father and Sister
Trevelyan on the other, leaving Primrose to the Brigadier and one each
of the little budgerigars to Montgomery and Mr Candy. In this arrangement Primrose was kept as near to Mr Candy as possible and as far from
Sister Trevelyan as could be without seeming outright rude. Ma thought
there was a bit of jealousy there.

And well there might be, she thought. Sister Trevelyan looked
stunningly attractive in a simple pure white dress that was deceptively
angelic, with its silver waist chain and simple neckline. So much so that
Ma wondered if she'd done the right thing in putting her next to Sir John,
who she had now decided was not only uncommonly handsome but had
quite a look in his eye. Took after Angela, she shouldn't wonder, and was
quick to note that quite half the time Sir John seemed to be eating with
only one hand, so that Ma shrewdly wondered what he was doing with
the other.

She needn't have wondered at all.

'If you do that again,' Sister Trevelyan whispered, 'I shall scream.'

'Scream.'

Sister Trevelyan thought it prudent not to scream.

'I thought,' Sir John said, 'you came from down under?'

'Yes, but not down under there!'

Presently Ma, shrewdly grasping that much more than mere eating and
drinking was going on, lifted her glass and said:

'Well, cheers! everybody. Nice to have you all here. Lovely. Cheers.'

Among the returning chorus of cheers the voice of the Brigadier could
be heard saying 'Bingo!' and a crescendo of twitterings came from the Miss
Barnwells. The only absent voice was that of Pop, who sat staring at a half
empty glass of ginger ale, a fact that touched Ma so much that she said
pointedly to Sister Trevelyan:

'What about it, Sister? What about a drop of Chambolle for Pop? Just a glass? Just one?'

Oh yes! yes indeed, the Miss Barnwells prattled. After all it was the Cause. Mr Larkin had been so terribly, terribly generous, to which Edith Pilchester added:

'Oh! yes, *please*. Just a teeny, teeny one. It seems so unfair.'

'What about it, Sister?' Ma said.

'Well, since I am not really on duty today,' Sister Trevelyan said, having been pinched so often by Sir John that she was now beginning to feel almost neglected when it didn't happen, 'just one glass. Just one small glass. But not a word to Dr O'Connor, otherwise my head will be on the block.'

Laughing with delight, Ma filled a glass with Chambolle Musigny and passed it over to Pop. At long, long last his period of *purdah* too was over. He could drink at last. Life was about to be good again.

With the word 'Cheers!' falling from his lips almost as a prayer of thanks Pop raised the glass, sipped at it and put it down again, his face wry.

'Something wrong?' Ma said. 'Not corked, is it?'

Pop hesitated, licked his lips and then tasted the wine again.

'Perfick,' he said. 'Only I don't like the taste, that's all.'

Did he mind? Ma said. He didn't *what*?

'Don't like it, that's all, Ma. Don't like the taste. Tastes funny.'

Ma, struck speechless for the third time that morning, told herself she would go to the bone-house. She didn't for the life of her know what things were coming to.

'Suppose when you've been off a thing all that long you sort of lose the urge for it or summat,' Pop said. 'Suppose you can do without it.'

Oh! you did, did you? Ma thought, thinking of other things and hoping that what applied to wine wouldn't apply to letting Nature take its course in other directions. Pop not liking the *taste*? It really had her be-jiggered.

'Great pity not to savour this excellent vintage,' Sir John said, at the same time savouring the vintage of Sister Trevelyan somewhere in the region of the left upper thigh. 'Beautiful bouquet.'

Future looked black, Ma thought. She half-wished she hadn't let her place next to Sir John be taken over by Phyllida, who in true feminine Larkin fashion had insisted on sitting next to him instead of Ma. After all there was no doubt he was a bit of a dog. She was very near tempted to start making up to him herself. The curled half-grey, half-blond hair, thick and rather long about the ears, together with the lamb-chop whiskers, the beautiful cultured aristocratic voice and the grey-blue eyes that were never still: it wouldn't take anybody long to get a bit worked up, Ma thought.

'Interested in gardening, Sir John?' Ma said, just to see what happened.

Well, yes, he was, Sir John said, intensely: it was one of his hobbies, he confessed, contriving at the same time to pursue another one of them with Sister Trevelyan.

'Good. You must come and see mine after lunch.'

'Splendid. Delighted.'

As the meal went on and on it struck the little Miss Barnwells and also Miss Pilchester and even Mr Candy and Ma, that it was very curious that no mention had been made of the Cause. This, after all, was largely what the lunch was about: to stave off the invading forces of treacherous bureaucracy and so on, to keep the village and Pop's property inviolate and in all ways to defend the Realm and the Cause. Everybody, rather like Ma, had certain confused ideas as to what the functions of a Queen's Counsel were and half wondered if they ought not to set up a committee there and then, appoint Sir John as chairman and then hear the case for the defence put in true expert legal fashion.

They were however so shy as to be utterly unable to put these thoughts into words and it was finally left to the Brigadier to broach the subject, which he did by holding up his sixth or seventh glass of Chambolle Musigny, looking through it with fruity ardour at Angela Snow and then saying:

'I understand, sir, that you've been good enough to take up the brief on our behalf. Noble gesture.'

The Brigadier's few cryptic words had the immediate effect of producing no reply whatever from Sir John. At the same time there was a positive torrent of explanation and comments from the little Miss Barnwells, Edith Pilchester and even Ma and Mr Candy. Road, tunnel, Common Market, Rome, Island, England's Green and Pleasant Land: the chorus wasn't merely one of explanation and comments but one of protest, indignation and, on Edith Pilchester's part, of righteous fervour amounting almost to wrath.

'I have even been able to discover that we are probably on *Holy ground.* A Consecrated Place.'

'' 'ear, 'ear,' Pop said. It pleased and flattered him greatly that his house, his land and his junk-yard might well be, as Mr Candy had intimated, on Sacred Ground.

'What we all feel is that the enemy is *near*,' Miss Pilchester said. 'We must act *swiftly*.'

At this point Sir John, whose mind had throughout lunch been, exactly as one hand had been, on other things, now seemed to take a desultory interest in the general proceedings.

'Really?' he said. He spoke in the most casual of voices and that languid aristocratic drawl that Pop had always loved in Angela Snow. '*Swiftly?* I should have thought quite the contrary.'

'Oh! no, *swiftly, swiftly,*' Miss Pilchester said. 'After all, "if 'twere done it were well that it" – Oh! yes, the quicker the better.'

Sir John smiled indulgently.

'No, no,' he said. 'What we need is a little Jarndyce and Jarndyce.'

'*Bleak House,*' Primrose said with flashing promptitude.

Bleak it would be too, Ma thought, if they had a road right through it and Pop no more in the mood for a glass of wine and the things that mattered. Jaundice was right. She'd heard there was a lot of it about.

Pop too had slightly misheard the words. *Jaundice and Jaundice?* He didn't want to catch that on top of everything else.

'"Jarndyce and Jarndyce drones on."' quoted Primrose with that endless knowledge of literature that had more than once had Mr Candy tied in knots both of emotion and excess. '"Jarndyce and Jarndyce has passed into a joke. The legion of bills in the suit have been transformed into mere bills of mortality."'

Pop was once again stunned by the marvels of education. He'd never heard anything like it. Clearly nobody else had, either. There was dead silence all round the table.

It was broken at last by Sir John, making a remark of such inconsequence that Ma suddenly thought he must be slightly off-course or something.

'Mrs Larkin, in which direction is your garden? The flower garden, I mean?'

Well, it was over there, Ma said, very mystified but at the same time wondering if this wasn't the chance she'd been waiting for. Why?

Without pausing to say why, Sir John rose from the table, took a swift draught of Chambolle Musigny and promptly disappeared in the direction of the garden.

Two or three minutes later he came back with a single scarlet flower in his hand. Then, rather to Sister Trevelyan's disappointment, he changed places with Phyllida and sat down next to Ma.

'Mrs Larkin,' he said, holding up the flower to Ma, 'I want you to tell me what flower this is.'

'It's a zinnia, of course.'

'Zinnia. Are you sure?'

'Of course I'm sure. After all, one of our twins is named Zinnia.'

'How do you know it's a zinnia?'

'Well, that's what it always has been. That's what I was always told.'

'And what is the name of the other twin?'

'Petunia.'

'And do you know one from the other? Zinnia from Petunia?'

'Well, I do, but Pop doesn't. He never sees them in the bath.'

'Never sees them in the bath, eh? Well, never mind. The point is you know a zinnia from a petunia?'

'Of course I do. Like knowing what a buttercup is.'

'Like knowing what a buttercup is? But this, you say, is a zinnia?'

'Yes.'

'Good. It's a zinnia because someone told you it was a zinnia, somewhere and at some time. And because you know one from the other. And why is it called a zinnia and not, for example, a petunia?'

Ma, very confused, confessed she didn't know. She could only suppose it was called a zinnia because it came from the country of Zinnia, wherever that was. Next to Zambia or somewhere, she shouldn't wonder. They changed the names of places and countries so often nowadays.

'There is no country called Zinnia.'

'No?'

'No. But in the sixteenth century there was a Polish author named Adam Sdizianskya von Zuluzian. What would you say if I told you that it was after him that the zinnia is named?'

'Well, I suppose I'd believe you.'

'You'd believe me. Why?'

'Well, if you say so.'

'If I say so.' Sir John once again smiled with both charm and indulgence, actually patting Ma on the cheek. 'But I didn't say so.'

'Oh! but you did.'

'No, no, dear Mrs Larkin, I did not. What I did say was "What would *you* say if I told you that it *was* after him that the zinnia is named?"'

'Oh! dear.'

'Exactly. In fact the zinnia is named after J. G. Zinn, a Professor of Botany.'

The entire lunch party having been stunned to utter silence by this display of argument and erudition the words which came from Primrose to break it fell on everybody like an explosion.

'In fact Jarndyce and Jarndyce,' she said, 'all over again.'

563

'Precisely,' Sir John said. 'By the way, who is that young lady?'

'That's our Primrose,' Ma said. 'She should have gone to University by rights.'

'University my Aunt Nellie. Never spoil a natural talent,' Sir John said and then gave Primrose such a handsome, fervent look of appraisal that Sister Trevelyan, Mariette, Ma, and Mr Candy were all jealous at the same time.

'Always quoting from the poets and all that,' Pop said. Ever ready to praise the virtues and marvels of education he nevertheless now found himself utterly out of his depth. He didn't catch on at all. What the pipe had Jaundice and Jaundice got to do with zinnias, professors and Polish poets? If he'd been drinking it might have explained it, but he was stone-cold sober.

'Always quoting the poets, eh?' Sir John said. 'Well, let's see if she can finish this quotation. "In delay there lies –"'

'"No plenty,"' Primrose said promptly, at the same time giving Mr Candy a melting look that scorched his vital parts as warmly and richly as another glass of Chambolle Musigny.

'"Then come and kiss me sweet and twenty."'

'True?' Sir John said, 'or false?'

'True in one sense,' Primrose said with that convincing look of intelligence and seduction that had long since led Mr Candy down the road of excess, 'but not in another.'

'Explain.'

Primrose promptly did so by further quotation:

'True in the sense "that such a thing might happen when the sky rained potatoes – or when we get through Jarndyce and Jarndyce".'

'Clever girl. Exactly.'

The Brigadier was another one who now confessed to himself that he was utterly out of his depth. Damme, what was this? Some kind of outflanking movement? A sort of verbal ambush? Or what? Damned odd tactics.

'If I may say so,' Miss Pilchester said, being also lost in verbal mystification, 'we don't seem to be getting very far. I don't know if you got what I said about the *Holy Place* – the Consecrated Ground – but it seems to me to be a point.'

It was now Mr Charlton, as so often in the past, who opened the doors to understanding. Marvellous feller, Charley boy, Pop told himself almost before Charley opened his mouth, lost in premature admiration.

'Ah! but the point is that we're not getting very far,' Mr Charlton said, 'because we don't want to get very far. Right, Sir John?'

'Admirably correct.'

'Or, what, in other words,' Primrose said, 'Shakespeare called "The Law's delays".'

Here Pop struck the table a shuddering blow with his open hand. He'd catched on now. Marvellous feller too, Sir John. There was more to that head than lamb-chop whiskers.

'Have a cigar, Sir John? Havanas. The best. Glass o' port? Vintage. Iced or warm?'

Ma, who had been no little bewildered by it all herself, promptly gave Pop one of her severe looks and said it wasn't time for port and cigars yet. They still had afters to come: the Christmas pudding and brandy and all that. She hoped Pop wasn't going to tell her he didn't like the taste of brandy on the pud now, was he? That *would* be the day, what with one thing and another.

The fires of Havanas and brandy on the pudding having at last been lit, Primrose was moved to quote yet again:

'"We shall this day light such a candle by God's grace in England –"'

to which the Brigadier, caressing with bucolic tenderness the rim of his wine-glass, filled for the tenth time to overflowing, murmured a fervent 'Hear, hear! They shall not pass.'

With the arrival of the port, poured with rich and characteristic generosity by Pop into big crimson goblets, Sir John proceeded to move back to his position side by side with Sister Trevelyan where he went through the mesmerizing act of caressing her thigh with one hand and alternately holding port and cigar with the other, while at the same time explaining to the still mystified Miss Barnwells and Miss Pilchester what exactly might constitute the law's delays.

'We shall go back in Time. We shall go sideways in Time. We shall go upside down in Time. Even underground in Time. We shall invoke statutes, quote Scripture, split hairs, even pause to pick daisies. Holy Well? – splendid. We shall quote Chaucer, lead in the Pilgrims, even trail the blood of Thomas a'Becket. What *is* will appear not to be. What *wasn't* we shall have to make sure *is*. Where there is no obstacle we will most certainly put one. Where one *is* we shall see that it's lost. A day in our courts, in fact, will be better than a thousand. Won't it, Sister Trevelyan?'

It already had been, Sister Trevelyan thought.

'And when we have reached the point of no return, or think we have, we shall surprise everyone by going back to where we started.'

It wouldn't surprise her, Sister Trevelyan thought. The point of no return had been reached some considerable time ago. Moreover it was her guess that any moment Sir John would be back there again.

How long this process of seduction, verbal and otherwise, might have gone on under the tender shade of the walnut tree, on which the young walnuts already hung in broken August sunshine like soft green plums, it was impossible to say. The silence and softness of the afternoon were by now woven into a web of embalment no less enrapturing than the words of the handsome Queen's Counsel, so that somewhere about mid afternoon Primrose was moved again to quotation.

'"A drowsy numbness pains my sense,"' she whispered to Mr Candy and quietly led him away.

As Ma watched the two of them drifting away towards the house she was suddenly yet again astonished by the sight of someone in the garden who appeared not to have been invited: another of those Sunday moochers, she didn't doubt, looking for a bargain.

Some moments later Mr Charlton, jumping suddenly up, told her otherwise.

'Good God, it's that man from the Ministry. I clean forgot. He said he might drop in one Sunday on the way back from visiting his sister in Brighton. Leave it to me – I'll get rid of him.'

'No, no, don't get rid of him,' Sir John said in that affable aristocratic voice that was so like that of Angela's, 'invite him over. After all, the spider hath had victories no less renowned than wasps.'

'That's what we call his whipped-cream voice,' Angela told Pop in a whisper. 'Creams 'em first. Whips 'em afterwards.'

A minute later a small, grey-haired, slightly balding man of fifty-five or so, lean, harassed and almost haggard, a little nervous and apologetic at having broken in on a family Sunday afternoon, joined the lunch table, where Pop, although refraining from striking him on the back in greeting, nevertheless offered him cigar, sherry, gin, brandy, vodka and port all in one breath, adding that he was afraid he didn't know his name?

'Harrington.'

'Right, Mr Harrington, sit you here. Take the load off your feet. What can we do for you?'

'Oh! very little actually. It's more of a courtesy call. I did call once before but unfortunately you were *hors de combat*. I hope you're feeling better?'

Pop, about to say that he was as fit as a flea, altered his mind and said middling instead and thrust into Mr Harrington's hand a goblet of iced sherry containing about half a bottle.

'Cheers!' Pop said. 'Bottoms up. Where are you from again?'

'The Ministry.'

At this point Sir John took over. His voice, as Angela herself had pointed out, was as smooth as whipped cream.

'What Ministry, may I ask, is that?'

'Transport.'

'Ah! Sing-Sing,' Sir John said, giving the Ministry the pet name by which it was known to its unfortunate occupants in London. 'So you work on Sundays now? Admirable innovation.'

'Well, not actually, no – yes and no – if –'

'Well, do you or don't you?'

'Well, no actually. I sort of acted on my own initiative.'

'So they actually let Civil Servants act on their own initiative nowadays, do they? Good.'

'Well, it isn't work, really.'

'Then what is it?'

'Well, it's – well there's this proposed – there's to be this preliminary inquiry –'

'Into what?'

'Well, not into anything yet.'

'Then why inquire?'

'Well, in due course – there may be – this area may be under consideration for –'

'Ah! the road. Yes, we've been chatting up about that.' With the handsomest of smiles Sir John seemed to become aware, as it were for the first time, of Miss Pilchester. 'You haven't met our local historian, have you? Miss Pilchester. Awfully good port, isn't it?'

'Actually I haven't tried it yet. I've got sherry.'

'Oh! but you must. It's sublime. Cockburns, '39. You simply can't get it any more. There just isn't any to be had.'

Instantly Pop handed Mr Harrington a large glass of port, which Mr Harrington tried, pronouncing it to be quite unlike anything he had ever tasted before, a remark that Sir John completely and coolly ignored.

'Ah! yes. Our local historian, Miss Pilchester,' Sir John said. 'She knows this part of the world inside out, don't you, Miss Pilchester?'

Thus flattered, Miss Pilchester could only fluff with indecision, unable to frame a word.

'From the time of Caesar's legions onwards. Romans, Pilgrims, Civil

War, Napoleonic War – she knows it all. I even swear she calls the blades of grass by their Christian, or even Roman, names.'

Mr Harrington, sipping now at iced sherry and then tentatively at the sublime excellence of the port, was suitably impressed.

'So you're from the Ministry?' Sir John said with the creamiest affability.

'Yes, I am, yes.'

'How do I know?'

'Well, I am, you know.'

'But I don't know.'

'But I said I was.'

'Which is not, of course, the same thing.'

'But it is.'

'I'm delighted to hear it. Have you your authority with you?'

'Well, no, actually not. I'm on leave for a few days.'

'Oh! yes? For all I know you may be either the Dean of St Paul's or the landlord of The Pig and Whistle in Lambeth, always supposing there is a Pig and Whistle in Lambeth.'

'I am not the landlord of The Pig and Whistle in Lambeth.'

'No? How do I know?'

'I just am not, that's all.'

'There again, can you prove otherwise?'

'Well, I'm afraid I can't if you put it like that.'

'I do put it like that. Beautiful port, isn't it? Nectar. When you think that there simply isn't any vintage port left. Except in a few private cellars. Like that of Mr Larkin here.'

'It's absolutely splendid.'

'Good. Have some more. You've lunched, I trust?'

Mr Harrington, who had stopped for a small packet of potato crisps, a half pint of bitter and a wash at a pub some miles farther down the road to the coast, was obliged to confess that he hadn't really.

'Oh! what a shame,' Ma said. 'We can't have that. I'll fetch you a mite of cold.'

The mite of cold turned out to be a complete wing of turkey fortified by a slab of breast and a pile of pink cold ham with salad, French beans and potatoes. Pop fortified it further by a glass of Chambolle Musigny, which he assured Mr Harrington was even better vintage than the port. It was the tops. Thus embalmed with food and wine Mr Harrington had scarcely another word to say.

The rest of the afternoon, and indeed the early evening, belonged almost wholly to Sir John. In a blue haze of cigar smoke, in tender dappled walnut shade, he held the company bewitched. He extracted from a wide-eyed Miss Pilchester thoughts that had never been hers. He beguiled her first into uttering truths that she knew to be falsehoods; then into lies which were made to seem like heaven-blessed truths. He besought her to remember the unfortunate army of Roman legionaries that had sunk and perished across the very meadows that now surrounded the Larkin domain: meadows of bottomless mire, fathomless traps which wouldn't support a train of beetles, still less an army, the entire establishment of which had perished as in a quick-mire, direly suffocated in mud.

He begged her further to remember the band of pilgrims that had been slaughtered even as they prayed and drank at the Holy Well, so that the well ran bright with the blood of the innocent and pious and was in consequence for ever cursed. He urged her to recite chapter and verse for those spies of Napoleon's found skulking in an osier bed, not two hundred yards away, from which they were taken on a far distant fine May morning and, to the sound of mocking cuckoos, hanged, drawn and quartered. Since earliest times the dark lustre of evil had lain on the adjacent land. Those who had come to violate it had themselves been violated. It had always been so and, he feared and suspected, always would be.

'And by the way, Mr Larkin, where did you get this excellent port?'

Pop said he'd got it from a former neighbour of his, Mr Jerebohm, city gent. Pop had sold him Gore Court, the big house down the road, since when nothing but bad luck, and then disaster, had followed him. Bluff Court was really Pop's name for the house, on account of its having formerly been owned by Sir George Bluff-Gore, who couldn't afford to keep it up and had pigged it out in a keeper's cottage instead until he had sold the big house to Pop, in despair.

'Couldn't get servants. Couldn't heat the place. Raised thousands of pheasants and never hardly shot one. Rode to hounds and always fell off his horse. Climbed over a gate one day with his gun and very near shot his foot orf. Couldn't keep the mice down. Remember the mice, Ma?'

Ma, laughing like jelly, remembered the mice. How could she ever forget them? Poor Pinkie, Mrs Jerebohm, had fifty traps going at a time and still found two in her bed and another in a rice pudding one day.

'Oh! in the end they gave it up,' Pop said. 'Went back to London. I bought the whole place back from them, lock, stock and barrel. Port, cellars an' all.'

'Very little of the port, I suppose? It's getting mighty scarce nowadays.'

Oh! he didn't know, Pop said. Hadn't counted it up just lately. Fifty cases or more he shouldn't wonder. Dows, Taylors, Fonseca, Cockburn – the whole shoot. Some as far back as '27. There was a nice lot of Chambolle and Vosne Romane, too. He'd given a fair price for it though, mind you. Sort of slipped it in with the price of the house.

'And that reminds me,' Sir John said in that smooth languid voice of his so well described by Angela as being like whipped cream, 'who is your immediate superior at Sing-Sing, Mr Harrington?'

'Fortescue.'

'Ah! of course. I know him. He's a member of my club. Great port man too. Swear he hasn't seen much like this for a long time.'

'Very good taste in port, Mr Jerebohm,' Ma said. 'I'll say that for him.'

'I suppose we couldn't spare Fortescue a case, could we, Mr Larkin? Excellent man to have on our side.'

Mr Harrington was seen to grow uneasy. Sending gifts of port to his immediate superior? Dangerous ground. There was after all such a thing as the Corrupt Practices Act.

'And perhaps a case of the Chambolle for Mr Harrington?'

'Of course. Perfick. Why not?'

Mr Harrison, bewitched and embalmed not only by Sir John's persuasive, creamy voice and manner, was also feeling heated, all too well-fed, uncertain and very dizzy.

'Montgomery, put a case of the old Chambolle into Mr Harrington's car, will you, wherever it is. Where is your car, Mr Harrington?'

Mr Harrington had neither the time nor will to answer before Sir John cut in with a remark of the smoothest innocence:

'And is anyone in the house? I mean Gore Court, now, Mr Larkin? You've sold it again?'

Pop said he'd sold it again about three months ago. Fair profit. Going to be a Horticultural Research place. House and twenty acres. Part of the new University.

'Really?' Sir John suddenly looked as if he'd seen a vision or stumbled on a diamond mine. 'Really?'

'Education on the doorstep now,' Ma said. 'Wherever you go it's education.'

'Education,' Sir John murmured as in a ruminative dream. 'Education.'

And then abruptly, off in one of those disconcerting tangents that Pop found so fascinating in Angela, he suddenly rose from the table and said:

'You were going to show me your garden, weren't you, Mrs Larkin? What have you got in it, now? I'm afraid mine's nearly over.'

Oh! she'd got dahlias, phloxes, fuchsias, petunias, gladioli, Ma said, and zinnias of course. And lilies. Ma was immensely proud of her lilies. They came from Japan. She had raised them all herself. From seed.

'Show me.'

Sir John extended his arm in a manner absolutely befitting, as Ma saw it, a Queen's Counsel, and Ma in turn accepted it almost as if for once, briefly, in her oyster satin, she was a queen herself: a gesture that at once aroused in Sister Trevelyan, Mariette, Miss Pilchester and even the little Miss Barnwells varying spasms of jealousy. Nor did Ma fail to note that there was also a glint of it in Pop's eye, a fact for which she wasn't in the least bit sorry.

And where are these lilies, Mrs Larkin?

'Right over the far side of the garden.'

As she and Sir John strolled slowly through paths lined with phloxes, dahlias, fuchsias, tobacco plants and all the flowers Ma loved, she suddenly remembered that word education. Funny how it was always cropping up. You couldn't get away from it nowadays.

Nor had she failed to notice how creamily satisfied Sir John had seemed about the word: so much so that he now repeated it, almost smacking his lips, as over a fresh glass of even more excellent port.

'Education, yes, Mrs Larkin. Education.'

'You think it's all that important?' Ma said. She was bound to confess she herself very often didn't.

'In this case, yes. We are back, Mrs Larkin, with Jarndyce and Jarndyce. Our old friends.'

Oh! were they? Ma said. And what had they got to do with it?

'On the one hand the Jarndyce of the Ministry of Transport, on the other the Jarndyce of the Ministry of Education.'

Ma confessed she didn't quite get it.

'No? As your dear clever little daughter said, when you get Jarndyce v. Jarndyce you can bet your sweet life it'll go on until it rains potatoes from the sky.'

Ah! they were clever, these Queen's Counsel, Ma told herself. No wonder Her Majesty had so many of them around her, giving her advice.

'And now the lilies. Let us consider how they grow. Where are the lilies?'

Well, they were, Ma said, up against the seat by the wall. She waved a big, fat admiring hand, the fingers of which flowered as opulently with rings as the lilies with heads of flower. They looked, the lilies, Ma often thought, like a crowd of Eastern emperors, all in Turks' caps, gold and white and pink and copper and lime-green and orange and sulphur. A bit like Solomon in all his glory.

Then, as Ma and Sir John stood gazing at the lilies in admiration and on Sir John's part with no little envy, Primrose and Mr Candy suddenly appeared through the garden gate that led from the fields beyond.

'Oh! there you are,' Ma said. 'Just been talking to Sir John about your old friends Jarndyce and Jarndyce.'

'Oh! yes?'

'Yes, Sir John says he don't think we need to worry our loaves about the road till 1990 or thereabouts, Jarndyce and Jarndyce'll see to that.'

It was time for Primrose to come up with Blake again; and she instantly did:

'"Improvement makes straight roads; but the crooked roads without Improvement are the roads of Genius."'

'I'm not sure if I care for that word crooked,' Sir John said, 'but I'll accept the genius,' and promptly gave Primrose a look of such seductive smoothness that Mr Candy at once felt wretchedly jealous and was slightly dismayed to hear Primrose say:

'Are we having supper in the garden, Ma? If so how many will we be? Then Mr Candy and I can start getting things ready.'

'Feels a bit like thunder, I think, don't you?' Ma said. 'Lots of these little thunder flies about.'

'Well, we can get everything ready anyway,' Primrose said. 'If it doesn't rain we'll eat outside. If it does – well, how many will we be anyway?'

Oh! they'd be the same as lunch, Ma supposed. That's if Sir John stayed. Would Sir John care to stay?

'Adore to. Utterly delighted,' Sir John said, sounding exactly like an echo of the smooth-voiced Angela. 'Absolutely nothing I'd like more.'

'Lovely,' Primrose said with a smoothness of her own and at once led an even more jealous Mr Candy away.

Alone in the garden with Ma, Sir John immediately began to praise the lilies with precisely the same extravagance he had previously bestowed on the vintage port. Incomparable. Sublime. Regal. Had a vintage of their own. Almost, as the dear Brigadier had said, of the Divine Order.

Entranced and flattered, Ma hardly knew what to do or say. Sir John at once solved part of this problem by suggesting that he and Ma sit down and admire the glorious trumpets and turks' caps that she, in her clever way, had raised from seed. Mrs Larkin really had green fingers.

'They're quite majestic, aren't they? How clever you are, Mrs Larkin. One really feels one ought to pay court to them.'

Court – lovely word, Ma thought. Majestic – she liked that very much too. After all you rather expected words like that from a Queen's Counsel.

'You really must tell me where you get the seed from, Mrs Larkin,' Sir John said and at the same time gave Ma's right thigh, or the extreme rim of it, a dexterous caress, like the movement of a slow warm iron across a smooth ironing board.

Ma pretended to take no notice whatsoever.

'Japan,' she said.

'Ah! yes, you said so. Not too heavy a perfume.'

'Not now. But you wait till it gets dark,' Ma said, at which Sir John repeated the smooth, dexterous caress across her thigh, as if hoping it soon would be.

Ma sniffed at the air, not for the immediate purpose of drinking in the scent of lilies but at the prospect of thunder.

'It's getting heavy like, don't you think? I mean the air,' she said. 'I do hope we don't get a storm.'

'Don't think so. It'll probably go along the hills,' Sir John said and softly proceeded to go along the hills himself, in the region of Ma's right shoulder.

'I think I ought to go upstairs and see that all the windows are shut,' Ma suddenly said. 'In case it comes a storm.'

'Is there that hurry?'

'Oh! better to be safe than sorry,' Ma said and swung herself deftly away, though not without calling over her shoulder that she'd be back soon. 'I've got plenty of young seedling lilies by the way if you'd like some. In that frame over there. Pick some out. You're very welcome.'

Smoothly Sir John murmured thanks and added that he adored young lilies, saying it in such a way that it seemed almost to refer to Ma, who was consequently honoured and delighted.

Upstairs Ma suddenly felt herself come over all hot and sticky. It wouldn't be a bad plan, she told herself, to change her oyster satin and get into something cooler. This she proceeded to do, at the same time dispensing with her slip, stockings and corsets, the latter having taken a tighter and tighter grip on her all day until now they had a positive and almost painful lock on her, creasing her ample flesh so that she could hardly breathe. With a figure like hers – 55–55–55 – you needed all the comfort you could get.

With much relief she finally got into a loose magenta-pink dress of rather low cut and short sleeves and at once felt a good deal refreshed. A generous dose of her favourite *Chanel No. 5* having drenched almost every part of her body she could reach she at last felt she smelled almost as sweetly as the lilies always did when they gave off their richest, heaviest perfume after dark.

By the time she got downstairs again the threat of thunder seemed less direct. Only a half-golden, half-murky premature twilight hung over the garden, slightly deepening under the big walnut-tree, where Primrose, Angela and Mariette had already laid the long table for supper.

'Candles,' Ma said, 'or these little lamps. Or both. Else we'll never see what we're eating.'

As the table was already grossly overladen with ham, cold duck, cold chicken, cold turkey, pork pies, cold sausages of several kinds and six sorts of cheeses, together with fruit and trifles and bread and pickles and salads and tarts and mousses and various other things, this seemed unlikely to happen, Mr Harrington thought.

Mr Harrington, an awfully confused and bewildered man in both mind and body, sat talking to Pop. His confusion rose from the fact that throughout the afternoon and evening he had asked himself the same question a thousand times and had never had an answer. The question, 'Why bother? Why such defence of a very ordinary, ramshackle, sloppy, almost derelict dump of a place as this?' referred to Pop's beloved paradise, where he and Ma had spent so much of their fruitful, unconstricted, happy lives. Mr Harrington, who had a few years yet to go before he could enjoy a frugal retirement and meagre pension, simply couldn't for the life of him understand the passionate, almost fanatical defence of such a dump. In his eyes and estimation it would have been far better bull-dozed swiftly away.

'Ah! you should be here in the spring,' Pop was saying to him. 'Perfick then, Mr Harrington. Blackbirds, nightingales, primroses, millions of bluebells – perfick bit of England. Perfick.'

The enthusiastic words fell from Pop's lips at the very moment when Ma was coming back from the house with Phyllida and little Oscar, the children carrying the candles, Ma bearing two small brass oil lamps. When Ma, at the urgent request of the children, lit both lamps and candles and set them on the supper table the glow of light fell close and bright on to the pink-magenta dress, its low cut revealing with startling pleasantness the vast cleft bosom smooth and olive above.

Very nice too, Pop thought. Primrose and bluebell, eh? He wondered if that pertickler mood of Ma's would ever come back?

'Beautiful, Mr Harrington, beautiful. Perfick,' Pop said, referring now not to Ma's revealing shape but again to his paradise in springtime.

Mr Harrington didn't doubt it was, but why? he kept asking himself, why? It was part of his job to go about the country in investigation of ministerial proposals to drive new and highly important roads through here, there and Heaven alone knew where else. It was his job, further, to attend public inquiries, listen to public objectors and try generally to cajole, argue, pacify and at last persuade people, if possible, to accept roads they all too often didn't want, which were often quite unnecessary and which would in all likelihood be inadequate and out of date by the time they were built. He had long been convinced that he had met every kind of objection and objector that existed on the face of the earth. Some of these he had persuaded; from others he had suffered defeat; of others he had made eternal enemies; from all he suffered the varying tortures and purgatories of frustration that had made him prematurely bald, prematurely grey, prematurely old and as often as not very nearly weary unto death. And they said, he sometimes told himself bitterly, that civil servants never worked. The wonder of it was that they were ever civil.

He had listened, in his time, to objectors wanting to save ancient cottages, historical court-houses, Palladian mansions, great avenues of limes, eighteenth-century follies, thirteenth-century bridges, precious farm-land, ye olde pubs and even ye olde tea-shoppes, pleasant private gardens, alms-houses, estates planned by Capability Brown, market crosses, great parks rich with oak-trees old when Henry VIII had reigned with licence and liberty, winding village streets, ornamental lakes, wrought-iron gates by Inigo Jones, exclusive schools, hallowed chapels, railway stations and even, on one occasion, an American airfield.

To someone or other all these had been important, precious, sweet, commemorative, even sacred. Like patience on a monument Mr Harrington had listened, unsmiling, ungrieved and always on the rim of despair, to all of them. And sometimes he had understood.

But not this: not the Larkin place. This, like the peace of God, passed all understanding.

'Another snifter, Mr Harrington? Sherry, gin? I make some very nice cocktails.'

Already replete and slightly heavy-headed from sherry, port and much burgundy Mr Harrington confessed that he thought he would settle for something soft, a dry ginger or something. He was rather thirsty.

'Red Bull,' Pop said with typical promptitude, 'just the thing. Long and harmless. I'll put plenty of ice in. That'll quench you like a charm.'

That was another thing that had Mr Harrington guessing. Where *did* it all come from? The lavish living, the vintage port, the expensive burgundy, the expensive taste combined with ghastly taste, the flamboyance and the vulgarity, the presence of the aristocratic Miss Snow and still more of her father, a Queen's Counsel. He wondered what *they* thought of it? and above all why *they* were here? It was really beyond all understanding.

'There you are, Mr Harrington. Mixed a good long double with plenty of ice. It'll go down like spring water.'

'Supper's ready!' Ma called.

A few moments later the whole company were again gathered under the walnut tree. The supper table, laden to the very edges, embroidered with faces above and about it, was golden with the light of lamps and candles. Ma presided at one end and Pop, rather like a sober shepherd with his flock, at the other.

Mr Charlton had decided that pink champagne, well-iced, would be the correct answer to all needs on such an evening of quiet, balmy sultriness and to this purpose had brought up an old foot-bath, in which a dozen bottles were now half-rising, half-floating in a small sea of icebergs.

'And give the children a drop,' Ma said, 'it won't hurt them.'

Ma had a theory that with alcohol, as with a number of other important things in life, it was better to start young. It would do you a lot less harm later.

The bountiful flow of pink iced champagne had the effect of making the company very gay. Beautiful thing to see, Pop told himself several times, watching the glow of faces in the candlelight: perfick. The little budgerigars chirped over their rose-pink glasses, Miss Pilchester giggled freely and often, the Brigadier hailed, with raised glass, everyone and everything, including the now dark summer night-sky, and Mr Harrington, suffering from the effect of cold pink champagne making its serpentine way into the already imposed spring water of Pop's Red Bull, was in a state of cross-eyed, wondrous stupefaction.

Some time later this became confusion worse confounded by the arrival of Phyllida, who said:

'Please may I sit on your knee?' The youngest of the Larkins, brilliantly red-haired, already a bright seductress, was on Mr Harrington's knee before he could answer, cuddling up to him, champagne glass in hand. 'Everybody else is sitting on everybody else's knee. Angela's sitting on the General's knee. Sister Trevelyan's sitting on Mr Charlton's. Miss Pilchester's sitting on Pop's. And Ma's sitting on – Oh! where's Ma gone? She was here a minute ago.'

Ma in fact was on the far side of the garden, by the lilies, with Sir John.

The air, sultry as ever, was over-rich with the perfume of lilies. Except for an occasional bat scooping overhead there was neither sound nor movement in the darkness.

'This is the time they always smell their best,' Ma said, touching one of the lilies as she and Sir John went down the path. 'So rich.'

'Ethereal,' Sir John said. 'Intoxicating.' Again something in the smooth compulsive way he said the words might have been referring to Ma. 'Celestial.'

'Did you take some seedlings for yourself?' Ma said. 'I said to take your pick.'

No, Sir John said, he confessed it had slipped his mind. Perhaps he might come and take his pick some other time?

'Any time,' Ma said. 'Any day suits me.'

Sir John, who was already sitting on the seat by the lilies, indicated with a pat of his hand that there was room for Ma there too. Unlike Mr Harrington, but like Angela, he understood, and also loved, the Larkin place. It seemed to him to be, among other things, part of the answer to a mad world. If it had to be defended he would defend it, with skill, eloquence, delay, subterfuge and if necessary with forms of knavery of which even Mr Harrington, in his ministerial innocence and experience, had never even dreamed.

But all those things were, as yet, far off. The immediate subject was Ma.

'You have such beautiful smooth skin, Mrs Larkin. Like one of those lily petals,' Sir John said and delicately ran his fingers up and down Ma's right thigh, an experience, a sort of trial run in Pop's language, that Ma neither resented nor found at all unpleasant.

Nor did she resent Sir John's next exercise in exploration, which was along her now bare right shoulder. Ma being of the great breadth she was it was impossible to put an arm round her completely and Sir John had consequently decided that the simplest and most rewarding tactics would be to approach, as the Brigadier might have said, in a right-flanking movement.

After several further preliminary exercises Sir John delicately drew Ma's head to his shoulder and kissed her full on her lips, expertly, deeply, warmly and as if inspired by immortal longings; the kiss lasting a very long time.

At the end of it Ma discovered, not completely to her surprise, that somehow, either by accident, design or a subtle combination of both, her right bosom had fallen out.

Sir John at once slipped a hand underneath it, with great delicacy, rather as if he might have been holding a large and precious goblet, eager to save it from falling.

Ma, unsurprised, said nothing. She was in fact thinking of Angela. There was nothing to be surprised about really, was there? It obviously ran in the family.

'You have the most beautiful breasts, Mrs Larkin.'

Oh! had she? Ma said, as if she had been totally unaware of such a blessing up to that moment.

'Very beautiful. Really they're so beautiful.'

Ma actually laughed, softly. How did he know? They? He'd only got one out yet.

'A situation that can soon be remedied no doubt,' Sir John said and proceeded to turn his attention to Ma's other breast.

'Oh! I shouldn't bother with that one. It always rains when that one comes out,' Ma said and deftly slipped the other bosom back into its rightful place again.

Inspired by these proceedings and several further warm, long and impassioned kisses Ma started to wonder. What would happen if she went a bit further, sort of? Any harm? Might be nice. She rather felt in that mood. After all she was, like Pop, a bit short of practice these days.

Then, she told herself, half in and half out of a seductive dream, perhaps she'd better watch it after all? Supposing something did happen? – it was no use thinking about the Pill. She never took it anyway. Nor was it any use asking Mariette, who never took it either. And she didn't for a minute suppose it was much good asking Edith if she had one on her anywhere. The Miss Barnwells were a dead loss too. Nor could she very well ask Angela a question like that, even if there was time, which there now quite obviously wasn't.

'Mrs Larkin, this has been one of the most enthralling, delicious experiences of my life.'

Ma had to confess that she didn't think it was too bad herself. Talk about practice – this was as near the real thing as she'd been for a long, long time.

'And tell me something. Why does it always rain when the other one comes out?'

'Oh! that's my little secret,' Ma said. She wasn't, she told herself, going to share that with anybody, even Sir John. 'You don't want it to rain, do you?'

'Not one bit. I want it to stay like this all night. All night long. You'd like that too?'

Ma was about to confess that she would indeed, it was very much in her line, and was just giving a deep ecstatic sigh which Sir John in turn was about to construe as one of surrender, when she thought she saw a star fall at the other end of the garden. Then the light of it seemed to hesitate, shimmered a little for a moment or two and then started to move along the path towards her, the lilies and Sir John.

A moment later she realized that the star was a lamp, carried by Phyllida and little Oscar.

'Ma,' they said, their eyes bright from lamplight and their voices equally bright from pink champagne, 'Pop sent us to find you. He says it's getting late and he wants to go to bed.'

'No peace for the wicked,' Ma said and, half-wished, embalmed in the deep rich night-fragrance of lilies, that she had been after all.

· 11 ·

'Very nice day, Pop.'

'Lovely. Perfick.'

'Sorry you didn't like the wine though.'

'Well, it sort of tasted funny.'

'Oh? Did it? You had me worried.'

'Oh! not to worry. It'll come back.'

Ma said she was more than glad to hear it.

Upstairs the air was still warm and sultry, though by now the sky had cleared, so that many stars were shining with deep August richness. Some of these seemed to be reflected down below, under the walnut tree, where a few of the guests still remained, talking in the light of lamps and candles, the flames of which occasionally flickered in the slightest turn of air.

'Quite a bit of a character, Angela's father,' Pop said.

Quite a bit of a character, Ma agreed, quite a bit of a character.

'Spot him at lunch-time? With Sister Trevelyan? Something going on there.'

'Oh?' Ma said serenely, not merely as if greatly surprised but at the same time as if not knowing what the something was even if it had been going on.

'You can see where Angela gets it from.'

'Well, you should know.'

Dreamily musing for another moment or two, Ma remembered the lilies, the heavenly scent of them and how Sir John had said her skin had been so like their petals. What with one thing and another it was enough to put her into one of her primrose-and-bluebell moods; and a quiet deep tremor crept through her.

'Unzip me, will you? I think I'm going to bed too.'

Pop dutifully unzipped Ma's dress, saying at the same time how much he'd liked the oyster satin. It didn't exactly have the effect of slimming Ma, but it made her look sort of – well, younger.

Ma merely murmured gently in acceptance of this flattery and then, having been unzipped, let the pink-magenta dress fall to the bedroom floor.

Rather to Pop's surprise there was neither slip nor corset underneath it and, thus deprived of watching the fascinating process of Ma undressing completely, he stood for a few moments speechless.

'Oh! younger, eh? We *are* coming on, aren't we? Just as well, because I've got something to tell you.'

Ma now stood completely naked in the middle of the bedroom, making no attempt, also to Pop's surprise, of searching for her nightdress.

Oh? Pop said, what had she got to tell?

'It's about our Primrose.'

Oh! yes? What about Primrose?

'She fell.'

Perfick, Pop said, perfick. Was she sure?

'Sure? Of course she's sure. She's had one of those pregnancy tests.'

Oh! yes? Pop said. He'd often wondered about them. You saw them advertised a lot nowadays. How did they work it? Drop a tablet in and if it fizzed a girl was preggy, if it didn't she wasn't? How had she let it get that far anyway?

'*How?*' Ma said. '*How?* You asked me that once before. What do you mean, *how?*'

He didn't mean that, Pop said. He meant he didn't think they fell nowadays, what with the Pill and all that.

'Oh! Mr Candy doesn't approve of the Pill.'

Mr Candy! Good Gawd Almighty, Pop said, whatever was the Church coming to?

'It's coming to not approving of the Pill, that's what it's coming to.'

Mr Candy, eh? Pop mused. Not approving of the Pill, eh? Liked it neat, did he?

'Well, why not? I've never known you take water with it yet.'

This discussion had Pop so fascinated that he partly if not completely lost sight of the fact that Ma was standing in the middle of the bedroom stark naked. He even forgot about the business of Ma's undressing: a process which, though in itself always fascinating, lacked the complications of dressing, in which the art of getting one bosom in before the other fell out again always struck him as being very like the English weather. You never knew if it was going to rain or shine next.

Well, he kept saying, Mr Candy, eh? Mr Candy. Church in the family now. He supposed they'd have to start behaving themselves now, would they?

'All depends what you mean by behave.'

The Church, the Army, the Income Tax, Queen's Counsel: good

gracious, Ma thought, there wasn't much difference in it, was there, when it came down to brass tacks?

Mr Candy, eh? The Reverend Candy. Pop had to confess he'd never thought Mr Candy had it in him.

'Oh! he had it in him all right,' Ma said. 'It just took our Primrose to get it out.'

Pop, still amazed, said yet again that he wondered how she'd managed it.

To his infinite astonishment Ma said she wouldn't be at all surprised if it wasn't education. She'd always said you never knew where it would land you if you let it get on top of you. There was altogether too much of it about nowadays.

'Well, are you coming in?'

This question, coming with total unexpectedness, out of darkness, took Pop utterly by surprise. Coming in where?

'Well, I'm in here, aren't I?' Ma said, speaking from the bed.

Totally unprepared for this question, as he had been for much that had preceded it, Pop could only ask Ma if she wasn't still going to sleep in the separate bedroom?

'Don't like that bed in there. The springs have gone.'

A moment or two later Ma was enfolding Pop into the great soft olive continent of her body. It was warm. Outside the August sky was brilliant with many stars.

'Well, how's that?' Ma said. 'Nice?'

'Perfick.'

Ma gave a great sigh, put her rich luscious lips on Pop's, gently lifted one of his hands to her left bosom, hoped it wouldn't rain before morning and said:

'Well, you know what they always say, don't you?'

Well, Pop said, what did they say?

'A little of what you fancy –'

That was a fact, Pop said, and at once proceeded to demonstrate, to the best of his ability, in spite of long lack of practice, the eternal truth of the words.